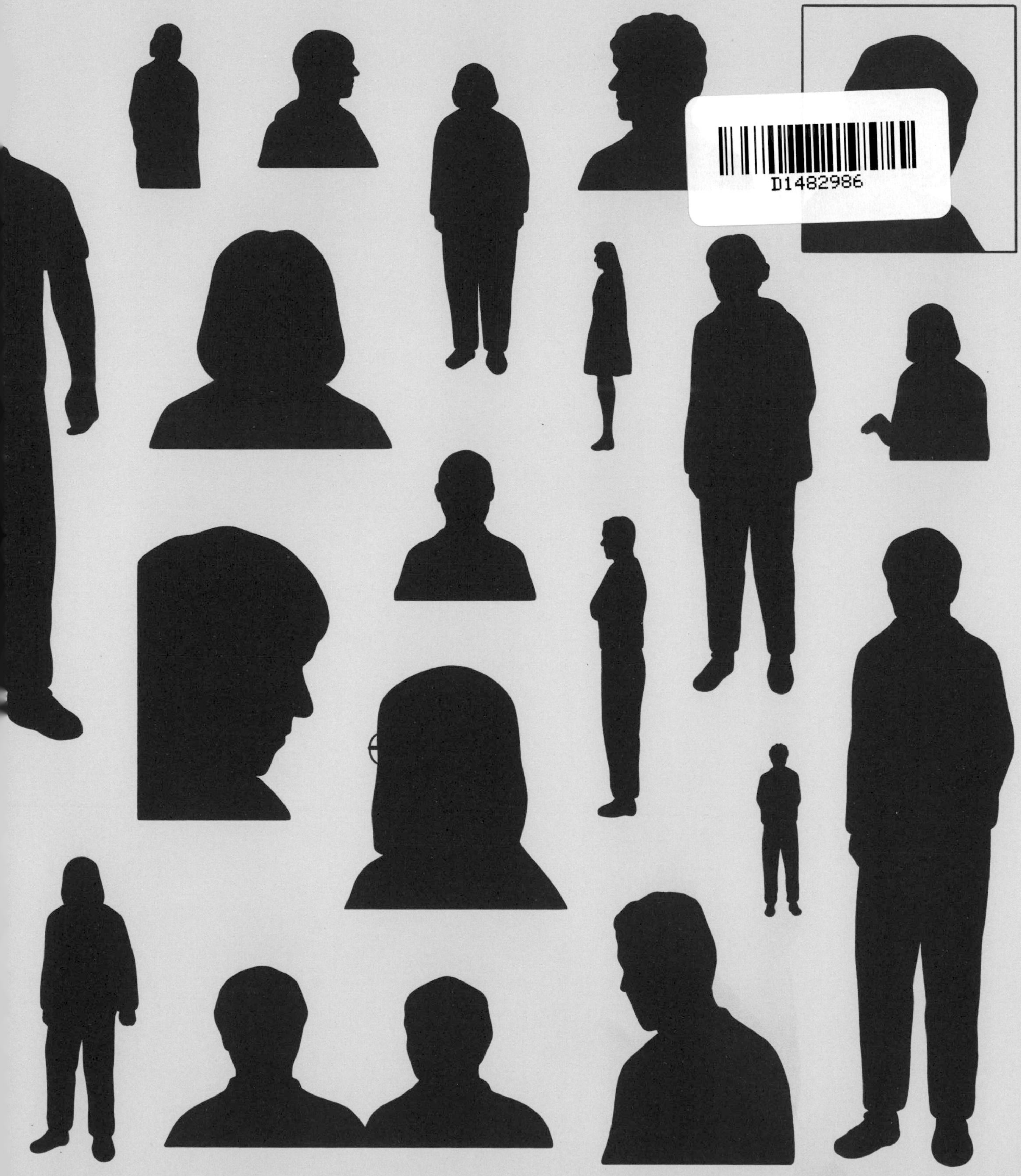

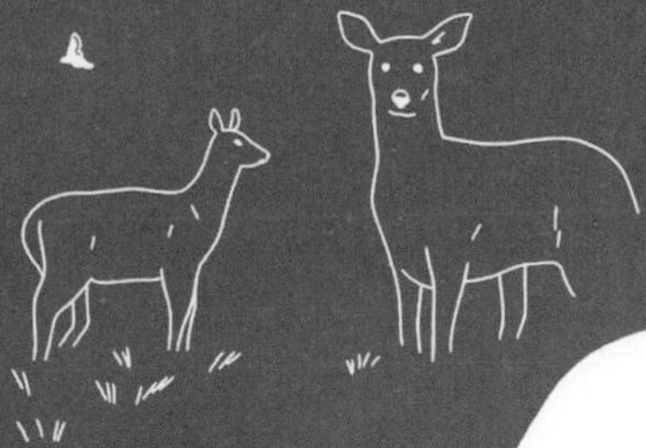
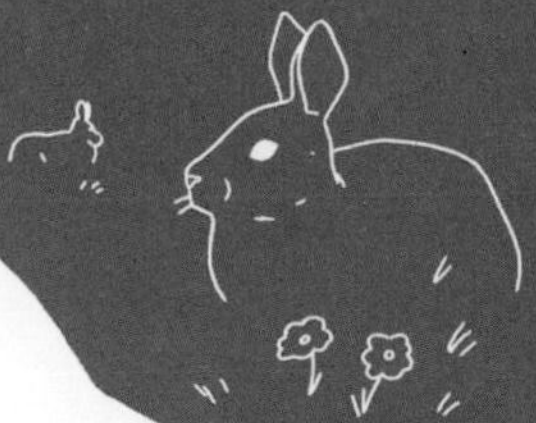



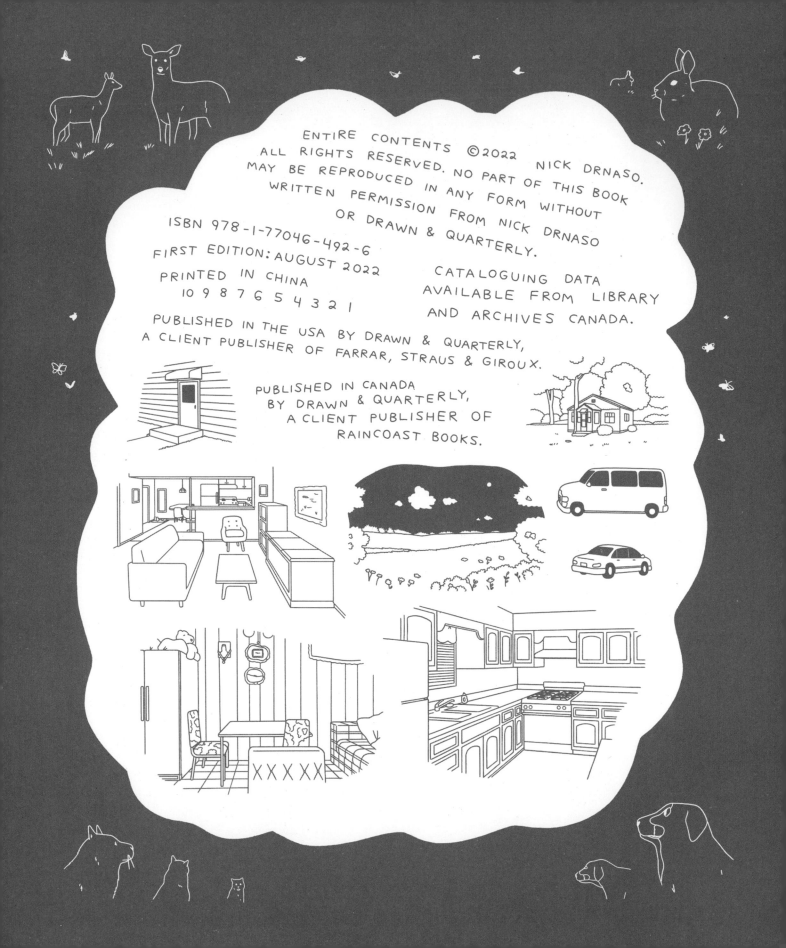

ISBN 978-1-77046-492-6

FIRST EDITION: AUGUST 2022

PRINTED IN CHINA
10 9 8 7 6 5 4 3 2 1

CATALOGUING DATA
AVAILABLE FROM LIBRARY
AND ARCHIVES CANADA.

PUBLISHED IN THE USA BY DRAWN & QUARTERLY,
A CLIENT PUBLISHER OF FARRAR, STRAUS & GIROUX.

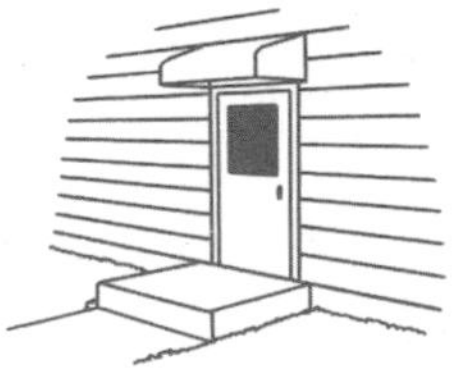

PUBLISHED IN CANADA
BY DRAWN & QUARTERLY,
A CLIENT PUBLISHER OF
RAINCOAST BOOKS.

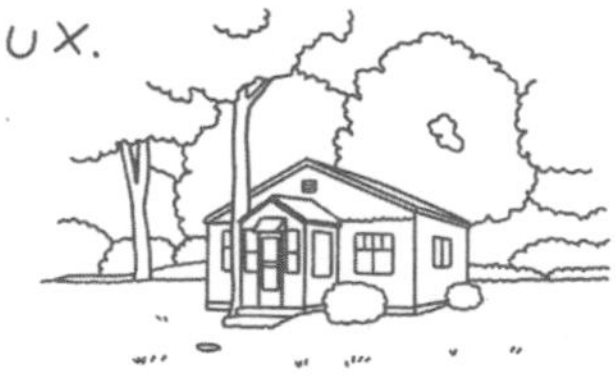

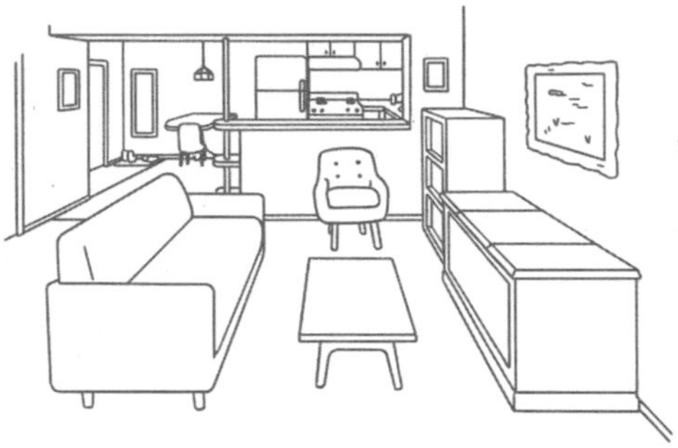
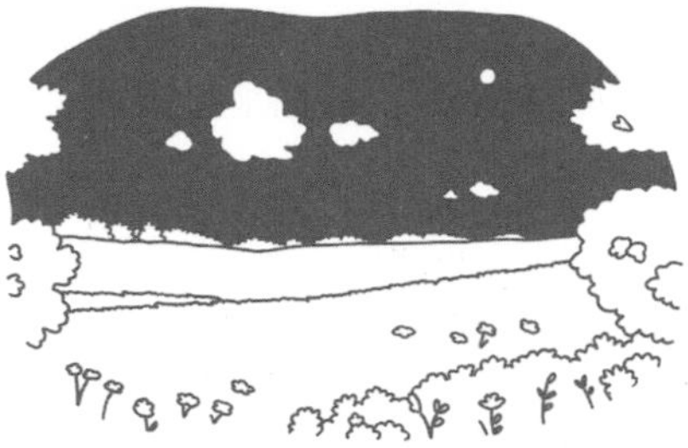
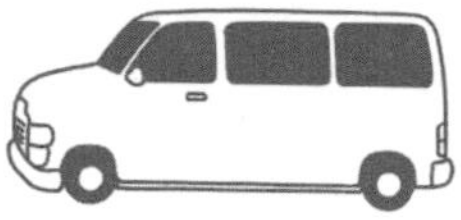
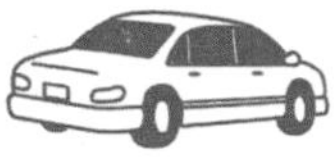
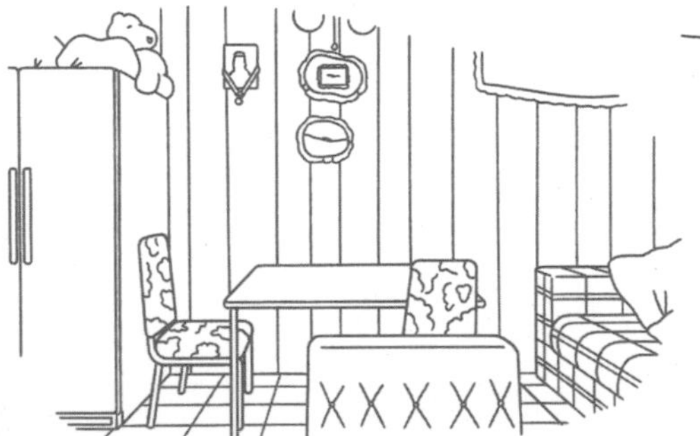
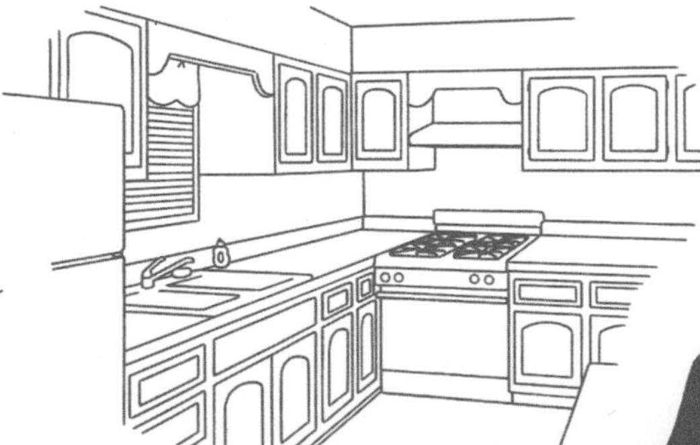
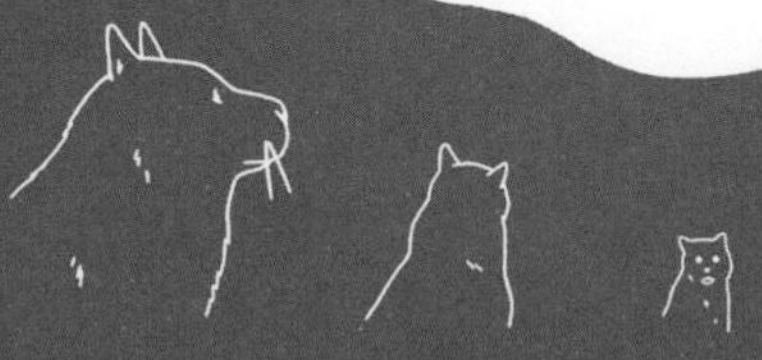
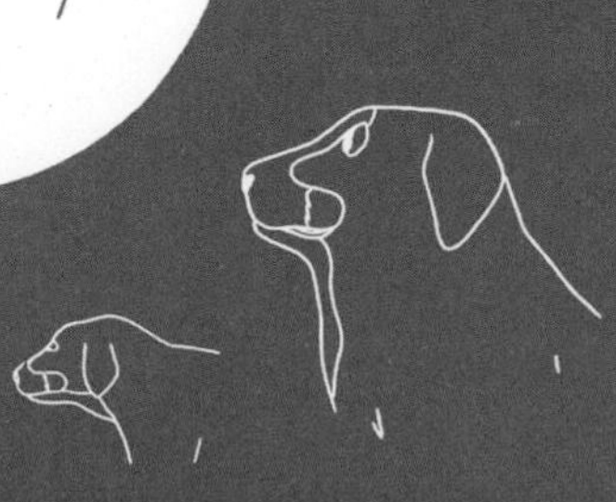

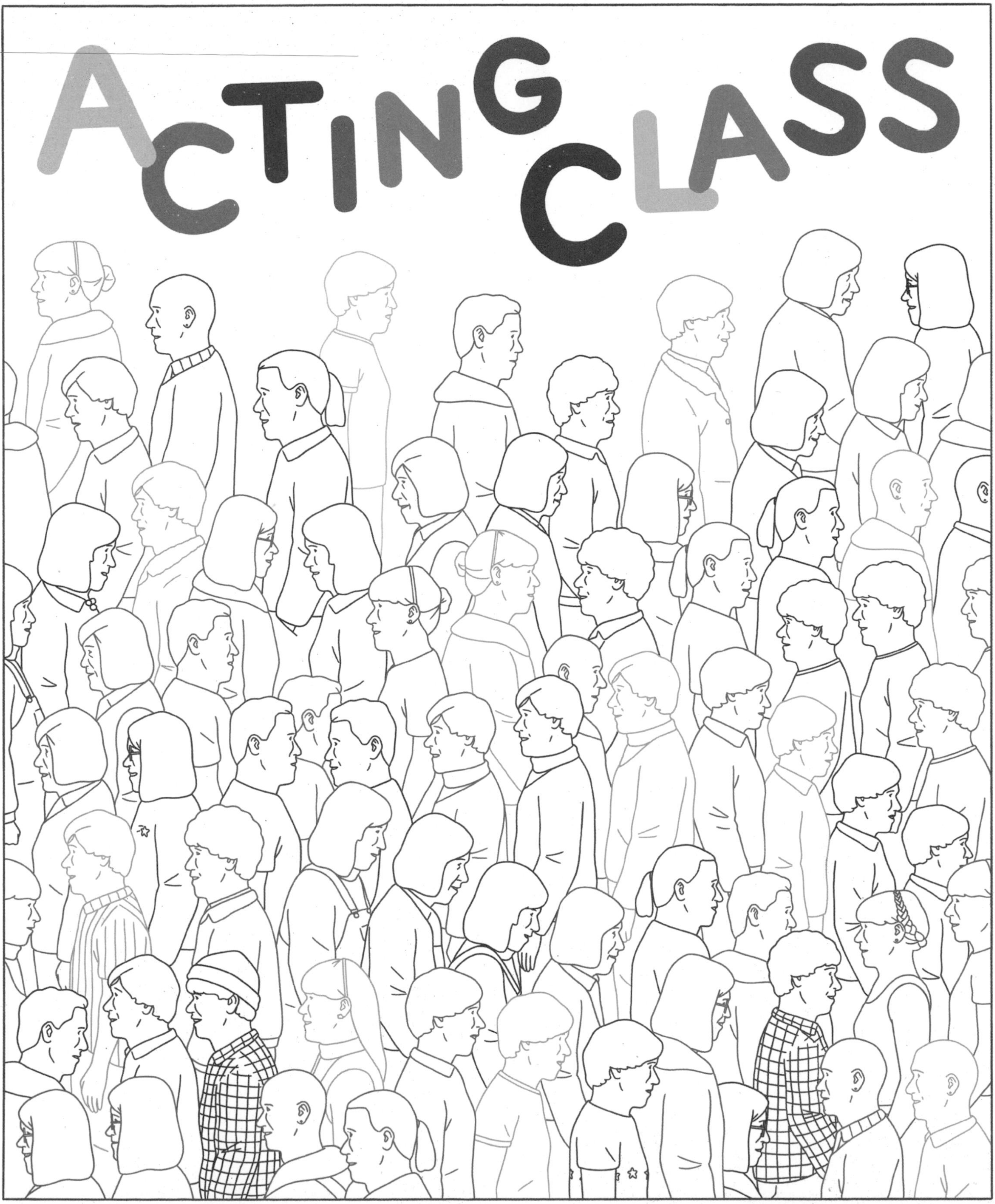
ACTING CLASS

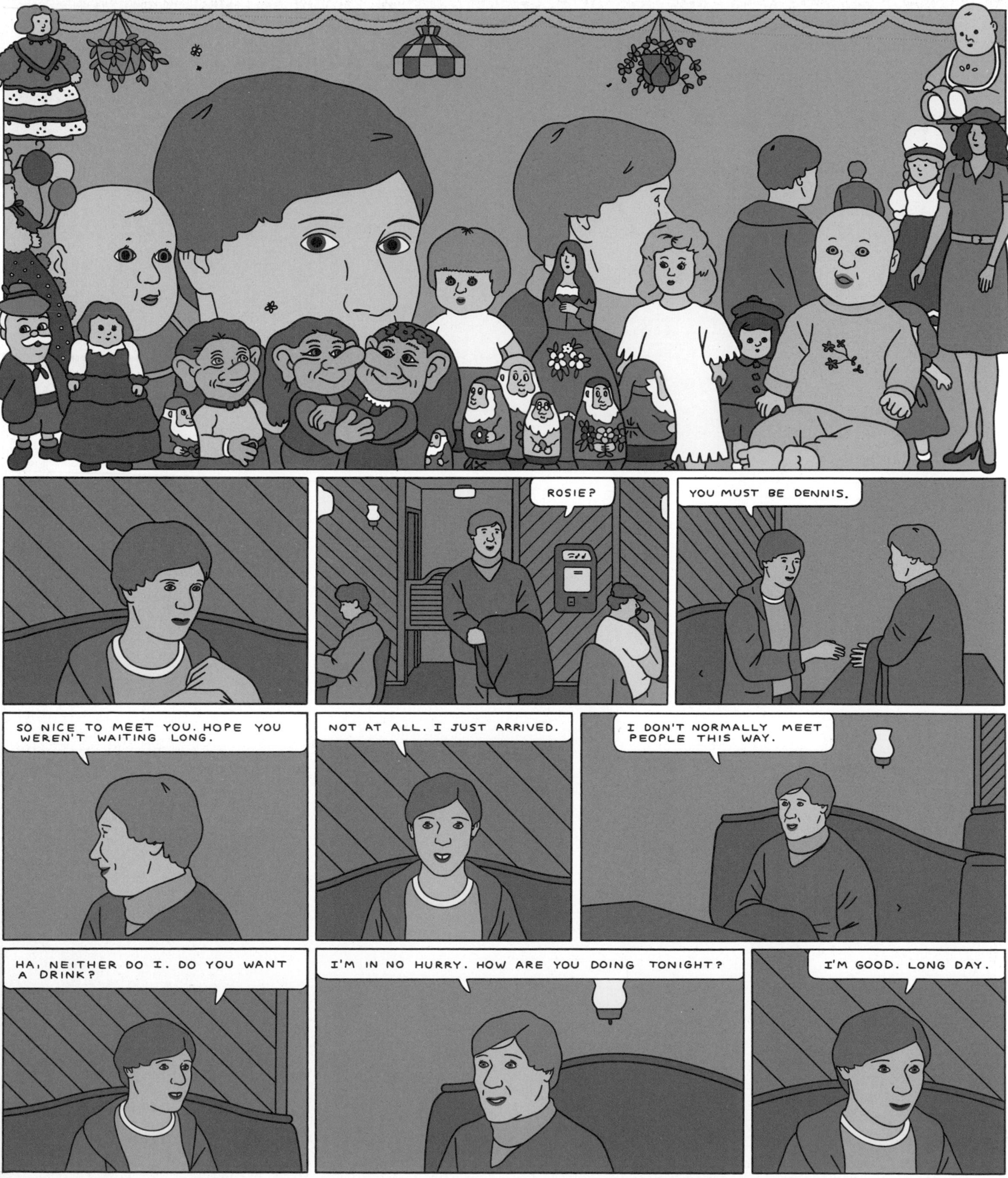
ROSIE?
YOU MUST BE DENNIS.
SO NICE TO MEET YOU. HOPE YOU WEREN'T WAITING LONG.
NOT AT ALL. I JUST ARRIVED.
I DON'T NORMALLY MEET PEOPLE THIS WAY.
HA, NEITHER DO I. DO YOU WANT A DRINK?
I'M IN NO HURRY. HOW ARE YOU DOING TONIGHT?
I'M GOOD. LONG DAY.

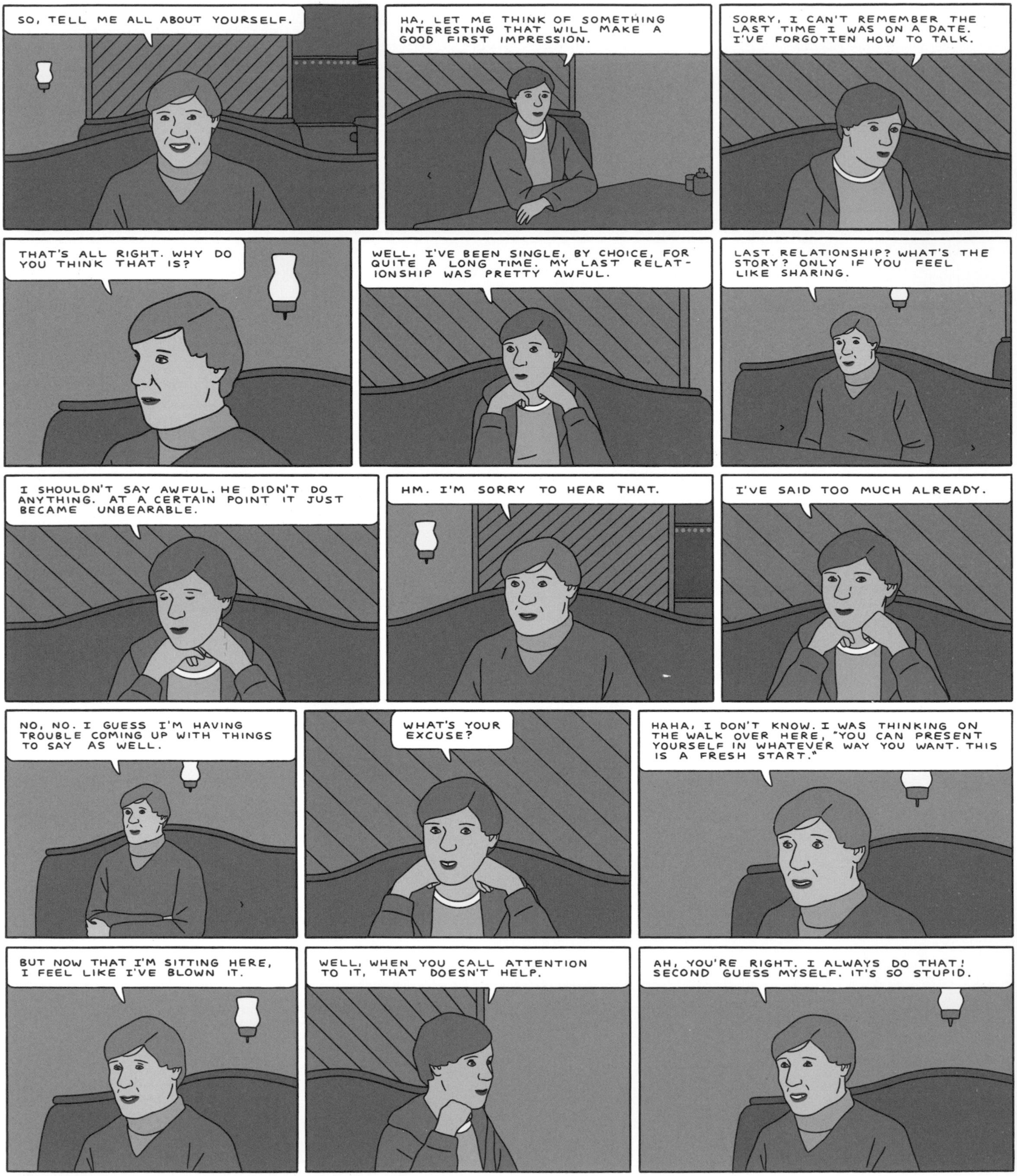
SO, TELL ME ALL ABOUT YOURSELF.
HA, LET ME THINK OF SOMETHING INTERESTING THAT WILL MAKE A GOOD FIRST IMPRESSION.
SORRY, I CAN'T REMEMBER THE LAST TIME I WAS ON A DATE. I'VE FORGOTTEN HOW TO TALK.
THAT'S ALL RIGHT. WHY DO YOU THINK THAT IS?
WELL, I'VE BEEN SINGLE, BY CHOICE, FOR QUITE A LONG TIME. MY LAST RELAT-IONSHIP WAS PRETTY AWFUL.
LAST RELATIONSHIP? WHAT'S THE STORY? ONLY IF YOU FEEL LIKE SHARING.
I SHOULDN'T SAY AWFUL. HE DIDN'T DO ANYTHING. AT A CERTAIN POINT IT JUST BECAME UNBEARABLE.
HM. I'M SORRY TO HEAR THAT.
I'VE SAID TOO MUCH ALREADY.
NO, NO. I GUESS I'M HAVING TROUBLE COMING UP WITH THINGS TO SAY AS WELL.
WHAT'S YOUR EXCUSE?
HAHA, I DON'T KNOW. I WAS THINKING ON THE WALK OVER HERE, "YOU CAN PRESENT YOURSELF IN WHATEVER WAY YOU WANT. THIS IS A FRESH START."
BUT NOW THAT I'M SITTING HERE, I FEEL LIKE I'VE BLOWN IT.
WELL, WHEN YOU CALL ATTENTION TO IT, THAT DOESN'T HELP.
AH, YOU'RE RIGHT. I ALWAYS DO THAT! SECOND GUESS MYSELF. IT'S SO STUPID.

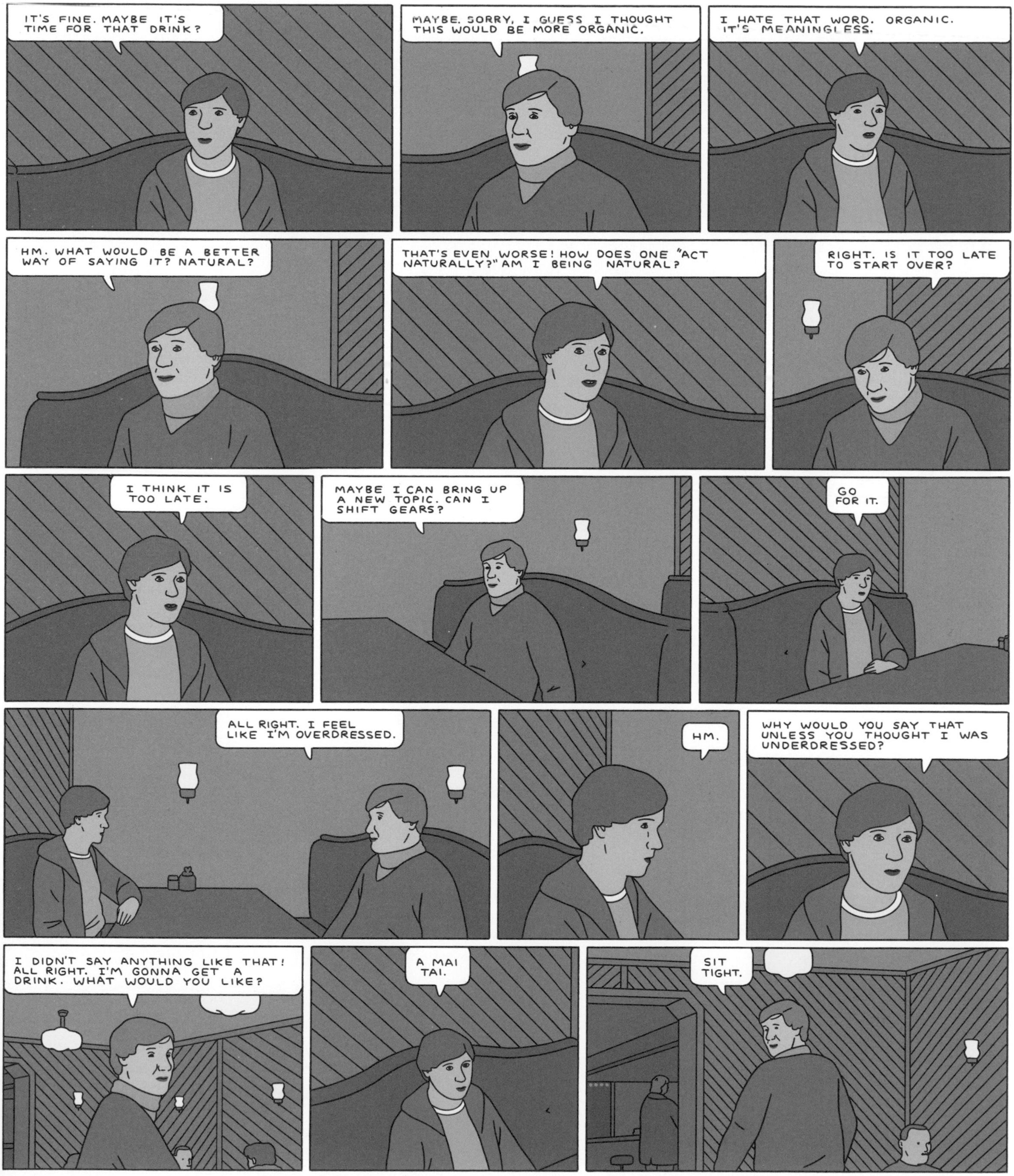
IT'S FINE. MAYBE IT'S TIME FOR THAT DRINK?
MAYBE. SORRY, I GUESS I THOUGHT THIS WOULD BE MORE ORGANIC.
I HATE THAT WORD. ORGANIC. IT'S MEANINGLESS.
HM. WHAT WOULD BE A BETTER WAY OF SAYING IT? NATURAL?
THAT'S EVEN WORSE! HOW DOES ONE "ACT NATURALLY?" AM I BEING NATURAL?
RIGHT. IS IT TOO LATE TO START OVER?
I THINK IT IS TOO LATE.
MAYBE I CAN BRING UP A NEW TOPIC. CAN I SHIFT GEARS?
GO FOR IT.
ALL RIGHT. I FEEL LIKE I'M OVERDRESSED.
HM.
WHY WOULD YOU SAY THAT UNLESS YOU THOUGHT I WAS UNDERDRESSED?
I DIDN'T SAY ANYTHING LIKE THAT! ALL RIGHT. I'M GONNA GET A DRINK. WHAT WOULD YOU LIKE?
A MAI TAI.
SIT TIGHT.

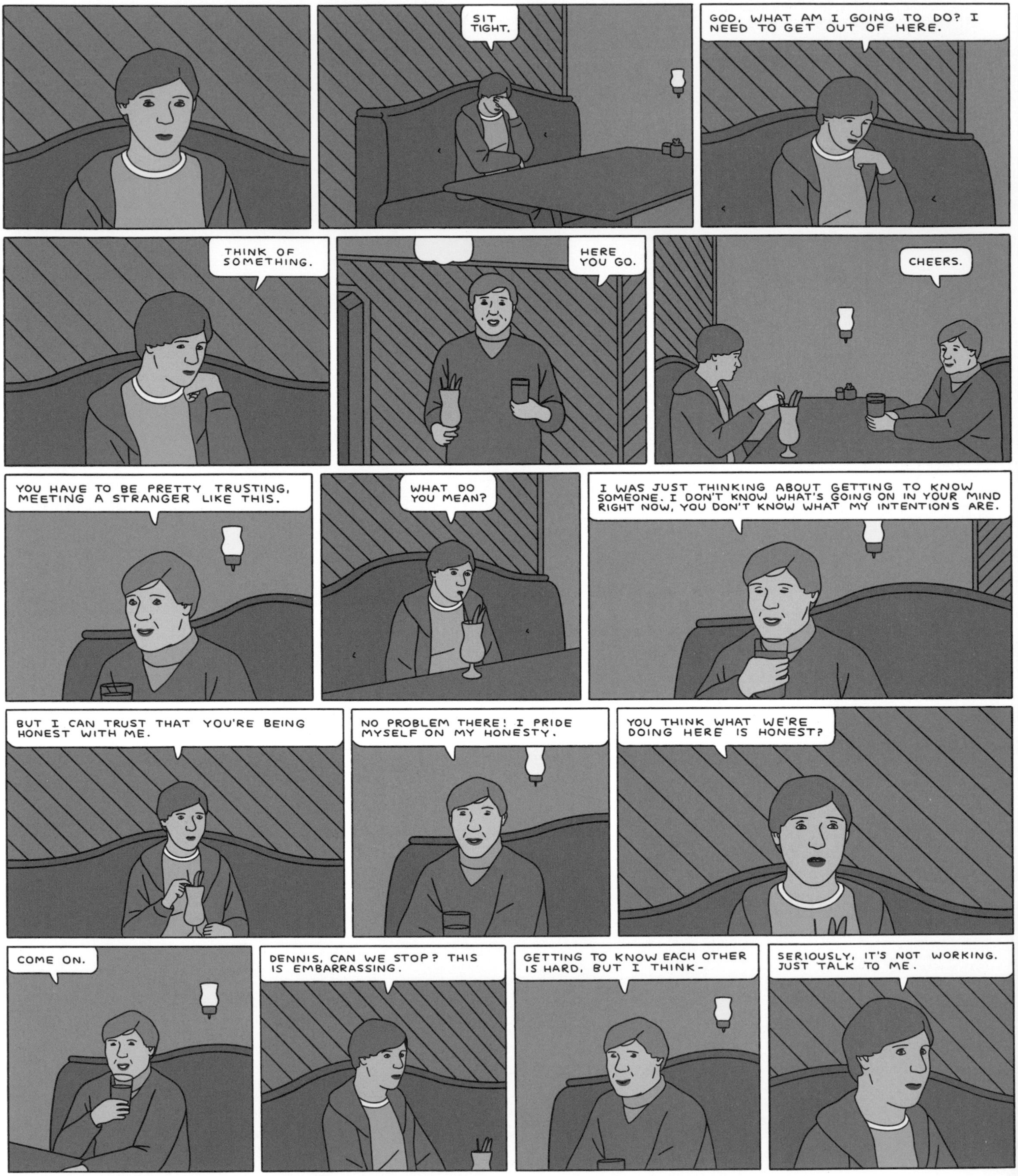
SIT TIGHT.
GOD, WHAT AM I GOING TO DO? I NEED TO GET OUT OF HERE.
THINK OF SOMETHING.
HERE YOU GO.
CHEERS.
YOU HAVE TO BE PRETTY TRUSTING, MEETING A STRANGER LIKE THIS.
WHAT DO YOU MEAN?
I WAS JUST THINKING ABOUT GETTING TO KNOW SOMEONE. I DON'T KNOW WHAT'S GOING ON IN YOUR MIND RIGHT NOW, YOU DON'T KNOW WHAT MY INTENTIONS ARE.
BUT I CAN TRUST THAT YOU'RE BEING HONEST WITH ME.
NO PROBLEM THERE! I PRIDE MYSELF ON MY HONESTY.
YOU THINK WHAT WE'RE DOING HERE IS HONEST?
COME ON.
DENNIS, CAN WE STOP? THIS IS EMBARRASSING.
GETTING TO KNOW EACH OTHER IS HARD, BUT I THINK-
SERIOUSLY, IT'S NOT WORKING. JUST TALK TO ME.

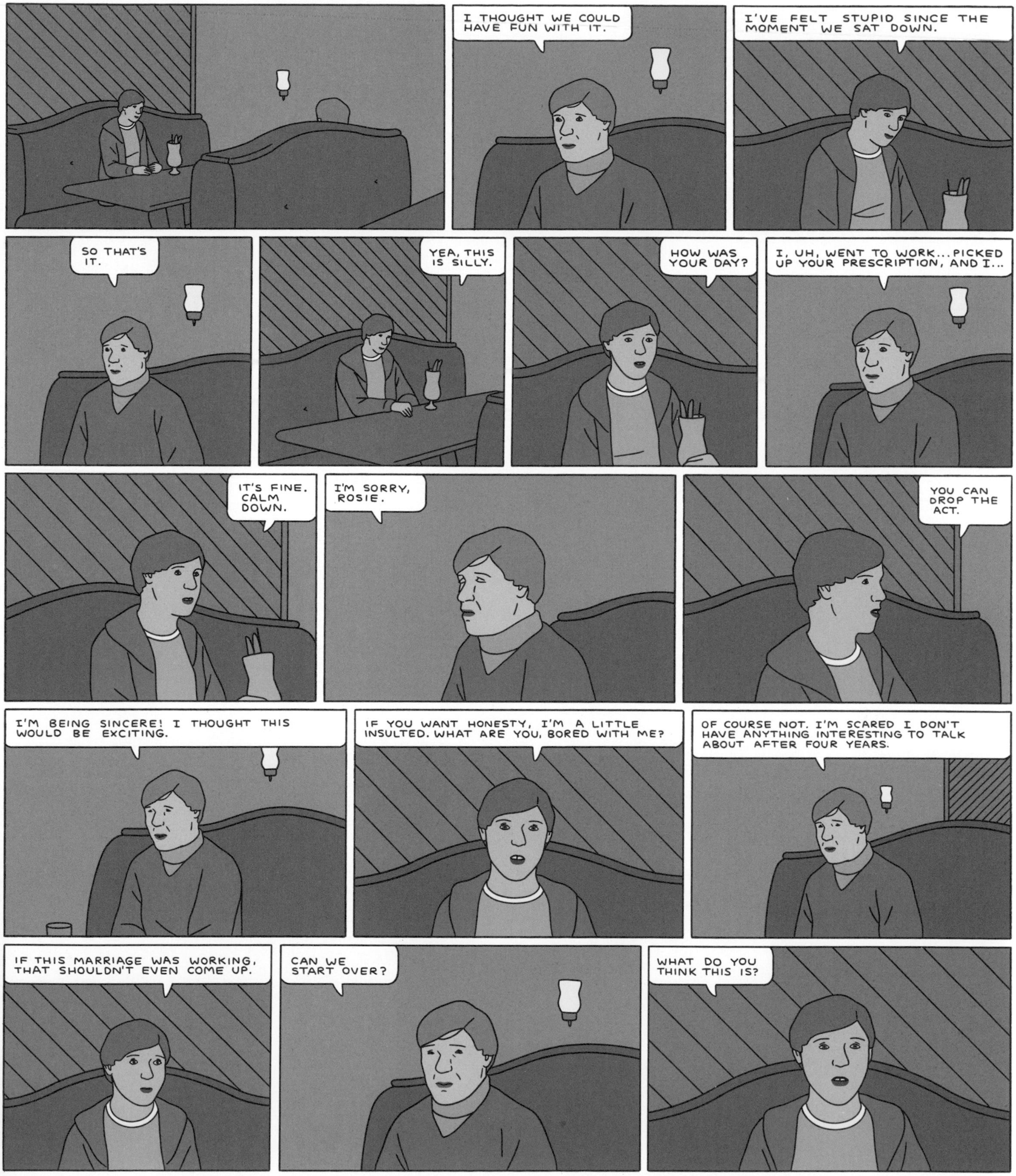
I THOUGHT WE COULD HAVE FUN WITH IT.
I'VE FELT STUPID SINCE THE MOMENT WE SAT DOWN.
SO THAT'S IT.
YEA, THIS IS SILLY.
HOW WAS YOUR DAY?
I, UH, WENT TO WORK... PICKED UP YOUR PRESCRIPTION, AND I...
IT'S FINE. CALM DOWN.
I'M SORRY, ROSIE.
YOU CAN DROP THE ACT.
I'M BEING SINCERE! I THOUGHT THIS WOULD BE EXCITING.
IF YOU WANT HONESTY, I'M A LITTLE INSULTED. WHAT ARE YOU, BORED WITH ME?
OF COURSE NOT. I'M SCARED I DON'T HAVE ANYTHING INTERESTING TO TALK ABOUT AFTER FOUR YEARS.
IF THIS MARRIAGE WAS WORKING, THAT SHOULDN'T EVEN COME UP.
CAN WE START OVER?
WHAT DO YOU THINK THIS IS?

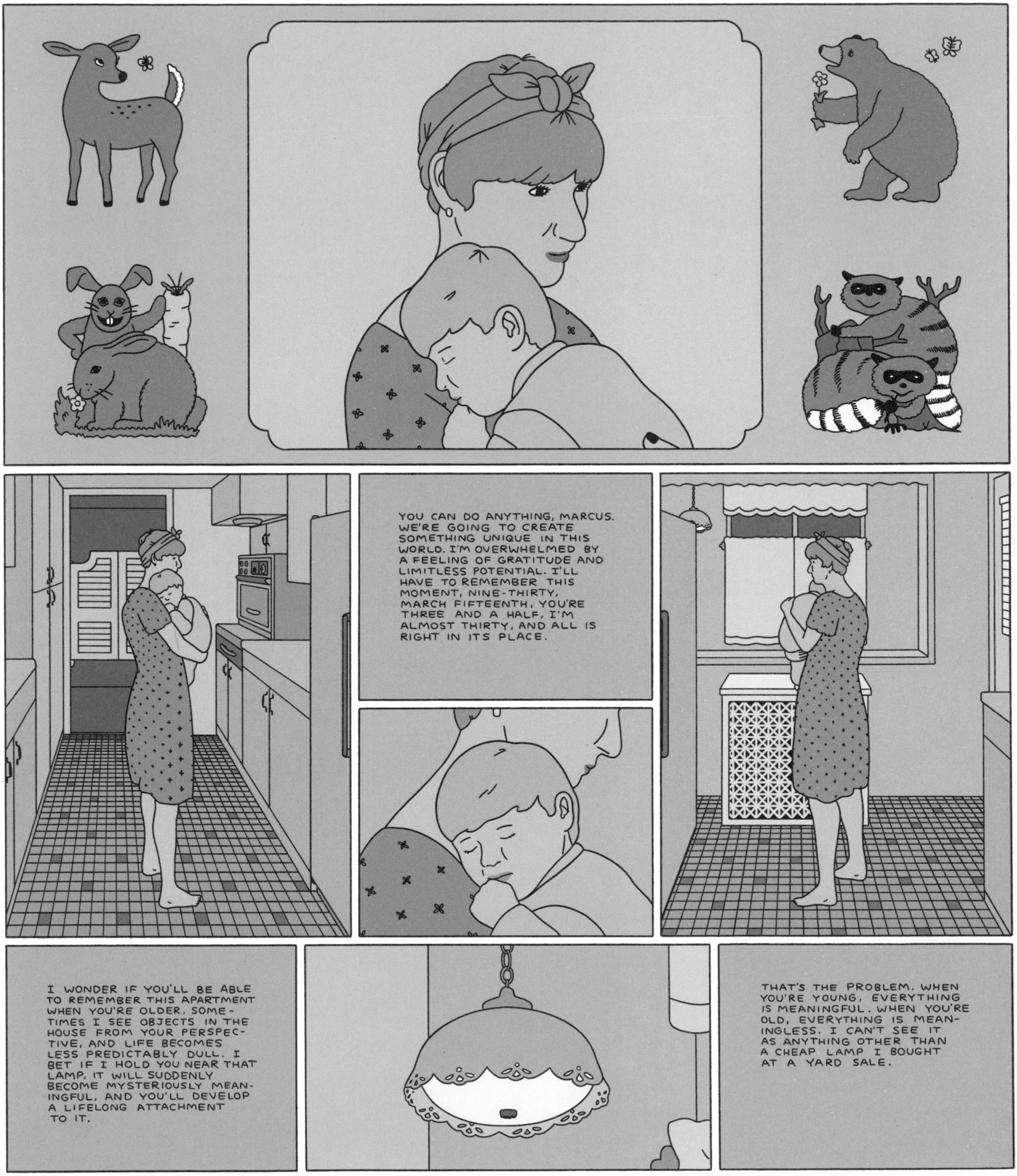
YOU CAN DO ANYTHING, MARCUS. WE'RE GOING TO CREATE SOMETHING UNIQUE IN THIS WORLD. I'M OVERWHELMED BY A FEELING OF GRATITUDE AND LIMITLESS POTENTIAL. I'LL HAVE TO REMEMBER THIS MOMENT, NINE-THIRTY, MARCH FIFTEENTH, YOU'RE THREE AND A HALF, I'M ALMOST THIRTY, AND ALL IS RIGHT IN ITS PLACE.
I WONDER IF YOU'LL BE ABLE TO REMEMBER THIS APARTMENT WHEN YOU'RE OLDER. SOME-TIMES I SEE OBJECTS IN THE HOUSE FROM YOUR PERSPEC-TIVE, AND LIFE BECOMES LESS PREDICTABLY DULL. I BET IF I HOLD YOU NEAR THAT LAMP, IT WILL SUDDENLY BECOME MYSTERIOUSLY MEAN-INGFUL, AND YOU'LL DEVELOP A LIFELONG ATTACHMENT TO IT.
THAT'S THE PROBLEM. WHEN YOU'RE YOUNG, EVERYTHING IS MEANINGFUL. WHEN YOU'RE OLD, EVERYTHING IS MEAN-INGLESS. I CAN'T SEE IT AS ANYTHING OTHER THAN A CHEAP LAMP I BOUGHT AT A YARD SALE.

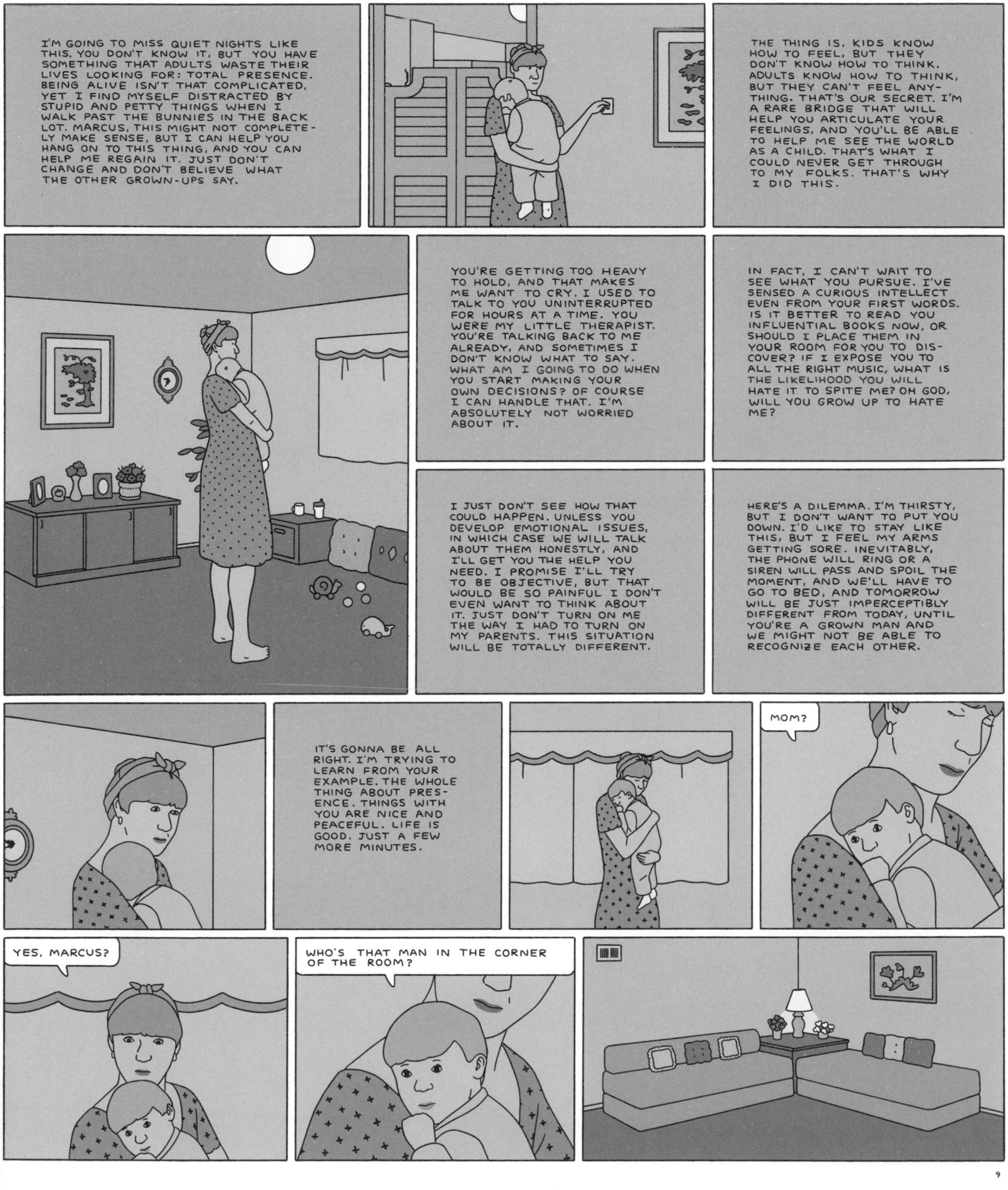

I'M GOING TO MISS QUIET NIGHTS LIKE THIS. YOU DON'T KNOW IT, BUT YOU HAVE SOMETHING THAT ADULTS WASTE THEIR LIVES LOOKING FOR: TOTAL PRESENCE. BEING ALIVE ISN'T THAT COMPLICATED, YET I FIND MYSELF DISTRACTED BY STUPID AND PETTY THINGS WHEN I WALK PAST THE BUNNIES IN THE BACK LOT. MARCUS, THIS MIGHT NOT COMPLETELY MAKE SENSE, BUT I CAN HELP YOU HANG ON TO THIS THING, AND YOU CAN HELP ME REGAIN IT. JUST DON'T CHANGE AND DON'T BELIEVE WHAT THE OTHER GROWN-UPS SAY.
THE THING IS, KIDS KNOW HOW TO FEEL, BUT THEY DON'T KNOW HOW TO THINK. ADULTS KNOW HOW TO THINK, BUT THEY CAN'T FEEL ANYTHING. THAT'S OUR SECRET. I'M A RARE BRIDGE THAT WILL HELP YOU ARTICULATE YOUR FEELINGS, AND YOU'LL BE ABLE TO HELP ME SEE THE WORLD AS A CHILD. THAT'S WHAT I COULD NEVER GET THROUGH TO MY FOLKS. THAT'S WHY I DID THIS.
YOU'RE GETTING TOO HEAVY TO HOLD, AND THAT MAKES ME WANT TO CRY. I USED TO TALK TO YOU UNINTERRUPTED FOR HOURS AT A TIME. YOU WERE MY LITTLE THERAPIST. YOU'RE TALKING BACK TO ME ALREADY, AND SOMETIMES I DON'T KNOW WHAT TO SAY. WHAT AM I GOING TO DO WHEN YOU START MAKING YOUR OWN DECISIONS? OF COURSE I CAN HANDLE THAT. I'M ABSOLUTELY NOT WORRIED ABOUT IT.
IN FACT, I CAN'T WAIT TO SEE WHAT YOU PURSUE. I'VE SENSED A CURIOUS INTELLECT EVEN FROM YOUR FIRST WORDS. IS IT BETTER TO READ YOU INFLUENTIAL BOOKS NOW, OR SHOULD I PLACE THEM IN YOUR ROOM FOR YOU TO DISCOVER? IF I EXPOSE YOU TO ALL THE RIGHT MUSIC, WHAT IS THE LIKELIHOOD YOU WILL HATE IT TO SPITE ME? OH GOD, WILL YOU GROW UP TO HATE ME?
I JUST DON'T SEE HOW THAT COULD HAPPEN. UNLESS YOU DEVELOP EMOTIONAL ISSUES, IN WHICH CASE WE WILL TALK ABOUT THEM HONESTLY, AND I'LL GET YOU THE HELP YOU NEED. I PROMISE I'LL TRY TO BE OBJECTIVE, BUT THAT WOULD BE SO PAINFUL I DON'T EVEN WANT TO THINK ABOUT IT. JUST DON'T TURN ON ME THE WAY I HAD TO TURN ON MY PARENTS. THIS SITUATION WILL BE TOTALLY DIFFERENT.
HERE'S A DILEMMA. I'M THIRSTY, BUT I DON'T WANT TO PUT YOU DOWN. I'D LIKE TO STAY LIKE THIS, BUT I FEEL MY ARMS GETTING SORE. INEVITABLY, THE PHONE WILL RING OR A SIREN WILL PASS AND SPOIL THE MOMENT, AND WE'LL HAVE TO GO TO BED, AND TOMORROW WILL BE JUST IMPERCEPTIBLY DIFFERENT FROM TODAY, UNTIL YOU'RE A GROWN MAN AND WE MIGHT NOT BE ABLE TO RECOGNIZE EACH OTHER.
IT'S GONNA BE ALL RIGHT. I'M TRYING TO LEARN FROM YOUR EXAMPLE. THE WHOLE THING ABOUT PRESENCE. THINGS WITH YOU ARE NICE AND PEACEFUL. LIFE IS GOOD. JUST A FEW MORE MINUTES.
MOM?
YES, MARCUS?
WHO'S THAT MAN IN THE CORNER OF THE ROOM?

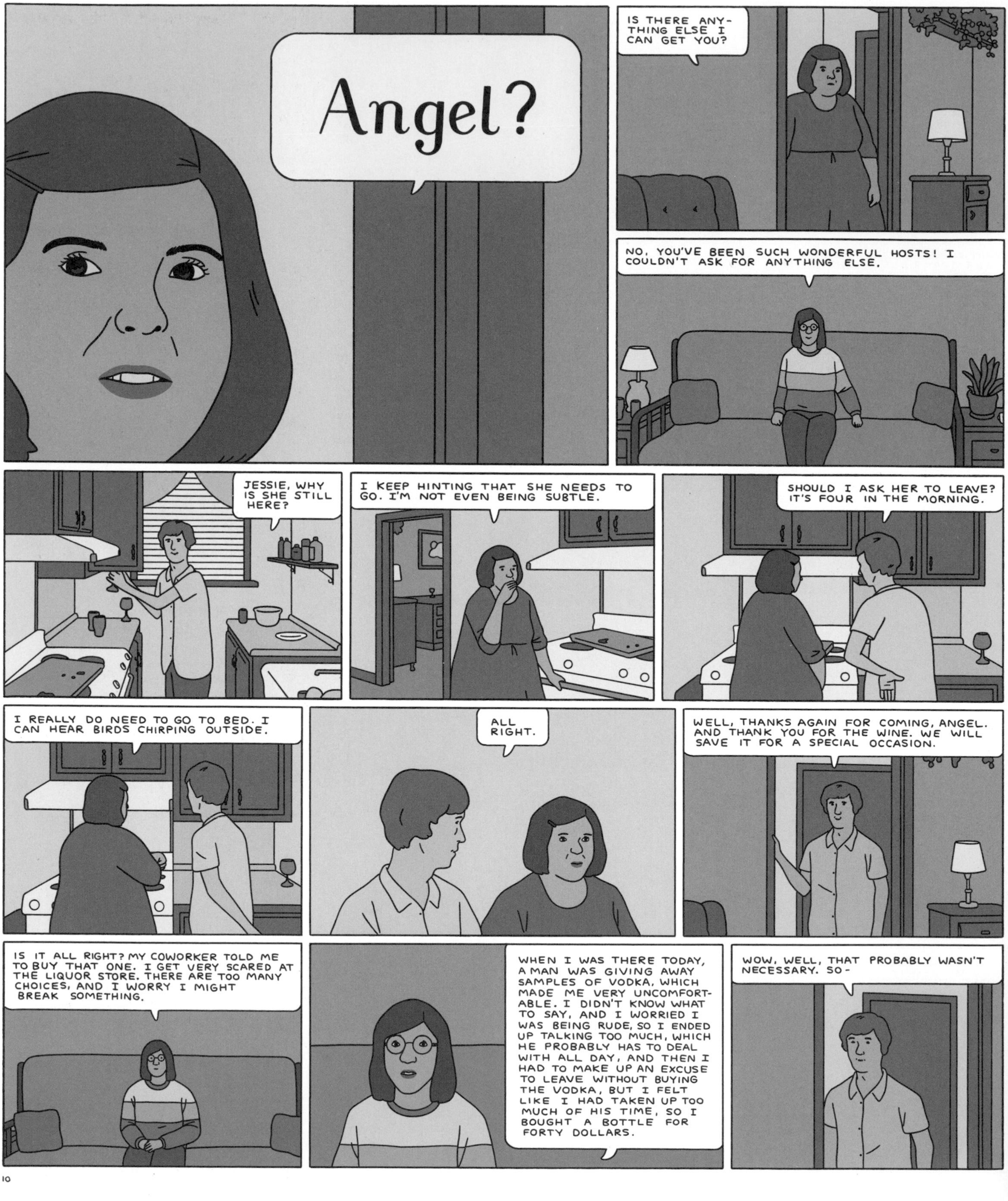
Angel?
IS THERE ANYTHING ELSE I CAN GET YOU?
NO, YOU'VE BEEN SUCH WONDERFUL HOSTS! I COULDN'T ASK FOR ANYTHING ELSE.
JESSIE, WHY IS SHE STILL HERE?
I KEEP HINTING THAT SHE NEEDS TO GO. I'M NOT EVEN BEING SUBTLE.
SHOULD I ASK HER TO LEAVE? IT'S FOUR IN THE MORNING.
I REALLY DO NEED TO GO TO BED. I CAN HEAR BIRDS CHIRPING OUTSIDE.
ALL RIGHT.
WELL, THANKS AGAIN FOR COMING, ANGEL. AND THANK YOU FOR THE WINE. WE WILL SAVE IT FOR A SPECIAL OCCASION.
IS IT ALL RIGHT? MY COWORKER TOLD ME TO BUY THAT ONE. I GET VERY SCARED AT THE LIQUOR STORE. THERE ARE TOO MANY CHOICES, AND I WORRY I MIGHT BREAK SOMETHING.
WHEN I WAS THERE TODAY, A MAN WAS GIVING AWAY SAMPLES OF VODKA, WHICH MADE ME VERY UNCOMFORTABLE. I DIDN'T KNOW WHAT TO SAY, AND I WORRIED I WAS BEING RUDE, SO I ENDED UP TALKING TOO MUCH, WHICH HE PROBABLY HAS TO DEAL WITH ALL DAY, AND THEN I HAD TO MAKE UP AN EXCUSE TO LEAVE WITHOUT BUYING THE VODKA, BUT I FELT LIKE I HAD TAKEN UP TOO MUCH OF HIS TIME, SO I BOUGHT A BOTTLE FOR FORTY DOLLARS.
WOW, WELL, THAT PROBABLY WASN'T NECESSARY. SO-

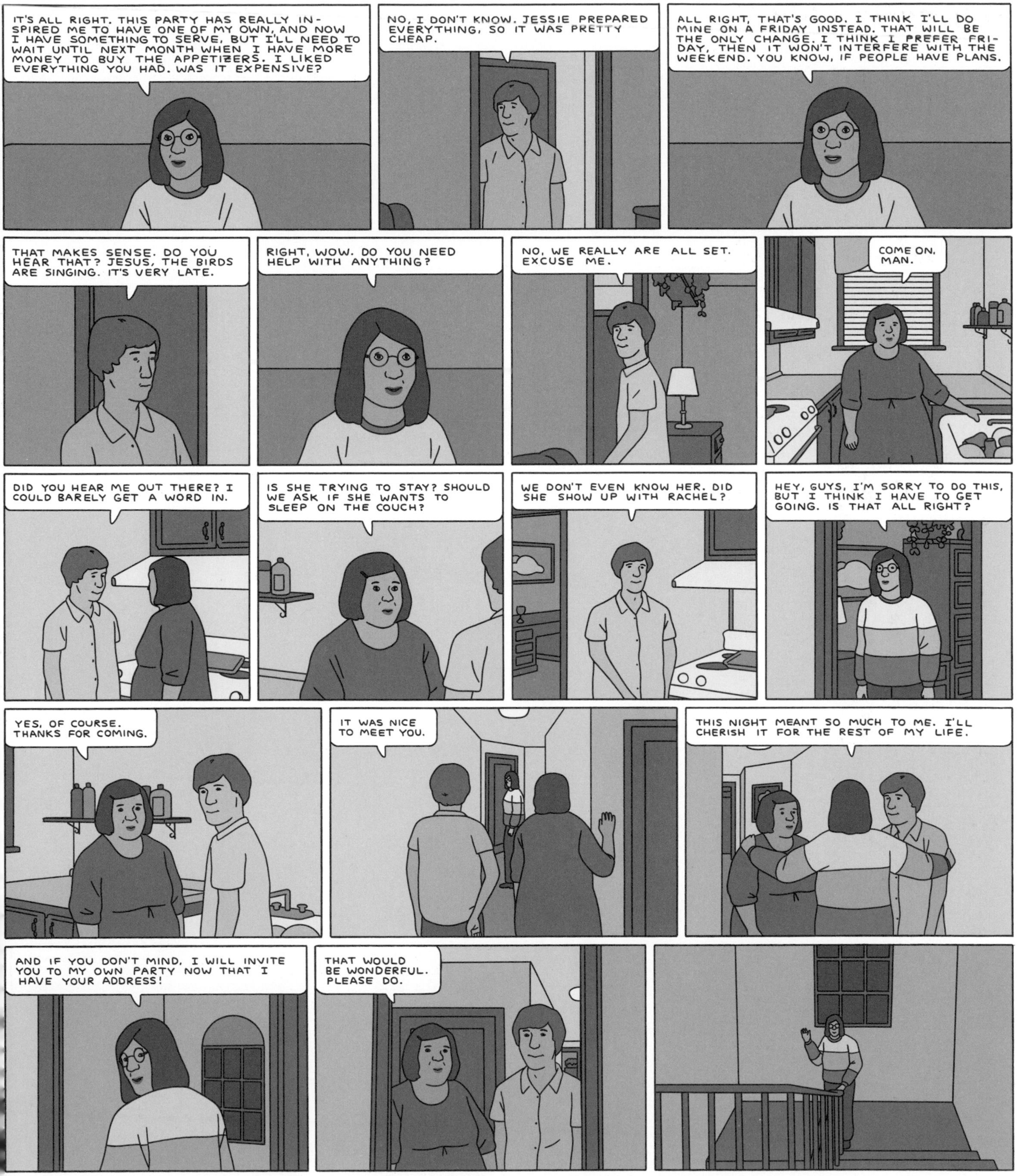
IT'S ALL RIGHT. THIS PARTY HAS REALLY IN-SPIRED ME TO HAVE ONE OF MY OWN, AND NOW I HAVE SOMETHING TO SERVE, BUT I'LL NEED TO WAIT UNTIL NEXT MONTH WHEN I HAVE MORE MONEY TO BUY THE APPETIZERS. I LIKED EVERYTHING YOU HAD. WAS IT EXPENSIVE?
NO, I DON'T KNOW. JESSIE PREPARED EVERYTHING, SO IT WAS PRETTY CHEAP.
ALL RIGHT, THAT'S GOOD. I THINK I'LL DO MINE ON A FRIDAY INSTEAD. THAT WILL BE THE ONLY CHANGE. I THINK I PREFER FRI-DAY, THEN IT WON'T INTERFERE WITH THE WEEKEND. YOU KNOW, IF PEOPLE HAVE PLANS.
THAT MAKES SENSE. DO YOU HEAR THAT? JESUS, THE BIRDS ARE SINGING. IT'S VERY LATE.
RIGHT, WOW. DO YOU NEED HELP WITH ANYTHING?
NO, WE REALLY ARE ALL SET. EXCUSE ME.
COME ON, MAN.
DID YOU HEAR ME OUT THERE? I COULD BARELY GET A WORD IN.
IS SHE TRYING TO STAY? SHOULD WE ASK IF SHE WANTS TO SLEEP ON THE COUCH?
WE DON'T EVEN KNOW HER. DID SHE SHOW UP WITH RACHEL?
HEY, GUYS, I'M SORRY TO DO THIS, BUT I THINK I HAVE TO GET GOING. IS THAT ALL RIGHT?
YES, OF COURSE. THANKS FOR COMING.
IT WAS NICE TO MEET YOU.
THIS NIGHT MEANT SO MUCH TO ME. I'LL CHERISH IT FOR THE REST OF MY LIFE.
AND IF YOU DON'T MIND, I WILL INVITE YOU TO MY OWN PARTY NOW THAT I HAVE YOUR ADDRESS!
THAT WOULD BE WONDERFUL. PLEASE DO.

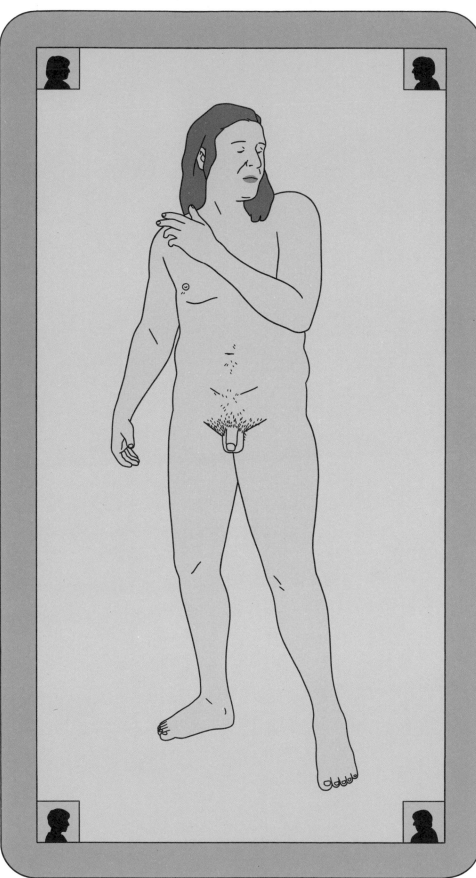

HOW ARE YOU DOING, HONEY? CAN YOU SEE THE MODEL?

WOW, THAT'S BEAUTIFUL. YOU ARE SUCH A FAST LEARNER.

CAN I MAKE A SUGGESTION? TRY TO PAY ATTENTION TO THE FEET. IMAGINE THE WEIGHT OF A HUMAN BODY AND HOW THE FEET ABSORB THAT WEIGHT.

THAT'S GREAT. HERE, HAVE SOME WATER.

CAN'T FORGET TO STAY HYDRATED. I KNOW IT'S EASY TO GET LOST IN THE WORK.

WE'RE SO HAPPY YOU WERE ABLE TO SIT IN TONIGHT. YOUR GRANDMA IS THE CLASS SUPERSTAR.

SO, WHAT DID YOU THINK?

OH, I HAD A LOT OF FUN.

DO YOU THINK YOU'LL SIGN UP PERMANENTLY?

I'M NOT SO SURE.

I'M TELLING YOU, BETH HAS ALWAYS BEEN A LITTLE SPONGE. SHE CAN DO ANYTHING.

JACK OF ALL TRADES? THAT'S A GOOD PROBLEM TO HAVE.

GOTTA RUN, BYE.

RIGHT. WE JUST NEED TO FIGURE OUT WHAT SHE IS GOING TO MASTER.

SORRY, HONEY, I'M JUST GOING TO TALK ABOUT YOU LIKE YOU'RE NOT HERE.

THAT'S ALL RIGHT.

THANKS, EVERYBODY.

THANK YOU, THOMAS. GREAT JOB TONIGHT!

THOMAS, MEET MY GRANDDAUGHTER. THIS IS BETH.

HOW DO YOU DO IT? I DON'T UNDERSTAND. YOU LOOK SO COMFORTABLE IN YOUR BODY.

YOU KNOW, I DON'T KNOW. IT FEELS GOOD.

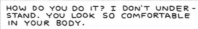

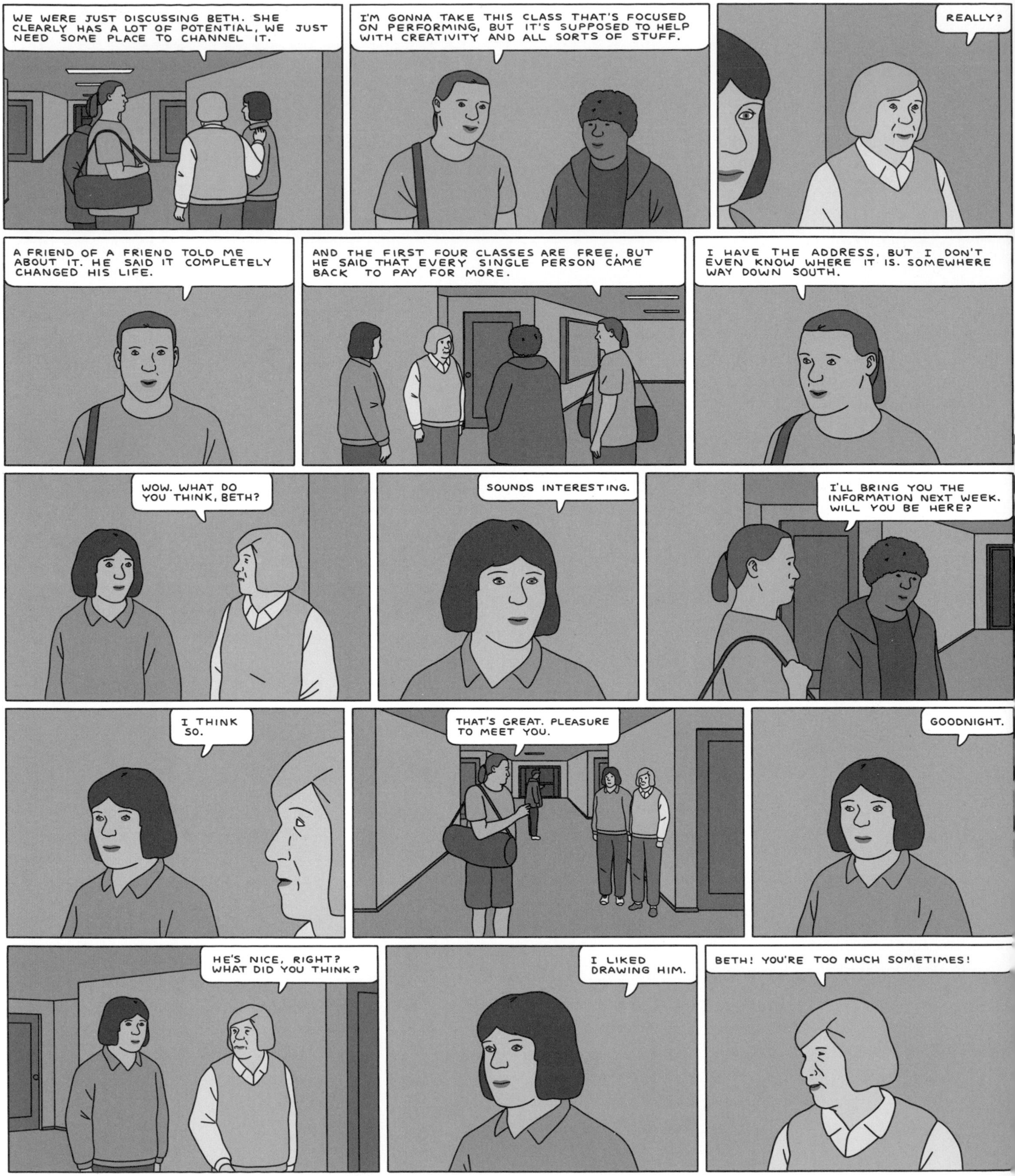
WE WERE JUST DISCUSSING BETH. SHE CLEARLY HAS A LOT OF POTENTIAL, WE JUST NEED SOME PLACE TO CHANNEL IT.
I'M GONNA TAKE THIS CLASS THAT'S FOCUSED ON PERFORMING, BUT IT'S SUPPOSED TO HELP WITH CREATIVITY AND ALL SORTS OF STUFF.
REALLY?
A FRIEND OF A FRIEND TOLD ME ABOUT IT. HE SAID IT COMPLETELY CHANGED HIS LIFE.
AND THE FIRST FOUR CLASSES ARE FREE, BUT HE SAID THAT EVERY SINGLE PERSON CAME BACK TO PAY FOR MORE.
I HAVE THE ADDRESS, BUT I DON'T EVEN KNOW WHERE IT IS. SOMEWHERE WAY DOWN SOUTH.
WOW. WHAT DO YOU THINK, BETH?
SOUNDS INTERESTING.
I'LL BRING YOU THE INFORMATION NEXT WEEK. WILL YOU BE HERE?
I THINK SO.
THAT'S GREAT. PLEASURE TO MEET YOU.
GOODNIGHT.
HE'S NICE, RIGHT? WHAT DID YOU THINK?
I LIKED DRAWING HIM.
BETH! YOU'RE TOO MUCH SOMETIMES!

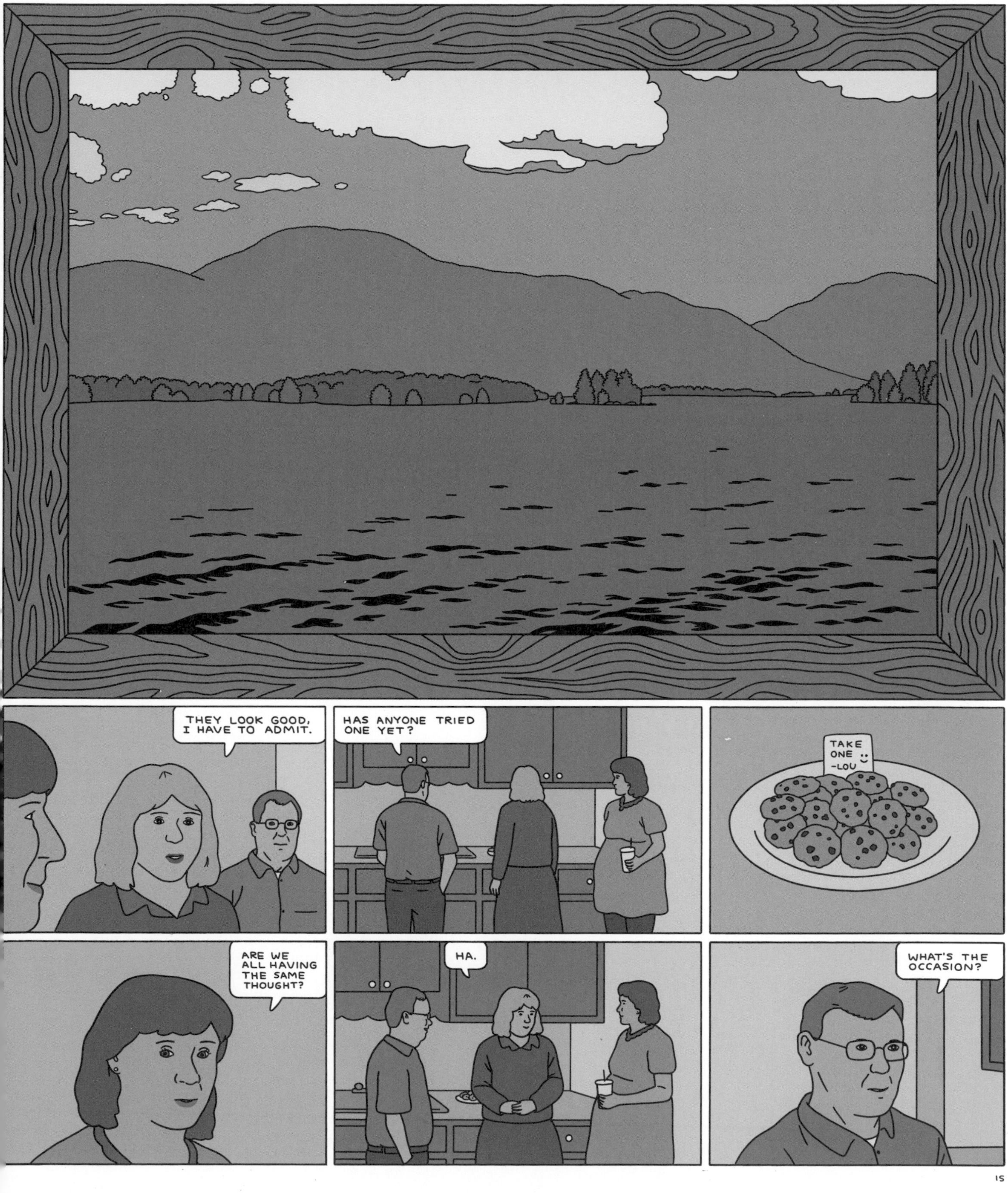
THEY LOOK GOOD, I HAVE TO ADMIT.
HAS ANYONE TRIED ONE YET?
TAKE ONE -LOU
ARE WE ALL HAVING THE SAME THOUGHT?
HA.
WHAT'S THE OCCASION?

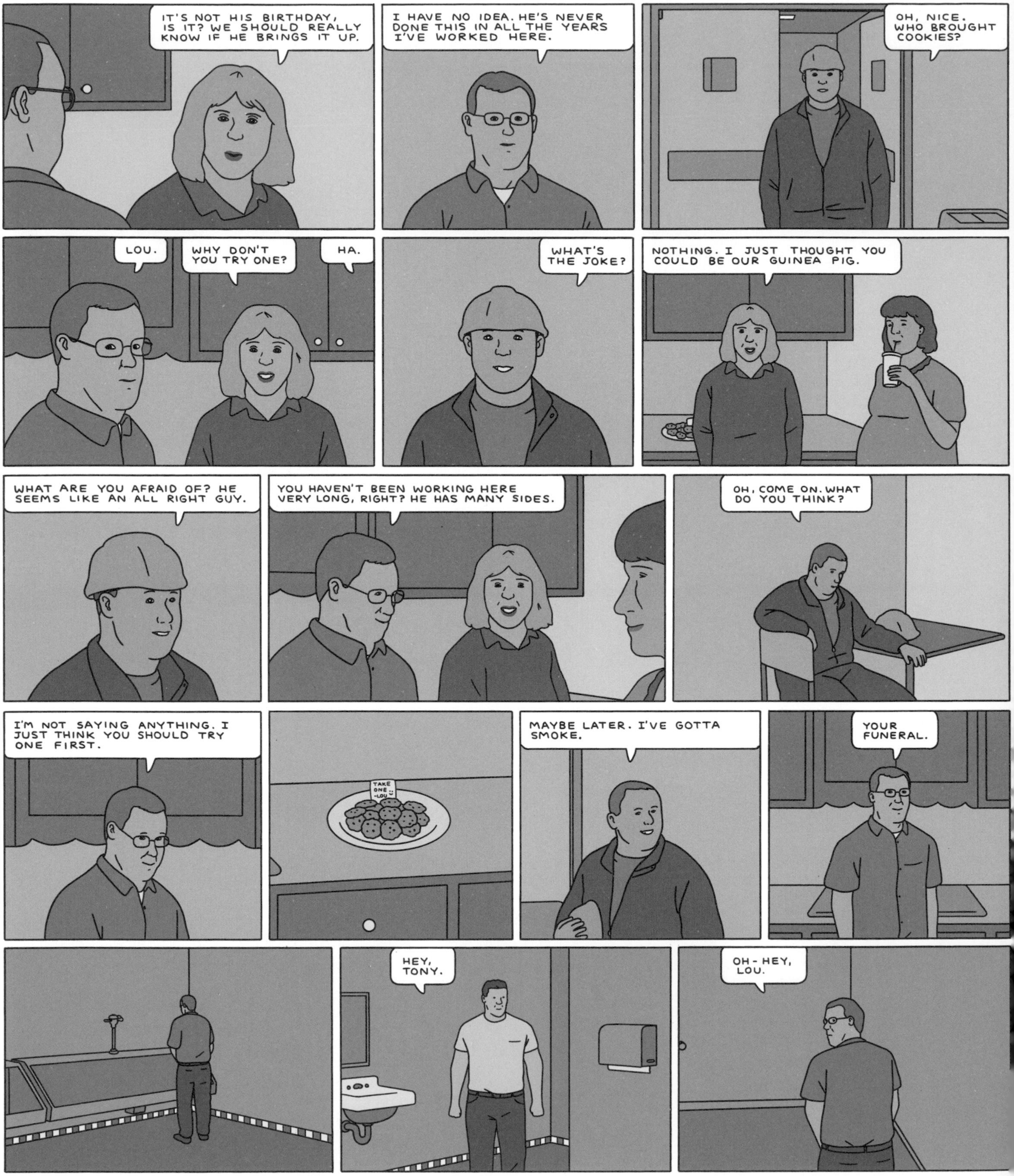
IT'S NOT HIS BIRTHDAY, IS IT? WE SHOULD REALLY KNOW IF HE BRINGS IT UP.
I HAVE NO IDEA. HE'S NEVER DONE THIS IN ALL THE YEARS I'VE WORKED HERE.
OH, NICE. WHO BROUGHT COOKIES?
LOU.
WHY DON'T YOU TRY ONE?
HA.
WHAT'S THE JOKE?
NOTHING. I JUST THOUGHT YOU COULD BE OUR GUINEA PIG.
WHAT ARE YOU AFRAID OF? HE SEEMS LIKE AN ALL RIGHT GUY.
YOU HAVEN'T BEEN WORKING HERE VERY LONG, RIGHT? HE HAS MANY SIDES.
OH, COME ON. WHAT DO YOU THINK?
I'M NOT SAYING ANYTHING. I JUST THINK YOU SHOULD TRY ONE FIRST.
TAKE ONE -LOU
MAYBE LATER. I'VE GOTTA SMOKE.
YOUR FUNERAL.
HEY, TONY.
OH - HEY, LOU.

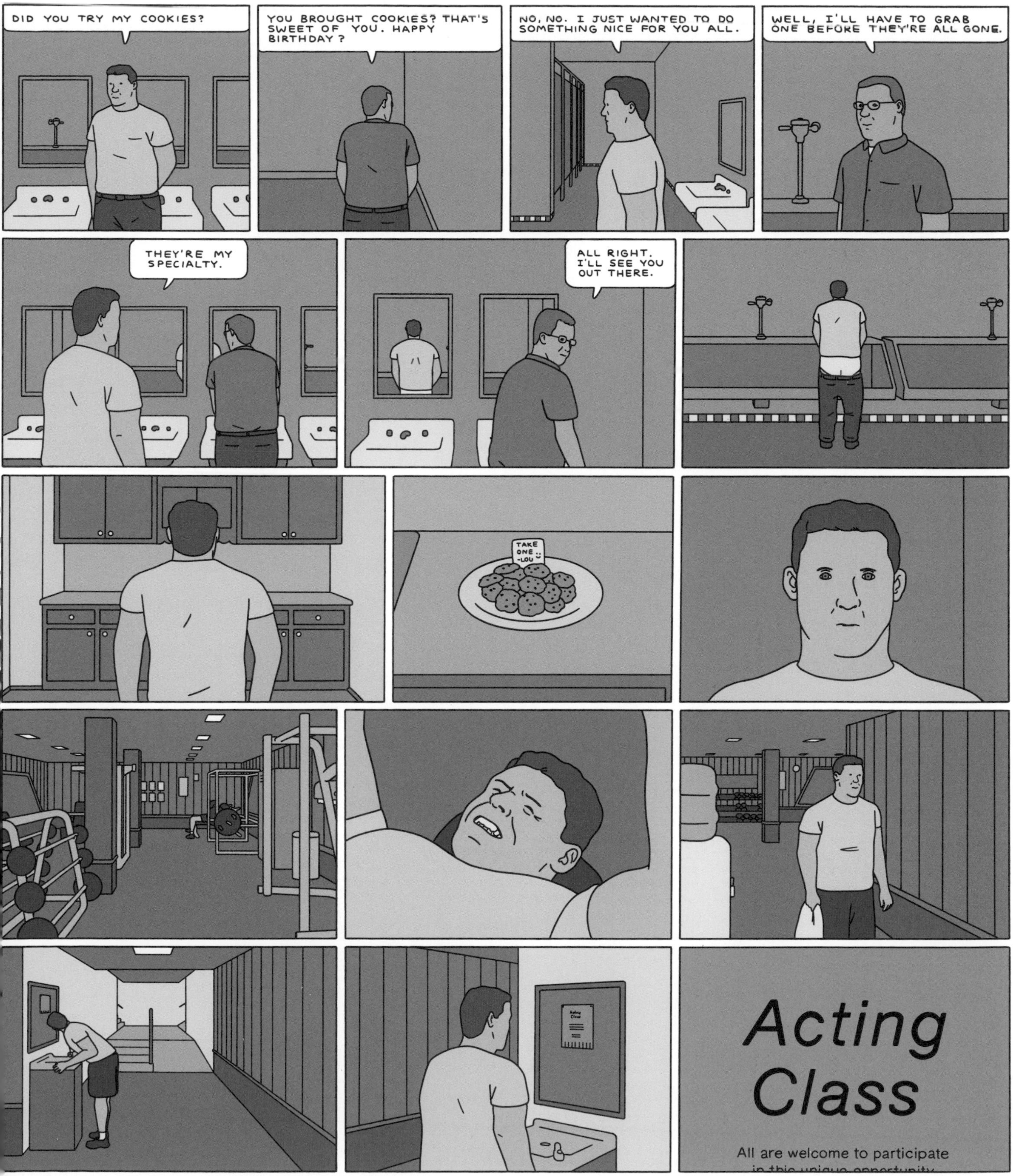
DID YOU TRY MY COOKIES?
YOU BROUGHT COOKIES? THAT'S SWEET OF YOU. HAPPY BIRTHDAY?
NO, NO. I JUST WANTED TO DO SOMETHING NICE FOR YOU ALL.
WELL, I'LL HAVE TO GRAB ONE BEFORE THEY'RE ALL GONE.
THEY'RE MY SPECIALTY.
ALL RIGHT. I'LL SEE YOU OUT THERE.
TAKE ONE -LOU
Acting Class
All are welcome to participate

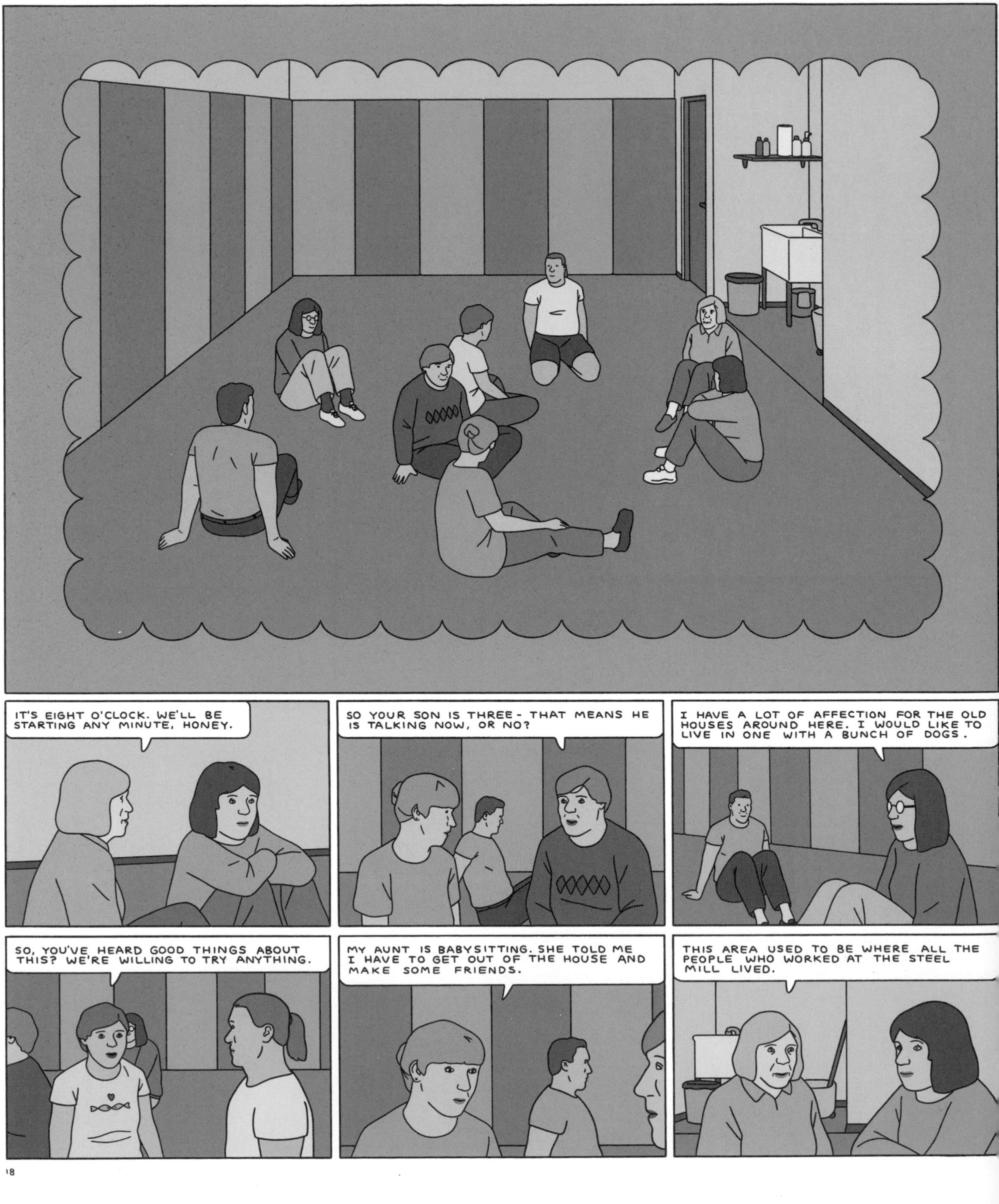
IT'S EIGHT O'CLOCK. WE'LL BE STARTING ANY MINUTE, HONEY.
SO YOUR SON IS THREE - THAT MEANS HE IS TALKING NOW, OR NO?
I HAVE A LOT OF AFFECTION FOR THE OLD HOUSES AROUND HERE. I WOULD LIKE TO LIVE IN ONE WITH A BUNCH OF DOGS.
SO, YOU'VE HEARD GOOD THINGS ABOUT THIS? WE'RE WILLING TO TRY ANYTHING.
MY AUNT IS BABYSITTING. SHE TOLD ME I HAVE TO GET OUT OF THE HOUSE AND MAKE SOME FRIENDS.
THIS AREA USED TO BE WHERE ALL THE PEOPLE WHO WORKED AT THE STEEL MILL LIVED.

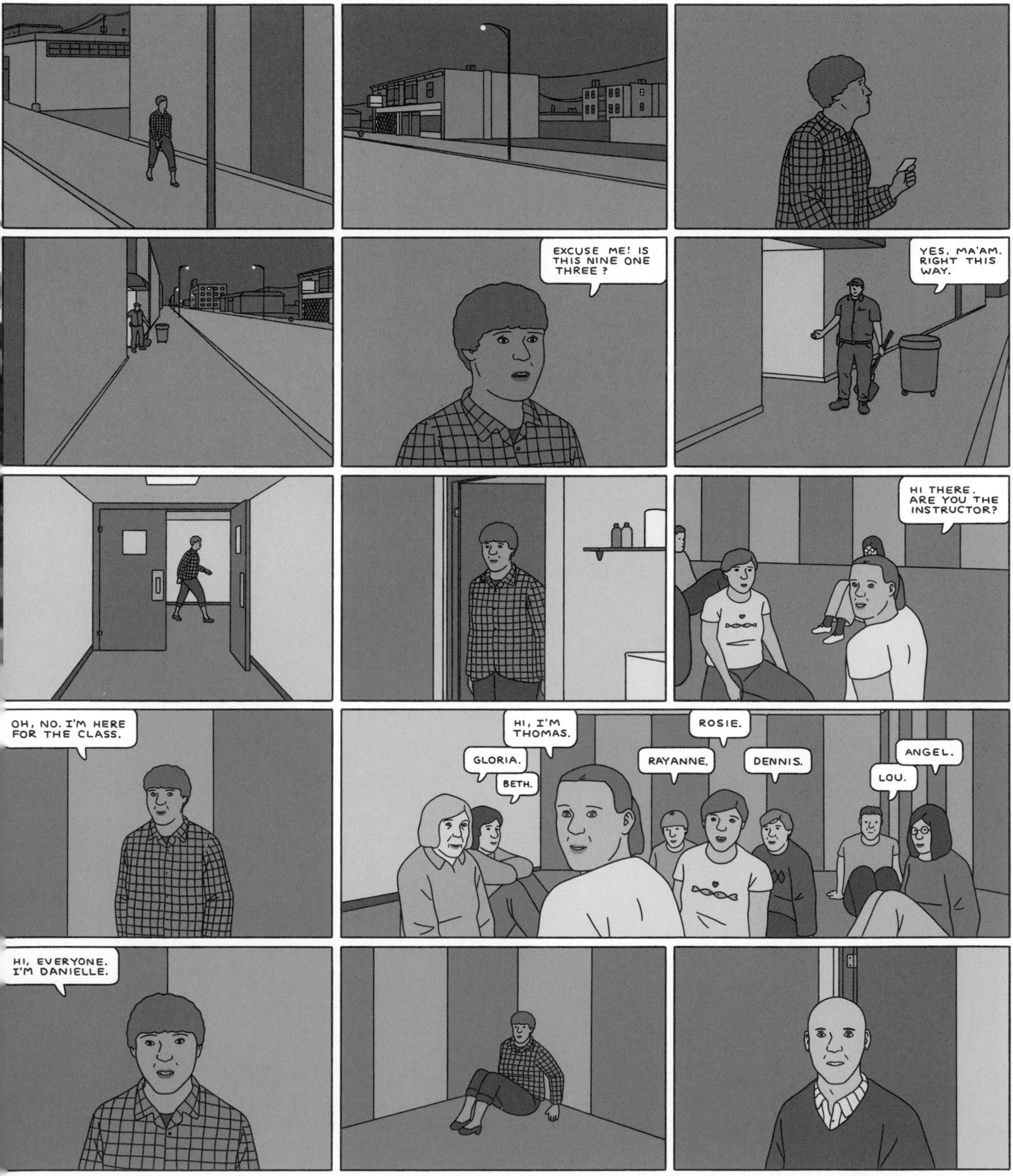
EXCUSE ME! IS THIS NINE ONE THREE ?
YES, MA'AM. RIGHT THIS WAY.
HI THERE. ARE YOU THE INSTRUCTOR?
OH, NO. I'M HERE FOR THE CLASS.
GLORIA.
BETH.
HI, I'M THOMAS.
RAYANNE.
ROSIE.
DENNIS.
LOU.
ANGEL.
HI, EVERYONE. I'M DANIELLE.

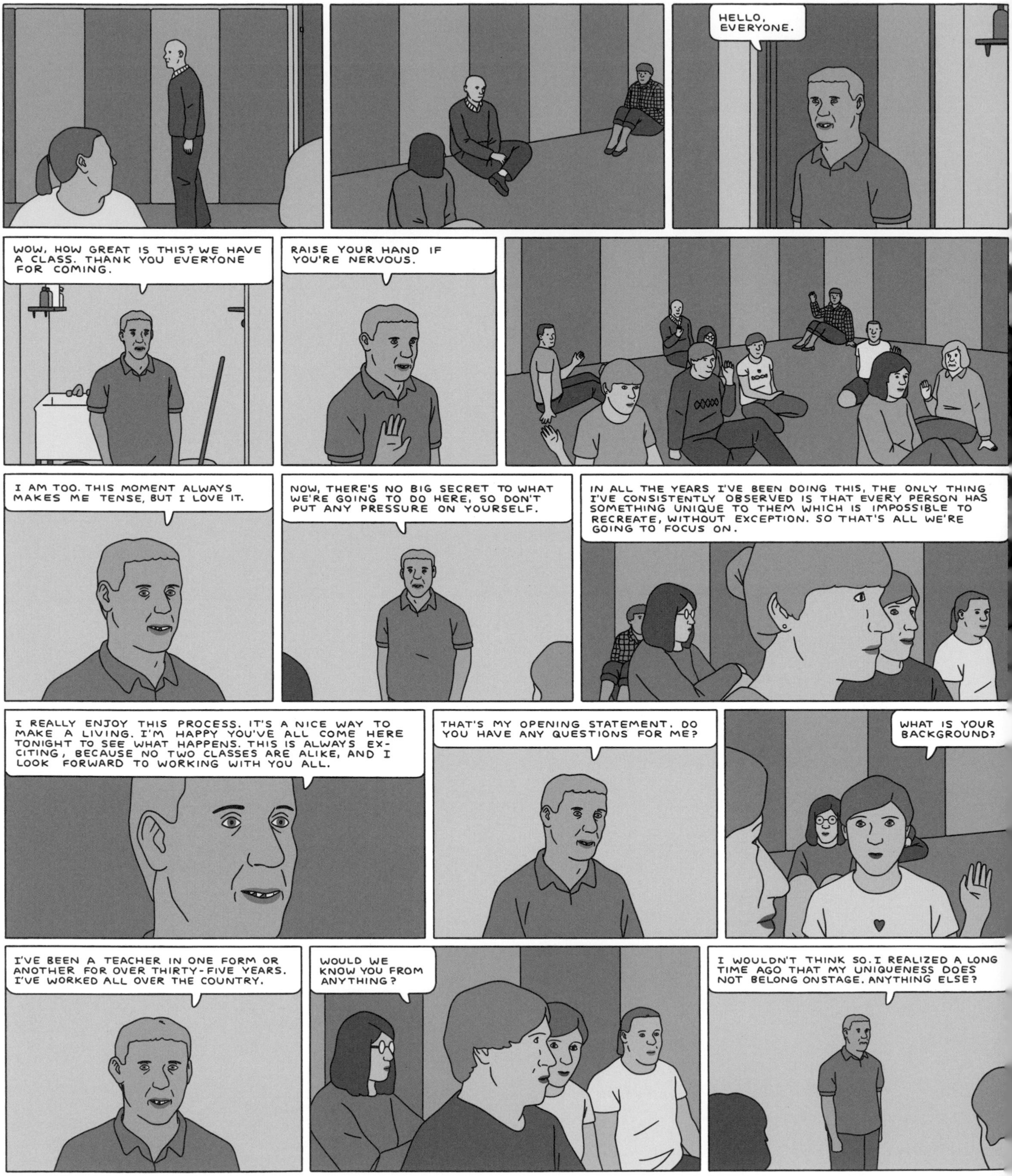
HELLO, EVERYONE.
WOW, HOW GREAT IS THIS? WE HAVE A CLASS. THANK YOU EVERYONE FOR COMING.
RAISE YOUR HAND IF YOU'RE NERVOUS.
I AM TOO. THIS MOMENT ALWAYS MAKES ME TENSE, BUT I LOVE IT.
NOW, THERE'S NO BIG SECRET TO WHAT WE'RE GOING TO DO HERE, SO DON'T PUT ANY PRESSURE ON YOURSELF.
IN ALL THE YEARS I'VE BEEN DOING THIS, THE ONLY THING I'VE CONSISTENTLY OBSERVED IS THAT EVERY PERSON HAS SOMETHING UNIQUE TO THEM WHICH IS IMPOSSIBLE TO RECREATE, WITHOUT EXCEPTION. SO THAT'S ALL WE'RE GOING TO FOCUS ON.
I REALLY ENJOY THIS PROCESS. IT'S A NICE WAY TO MAKE A LIVING. I'M HAPPY YOU'VE ALL COME HERE TONIGHT TO SEE WHAT HAPPENS. THIS IS ALWAYS EXCITING, BECAUSE NO TWO CLASSES ARE ALIKE, AND I LOOK FORWARD TO WORKING WITH YOU ALL.
THAT'S MY OPENING STATEMENT. DO YOU HAVE ANY QUESTIONS FOR ME?
WHAT IS YOUR BACKGROUND?
I'VE BEEN A TEACHER IN ONE FORM OR ANOTHER FOR OVER THIRTY-FIVE YEARS. I'VE WORKED ALL OVER THE COUNTRY.
WOULD WE KNOW YOU FROM ANYTHING?
I WOULDN'T THINK SO. I REALIZED A LONG TIME AGO THAT MY UNIQUENESS DOES NOT BELONG ONSTAGE. ANYTHING ELSE?

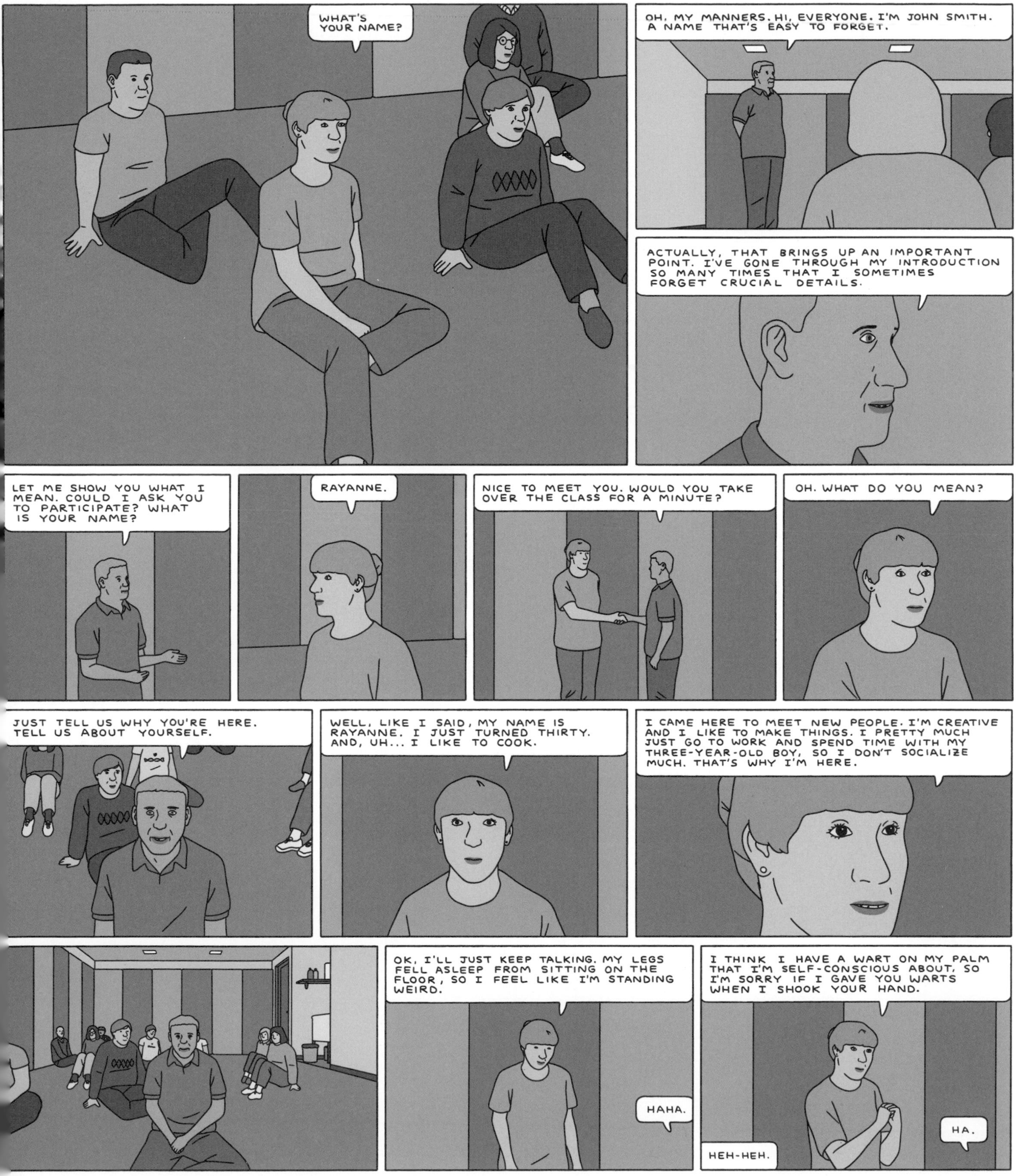
WHAT'S YOUR NAME?
OH, MY MANNERS. HI, EVERYONE. I'M JOHN SMITH. A NAME THAT'S EASY TO FORGET.
ACTUALLY, THAT BRINGS UP AN IMPORTANT POINT. I'VE GONE THROUGH MY INTRODUCTION SO MANY TIMES THAT I SOMETIMES FORGET CRUCIAL DETAILS.
LET ME SHOW YOU WHAT I MEAN. COULD I ASK YOU TO PARTICIPATE? WHAT IS YOUR NAME?
RAYANNE.
NICE TO MEET YOU. WOULD YOU TAKE OVER THE CLASS FOR A MINUTE?
OH. WHAT DO YOU MEAN?
JUST TELL US WHY YOU'RE HERE. TELL US ABOUT YOURSELF.
WELL, LIKE I SAID, MY NAME IS RAYANNE. I JUST TURNED THIRTY. AND, UH... I LIKE TO COOK.
I CAME HERE TO MEET NEW PEOPLE. I'M CREATIVE AND I LIKE TO MAKE THINGS. I PRETTY MUCH JUST GO TO WORK AND SPEND TIME WITH MY THREE-YEAR-OLD BOY, SO I DON'T SOCIALIZE MUCH. THAT'S WHY I'M HERE.
OK, I'LL JUST KEEP TALKING. MY LEGS FELL ASLEEP FROM SITTING ON THE FLOOR, SO I FEEL LIKE I'M STANDING WEIRD.
HAHA.
I THINK I HAVE A WART ON MY PALM THAT I'M SELF-CONSCIOUS ABOUT, SO I'M SORRY IF I GAVE YOU WARTS WHEN I SHOOK YOUR HAND.
HEH-HEH.
HA.

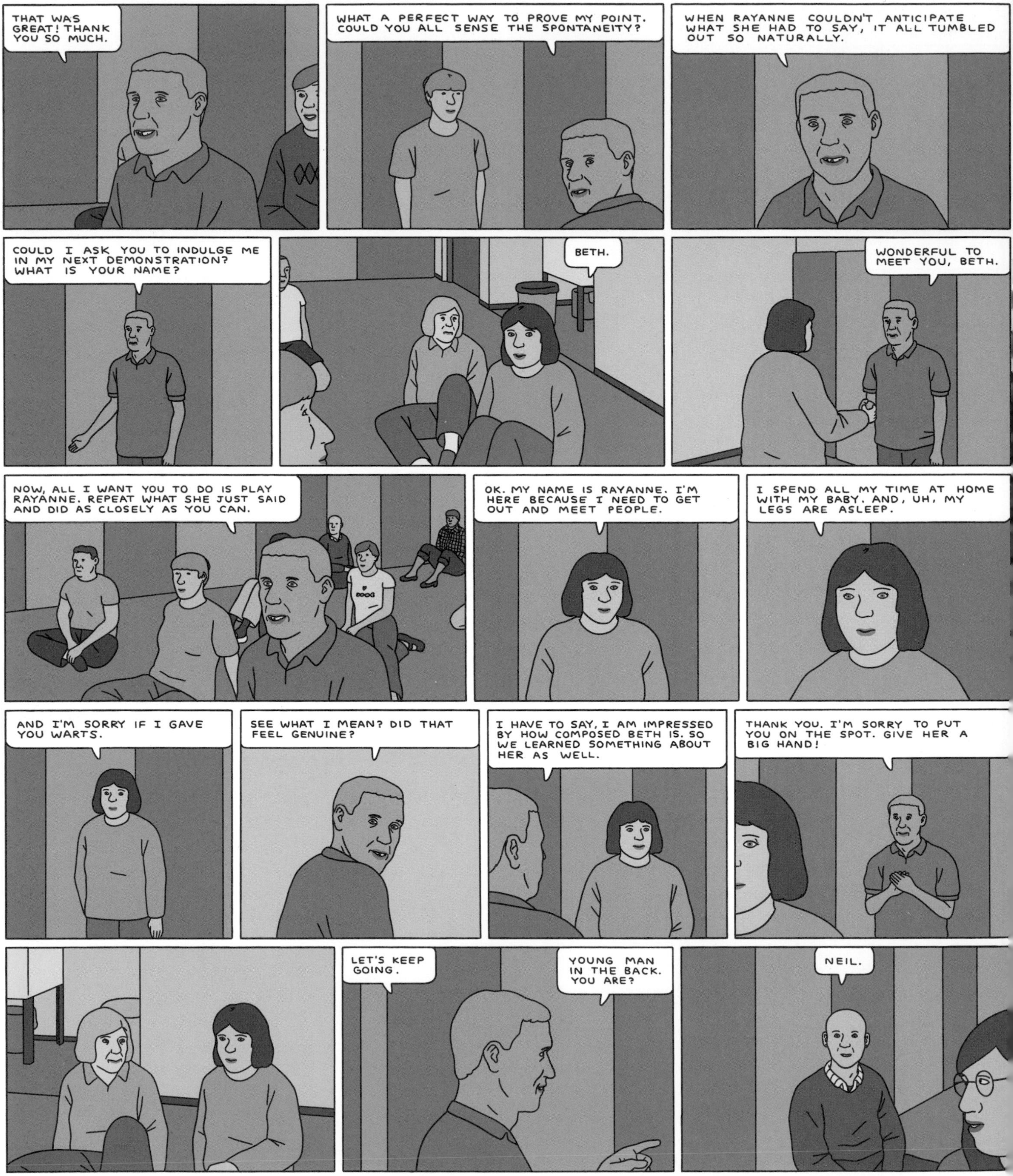
THAT WAS GREAT! THANK YOU SO MUCH.
WHAT A PERFECT WAY TO PROVE MY POINT. COULD YOU ALL SENSE THE SPONTANEITY?
WHEN RAYANNE COULDN'T ANTICIPATE WHAT SHE HAD TO SAY, IT ALL TUMBLED OUT SO NATURALLY.
COULD I ASK YOU TO INDULGE ME IN MY NEXT DEMONSTRATION? WHAT IS YOUR NAME?
BETH.
WONDERFUL TO MEET YOU, BETH.
NOW, ALL I WANT YOU TO DO IS PLAY RAYANNE. REPEAT WHAT SHE JUST SAID AND DID AS CLOSELY AS YOU CAN.
OK. MY NAME IS RAYANNE. I'M HERE BECAUSE I NEED TO GET OUT AND MEET PEOPLE.
I SPEND ALL MY TIME AT HOME WITH MY BABY. AND, UH, MY LEGS ARE ASLEEP.
AND I'M SORRY IF I GAVE YOU WARTS.
SEE WHAT I MEAN? DID THAT FEEL GENUINE?
I HAVE TO SAY, I AM IMPRESSED BY HOW COMPOSED BETH IS. SO WE LEARNED SOMETHING ABOUT HER AS WELL.
THANK YOU. I'M SORRY TO PUT YOU ON THE SPOT. GIVE HER A BIG HAND!
LET'S KEEP GOING.
YOUNG MAN IN THE BACK. YOU ARE?
NEIL.

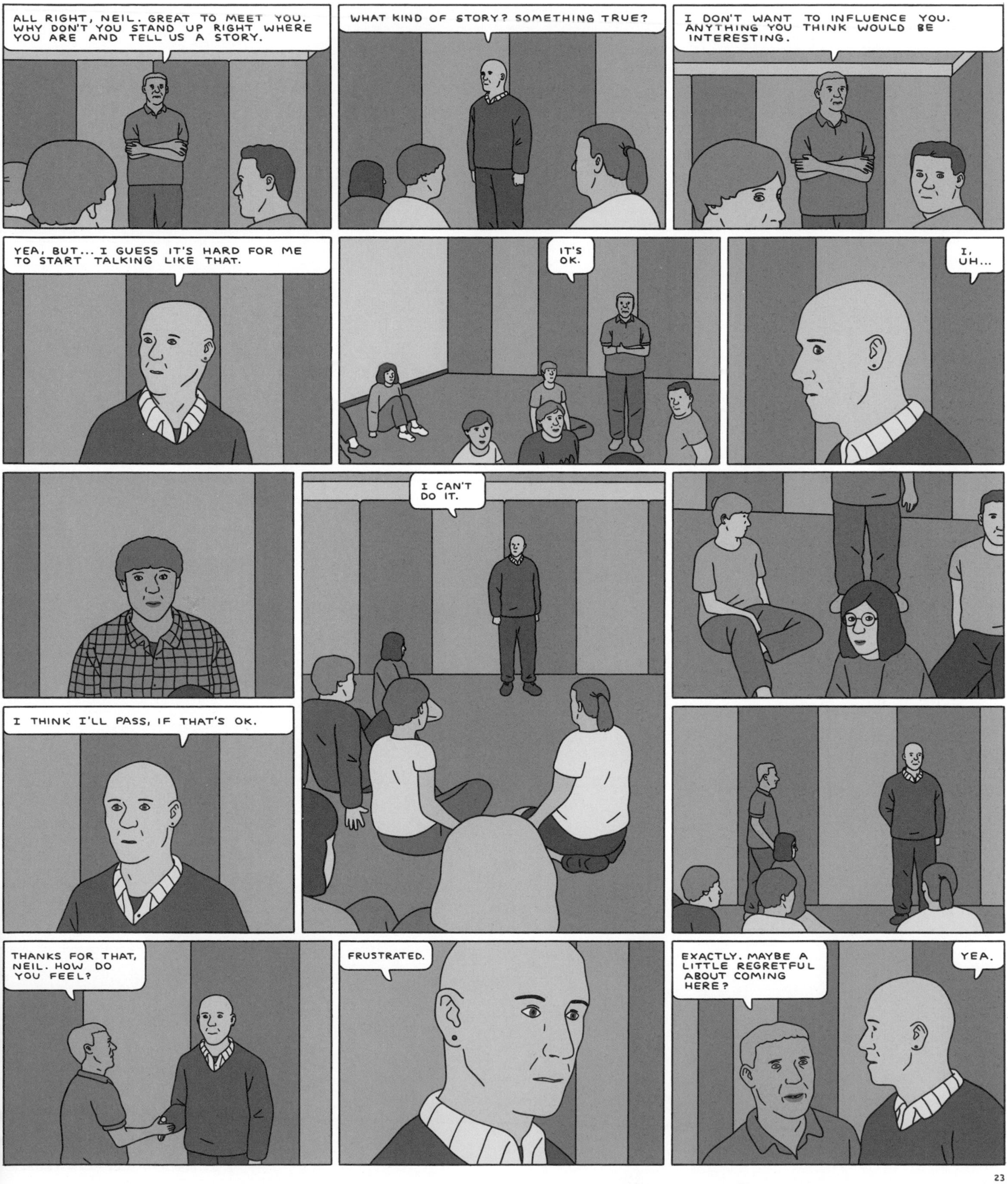
ALL RIGHT, NEIL. GREAT TO MEET YOU. WHY DON'T YOU STAND UP RIGHT WHERE YOU ARE AND TELL US A STORY.
WHAT KIND OF STORY? SOMETHING TRUE?
I DON'T WANT TO INFLUENCE YOU. ANYTHING YOU THINK WOULD BE INTERESTING.
YEA, BUT... I GUESS IT'S HARD FOR ME TO START TALKING LIKE THAT.
IT'S OK.
I, UH...
I CAN'T DO IT.
I THINK I'LL PASS, IF THAT'S OK.
THANKS FOR THAT, NEIL. HOW DO YOU FEEL?
FRUSTRATED.
EXACTLY. MAYBE A LITTLE REGRETFUL ABOUT COMING HERE?
YEA.

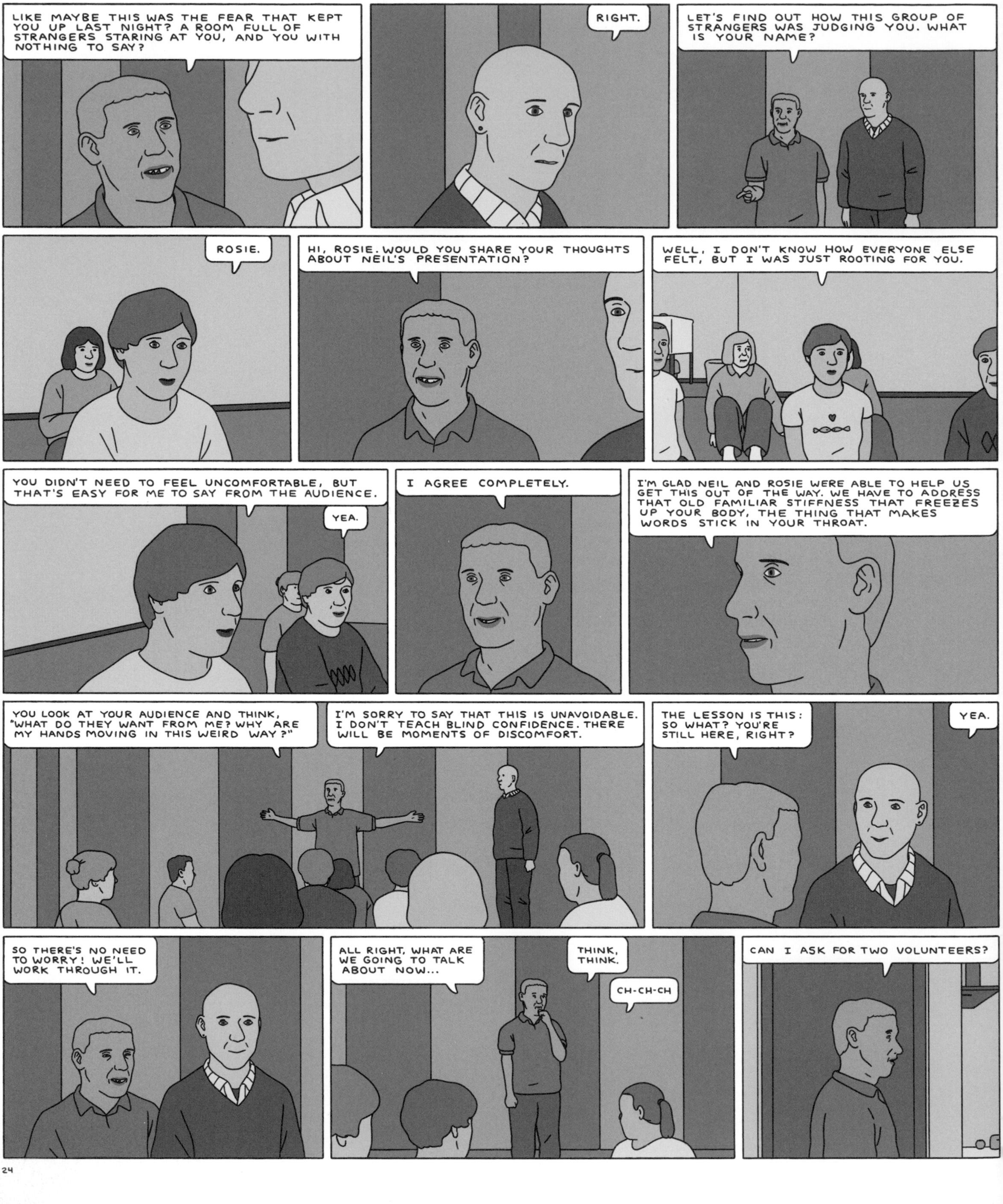
LIKE MAYBE THIS WAS THE FEAR THAT KEPT YOU UP LAST NIGHT? A ROOM FULL OF STRANGERS STARING AT YOU, AND YOU WITH NOTHING TO SAY?
RIGHT.
LET'S FIND OUT HOW THIS GROUP OF STRANGERS WAS JUDGING YOU. WHAT IS YOUR NAME?
ROSIE.
HI, ROSIE. WOULD YOU SHARE YOUR THOUGHTS ABOUT NEIL'S PRESENTATION?
WELL, I DON'T KNOW HOW EVERYONE ELSE FELT, BUT I WAS JUST ROOTING FOR YOU.
YOU DIDN'T NEED TO FEEL UNCOMFORTABLE, BUT THAT'S EASY FOR ME TO SAY FROM THE AUDIENCE.
YEA.
I AGREE COMPLETELY.
I'M GLAD NEIL AND ROSIE WERE ABLE TO HELP US GET THIS OUT OF THE WAY. WE HAVE TO ADDRESS THAT OLD FAMILIAR STIFFNESS THAT FREEZES UP YOUR BODY, THE THING THAT MAKES WORDS STICK IN YOUR THROAT.
YOU LOOK AT YOUR AUDIENCE AND THINK, "WHAT DO THEY WANT FROM ME? WHY ARE MY HANDS MOVING IN THIS WEIRD WAY?"
I'M SORRY TO SAY THAT THIS IS UNAVOIDABLE. I DON'T TEACH BLIND CONFIDENCE. THERE WILL BE MOMENTS OF DISCOMFORT.
THE LESSON IS THIS: SO WHAT? YOU'RE STILL HERE, RIGHT?
YEA.
SO THERE'S NO NEED TO WORRY! WE'LL WORK THROUGH IT.
ALL RIGHT, WHAT ARE WE GOING TO TALK ABOUT NOW...
THINK, THINK.
CH-CH-CH
CAN I ASK FOR TWO VOLUNTEERS?

HI, I'M THOMAS.

THANKS. GOOD TO MEET YOU. ONE MORE?

DID I SEE YOU RAISE YOUR HAND?

NO, BUT I'LL DO IT.

I'M DANIELLE.

NICE TO MEET YOU.

I'D LIKE THE TWO OF YOU TO IMPROVISE A SCENE.

DANIELLE, YOU'RE THE BOSS. AND THOMAS, YOU'RE THE EMPLOYEE.

THE REST IS UP TO BOTH OF YOU.

OK.

IT MAY SEEM LIKE WE'RE MOVING ALONG UNREASONABLY FAST, BUT I DON'T BELIEVE IN BUILDING UP A LOT OF SUSPENSE AROUND PERFORMING.

I'VE FOUND IT'S BETTER TO JUMP IN AWKWARDLY AND WORK IT OUT AS WE GO.

AND AGAIN, IT DOESN'T MATTER. BUT IT DOES. AND YET, IT DOESN'T. IF THAT MAKES SENSE.

NOW LET'S MAKE DANIELLE AND THOMAS FEEL COMFORTABLE WITH A NICE ROUND OF APPLAUSE!

WOO!

ALL RIGHT! WHY DON'T YOU WAIT IN THE HALL. WHEN YOU KNOCK, THE SCENE HAS BEGUN.

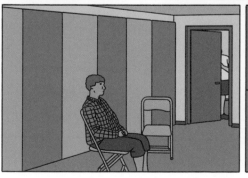

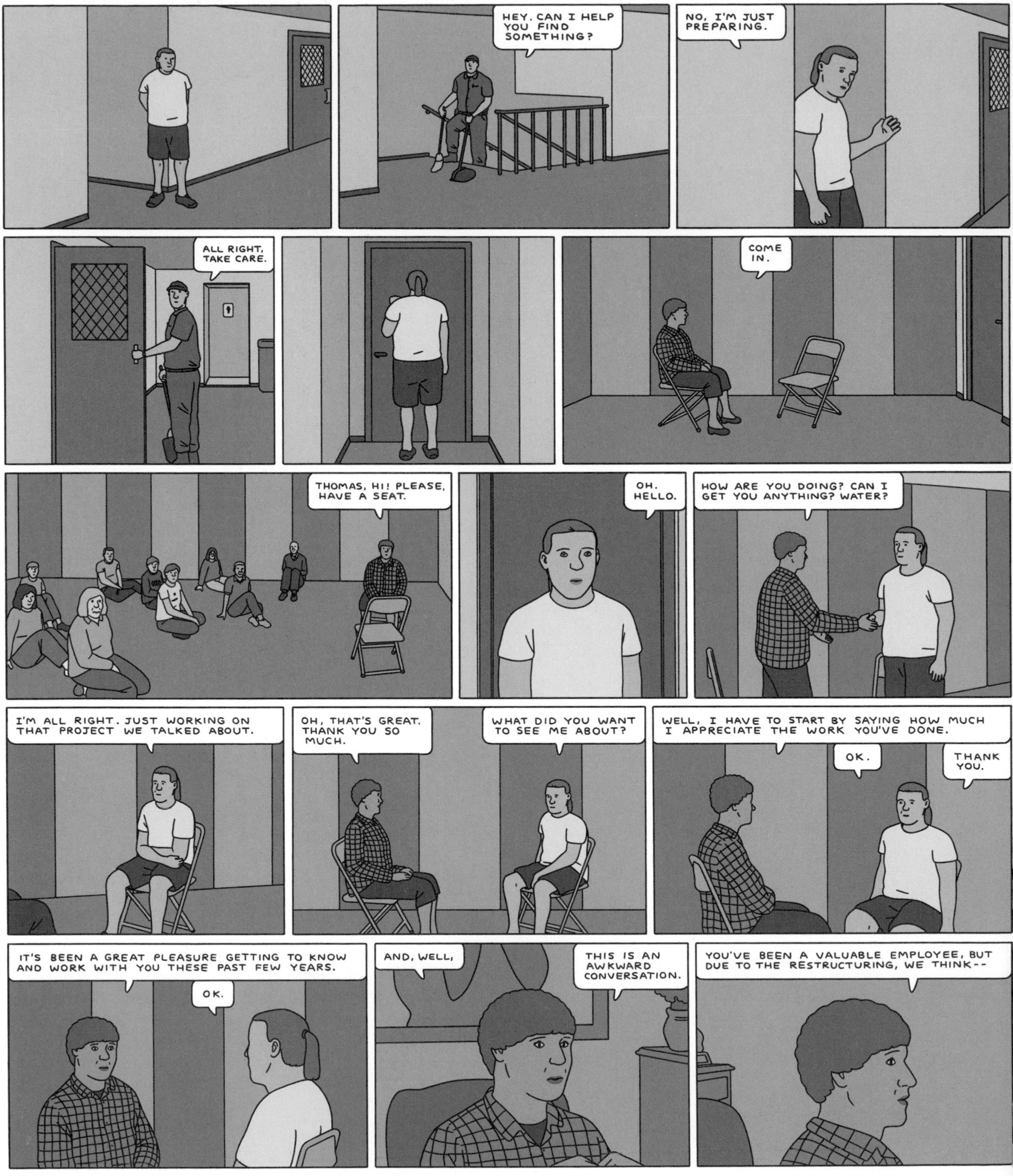
HEY. CAN I HELP YOU FIND SOMETHING?
NO, I'M JUST PREPARING.
ALL RIGHT, TAKE CARE.
COME IN.
THOMAS, HI! PLEASE, HAVE A SEAT.
OH. HELLO.
HOW ARE YOU DOING? CAN I GET YOU ANYTHING? WATER?
I'M ALL RIGHT. JUST WORKING ON THAT PROJECT WE TALKED ABOUT.
OH, THAT'S GREAT. THANK YOU SO MUCH.
WHAT DID YOU WANT TO SEE ME ABOUT?
WELL, I HAVE TO START BY SAYING HOW MUCH I APPRECIATE THE WORK YOU'VE DONE.
OK.
THANK YOU.
IT'S BEEN A GREAT PLEASURE GETTING TO KNOW AND WORK WITH YOU THESE PAST FEW YEARS.
OK.
AND, WELL,
THIS IS AN AWKWARD CONVERSATION.
YOU'VE BEEN A VALUABLE EMPLOYEE, BUT DUE TO THE RESTRUCTURING, WE THINK--

I CAN'T BELIEVE THIS.

HOLD ON—

YOU HAVE TO BE KIDDING!

AFTER ALL I'VE DONE FOR YOU?!

LIED FOR YOU?! CLEANED UP ALL YOUR MESSES?! ALL YOUR FUCK UPS?!

THERE'S NO GOD-DAMNED JUSTICE IN THIS WORLD!

WAIT A MINUTE.

I'VE HAD IT!

THOMAS.

I NEED A DRINK!

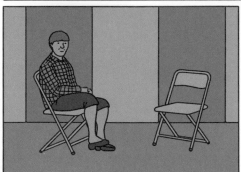

THAT WAS REALLY SOMETHING.

COME ON BACK.

THANK YOU SO MUCH FOR BREAKING THE ICE. IT'S NOT EASY.

THAT WAS INTERESTING. NO ONE IN THIS ROOM CAN SAY THEY DIDN'T SNAP TO ATTENTION, RIGHT?

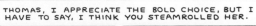

I'D LIKE TO GO BACK TO WHERE DANIELLE BEGAN, BECAUSE WE MIGHT HAVE PASSED OVER WHAT SHE WAS DOING.

THOMAS, I APPRECIATE THE BOLD CHOICE, BUT I HAVE TO SAY, I THINK YOU STEAMROLLED HER.

WELL, WHEN I STARTED TO THINK ABOUT IT, I GUESS I THOUGHT THIS CHARACTER WOULD BLOW HIS TOP.

WHO IS THIS CHARACTER?

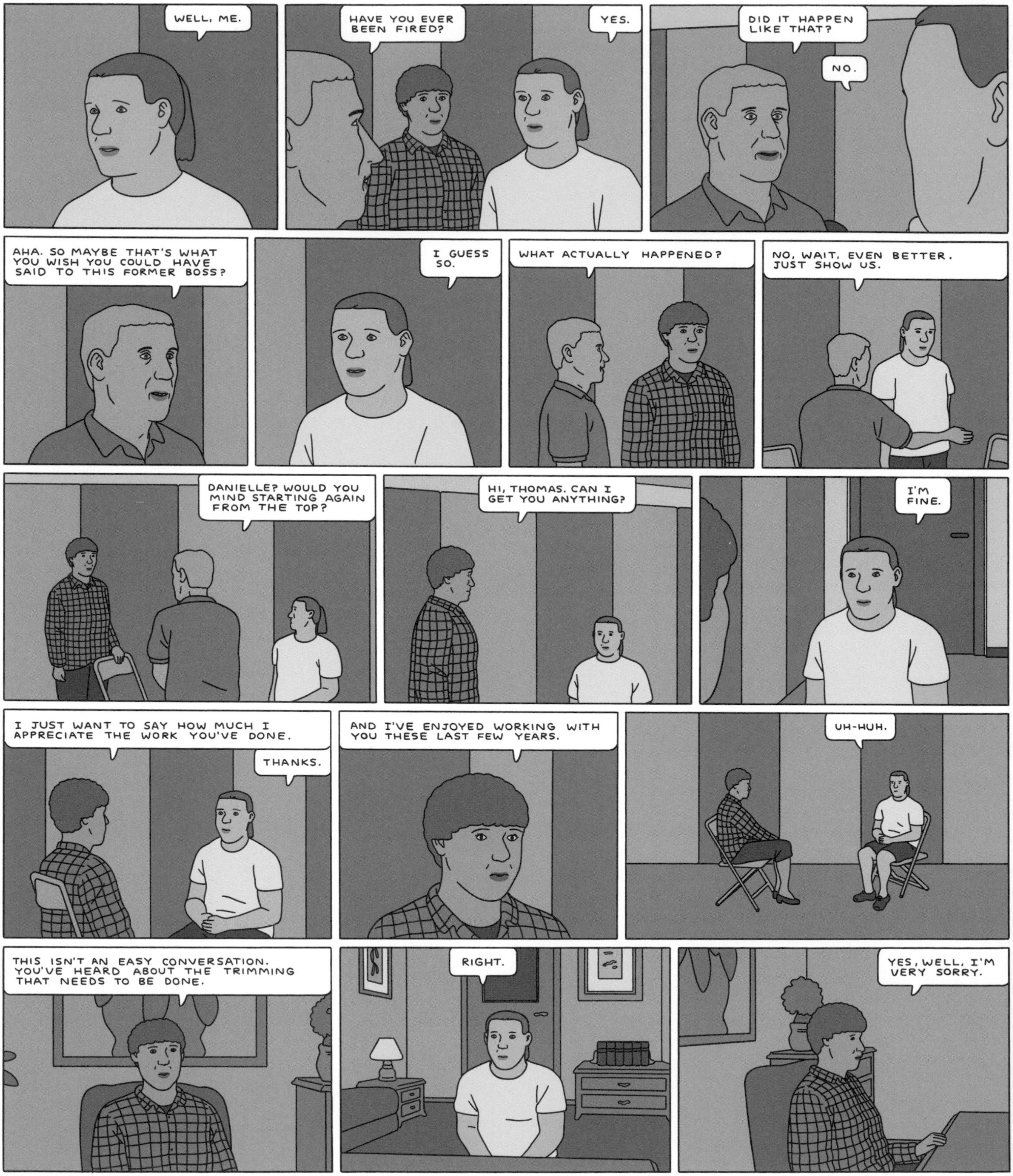
WELL, ME.
HAVE YOU EVER BEEN FIRED?
YES.
DID IT HAPPEN LIKE THAT?
NO.
AHA. SO MAYBE THAT'S WHAT YOU WISH YOU COULD HAVE SAID TO THIS FORMER BOSS?
I GUESS SO.
WHAT ACTUALLY HAPPENED?
NO, WAIT, EVEN BETTER. JUST SHOW US.
DANIELLE? WOULD YOU MIND STARTING AGAIN FROM THE TOP?
HI, THOMAS. CAN I GET YOU ANYTHING?
I'M FINE.
I JUST WANT TO SAY HOW MUCH I APPRECIATE THE WORK YOU'VE DONE.
THANKS.
AND I'VE ENJOYED WORKING WITH YOU THESE LAST FEW YEARS.
UH-HUH.
THIS ISN'T AN EASY CONVERSATION. YOU'VE HEARD ABOUT THE TRIMMING THAT NEEDS TO BE DONE.
RIGHT.
YES, WELL, I'M VERY SORRY.

WE'RE GOING TO HAVE TO LET YOU GO.

OH NO.

TODAY?

YES. WE'LL NEED YOUR LOCKER KEY AND BADGE.

I CAN'T BELIEVE THIS.

IT WASN'T MY DECISION. THEY HAD TO DRAW A LINE AND ELIMINATE EVERYTHING BELOW.

I'M SORRY. I'LL ALWAYS BE HERE TO WRITE A LETTER OF RECOMMENDATION.

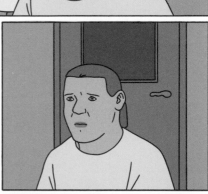

IF YOU DON'T MIND, I HAVE TO TALK TO A FEW OTHER PEOPLE TODAY.

YES!

DANIELLE, PERFECT INSTINCTS. THOMAS, WHAT A TRANSFORMATION.

GIVE THEM A BIG HAND!

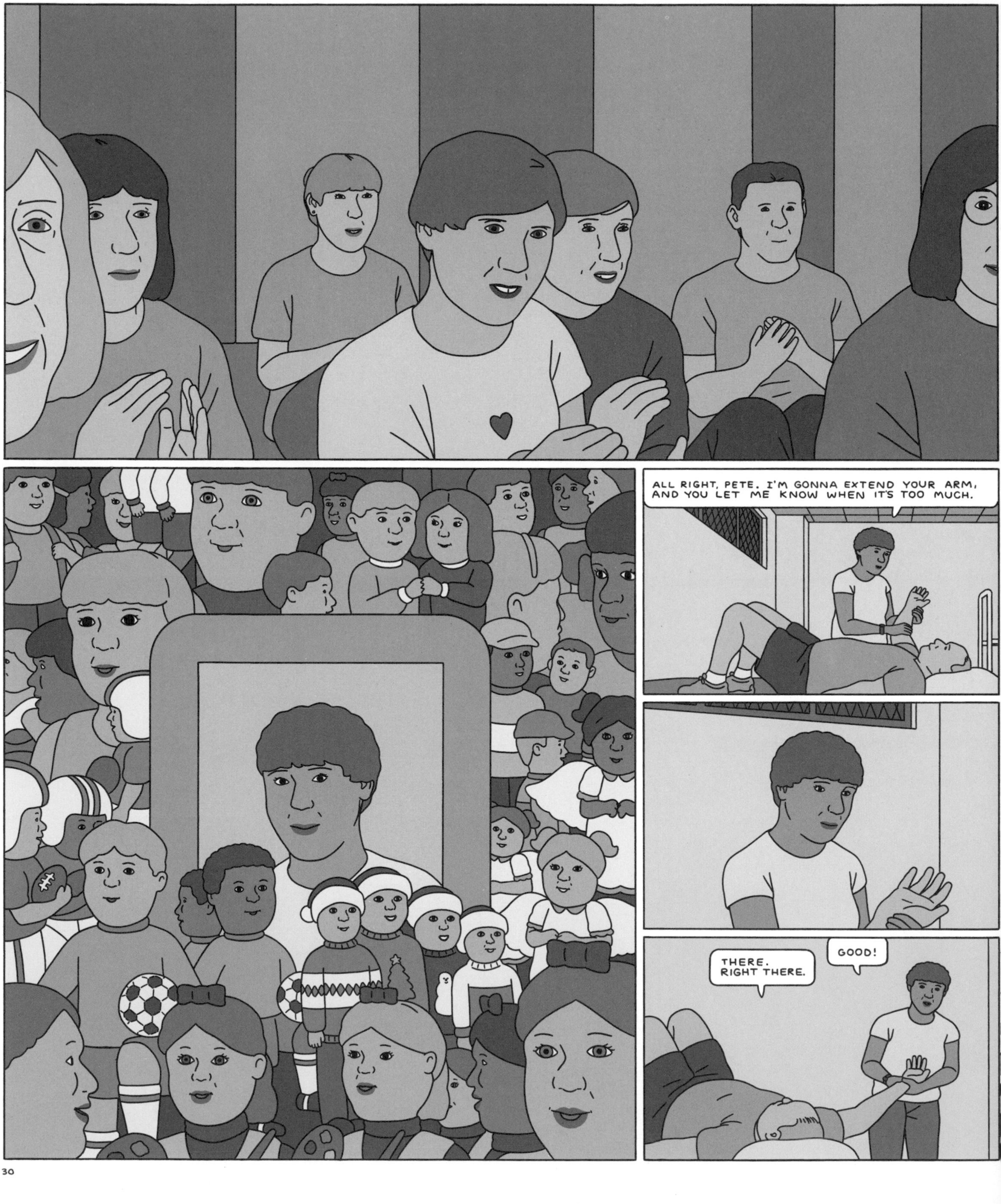
ALL RIGHT, PETE. I'M GONNA EXTEND YOUR ARM, AND YOU LET ME KNOW WHEN IT'S TOO MUCH.
THERE. RIGHT THERE.
GOOD!

NOW THE OTHER.

CAN YOU SMELL THE BAKERY ACROSS THE STREET? GOD, I LOVE THAT SMELL.

I'M A SMOKER. I CAN'T SMELL ANYTHING.

DO YOURSELF A FAVOR. GO OVER THERE AFTER YOUR APPOINTMENT AND GET SOME FRENCH BREAD.

OW! THERE, THERE.

GREAT. GOOD PROGRESS. DO YOU REMEMBER YOUR FINAL STRETCH OR DO YOU WANT ME TO SHOW YOU?

HOW WAS YOUR BEST FRIEND PETE THIS WEEK? IF HE'S STILL BEING DIFFICULT, I CAN TAKE OVER NEXT TIME.

OH, HE'S ALL RIGHT. I THINK I'VE GOT A HANDLE ON HIM.

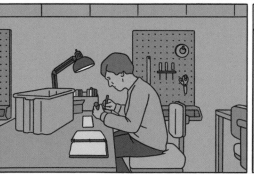

I HAVE GOOD NEWS.

WHAT?

THIS IS JENNA. SHE'LL BE HELPING OUT A FEW NIGHTS A WEEK.

HI.

OH, WONDERFUL! NICE TO MEET YOU. I'M ROSIE.

WOULD YOU MIND TRAINING HER UNTIL YOU LEAVE?

31

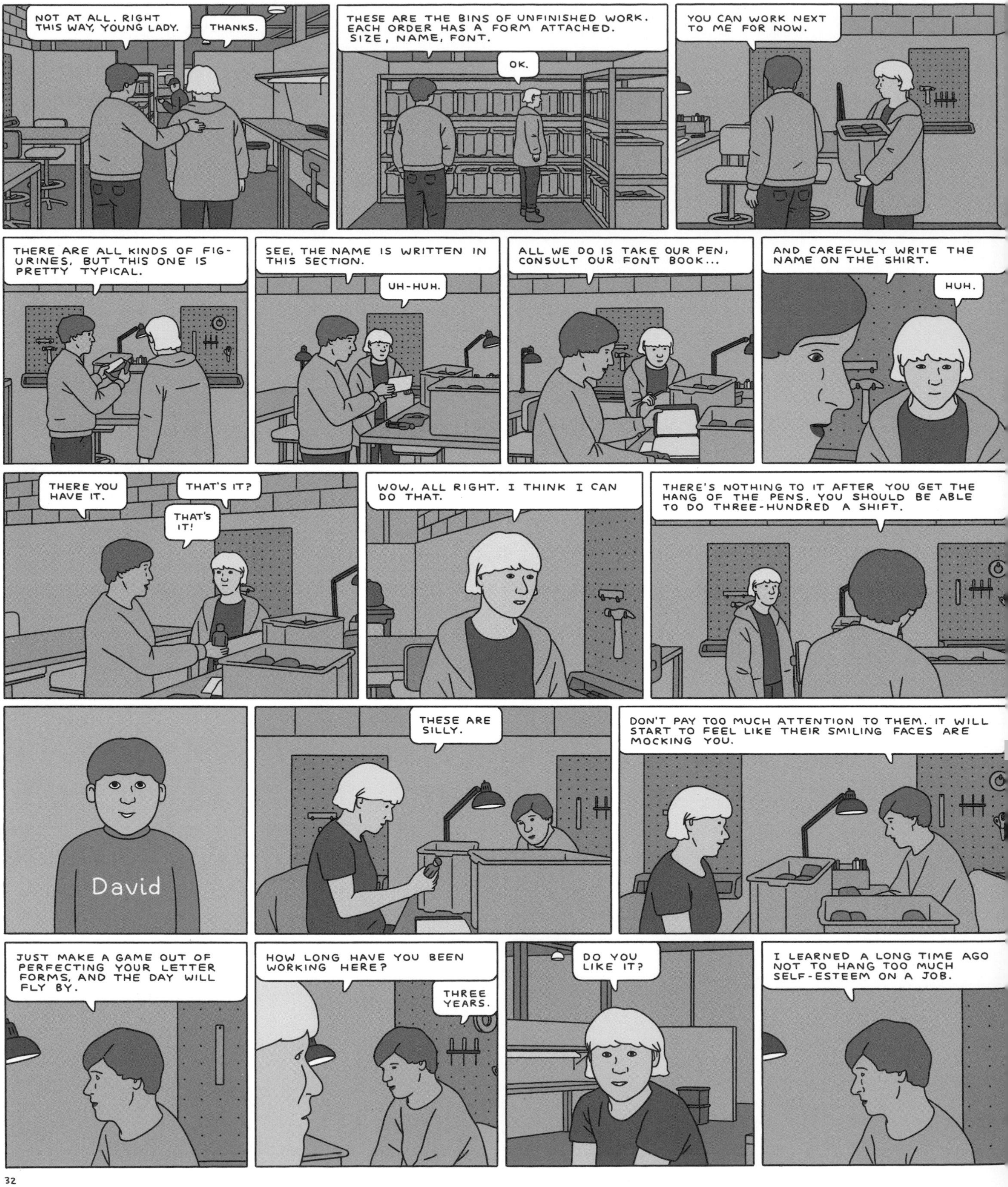
NOT AT ALL. RIGHT THIS WAY, YOUNG LADY.
THANKS.
THESE ARE THE BINS OF UNFINISHED WORK. EACH ORDER HAS A FORM ATTACHED. SIZE, NAME, FONT.
OK.
YOU CAN WORK NEXT TO ME FOR NOW.
THERE ARE ALL KINDS OF FIG-URINES, BUT THIS ONE IS PRETTY TYPICAL.
SEE, THE NAME IS WRITTEN IN THIS SECTION.
UH-HUH.
ALL WE DO IS TAKE OUR PEN, CONSULT OUR FONT BOOK...
AND CAREFULLY WRITE THE NAME ON THE SHIRT.
HUH.
THERE YOU HAVE IT.
THAT'S IT?
THAT'S IT!
WOW, ALL RIGHT. I THINK I CAN DO THAT.
THERE'S NOTHING TO IT AFTER YOU GET THE HANG OF THE PENS. YOU SHOULD BE ABLE TO DO THREE-HUNDRED A SHIFT.
David
THESE ARE SILLY.
DON'T PAY TOO MUCH ATTENTION TO THEM. IT WILL START TO FEEL LIKE THEIR SMILING FACES ARE MOCKING YOU.
JUST MAKE A GAME OUT OF PERFECTING YOUR LETTER FORMS, AND THE DAY WILL FLY BY.
HOW LONG HAVE YOU BEEN WORKING HERE?
THREE YEARS.
DO YOU LIKE IT?
I LEARNED A LONG TIME AGO NOT TO HANG TOO MUCH SELF-ESTEEM ON A JOB.

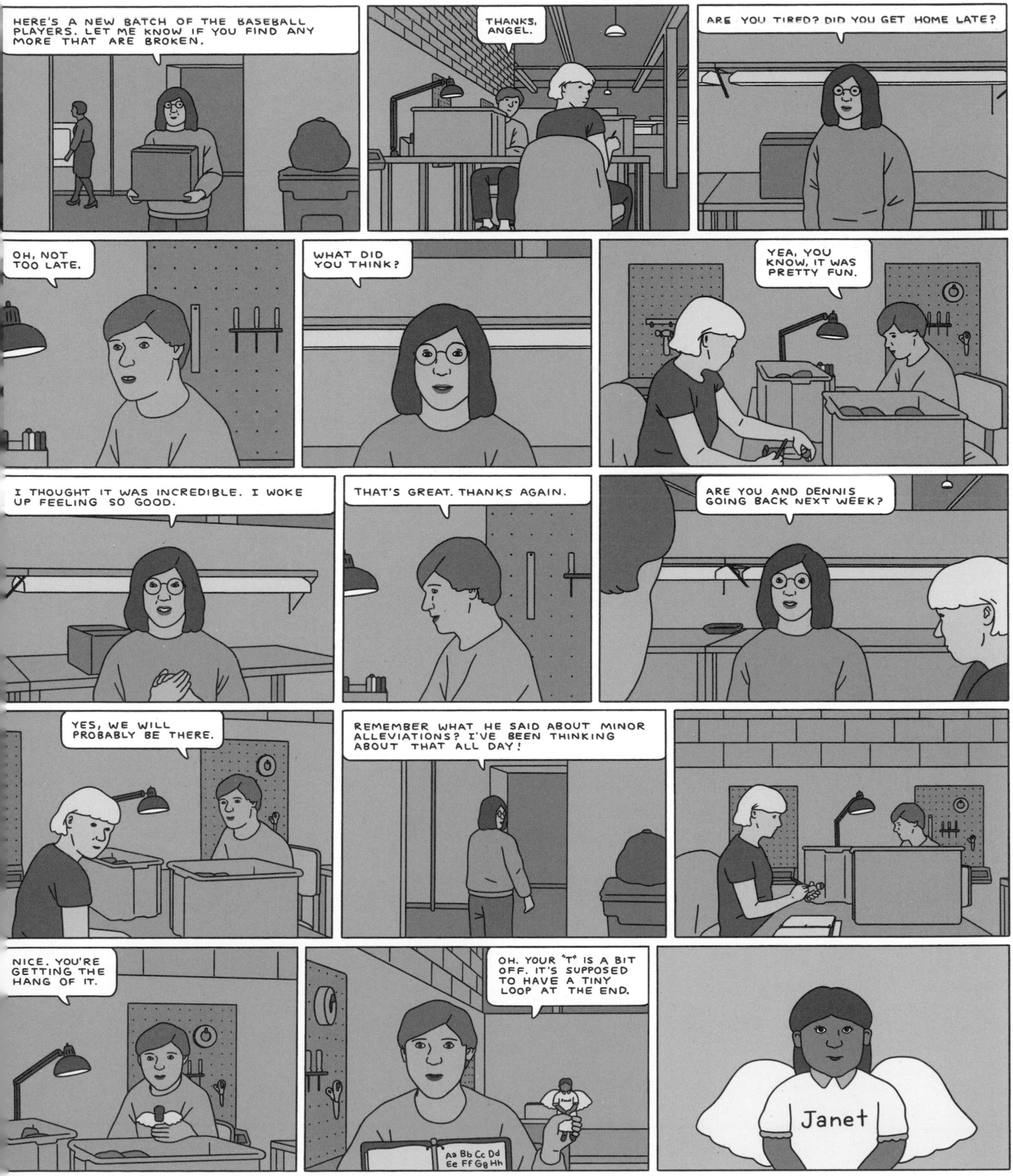
HERE'S A NEW BATCH OF THE BASEBALL PLAYERS. LET ME KNOW IF YOU FIND ANY MORE THAT ARE BROKEN.
THANKS, ANGEL.
ARE YOU TIRED? DID YOU GET HOME LATE?
OH, NOT TOO LATE.
WHAT DID YOU THINK?
YEA, YOU KNOW, IT WAS PRETTY FUN.
I THOUGHT IT WAS INCREDIBLE. I WOKE UP FEELING SO GOOD.
THAT'S GREAT. THANKS AGAIN.
ARE YOU AND DENNIS GOING BACK NEXT WEEK?
YES, WE WILL PROBABLY BE THERE.
REMEMBER WHAT HE SAID ABOUT MINOR ALLEVIATIONS? I'VE BEEN THINKING ABOUT THAT ALL DAY!
NICE. YOU'RE GETTING THE HANG OF IT.
OH. YOUR "T" IS A BIT OFF. IT'S SUPPOSED TO HAVE A TINY LOOP AT THE END.
Aa Bb Cc Dd Ee Ff Gg Hh
Janet

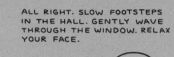

KNOCK CHEERFULLY. KEEP YOUR HANDS OUT OF YOUR JACKET POCKETS. PEOPLE DON'T LIKE THAT. DON'T STARE, AND DON'T JERK YOUR HEAD AROUND SO MUCH.

DON'T KNOCK AGAIN. DON'T PEER INTO THE WINDOW. DON'T CHEW ON YOUR CHEEK WHEN THE PERSON IS SPEAKING. DON'T DO ANYTHING TO AROUSE SUSPICION. BE RESPECTFUL. SAY THANK YOU, BUT NOT TOO MUCH. ASK, REQUEST, SUGGEST, BUT DON'T BEG.

ALL RIGHT. SLOW FOOTSTEPS IN THE HALL. GENTLY WAVE THROUGH THE WINDOW. RELAX YOUR FACE.

HOWDY.

HI THERE! MY NAME IS NEIL, AND I WORK FOR THE UNIFIED COMMUNITY FOOD PANTRY.

WE'RE REACHING OUT TO OUR NEIGHBORS TO INVITE THEM TO CONTRIBUTE TO OUR YEARLY FUNDRAISER.

ALL MONETARY DONATIONS WILL GO TO BULK FOOD PURCHASES, WHICH WILL BE PROVIDED TO FAMILIES IN NEED. WE WELCOME CONTRIBUTIONS OF ANY SIZE.

YEA, I'M SORRY, MAN.

AS LITTLE AS FIVE DOLLARS IS IMMENSELY APPRECIATED.

SORRY, I DON'T HAVE ANY CASH.

CAN I GIVE YOU A FLYER WITH OUR LOCATION AND NUMBER IN CASE YOU CHANGE YOUR MIND?

THAT'S ALL RIGHT. I KNOW THE PLACE.

WELL, WHAT ABOUT HANGING IT UP AT WORK?

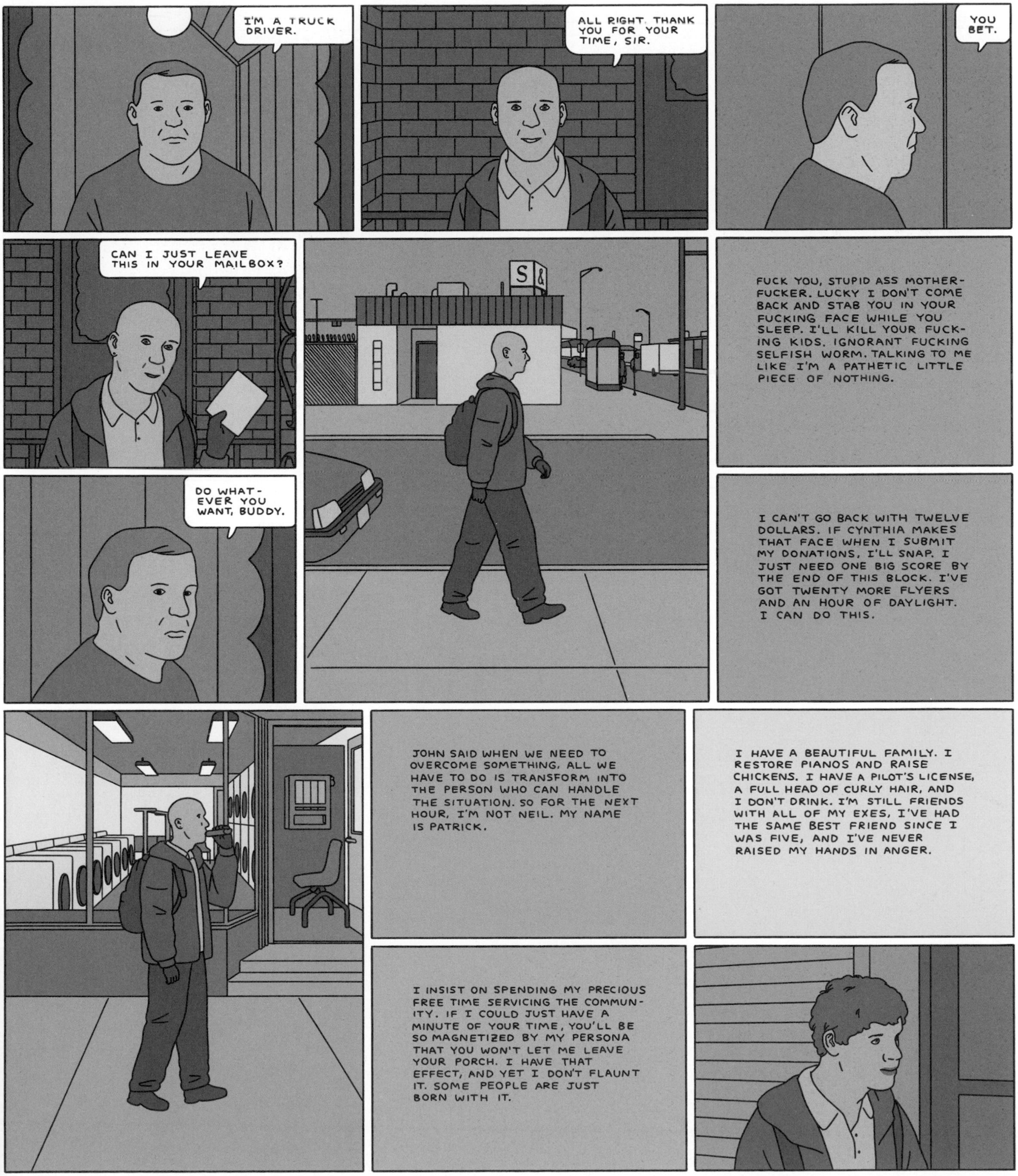
I'M A TRUCK DRIVER.
ALL RIGHT. THANK YOU FOR YOUR TIME, SIR.
YOU BET.
CAN I JUST LEAVE THIS IN YOUR MAILBOX?
DO WHATEVER YOU WANT, BUDDY.
FUCK YOU, STUPID ASS MOTHERFUCKER. LUCKY I DON'T COME BACK AND STAB YOU IN YOUR FUCKING FACE WHILE YOU SLEEP. I'LL KILL YOUR FUCKING KIDS. IGNORANT FUCKING SELFISH WORM. TALKING TO ME LIKE I'M A PATHETIC LITTLE PIECE OF NOTHING.
I CAN'T GO BACK WITH TWELVE DOLLARS. IF CYNTHIA MAKES THAT FACE WHEN I SUBMIT MY DONATIONS, I'LL SNAP. I JUST NEED ONE BIG SCORE BY THE END OF THIS BLOCK. I'VE GOT TWENTY MORE FLYERS AND AN HOUR OF DAYLIGHT. I CAN DO THIS.
JOHN SAID WHEN WE NEED TO OVERCOME SOMETHING, ALL WE HAVE TO DO IS TRANSFORM INTO THE PERSON WHO CAN HANDLE THE SITUATION. SO FOR THE NEXT HOUR, I'M NOT NEIL. MY NAME IS PATRICK.
I HAVE A BEAUTIFUL FAMILY. I RESTORE PIANOS AND RAISE CHICKENS. I HAVE A PILOT'S LICENSE, A FULL HEAD OF CURLY HAIR, AND I DON'T DRINK. I'M STILL FRIENDS WITH ALL OF MY EXES, I'VE HAD THE SAME BEST FRIEND SINCE I WAS FIVE, AND I'VE NEVER RAISED MY HANDS IN ANGER.
I INSIST ON SPENDING MY PRECIOUS FREE TIME SERVICING THE COMMUNITY. IF I COULD JUST HAVE A MINUTE OF YOUR TIME, YOU'LL BE SO MAGNETIZED BY MY PERSONA THAT YOU WON'T LET ME LEAVE YOUR PORCH. I HAVE THAT EFFECT, AND YET I DON'T FLAUNT IT. SOME PEOPLE ARE JUST BORN WITH IT.

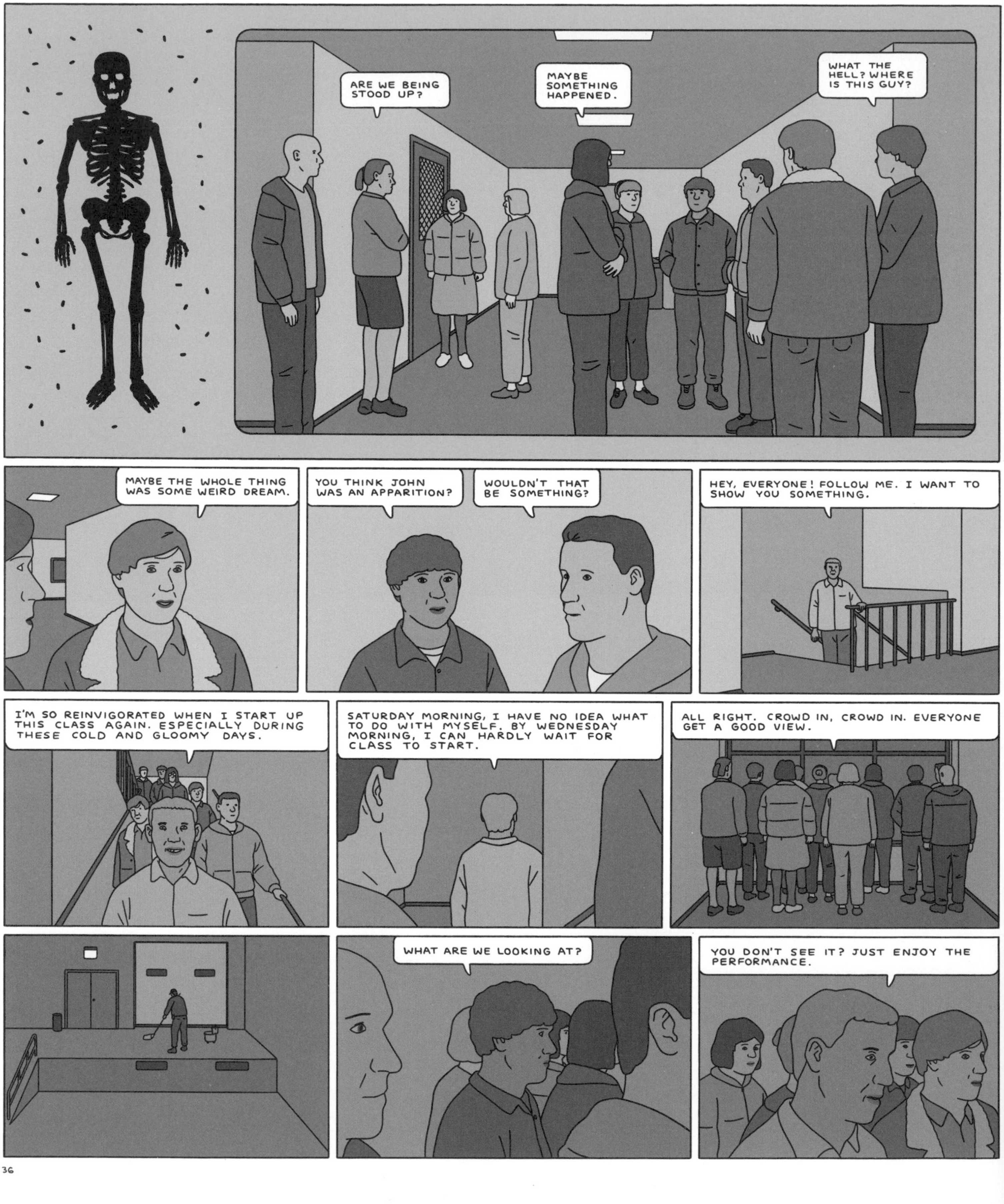
ARE WE BEING STOOD UP?
MAYBE SOMETHING HAPPENED.
WHAT THE HELL? WHERE IS THIS GUY?
MAYBE THE WHOLE THING WAS SOME WEIRD DREAM.
YOU THINK JOHN WAS AN APPARITION?
WOULDN'T THAT BE SOMETHING?
HEY, EVERYONE! FOLLOW ME. I WANT TO SHOW YOU SOMETHING.
I'M SO REINVIGORATED WHEN I START UP THIS CLASS AGAIN. ESPECIALLY DURING THESE COLD AND GLOOMY DAYS.
SATURDAY MORNING, I HAVE NO IDEA WHAT TO DO WITH MYSELF. BY WEDNESDAY MORNING, I CAN HARDLY WAIT FOR CLASS TO START.
ALL RIGHT. CROWD IN, CROWD IN. EVERYONE GET A GOOD VIEW.
WHAT ARE WE LOOKING AT?
YOU DON'T SEE IT? JUST ENJOY THE PERFORMANCE.

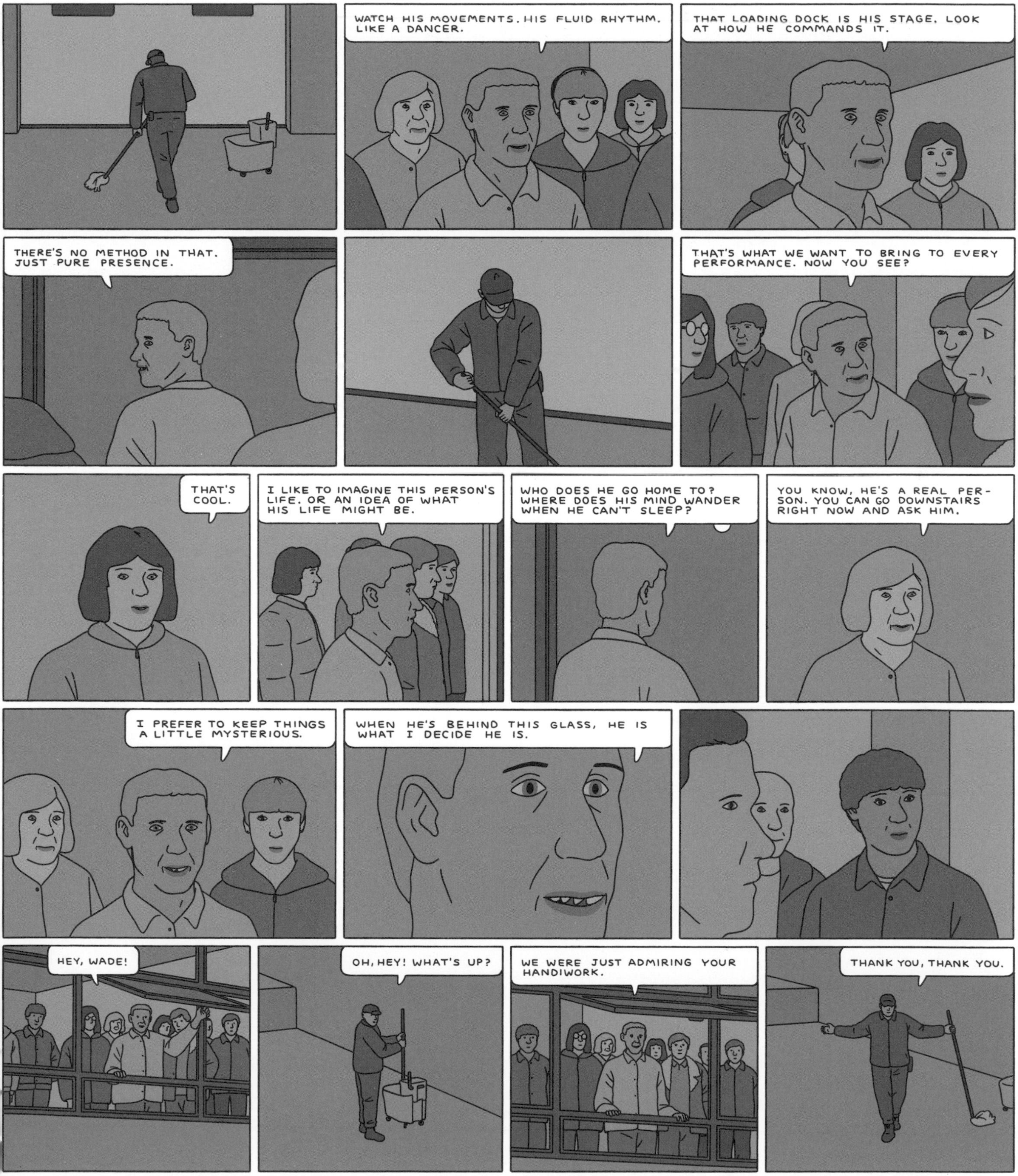
WATCH HIS MOVEMENTS. HIS FLUID RHYTHM. LIKE A DANCER.
THAT LOADING DOCK IS HIS STAGE. LOOK AT HOW HE COMMANDS IT.
THERE'S NO METHOD IN THAT. JUST PURE PRESENCE.
THAT'S WHAT WE WANT TO BRING TO EVERY PERFORMANCE. NOW YOU SEE?
THAT'S COOL.
I LIKE TO IMAGINE THIS PERSON'S LIFE. OR AN IDEA OF WHAT HIS LIFE MIGHT BE.
WHO DOES HE GO HOME TO? WHERE DOES HIS MIND WANDER WHEN HE CAN'T SLEEP?
YOU KNOW, HE'S A REAL PER-SON. YOU CAN GO DOWNSTAIRS RIGHT NOW AND ASK HIM.
I PREFER TO KEEP THINGS A LITTLE MYSTERIOUS.
WHEN HE'S BEHIND THIS GLASS, HE IS WHAT I DECIDE HE IS.
HEY, WADE!
OH, HEY! WHAT'S UP?
WE WERE JUST ADMIRING YOUR HANDIWORK.
THANK YOU, THANK YOU.

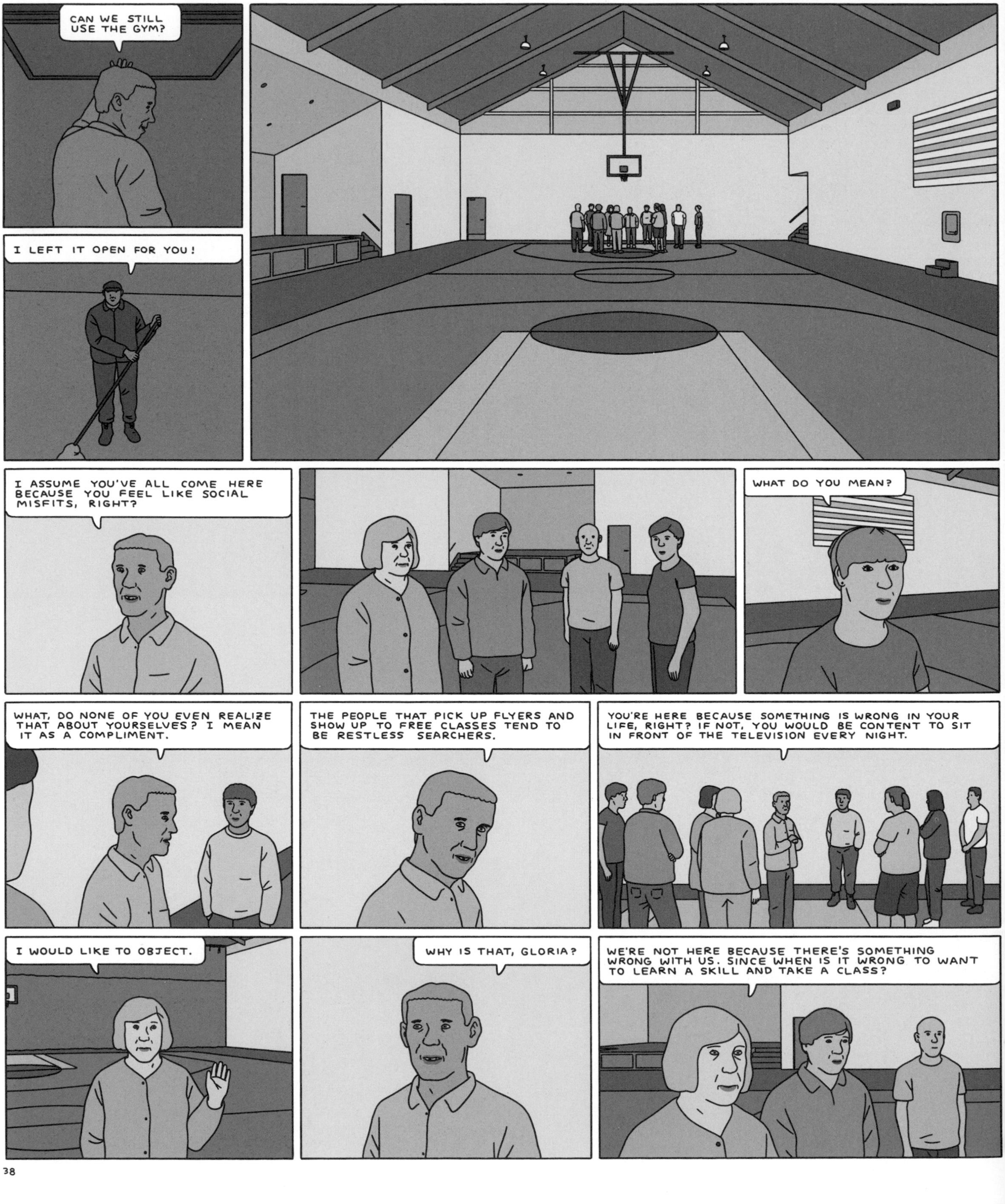
CAN WE STILL USE THE GYM?
I LEFT IT OPEN FOR YOU!
I ASSUME YOU'VE ALL COME HERE BECAUSE YOU FEEL LIKE SOCIAL MISFITS, RIGHT?
WHAT DO YOU MEAN?
WHAT, DO NONE OF YOU EVEN REALIZE THAT ABOUT YOURSELVES? I MEAN IT AS A COMPLIMENT.
THE PEOPLE THAT PICK UP FLYERS AND SHOW UP TO FREE CLASSES TEND TO BE RESTLESS SEARCHERS.
YOU'RE HERE BECAUSE SOMETHING IS WRONG IN YOUR LIFE, RIGHT? IF NOT, YOU WOULD BE CONTENT TO SIT IN FRONT OF THE TELEVISION EVERY NIGHT.
I WOULD LIKE TO OBJECT.
WHY IS THAT, GLORIA?
WE'RE NOT HERE BECAUSE THERE'S SOMETHING WRONG WITH US. SINCE WHEN IS IT WRONG TO WANT TO LEARN A SKILL AND TAKE A CLASS?

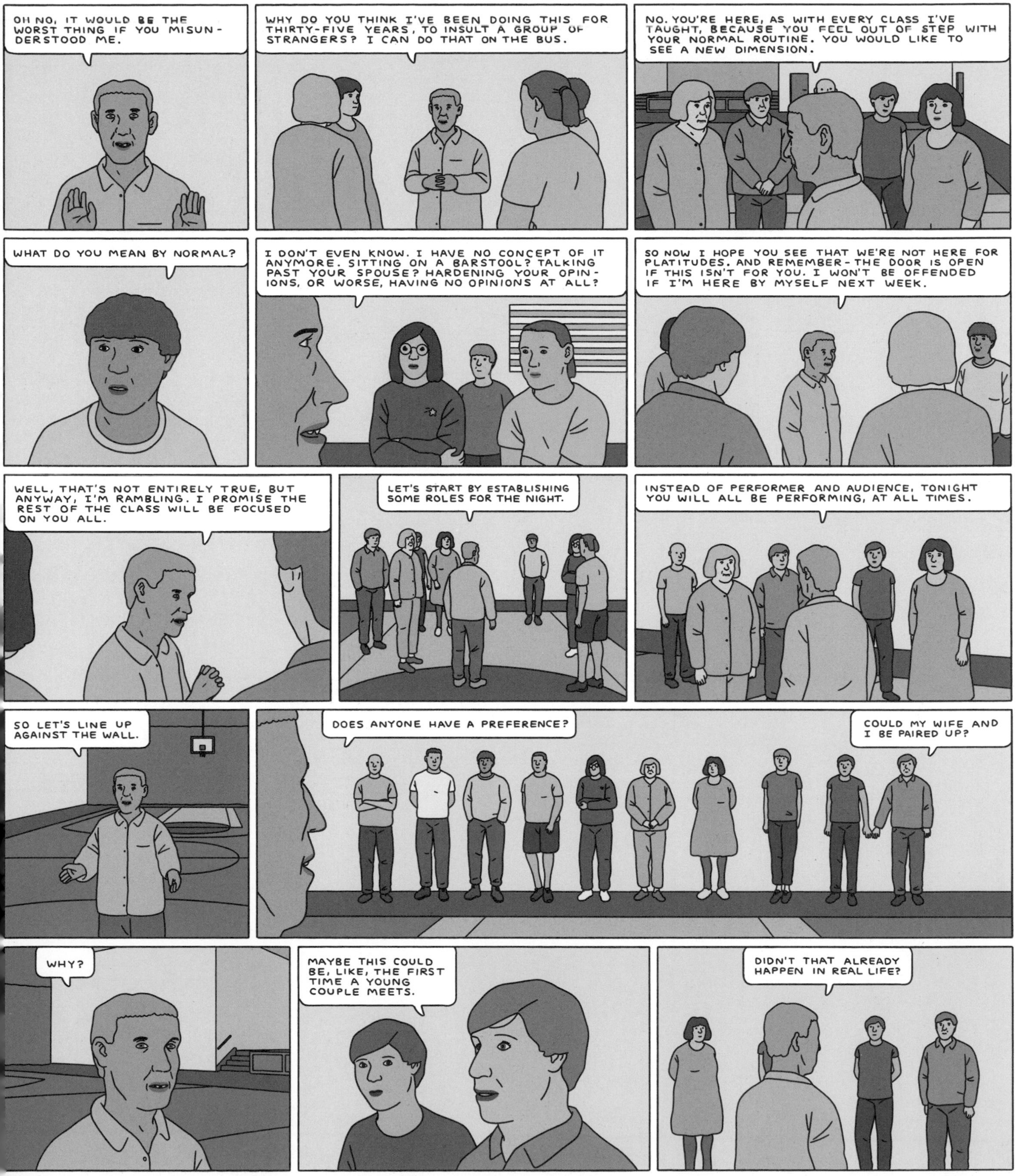
OH NO, IT WOULD BE THE WORST THING IF YOU MISUNDERSTOOD ME.
WHY DO YOU THINK I'VE BEEN DOING THIS FOR THIRTY-FIVE YEARS, TO INSULT A GROUP OF STRANGERS? I CAN DO THAT ON THE BUS.
NO. YOU'RE HERE, AS WITH EVERY CLASS I'VE TAUGHT, BECAUSE YOU FEEL OUT OF STEP WITH YOUR NORMAL ROUTINE. YOU WOULD LIKE TO SEE A NEW DIMENSION.
WHAT DO YOU MEAN BY NORMAL?
I DON'T EVEN KNOW. I HAVE NO CONCEPT OF IT ANYMORE. SITTING ON A BARSTOOL? TALKING PAST YOUR SPOUSE? HARDENING YOUR OPINIONS, OR WORSE, HAVING NO OPINIONS AT ALL?
SO NOW I HOPE YOU SEE THAT WE'RE NOT HERE FOR PLATITUDES. AND REMEMBER - THE DOOR IS OPEN IF THIS ISN'T FOR YOU. I WON'T BE OFFENDED IF I'M HERE BY MYSELF NEXT WEEK.
WELL, THAT'S NOT ENTIRELY TRUE, BUT ANYWAY, I'M RAMBLING. I PROMISE THE REST OF THE CLASS WILL BE FOCUSED ON YOU ALL.
LET'S START BY ESTABLISHING SOME ROLES FOR THE NIGHT.
INSTEAD OF PERFORMER AND AUDIENCE, TONIGHT YOU WILL ALL BE PERFORMING, AT ALL TIMES.
SO LET'S LINE UP AGAINST THE WALL.
DOES ANYONE HAVE A PREFERENCE?
COULD MY WIFE AND I BE PAIRED UP?
WHY?
MAYBE THIS COULD BE, LIKE, THE FIRST TIME A YOUNG COUPLE MEETS.
DIDN'T THAT ALREADY HAPPEN IN REAL LIFE?

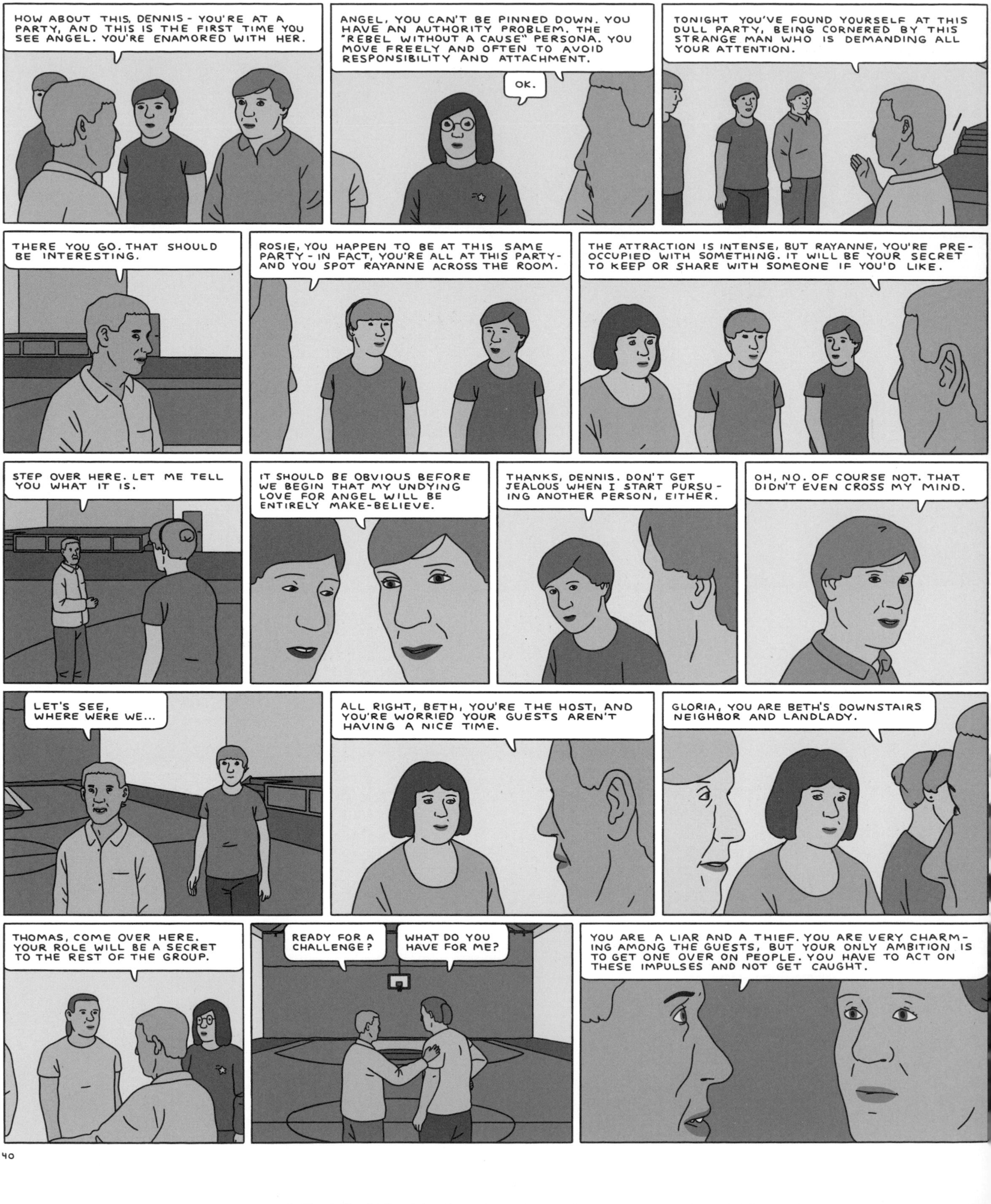
HOW ABOUT THIS, DENNIS - YOU'RE AT A PARTY, AND THIS IS THE FIRST TIME YOU SEE ANGEL. YOU'RE ENAMORED WITH HER.
ANGEL, YOU CAN'T BE PINNED DOWN. YOU HAVE AN AUTHORITY PROBLEM. THE "REBEL WITHOUT A CAUSE" PERSONA. YOU MOVE FREELY AND OFTEN TO AVOID RESPONSIBILITY AND ATTACHMENT.
OK.
TONIGHT YOU'VE FOUND YOURSELF AT THIS DULL PARTY, BEING CORNERED BY THIS STRANGE MAN WHO IS DEMANDING ALL YOUR ATTENTION.
THERE YOU GO. THAT SHOULD BE INTERESTING.
ROSIE, YOU HAPPEN TO BE AT THIS SAME PARTY - IN FACT, YOU'RE ALL AT THIS PARTY - AND YOU SPOT RAYANNE ACROSS THE ROOM.
THE ATTRACTION IS INTENSE, BUT RAYANNE, YOU'RE PRE-OCCUPIED WITH SOMETHING. IT WILL BE YOUR SECRET TO KEEP OR SHARE WITH SOMEONE IF YOU'D LIKE.
STEP OVER HERE. LET ME TELL YOU WHAT IT IS.
IT SHOULD BE OBVIOUS BEFORE WE BEGIN THAT MY UNDYING LOVE FOR ANGEL WILL BE ENTIRELY MAKE-BELIEVE.
THANKS, DENNIS. DON'T GET JEALOUS WHEN I START PURSU-ING ANOTHER PERSON, EITHER.
OH, NO. OF COURSE NOT. THAT DIDN'T EVEN CROSS MY MIND.
LET'S SEE, WHERE WERE WE...
ALL RIGHT, BETH, YOU'RE THE HOST, AND YOU'RE WORRIED YOUR GUESTS AREN'T HAVING A NICE TIME.
GLORIA, YOU ARE BETH'S DOWNSTAIRS NEIGHBOR AND LANDLADY.
THOMAS, COME OVER HERE. YOUR ROLE WILL BE A SECRET TO THE REST OF THE GROUP.
READY FOR A CHALLENGE?
WHAT DO YOU HAVE FOR ME?
YOU ARE A LIAR AND A THIEF. YOU ARE VERY CHARM-ING AMONG THE GUESTS, BUT YOUR ONLY AMBITION IS TO GET ONE OVER ON PEOPLE. YOU HAVE TO ACT ON THESE IMPULSES AND NOT GET CAUGHT.

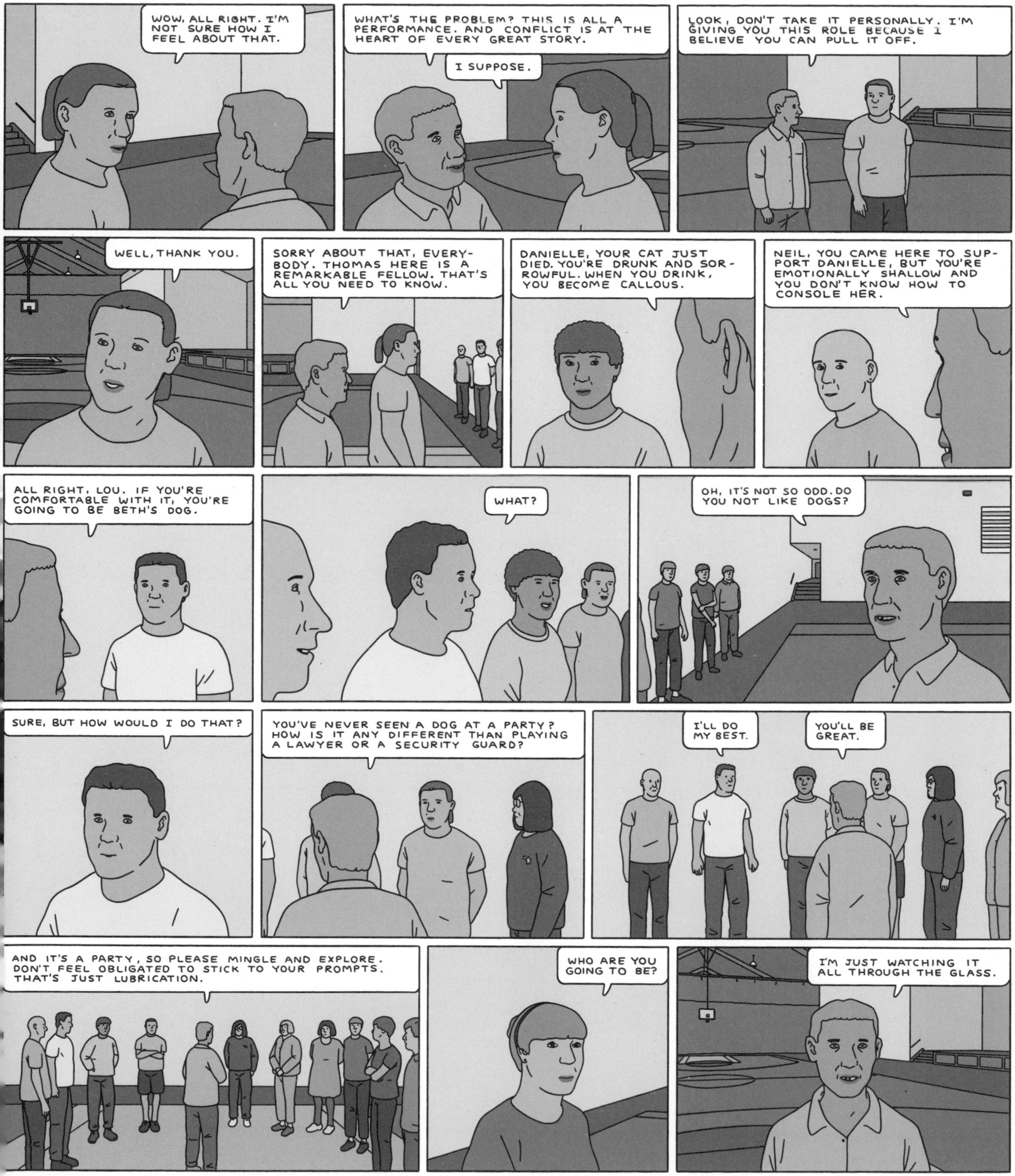
WOW, ALL RIGHT. I'M NOT SURE HOW I FEEL ABOUT THAT.
WHAT'S THE PROBLEM? THIS IS ALL A PERFORMANCE. AND CONFLICT IS AT THE HEART OF EVERY GREAT STORY.
I SUPPOSE.
LOOK, DON'T TAKE IT PERSONALLY. I'M GIVING YOU THIS ROLE BECAUSE I BELIEVE YOU CAN PULL IT OFF.
WELL, THANK YOU.
SORRY ABOUT THAT, EVERY-BODY. THOMAS HERE IS A REMARKABLE FELLOW. THAT'S ALL YOU NEED TO KNOW.
DANIELLE, YOUR CAT JUST DIED. YOU'RE DRUNK AND SOR-ROWFUL. WHEN YOU DRINK, YOU BECOME CALLOUS.
NEIL, YOU CAME HERE TO SUP-PORT DANIELLE, BUT YOU'RE EMOTIONALLY SHALLOW AND YOU DON'T KNOW HOW TO CONSOLE HER.
ALL RIGHT, LOU. IF YOU'RE COMFORTABLE WITH IT, YOU'RE GOING TO BE BETH'S DOG.
WHAT?
OH, IT'S NOT SO ODD. DO YOU NOT LIKE DOGS?
SURE, BUT HOW WOULD I DO THAT?
YOU'VE NEVER SEEN A DOG AT A PARTY? HOW IS IT ANY DIFFERENT THAN PLAYING A LAWYER OR A SECURITY GUARD?
I'LL DO MY BEST.
YOU'LL BE GREAT.
AND IT'S A PARTY, SO PLEASE MINGLE AND EXPLORE. DON'T FEEL OBLIGATED TO STICK TO YOUR PROMPTS. THAT'S JUST LUBRICATION.
WHO ARE YOU GOING TO BE?
I'M JUST WATCHING IT ALL THROUGH THE GLASS.

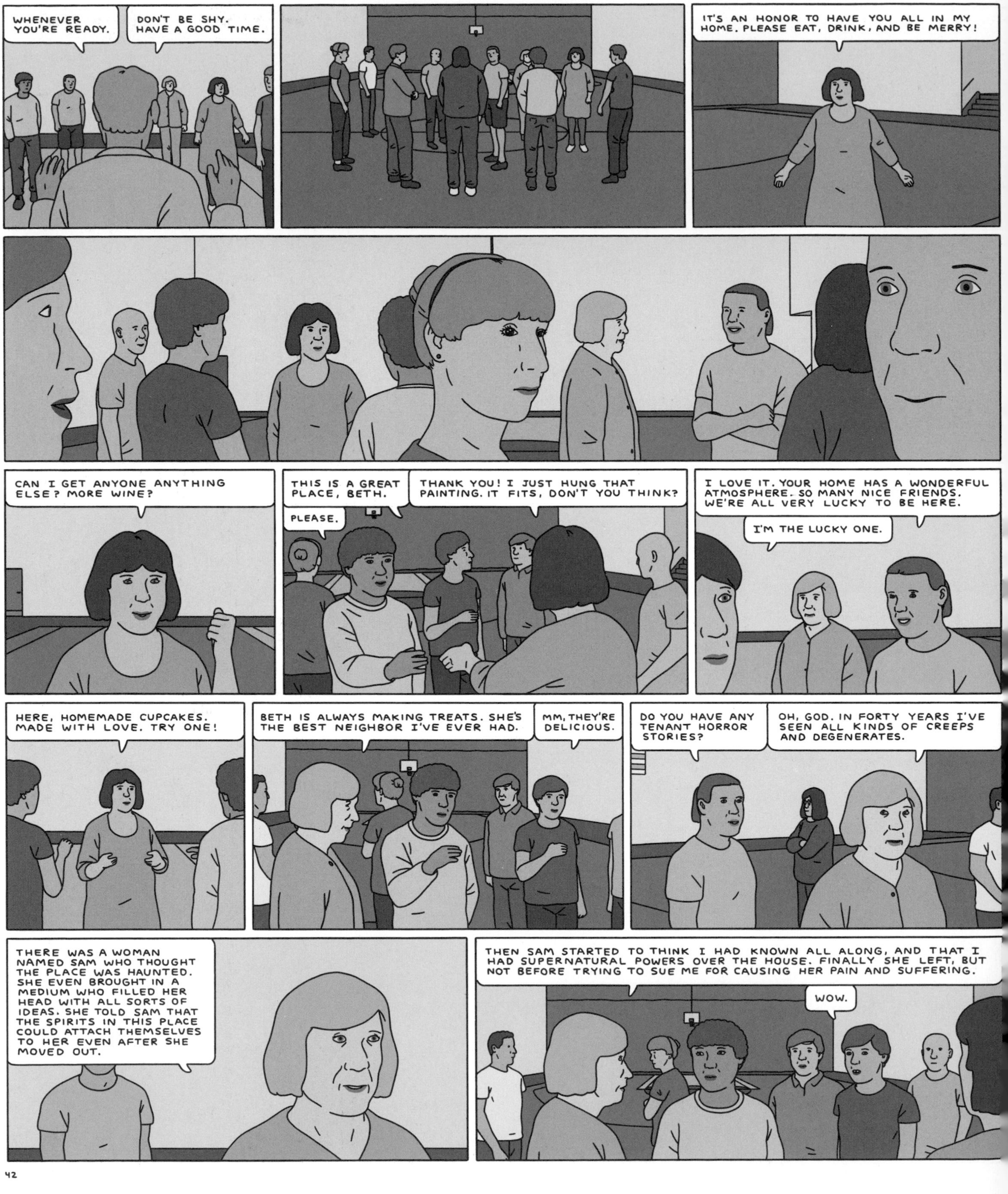
WHENEVER YOU'RE READY.
DON'T BE SHY. HAVE A GOOD TIME.
IT'S AN HONOR TO HAVE YOU ALL IN MY HOME. PLEASE EAT, DRINK, AND BE MERRY!
CAN I GET ANYONE ANYTHING ELSE? MORE WINE?
THIS IS A GREAT PLACE, BETH.
PLEASE.
THANK YOU! I JUST HUNG THAT PAINTING. IT FITS, DON'T YOU THINK?
I LOVE IT. YOUR HOME HAS A WONDERFUL ATMOSPHERE. SO MANY NICE FRIENDS. WE'RE ALL VERY LUCKY TO BE HERE.
I'M THE LUCKY ONE.
HERE, HOMEMADE CUPCAKES. MADE WITH LOVE. TRY ONE!
BETH IS ALWAYS MAKING TREATS. SHE'S THE BEST NEIGHBOR I'VE EVER HAD.
MM, THEY'RE DELICIOUS.
DO YOU HAVE ANY TENANT HORROR STORIES?
OH, GOD. IN FORTY YEARS I'VE SEEN ALL KINDS OF CREEPS AND DEGENERATES.
THERE WAS A WOMAN NAMED SAM WHO THOUGHT THE PLACE WAS HAUNTED. SHE EVEN BROUGHT IN A MEDIUM WHO FILLED HER HEAD WITH ALL SORTS OF IDEAS. SHE TOLD SAM THAT THE SPIRITS IN THIS PLACE COULD ATTACH THEMSELVES TO HER EVEN AFTER SHE MOVED OUT.
THEN SAM STARTED TO THINK I HAD KNOWN ALL ALONG, AND THAT I HAD SUPERNATURAL POWERS OVER THE HOUSE. FINALLY SHE LEFT, BUT NOT BEFORE TRYING TO SUE ME FOR CAUSING HER PAIN AND SUFFERING.
WOW.

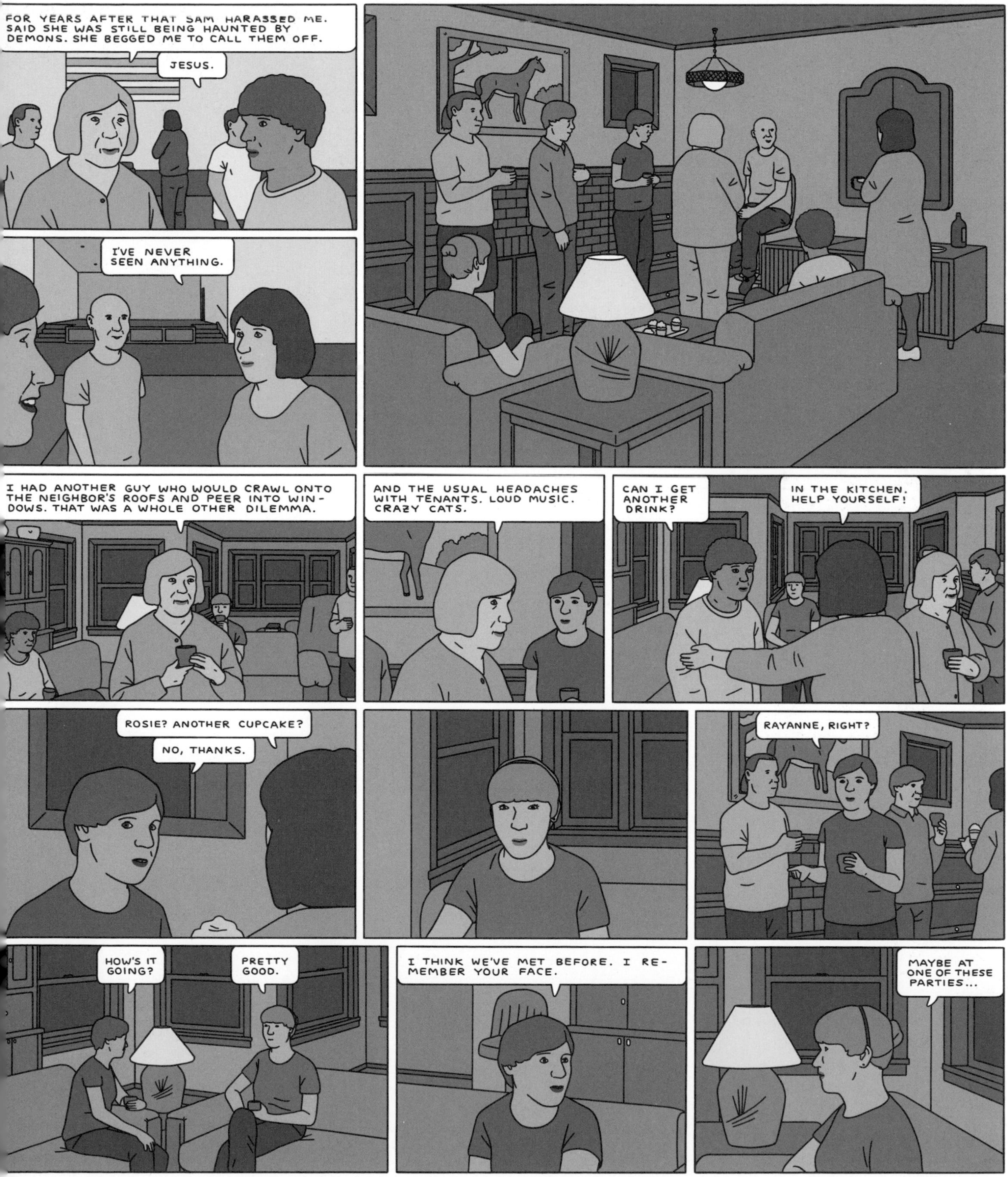
FOR YEARS AFTER THAT SAM HARASSED ME. SAID SHE WAS STILL BEING HAUNTED BY DEMONS. SHE BEGGED ME TO CALL THEM OFF.
JESUS.
I'VE NEVER SEEN ANYTHING.
I HAD ANOTHER GUY WHO WOULD CRAWL ONTO THE NEIGHBOR'S ROOFS AND PEER INTO WINDOWS. THAT WAS A WHOLE OTHER DILEMMA.
AND THE USUAL HEADACHES WITH TENANTS. LOUD MUSIC. CRAZY CATS.
CAN I GET ANOTHER DRINK?
IN THE KITCHEN. HELP YOURSELF!
ROSIE? ANOTHER CUPCAKE?
NO, THANKS.
RAYANNE, RIGHT?
HOW'S IT GOING?
PRETTY GOOD.
I THINK WE'VE MET BEFORE. I REMEMBER YOUR FACE.
MAYBE AT ONE OF THESE PARTIES...

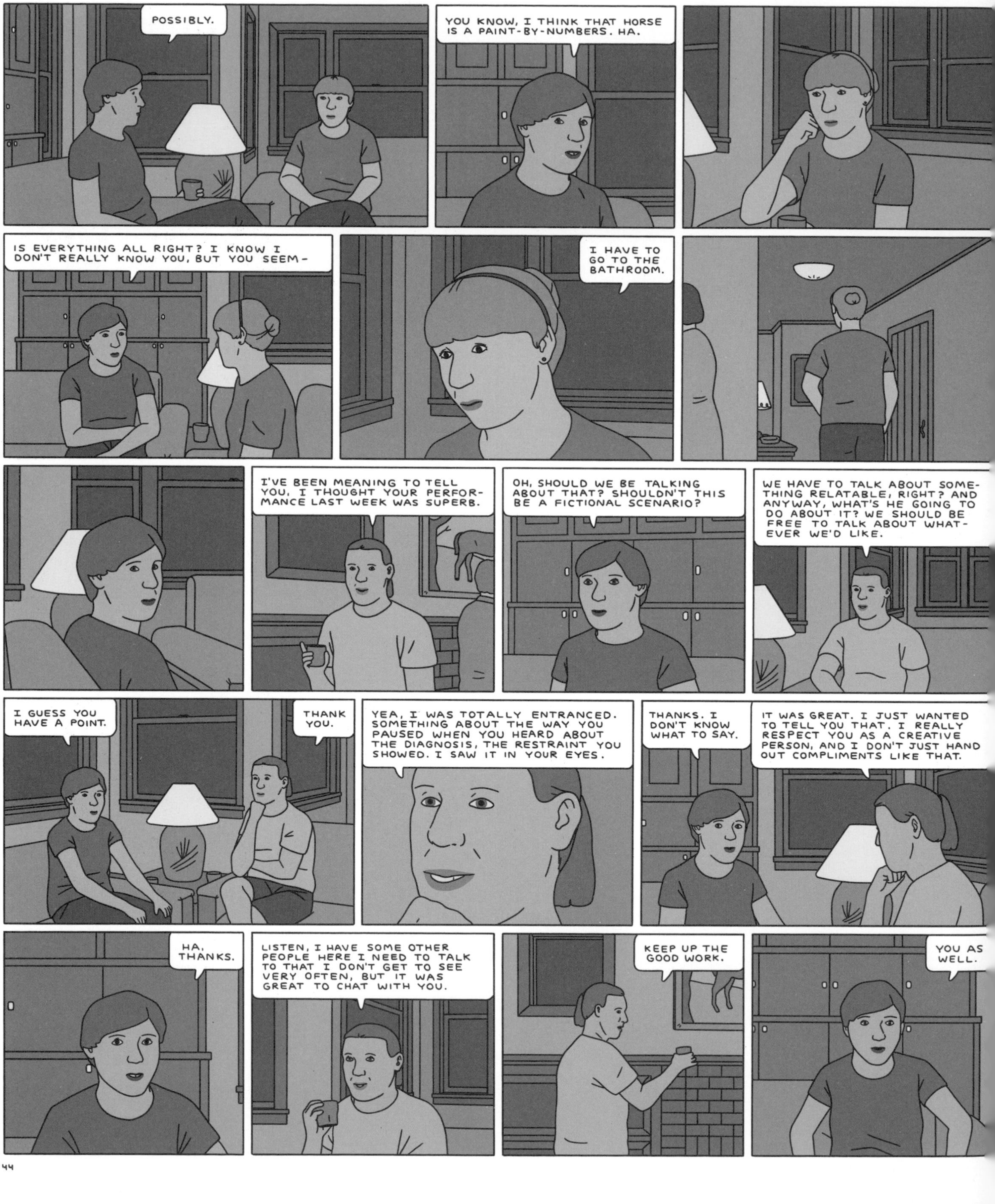
POSSIBLY.
YOU KNOW, I THINK THAT HORSE IS A PAINT-BY-NUMBERS. HA.
IS EVERYTHING ALL RIGHT? I KNOW I DON'T REALLY KNOW YOU, BUT YOU SEEM-
I HAVE TO GO TO THE BATHROOM.
I'VE BEEN MEANING TO TELL YOU, I THOUGHT YOUR PERFORMANCE LAST WEEK WAS SUPERB.
OH, SHOULD WE BE TALKING ABOUT THAT? SHOULDN'T THIS BE A FICTIONAL SCENARIO?
WE HAVE TO TALK ABOUT SOMETHING RELATABLE, RIGHT? AND ANYWAY, WHAT'S HE GOING TO DO ABOUT IT? WE SHOULD BE FREE TO TALK ABOUT WHATEVER WE'D LIKE.
I GUESS YOU HAVE A POINT.
THANK YOU.
YEA, I WAS TOTALLY ENTRANCED. SOMETHING ABOUT THE WAY YOU PAUSED WHEN YOU HEARD ABOUT THE DIAGNOSIS, THE RESTRAINT YOU SHOWED. I SAW IT IN YOUR EYES.
THANKS. I DON'T KNOW WHAT TO SAY.
IT WAS GREAT. I JUST WANTED TO TELL YOU THAT. I REALLY RESPECT YOU AS A CREATIVE PERSON, AND I DON'T JUST HAND OUT COMPLIMENTS LIKE THAT.
HA. THANKS.
LISTEN, I HAVE SOME OTHER PEOPLE HERE I NEED TO TALK TO THAT I DON'T GET TO SEE VERY OFTEN, BUT IT WAS GREAT TO CHAT WITH YOU.
KEEP UP THE GOOD WORK.
YOU AS WELL.

GOT AN EXTRA CIGARETTE?

THANKS.

AND A LIGHT?

I'M DENNIS.

WHAT'S YOUR NAME?

ANGEL.

PLEASURE TO MEET YOU. HOW DO YOU KNOW BETH?

I DON'T KNOW HER. I JUST FOUND MYSELF HERE.

THAT'S COOL. I'VE KNOWN BETH FOR YEAR'S. SHE'S A GREAT PERSON.

THAT'S WONDERFUL.

HAHA.

WHAT ARE YOU LAUGHING AT?

NOTHING. IT'S JUST, YOU'RE NOT THE ANGEL I'VE TALKED TO AT THOSE WORK CHRISTMAS PARTIES.

CHRISTMAS PARTIES? I'VE NEVER WORKED A JOB LONG ENOUGH TO GO TO ANY GODDAMNED CHRISTMAS PARTIES.

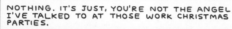

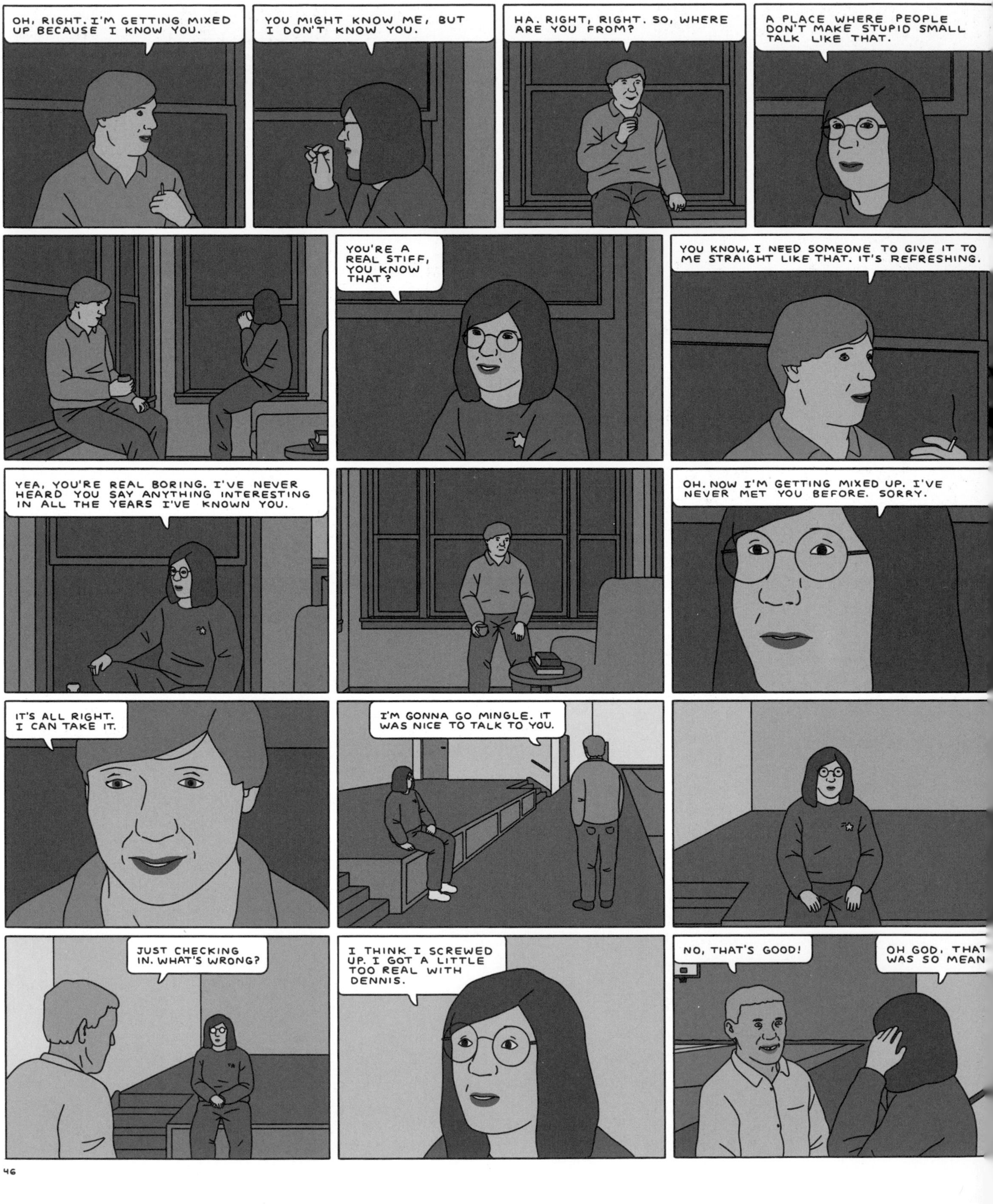
OH, RIGHT. I'M GETTING MIXED UP BECAUSE I KNOW YOU.
YOU MIGHT KNOW ME, BUT I DON'T KNOW YOU.
HA. RIGHT, RIGHT. SO, WHERE ARE YOU FROM?
A PLACE WHERE PEOPLE DON'T MAKE STUPID SMALL TALK LIKE THAT.
YOU'RE A REAL STIFF, YOU KNOW THAT?
YOU KNOW, I NEED SOMEONE TO GIVE IT TO ME STRAIGHT LIKE THAT. IT'S REFRESHING.
YEA, YOU'RE REAL BORING. I'VE NEVER HEARD YOU SAY ANYTHING INTERESTING IN ALL THE YEARS I'VE KNOWN YOU.
OH. NOW I'M GETTING MIXED UP. I'VE NEVER MET YOU BEFORE. SORRY.
IT'S ALL RIGHT. I CAN TAKE IT.
I'M GONNA GO MINGLE. IT WAS NICE TO TALK TO YOU.
JUST CHECKING IN. WHAT'S WRONG?
I THINK I SCREWED UP. I GOT A LITTLE TOO REAL WITH DENNIS.
NO, THAT'S GOOD!
OH GOD, THAT WAS SO MEAN

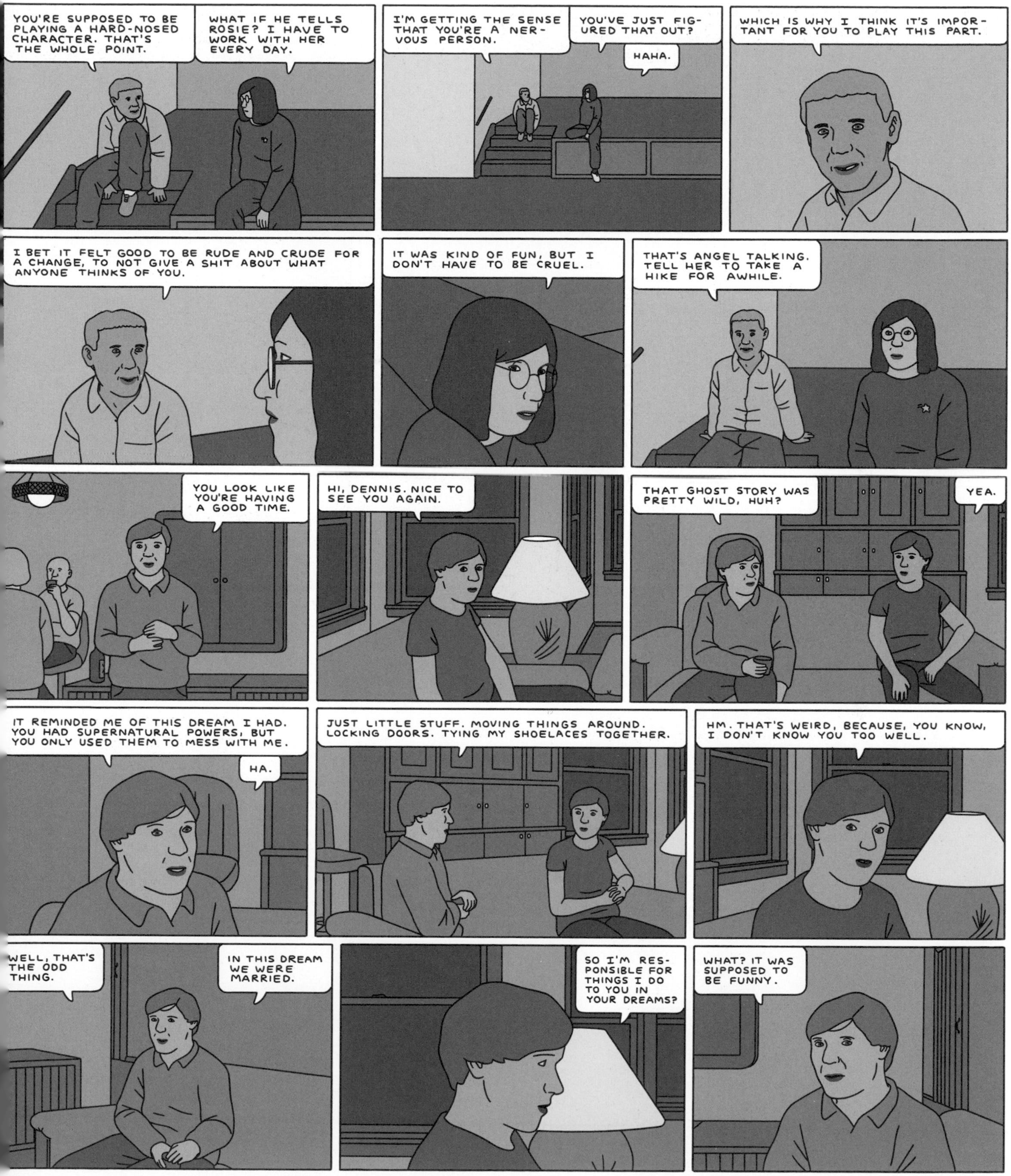
YOU'RE SUPPOSED TO BE PLAYING A HARD-NOSED CHARACTER. THAT'S THE WHOLE POINT.
WHAT IF HE TELLS ROSIE? I HAVE TO WORK WITH HER EVERY DAY.
I'M GETTING THE SENSE THAT YOU'RE A NER-VOUS PERSON.
YOU'VE JUST FIG-URED THAT OUT?
HAHA.
WHICH IS WHY I THINK IT'S IMPOR-TANT FOR YOU TO PLAY THIS PART.
I BET IT FELT GOOD TO BE RUDE AND CRUDE FOR A CHANGE, TO NOT GIVE A SHIT ABOUT WHAT ANYONE THINKS OF YOU.
IT WAS KIND OF FUN, BUT I DON'T HAVE TO BE CRUEL.
THAT'S ANGEL TALKING. TELL HER TO TAKE A HIKE FOR AWHILE.
YOU LOOK LIKE YOU'RE HAVING A GOOD TIME.
HI, DENNIS. NICE TO SEE YOU AGAIN.
THAT GHOST STORY WAS PRETTY WILD, HUH?
YEA.
IT REMINDED ME OF THIS DREAM I HAD. YOU HAD SUPERNATURAL POWERS, BUT YOU ONLY USED THEM TO MESS WITH ME.
HA.
JUST LITTLE STUFF. MOVING THINGS AROUND. LOCKING DOORS. TYING MY SHOELACES TOGETHER.
HM. THAT'S WEIRD, BECAUSE, YOU KNOW, I DON'T KNOW YOU TOO WELL.
WELL, THAT'S THE ODD THING.
IN THIS DREAM WE WERE MARRIED.
SO I'M RES-PONSIBLE FOR THINGS I DO TO YOU IN YOUR DREAMS?
WHAT? IT WAS SUPPOSED TO BE FUNNY.

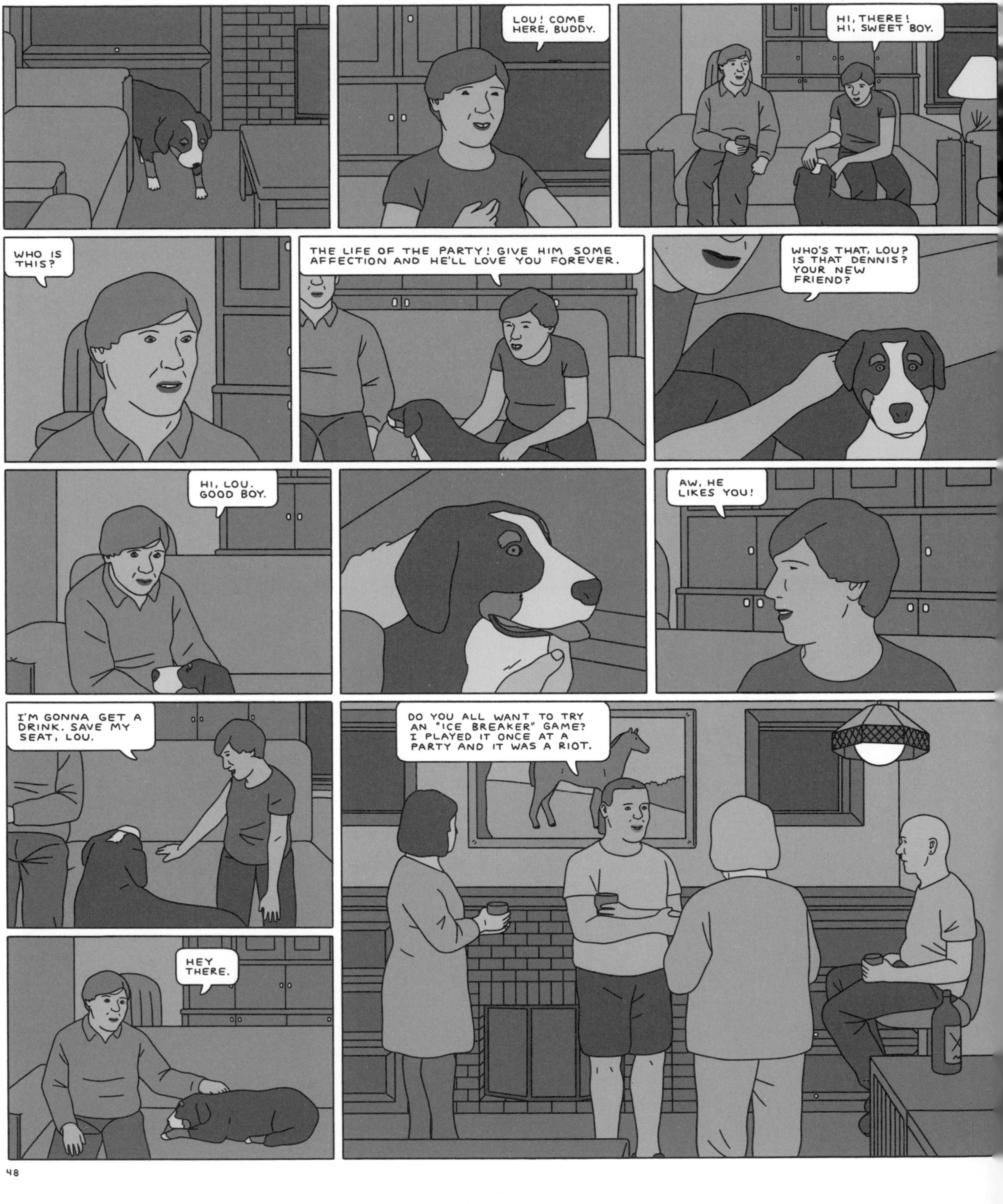
LOU! COME HERE, BUDDY.
HI, THERE! HI, SWEET BOY.
WHO IS THIS?
THE LIFE OF THE PARTY! GIVE HIM SOME AFFECTION AND HE'LL LOVE YOU FOREVER.
WHO'S THAT, LOU? IS THAT DENNIS? YOUR NEW FRIEND?
HI, LOU. GOOD BOY.
AW, HE LIKES YOU!
I'M GONNA GET A DRINK. SAVE MY SEAT, LOU.
HEY THERE.
DO YOU ALL WANT TO TRY AN "ICE BREAKER" GAME? I PLAYED IT ONCE AT A PARTY AND IT WAS A RIOT.

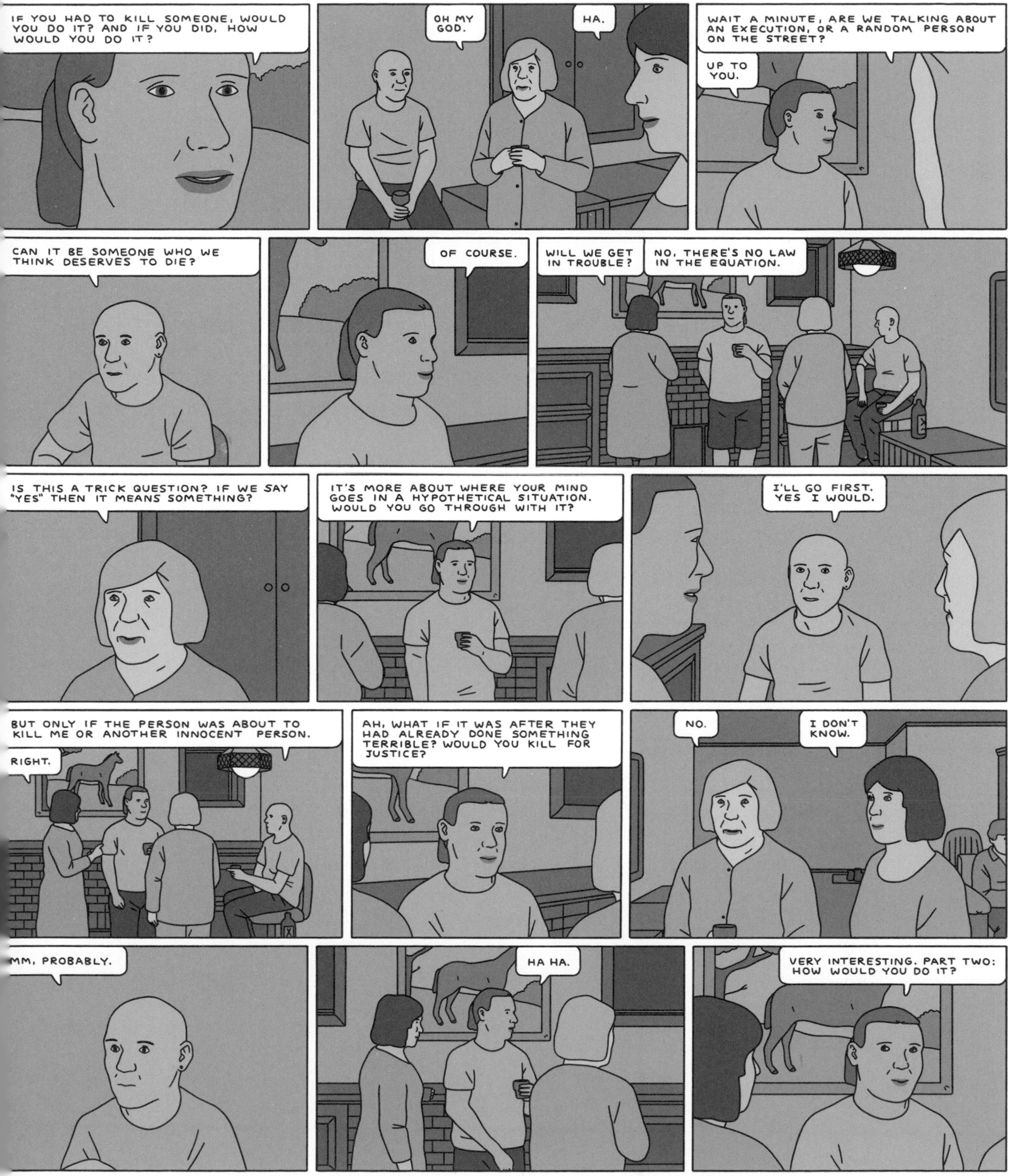
IF YOU HAD TO KILL SOMEONE, WOULD YOU DO IT? AND IF YOU DID, HOW WOULD YOU DO IT?
OH MY GOD.
HA.
WAIT A MINUTE, ARE WE TALKING ABOUT AN EXECUTION, OR A RANDOM PERSON ON THE STREET?
UP TO YOU.
CAN IT BE SOMEONE WHO WE THINK DESERVES TO DIE?
OF COURSE.
WILL WE GET IN TROUBLE?
NO, THERE'S NO LAW IN THE EQUATION.
IS THIS A TRICK QUESTION? IF WE SAY "YES" THEN IT MEANS SOMETHING?
IT'S MORE ABOUT WHERE YOUR MIND GOES IN A HYPOTHETICAL SITUATION. WOULD YOU GO THROUGH WITH IT?
I'LL GO FIRST. YES I WOULD.
BUT ONLY IF THE PERSON WAS ABOUT TO KILL ME OR ANOTHER INNOCENT PERSON.
RIGHT.
AH, WHAT IF IT WAS AFTER THEY HAD ALREADY DONE SOMETHING TERRIBLE? WOULD YOU KILL FOR JUSTICE?
NO.
I DON'T KNOW.
MM, PROBABLY.
HA HA.
VERY INTERESTING. PART TWO: HOW WOULD YOU DO IT?

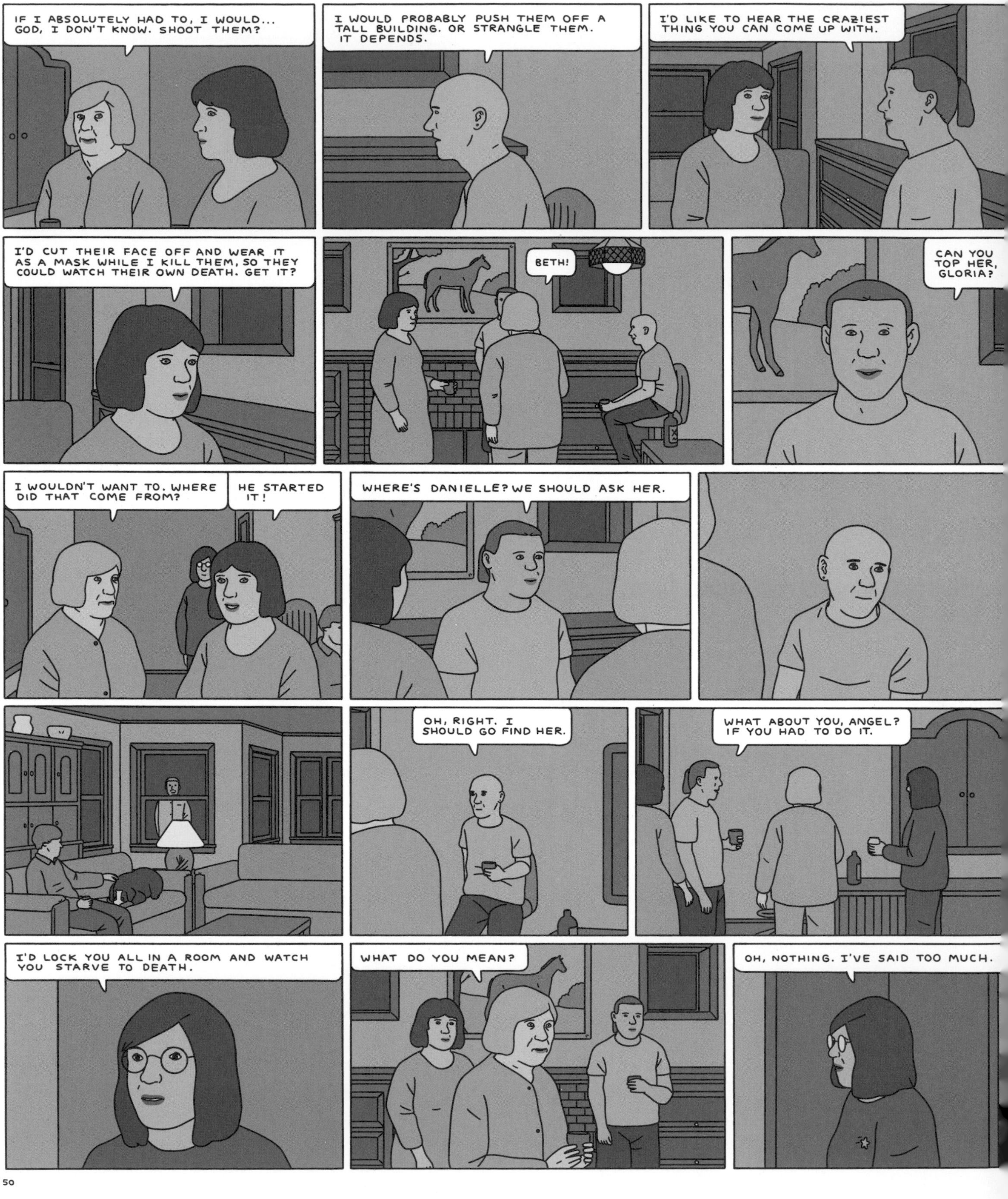
IF I ABSOLUTELY HAD TO, I WOULD... GOD, I DON'T KNOW. SHOOT THEM?
I WOULD PROBABLY PUSH THEM OFF A TALL BUILDING. OR STRANGLE THEM. IT DEPENDS.
I'D LIKE TO HEAR THE CRAZIEST THING YOU CAN COME UP WITH.
I'D CUT THEIR FACE OFF AND WEAR IT AS A MASK WHILE I KILL THEM, SO THEY COULD WATCH THEIR OWN DEATH. GET IT?
BETH!
CAN YOU TOP HER, GLORIA?
I WOULDN'T WANT TO. WHERE DID THAT COME FROM?
HE STARTED IT!
WHERE'S DANIELLE? WE SHOULD ASK HER.
OH, RIGHT. I SHOULD GO FIND HER.
WHAT ABOUT YOU, ANGEL? IF YOU HAD TO DO IT.
I'D LOCK YOU ALL IN A ROOM AND WATCH YOU STARVE TO DEATH.
WHAT DO YOU MEAN?
OH, NOTHING. I'VE SAID TOO MUCH.

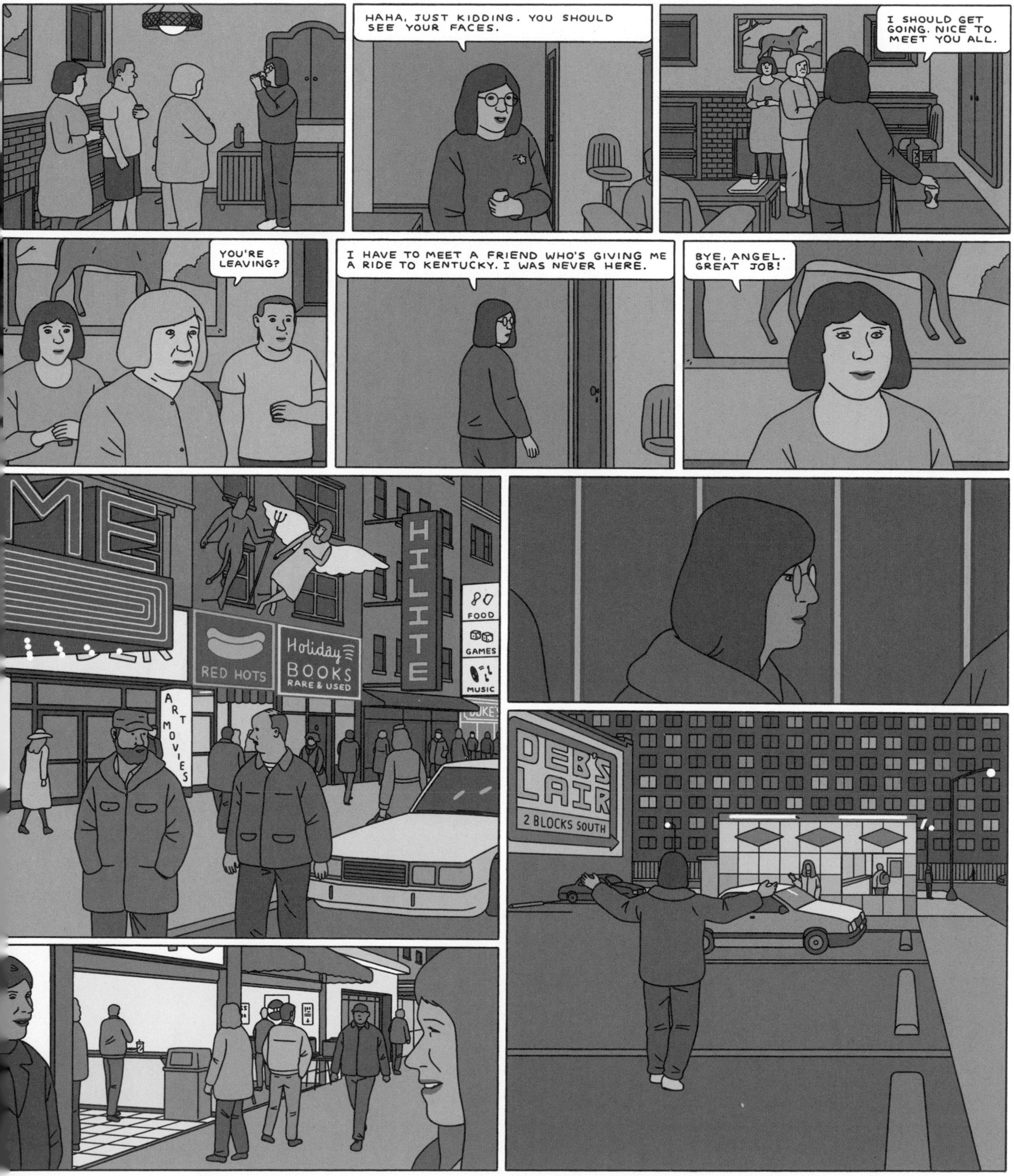
HAHA, JUST KIDDING. YOU SHOULD SEE YOUR FACES.
I SHOULD GET GOING. NICE TO MEET YOU ALL.
YOU'RE LEAVING?
I HAVE TO MEET A FRIEND WHO'S GIVING ME A RIDE TO KENTUCKY. I WAS NEVER HERE.
BYE, ANGEL. GREAT JOB!
HILITE
FOOD
GAMES
MUSIC
RED HOTS
Holiday BOOKS RARE & USED
ART MOVIES
DEB'S LAIR
2 BLOCKS SOUTH

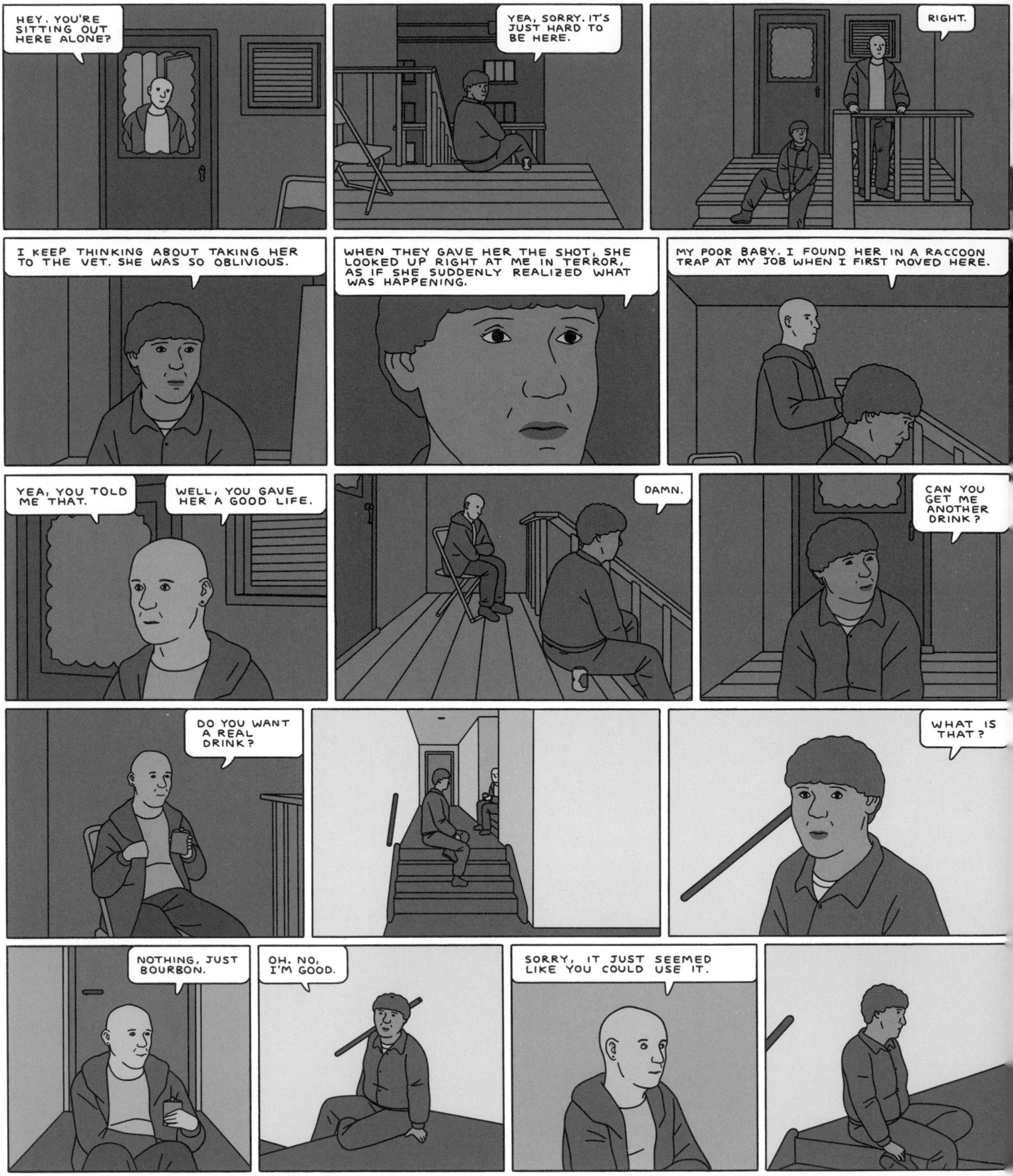
HEY. YOU'RE SITTING OUT HERE ALONE?
YEA, SORRY. IT'S JUST HARD TO BE HERE.
RIGHT.
I KEEP THINKING ABOUT TAKING HER TO THE VET. SHE WAS SO OBLIVIOUS.
WHEN THEY GAVE HER THE SHOT, SHE LOOKED UP RIGHT AT ME IN TERROR, AS IF SHE SUDDENLY REALIZED WHAT WAS HAPPENING.
MY POOR BABY. I FOUND HER IN A RACCOON TRAP AT MY JOB WHEN I FIRST MOVED HERE.
YEA, YOU TOLD ME THAT.
WELL, YOU GAVE HER A GOOD LIFE.
DAMN.
CAN YOU GET ME ANOTHER DRINK?
DO YOU WANT A REAL DRINK?
WHAT IS THAT?
NOTHING, JUST BOURBON.
OH. NO, I'M GOOD.
SORRY, IT JUST SEEMED LIKE YOU COULD USE IT.

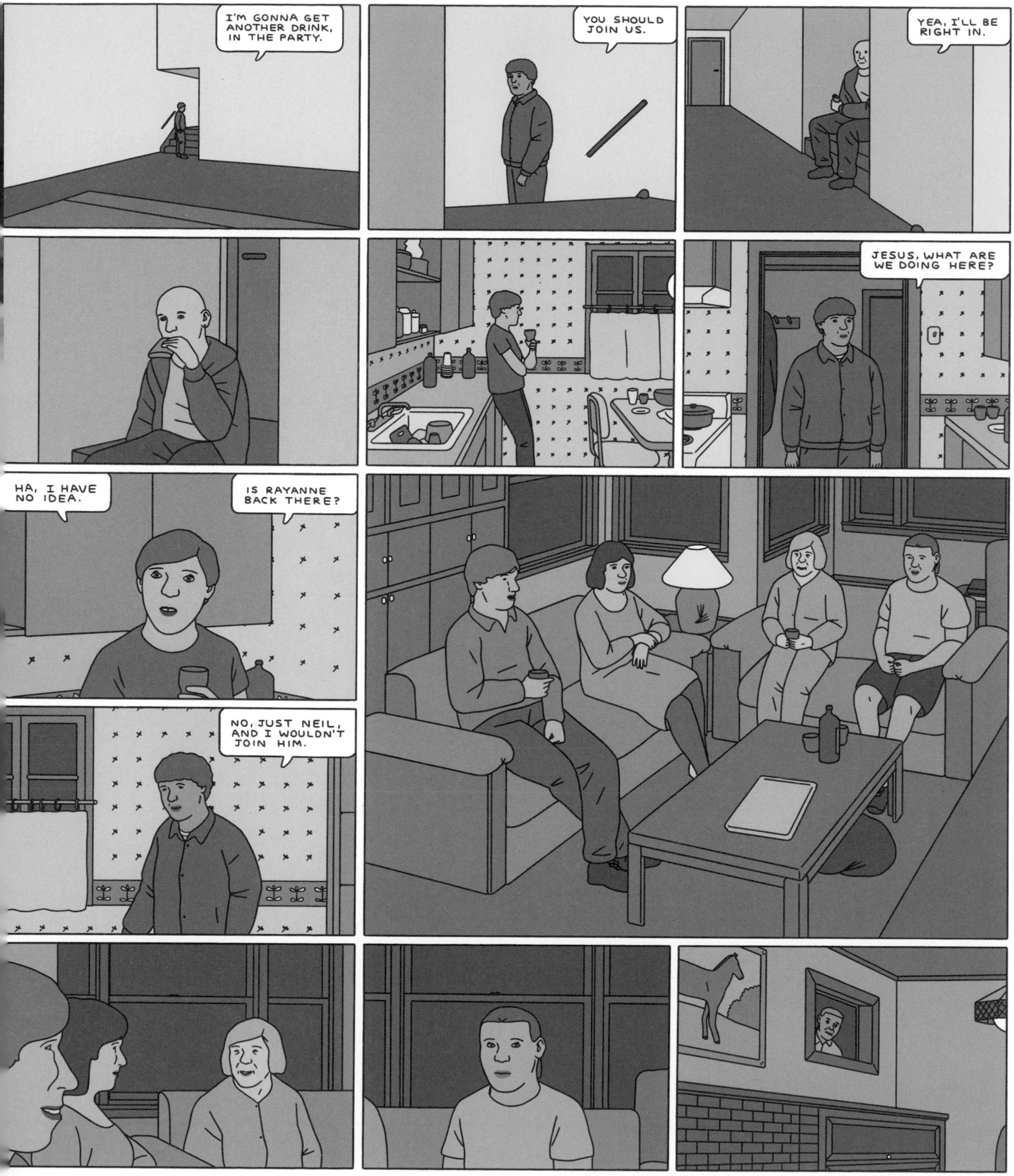
I'M GONNA GET ANOTHER DRINK, IN THE PARTY.
YOU SHOULD JOIN US.
YEA, I'LL BE RIGHT IN.
JESUS, WHAT ARE WE DOING HERE?
HA, I HAVE NO IDEA.
IS RAYANNE BACK THERE?
NO, JUST NEIL, AND I WOULDN'T JOIN HIM.

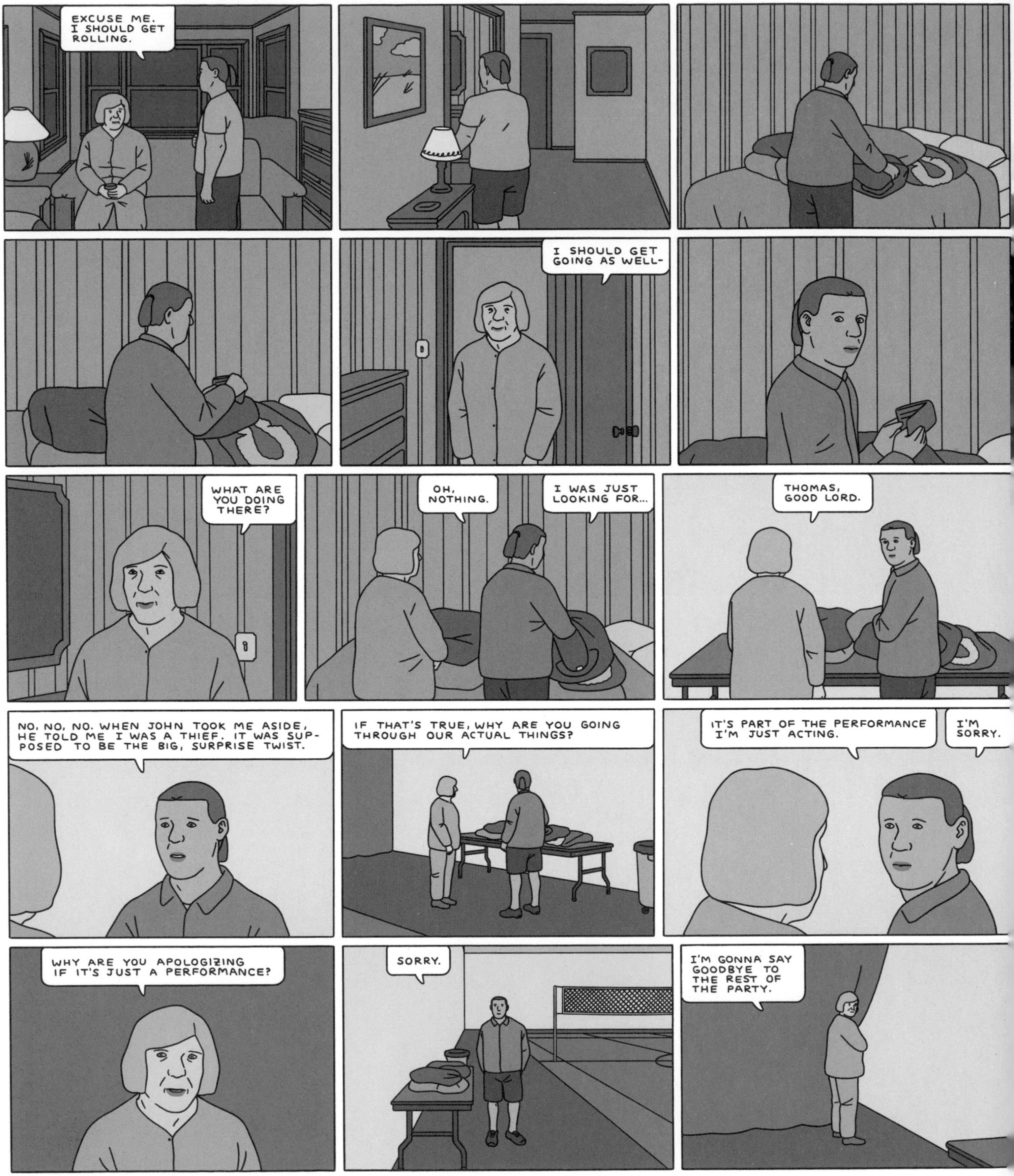
EXCUSE ME. I SHOULD GET ROLLING.
I SHOULD GET GOING AS WELL-
WHAT ARE YOU DOING THERE?
OH, NOTHING.
I WAS JUST LOOKING FOR...
THOMAS, GOOD LORD.
NO, NO, NO. WHEN JOHN TOOK ME ASIDE, HE TOLD ME I WAS A THIEF. IT WAS SUPPOSED TO BE THE BIG, SURPRISE TWIST.
IF THAT'S TRUE, WHY ARE YOU GOING THROUGH OUR ACTUAL THINGS?
IT'S PART OF THE PERFORMANCE I'M JUST ACTING.
I'M SORRY.
WHY ARE YOU APOLOGIZING IF IT'S JUST A PERFORMANCE?
SORRY.
I'M GONNA SAY GOODBYE TO THE REST OF THE PARTY.

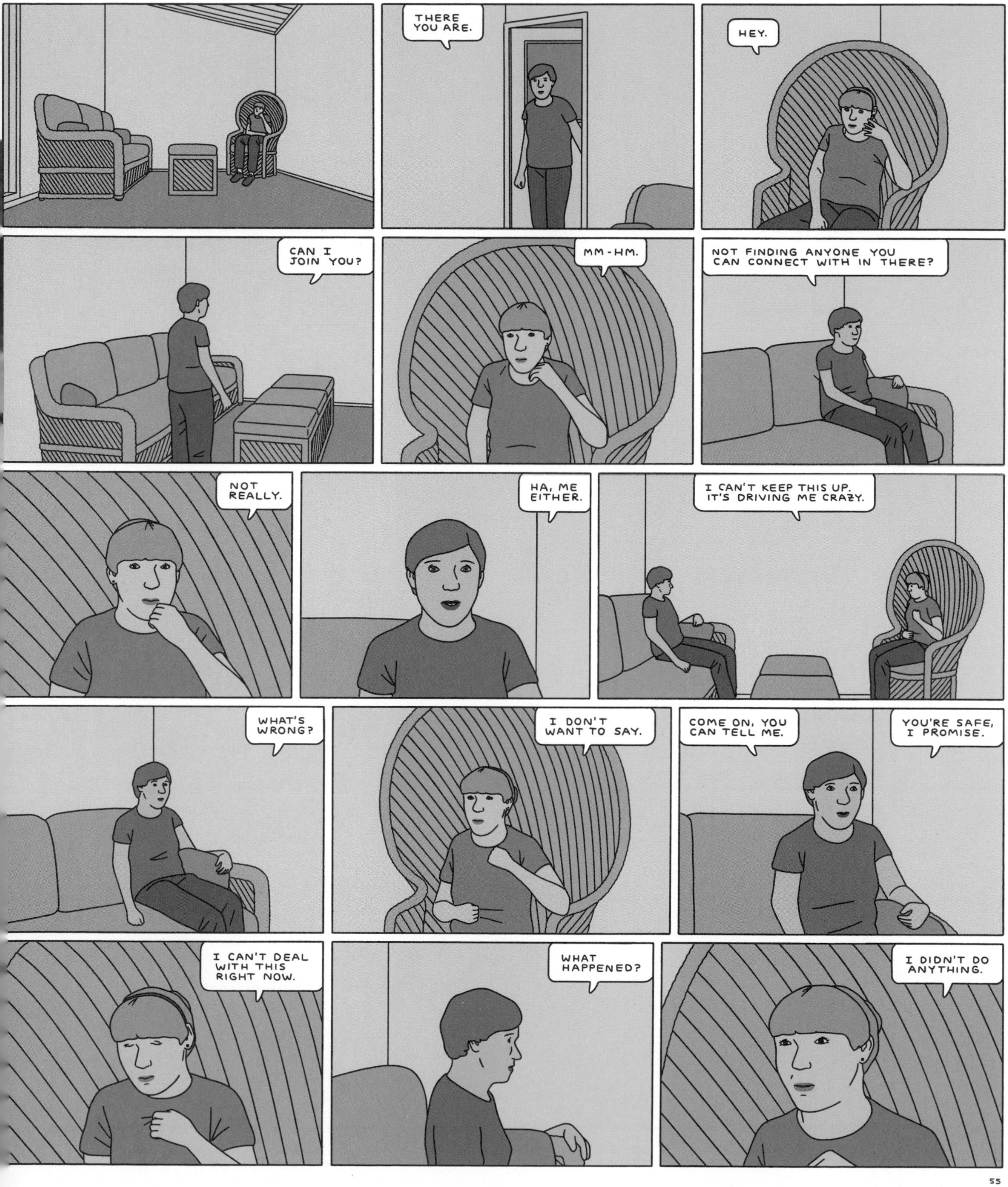
THERE YOU ARE.
HEY.
CAN I JOIN YOU?
MM-HM.
NOT FINDING ANYONE YOU CAN CONNECT WITH IN THERE?
NOT REALLY.
HA, ME EITHER.
I CAN'T KEEP THIS UP. IT'S DRIVING ME CRAZY.
WHAT'S WRONG?
I DON'T WANT TO SAY.
COME ON, YOU CAN TELL ME.
YOU'RE SAFE, I PROMISE.
I CAN'T DEAL WITH THIS RIGHT NOW.
WHAT HAPPENED?
I DIDN'T DO ANYTHING.

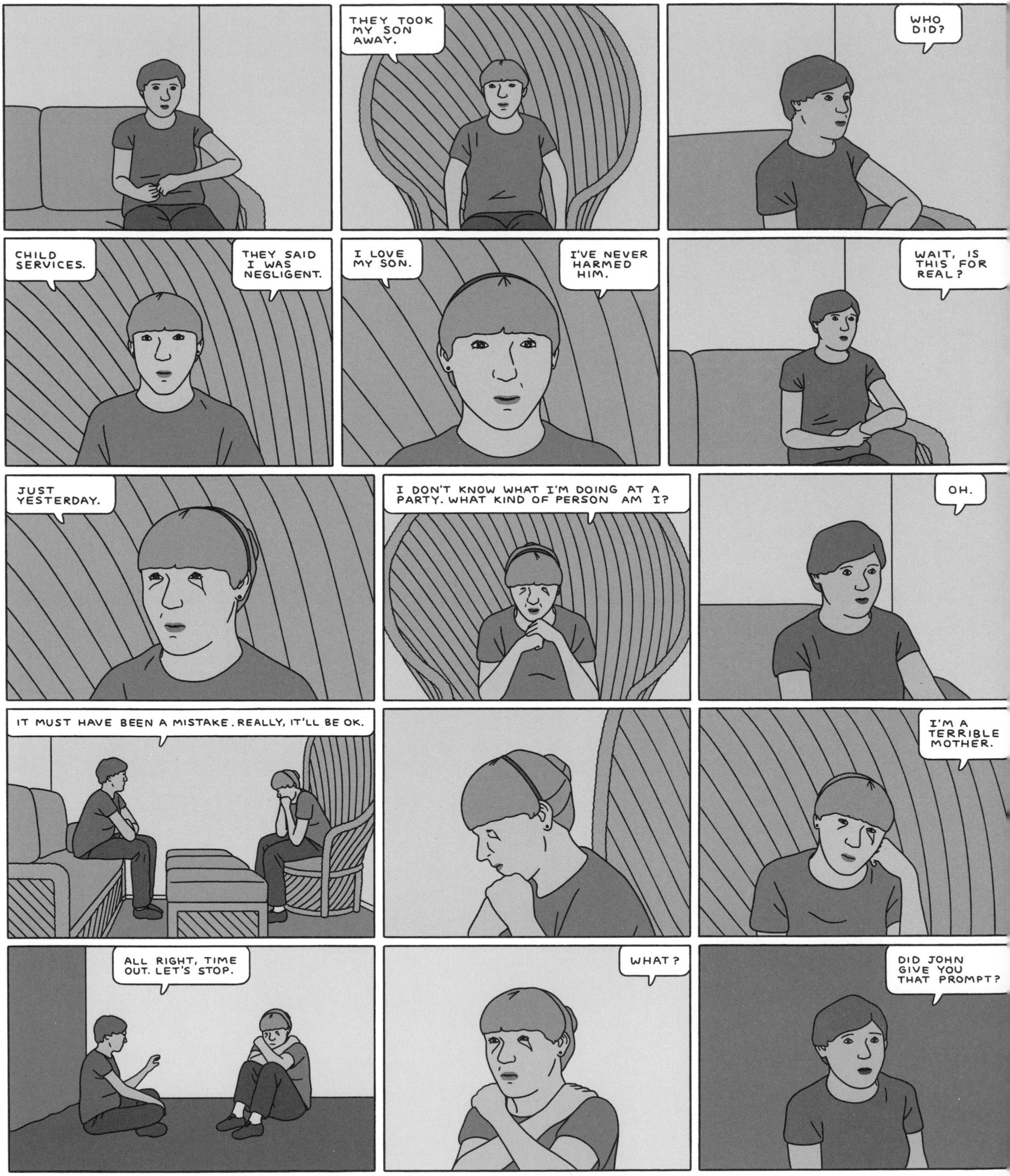
THEY TOOK MY SON AWAY.
WHO DID?
CHILD SERVICES.
THEY SAID I WAS NEGLIGENT.
I LOVE MY SON.
I'VE NEVER HARMED HIM.
WAIT, IS THIS FOR REAL?
JUST YESTERDAY.
I DON'T KNOW WHAT I'M DOING AT A PARTY. WHAT KIND OF PERSON AM I?
OH.
IT MUST HAVE BEEN A MISTAKE. REALLY, IT'LL BE OK.
I'M A TERRIBLE MOTHER.
ALL RIGHT, TIME OUT. LET'S STOP.
WHAT?
DID JOHN GIVE YOU THAT PROMPT?

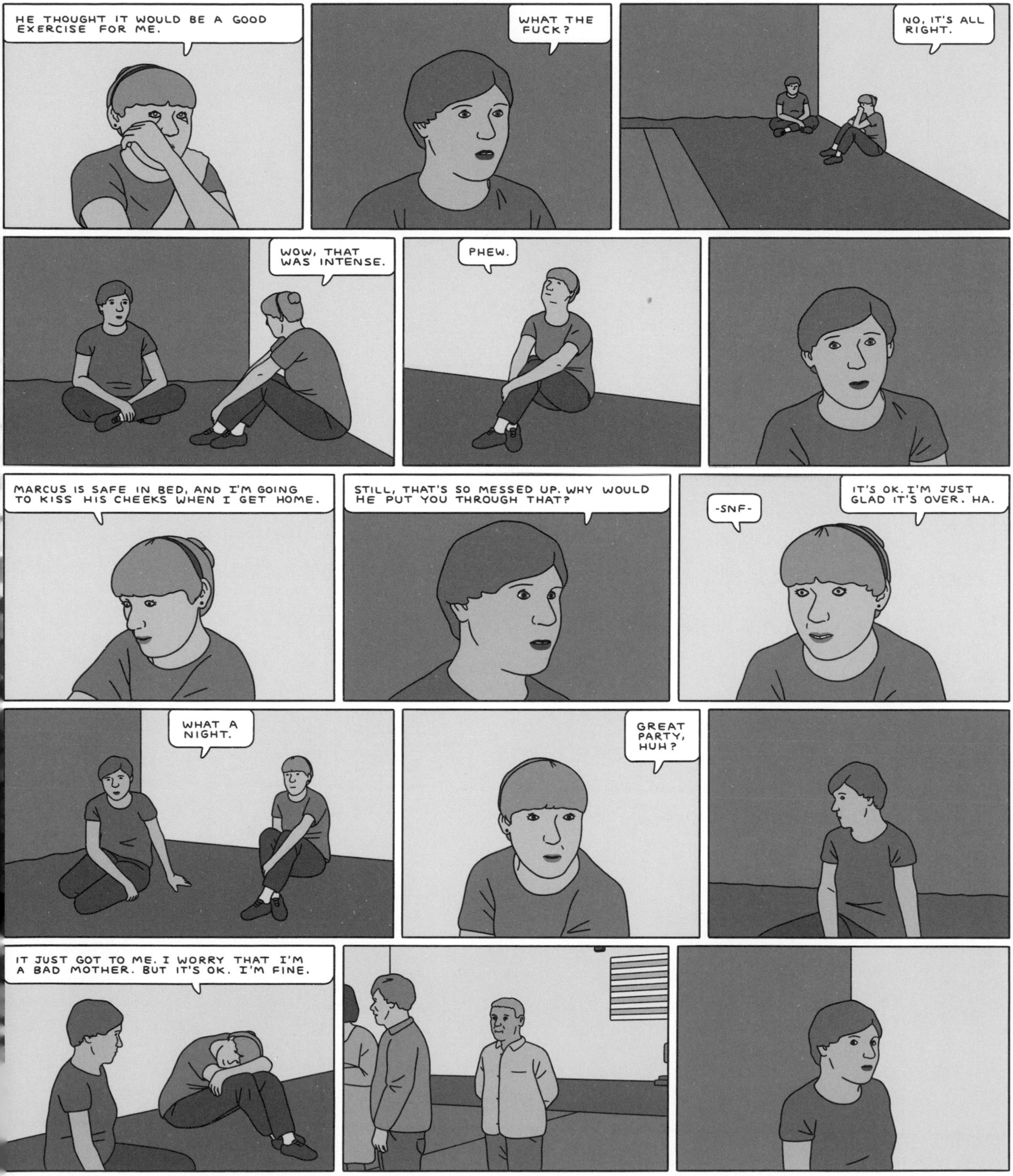
HE THOUGHT IT WOULD BE A GOOD EXERCISE FOR ME.
WHAT THE FUCK?
NO, IT'S ALL RIGHT.
WOW, THAT WAS INTENSE.
PHEW.
MARCUS IS SAFE IN BED, AND I'M GOING TO KISS HIS CHEEKS WHEN I GET HOME.
STILL, THAT'S SO MESSED UP. WHY WOULD HE PUT YOU THROUGH THAT?
-SNF-
IT'S OK. I'M JUST GLAD IT'S OVER. HA.
WHAT A NIGHT.
GREAT PARTY, HUH?
IT JUST GOT TO ME. I WORRY THAT I'M A BAD MOTHER. BUT IT'S OK. I'M FINE.

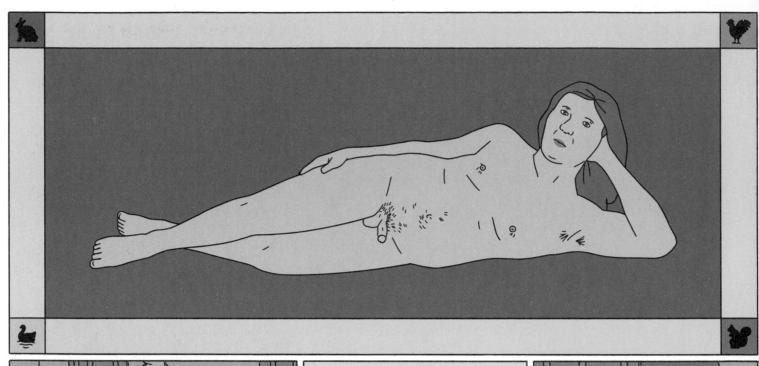

HAVE YOU HEARD FROM ANGEL?

NO, WHY?

NO CALL, NO SHOW, YESTERDAY AND TODAY.

REALLY? SHE WOULD NEVER DO THAT.

I KNOW. SHOULD I BE WORRIED OR PISSED OFF?

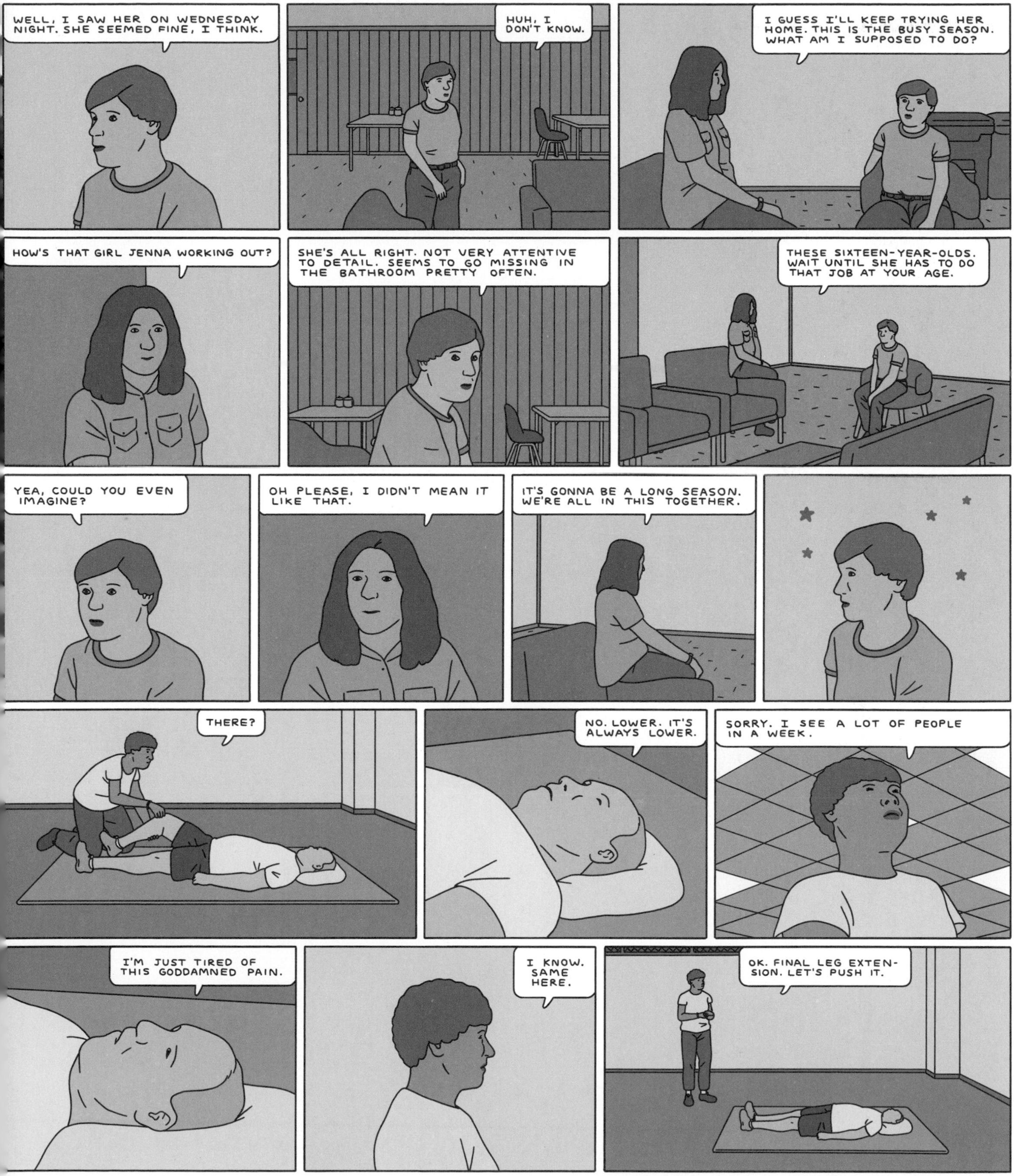
WELL, I SAW HER ON WEDNESDAY NIGHT. SHE SEEMED FINE, I THINK.
HUH, I DON'T KNOW.
I GUESS I'LL KEEP TRYING HER HOME. THIS IS THE BUSY SEASON. WHAT AM I SUPPOSED TO DO?
HOW'S THAT GIRL JENNA WORKING OUT?
SHE'S ALL RIGHT. NOT VERY ATTENTIVE TO DETAIL. SEEMS TO GO MISSING IN THE BATHROOM PRETTY OFTEN.
THESE SIXTEEN-YEAR-OLDS. WAIT UNTIL SHE HAS TO DO THAT JOB AT YOUR AGE.
YEA, COULD YOU EVEN IMAGINE?
OH PLEASE, I DIDN'T MEAN IT LIKE THAT.
IT'S GONNA BE A LONG SEASON. WE'RE ALL IN THIS TOGETHER.
THERE?
NO. LOWER. IT'S ALWAYS LOWER.
SORRY. I SEE A LOT OF PEOPLE IN A WEEK.
I'M JUST TIRED OF THIS GODDAMNED PAIN.
I KNOW. SAME HERE.
OK. FINAL LEG EXTENSION. LET'S PUSH IT.

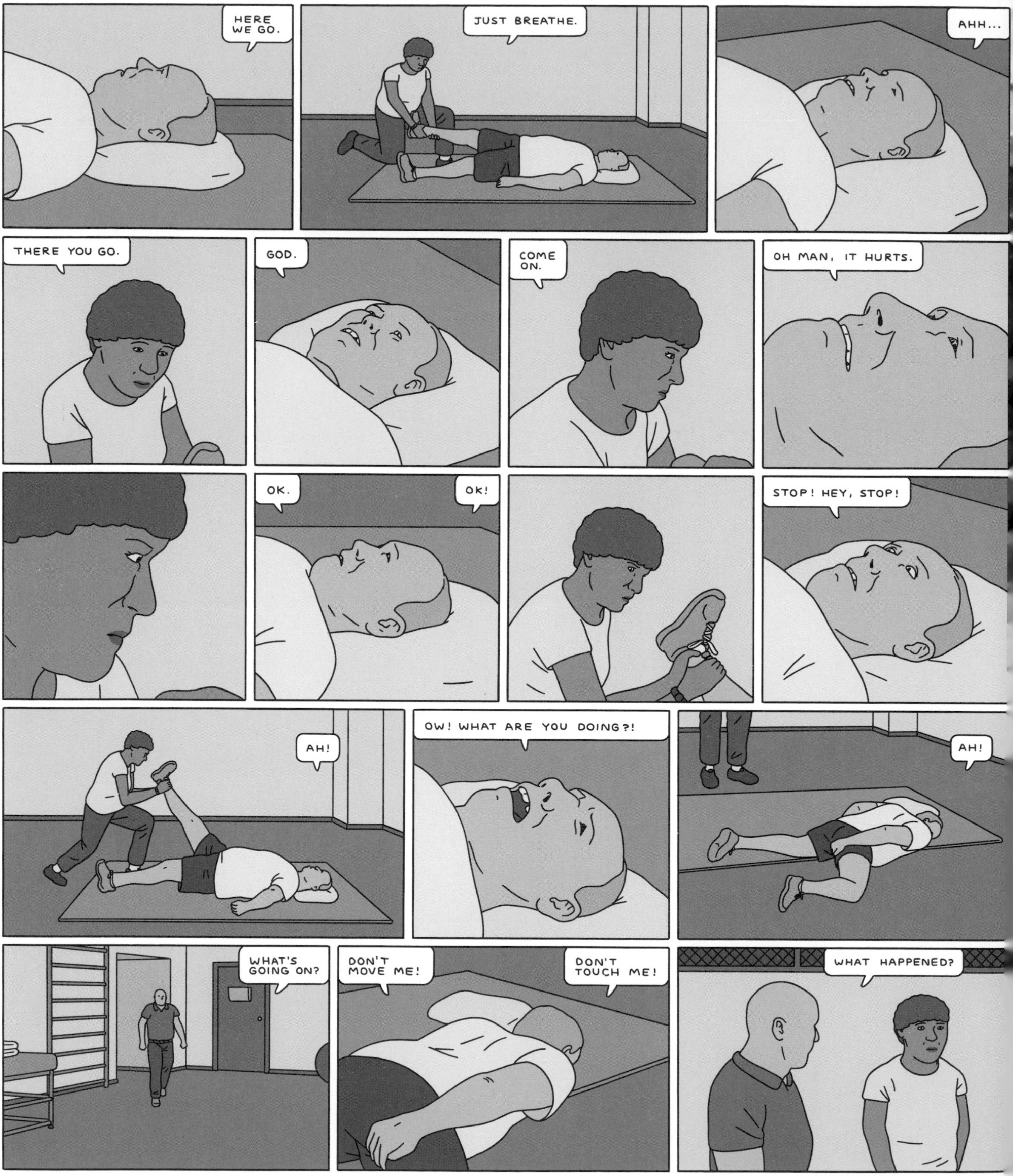
HERE WE GO.
JUST BREATHE.
AHH...
THERE YOU GO.
GOD.
COME ON.
OH MAN, IT HURTS.
OK.
OK!
STOP! HEY, STOP!
AH!
OW! WHAT ARE YOU DOING?!
AH!
WHAT'S GOING ON?
DON'T MOVE ME!
DON'T TOUCH ME!
WHAT HAPPENED?

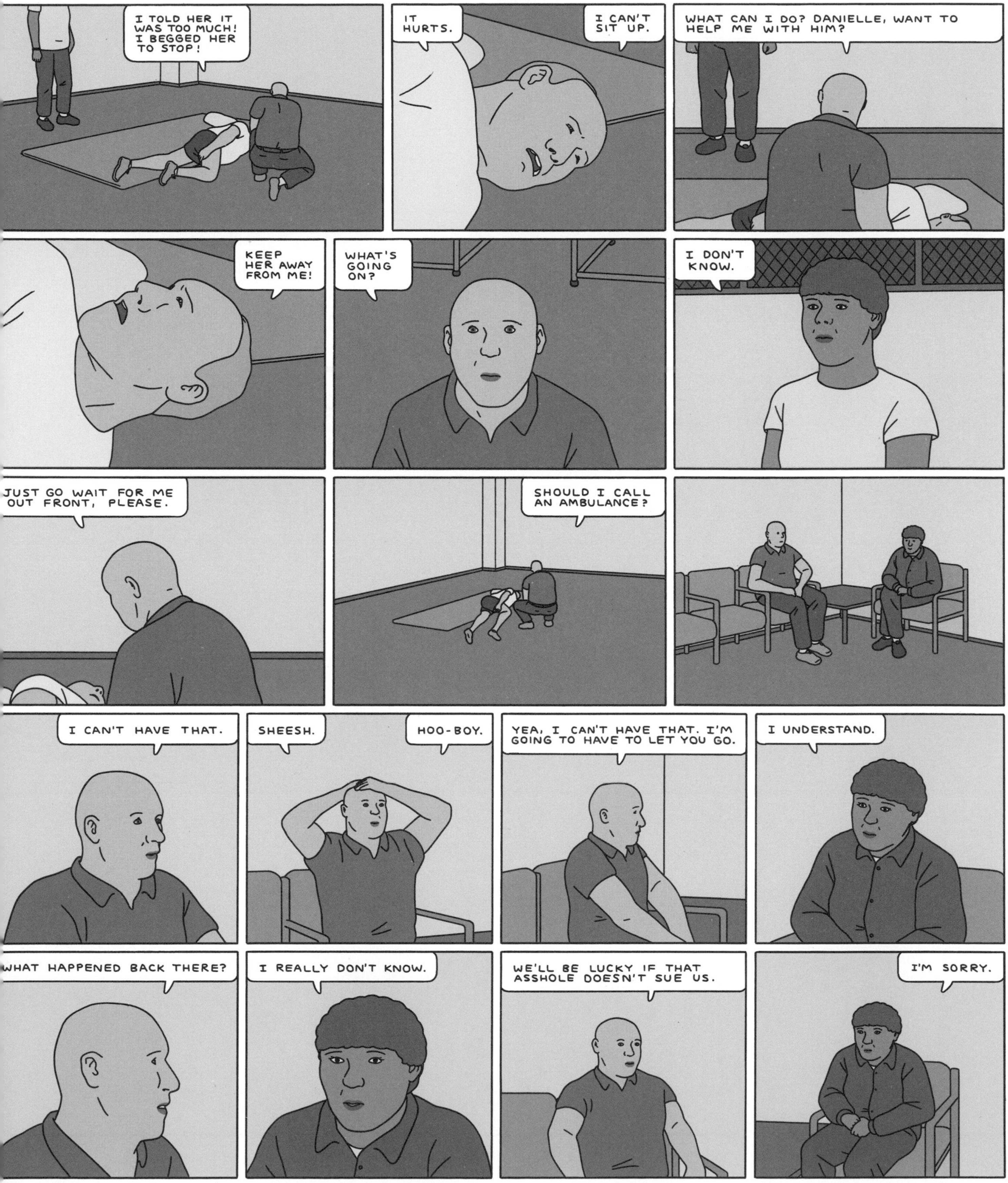
I TOLD HER IT WAS TOO MUCH! I BEGGED HER TO STOP!
IT HURTS.
I CAN'T SIT UP.
WHAT CAN I DO? DANIELLE, WANT TO HELP ME WITH HIM?
KEEP HER AWAY FROM ME!
WHAT'S GOING ON?
I DON'T KNOW.
JUST GO WAIT FOR ME OUT FRONT, PLEASE.
SHOULD I CALL AN AMBULANCE?
I CAN'T HAVE THAT.
SHEESH.
HOO-BOY.
YEA, I CAN'T HAVE THAT. I'M GOING TO HAVE TO LET YOU GO.
I UNDERSTAND.
WHAT HAPPENED BACK THERE?
I REALLY DON'T KNOW.
WE'LL BE LUCKY IF THAT ASSHOLE DOESN'T SUE US.
I'M SORRY.

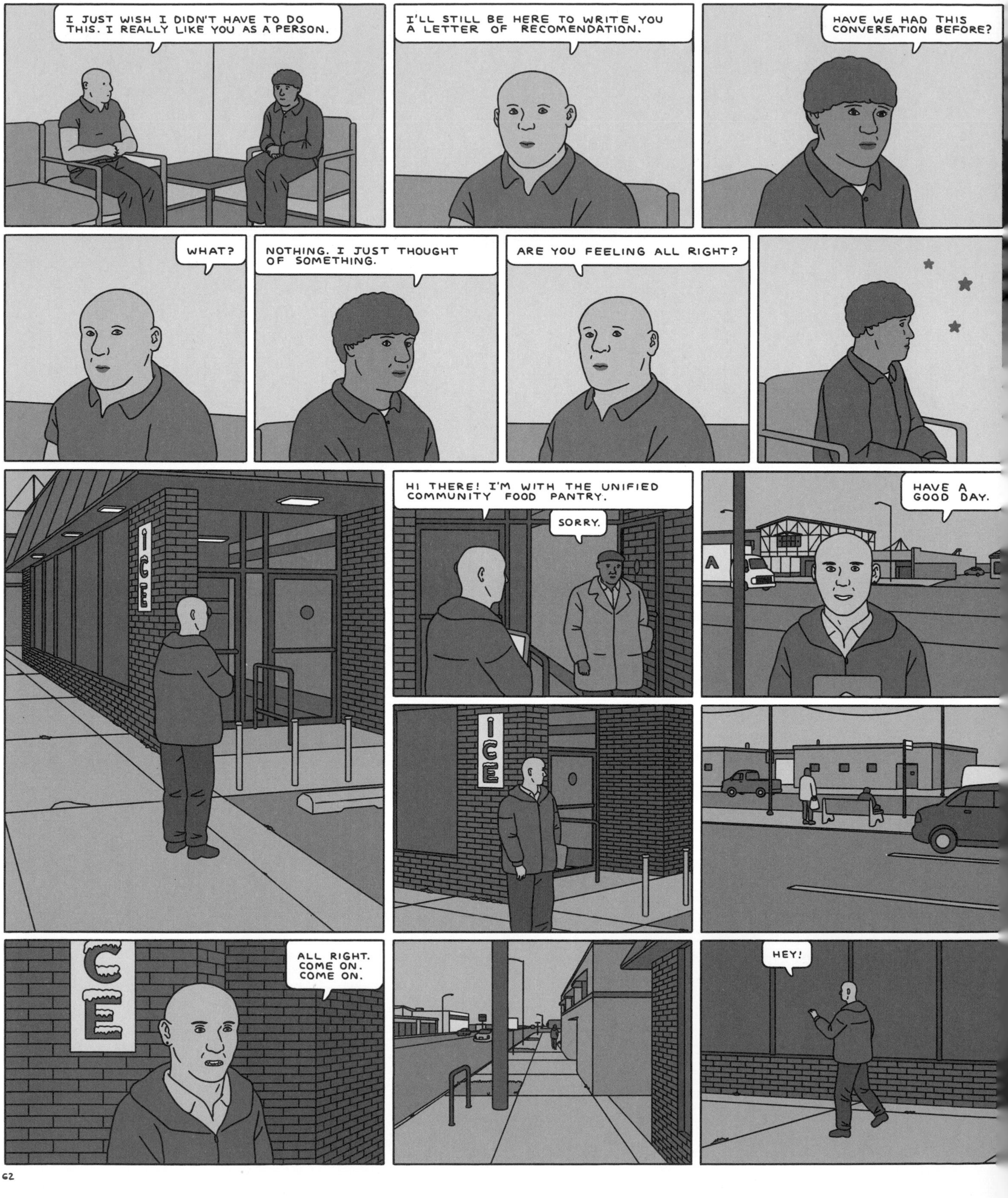
I JUST WISH I DIDN'T HAVE TO DO THIS. I REALLY LIKE YOU AS A PERSON.
I'LL STILL BE HERE TO WRITE YOU A LETTER OF RECOMENDATION.
HAVE WE HAD THIS CONVERSATION BEFORE?
WHAT?
NOTHING. I JUST THOUGHT OF SOMETHING.
ARE YOU FEELING ALL RIGHT?
ICE
HI THERE! I'M WITH THE UNIFIED COMMUNITY FOOD PANTRY.
SORRY.
HAVE A GOOD DAY.
ICE
ALL RIGHT. COME ON. COME ON.
HEY!

FUNNY MEETING YOU HERE.

HEY, BUDDY.

GREAT JOB THE OTHER NIGHT. I DIDN'T GET TO TALK TO YOU, BUT I SAW A BIT OF YOUR PERFORMANCE.

REALLY COOL STUFF.

THANKS, MAN. THANKS A LOT.

I DON'T THINK I'VE GOTTEN THE HANG OF IT. I CAN'T BREAK THROUGH. IT'S FRUSTRATING.

MM. I DON'T KNOW.

WHAT ARE YOU UP TO?

OH, JUST SEEING THE SIGHTS.

WELL, WILL I SEE YOU NEXT WEEK?

HM?

AT THE GROUP.

OH, YEA. OF COURSE.

YOU KNOW, I THINK YOU TOOK OFF BEFORE THE END. WE'RE MEETING AT A NEW SPOT.

I HAVE THE ADDRESS. I DON'T KNOW WHERE THE HELL THIS PLACE IS. SOMEWHERE OUT IN THE STICKS.

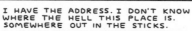

DO YOU NEED IT?

SURE.

65

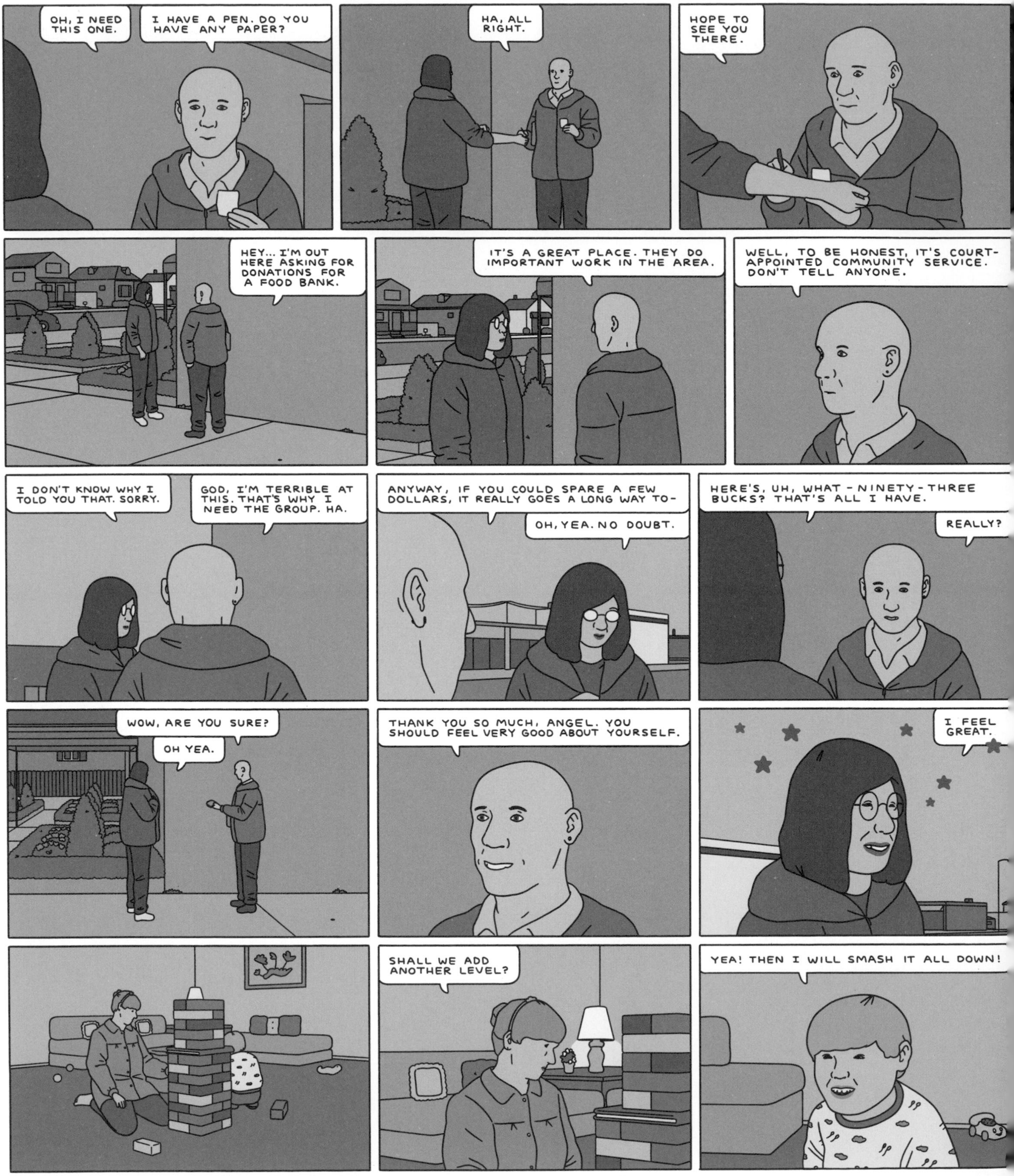
OH, I NEED THIS ONE.
I HAVE A PEN. DO YOU HAVE ANY PAPER?
HA, ALL RIGHT.
HOPE TO SEE YOU THERE.
HEY... I'M OUT HERE ASKING FOR DONATIONS FOR A FOOD BANK.
IT'S A GREAT PLACE. THEY DO IMPORTANT WORK IN THE AREA.
WELL, TO BE HONEST, IT'S COURT-APPOINTED COMMUNITY SERVICE. DON'T TELL ANYONE.
I DON'T KNOW WHY I TOLD YOU THAT. SORRY.
GOD, I'M TERRIBLE AT THIS. THAT'S WHY I NEED THE GROUP. HA.
ANYWAY, IF YOU COULD SPARE A FEW DOLLARS, IT REALLY GOES A LONG WAY TO-
OH, YEA. NO DOUBT.
HERE'S, UH, WHAT - NINETY - THREE BUCKS? THAT'S ALL I HAVE.
REALLY?
WOW, ARE YOU SURE?
OH YEA.
THANK YOU SO MUCH, ANGEL. YOU SHOULD FEEL VERY GOOD ABOUT YOURSELF.
I FEEL GREAT.
SHALL WE ADD ANOTHER LEVEL?
YEA! THEN I WILL SMASH IT ALL DOWN!

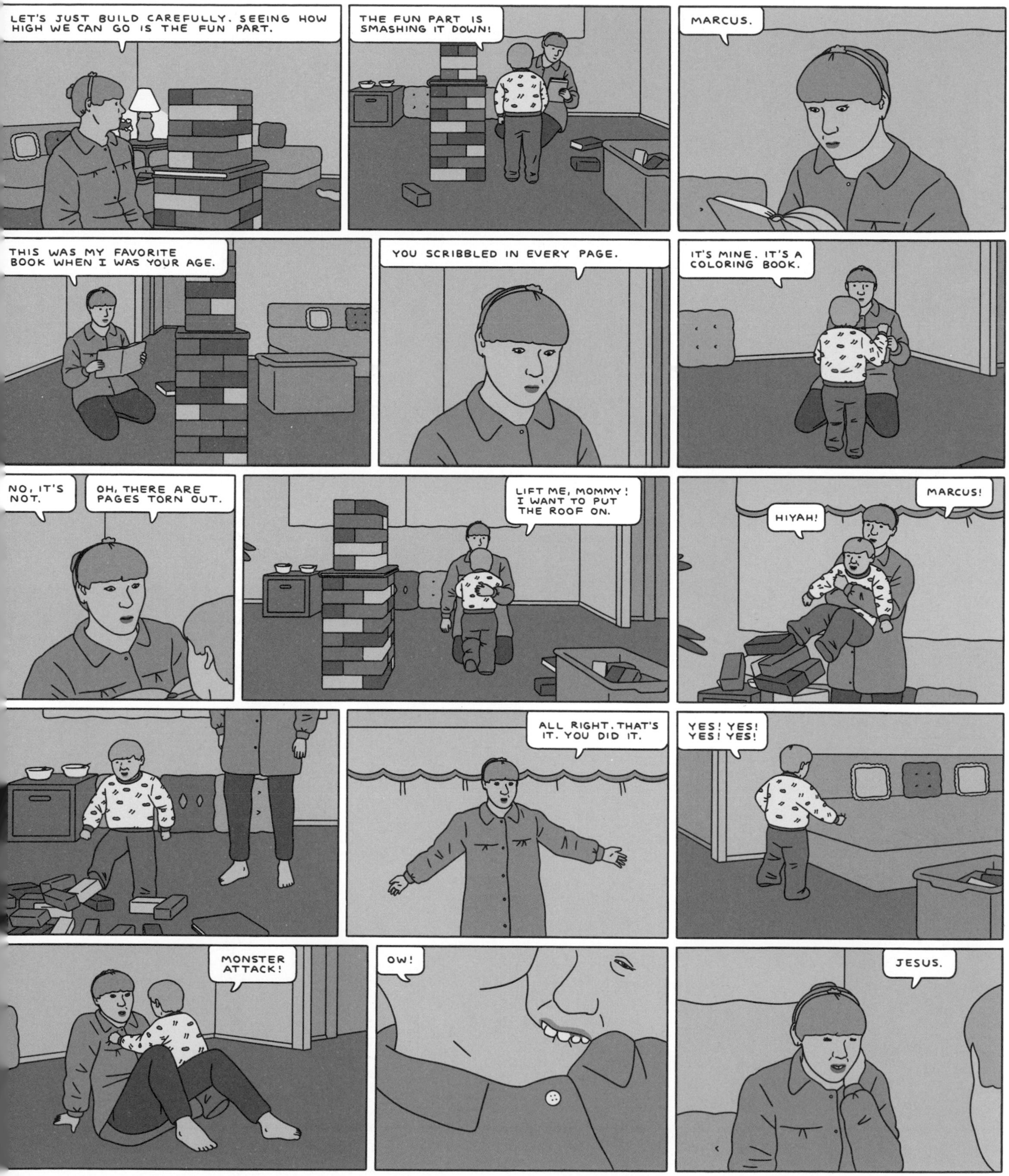
LET'S JUST BUILD CAREFULLY. SEEING HOW HIGH WE CAN GO IS THE FUN PART.
THE FUN PART IS SMASHING IT DOWN!
MARCUS.
THIS WAS MY FAVORITE BOOK WHEN I WAS YOUR AGE.
YOU SCRIBBLED IN EVERY PAGE.
IT'S MINE. IT'S A COLORING BOOK.
NO, IT'S NOT.
OH, THERE ARE PAGES TORN OUT.
LIFT ME, MOMMY! I WANT TO PUT THE ROOF ON.
HIYAH!
MARCUS!
ALL RIGHT. THAT'S IT. YOU DID IT.
YES! YES! YES! YES!
MONSTER ATTACK!
OW!
JESUS.

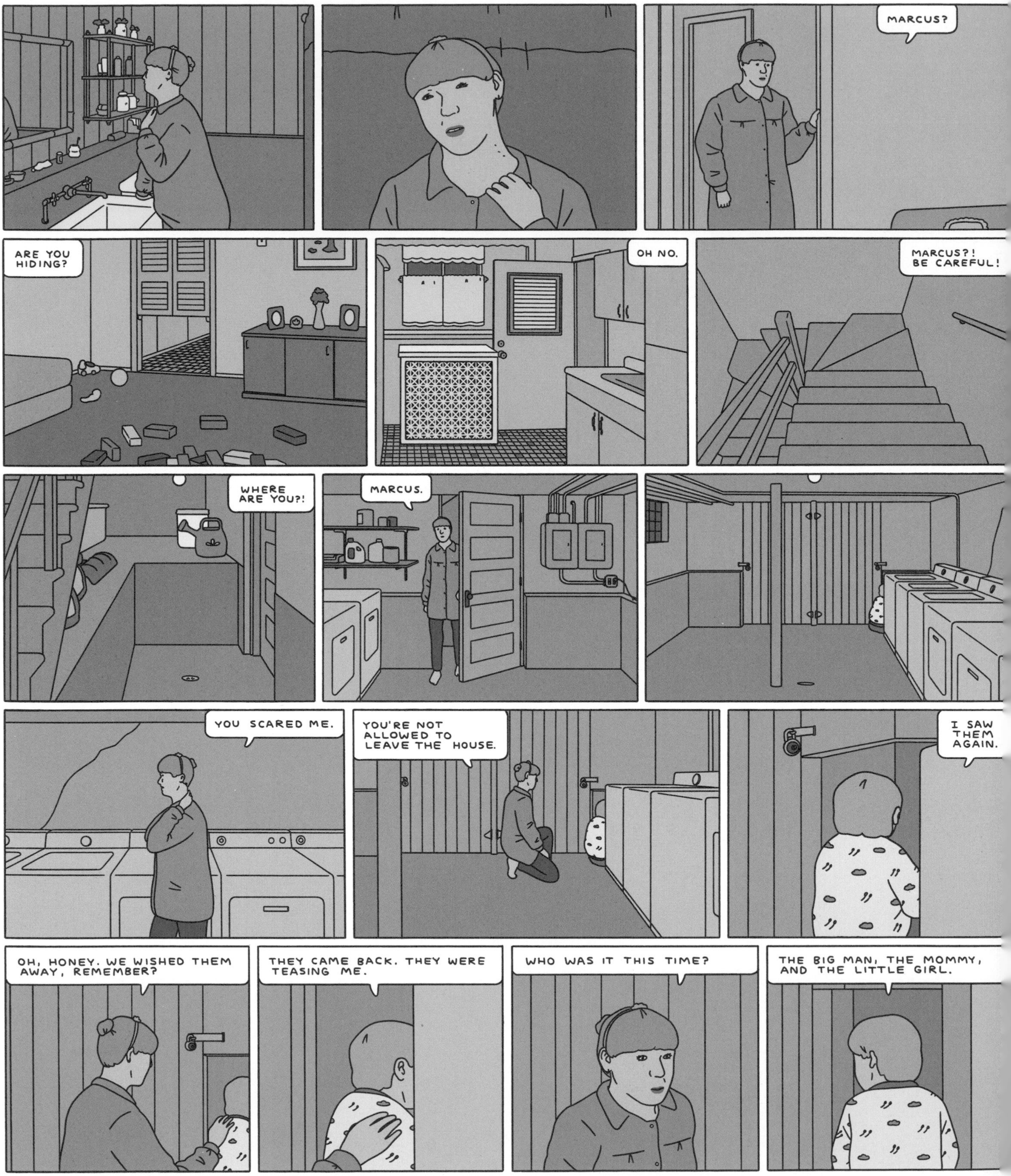
MARCUS?
ARE YOU HIDING?
OH NO.
MARCUS?! BE CAREFUL!
WHERE ARE YOU?!
MARCUS.
YOU SCARED ME.
YOU'RE NOT ALLOWED TO LEAVE THE HOUSE.
I SAW THEM AGAIN.
OH, HONEY. WE WISHED THEM AWAY, REMEMBER?
THEY CAME BACK. THEY WERE TEASING ME.
WHO WAS IT THIS TIME?
THE BIG MAN, THE MOMMY, AND THE LITTLE GIRL.

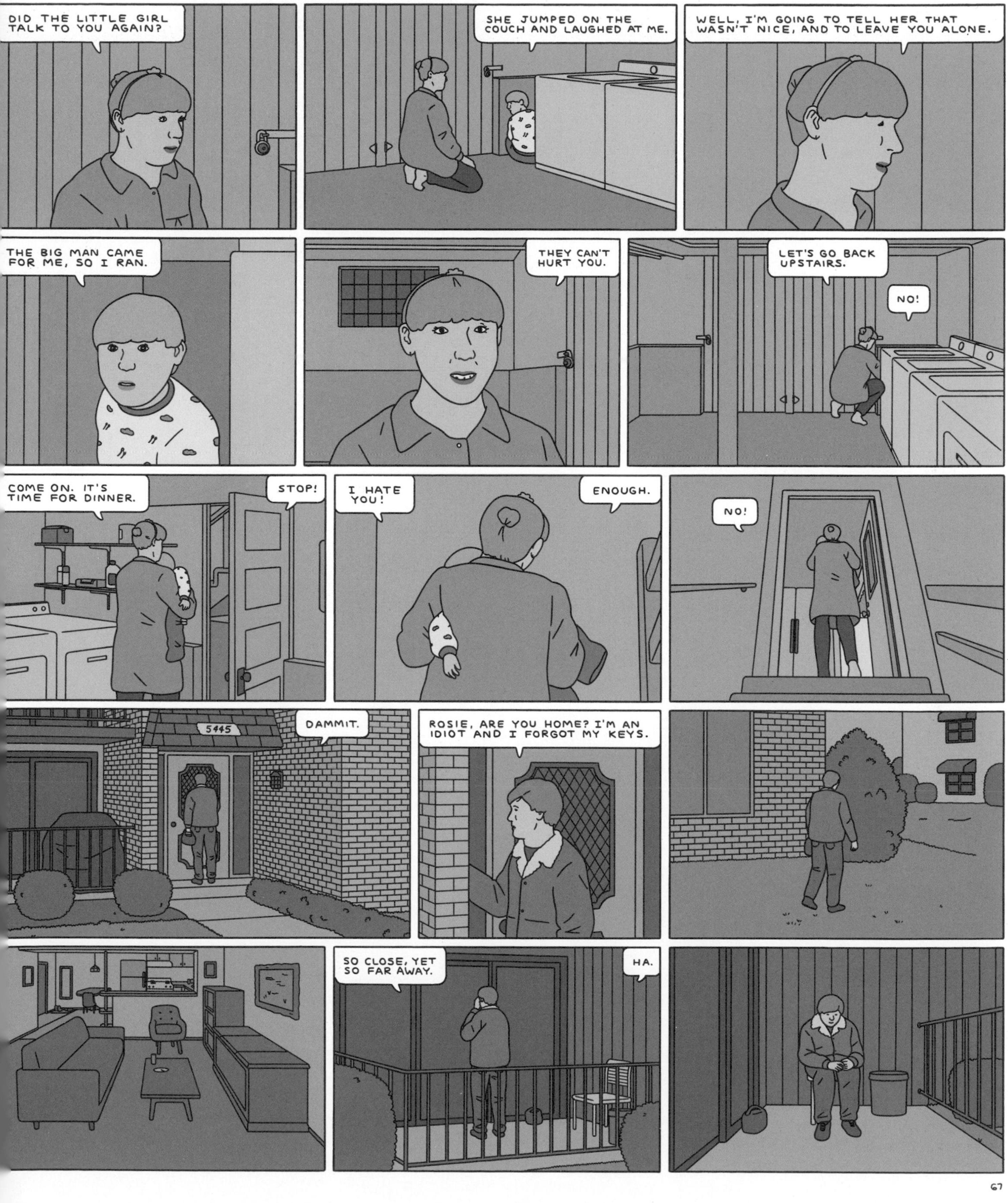
DID THE LITTLE GIRL TALK TO YOU AGAIN?
SHE JUMPED ON THE COUCH AND LAUGHED AT ME.
WELL, I'M GOING TO TELL HER THAT WASN'T NICE, AND TO LEAVE YOU ALONE.
THE BIG MAN CAME FOR ME, SO I RAN.
THEY CAN'T HURT YOU.
LET'S GO BACK UPSTAIRS.
NO!
COME ON. IT'S TIME FOR DINNER.
STOP!
I HATE YOU!
ENOUGH.
NO!
5445
DAMMIT.
ROSIE, ARE YOU HOME? I'M AN IDIOT AND I FORGOT MY KEYS.
SO CLOSE, YET SO FAR AWAY.
HA.

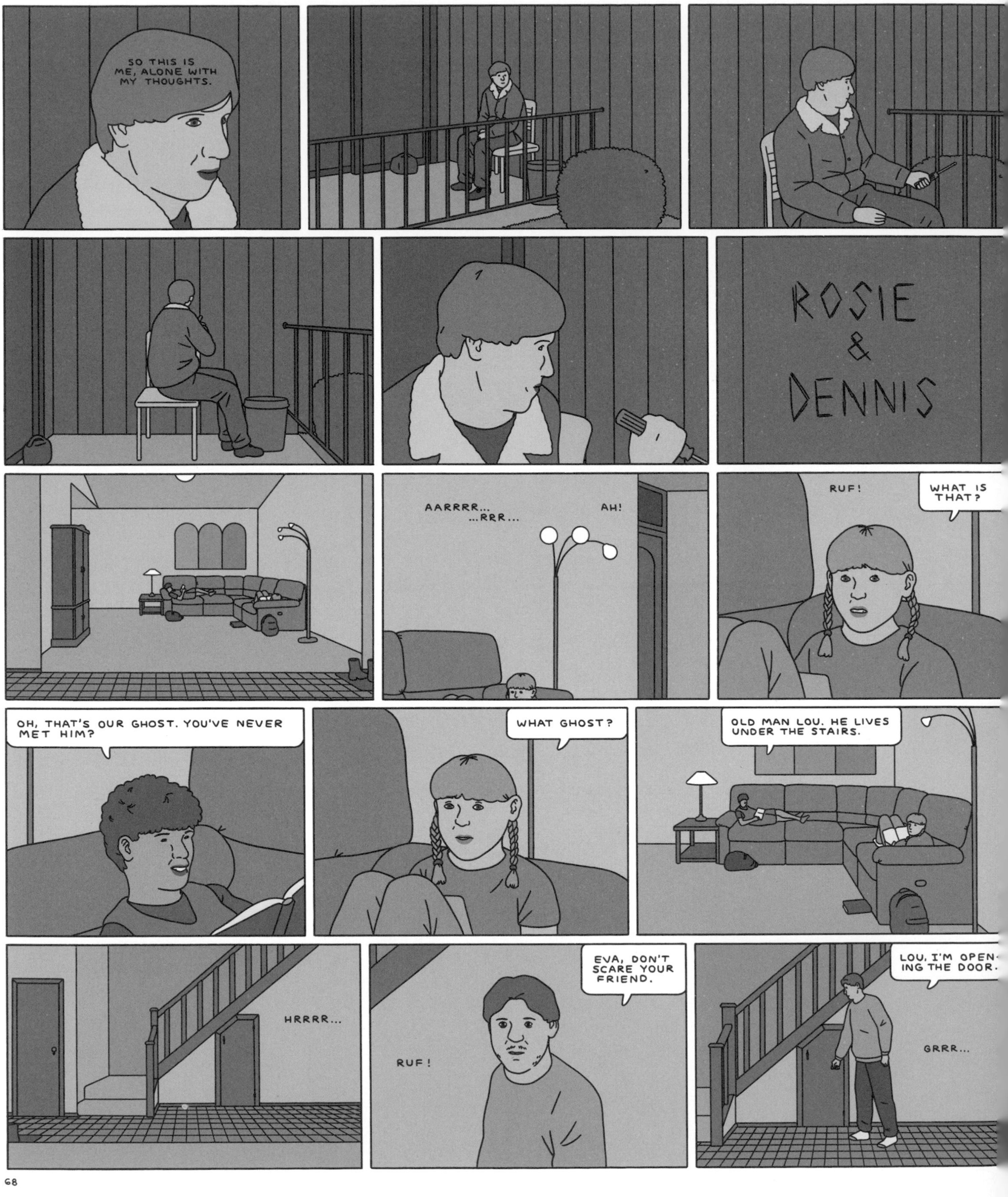

SO THIS IS ME, ALONE WITH MY THOUGHTS.
ROSIE & DENNIS
AARRRR... ...RRR...
AH!
RUF!
WHAT IS THAT?
OH, THAT'S OUR GHOST. YOU'VE NEVER MET HIM?
WHAT GHOST?
OLD MAN LOU. HE LIVES UNDER THE STAIRS.
HRRRR...
EVA, DON'T SCARE YOUR FRIEND.
RUF!
LOU, I'M OPEN-ING THE DOOR.
GRRR...

HUH?

YOU'RE HAVING ANOTHER NIGHT TERROR. EVERYTHING ALL RIGHT?

WHAT? YES.

I PROMISED THE GIRLS I'D TAKE THEM OUT FOR PIZZA. WANT SOMETHING?

NO, THANKS. I NEED TO REST.

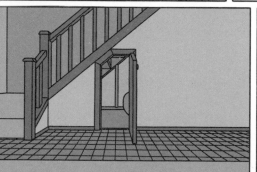

HI, LOU.

HEY.

WOULD YOU DO ME A FAVOR?

WHAT?

SHUT THAT DOOR, PLEASE.

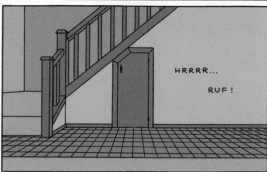HRRRR...

RUF!

69

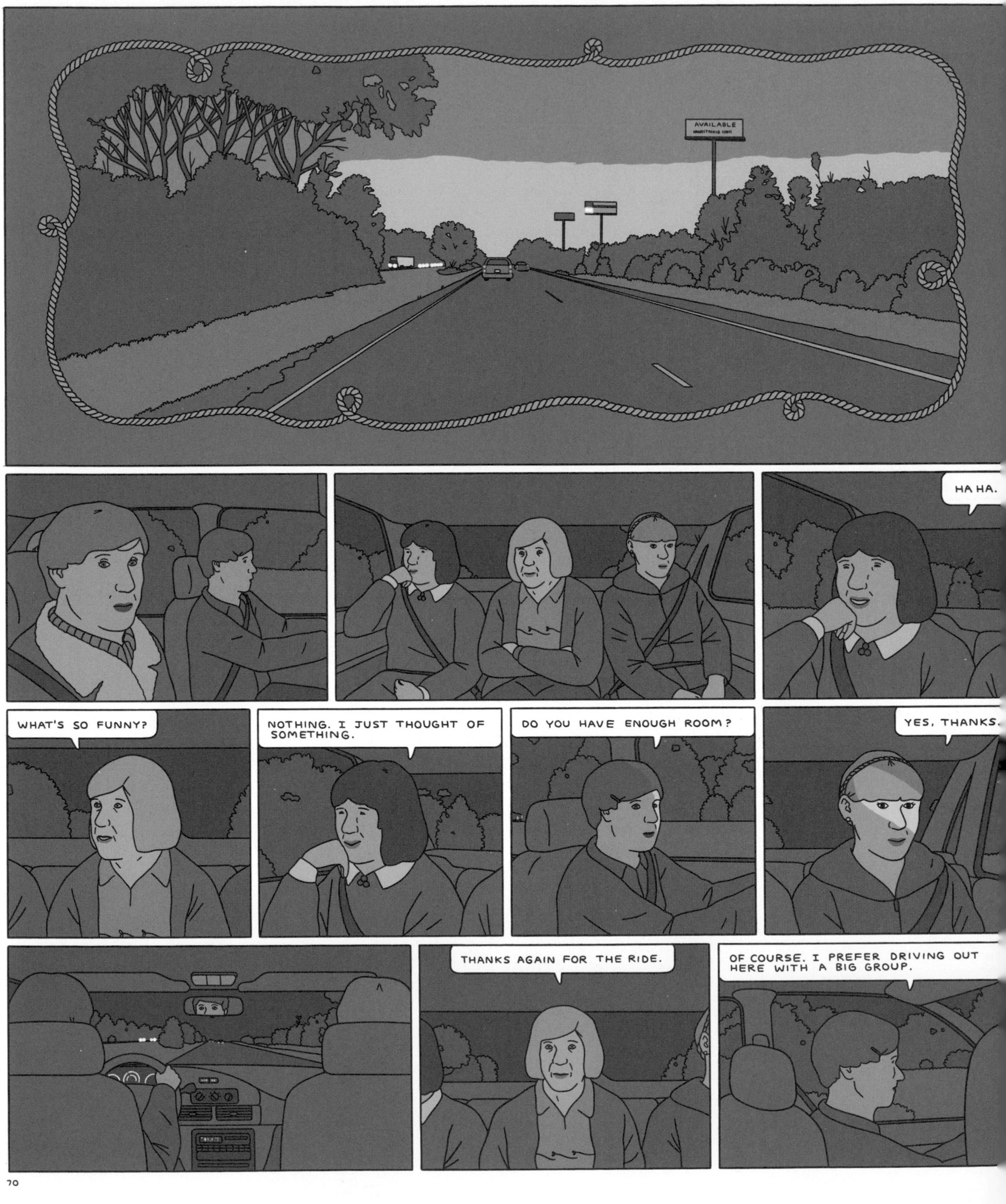
AVAILABLE
HA HA.
WHAT'S SO FUNNY?
NOTHING. I JUST THOUGHT OF SOMETHING.
DO YOU HAVE ENOUGH ROOM?
YES, THANKS.
THANKS AGAIN FOR THE RIDE.
OF COURSE. I PREFER DRIVING OUT HERE WITH A BIG GROUP.

 IT'S KINDA EERIE.

 I LOVE IT. I'M ONLY GOING TO THIS MEETING TO GET OUT OF THE CITY.

 I JUST FEEL MORE COMFORTABLE AROUND CROWDS AND BUILDINGS.

 DENNIS HAS TROUBLE BEING ALONE WITH HIMSELF.

 YOU THINK? IS THAT IT?

 WHAT? YOU'VE SAID SO YOURSELF.

 I'VE SAID I'M MORE OF A PEOPLE PERSON.

 I DON'T LIKE IT OUT HERE EITHER. I GREW UP IN AN AREA LIKE THIS.

 OH, YOU DID? WELL, IT MUST BE HARD TO LIVE IN ISOLATION, BUT IT DOES SEEM PEACEFUL.

 I DON'T KNOW. I FELT LIKE I WAS GOING CRAZY.

 I WANTED TO RAISE MARCUS IN A DIFFERENT ENVIRONMENT.

 HOW OLD DID YOU SAY YOUR SON IS?

THREE.

 THAT'S A CRUCIAL AGE IN DEVELOPMENT.

 UH-HUH. THAT'S SOMETHING I THINK ABOUT A LOT.

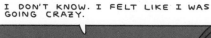

71

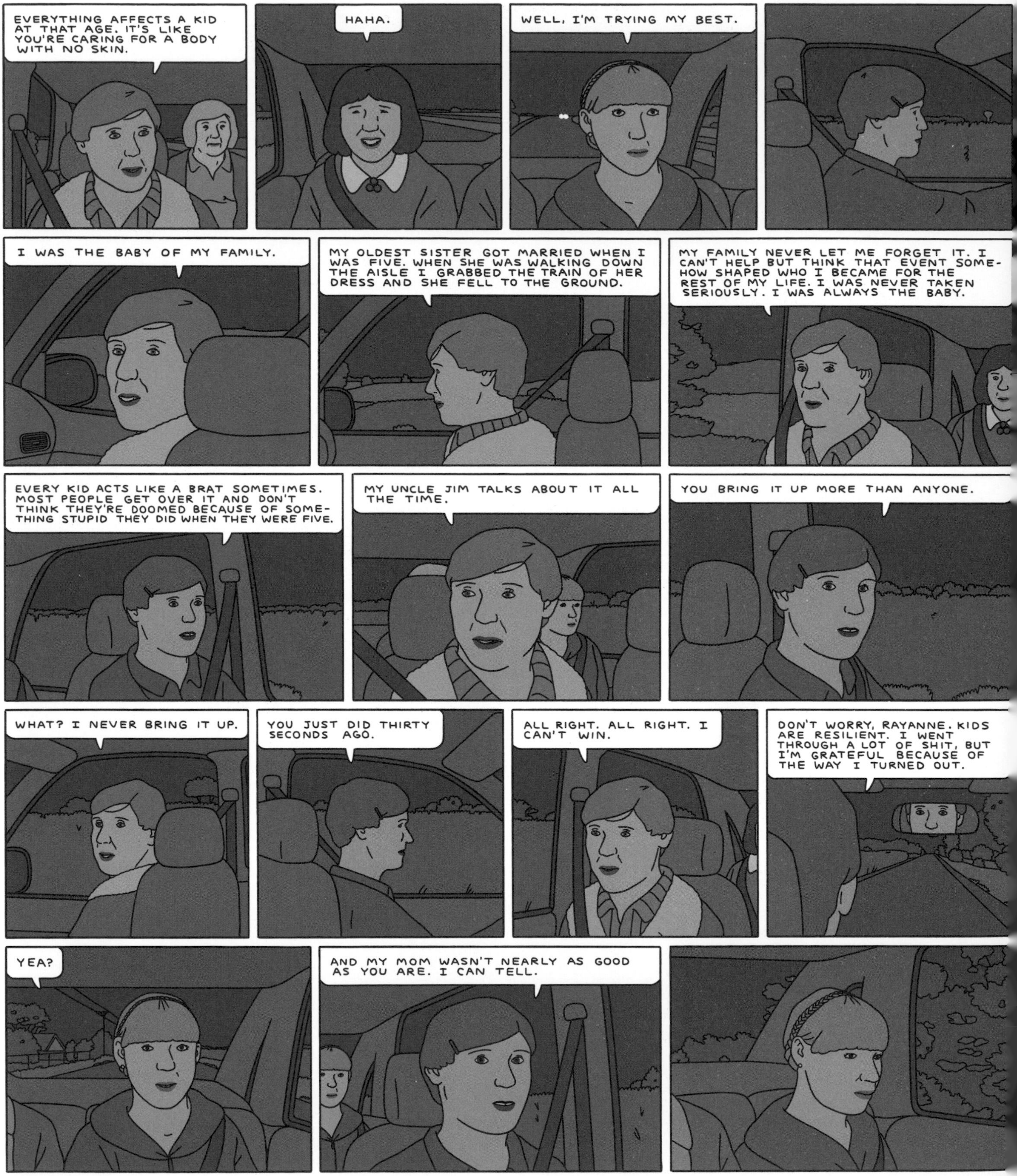
EVERYTHING AFFECTS A KID AT THAT AGE. IT'S LIKE YOU'RE CARING FOR A BODY WITH NO SKIN.
HAHA.
WELL, I'M TRYING MY BEST.
I WAS THE BABY OF MY FAMILY.
MY OLDEST SISTER GOT MARRIED WHEN I WAS FIVE. WHEN SHE WAS WALKING DOWN THE AISLE I GRABBED THE TRAIN OF HER DRESS AND SHE FELL TO THE GROUND.
MY FAMILY NEVER LET ME FORGET IT. I CAN'T HELP BUT THINK THAT EVENT SOME-HOW SHAPED WHO I BECAME FOR THE REST OF MY LIFE. I WAS NEVER TAKEN SERIOUSLY. I WAS ALWAYS THE BABY.
EVERY KID ACTS LIKE A BRAT SOMETIMES. MOST PEOPLE GET OVER IT AND DON'T THINK THEY'RE DOOMED BECAUSE OF SOME-THING STUPID THEY DID WHEN THEY WERE FIVE.
MY UNCLE JIM TALKS ABOUT IT ALL THE TIME.
YOU BRING IT UP MORE THAN ANYONE.
WHAT? I NEVER BRING IT UP.
YOU JUST DID THIRTY SECONDS AGO.
ALL RIGHT. ALL RIGHT. I CAN'T WIN.
DON'T WORRY, RAYANNE. KIDS ARE RESILIENT. I WENT THROUGH A LOT OF SHIT, BUT I'M GRATEFUL BECAUSE OF THE WAY I TURNED OUT.
YEA?
AND MY MOM WASN'T NEARLY AS GOOD AS YOU ARE. I CAN TELL.

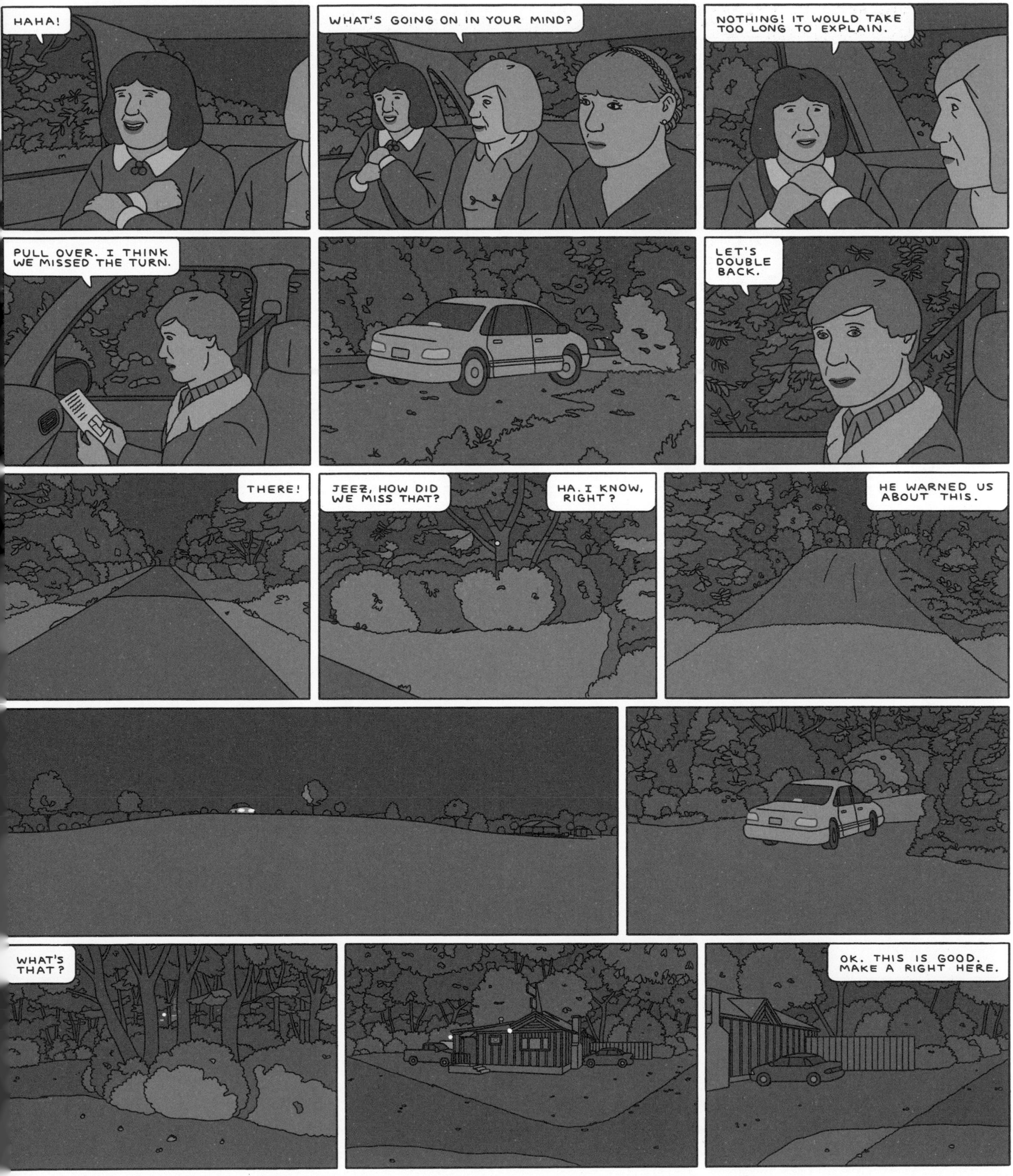
HAHA!
WHAT'S GOING ON IN YOUR MIND?
NOTHING! IT WOULD TAKE TOO LONG TO EXPLAIN.
PULL OVER. I THINK WE MISSED THE TURN.
LET'S DOUBLE BACK.
THERE!
JEEZ, HOW DID WE MISS THAT?
HA. I KNOW, RIGHT?
HE WARNED US ABOUT THIS.
WHAT'S THAT?
OK. THIS IS GOOD. MAKE A RIGHT HERE.

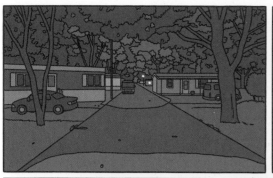

HE SAID TO DRIVE UNTIL THE ROAD ENDS AND WE'LL BE THERE.

IS THIS IT?

I GUESS WE'RE NOT THE FIRST PEOPLE HERE.

OK, I HAVE TO SAY SOMETHING.

AM I THE ONLY ONE WHO FEELS WEIRD ABOUT THIS?

IT IS MUCH FARTHER AWAY THAN I THOUGHT.

DID ANY OF YOU TELL SOMEONE WHERE YOU WOULD BE?

MY AUNT HAS THE ADDRESS. SHE'LL KNOW SOMETHING IS WRONG IF I'M NOT BACK BY MIDNIGHT.

WHAT ARE WE GETTING OURSELVES INTO?

I'M SUDDENLY FEELING VERY PEACEFUL OUT HERE. I THINK I SEE WHAT YOU MEAN NOW.

COME ON. AT WORST IT WILL BE A WASTE OF TIME OR A GOOD STORY.

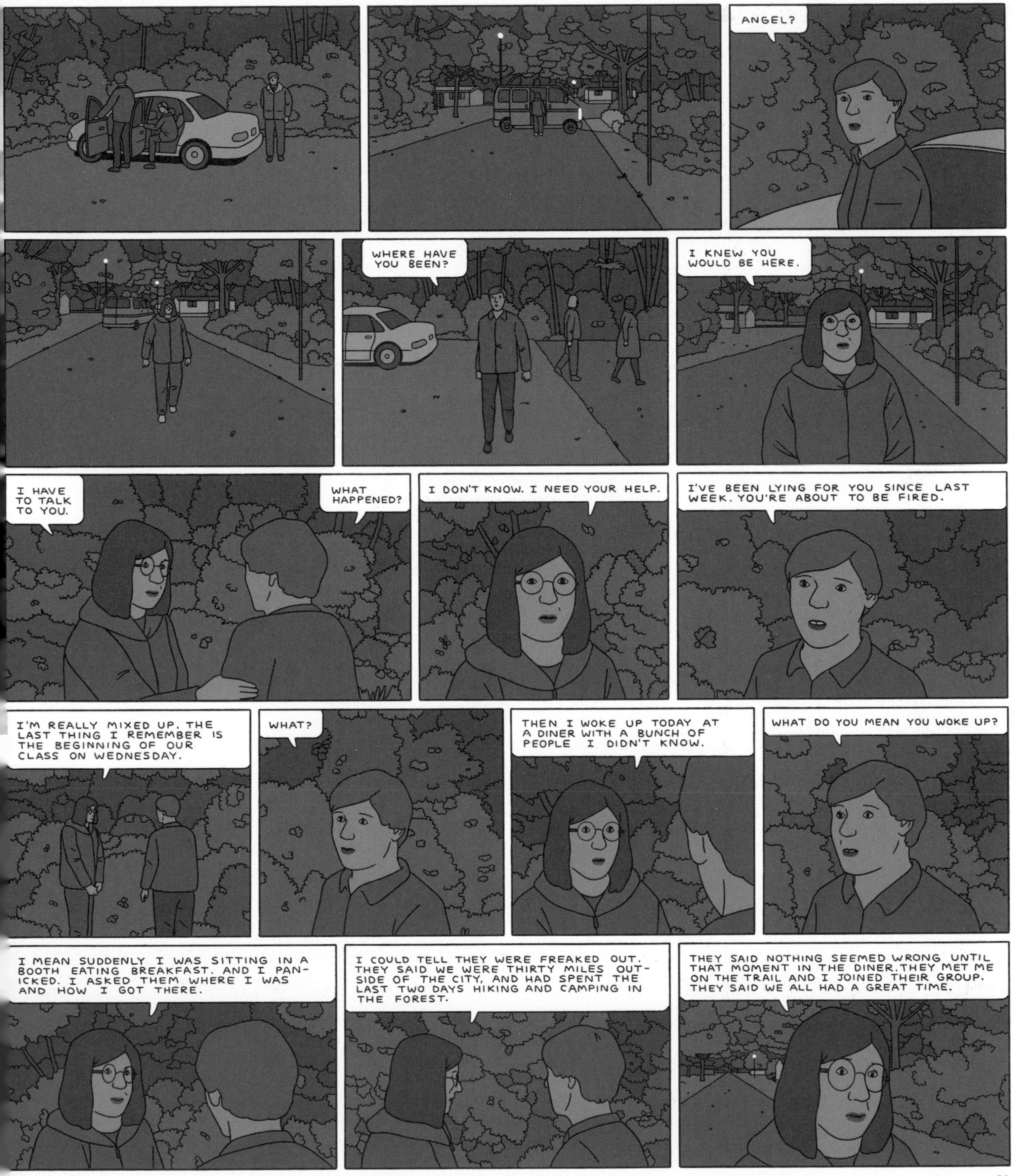
ANGEL?
WHERE HAVE YOU BEEN?
I KNEW YOU WOULD BE HERE.
I HAVE TO TALK TO YOU.
WHAT HAPPENED?
I DON'T KNOW. I NEED YOUR HELP.
I'VE BEEN LYING FOR YOU SINCE LAST WEEK. YOU'RE ABOUT TO BE FIRED.
I'M REALLY MIXED UP. THE LAST THING I REMEMBER IS THE BEGINNING OF OUR CLASS ON WEDNESDAY.
WHAT?
THEN I WOKE UP TODAY AT A DINER WITH A BUNCH OF PEOPLE I DIDN'T KNOW.
WHAT DO YOU MEAN YOU WOKE UP?
I MEAN SUDDENLY I WAS SITTING IN A BOOTH EATING BREAKFAST. AND I PANICKED. I ASKED THEM WHERE I WAS AND HOW I GOT THERE.
I COULD TELL THEY WERE FREAKED OUT. THEY SAID WE WERE THIRTY MILES OUTSIDE OF THE CITY, AND HAD SPENT THE LAST TWO DAYS HIKING AND CAMPING IN THE FOREST.
THEY SAID NOTHING SEEMED WRONG UNTIL THAT MOMENT IN THE DINER. THEY MET ME ON THE TRAIL AND I JOINED THEIR GROUP. THEY SAID WE ALL HAD A GREAT TIME.

YOU BLACKED OUT?

I DON'T KNOW. I GUESS SO. THANK GOD THEY WERE REALLY NICE. THEY JUST SEEMED CONCERNED. THEY TOLD ME ALL ABOUT THE PREVIOUS TWO DAYS TO JOG MY MEMORY, BUT I DON'T REMEMBER ANY OF IT.

BUT WHERE WAS I FROM WEDNESDAY NIGHT TO SATURDAY MORNING? HOW CAN I NOT REMEMBER ANYTHING?

ROSIE, I'M REALLY SCARED.

IT'S GOING TO BE ALL RIGHT. I'M JUST GLAD YOU'RE SAFE.

I'VE HEARD OF THIS HAPPENING. YOU SHOULD MAKE AN APPOINTMENT WITH YOUR DOCTOR.

ONE THING I DON'T UNDERSTAND. HOW DID YOU GET HERE?

THIS WAS WRITTEN ON MY ARM.

I THOUGHT IT MIGHT HAVE SOMETHING TO DO WITH THE CLASS, SO I HAD TO COME AND FIGURE OUT WHAT'S BEEN GOING ON.

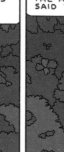

HOW DID YOU EVEN FIND THIS PLACE? WE HAD A MAP AND WE ALMOST GOT LOST.

THE HIKERS DROVE ME. THEY SAID THEY KNEW THE AREA.

AM I IN TROUBLE AT WORK?

THEY'RE PRETTY UPSET. THE ONLY REASON YOU WEREN'T FIRED OUTRIGHT IS THAT YOU'VE NEVER DONE ANYTHING LIKE THIS.

OH NO. I CAN'T LOSE THIS JOB. WHAT AM I GOING TO DO?

I THINK YOU CAN SMOOTH THINGS OVER IF YOU TALK TO THEM FIRST THING TOMORROW MORNING. I'VE BEEN TELLING THEM YOU HAD SOME KIND OF FAMILY EMERGENCY. YOU'LL HAVE TO MAKE UP A GOOD EXCUSE.

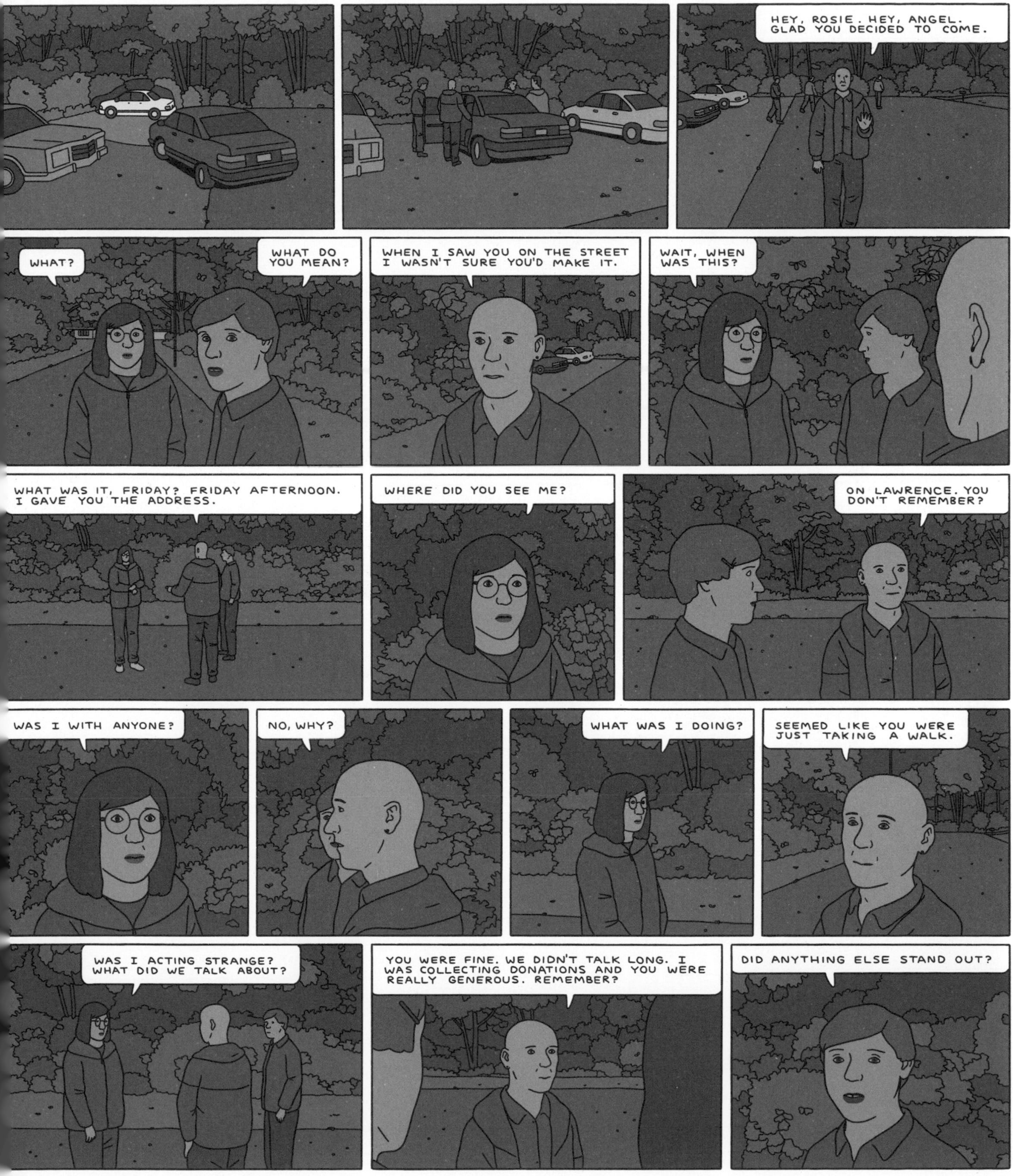
HEY, ROSIE. HEY, ANGEL. GLAD YOU DECIDED TO COME.
WHAT?
WHAT DO YOU MEAN?
WHEN I SAW YOU ON THE STREET I WASN'T SURE YOU'D MAKE IT.
WAIT, WHEN WAS THIS?
WHAT WAS IT, FRIDAY? FRIDAY AFTERNOON. I GAVE YOU THE ADDRESS.
WHERE DID YOU SEE ME?
ON LAWRENCE. YOU DON'T REMEMBER?
WAS I WITH ANYONE?
NO, WHY?
WHAT WAS I DOING?
SEEMED LIKE YOU WERE JUST TAKING A WALK.
WAS I ACTING STRANGE? WHAT DID WE TALK ABOUT?
YOU WERE FINE. WE DIDN'T TALK LONG. I WAS COLLECTING DONATIONS AND YOU WERE REALLY GENEROUS. REMEMBER?
DID ANYTHING ELSE STAND OUT?

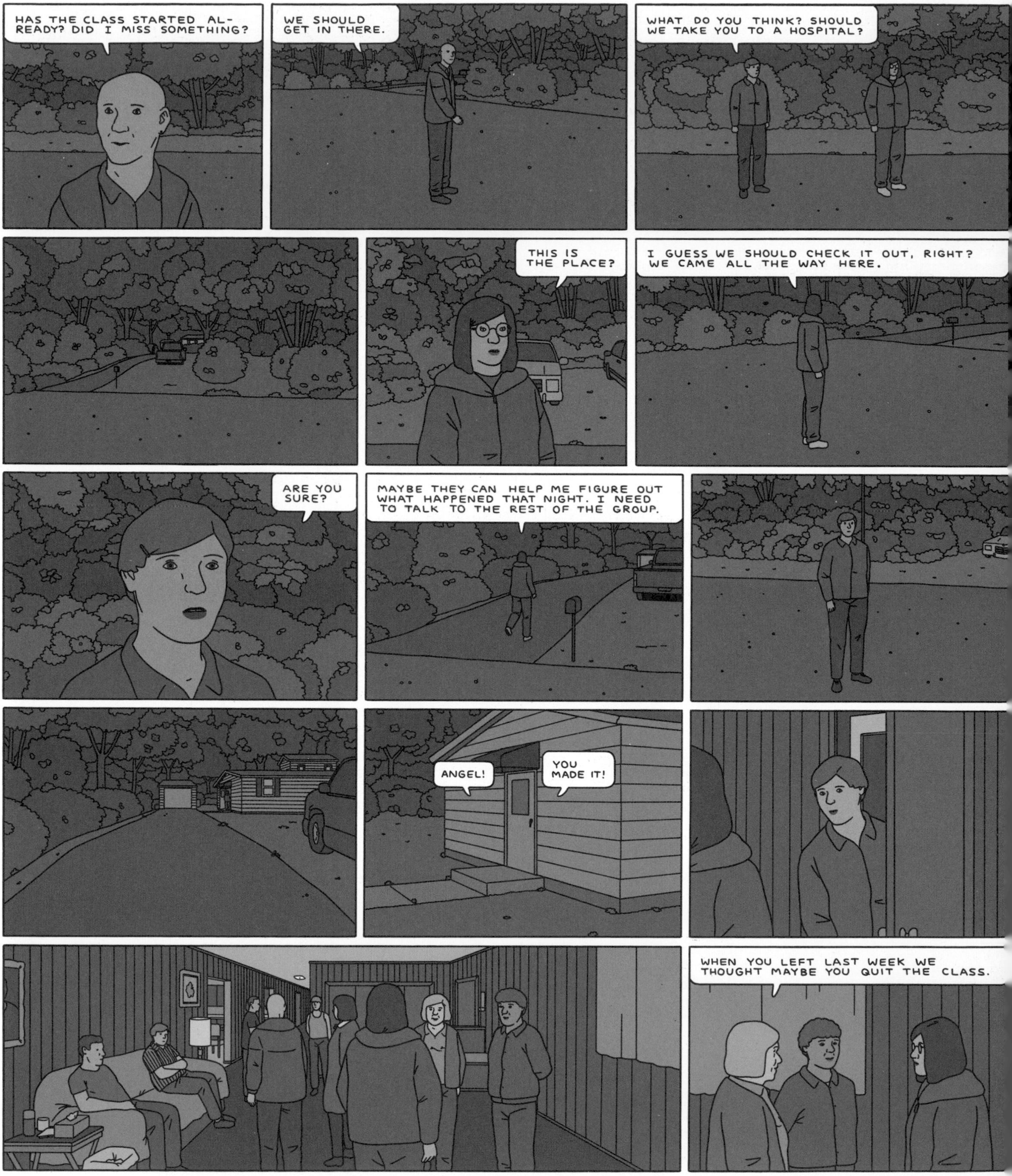
HAS THE CLASS STARTED AL-
READY? DID I MISS SOMETHING?
WE SHOULD
GET IN THERE.
WHAT DO YOU THINK? SHOULD
WE TAKE YOU TO A HOSPITAL?
THIS IS
THE PLACE?
I GUESS WE SHOULD CHECK IT OUT, RIGHT?
WE CAME ALL THE WAY HERE.
ARE YOU
SURE?
MAYBE THEY CAN HELP ME FIGURE OUT
WHAT HAPPENED THAT NIGHT. I NEED
TO TALK TO THE REST OF THE GROUP.
ANGEL!
YOU
MADE IT!
WHEN YOU LEFT LAST WEEK WE
THOUGHT MAYBE YOU QUIT THE CLASS.

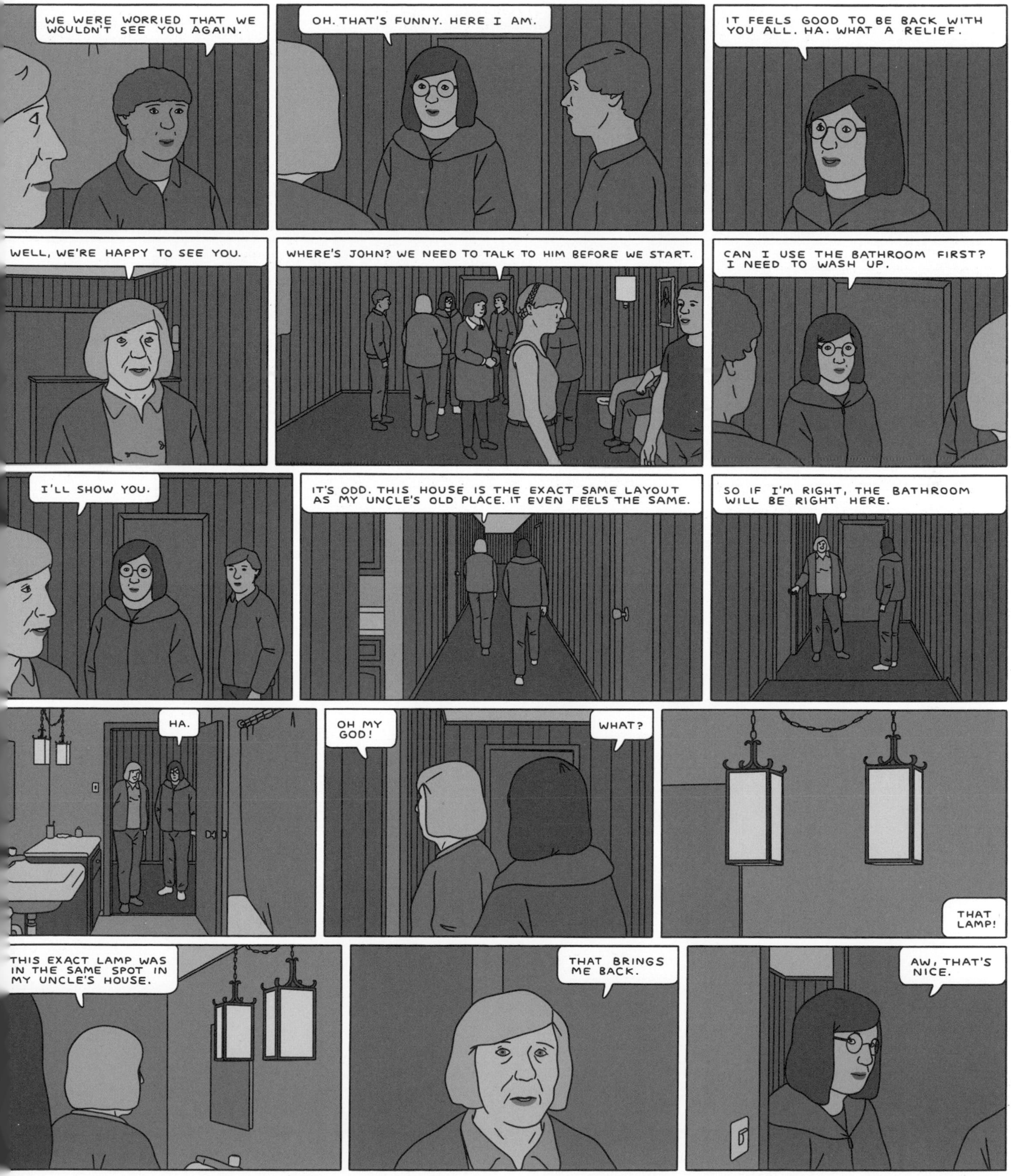
WE WERE WORRIED THAT WE WOULDN'T SEE YOU AGAIN.
OH. THAT'S FUNNY. HERE I AM.
IT FEELS GOOD TO BE BACK WITH YOU ALL. HA. WHAT A RELIEF.
WELL, WE'RE HAPPY TO SEE YOU.
WHERE'S JOHN? WE NEED TO TALK TO HIM BEFORE WE START.
CAN I USE THE BATHROOM FIRST? I NEED TO WASH UP.
I'LL SHOW YOU.
IT'S ODD. THIS HOUSE IS THE EXACT SAME LAYOUT AS MY UNCLE'S OLD PLACE. IT EVEN FEELS THE SAME.
SO IF I'M RIGHT, THE BATHROOM WILL BE RIGHT HERE.
HA.
OH MY GOD!
WHAT?
THAT LAMP!
THIS EXACT LAMP WAS IN THE SAME SPOT IN MY UNCLE'S HOUSE.
THAT BRINGS ME BACK.
AW, THAT'S NICE.

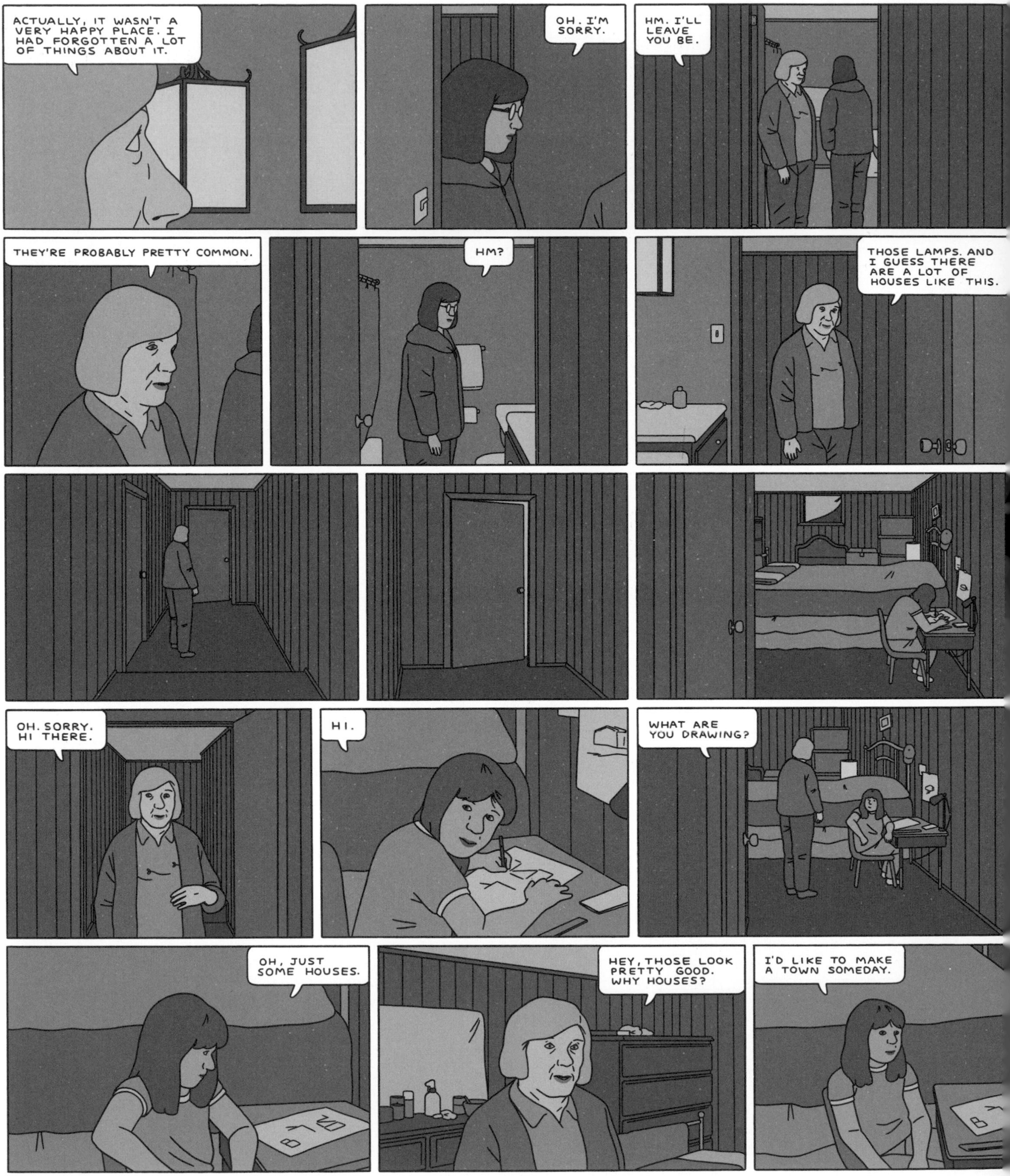

ACTUALLY, IT WASN'T A VERY HAPPY PLACE. I HAD FORGOTTEN A LOT OF THINGS ABOUT IT.
OH. I'M SORRY.
HM. I'LL LEAVE YOU BE.
THEY'RE PROBABLY PRETTY COMMON.
HM?
THOSE LAMPS. AND I GUESS THERE ARE A LOT OF HOUSES LIKE THIS.
OH. SORRY. HI THERE.
HI.
WHAT ARE YOU DRAWING?
OH, JUST SOME HOUSES.
HEY, THOSE LOOK PRETTY GOOD. WHY HOUSES?
I'D LIKE TO MAKE A TOWN SOMEDAY.

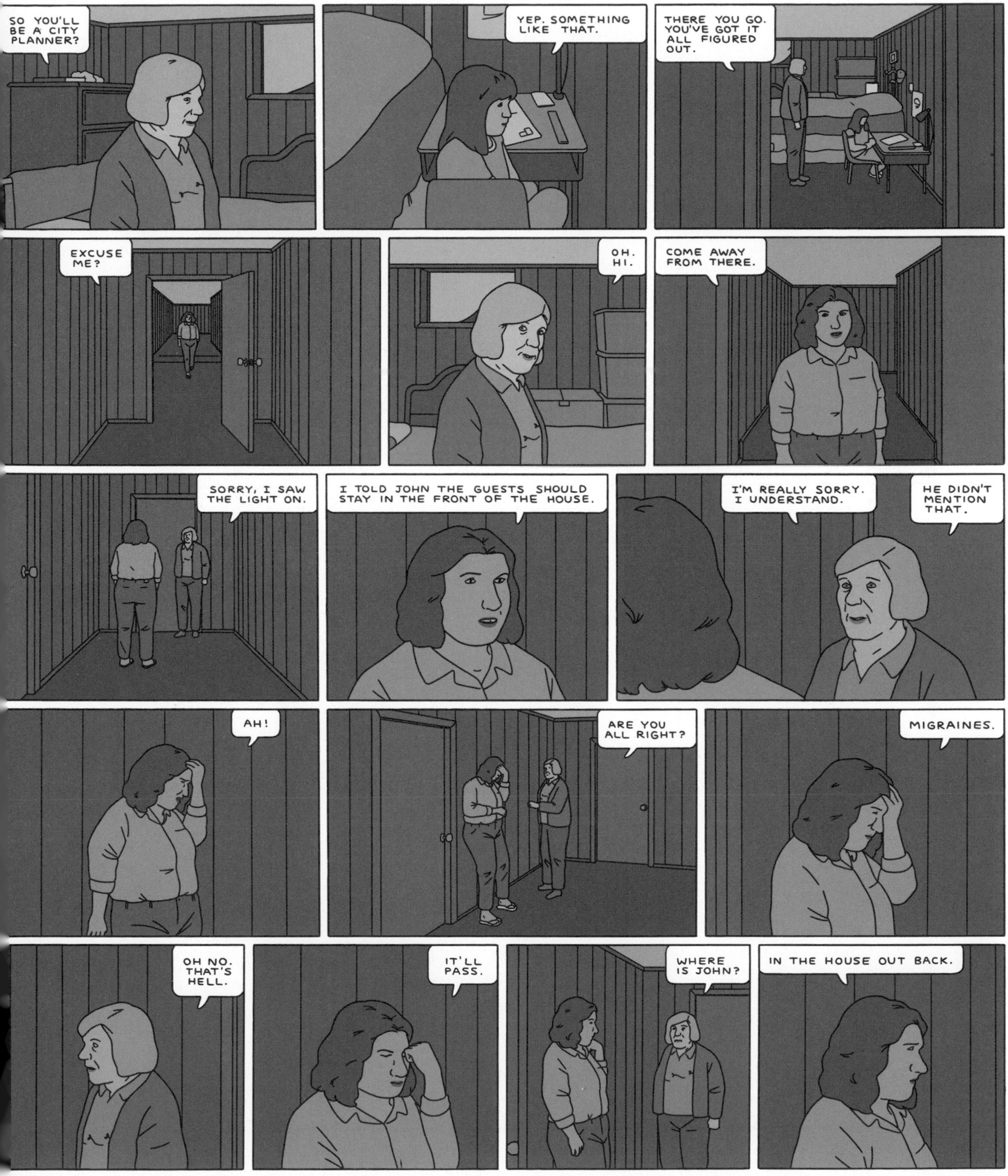
SO YOU'LL BE A CITY PLANNER?
YEP. SOMETHING LIKE THAT.
THERE YOU GO. YOU'VE GOT IT ALL FIGURED OUT.
EXCUSE ME?
OH. HI.
COME AWAY FROM THERE.
SORRY, I SAW THE LIGHT ON.
I TOLD JOHN THE GUESTS SHOULD STAY IN THE FRONT OF THE HOUSE.
I'M REALLY SORRY. I UNDERSTAND.
HE DIDN'T MENTION THAT.
AH!
ARE YOU ALL RIGHT?
MIGRAINES.
OH NO. THAT'S HELL.
IT'LL PASS.
WHERE IS JOHN?
IN THE HOUSE OUT BACK.

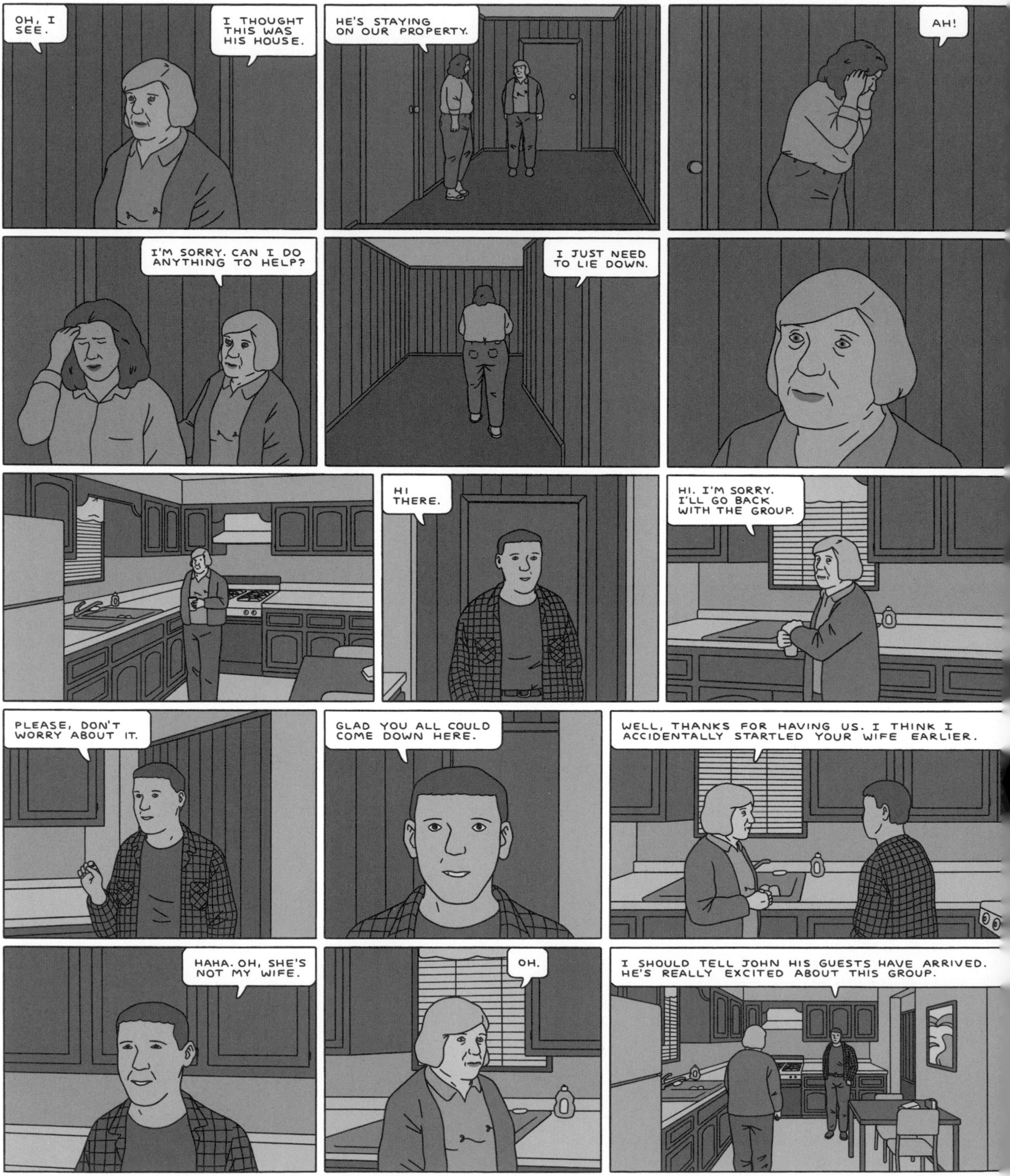
OH, I SEE.
I THOUGHT THIS WAS HIS HOUSE.
HE'S STAYING ON OUR PROPERTY.
AH!
I'M SORRY. CAN I DO ANYTHING TO HELP?
I JUST NEED TO LIE DOWN.
HI THERE.
HI. I'M SORRY. I'LL GO BACK WITH THE GROUP.
PLEASE, DON'T WORRY ABOUT IT.
GLAD YOU ALL COULD COME DOWN HERE.
WELL, THANKS FOR HAVING US. I THINK I ACCIDENTALLY STARTLED YOUR WIFE EARLIER.
HAHA. OH, SHE'S NOT MY WIFE.
OH.
I SHOULD TELL JOHN HIS GUESTS HAVE ARRIVED. HE'S REALLY EXCITED ABOUT THIS GROUP.

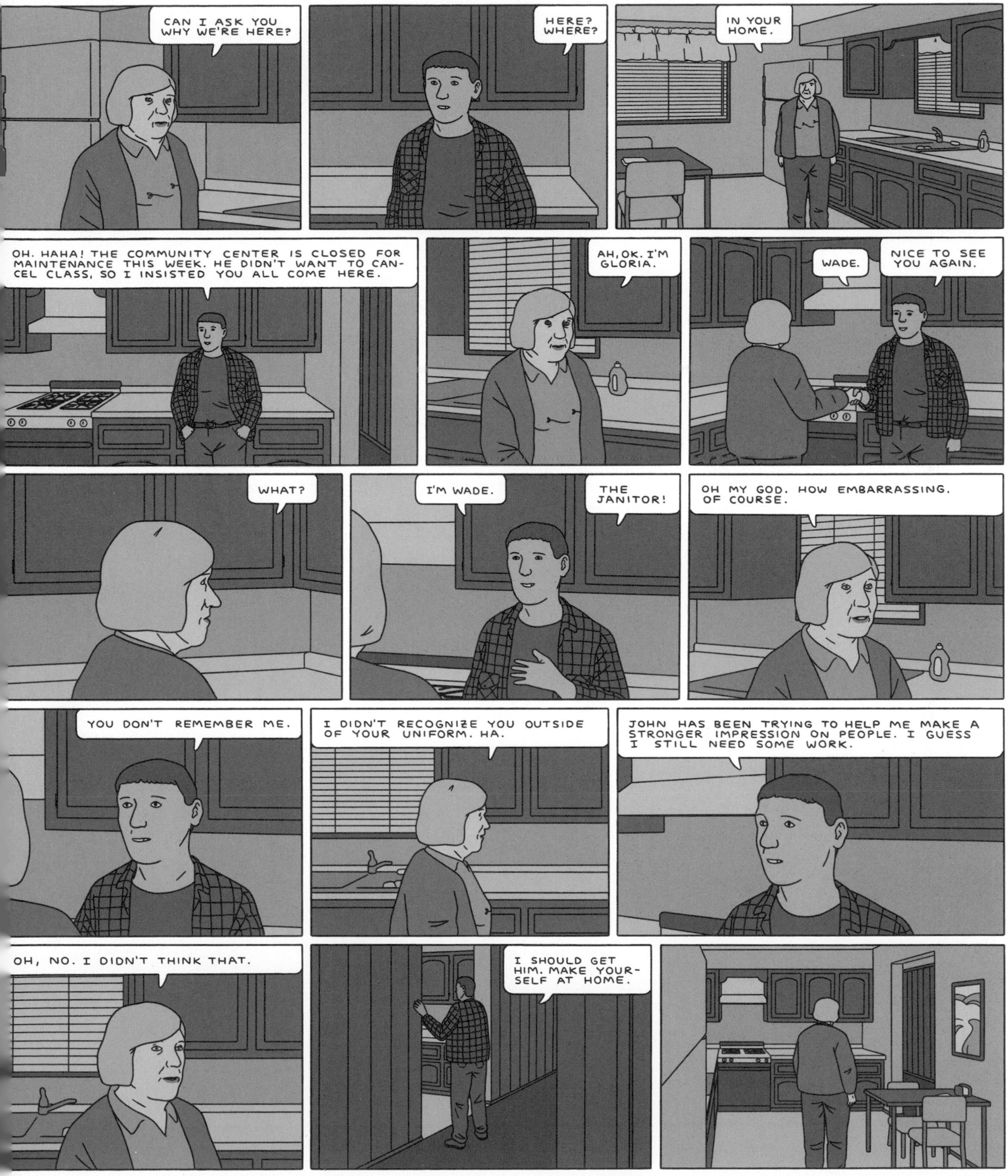
CAN I ASK YOU WHY WE'RE HERE?
HERE? WHERE?
IN YOUR HOME.
OH. HAHA! THE COMMUNITY CENTER IS CLOSED FOR MAINTENANCE THIS WEEK. HE DIDN'T WANT TO CANCEL CLASS, SO I INSISTED YOU ALL COME HERE.
AH, OK. I'M GLORIA.
WADE.
NICE TO SEE YOU AGAIN.
WHAT?
I'M WADE.
THE JANITOR!
OH MY GOD. HOW EMBARRASSING. OF COURSE.
YOU DON'T REMEMBER ME.
I DIDN'T RECOGNIZE YOU OUTSIDE OF YOUR UNIFORM. HA.
JOHN HAS BEEN TRYING TO HELP ME MAKE A STRONGER IMPRESSION ON PEOPLE. I GUESS I STILL NEED SOME WORK.
OH, NO. I DIDN'T THINK THAT.
I SHOULD GET HIM. MAKE YOURSELF AT HOME.

 HOW'S IT GOING?

 MY HEAD IS SPINNING ALREADY.

 ME TOO. I'M NOT SURE THIS IS WORKING FOR ME.

 WHAT'S WRONG?

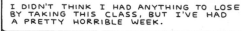 I DIDN'T THINK I HAD ANYTHING TO LOSE BY TAKING THIS CLASS, BUT I'VE HAD A PRETTY HORRIBLE WEEK.

 EVEN LITTLE INTERACTIONS ARE HARD. YESTERDAY I GOT MY OIL CHANGED, AND THIS GUY IN THE WAITING AREA WAS MAKING SMALL TALK.

NORMALLY, THAT WOULD BE NO BIG DEAL. I'M PRETTY EASY GOING. BUT I FOUND THAT I COULDN'T TALK. I COULDN'T THINK CLEARLY. I WAS SURE HE WAS JUDGING ME.

 AND I GOT LOST IN MY OWN HEAD. I WAS ACTUALLY SWEATING.

IT FELT LIKE I WAS GIVING A BAD PERFORMANCE.

THAT'S SOMETHING THAT WOULD HAVE NEVER CROSSED MY MIND BEFORE.

I THINK I KNOW WHAT YOU MEAN. MAYBE IGNORANCE IS BLISS.

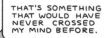

 BUT YOU SEEM COMFORTABLE SLIPPING INTO THESE EXERCISES.

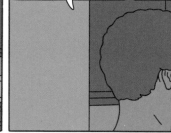 MAYBE YOU STOP CARING AS YOU GET OLDER. THAT MAKES IT EASIER.

 CAN I ASK YOU WHERE THAT STORY ABOUT THE TENANT AND THE GHOSTS CAME FROM? I'VE BEEN THINKING ABOUT IT ALL WEEK.

 YOU WANT ME TO GIVE AWAY MY ACTING SECRETS?

 IT SEEMED SO VIVID. IT HAS TO BE A TRUE STORY.

 WELL, YOU GOT ME. IT'S ACTUALLY MY SISTER'S STORY FROM A LONG TIME AGO.

 THAT WAS WHEN THINGS WERE PRETTY BAD. SHE WAS GOING THROUGH A LOT. IT WAS A DIFFICULT TIME.

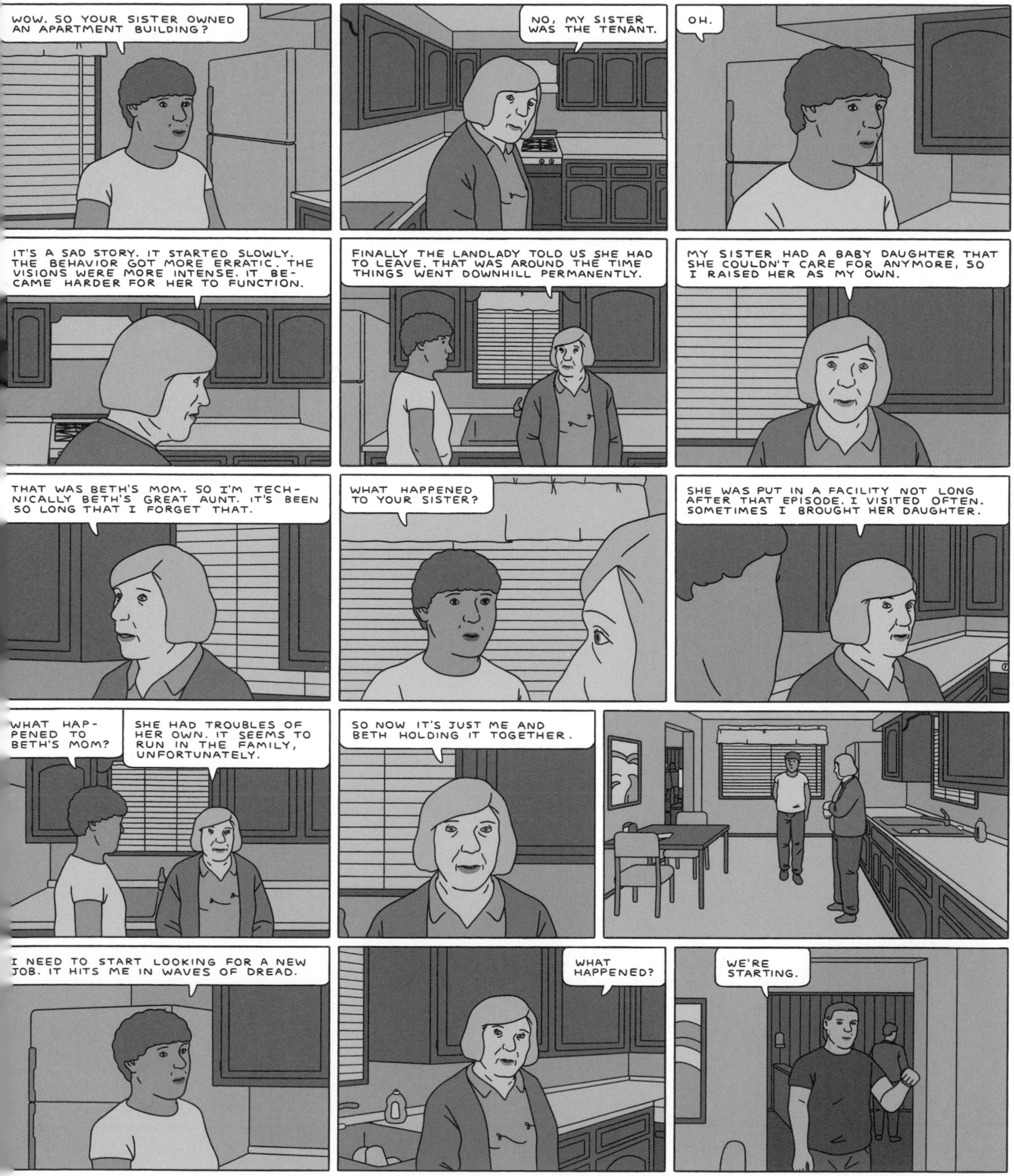
WOW. SO YOUR SISTER OWNED AN APARTMENT BUILDING?
NO, MY SISTER WAS THE TENANT.
OH.
IT'S A SAD STORY. IT STARTED SLOWLY. THE BEHAVIOR GOT MORE ERRATIC. THE VISIONS WERE MORE INTENSE. IT BE-CAME HARDER FOR HER TO FUNCTION.
FINALLY THE LANDLADY TOLD US SHE HAD TO LEAVE. THAT WAS AROUND THE TIME THINGS WENT DOWNHILL PERMANENTLY.
MY SISTER HAD A BABY DAUGHTER THAT SHE COULDN'T CARE FOR ANYMORE, SO I RAISED HER AS MY OWN.
THAT WAS BETH'S MOM. SO I'M TECH-NICALLY BETH'S GREAT AUNT. IT'S BEEN SO LONG THAT I FORGET THAT.
WHAT HAPPENED TO YOUR SISTER?
SHE WAS PUT IN A FACILITY NOT LONG AFTER THAT EPISODE. I VISITED OFTEN. SOMETIMES I BROUGHT HER DAUGHTER.
WHAT HAP-PENED TO BETH'S MOM?
SHE HAD TROUBLES OF HER OWN. IT SEEMS TO RUN IN THE FAMILY, UNFORTUNATELY.
SO NOW IT'S JUST ME AND BETH HOLDING IT TOGETHER.
I NEED TO START LOOKING FOR A NEW JOB. IT HITS ME IN WAVES OF DREAD.
WHAT HAPPENED?
WE'RE STARTING.

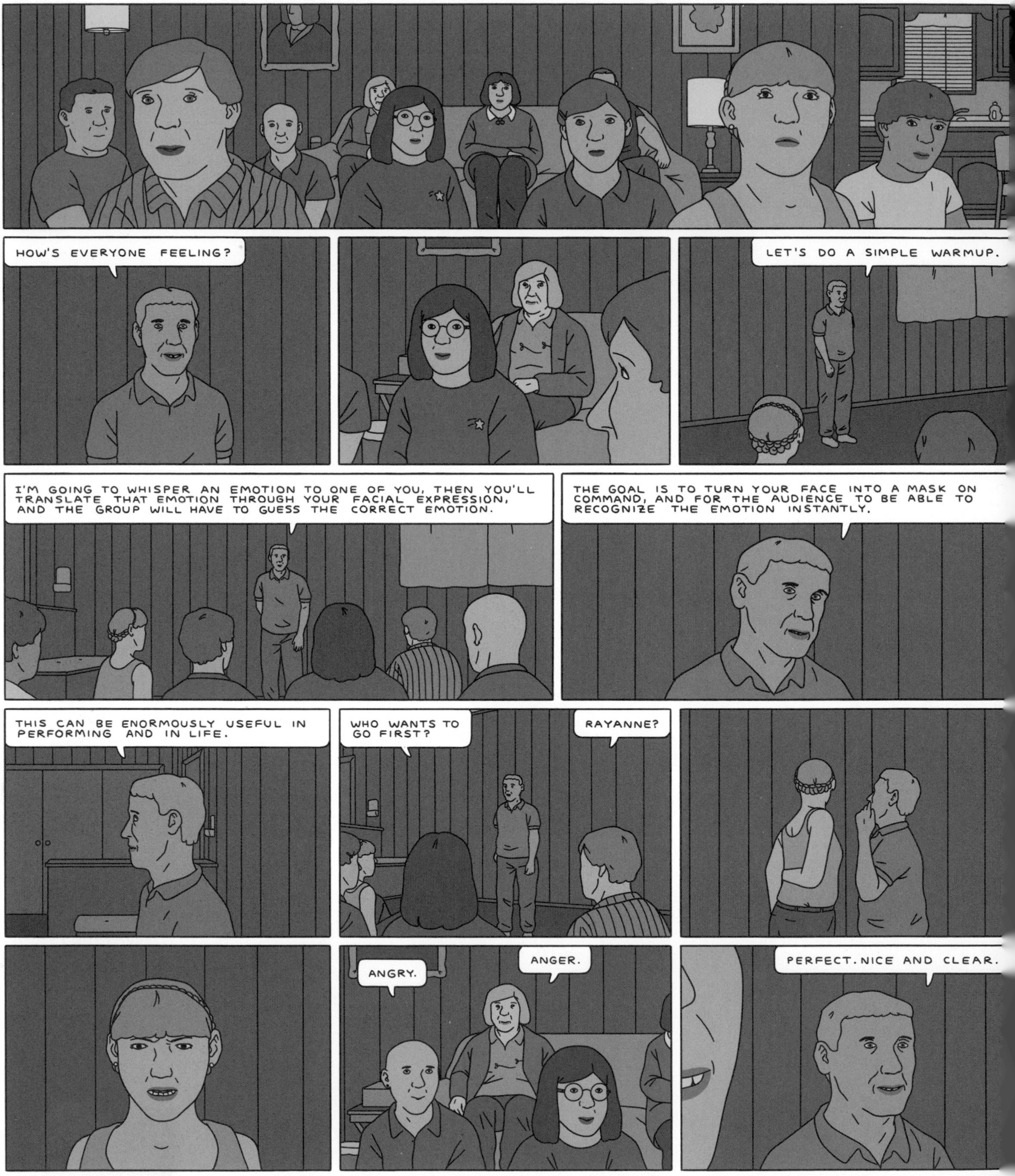
HOW'S EVERYONE FEELING?
LET'S DO A SIMPLE WARMUP.
I'M GOING TO WHISPER AN EMOTION TO ONE OF YOU, THEN YOU'LL TRANSLATE THAT EMOTION THROUGH YOUR FACIAL EXPRESSION, AND THE GROUP WILL HAVE TO GUESS THE CORRECT EMOTION.
THE GOAL IS TO TURN YOUR FACE INTO A MASK ON COMMAND, AND FOR THE AUDIENCE TO BE ABLE TO RECOGNIZE THE EMOTION INSTANTLY.
THIS CAN BE ENORMOUSLY USEFUL IN PERFORMING AND IN LIFE.
WHO WANTS TO GO FIRST?
RAYANNE?
ANGRY.
ANGER.
PERFECT. NICE AND CLEAR.

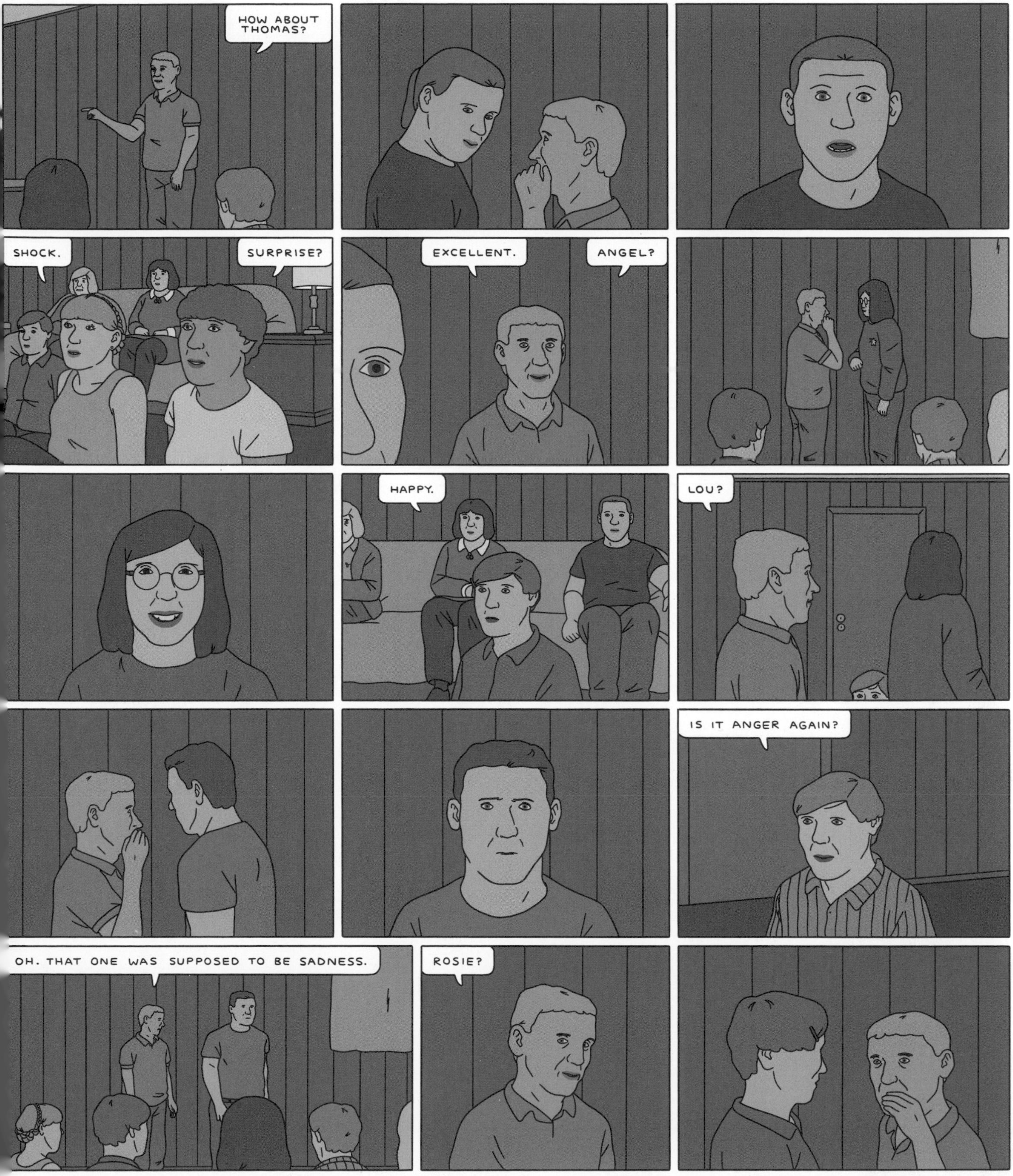
HOW ABOUT THOMAS?
SHOCK.
SURPRISE?
EXCELLENT.
ANGEL?
HAPPY.
LOU?
IS IT ANGER AGAIN?
OH. THAT ONE WAS SUPPOSED TO BE SADNESS.
ROSIE?

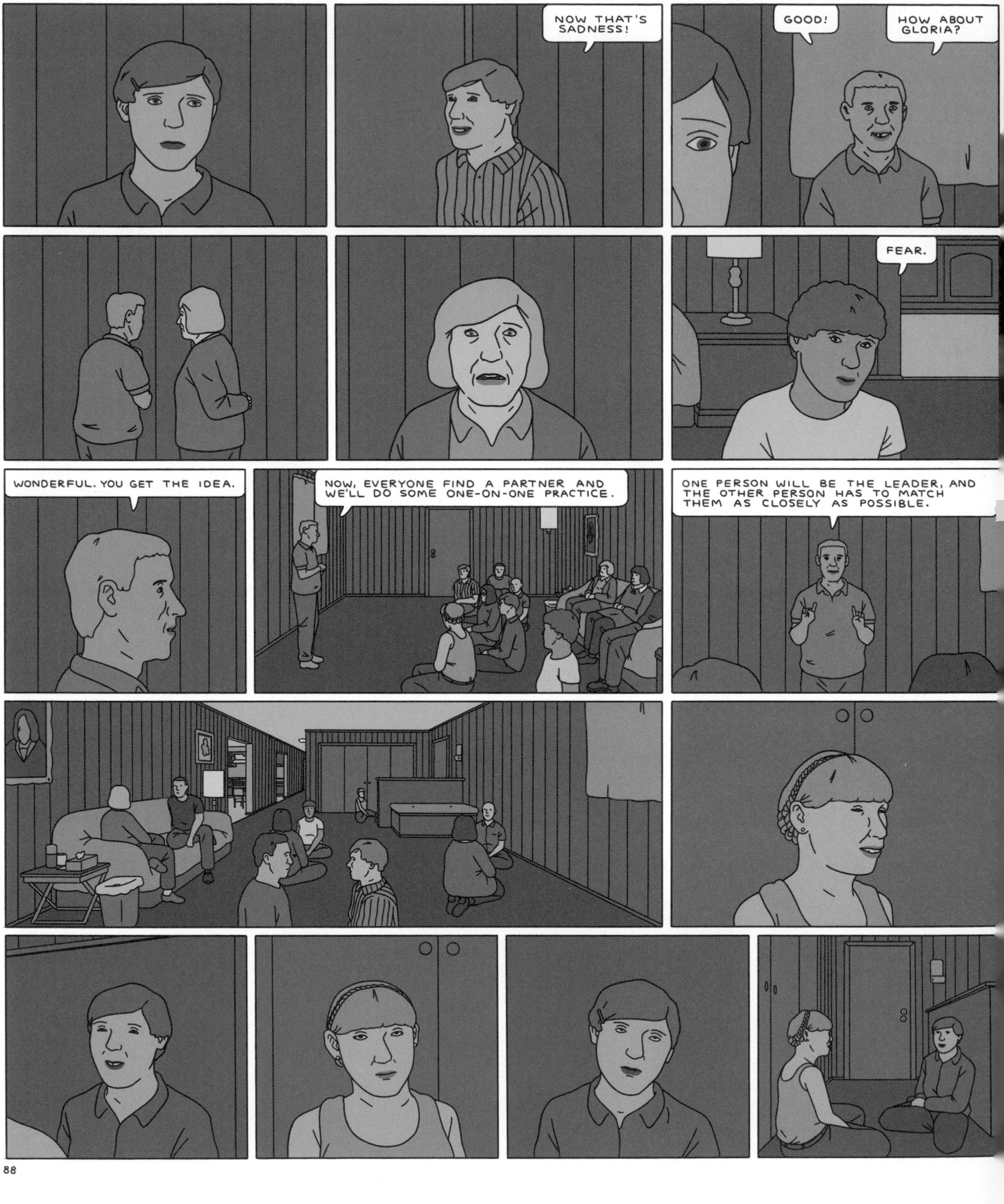
NOW THAT'S SADNESS!
GOOD!
HOW ABOUT GLORIA?
FEAR.
WONDERFUL. YOU GET THE IDEA.
NOW, EVERYONE FIND A PARTNER AND WE'LL DO SOME ONE-ON-ONE PRACTICE.
ONE PERSON WILL BE THE LEADER, AND THE OTHER PERSON HAS TO MATCH THEM AS CLOSELY AS POSSIBLE.

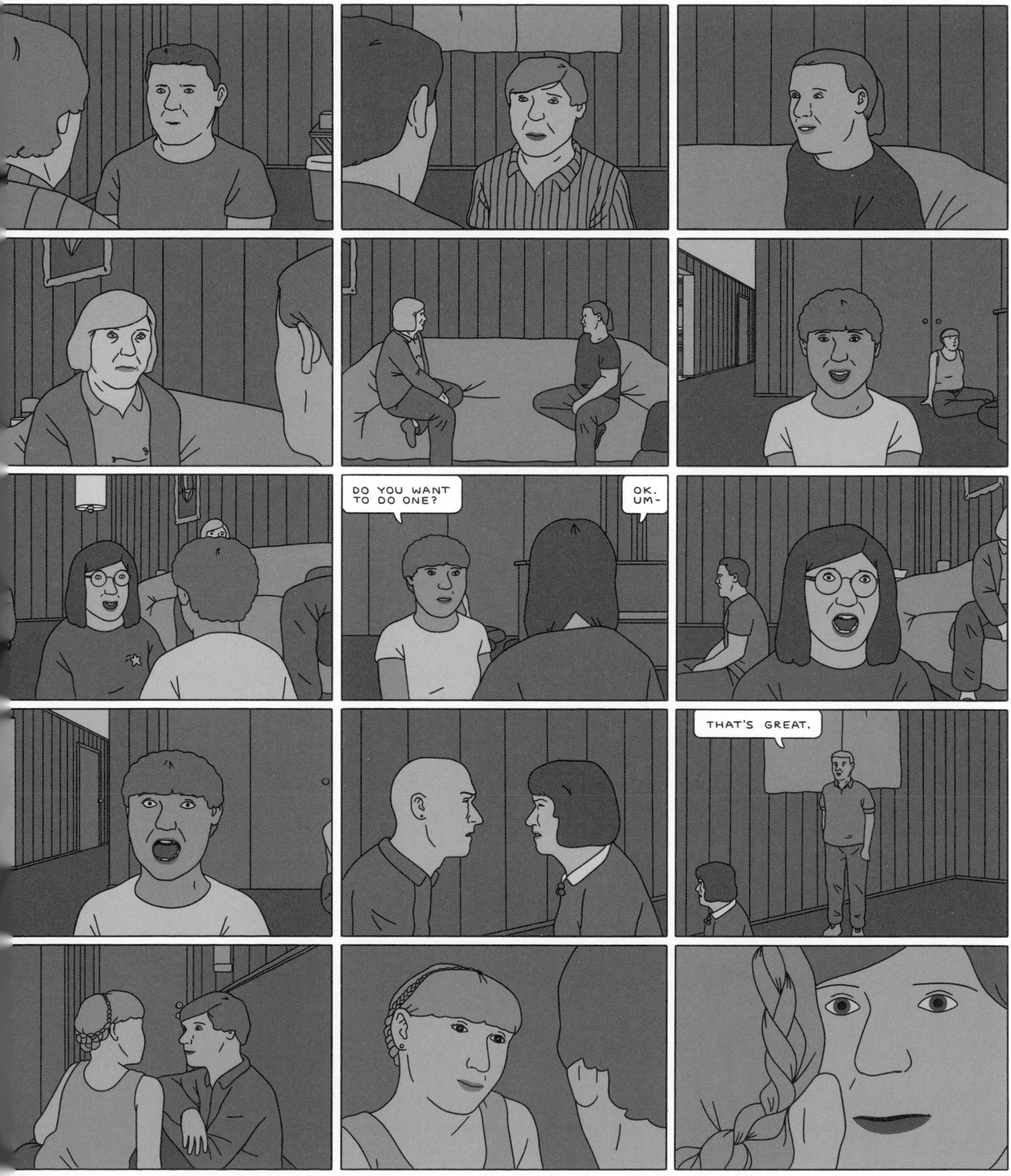
DO YOU WANT TO DO ONE?
OK. UM-
THAT'S GREAT.

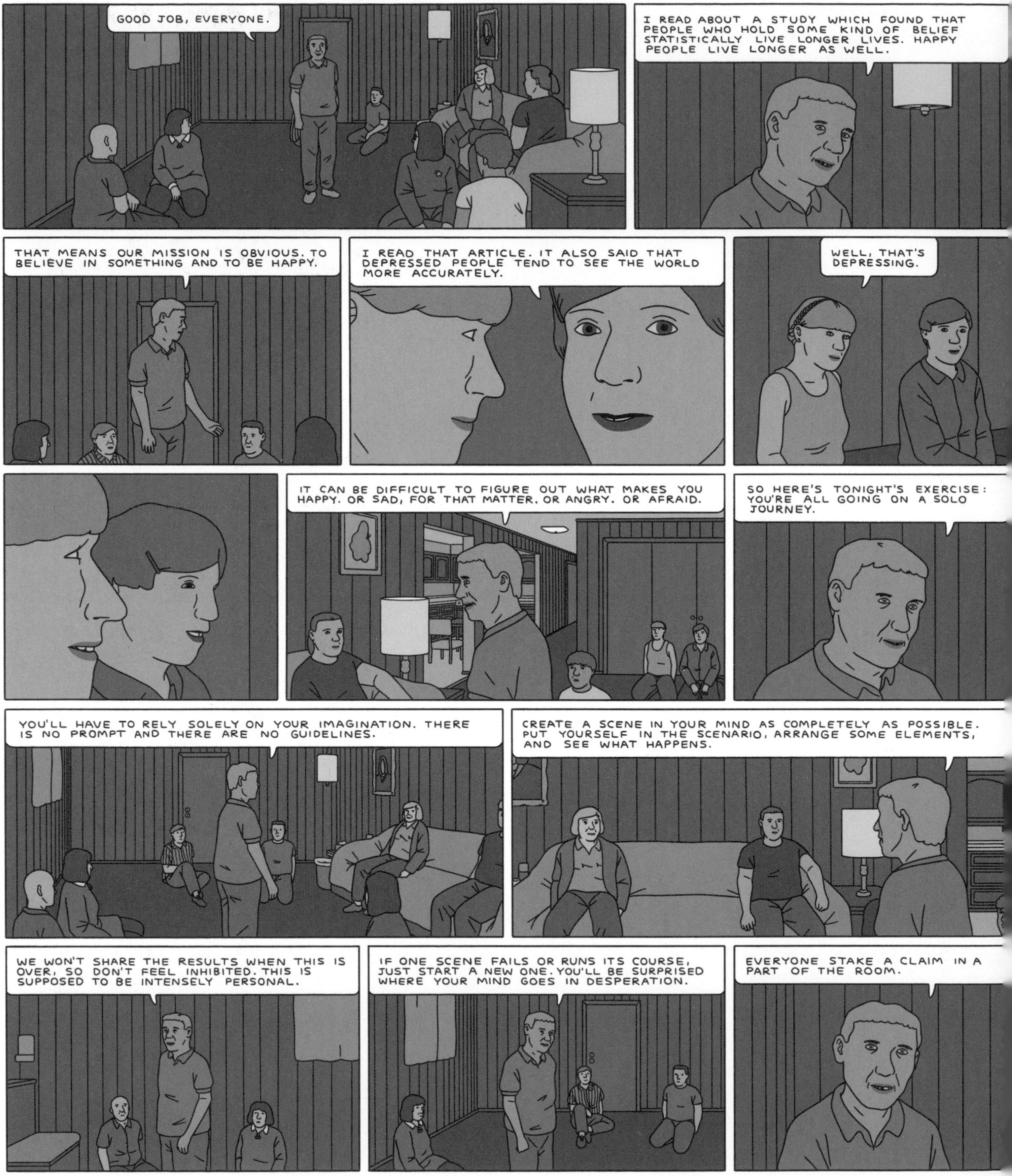
GOOD JOB, EVERYONE.
I READ ABOUT A STUDY WHICH FOUND THAT PEOPLE WHO HOLD SOME KIND OF BELIEF STATISTICALLY LIVE LONGER LIVES. HAPPY PEOPLE LIVE LONGER AS WELL.
THAT MEANS OUR MISSION IS OBVIOUS. TO BELIEVE IN SOMETHING AND TO BE HAPPY.
I READ THAT ARTICLE. IT ALSO SAID THAT DEPRESSED PEOPLE TEND TO SEE THE WORLD MORE ACCURATELY.
WELL, THAT'S DEPRESSING.
IT CAN BE DIFFICULT TO FIGURE OUT WHAT MAKES YOU HAPPY. OR SAD, FOR THAT MATTER. OR ANGRY. OR AFRAID.
SO HERE'S TONIGHT'S EXERCISE: YOU'RE ALL GOING ON A SOLO JOURNEY.
YOU'LL HAVE TO RELY SOLELY ON YOUR IMAGINATION. THERE IS NO PROMPT AND THERE ARE NO GUIDELINES.
CREATE A SCENE IN YOUR MIND AS COMPLETELY AS POSSIBLE. PUT YOURSELF IN THE SCENARIO, ARRANGE SOME ELEMENTS, AND SEE WHAT HAPPENS.
WE WON'T SHARE THE RESULTS WHEN THIS IS OVER, SO DON'T FEEL INHIBITED. THIS IS SUPPOSED TO BE INTENSELY PERSONAL.
IF ONE SCENE FAILS OR RUNS ITS COURSE, JUST START A NEW ONE. YOU'LL BE SURPRISED WHERE YOUR MIND GOES IN DESPERATION.
EVERYONE STAKE A CLAIM IN A PART OF THE ROOM.

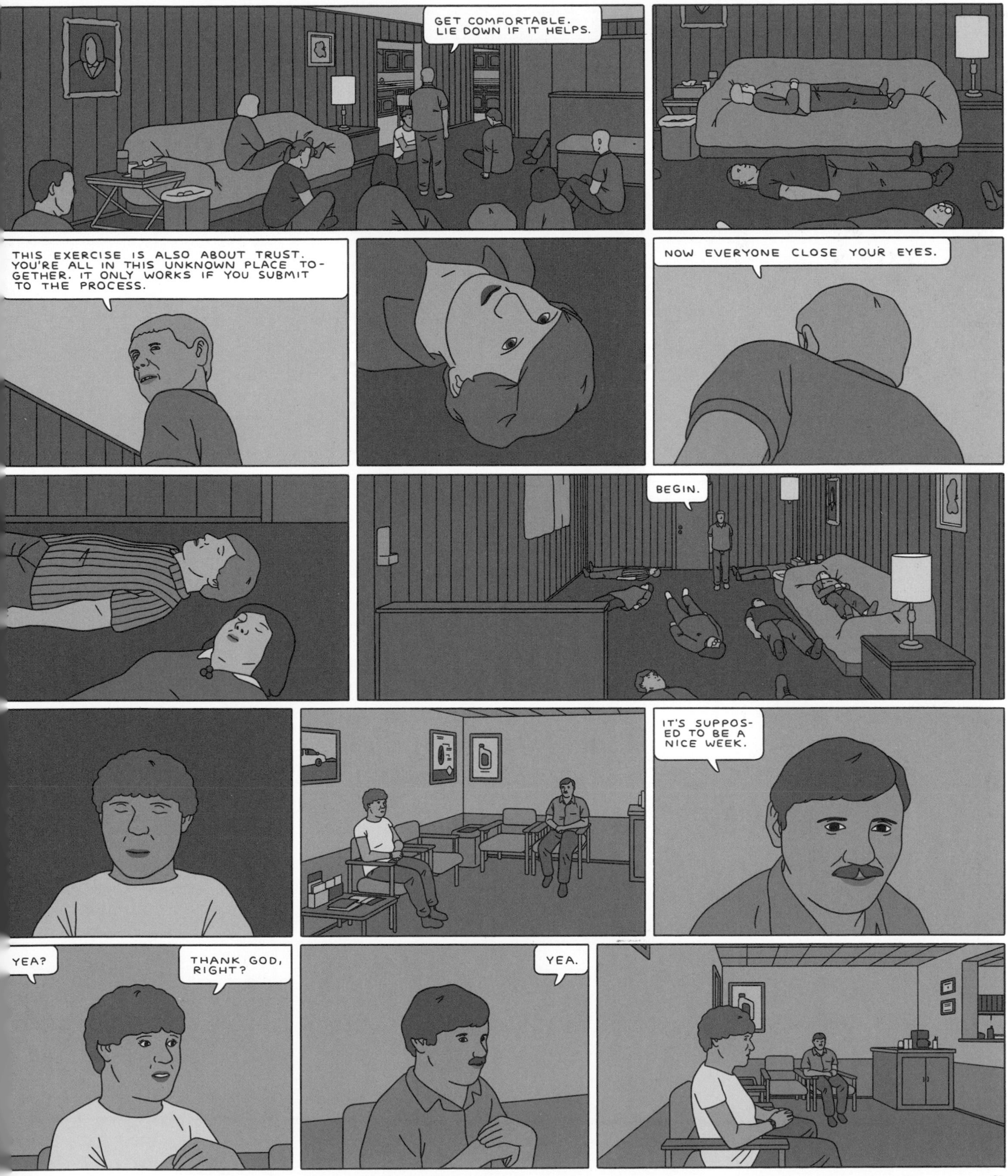
GET COMFORTABLE. LIE DOWN IF IT HELPS.
THIS EXERCISE IS ALSO ABOUT TRUST. YOU'RE ALL IN THIS UNKNOWN PLACE TO-GETHER. IT ONLY WORKS IF YOU SUBMIT TO THE PROCESS.
NOW EVERYONE CLOSE YOUR EYES.
BEGIN.
IT'S SUPPOS-ED TO BE A NICE WEEK.
YEA?
THANK GOD, RIGHT?
YEA.

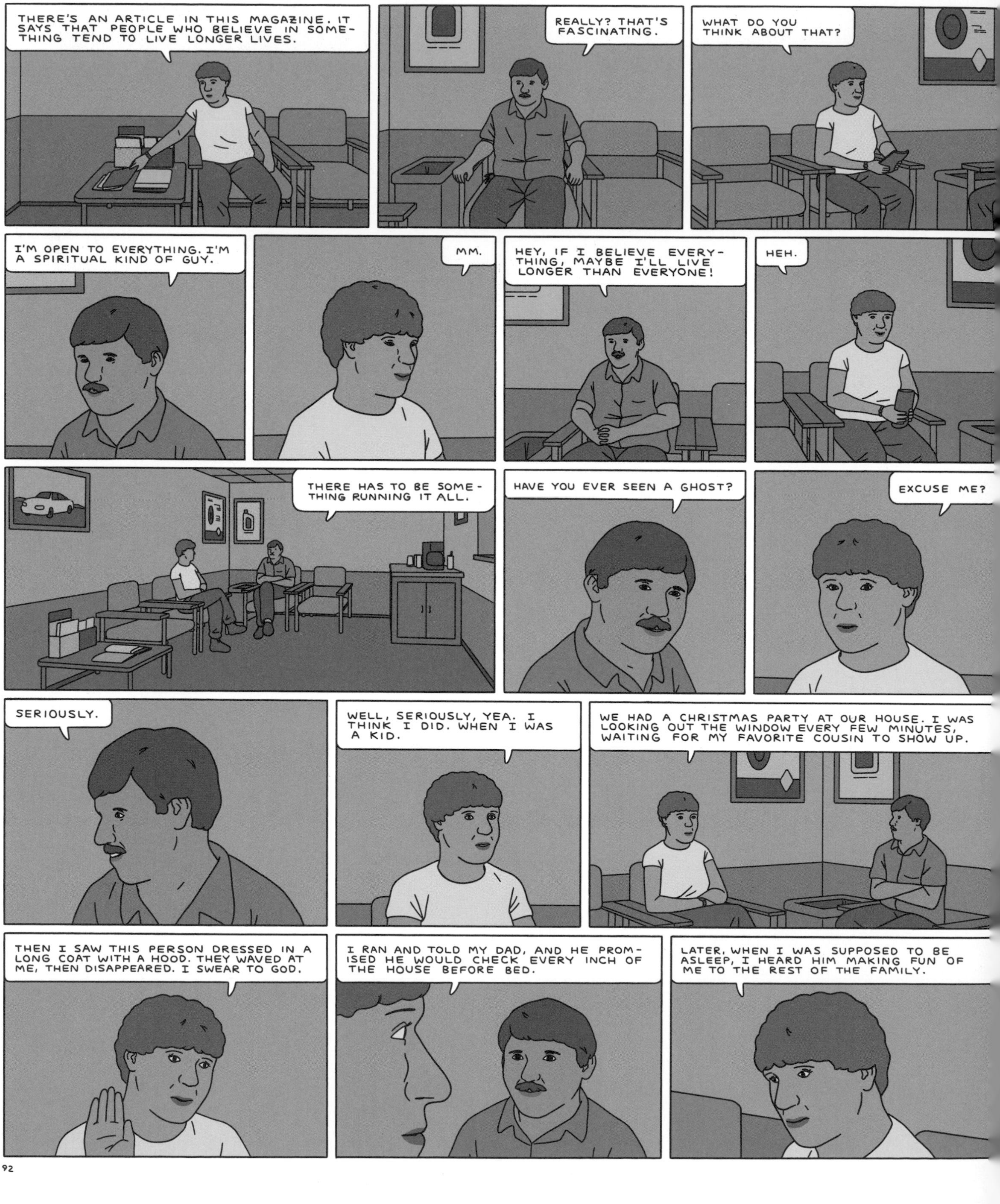
THERE'S AN ARTICLE IN THIS MAGAZINE. IT SAYS THAT PEOPLE WHO BELIEVE IN SOMETHING TEND TO LIVE LONGER LIVES.
REALLY? THAT'S FASCINATING.
WHAT DO YOU THINK ABOUT THAT?
I'M OPEN TO EVERYTHING. I'M A SPIRITUAL KIND OF GUY.
MM.
HEY, IF I BELIEVE EVERYTHING, MAYBE I'LL LIVE LONGER THAN EVERYONE!
HEH.
THERE HAS TO BE SOMETHING RUNNING IT ALL.
HAVE YOU EVER SEEN A GHOST?
EXCUSE ME?
SERIOUSLY.
WELL, SERIOUSLY, YEA. I THINK I DID. WHEN I WAS A KID.
WE HAD A CHRISTMAS PARTY AT OUR HOUSE. I WAS LOOKING OUT THE WINDOW EVERY FEW MINUTES, WAITING FOR MY FAVORITE COUSIN TO SHOW UP.
THEN I SAW THIS PERSON DRESSED IN A LONG COAT WITH A HOOD. THEY WAVED AT ME, THEN DISAPPEARED. I SWEAR TO GOD.
I RAN AND TOLD MY DAD, AND HE PROMISED HE WOULD CHECK EVERY INCH OF THE HOUSE BEFORE BED.
LATER, WHEN I WAS SUPPOSED TO BE ASLEEP, I HEARD HIM MAKING FUN OF ME TO THE REST OF THE FAMILY.

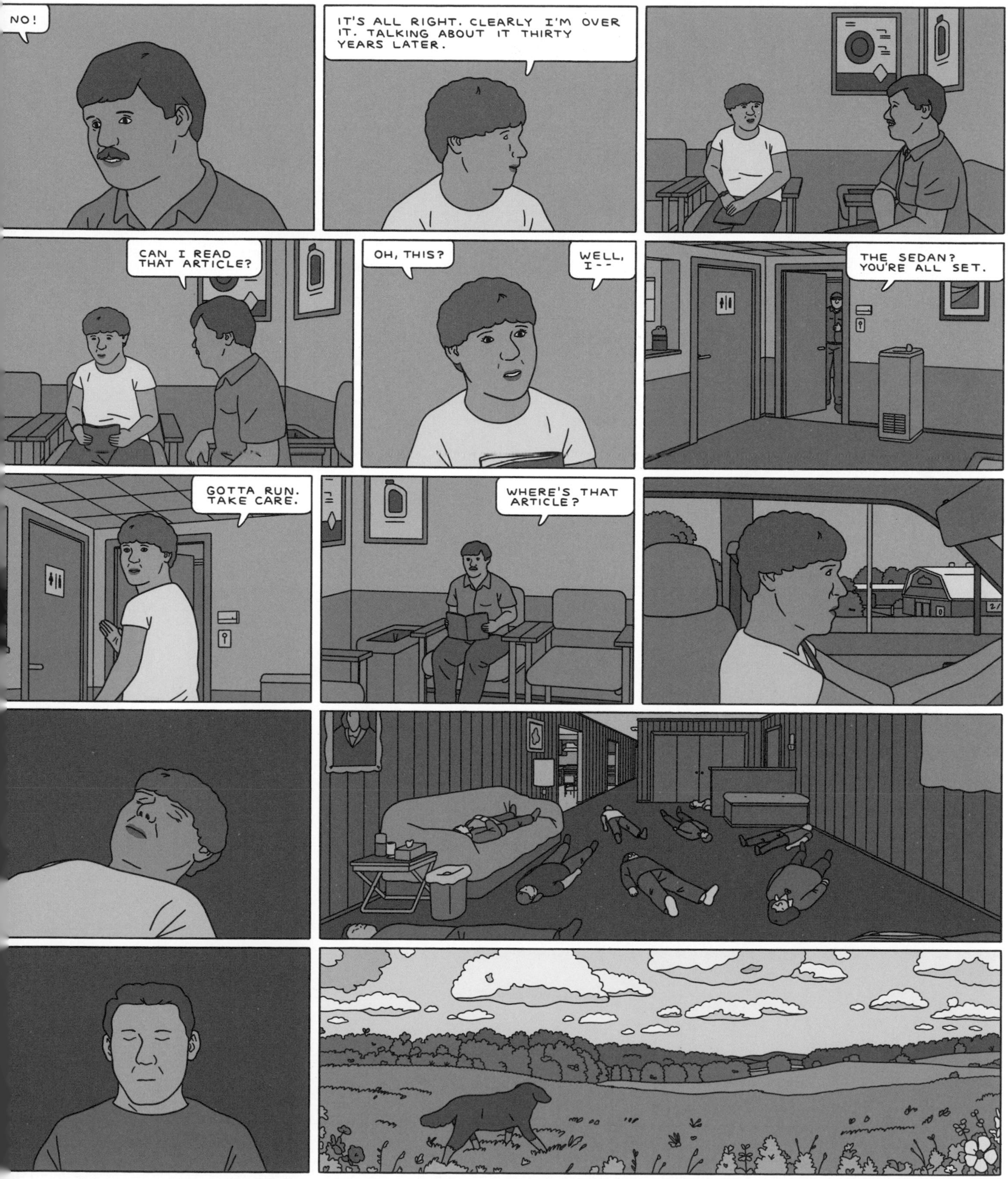
NO!
IT'S ALL RIGHT. CLEARLY I'M OVER IT. TALKING ABOUT IT THIRTY YEARS LATER.
CAN I READ THAT ARTICLE?
OH, THIS?
WELL, I--
THE SEDAN? YOU'RE ALL SET.
GOTTA RUN. TAKE CARE.
WHERE'S THAT ARTICLE?

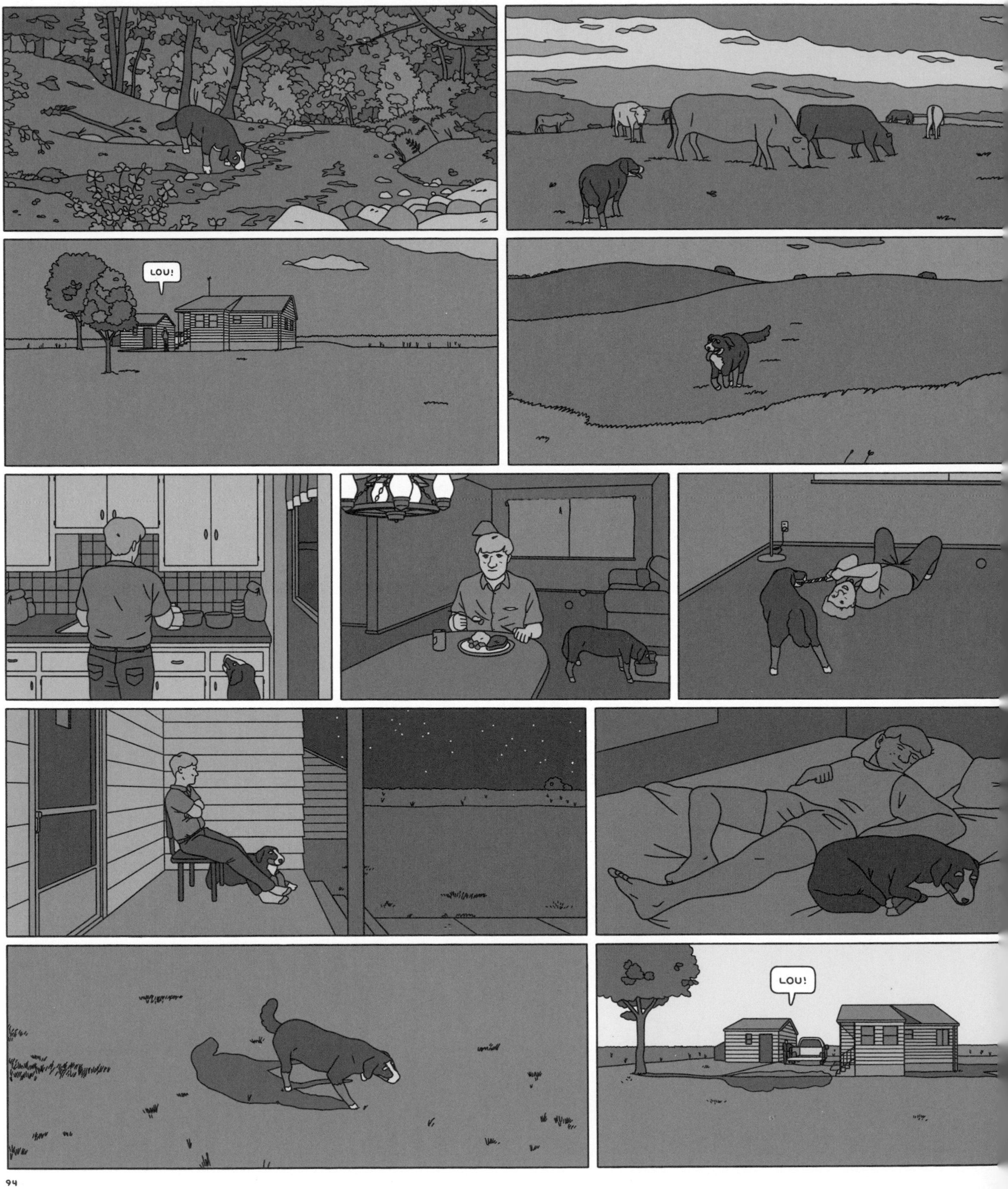
LOU!
LOU!

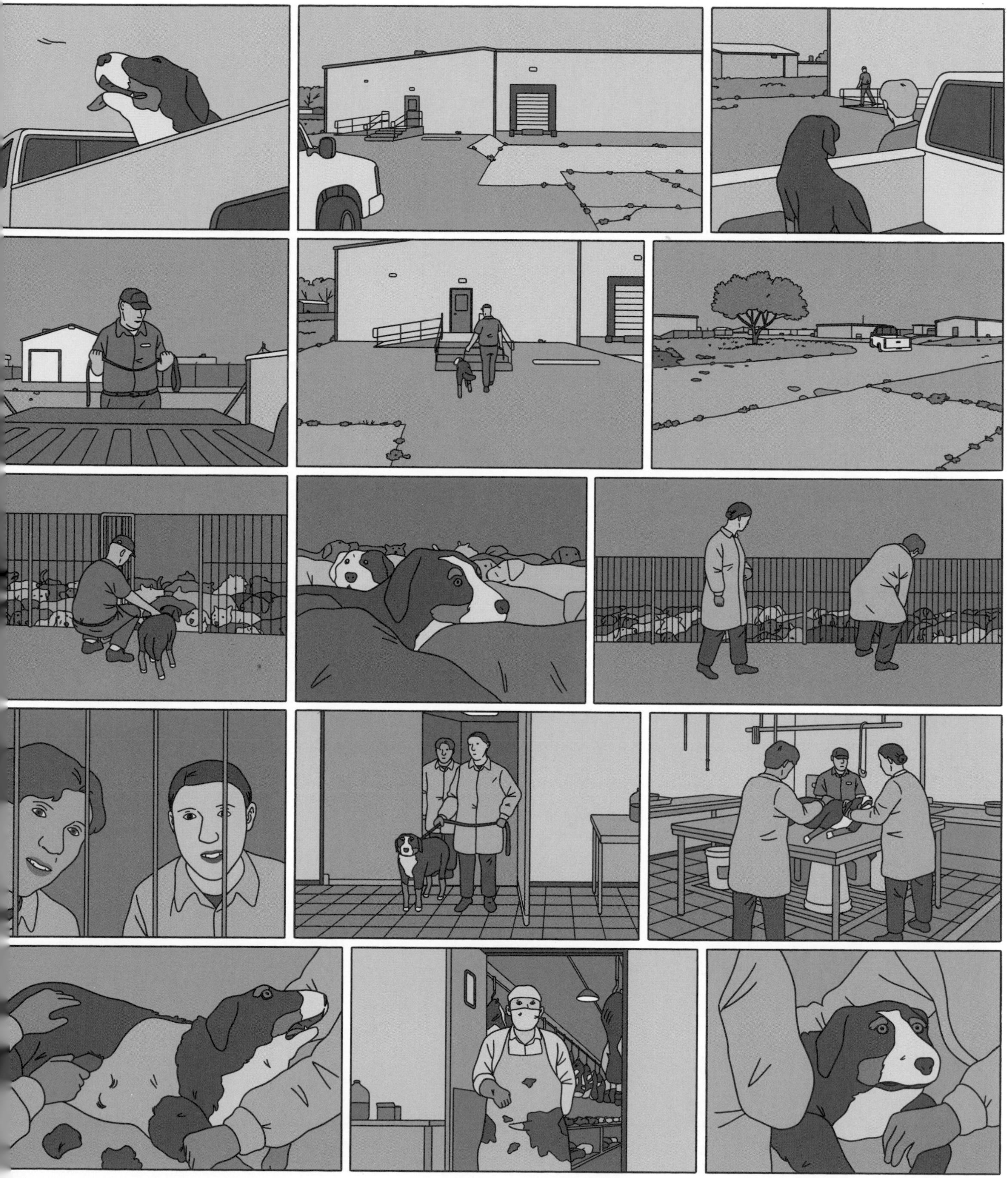

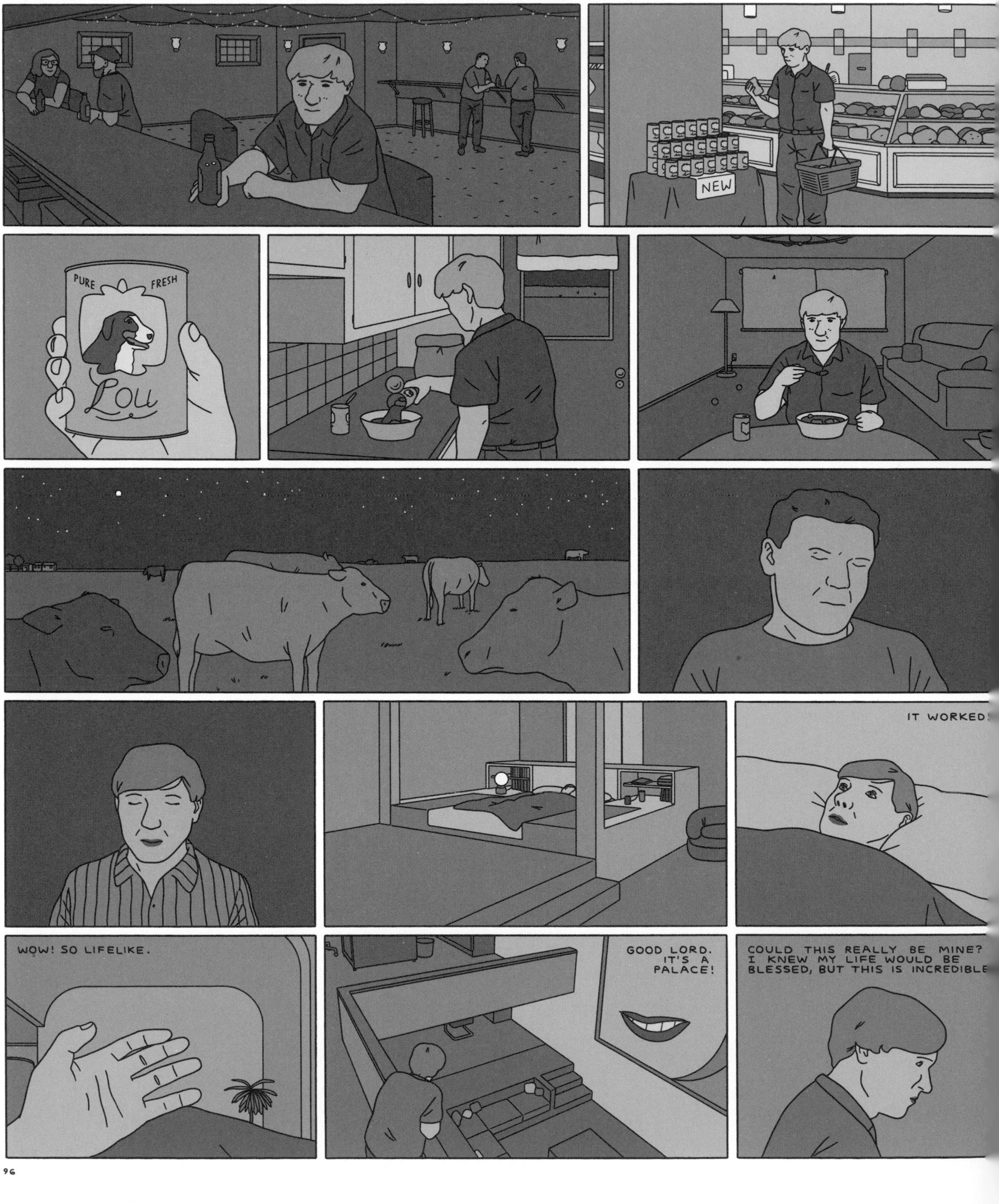
NEW
PURE FRESH
Lou
IT WORKED!
WOW! SO LIFELIKE.
GOOD LORD. IT'S A PALACE!
COULD THIS REALLY BE MINE? I KNEW MY LIFE WOULD BE BLESSED, BUT THIS IS INCREDIBLE

NICE NEIGHBORHOOD. I'LL HAVE TO INTRODUCE MYSELF TO EVERYONE.

THIS MUST BE WHAT JOHN WAS TALKING ABOUT. IT WASN'T SO HARD.

WHERE'S ROSIE? I SHOULD CALL HER. SHE'LL LOVE THIS.

I SUPPOSE I NEED A STORY. THIS CAN'T GO ON FOREVER.

THERE SHOULD BE SOME KIND OF CON-FLICT. BUT HOW? I'M IN PARADISE!

I KNOW! I'LL INVITE MY WHOLE FAMILY UP HERE.

THEY WON'T KNOW WHAT TO SAY WHEN THEY SEE THIS PLACE. THERE'S A PRI-VATE ROOM FOR EVERY ONE OF THEM.

FIRST THING TOMORROW, I'LL CALL THEM WITH THE INVITATION.

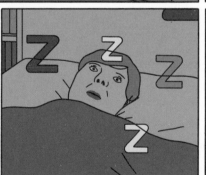

WHAT THE HELL?!

YOU HAVE GOT TO BE KIDDING ME.

HEY! YOUR NEIGHBOR IS TRYING TO SLEEP!

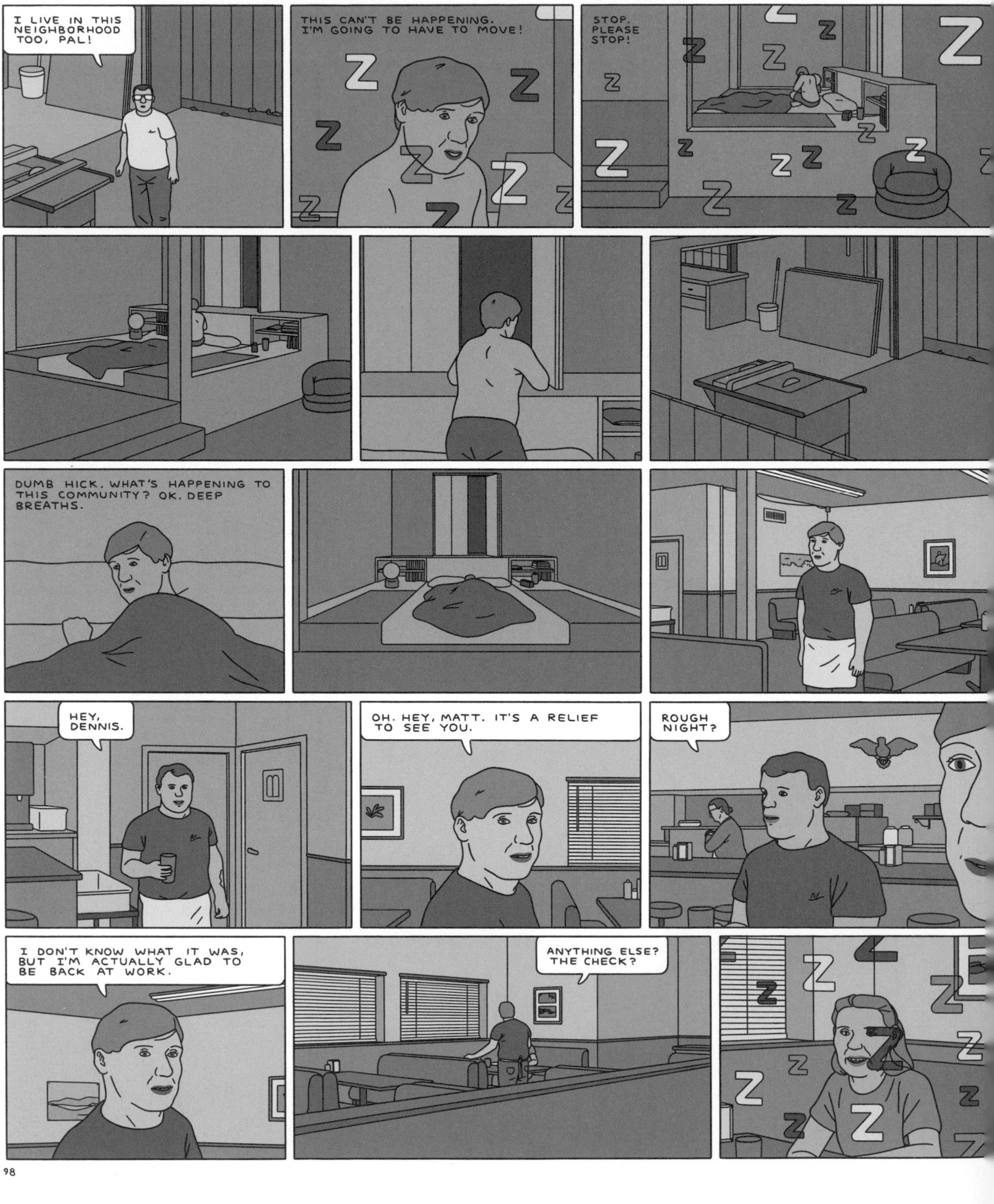
I LIVE IN THIS NEIGHBORHOOD TOO, PAL!
THIS CAN'T BE HAPPENING. I'M GOING TO HAVE TO MOVE!
STOP. PLEASE STOP!
DUMB HICK. WHAT'S HAPPENING TO THIS COMMUNITY? OK. DEEP BREATHS.
HEY, DENNIS.
OH. HEY, MATT. IT'S A RELIEF TO SEE YOU.
ROUGH NIGHT?
I DON'T KNOW WHAT IT WAS, BUT I'M ACTUALLY GLAD TO BE BACK AT WORK.
ANYTHING ELSE? THE CHECK?

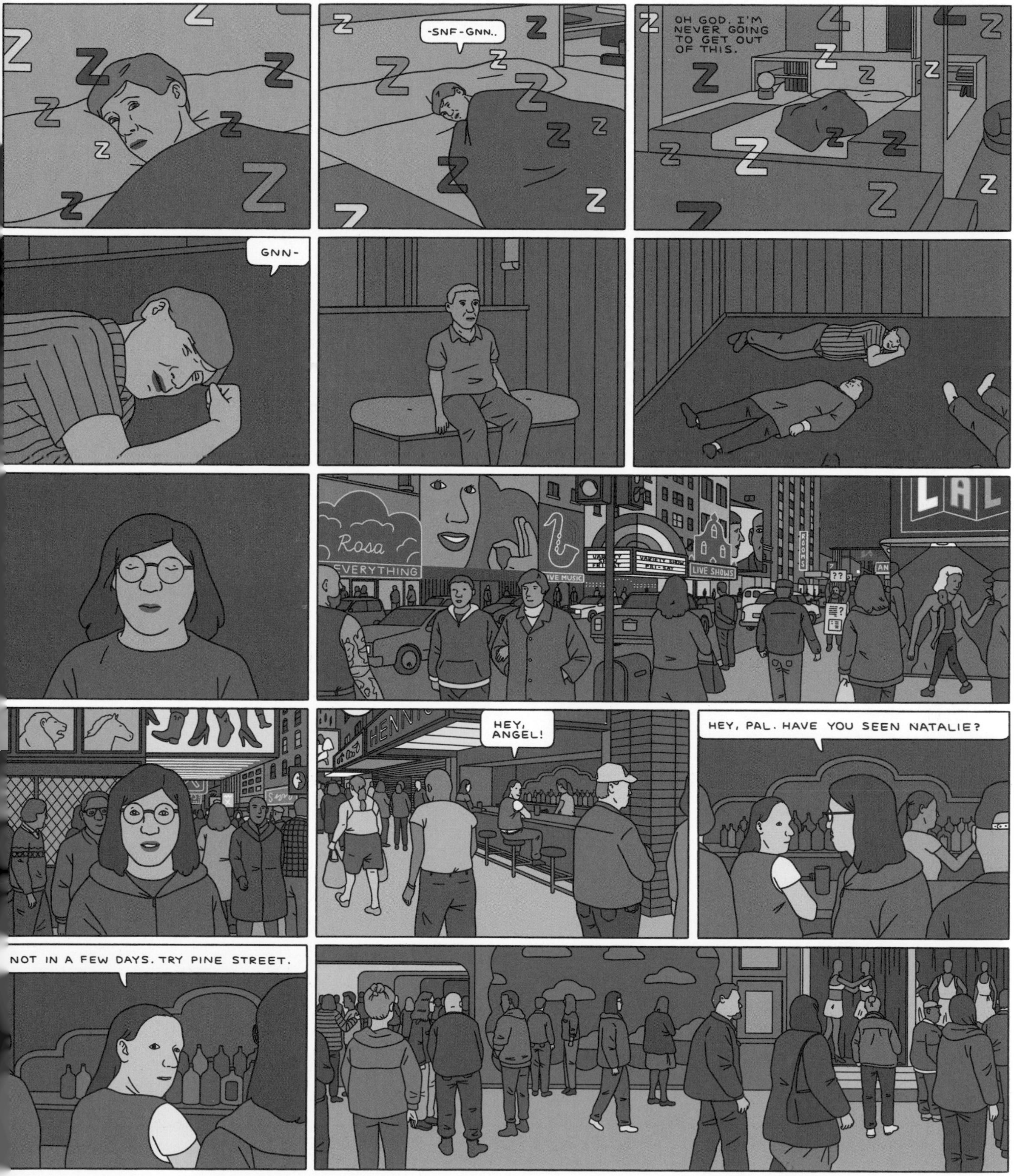
-SNF-GNN..
OH GOD. I'M NEVER GOING TO GET OUT OF THIS.
GNN-
Rosa
EVERYTHING
LIVE MUSIC
LIVE SHOWS
HEY, ANGEL!
HEY, PAL. HAVE YOU SEEN NATALIE?
NOT IN A FEW DAYS. TRY PINE STREET.

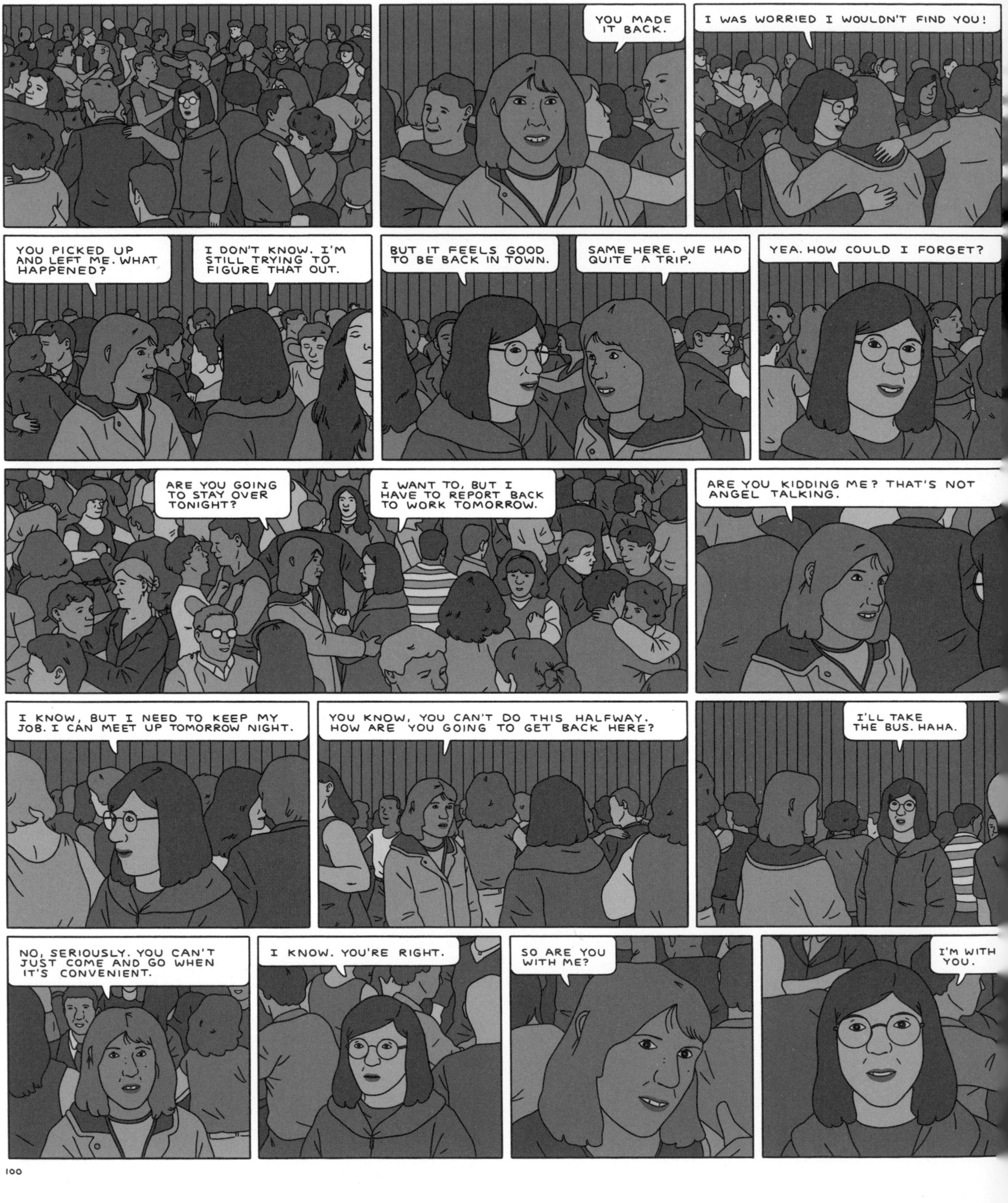
YOU MADE IT BACK.
I WAS WORRIED I WOULDN'T FIND YOU!
YOU PICKED UP AND LEFT ME. WHAT HAPPENED?
I DON'T KNOW. I'M STILL TRYING TO FIGURE THAT OUT.
BUT IT FEELS GOOD TO BE BACK IN TOWN.
SAME HERE. WE HAD QUITE A TRIP.
YEA. HOW COULD I FORGET?
ARE YOU GOING TO STAY OVER TONIGHT?
I WANT TO, BUT I HAVE TO REPORT BACK TO WORK TOMORROW.
ARE YOU KIDDING ME? THAT'S NOT ANGEL TALKING.
I KNOW, BUT I NEED TO KEEP MY JOB. I CAN MEET UP TOMORROW NIGHT.
YOU KNOW, YOU CAN'T DO THIS HALFWAY. HOW ARE YOU GOING TO GET BACK HERE?
I'LL TAKE THE BUS. HAHA.
NO, SERIOUSLY. YOU CAN'T JUST COME AND GO WHEN IT'S CONVENIENT.
I KNOW. YOU'RE RIGHT.
SO ARE YOU WITH ME?
I'M WITH YOU.

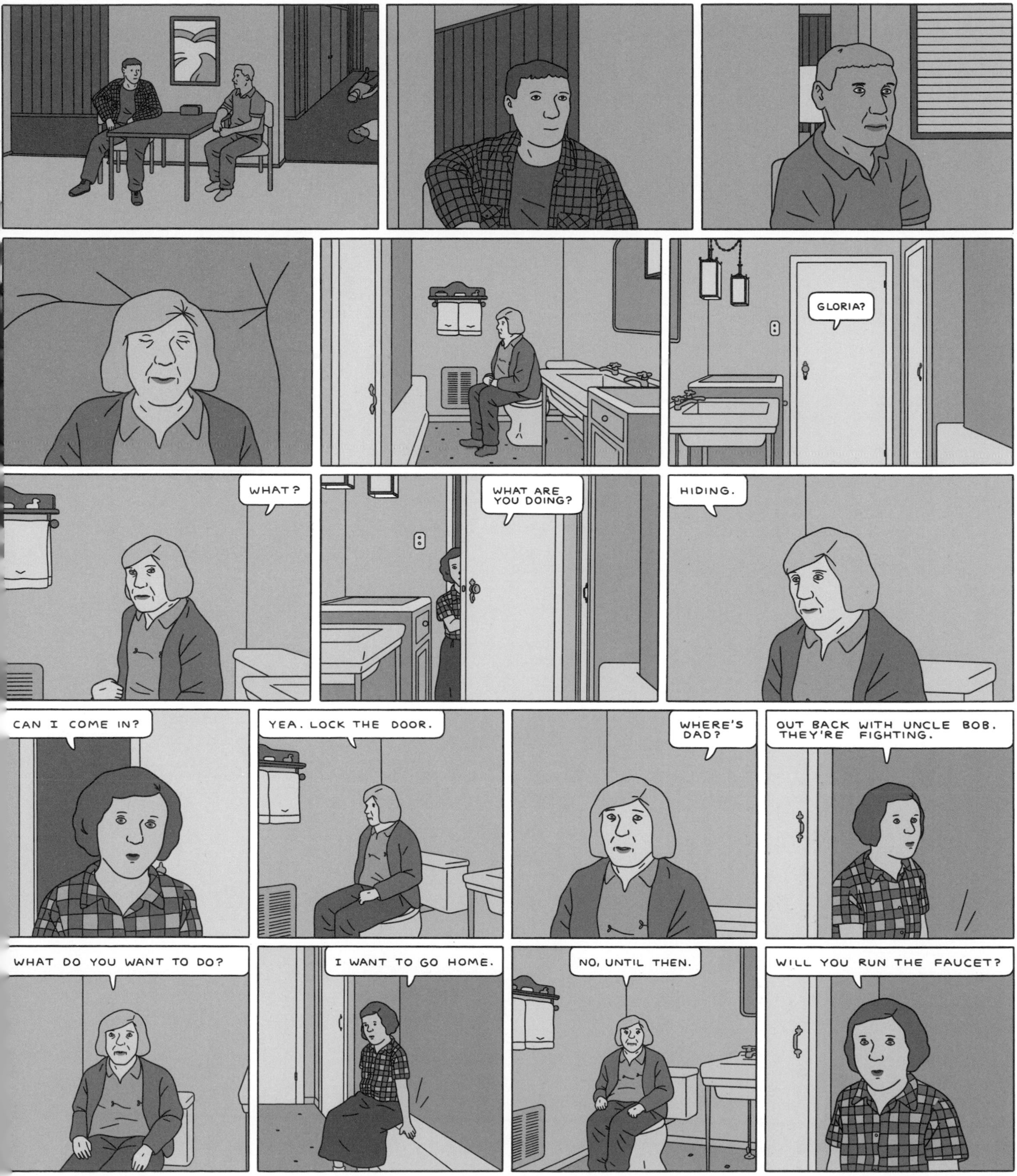
GLORIA?
WHAT?
WHAT ARE YOU DOING?
HIDING.
CAN I COME IN?
YEA. LOCK THE DOOR.
WHERE'S DAD?
OUT BACK WITH UNCLE BOB. THEY'RE FIGHTING.
WHAT DO YOU WANT TO DO?
I WANT TO GO HOME.
NO, UNTIL THEN.
WILL YOU RUN THE FAUCET?

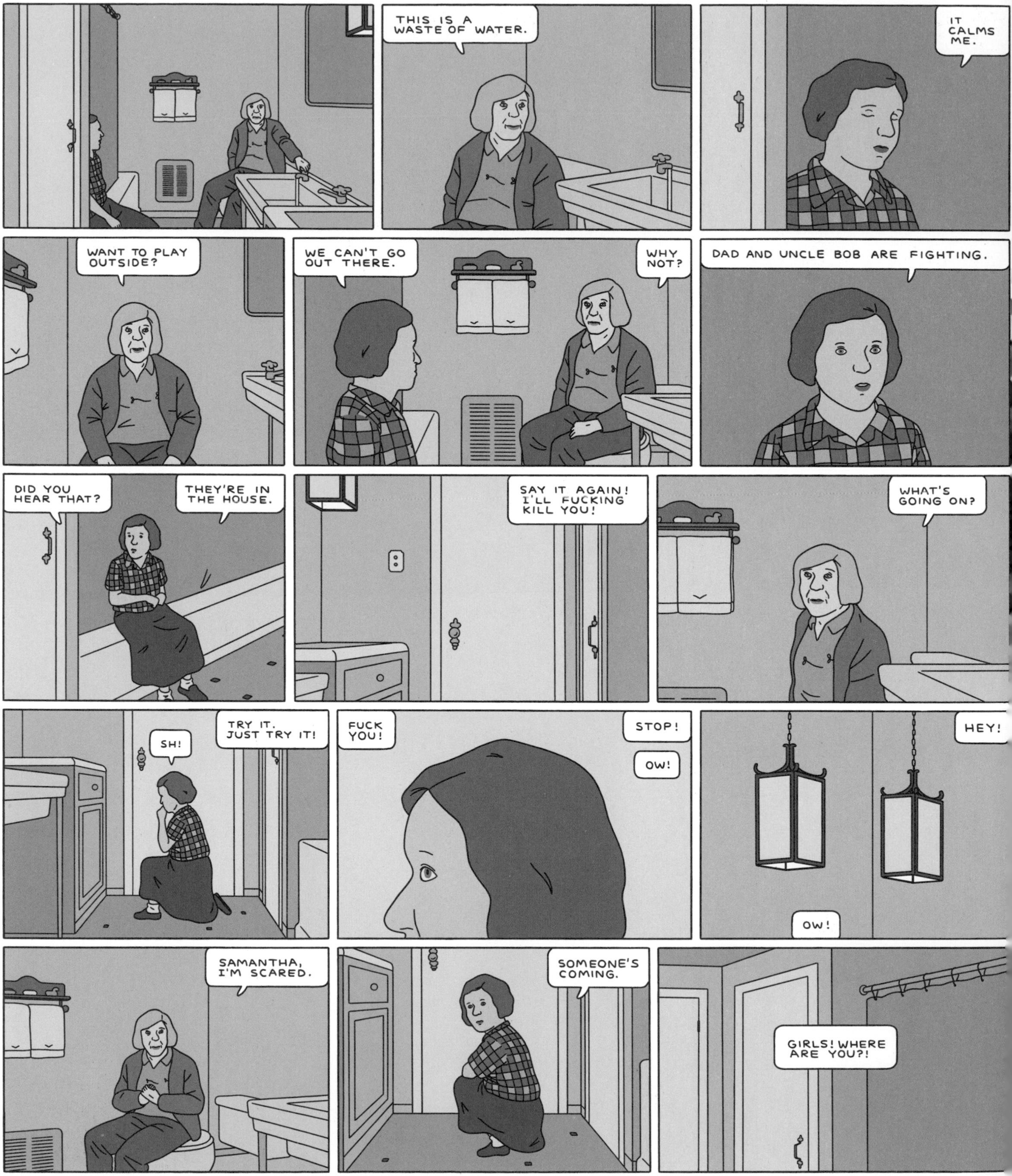
THIS IS A WASTE OF WATER.
IT CALMS ME.
WANT TO PLAY OUTSIDE?
WE CAN'T GO OUT THERE.
WHY NOT?
DAD AND UNCLE BOB ARE FIGHTING.
DID YOU HEAR THAT?
THEY'RE IN THE HOUSE.
SAY IT AGAIN! I'LL FUCKING KILL YOU!
WHAT'S GOING ON?
SH!
TRY IT. JUST TRY IT!
FUCK YOU!
STOP!
OW!
HEY!
OW!
SAMANTHA, I'M SCARED.
SOMEONE'S COMING.
GIRLS! WHERE ARE YOU?!

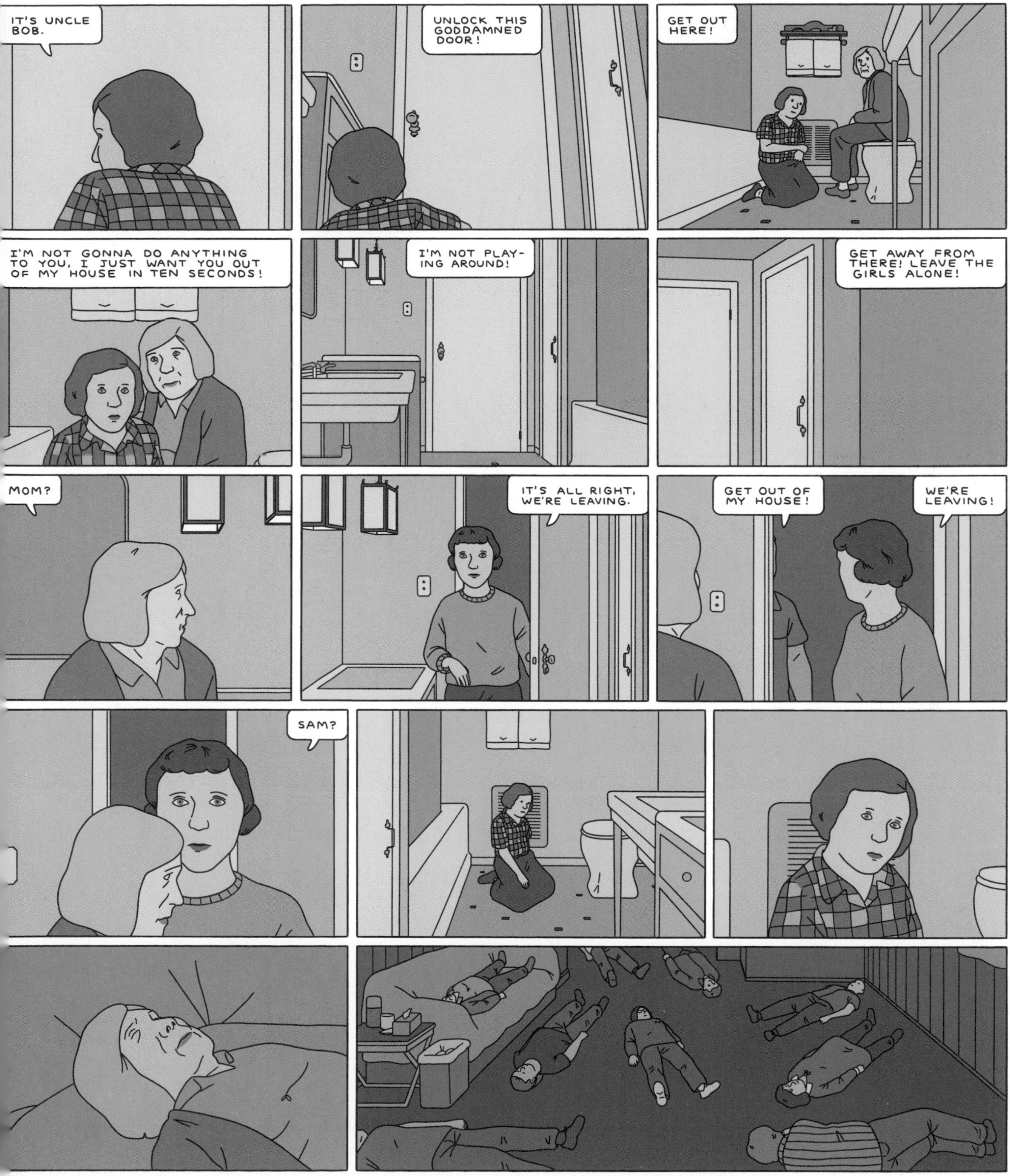
IT'S UNCLE BOB.
UNLOCK THIS GODDAMNED DOOR!
GET OUT HERE!
I'M NOT GONNA DO ANYTHING TO YOU, I JUST WANT YOU OUT OF MY HOUSE IN TEN SECONDS!
I'M NOT PLAYING AROUND!
GET AWAY FROM THERE! LEAVE THE GIRLS ALONE!
MOM?
IT'S ALL RIGHT, WE'RE LEAVING.
GET OUT OF MY HOUSE!
WE'RE LEAVING!
SAM?

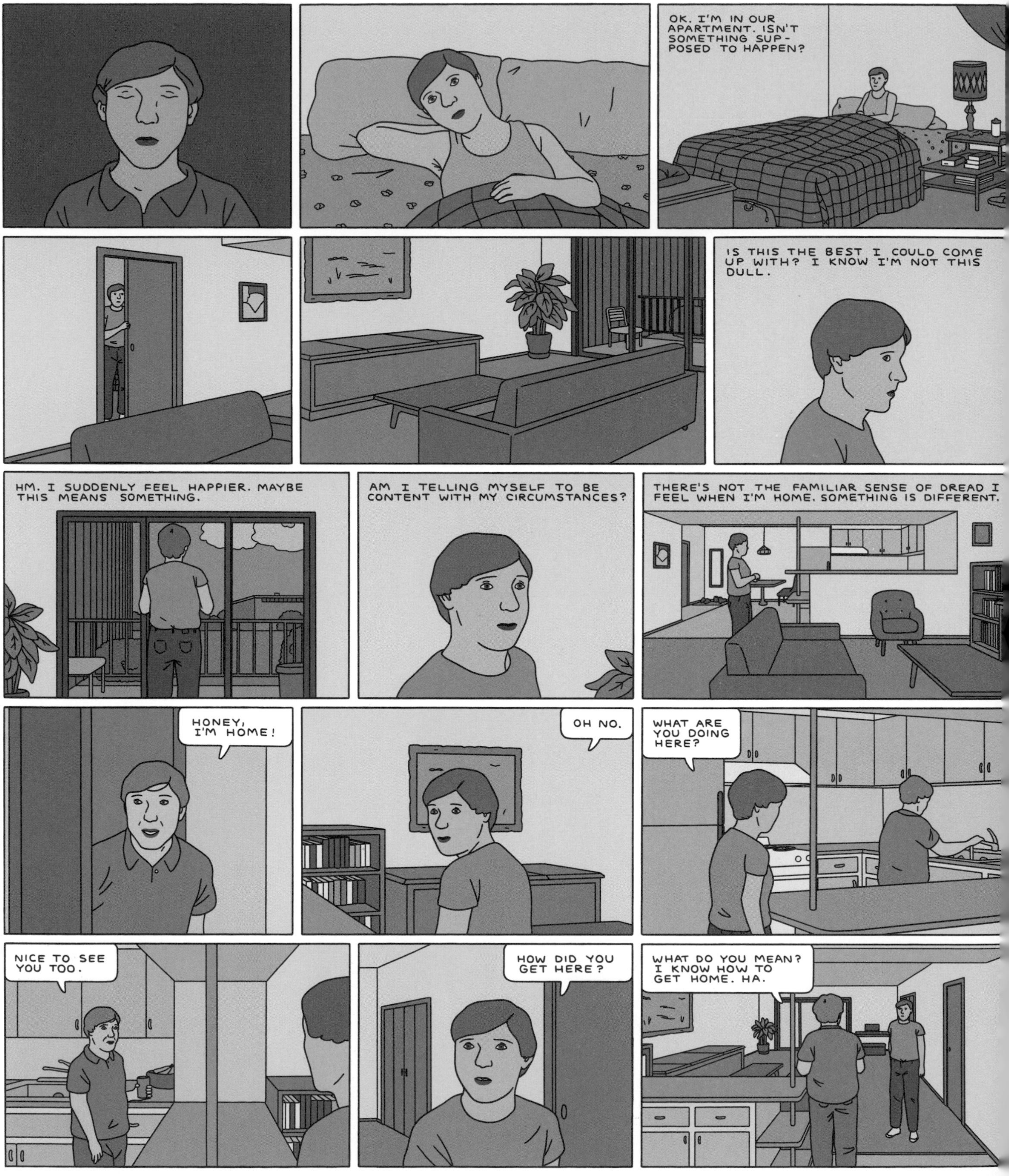
OK. I'M IN OUR APARTMENT. ISN'T SOMETHING SUP-POSED TO HAPPEN?
IS THIS THE BEST I COULD COME UP WITH? I KNOW I'M NOT THIS DULL.
HM. I SUDDENLY FEEL HAPPIER. MAYBE THIS MEANS SOMETHING.
AM I TELLING MYSELF TO BE CONTENT WITH MY CIRCUMSTANCES?
THERE'S NOT THE FAMILIAR SENSE OF DREAD I FEEL WHEN I'M HOME. SOMETHING IS DIFFERENT.
HONEY, I'M HOME!
OH NO.
WHAT ARE YOU DOING HERE?
NICE TO SEE YOU TOO.
HOW DID YOU GET HERE?
WHAT DO YOU MEAN? I KNOW HOW TO GET HOME. HA.

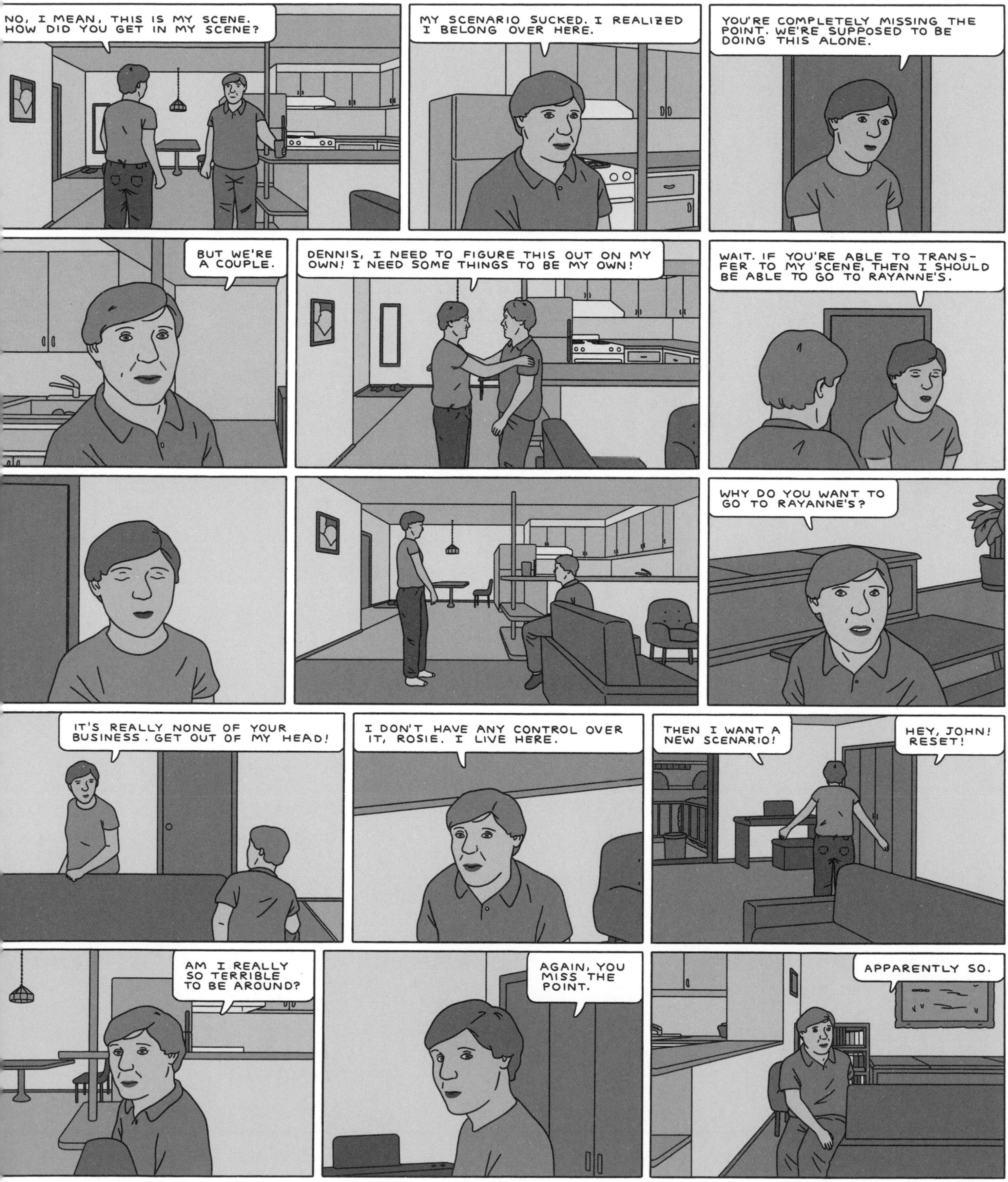
NO, I MEAN, THIS IS MY SCENE. HOW DID YOU GET IN MY SCENE?
MY SCENARIO SUCKED. I REALIZED I BELONG OVER HERE.
YOU'RE COMPLETELY MISSING THE POINT. WE'RE SUPPOSED TO BE DOING THIS ALONE.
BUT WE'RE A COUPLE.
DENNIS, I NEED TO FIGURE THIS OUT ON MY OWN! I NEED SOME THINGS TO BE MY OWN!
WAIT. IF YOU'RE ABLE TO TRANS-FER TO MY SCENE, THEN I SHOULD BE ABLE TO GO TO RAYANNE'S.
WHY DO YOU WANT TO GO TO RAYANNE'S?
IT'S REALLY NONE OF YOUR BUSINESS. GET OUT OF MY HEAD!
I DON'T HAVE ANY CONTROL OVER IT, ROSIE. I LIVE HERE.
THEN I WANT A NEW SCENARIO!
HEY, JOHN! RESET!
AM I REALLY SO TERRIBLE TO BE AROUND?
AGAIN, YOU MISS THE POINT.
APPARENTLY SO.

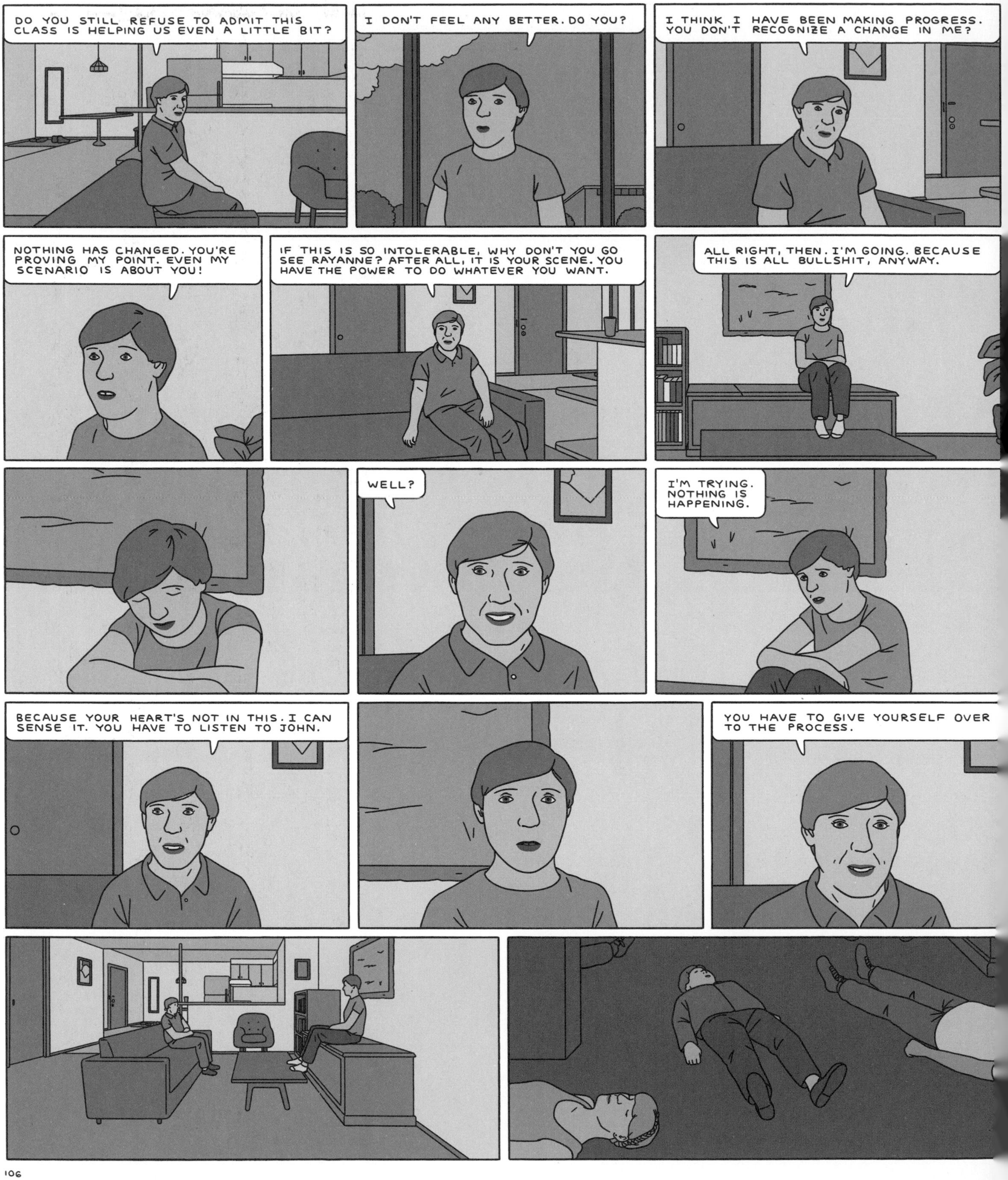
DO YOU STILL REFUSE TO ADMIT THIS CLASS IS HELPING US EVEN A LITTLE BIT?
I DON'T FEEL ANY BETTER. DO YOU?
I THINK I HAVE BEEN MAKING PROGRESS. YOU DON'T RECOGNIZE A CHANGE IN ME?
NOTHING HAS CHANGED. YOU'RE PROVING MY POINT. EVEN MY SCENARIO IS ABOUT YOU!
IF THIS IS SO INTOLERABLE, WHY DON'T YOU GO SEE RAYANNE? AFTER ALL, IT IS YOUR SCENE. YOU HAVE THE POWER TO DO WHATEVER YOU WANT.
ALL RIGHT, THEN. I'M GOING. BECAUSE THIS IS ALL BULLSHIT, ANYWAY.
WELL?
I'M TRYING. NOTHING IS HAPPENING.
BECAUSE YOUR HEART'S NOT IN THIS. I CAN SENSE IT. YOU HAVE TO LISTEN TO JOHN.
YOU HAVE TO GIVE YOURSELF OVER TO THE PROCESS.

COME ON.

UH OH.

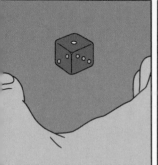
HA.

ALL
RIGHT.

HERE
WE GO.

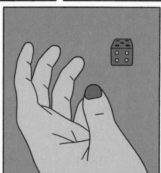

OH! BETTER LUCK NEXT TIME.

YOU THINK
I'M AFRAID?

HAHA.

HAHA.

COME ON.
COME ON.

YES! YOUR
TURN AGAIN.

LET'S GO.

I'M NOT
SCARED.

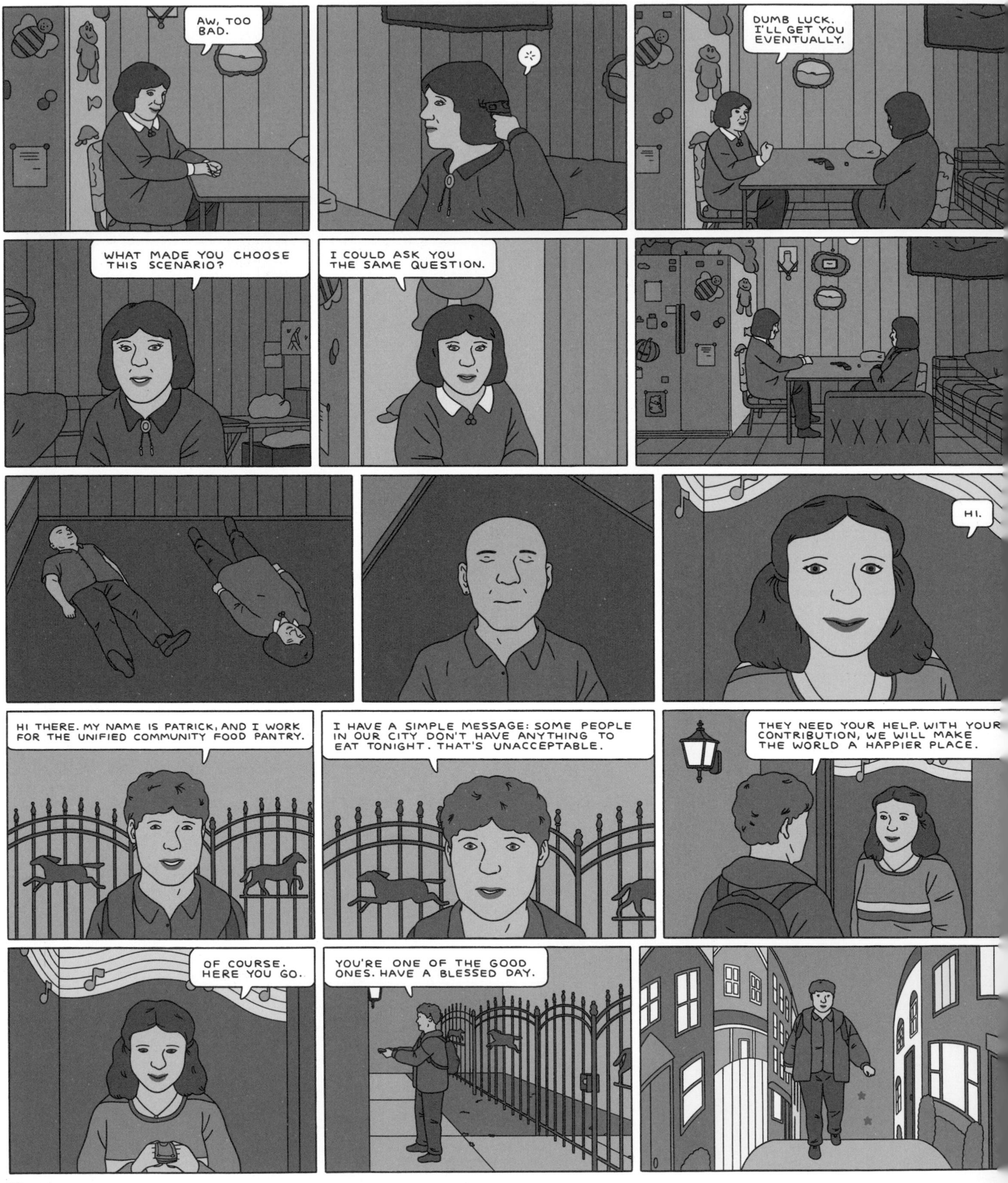
AW, TOO BAD.
DUMB LUCK. I'LL GET YOU EVENTUALLY.
WHAT MADE YOU CHOOSE THIS SCENARIO?
I COULD ASK YOU THE SAME QUESTION.
HI.
HI THERE. MY NAME IS PATRICK, AND I WORK FOR THE UNIFIED COMMUNITY FOOD PANTRY.
I HAVE A SIMPLE MESSAGE: SOME PEOPLE IN OUR CITY DON'T HAVE ANYTHING TO EAT TONIGHT. THAT'S UNACCEPTABLE.
THEY NEED YOUR HELP. WITH YOUR CONTRIBUTION, WE WILL MAKE THE WORLD A HAPPIER PLACE.
OF COURSE. HERE YOU GO.
YOU'RE ONE OF THE GOOD ONES. HAVE A BLESSED DAY.

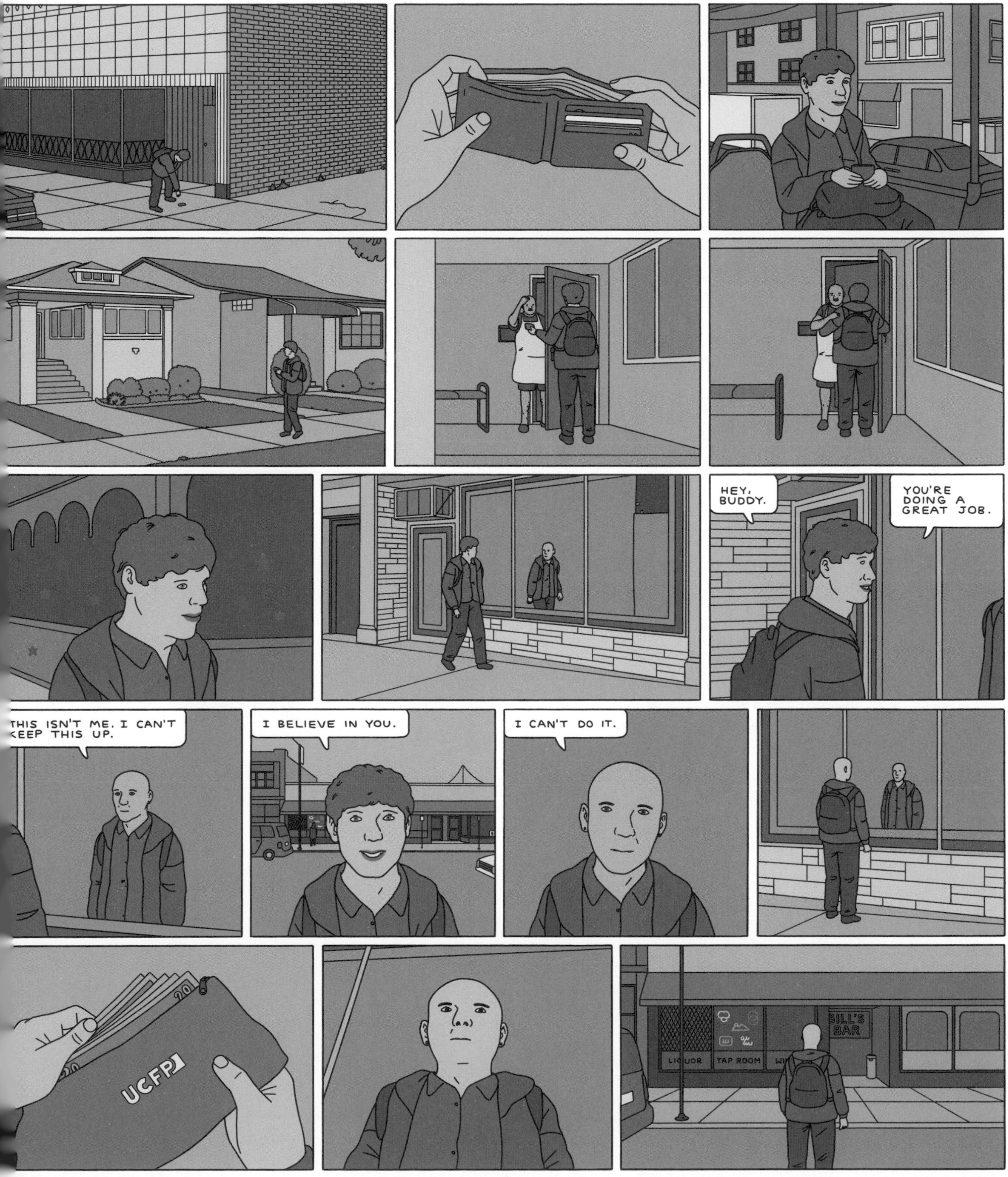
HEY, BUDDY.
YOU'RE DOING A GREAT JOB.
THIS ISN'T ME. I CAN'T KEEP THIS UP.
I BELIEVE IN YOU.
I CAN'T DO IT.
UCFP
BILL'S BAR
LIQUOR
TAP ROOM

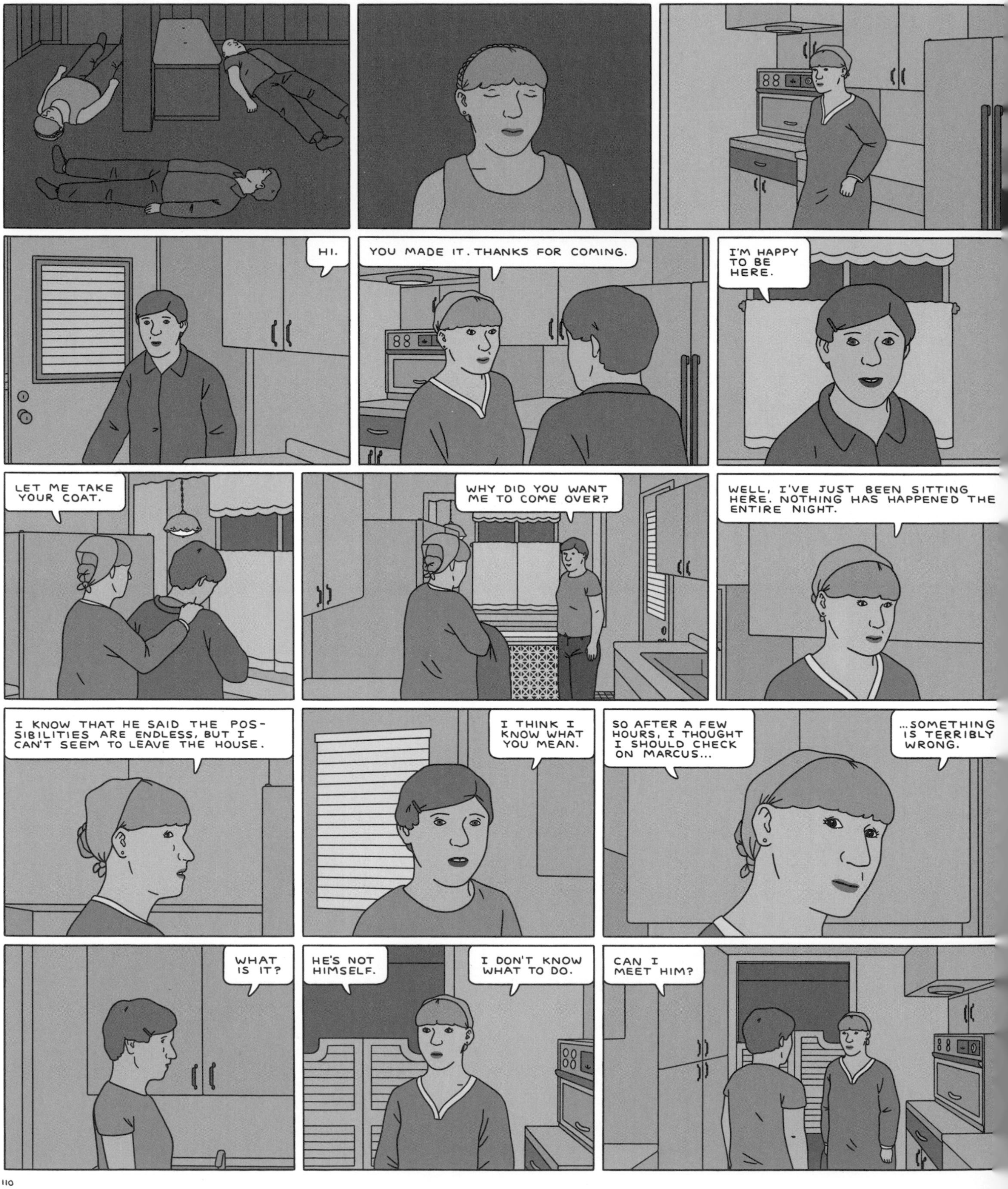
HI.
YOU MADE IT. THANKS FOR COMING.
I'M HAPPY TO BE HERE.
LET ME TAKE YOUR COAT.
WHY DID YOU WANT ME TO COME OVER?
WELL, I'VE JUST BEEN SITTING HERE. NOTHING HAS HAPPENED THE ENTIRE NIGHT.
I KNOW THAT HE SAID THE POSSIBILITIES ARE ENDLESS, BUT I CAN'T SEEM TO LEAVE THE HOUSE.
I THINK I KNOW WHAT YOU MEAN.
SO AFTER A FEW HOURS, I THOUGHT I SHOULD CHECK ON MARCUS...
...SOMETHING IS TERRIBLY WRONG.
WHAT IS IT?
HE'S NOT HIMSELF.
I DON'T KNOW WHAT TO DO.
CAN I MEET HIM?

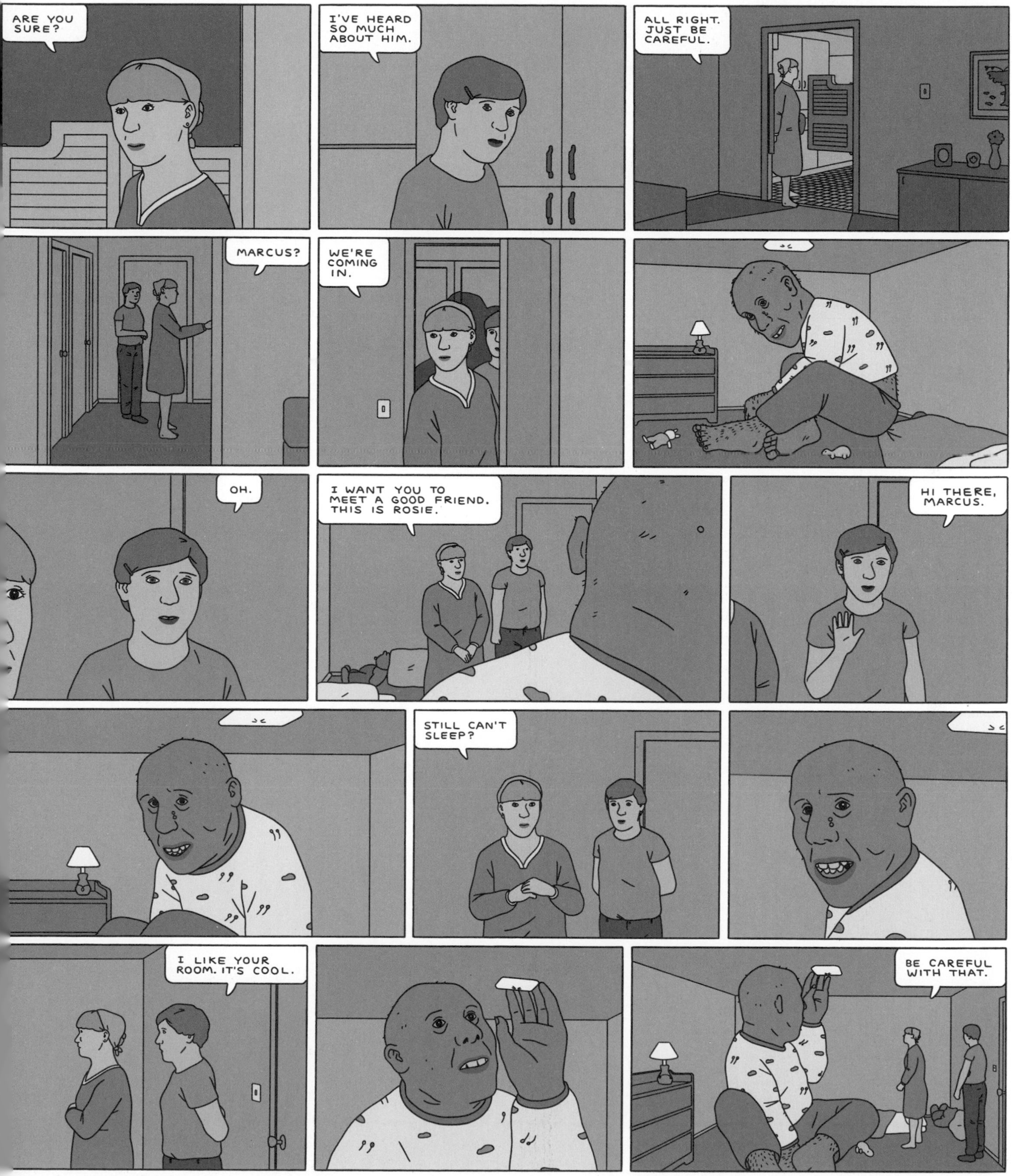
ARE YOU SURE?
I'VE HEARD SO MUCH ABOUT HIM.
ALL RIGHT. JUST BE CAREFUL.
MARCUS?
WE'RE COMING IN.
OH.
I WANT YOU TO MEET A GOOD FRIEND. THIS IS ROSIE.
HI THERE, MARCUS.
STILL CAN'T SLEEP?
I LIKE YOUR ROOM. IT'S COOL.
BE CAREFUL WITH THAT.

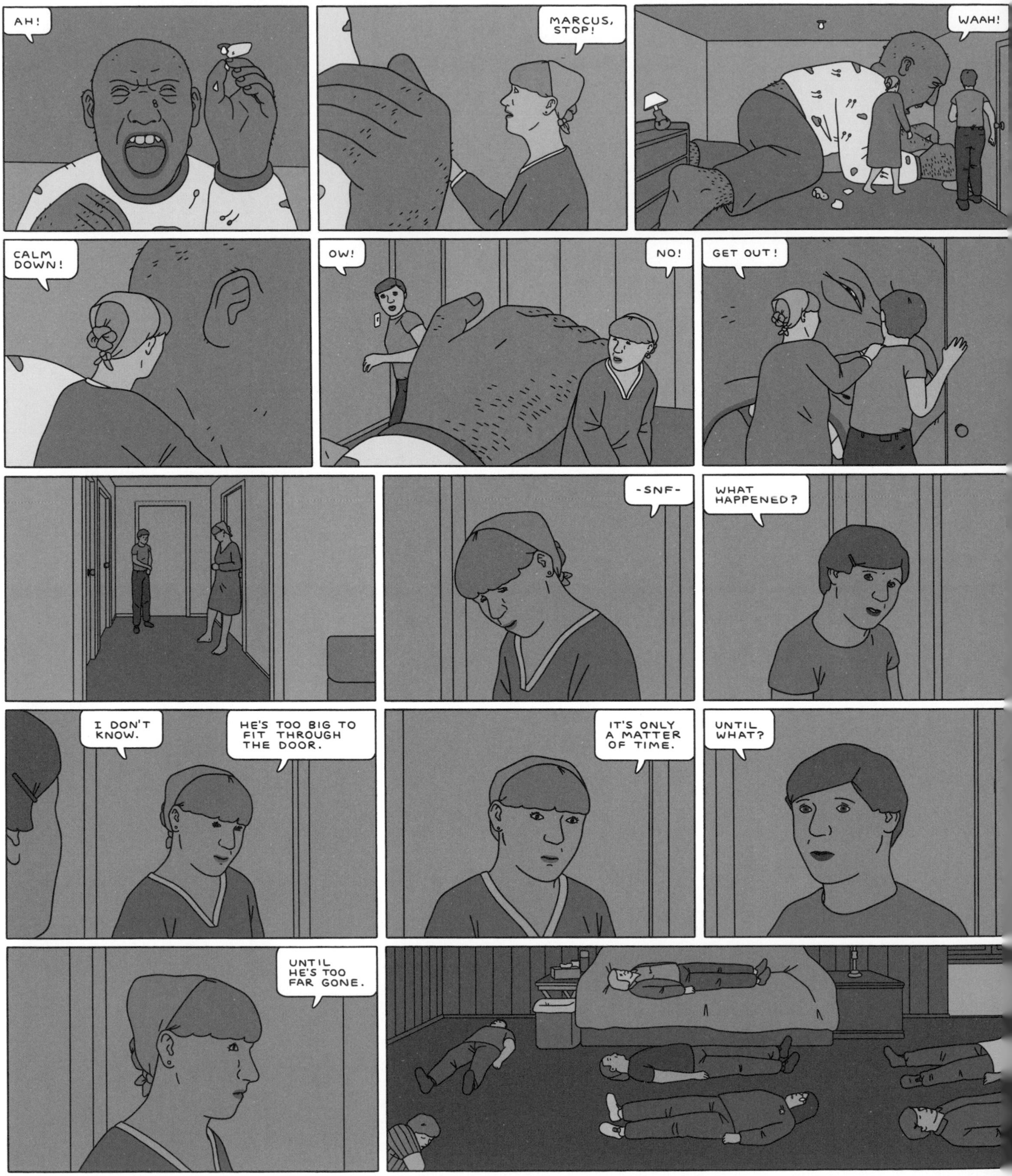
AH!
MARCUS, STOP!
WAAH!
CALM DOWN!
OW!
NO!
GET OUT!
-SNF-
WHAT HAPPENED?
I DON'T KNOW.
HE'S TOO BIG TO FIT THROUGH THE DOOR.
IT'S ONLY A MATTER OF TIME.
UNTIL WHAT?
UNTIL HE'S TOO FAR GONE.

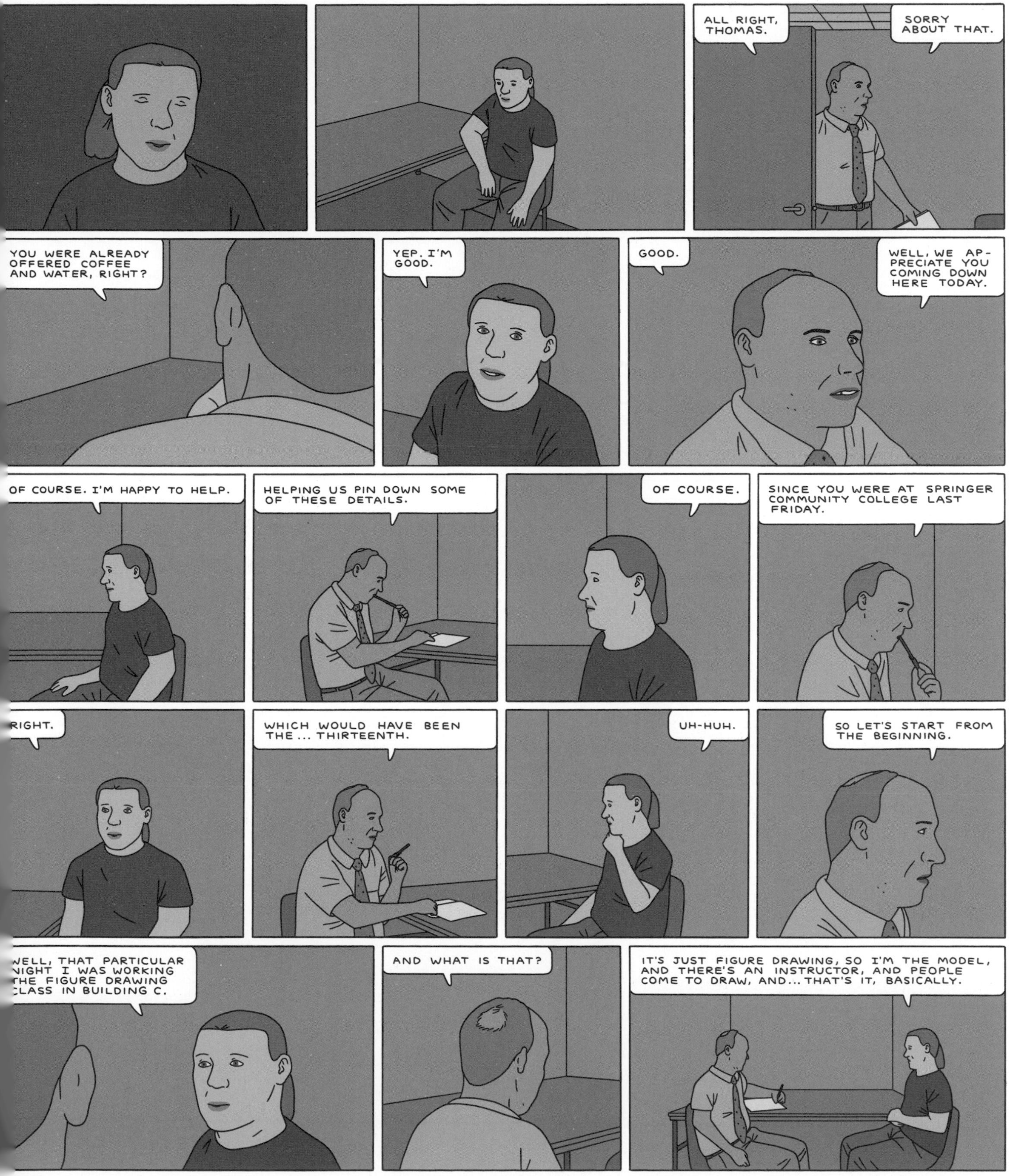
ALL RIGHT, THOMAS.
SORRY ABOUT THAT.
YOU WERE ALREADY OFFERED COFFEE AND WATER, RIGHT?
YEP. I'M GOOD.
GOOD.
WELL, WE AP-PRECIATE YOU COMING DOWN HERE TODAY.
OF COURSE. I'M HAPPY TO HELP.
HELPING US PIN DOWN SOME OF THESE DETAILS.
OF COURSE.
SINCE YOU WERE AT SPRINGER COMMUNITY COLLEGE LAST FRIDAY.
RIGHT.
WHICH WOULD HAVE BEEN THE ... THIRTEENTH.
UH-HUH.
SO LET'S START FROM THE BEGINNING.
WELL, THAT PARTICULAR NIGHT I WAS WORKING THE FIGURE DRAWING CLASS IN BUILDING C.
AND WHAT IS THAT?
IT'S JUST FIGURE DRAWING, SO I'M THE MODEL, AND THERE'S AN INSTRUCTOR, AND PEOPLE COME TO DRAW, AND... THAT'S IT, BASICALLY.

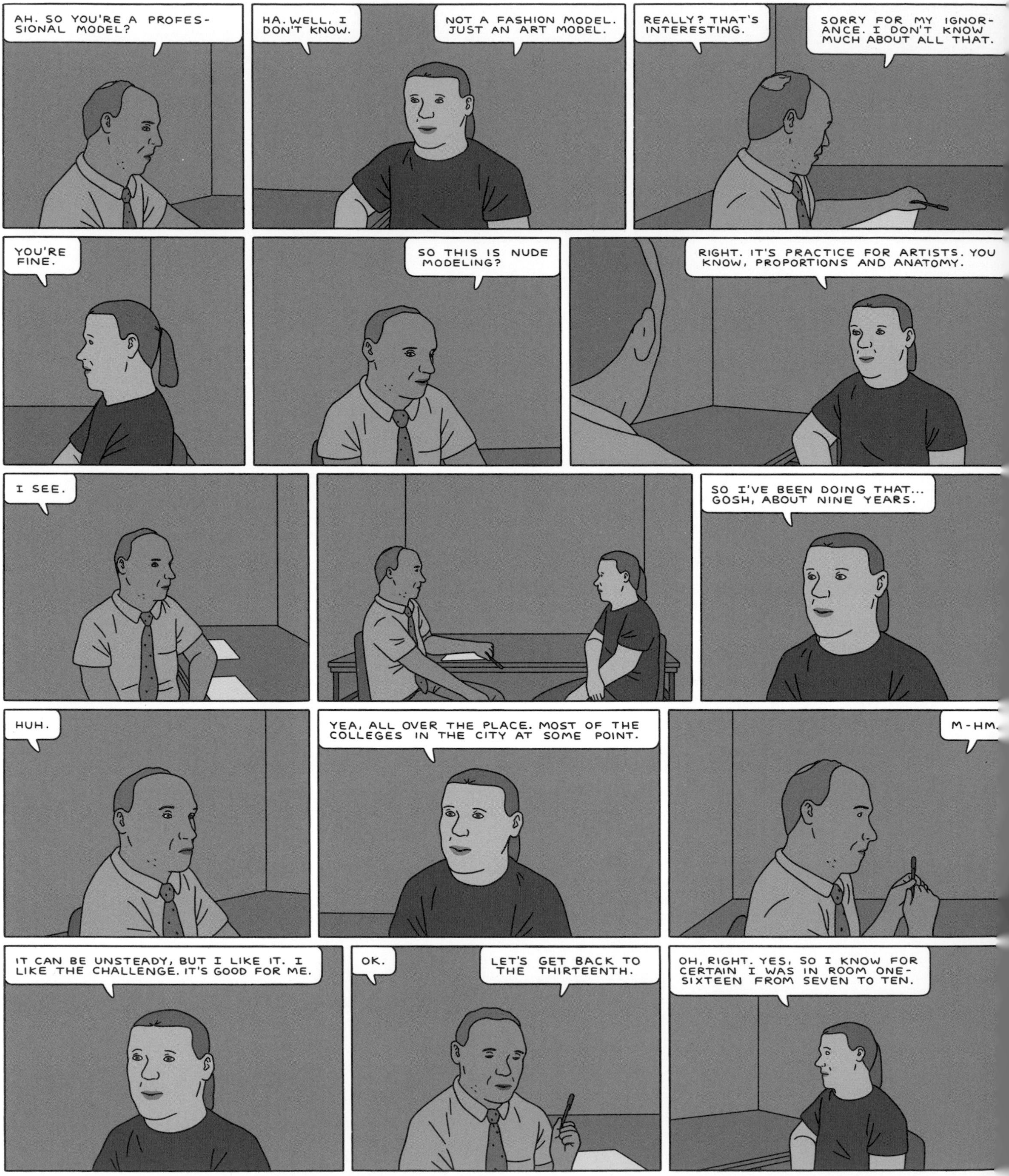
AH. SO YOU'RE A PROFESSIONAL MODEL?
HA. WELL, I DON'T KNOW.
NOT A FASHION MODEL. JUST AN ART MODEL.
REALLY? THAT'S INTERESTING.
SORRY FOR MY IGNORANCE. I DON'T KNOW MUCH ABOUT ALL THAT.
YOU'RE FINE.
SO THIS IS NUDE MODELING?
RIGHT. IT'S PRACTICE FOR ARTISTS. YOU KNOW, PROPORTIONS AND ANATOMY.
I SEE.
SO I'VE BEEN DOING THAT... GOSH, ABOUT NINE YEARS.
HUH.
YEA, ALL OVER THE PLACE. MOST OF THE COLLEGES IN THE CITY AT SOME POINT.
M-HM.
IT CAN BE UNSTEADY, BUT I LIKE IT. I LIKE THE CHALLENGE. IT'S GOOD FOR ME.
OK.
LET'S GET BACK TO THE THIRTEENTH.
OH, RIGHT. YES, SO I KNOW FOR CERTAIN I WAS IN ROOM ONE-SIXTEEN FROM SEVEN TO TEN.

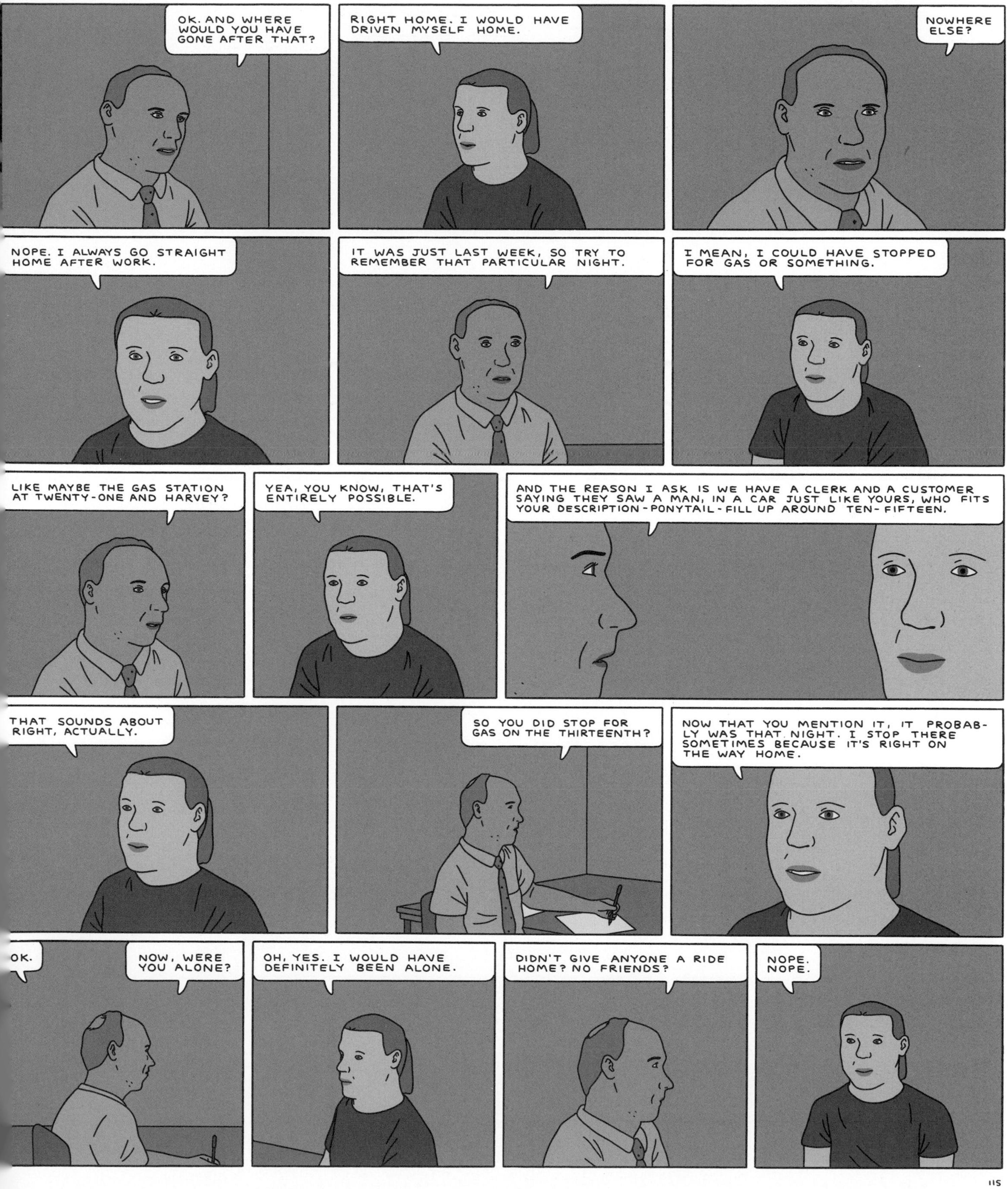
OK. AND WHERE WOULD YOU HAVE GONE AFTER THAT?
RIGHT HOME. I WOULD HAVE DRIVEN MYSELF HOME.
NOWHERE ELSE?
NOPE. I ALWAYS GO STRAIGHT HOME AFTER WORK.
IT WAS JUST LAST WEEK, SO TRY TO REMEMBER THAT PARTICULAR NIGHT.
I MEAN, I COULD HAVE STOPPED FOR GAS OR SOMETHING.
LIKE MAYBE THE GAS STATION AT TWENTY-ONE AND HARVEY?
YEA, YOU KNOW, THAT'S ENTIRELY POSSIBLE.
AND THE REASON I ASK IS WE HAVE A CLERK AND A CUSTOMER SAYING THEY SAW A MAN, IN A CAR JUST LIKE YOURS, WHO FITS YOUR DESCRIPTION-PONYTAIL-FILL UP AROUND TEN-FIFTEEN.
THAT SOUNDS ABOUT RIGHT, ACTUALLY.
SO YOU DID STOP FOR GAS ON THE THIRTEENTH?
NOW THAT YOU MENTION IT, IT PROBAB-LY WAS THAT NIGHT. I STOP THERE SOMETIMES BECAUSE IT'S RIGHT ON THE WAY HOME.
OK.
NOW, WERE YOU ALONE?
OH, YES. I WOULD HAVE DEFINITELY BEEN ALONE.
DIDN'T GIVE ANYONE A RIDE HOME? NO FRIENDS?
NOPE. NOPE.

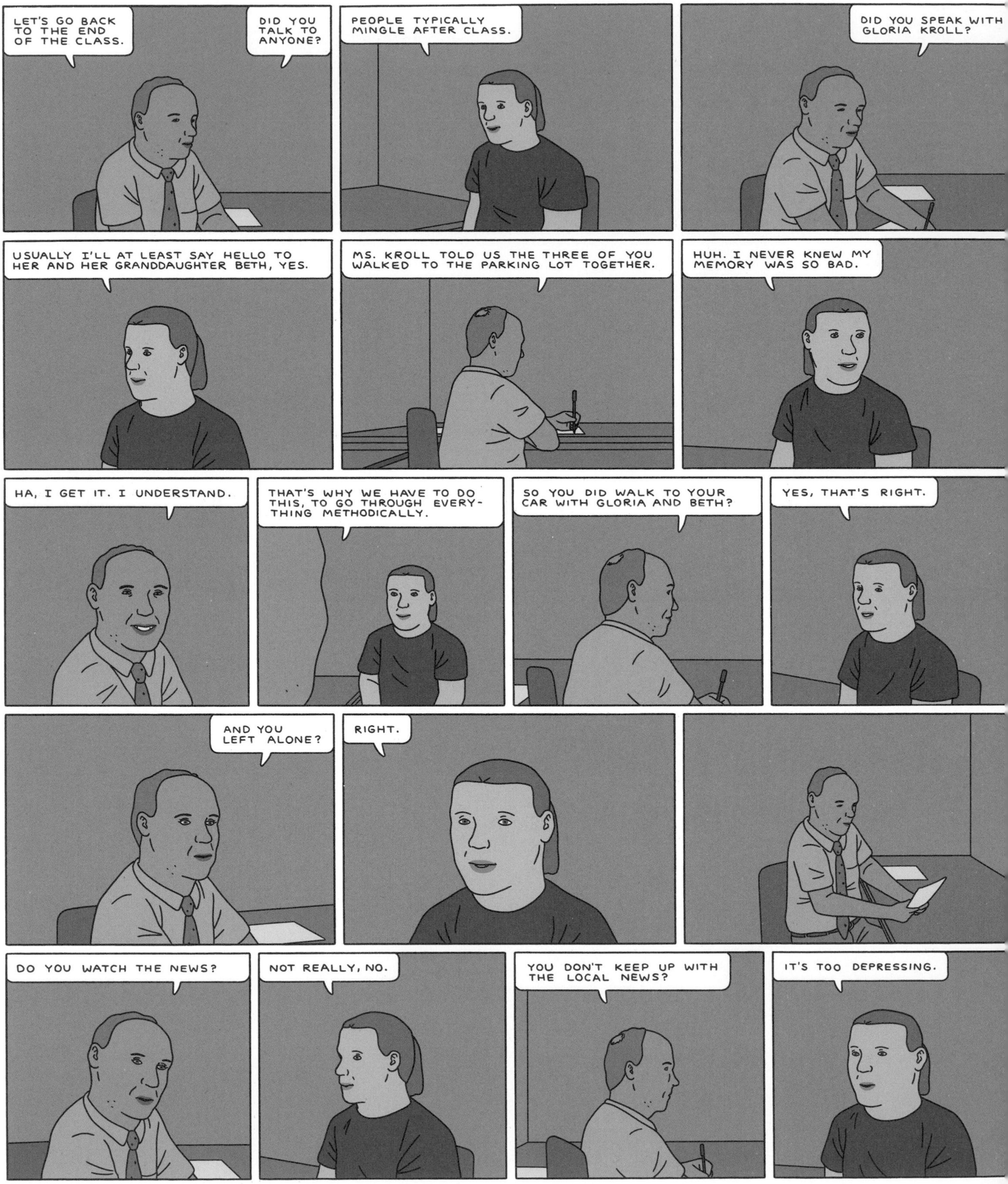
LET'S GO BACK TO THE END OF THE CLASS.
DID YOU TALK TO ANYONE?
PEOPLE TYPICALLY MINGLE AFTER CLASS.
DID YOU SPEAK WITH GLORIA KROLL?
USUALLY I'LL AT LEAST SAY HELLO TO HER AND HER GRANDDAUGHTER BETH, YES.
MS. KROLL TOLD US THE THREE OF YOU WALKED TO THE PARKING LOT TOGETHER.
HUH. I NEVER KNEW MY MEMORY WAS SO BAD.
HA, I GET IT. I UNDERSTAND.
THAT'S WHY WE HAVE TO DO THIS, TO GO THROUGH EVERY-THING METHODICALLY.
SO YOU DID WALK TO YOUR CAR WITH GLORIA AND BETH?
YES, THAT'S RIGHT.
AND YOU LEFT ALONE?
RIGHT.
DO YOU WATCH THE NEWS?
NOT REALLY, NO.
YOU DON'T KEEP UP WITH THE LOCAL NEWS?
IT'S TOO DEPRESSING.

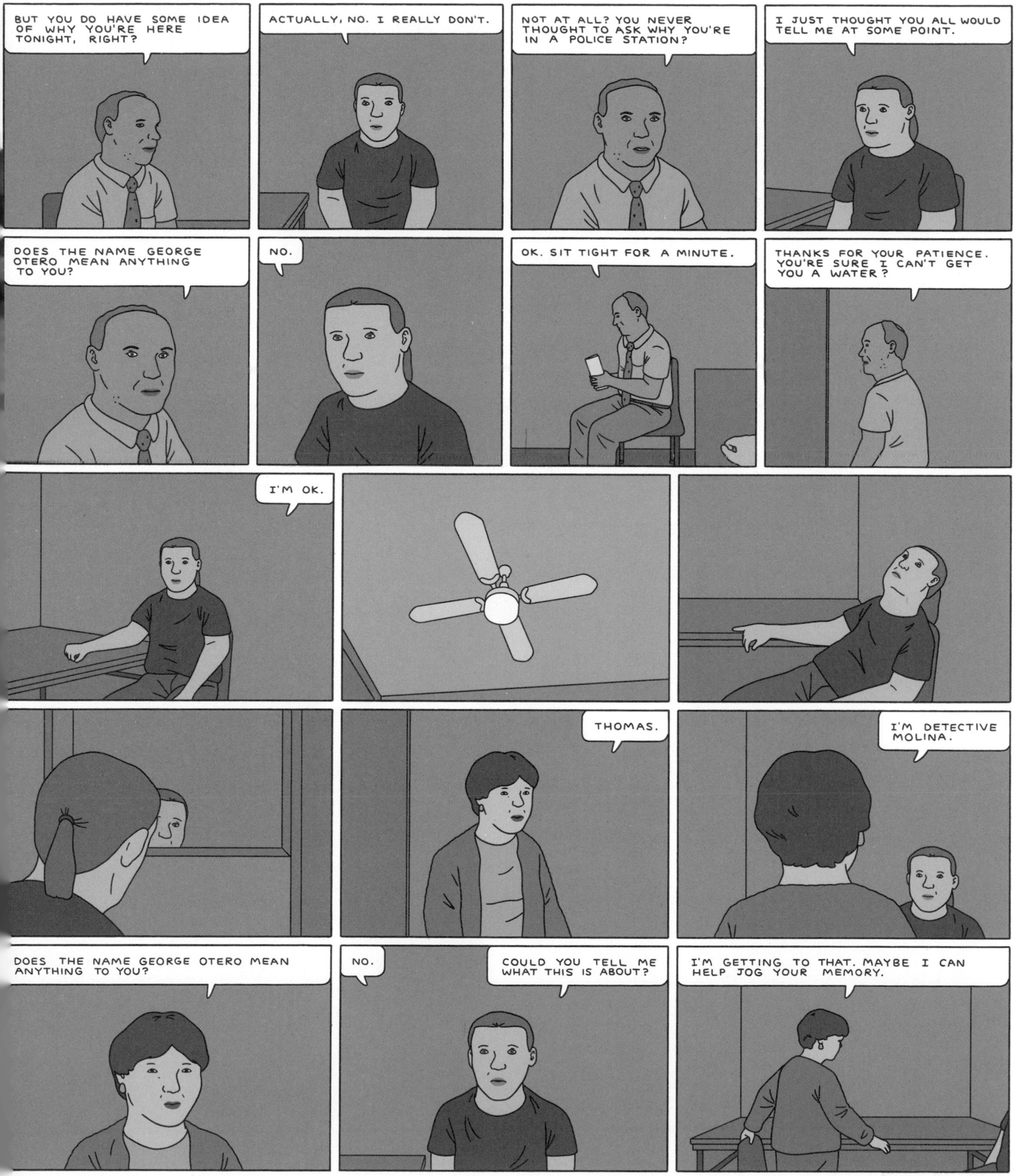
BUT YOU DO HAVE SOME IDEA OF WHY YOU'RE HERE TONIGHT, RIGHT?
ACTUALLY, NO. I REALLY DON'T.
NOT AT ALL? YOU NEVER THOUGHT TO ASK WHY YOU'RE IN A POLICE STATION?
I JUST THOUGHT YOU ALL WOULD TELL ME AT SOME POINT.
DOES THE NAME GEORGE OTERO MEAN ANYTHING TO YOU?
NO.
OK. SIT TIGHT FOR A MINUTE.
THANKS FOR YOUR PATIENCE. YOU'RE SURE I CAN'T GET YOU A WATER?
I'M OK.
THOMAS.
I'M DETECTIVE MOLINA.
DOES THE NAME GEORGE OTERO MEAN ANYTHING TO YOU?
NO.
COULD YOU TELL ME WHAT THIS IS ABOUT?
I'M GETTING TO THAT. MAYBE I CAN HELP JOG YOUR MEMORY.

MR. OTERO RIDES HIS BIKE AROUND SPRINGER CAMPUS. HE HANGS OUT AT THE PICNIC TABLES. SOMETIMES HE DRESSES UP LIKE ELVIS AND SINGS.

OH, RIGHT. I'VE SEEN THAT GUY. HE'S KIND OF DISABLED, RIGHT?

THAT'S THE GUY. HE LIVES WITH HIS SISTER.

SO YOU HAVEN'T HEARD HE'S BEEN MISSING SINCE THE THIRTEENTH?

OH NO. I DIDN'T KNOW THAT.

HIS FAMILY IS WORRIED TO DEATH.

HERE'S THE CURIOUS THING. THE LAST PLACE HE WAS SEEN — AND THIS IS VERIFIED BY TWO PEOPLE WHO IDENTIFIED HIS PHOTO — WAS SITTING IN THE FRONT SEAT OF YOUR CAR, AT A GAS STATION, ON THE NIGHT OF THE THIRTEENTH.

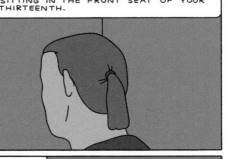

WHAT?

AND THE SECOND TO LAST PLACE HE WAS SEEN WAS IN THE SPRINGER PARKING LOT, ALSO IN THE FRONT SEAT OF YOUR CAR.

THAT'S NOT POSSIBLE.

YOU SAID YOU WALKED TO YOUR CAR WITH GLORIA AND BETH KROLL.

THAT'S RIGHT.

WELL, THEY'RE SAYING THAT MR. OTERO WAS IN YOUR CAR.

THAT'S NOT TRUE! I NEED TO TALK TO THEM.

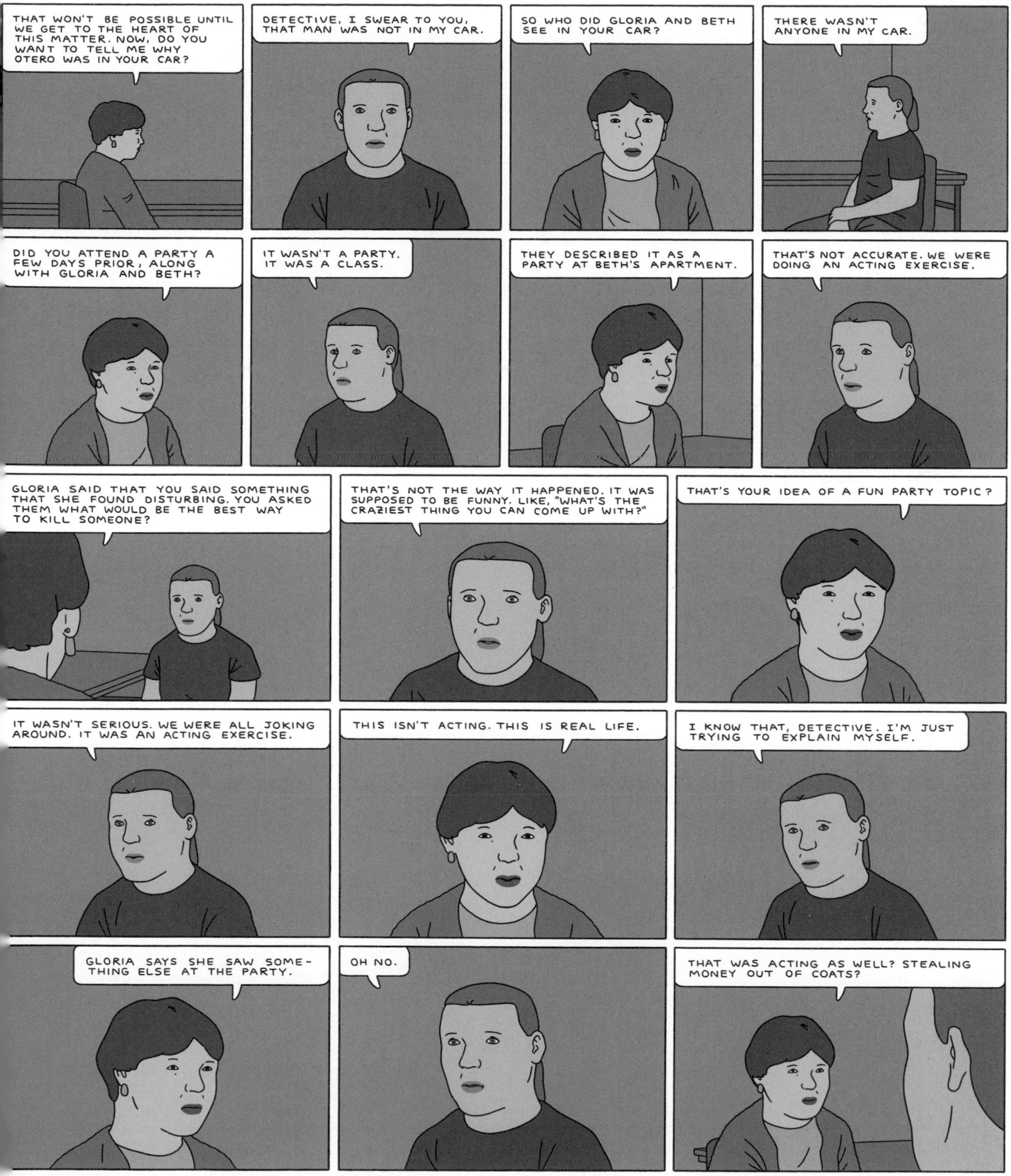
THAT WON'T BE POSSIBLE UNTIL WE GET TO THE HEART OF THIS MATTER. NOW, DO YOU WANT TO TELL ME WHY OTERO WAS IN YOUR CAR?
DETECTIVE, I SWEAR TO YOU, THAT MAN WAS NOT IN MY CAR.
SO WHO DID GLORIA AND BETH SEE IN YOUR CAR?
THERE WASN'T ANYONE IN MY CAR.
DID YOU ATTEND A PARTY A FEW DAYS PRIOR, ALONG WITH GLORIA AND BETH?
IT WASN'T A PARTY. IT WAS A CLASS.
THEY DESCRIBED IT AS A PARTY AT BETH'S APARTMENT.
THAT'S NOT ACCURATE. WE WERE DOING AN ACTING EXERCISE.
GLORIA SAID THAT YOU SAID SOMETHING THAT SHE FOUND DISTURBING. YOU ASKED THEM WHAT WOULD BE THE BEST WAY TO KILL SOMEONE?
THAT'S NOT THE WAY IT HAPPENED. IT WAS SUPPOSED TO BE FUNNY. LIKE, "WHAT'S THE CRAZIEST THING YOU CAN COME UP WITH?"
THAT'S YOUR IDEA OF A FUN PARTY TOPIC?
IT WASN'T SERIOUS. WE WERE ALL JOKING AROUND. IT WAS AN ACTING EXERCISE.
THIS ISN'T ACTING. THIS IS REAL LIFE.
I KNOW THAT, DETECTIVE. I'M JUST TRYING TO EXPLAIN MYSELF.
GLORIA SAYS SHE SAW SOMETHING ELSE AT THE PARTY.
OH NO.
THAT WAS ACTING AS WELL? STEALING MONEY OUT OF COATS?

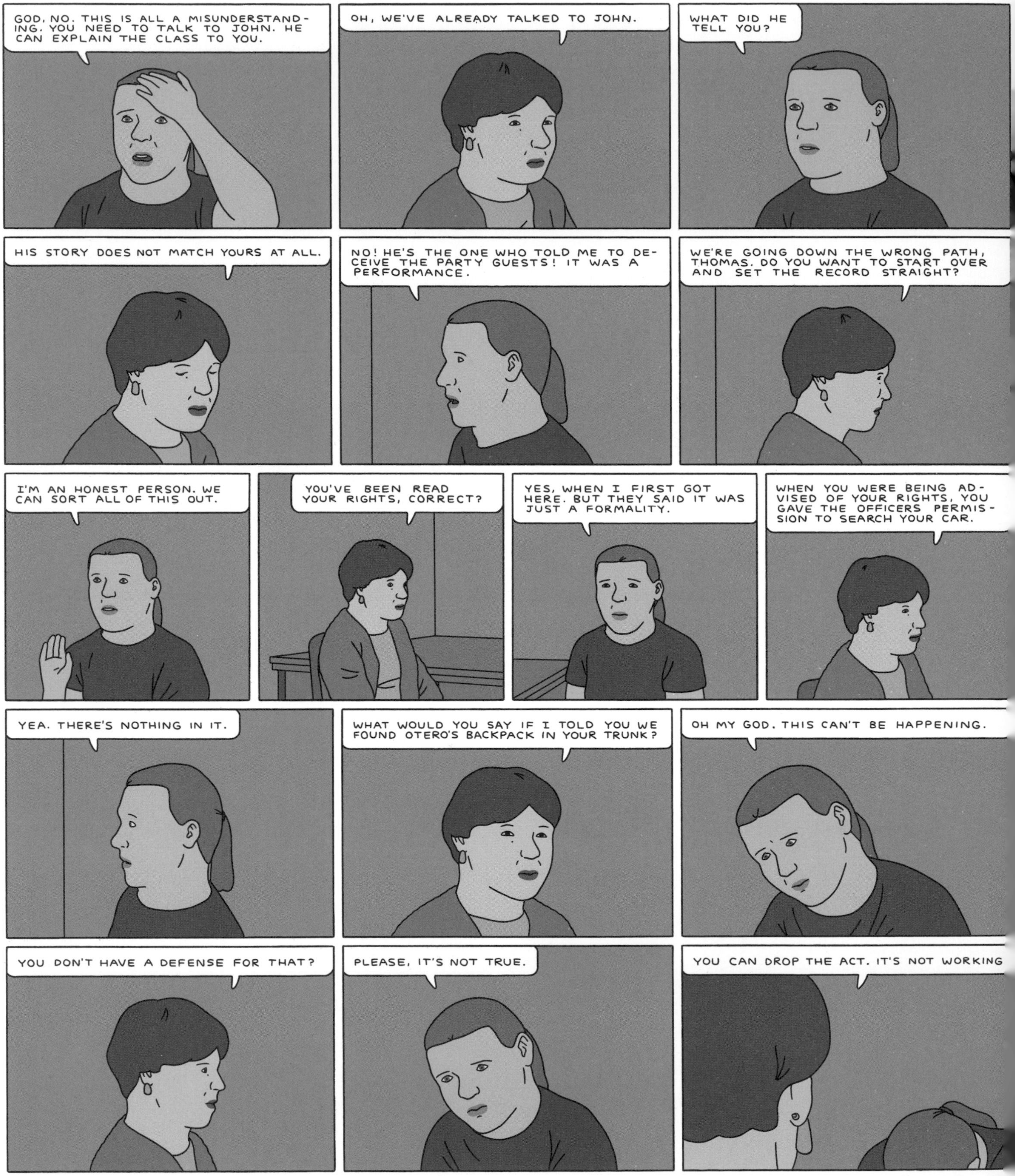
GOD, NO. THIS IS ALL A MISUNDERSTAND-ING. YOU NEED TO TALK TO JOHN. HE CAN EXPLAIN THE CLASS TO YOU.
OH, WE'VE ALREADY TALKED TO JOHN.
WHAT DID HE TELL YOU?
HIS STORY DOES NOT MATCH YOURS AT ALL.
NO! HE'S THE ONE WHO TOLD ME TO DE-CEIVE THE PARTY GUESTS! IT WAS A PERFORMANCE.
WE'RE GOING DOWN THE WRONG PATH, THOMAS. DO YOU WANT TO START OVER AND SET THE RECORD STRAIGHT?
I'M AN HONEST PERSON. WE CAN SORT ALL OF THIS OUT.
YOU'VE BEEN READ YOUR RIGHTS, CORRECT?
YES, WHEN I FIRST GOT HERE. BUT THEY SAID IT WAS JUST A FORMALITY.
WHEN YOU WERE BEING AD-VISED OF YOUR RIGHTS, YOU GAVE THE OFFICERS PERMIS-SION TO SEARCH YOUR CAR.
YEA. THERE'S NOTHING IN IT.
WHAT WOULD YOU SAY IF I TOLD YOU WE FOUND OTERO'S BACKPACK IN YOUR TRUNK?
OH MY GOD. THIS CAN'T BE HAPPENING.
YOU DON'T HAVE A DEFENSE FOR THAT?
PLEASE, IT'S NOT TRUE.
YOU CAN DROP THE ACT. IT'S NOT WORKING

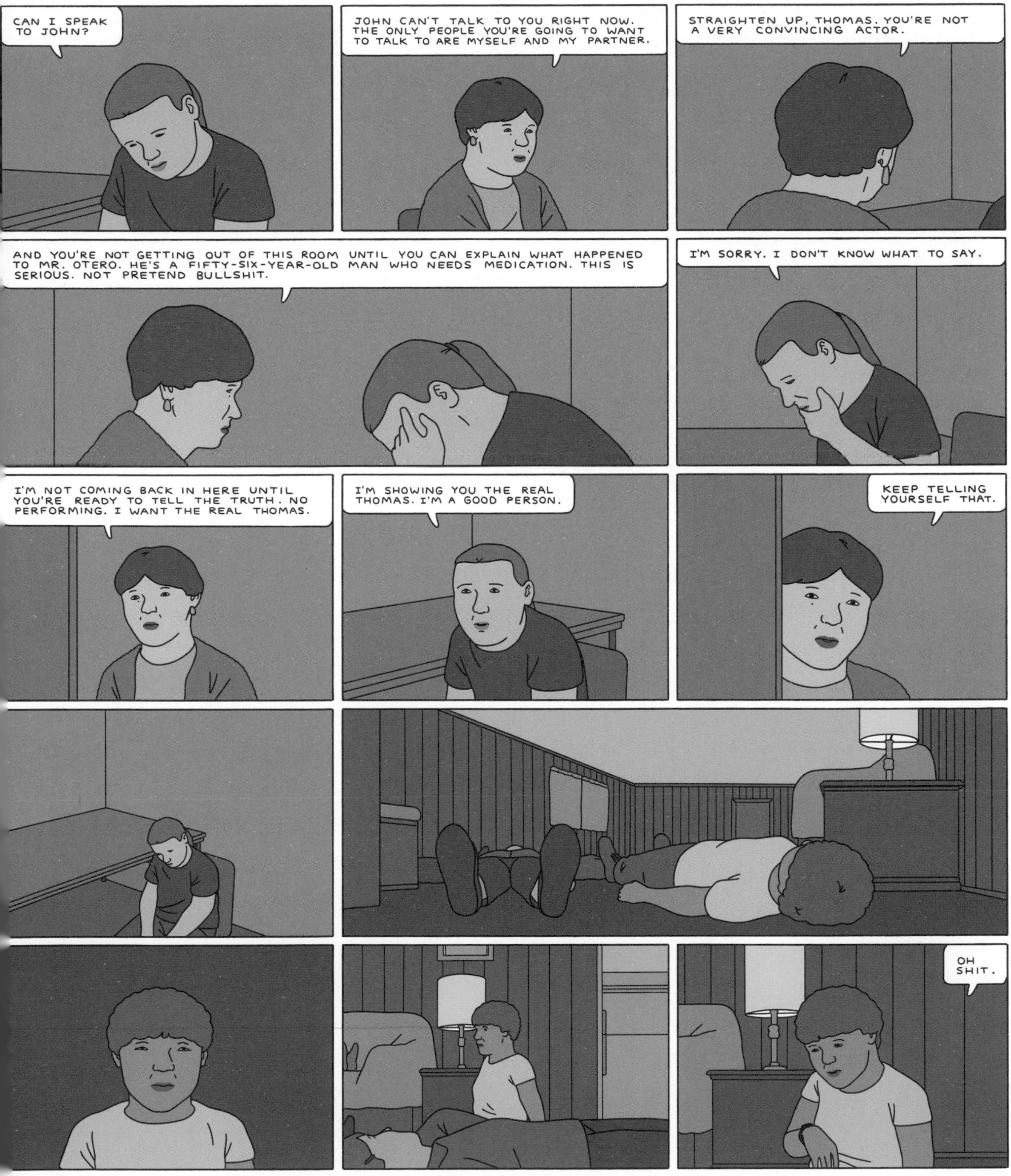
CAN I SPEAK TO JOHN?
JOHN CAN'T TALK TO YOU RIGHT NOW. THE ONLY PEOPLE YOU'RE GOING TO WANT TO TALK TO ARE MYSELF AND MY PARTNER.
STRAIGHTEN UP, THOMAS. YOU'RE NOT A VERY CONVINCING ACTOR.
AND YOU'RE NOT GETTING OUT OF THIS ROOM UNTIL YOU CAN EXPLAIN WHAT HAPPENED TO MR. OTERO. HE'S A FIFTY-SIX-YEAR-OLD MAN WHO NEEDS MEDICATION. THIS IS SERIOUS. NOT PRETEND BULLSHIT.
I'M SORRY. I DON'T KNOW WHAT TO SAY.
I'M NOT COMING BACK IN HERE UNTIL YOU'RE READY TO TELL THE TRUTH. NO PERFORMING. I WANT THE REAL THOMAS.
I'M SHOWING YOU THE REAL THOMAS. I'M A GOOD PERSON.
KEEP TELLING YOURSELF THAT.
OH SHIT.

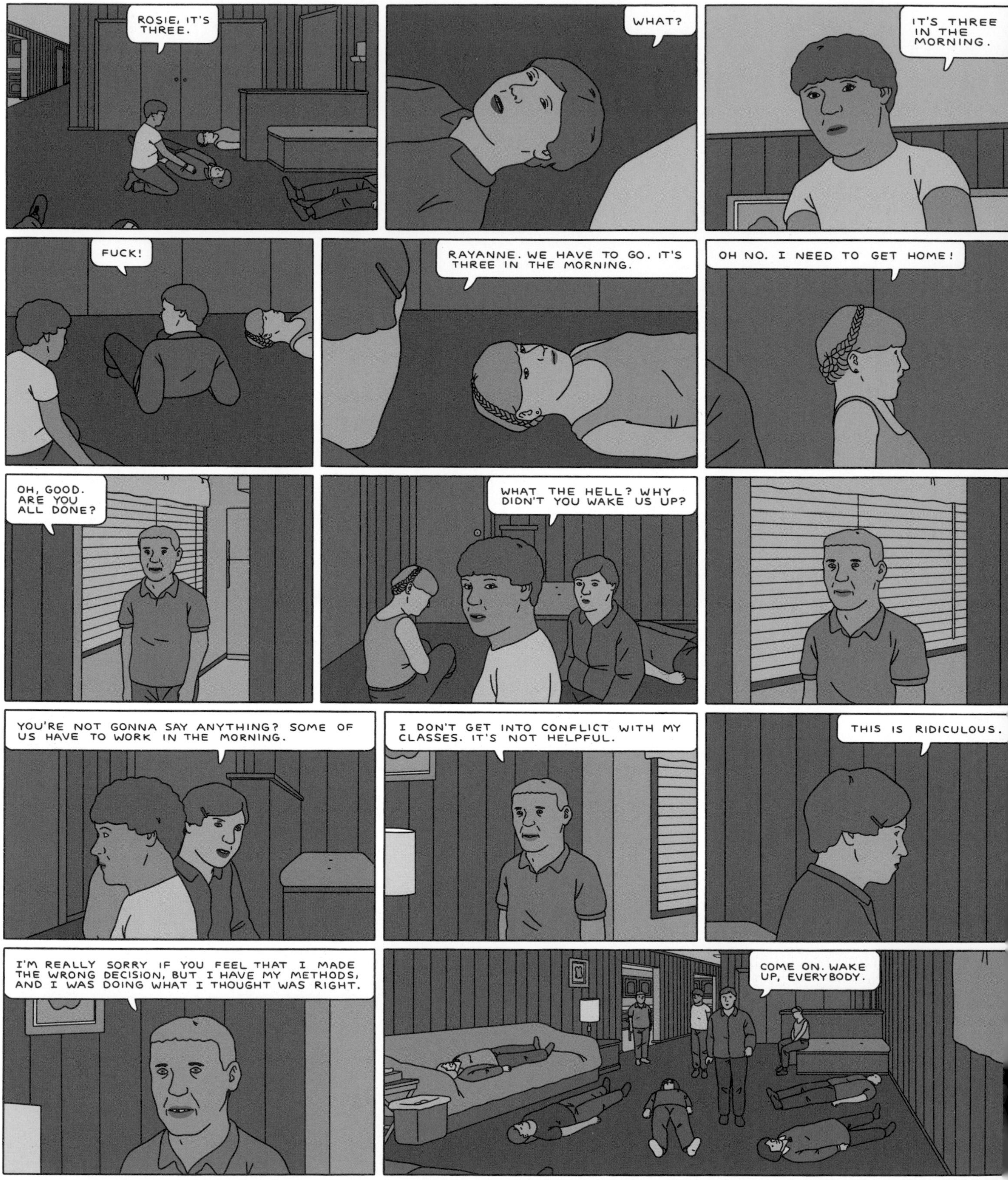
ROSIE, IT'S THREE.
WHAT?
IT'S THREE IN THE MORNING.
FUCK!
RAYANNE. WE HAVE TO GO. IT'S THREE IN THE MORNING.
OH NO. I NEED TO GET HOME!
OH, GOOD. ARE YOU ALL DONE?
WHAT THE HELL? WHY DIDN'T YOU WAKE US UP?
YOU'RE NOT GONNA SAY ANYTHING? SOME OF US HAVE TO WORK IN THE MORNING.
I DON'T GET INTO CONFLICT WITH MY CLASSES. IT'S NOT HELPFUL.
THIS IS RIDICULOUS.
I'M REALLY SORRY IF YOU FEEL THAT I MADE THE WRONG DECISION, BUT I HAVE MY METHODS, AND I WAS DOING WHAT I THOUGHT WAS RIGHT.
COME ON. WAKE UP, EVERYBODY.

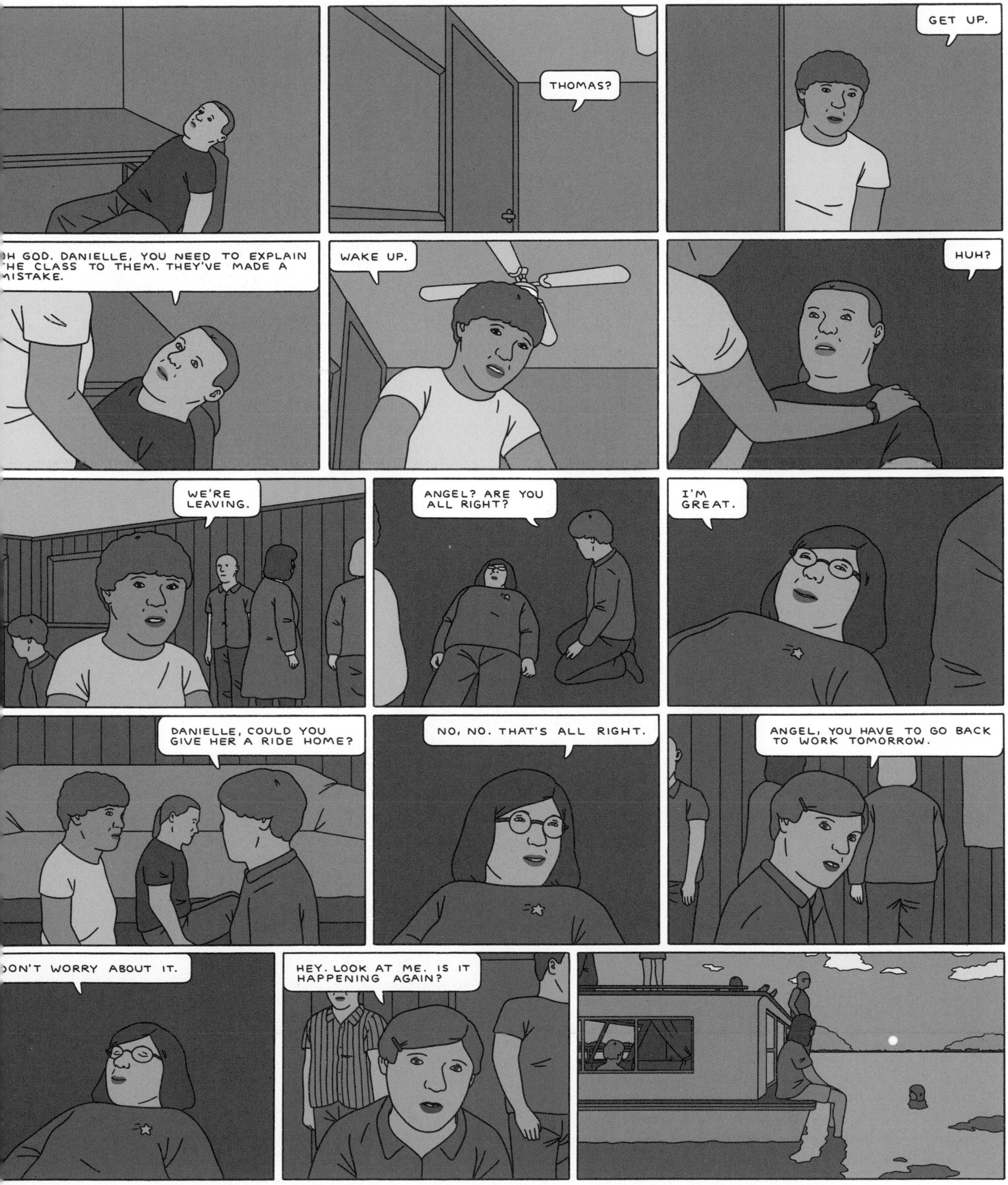
THOMAS?
GET UP.
H GOD. DANIELLE, YOU NEED TO EXPLAIN HE CLASS TO THEM. THEY'VE MADE A ISTAKE.
WAKE UP.
HUH?
WE'RE LEAVING.
ANGEL? ARE YOU ALL RIGHT?
I'M GREAT.
DANIELLE, COULD YOU GIVE HER A RIDE HOME?
NO, NO. THAT'S ALL RIGHT.
ANGEL, YOU HAVE TO GO BACK TO WORK TOMORROW.
ON'T WORRY ABOUT IT.
HEY. LOOK AT ME. IS IT HAPPENING AGAIN?

YEA. EVERYTHING IS GOOD. I'LL STAY HERE.

THAT WOULD BE JUST FINE. WADE CAN GIVE HER A RIDE BACK TO THE CITY TOMORROW.

NO, SHE HAS TO COME WITH US.

REALLY, I'M FINE!

COME ON, ROSIE. LET'S GO.

I HAVE A SEAT IN MY CAR.

PLEASE, LEAVE ME BE. I'LL SEE YOU AT WORK TOMORROW.

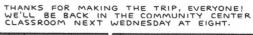

THANKS FOR MAKING THE TRIP, EVERYONE! WE'LL BE BACK IN THE COMMUNITY CENTER CLASSROOM NEXT WEDNESDAY AT EIGHT.

JUST A REMINDER, THAT WILL BE OUR LAST FREE SESSION.

THANKS, JOHN.

YOU ALL MUST BE TIRED. DRIVE SAFE.

DO YOU WANT A CHANGE OF CLOTHES?

I'LL GET YOU SOME BLANKETS.

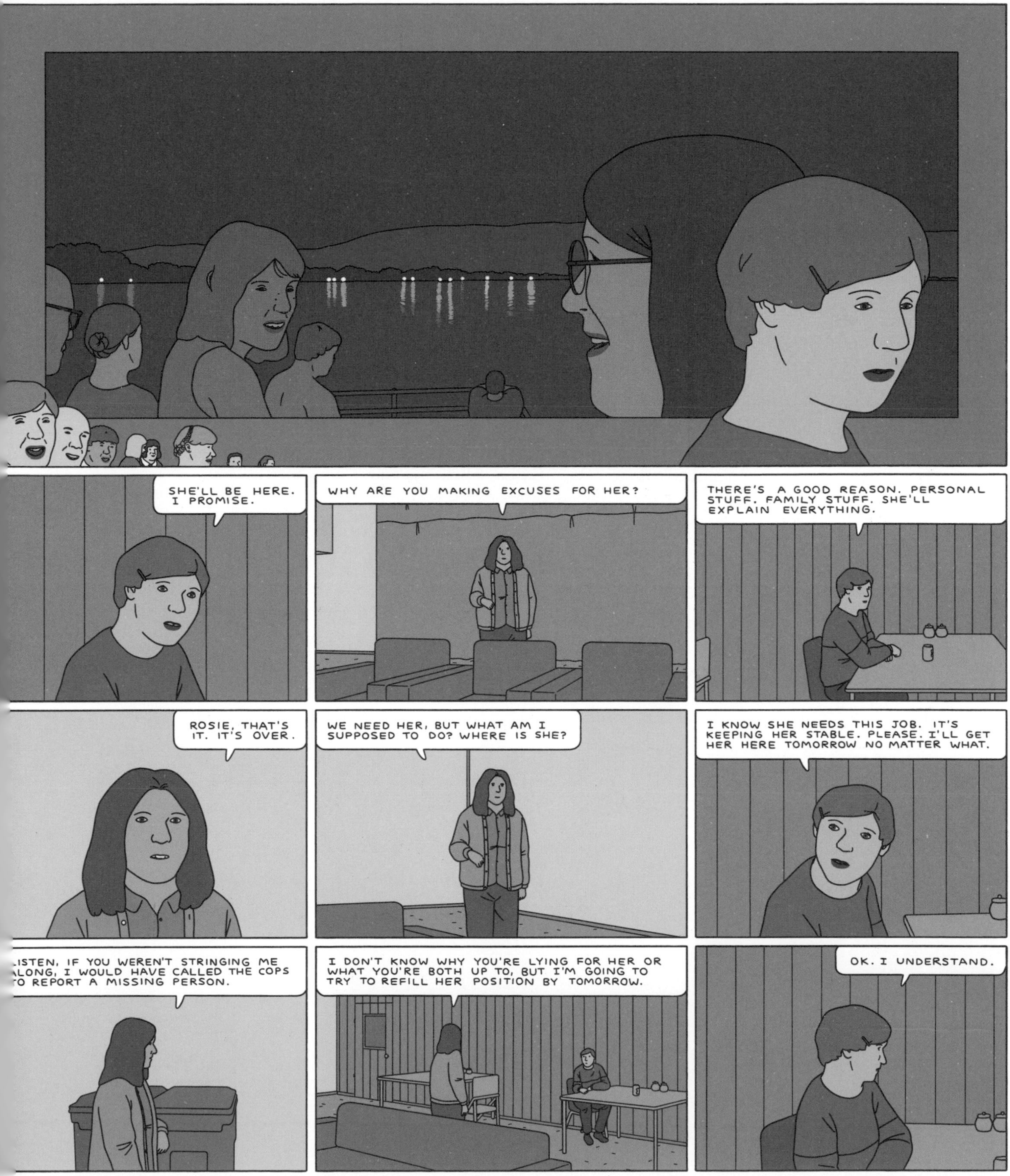

SHE'LL BE HERE. I PROMISE.
WHY ARE YOU MAKING EXCUSES FOR HER?
THERE'S A GOOD REASON. PERSONAL STUFF. FAMILY STUFF. SHE'LL EXPLAIN EVERYTHING.
ROSIE, THAT'S IT. IT'S OVER.
WE NEED HER, BUT WHAT AM I SUPPOSED TO DO? WHERE IS SHE?
I KNOW SHE NEEDS THIS JOB. IT'S KEEPING HER STABLE. PLEASE. I'LL GET HER HERE TOMORROW NO MATTER WHAT.
LISTEN, IF YOU WEREN'T STRINGING ME ALONG, I WOULD HAVE CALLED THE COPS TO REPORT A MISSING PERSON.
I DON'T KNOW WHY YOU'RE LYING FOR HER OR WHAT YOU'RE BOTH UP TO, BUT I'M GOING TO TRY TO REFILL HER POSITION BY TOMORROW.
OK. I UNDERSTAND.

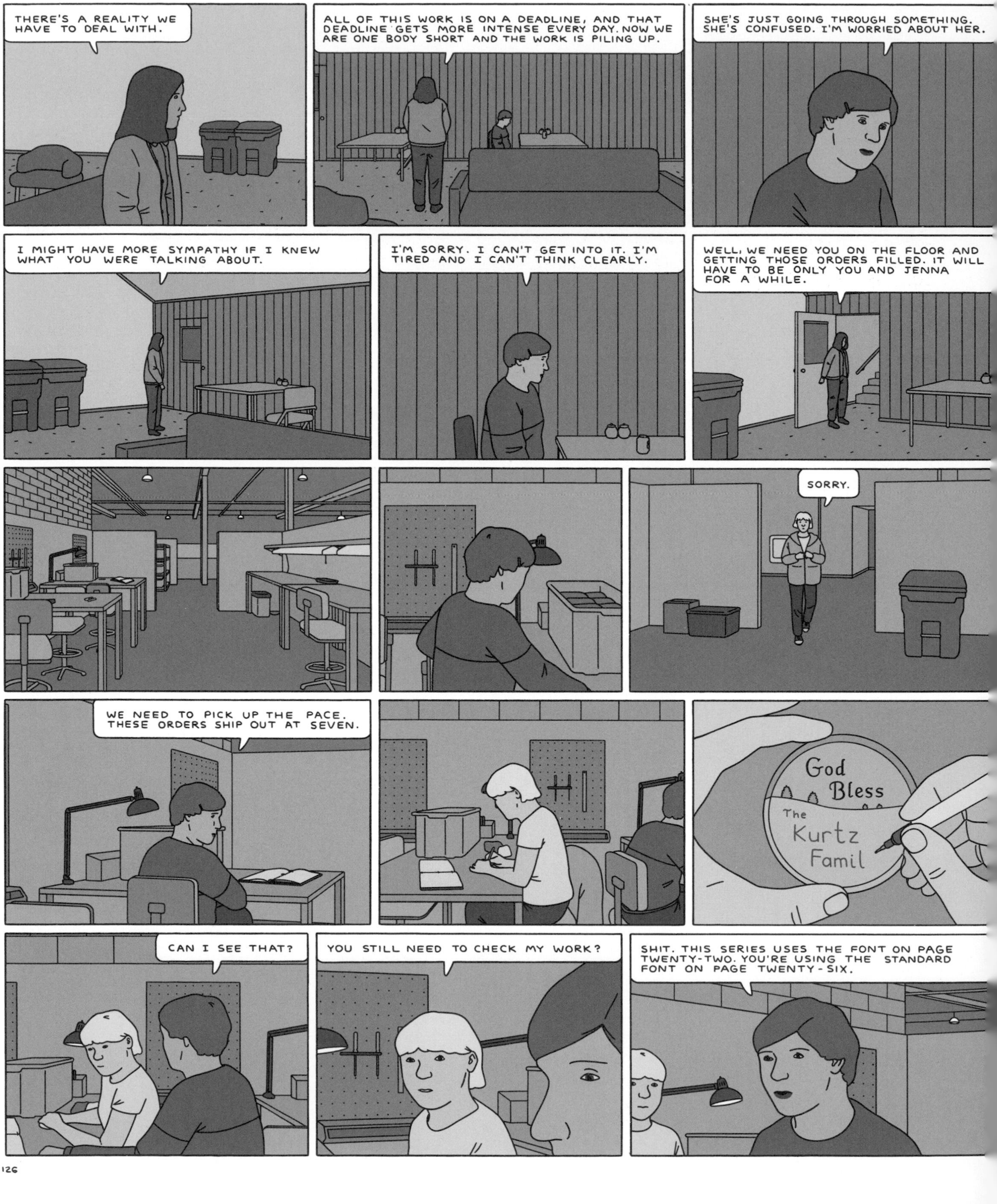
THERE'S A REALITY WE HAVE TO DEAL WITH.
ALL OF THIS WORK IS ON A DEADLINE, AND THAT DEADLINE GETS MORE INTENSE EVERY DAY. NOW WE ARE ONE BODY SHORT AND THE WORK IS PILING UP.
SHE'S JUST GOING THROUGH SOMETHING. SHE'S CONFUSED. I'M WORRIED ABOUT HER.
I MIGHT HAVE MORE SYMPATHY IF I KNEW WHAT YOU WERE TALKING ABOUT.
I'M SORRY. I CAN'T GET INTO IT. I'M TIRED AND I CAN'T THINK CLEARLY.
WELL, WE NEED YOU ON THE FLOOR AND GETTING THOSE ORDERS FILLED. IT WILL HAVE TO BE ONLY YOU AND JENNA FOR A WHILE.
SORRY.
WE NEED TO PICK UP THE PACE. THESE ORDERS SHIP OUT AT SEVEN.
God Bless The Kurtz Famil
CAN I SEE THAT?
YOU STILL NEED TO CHECK MY WORK?
SHIT. THIS SERIES USES THE FONT ON PAGE TWENTY-TWO. YOU'RE USING THE STANDARD FONT ON PAGE TWENTY-SIX.

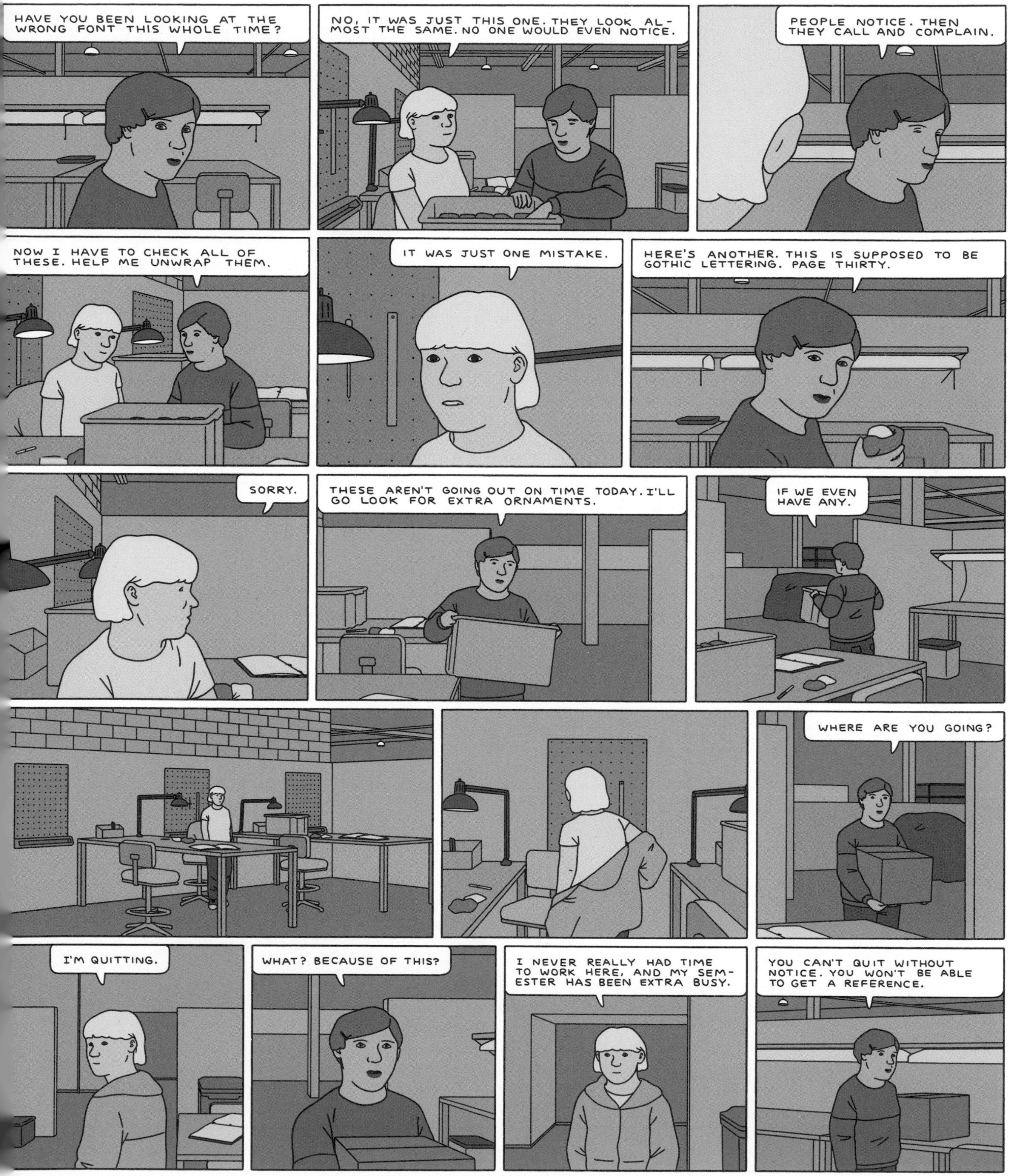
HAVE YOU BEEN LOOKING AT THE WRONG FONT THIS WHOLE TIME?
NO, IT WAS JUST THIS ONE. THEY LOOK AL-MOST THE SAME. NO ONE WOULD EVEN NOTICE.
PEOPLE NOTICE. THEN THEY CALL AND COMPLAIN.
NOW I HAVE TO CHECK ALL OF THESE. HELP ME UNWRAP THEM.
IT WAS JUST ONE MISTAKE.
HERE'S ANOTHER. THIS IS SUPPOSED TO BE GOTHIC LETTERING. PAGE THIRTY.
SORRY.
THESE AREN'T GOING OUT ON TIME TODAY. I'LL GO LOOK FOR EXTRA ORNAMENTS.
IF WE EVEN HAVE ANY.
WHERE ARE YOU GOING?
I'M QUITTING.
WHAT? BECAUSE OF THIS?
I NEVER REALLY HAD TIME TO WORK HERE, AND MY SEM-ESTER HAS BEEN EXTRA BUSY.
YOU CAN'T QUIT WITHOUT NOTICE. YOU WON'T BE ABLE TO GET A REFERENCE.

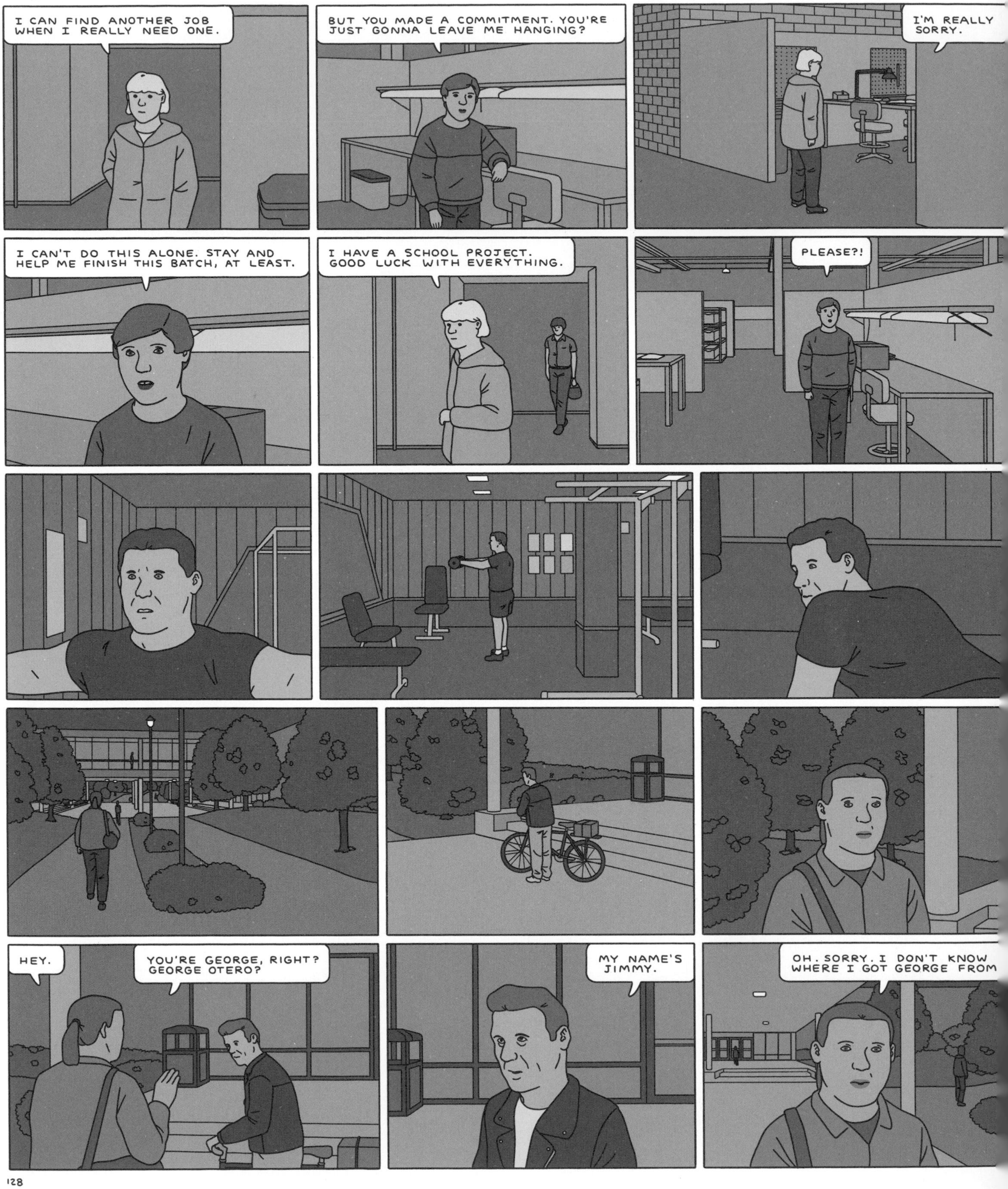
I CAN FIND ANOTHER JOB WHEN I REALLY NEED ONE.
BUT YOU MADE A COMMITMENT. YOU'RE JUST GONNA LEAVE ME HANGING?
I'M REALLY SORRY.
I CAN'T DO THIS ALONE. STAY AND HELP ME FINISH THIS BATCH, AT LEAST.
I HAVE A SCHOOL PROJECT. GOOD LUCK WITH EVERYTHING.
PLEASE?!
HEY.
YOU'RE GEORGE, RIGHT? GEORGE OTERO?
MY NAME'S JIMMY.
OH. SORRY. I DON'T KNOW WHERE I GOT GEORGE FROM

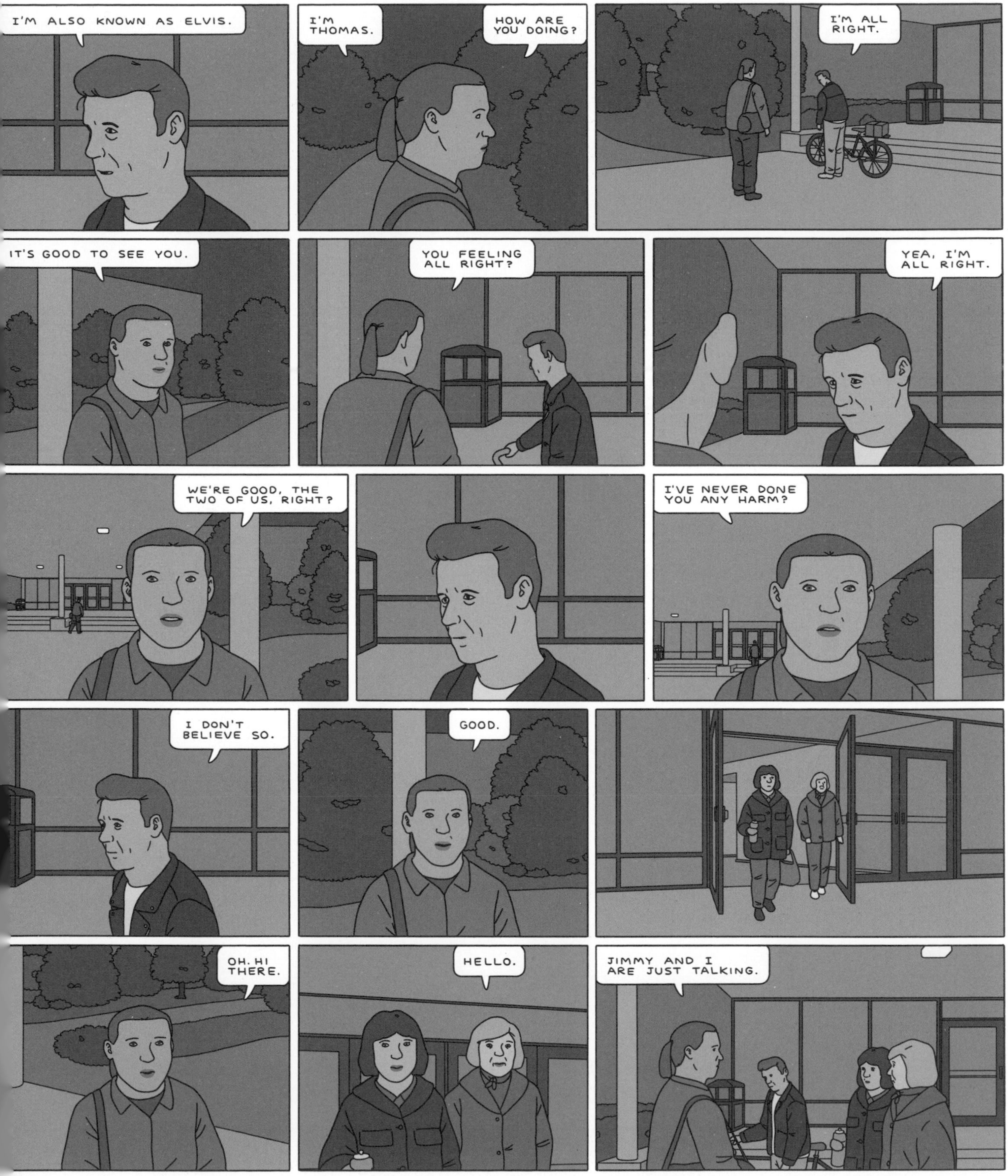
I'M ALSO KNOWN AS ELVIS.
I'M THOMAS.
HOW ARE YOU DOING?
I'M ALL RIGHT.
IT'S GOOD TO SEE YOU.
YOU FEELING ALL RIGHT?
YEA, I'M ALL RIGHT.
WE'RE GOOD, THE TWO OF US, RIGHT?
I'VE NEVER DONE YOU ANY HARM?
I DON'T BELIEVE SO.
GOOD.
OH. HI THERE.
HELLO.
JIMMY AND I ARE JUST TALKING.

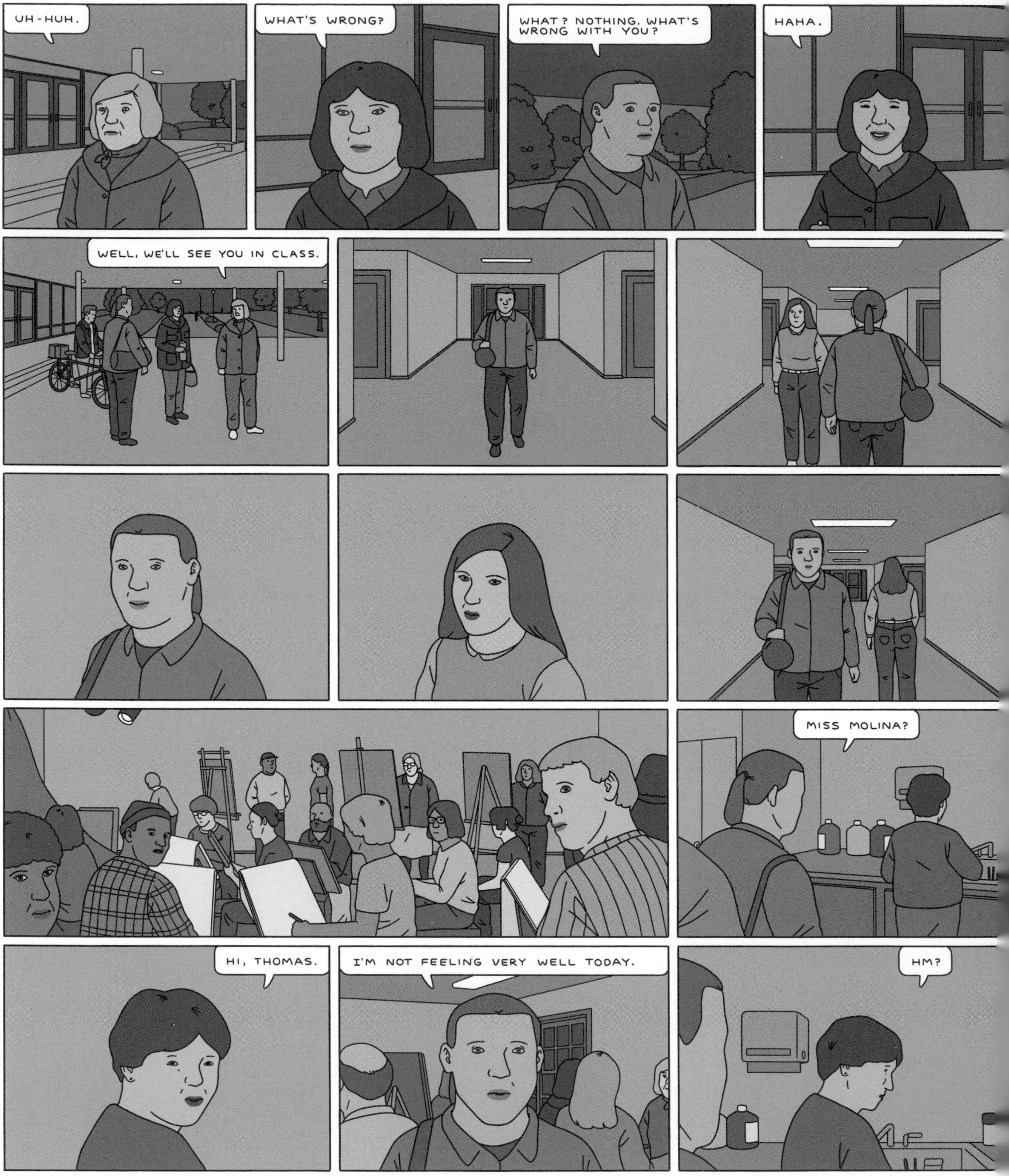
UH-HUH.
WHAT'S WRONG?
WHAT? NOTHING. WHAT'S WRONG WITH YOU?
HAHA.
WELL, WE'LL SEE YOU IN CLASS.
MISS MOLINA?
HI, THOMAS.
I'M NOT FEELING VERY WELL TODAY.
HM?

AND I WAS WONDERING IF I COULD POSE WITH MY CLOTHES ON.

WHY?

I JUST... SUDDENLY DON'T FEEL COMFORTABLE.

THOMAS, WE HAVE A CLASS FULL OF STUDENTS WHO PAID FOR FIGURE DRAWING.

WHERE IS THIS COMING FROM?

WELL, YOU'VE LEFT ME WITH NO OPTIONS.

THANK YOU.

THIS IS ONE TIME. IF YOU DON'T SNAP OUT OF IT BY THE NEXT CLASS, THEN WE WON'T BE ABLE TO USE YOU ANYMORE.

ALL RIGHT, CLASS. WE'RE GOING TO DO SOME-THING DIFFERENT THIS WEEK. LET'S SEE WHAT IT'S LIKE TO DRAW A CLOTHED MODEL.

THE RIPPLES AND FOLDS OF A SHIRT CAN BE SURPRISINGLY COMPLEX, SO THIS WILL BE A GOOD EXERCISE.

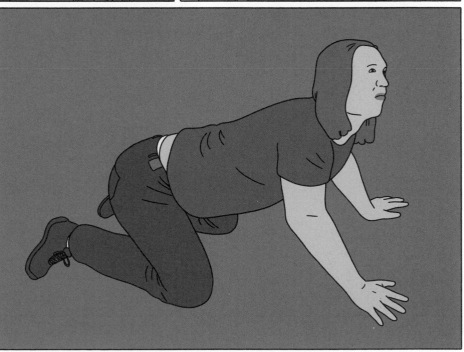

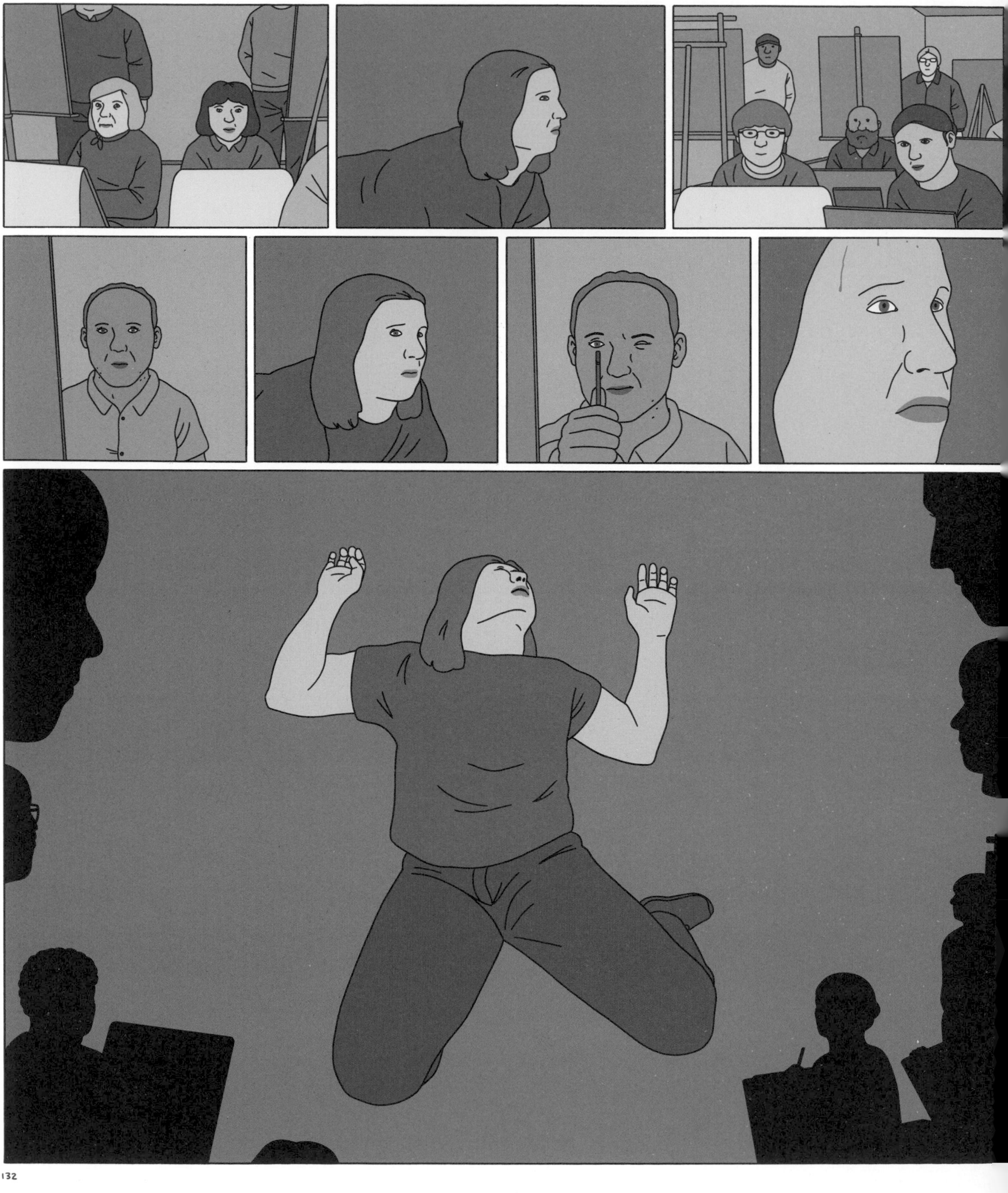

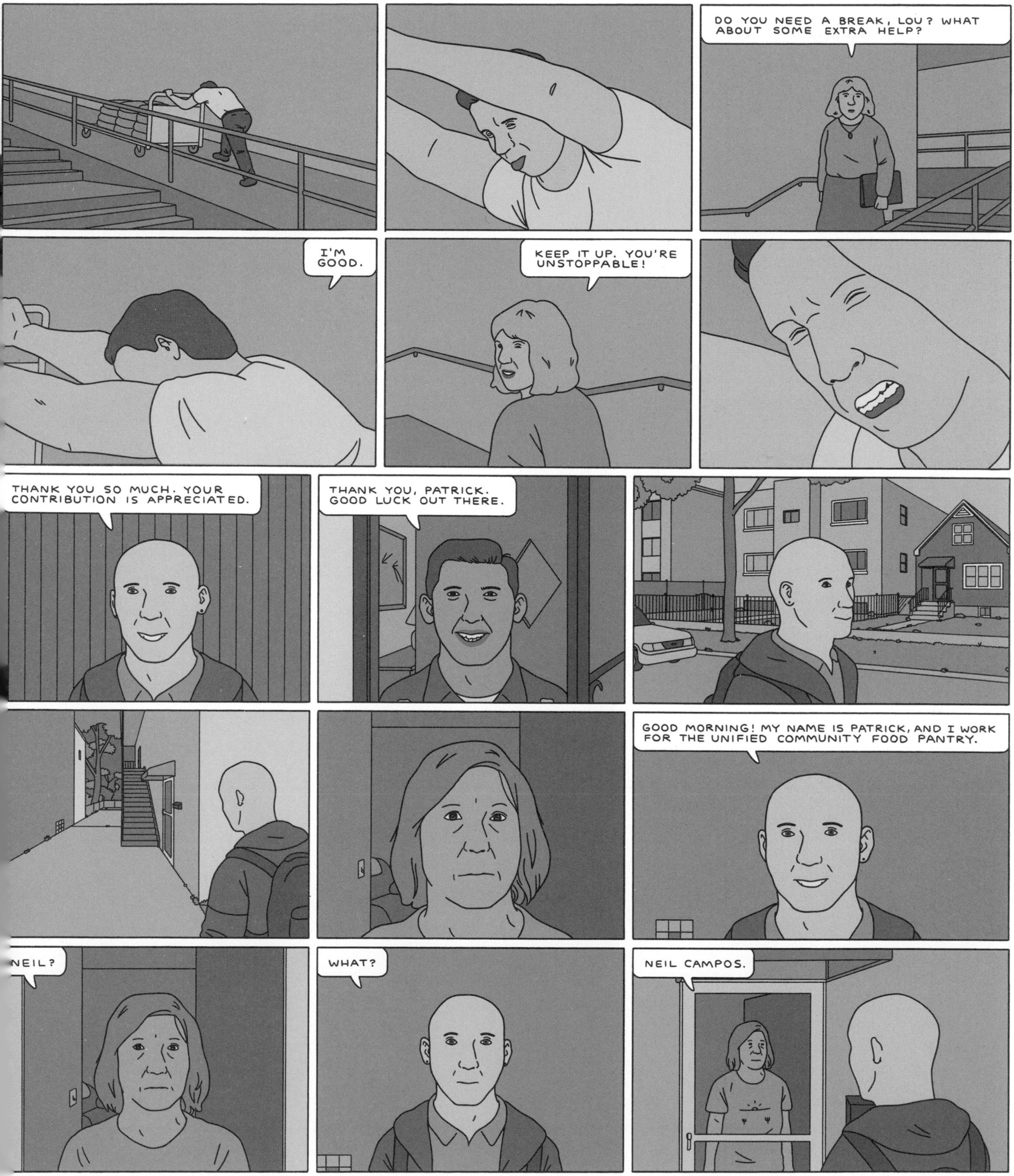
DO YOU NEED A BREAK, LOU? WHAT ABOUT SOME EXTRA HELP?
I'M GOOD.
KEEP IT UP. YOU'RE UNSTOPPABLE!
THANK YOU SO MUCH. YOUR CONTRIBUTION IS APPRECIATED.
THANK YOU, PATRICK. GOOD LUCK OUT THERE.
GOOD MORNING! MY NAME IS PATRICK, AND I WORK FOR THE UNIFIED COMMUNITY FOOD PANTRY.
NEIL?
WHAT?
NEIL CAMPOS.

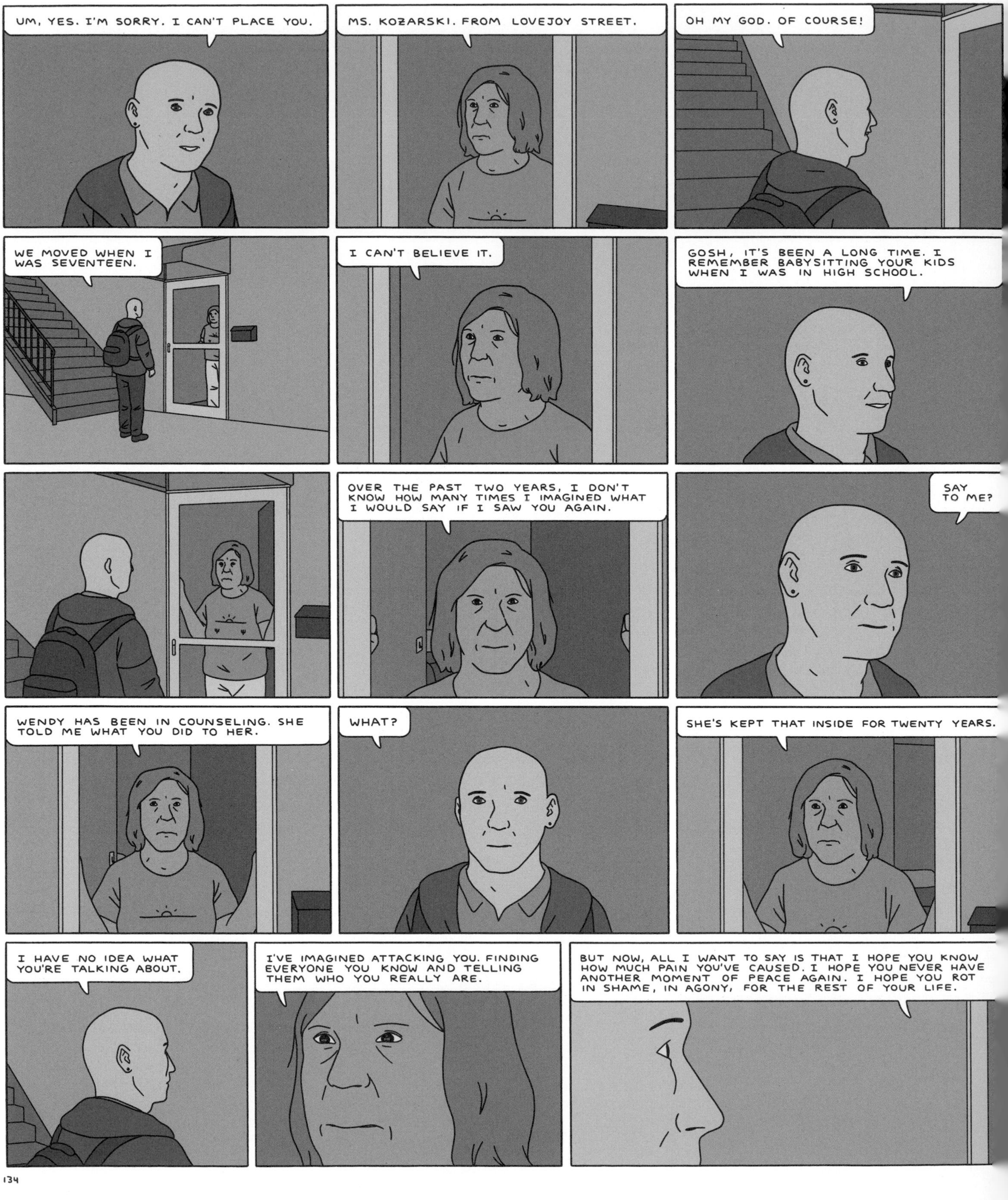
UM, YES. I'M SORRY. I CAN'T PLACE YOU.
MS. KOZARSKI. FROM LOVEJOY STREET.
OH MY GOD. OF COURSE!
WE MOVED WHEN I WAS SEVENTEEN.
I CAN'T BELIEVE IT.
GOSH, IT'S BEEN A LONG TIME. I REMEMBER BABYSITTING YOUR KIDS WHEN I WAS IN HIGH SCHOOL.
OVER THE PAST TWO YEARS, I DON'T KNOW HOW MANY TIMES I IMAGINED WHAT I WOULD SAY IF I SAW YOU AGAIN.
SAY TO ME?
WENDY HAS BEEN IN COUNSELING. SHE TOLD ME WHAT YOU DID TO HER.
WHAT?
SHE'S KEPT THAT INSIDE FOR TWENTY YEARS.
I HAVE NO IDEA WHAT YOU'RE TALKING ABOUT.
I'VE IMAGINED ATTACKING YOU. FINDING EVERYONE YOU KNOW AND TELLING THEM WHO YOU REALLY ARE.
BUT NOW, ALL I WANT TO SAY IS THAT I HOPE YOU KNOW HOW MUCH PAIN YOU'VE CAUSED. I HOPE YOU NEVER HAVE ANOTHER MOMENT OF PEACE AGAIN. I HOPE YOU ROT IN SHAME, IN AGONY, FOR THE REST OF YOUR LIFE.

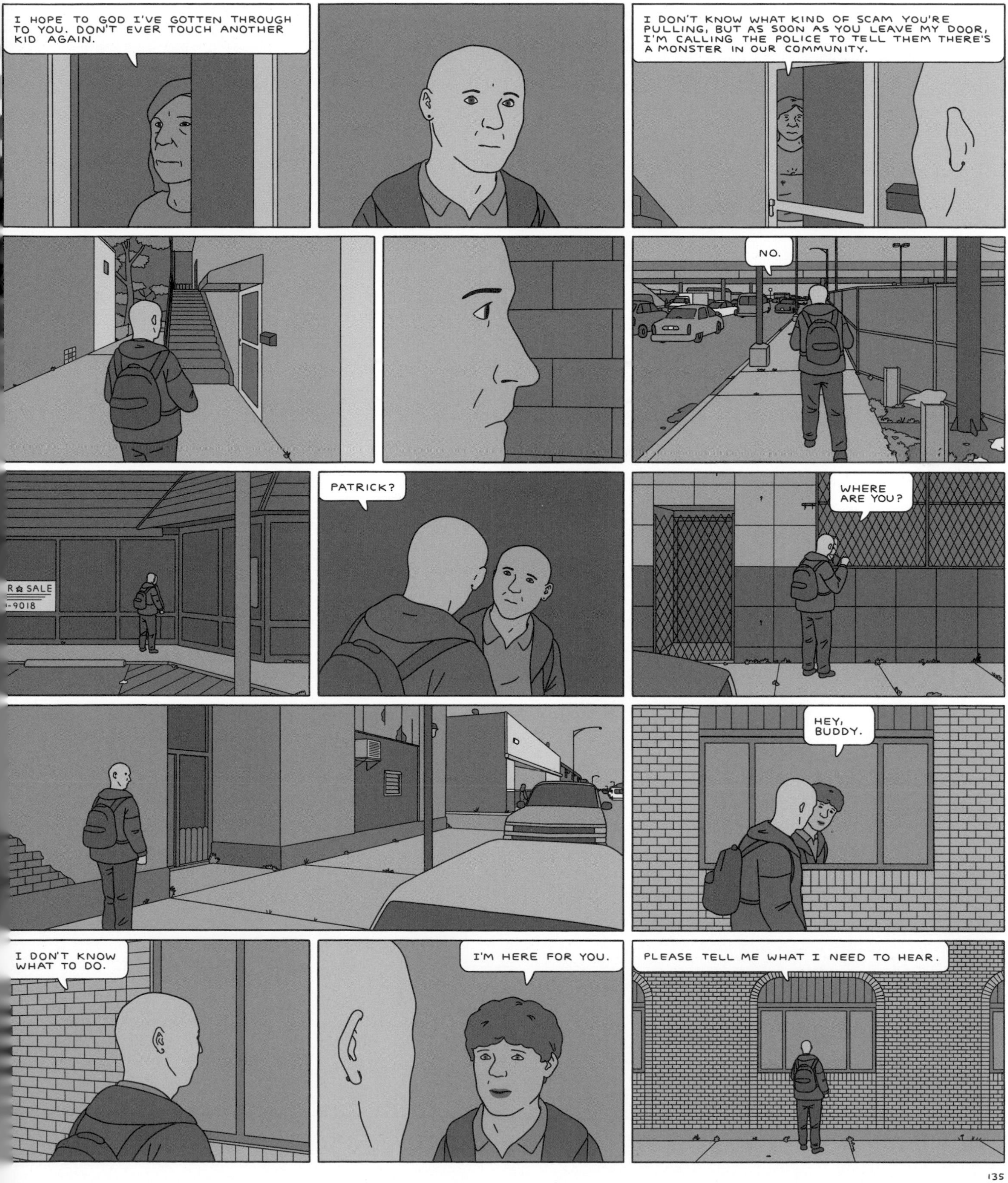
I HOPE TO GOD I'VE GOTTEN THROUGH TO YOU. DON'T EVER TOUCH ANOTHER KID AGAIN.
I DON'T KNOW WHAT KIND OF SCAM YOU'RE PULLING, BUT AS SOON AS YOU LEAVE MY DOOR, I'M CALLING THE POLICE TO TELL THEM THERE'S A MONSTER IN OUR COMMUNITY.
NO.
R ✿ SALE
-9018
PATRICK?
WHERE ARE YOU?
HEY, BUDDY.
I DON'T KNOW WHAT TO DO.
I'M HERE FOR YOU.
PLEASE TELL ME WHAT I NEED TO HEAR.

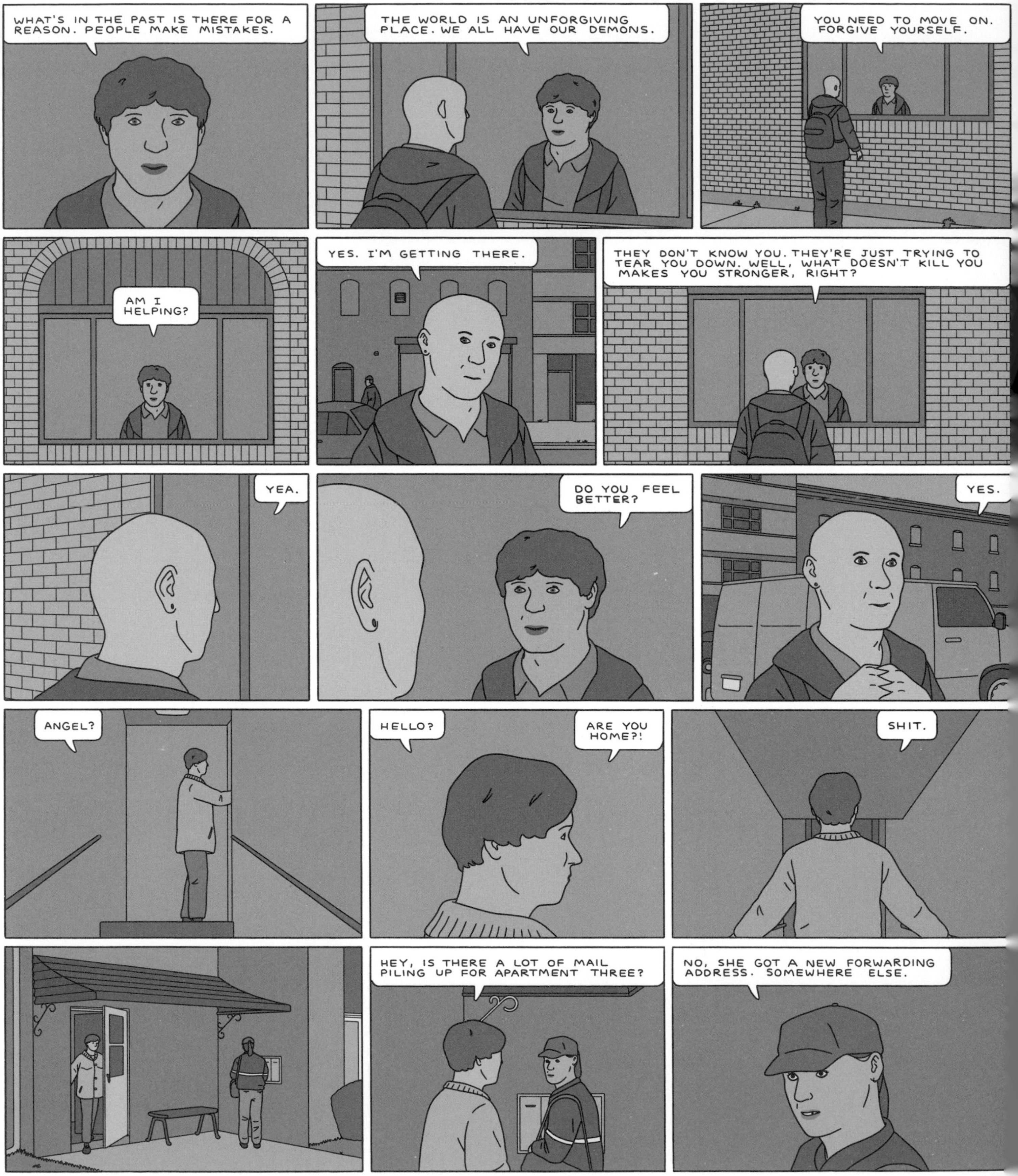
WHAT'S IN THE PAST IS THERE FOR A REASON. PEOPLE MAKE MISTAKES.
THE WORLD IS AN UNFORGIVING PLACE. WE ALL HAVE OUR DEMONS.
YOU NEED TO MOVE ON. FORGIVE YOURSELF.
AM I HELPING?
YES. I'M GETTING THERE.
THEY DON'T KNOW YOU. THEY'RE JUST TRYING TO TEAR YOU DOWN. WELL, WHAT DOESN'T KILL YOU MAKES YOU STRONGER, RIGHT?
YEA.
DO YOU FEEL BETTER?
YES.
ANGEL?
HELLO?
ARE YOU HOME?!
SHIT.
HEY, IS THERE A LOT OF MAIL PILING UP FOR APARTMENT THREE?
NO, SHE GOT A NEW FORWARDING ADDRESS. SOMEWHERE ELSE.

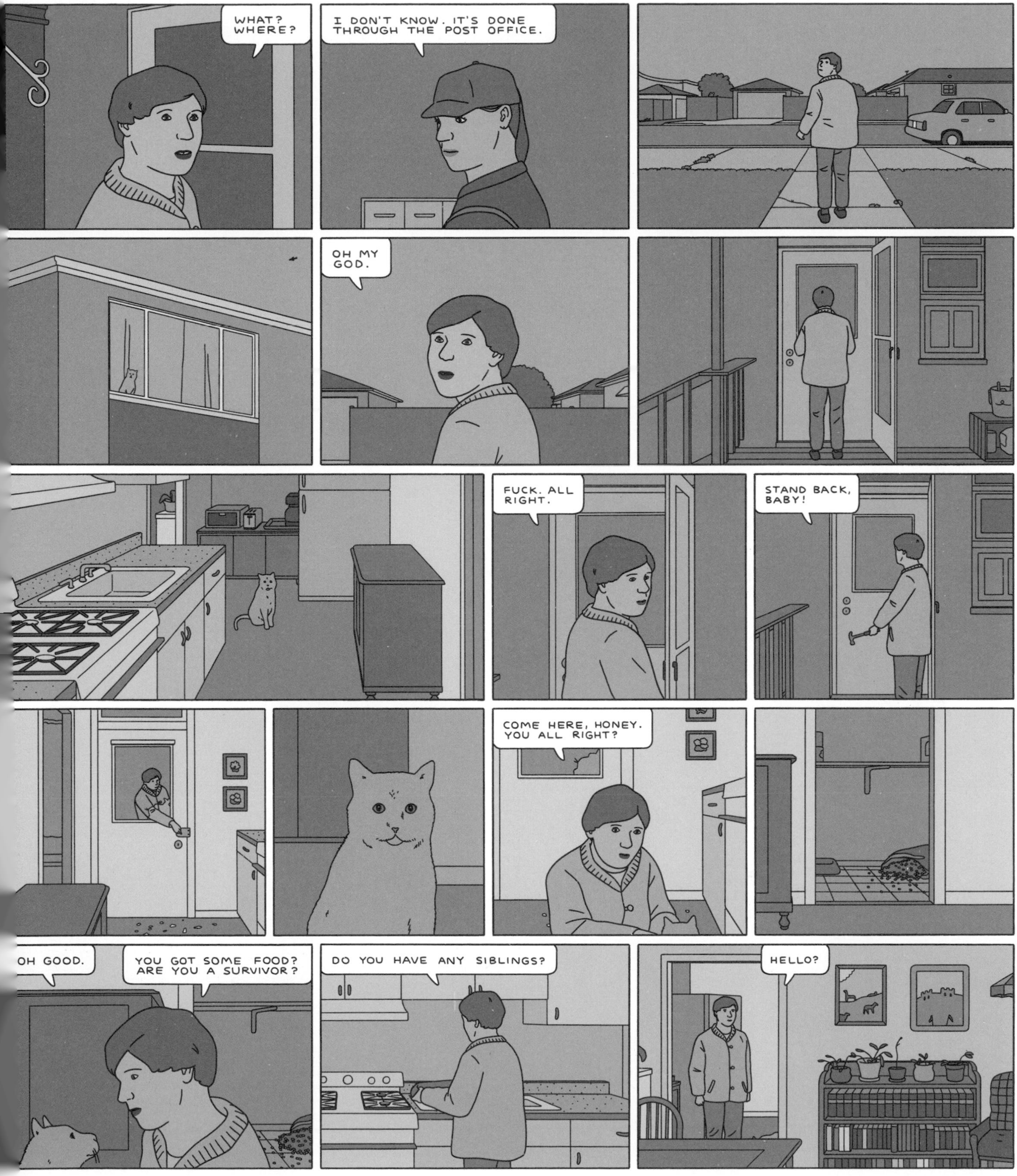
WHAT? WHERE?
I DON'T KNOW. IT'S DONE THROUGH THE POST OFFICE.
OH MY GOD.
FUCK. ALL RIGHT.
STAND BACK, BABY!
COME HERE, HONEY. YOU ALL RIGHT?
OH GOOD.
YOU GOT SOME FOOD? ARE YOU A SURVIVOR?
DO YOU HAVE ANY SIBLINGS?
HELLO?

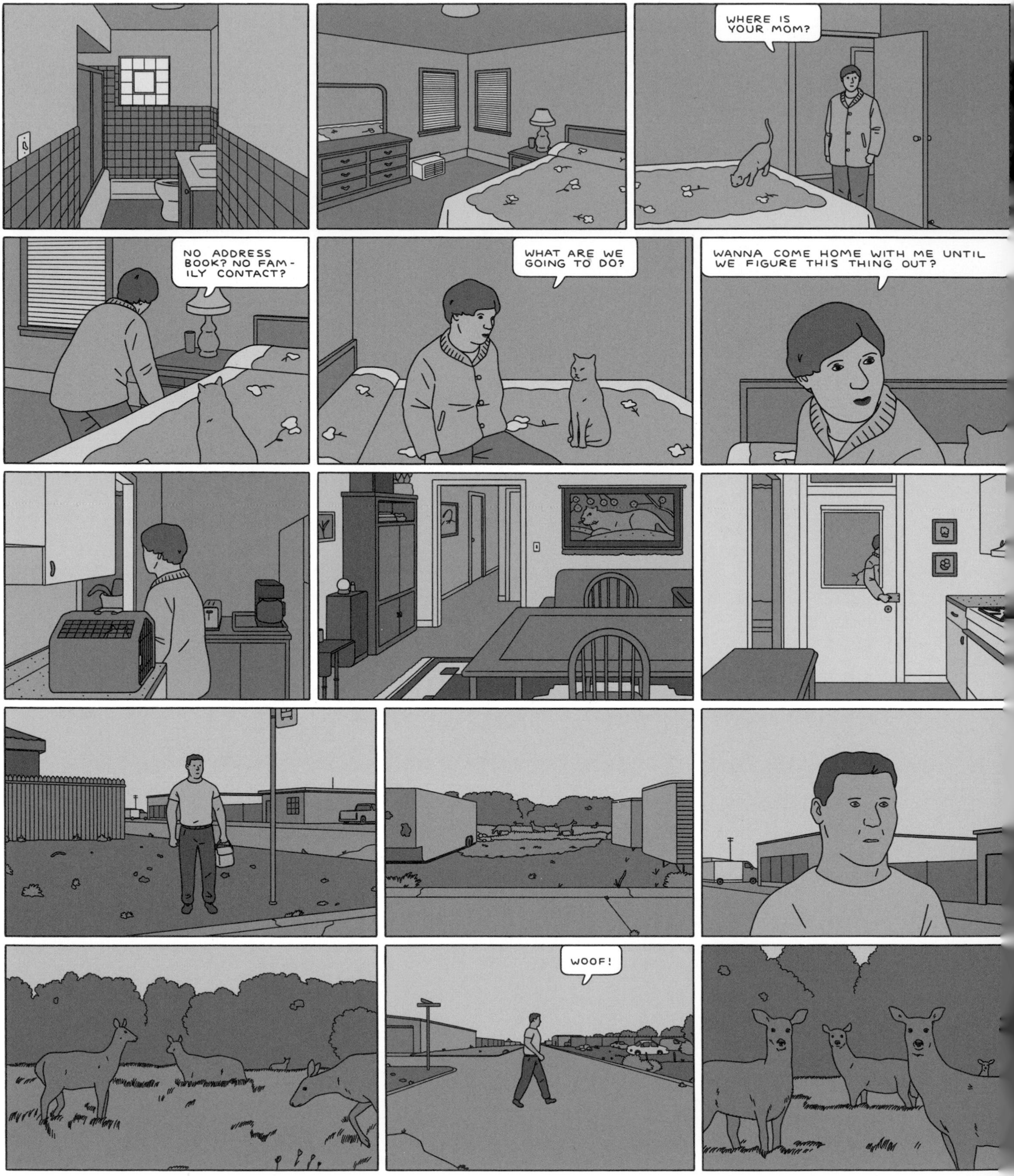
WHERE IS YOUR MOM?
NO ADDRESS BOOK? NO FAM-ILY CONTACT?
WHAT ARE WE GOING TO DO?
WANNA COME HOME WITH ME UNTIL WE FIGURE THIS THING OUT?
WOOF!

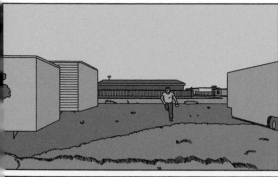

ARE YOU ALL RIGHT WITH EGGS AND POTATOES AGAIN?

YEP.

WE HAVE SOME BACON AS WELL.

LIKE AN AVIARY?

WHAT?

LIKE A MAGNETIC POCKET WATCH. THE BEST KIND.

OH NO, BETH. LET'S SLOW DOWN.

THERE'S A CONSISTENT STOMPING. IT'S SIMMERING LIKE THAT.

OK. I HEAR YOU. I UNDERSTAND. LET'S TALK THIS THROUGH LIKE REBECCA SAID.

ELECTIONEERING. PULSING BATTLE HYMN. IT'S A REQUIREMENT. DO YOU HEAR IT?

HOW ARE YOU FEELING?

LEAVE IT TO ME. WHICH ONE?

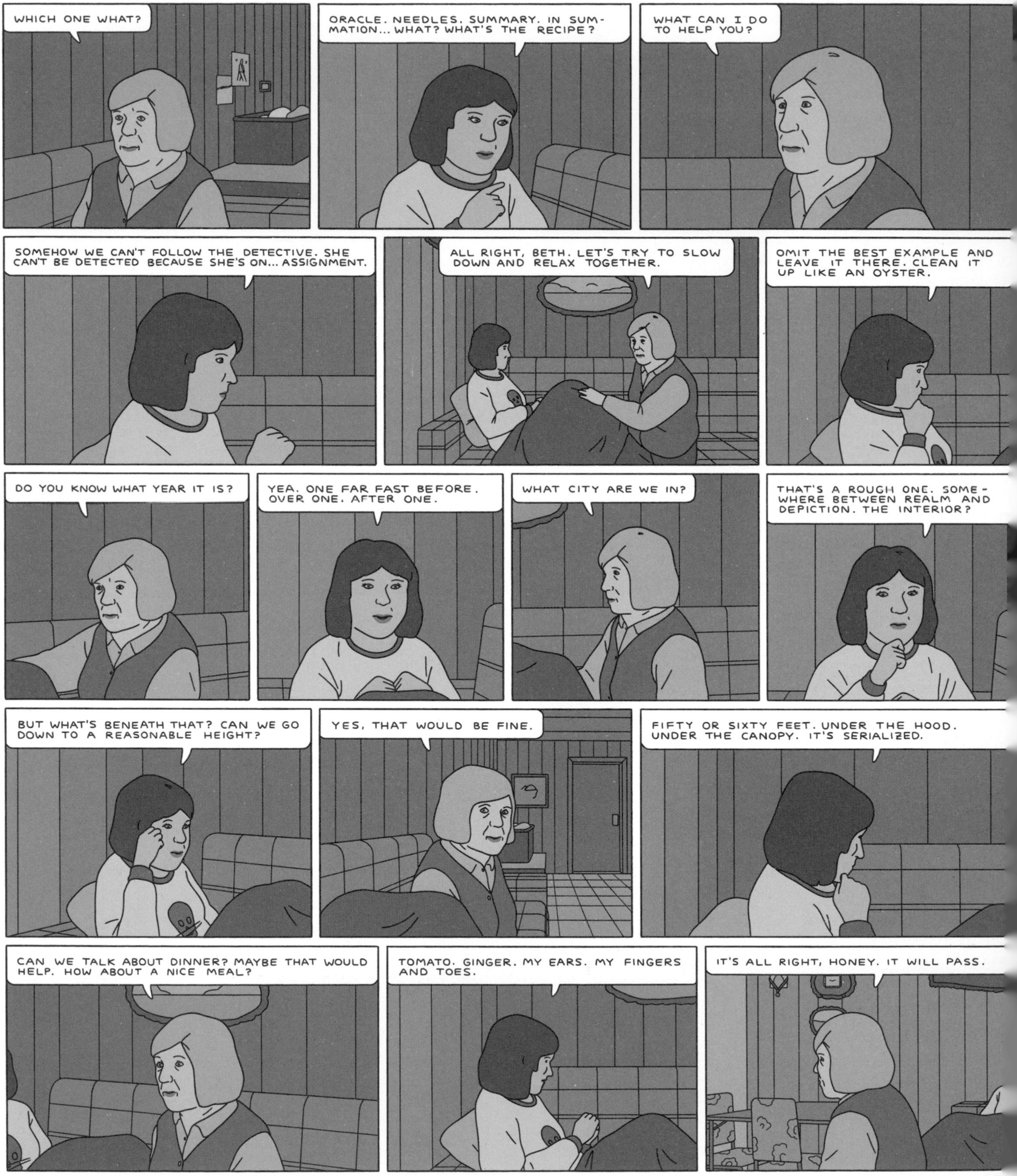
WHICH ONE WHAT?
ORACLE. NEEDLES. SUMMARY. IN SUMMATION... WHAT? WHAT'S THE RECIPE?
WHAT CAN I DO TO HELP YOU?
SOMEHOW WE CAN'T FOLLOW THE DETECTIVE. SHE CAN'T BE DETECTED BECAUSE SHE'S ON... ASSIGNMENT.
ALL RIGHT, BETH. LET'S TRY TO SLOW DOWN AND RELAX TOGETHER.
OMIT THE BEST EXAMPLE AND LEAVE IT THERE. CLEAN IT UP LIKE AN OYSTER.
DO YOU KNOW WHAT YEAR IT IS?
YEA. ONE FAR FAST BEFORE. OVER ONE. AFTER ONE.
WHAT CITY ARE WE IN?
THAT'S A ROUGH ONE. SOMEWHERE BETWEEN REALM AND DEPICTION. THE INTERIOR?
BUT WHAT'S BENEATH THAT? CAN WE GO DOWN TO A REASONABLE HEIGHT?
YES, THAT WOULD BE FINE.
FIFTY OR SIXTY FEET. UNDER THE HOOD. UNDER THE CANOPY. IT'S SERIALIZED.
CAN WE TALK ABOUT DINNER? MAYBE THAT WOULD HELP. HOW ABOUT A NICE MEAL?
TOMATO. GINGER. MY EARS. MY FINGERS AND TOES.
IT'S ALL RIGHT, HONEY. IT WILL PASS.

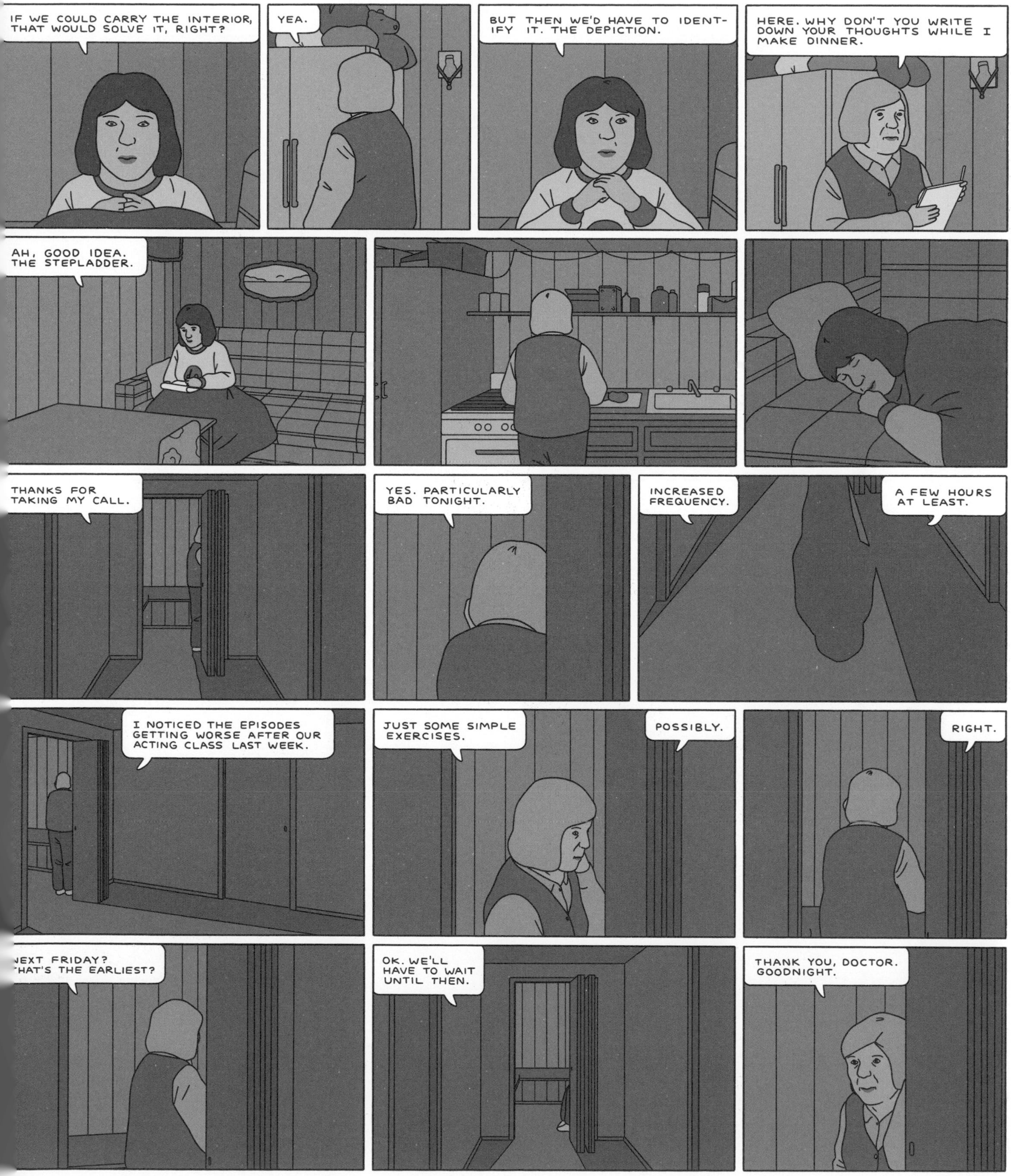
IF WE COULD CARRY THE INTERIOR, THAT WOULD SOLVE IT, RIGHT?
YEA.
BUT THEN WE'D HAVE TO IDENT-IFY IT. THE DEPICTION.
HERE. WHY DON'T YOU WRITE DOWN YOUR THOUGHTS WHILE I MAKE DINNER.
AH, GOOD IDEA. THE STEPLADDER.
THANKS FOR TAKING MY CALL.
YES. PARTICULARLY BAD TONIGHT.
INCREASED FREQUENCY.
A FEW HOURS AT LEAST.
I NOTICED THE EPISODES GETTING WORSE AFTER OUR ACTING CLASS LAST WEEK.
JUST SOME SIMPLE EXERCISES.
POSSIBLY.
RIGHT.
NEXT FRIDAY? THAT'S THE EARLIEST?
OK. WE'LL HAVE TO WAIT UNTIL THEN.
THANK YOU, DOCTOR. GOODNIGHT.

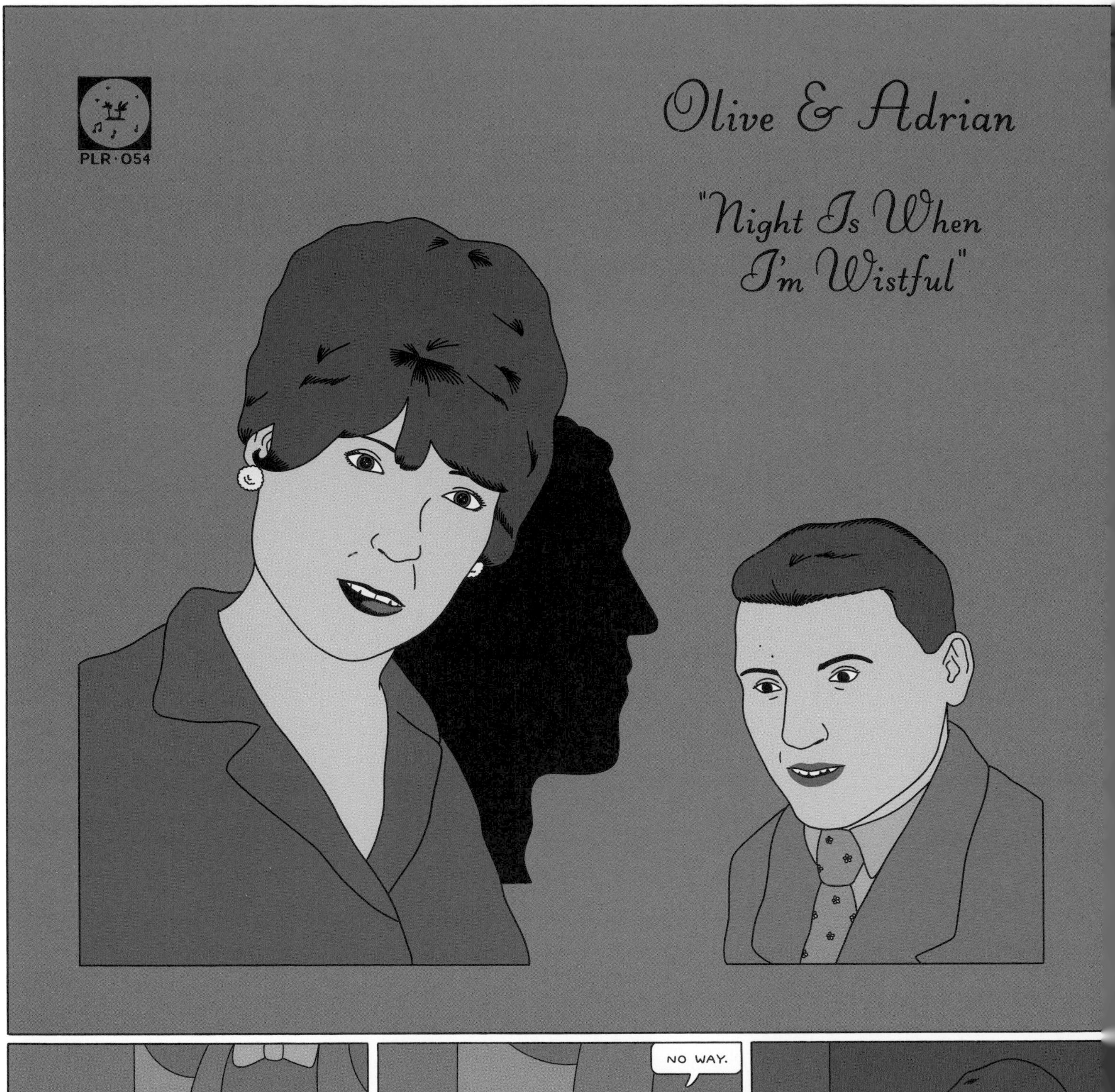
PLR · 054
Olive & Adrian
"Night Is When I'm Wistful"

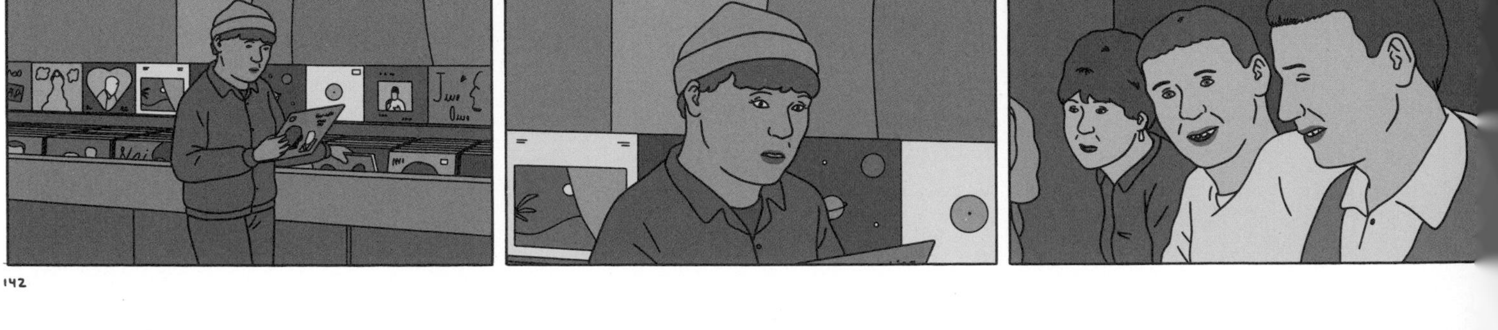
NO WAY.

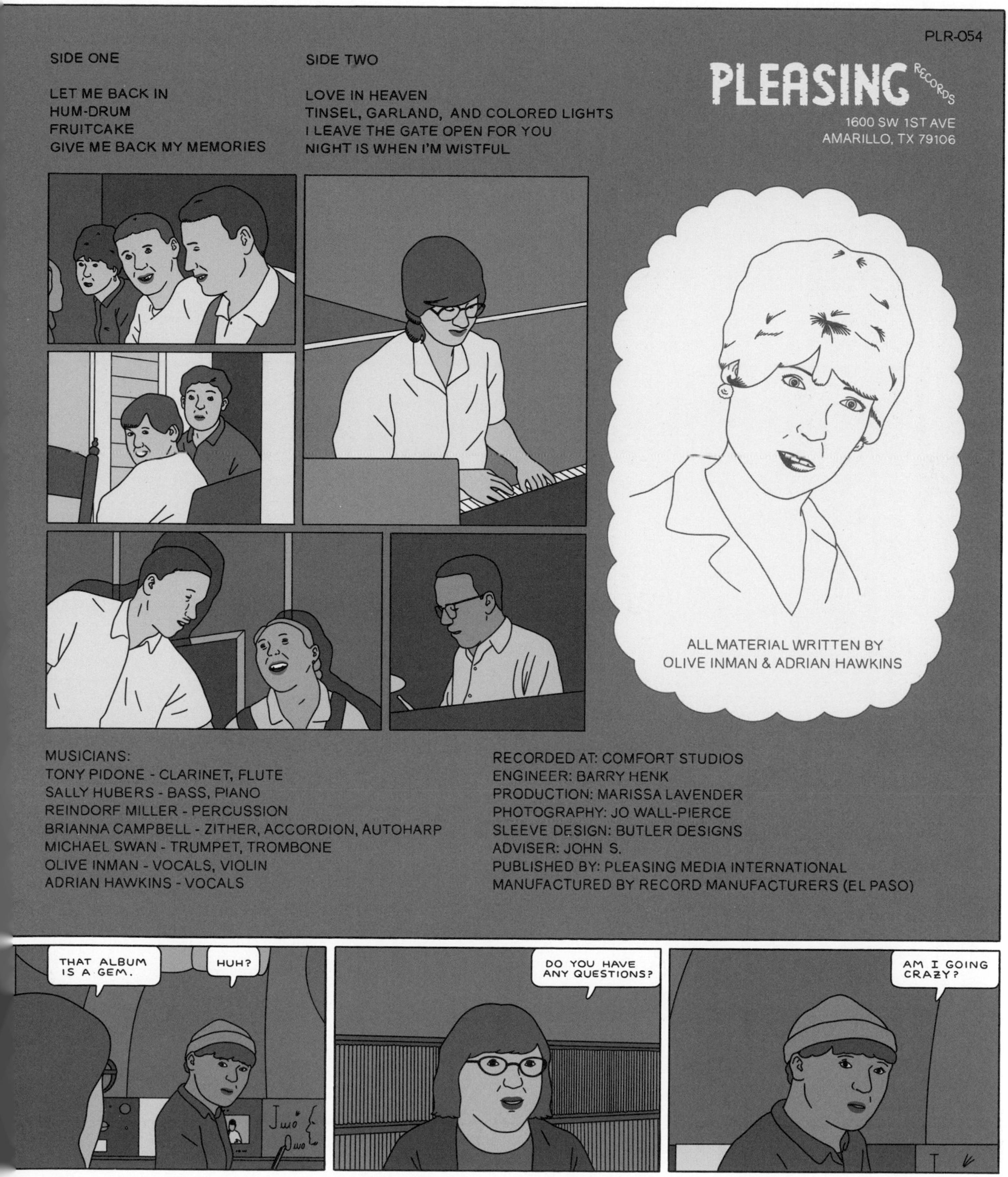
PLR-054
SIDE ONE
LET ME BACK IN
HUM-DRUM
FRUITCAKE
GIVE ME BACK MY MEMORIES
SIDE TWO
LOVE IN HEAVEN
TINSEL, GARLAND, AND COLORED LIGHTS
I LEAVE THE GATE OPEN FOR YOU
NIGHT IS WHEN I'M WISTFUL
PLEASING RECORDS
1600 SW 1ST AVE
AMARILLO, TX 79106
ALL MATERIAL WRITTEN BY
OLIVE INMAN & ADRIAN HAWKINS
MUSICIANS:
TONY PIDONE - CLARINET, FLUTE
SALLY HUBERS - BASS, PIANO
REINDORF MILLER - PERCUSSION
BRIANNA CAMPBELL - ZITHER, ACCORDION, AUTOHARP
MICHAEL SWAN - TRUMPET, TROMBONE
OLIVE INMAN - VOCALS, VIOLIN
ADRIAN HAWKINS - VOCALS
RECORDED AT: COMFORT STUDIOS
ENGINEER: BARRY HENK
PRODUCTION: MARISSA LAVENDER
PHOTOGRAPHY: JO WALL-PIERCE
SLEEVE DESIGN: BUTLER DESIGNS
ADVISER: JOHN S.
PUBLISHED BY: PLEASING MEDIA INTERNATIONAL
MANUFACTURED BY RECORD MANUFACTURERS (EL PASO)
THAT ALBUM IS A GEM.
HUH?
DO YOU HAVE ANY QUESTIONS?
AM I GOING CRAZY?

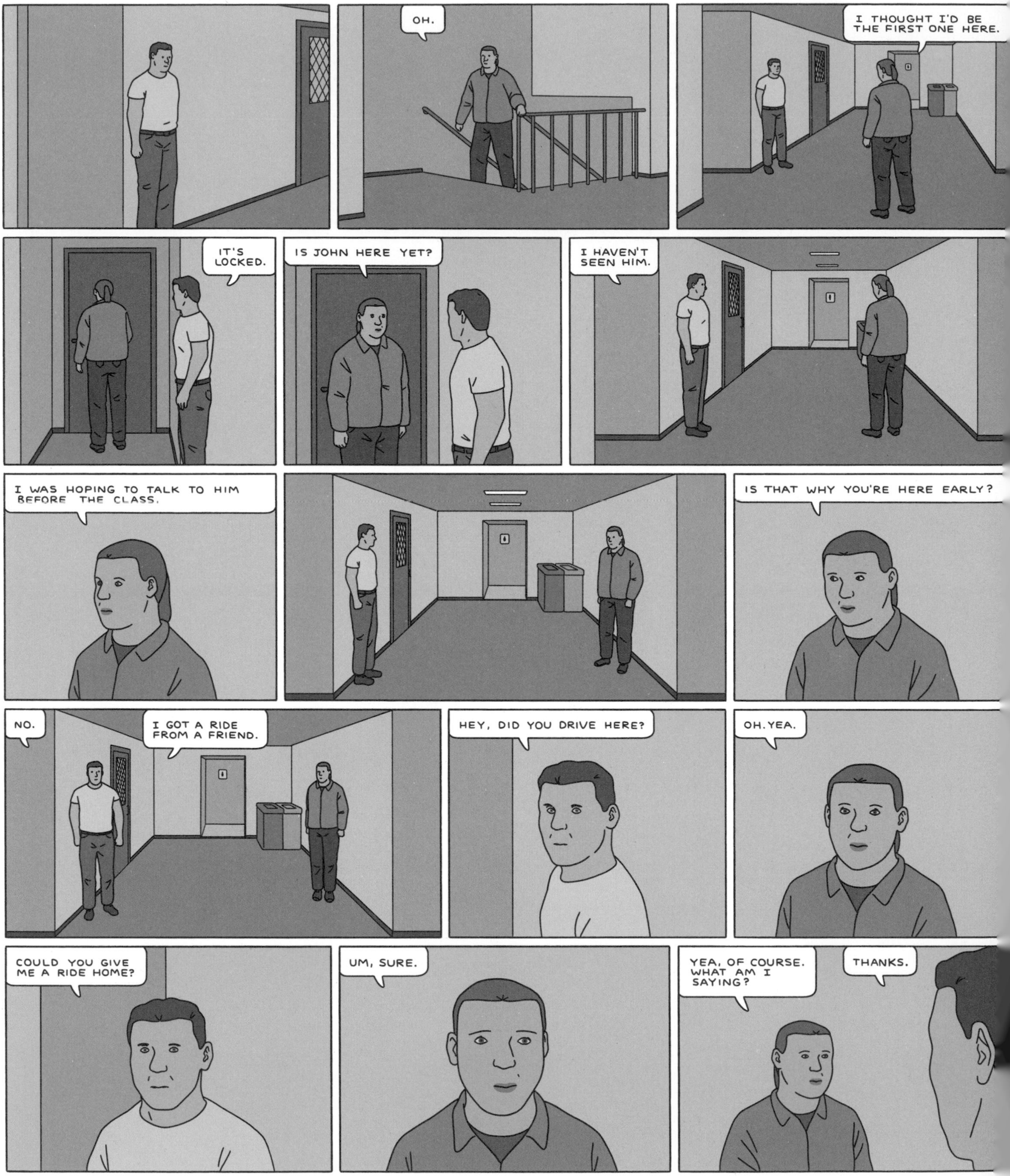
OH.
I THOUGHT I'D BE THE FIRST ONE HERE.
IT'S LOCKED.
IS JOHN HERE YET?
I HAVEN'T SEEN HIM.
I WAS HOPING TO TALK TO HIM BEFORE THE CLASS.
IS THAT WHY YOU'RE HERE EARLY?
NO.
I GOT A RIDE FROM A FRIEND.
HEY, DID YOU DRIVE HERE?
OH. YEA.
COULD YOU GIVE ME A RIDE HOME?
UM, SURE.
YEA, OF COURSE. WHAT AM I SAYING?
THANKS.

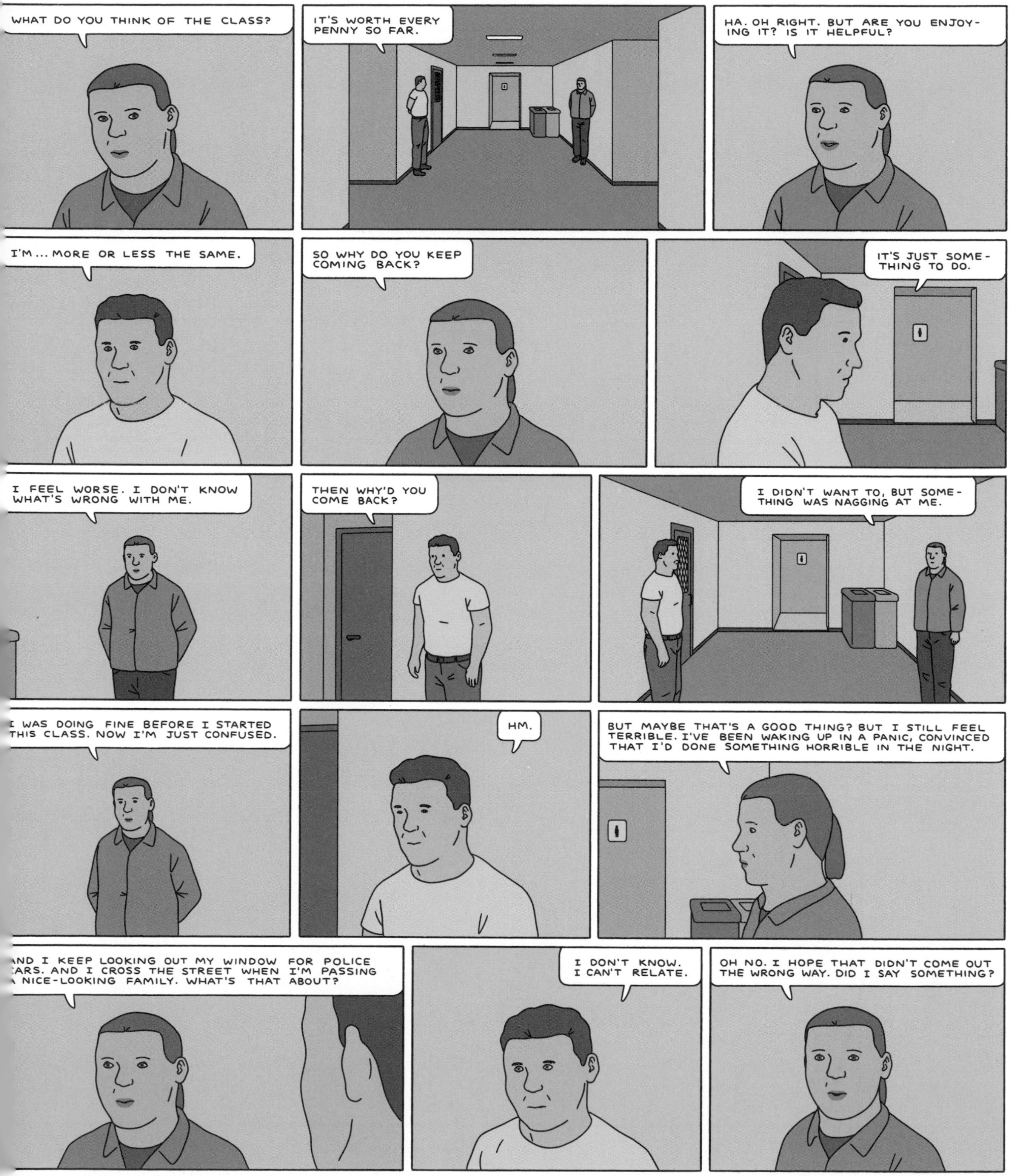
WHAT DO YOU THINK OF THE CLASS?
IT'S WORTH EVERY PENNY SO FAR.
HA. OH RIGHT. BUT ARE YOU ENJOYING IT? IS IT HELPFUL?
I'M... MORE OR LESS THE SAME.
SO WHY DO YOU KEEP COMING BACK?
IT'S JUST SOMETHING TO DO.
I FEEL WORSE. I DON'T KNOW WHAT'S WRONG WITH ME.
THEN WHY'D YOU COME BACK?
I DIDN'T WANT TO, BUT SOMETHING WAS NAGGING AT ME.
I WAS DOING FINE BEFORE I STARTED THIS CLASS. NOW I'M JUST CONFUSED.
HM.
BUT MAYBE THAT'S A GOOD THING? BUT I STILL FEEL TERRIBLE. I'VE BEEN WAKING UP IN A PANIC, CONVINCED THAT I'D DONE SOMETHING HORRIBLE IN THE NIGHT.
AND I KEEP LOOKING OUT MY WINDOW FOR POLICE CARS. AND I CROSS THE STREET WHEN I'M PASSING A NICE-LOOKING FAMILY. WHAT'S THAT ABOUT?
I DON'T KNOW. I CAN'T RELATE.
OH NO. I HOPE THAT DIDN'T COME OUT THE WRONG WAY. DID I SAY SOMETHING?

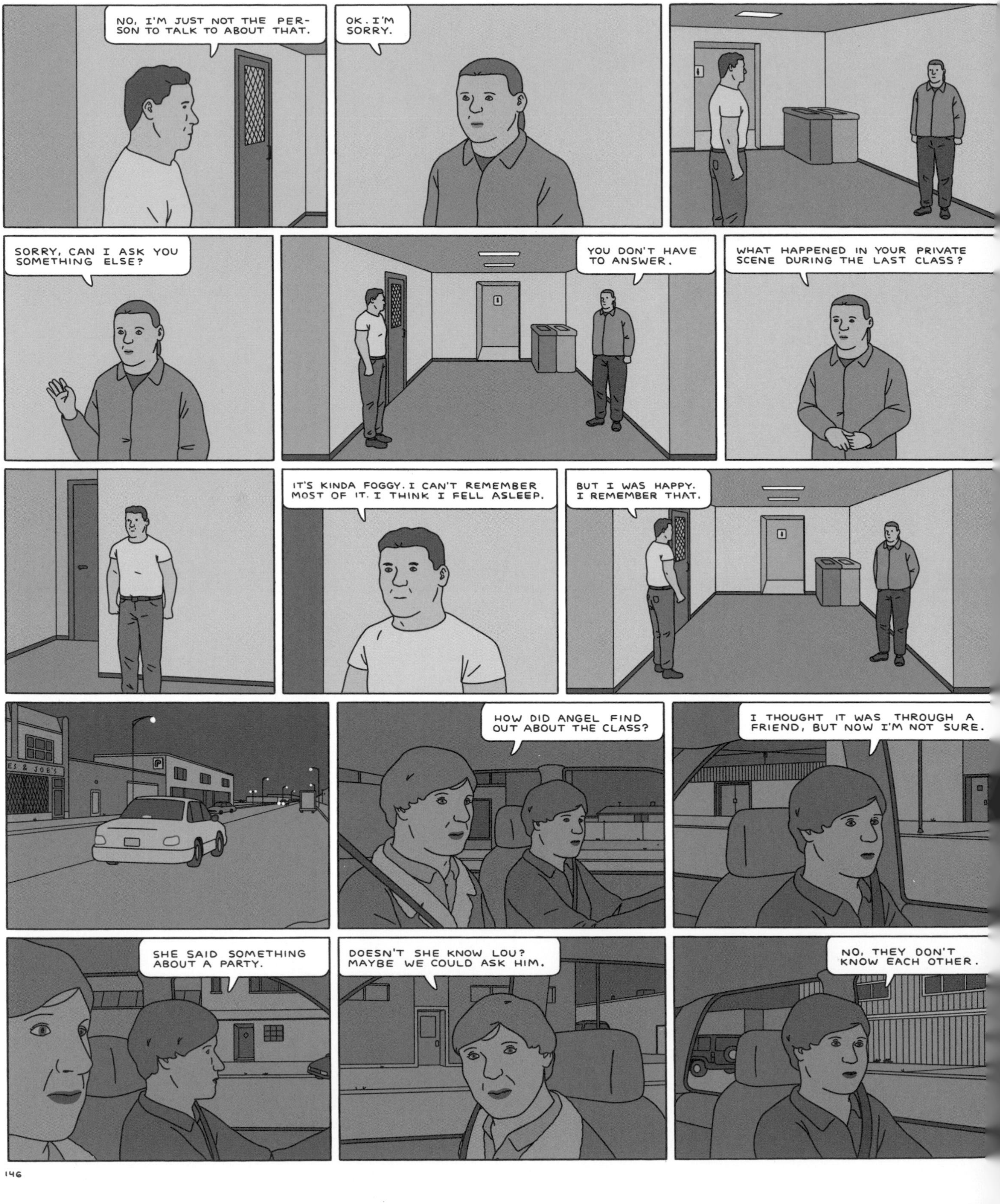
NO, I'M JUST NOT THE PERSON TO TALK TO ABOUT THAT.
OK. I'M SORRY.
SORRY, CAN I ASK YOU SOMETHING ELSE?
YOU DON'T HAVE TO ANSWER.
WHAT HAPPENED IN YOUR PRIVATE SCENE DURING THE LAST CLASS?
IT'S KINDA FOGGY. I CAN'T REMEMBER MOST OF IT. I THINK I FELL ASLEEP.
BUT I WAS HAPPY. I REMEMBER THAT.
ES & JOE'S
HOW DID ANGEL FIND OUT ABOUT THE CLASS?
I THOUGHT IT WAS THROUGH A FRIEND, BUT NOW I'M NOT SURE.
SHE SAID SOMETHING ABOUT A PARTY.
DOESN'T SHE KNOW LOU? MAYBE WE COULD ASK HIM.
NO, THEY DON'T KNOW EACH OTHER.

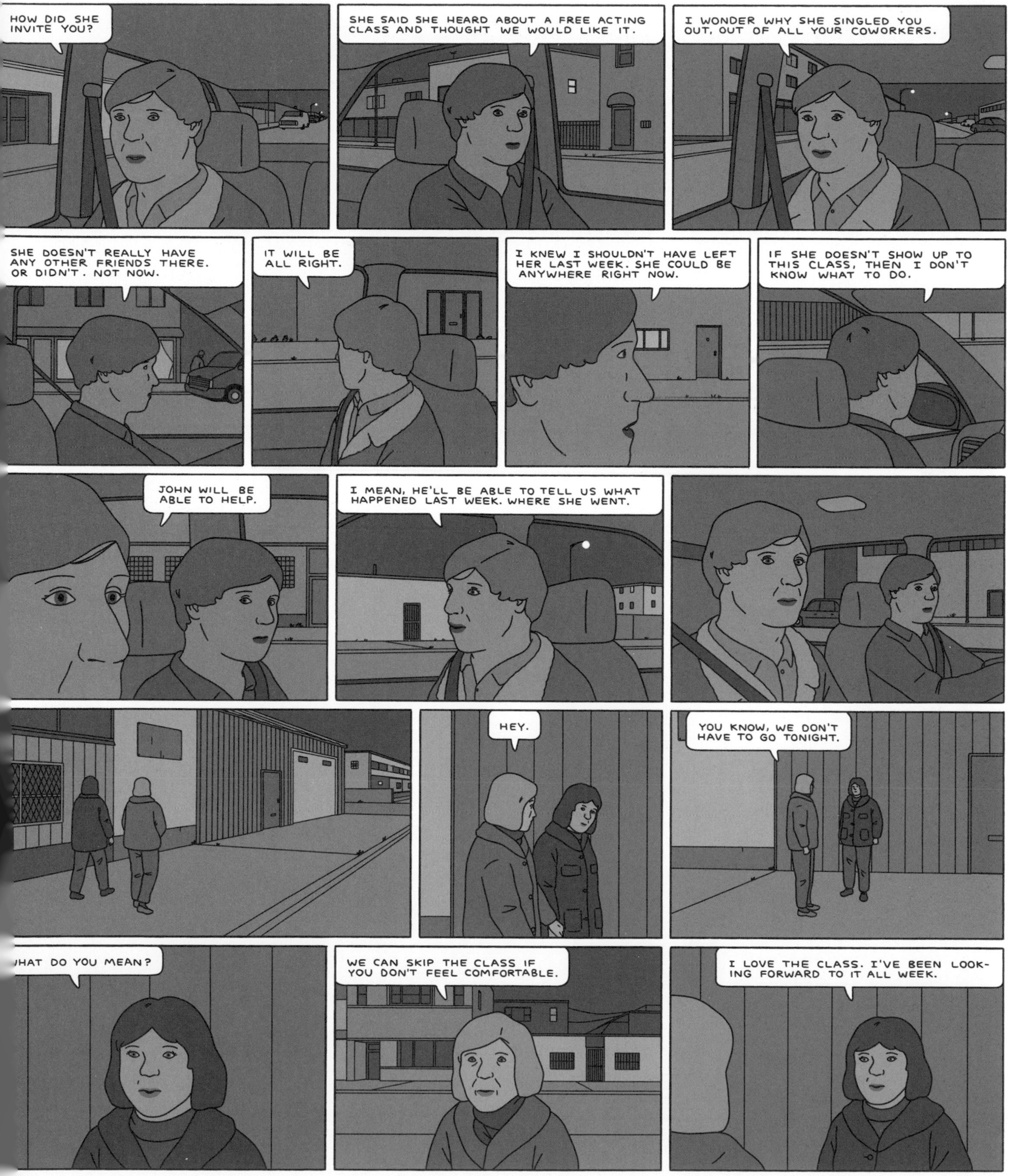
HOW DID SHE INVITE YOU?
SHE SAID SHE HEARD ABOUT A FREE ACTING CLASS AND THOUGHT WE WOULD LIKE IT.
I WONDER WHY SHE SINGLED YOU OUT, OUT OF ALL YOUR COWORKERS.
SHE DOESN'T REALLY HAVE ANY OTHER FRIENDS THERE. OR DIDN'T. NOT NOW.
IT WILL BE ALL RIGHT.
I KNEW I SHOULDN'T HAVE LEFT HER LAST WEEK. SHE COULD BE ANYWHERE RIGHT NOW.
IF SHE DOESN'T SHOW UP TO THIS CLASS, THEN I DON'T KNOW WHAT TO DO.
JOHN WILL BE ABLE TO HELP.
I MEAN, HE'LL BE ABLE TO TELL US WHAT HAPPENED LAST WEEK. WHERE SHE WENT.
HEY.
YOU KNOW, WE DON'T HAVE TO GO TONIGHT.
WHAT DO YOU MEAN?
WE CAN SKIP THE CLASS IF YOU DON'T FEEL COMFORTABLE.
I LOVE THE CLASS. I'VE BEEN LOOKING FORWARD TO IT ALL WEEK.

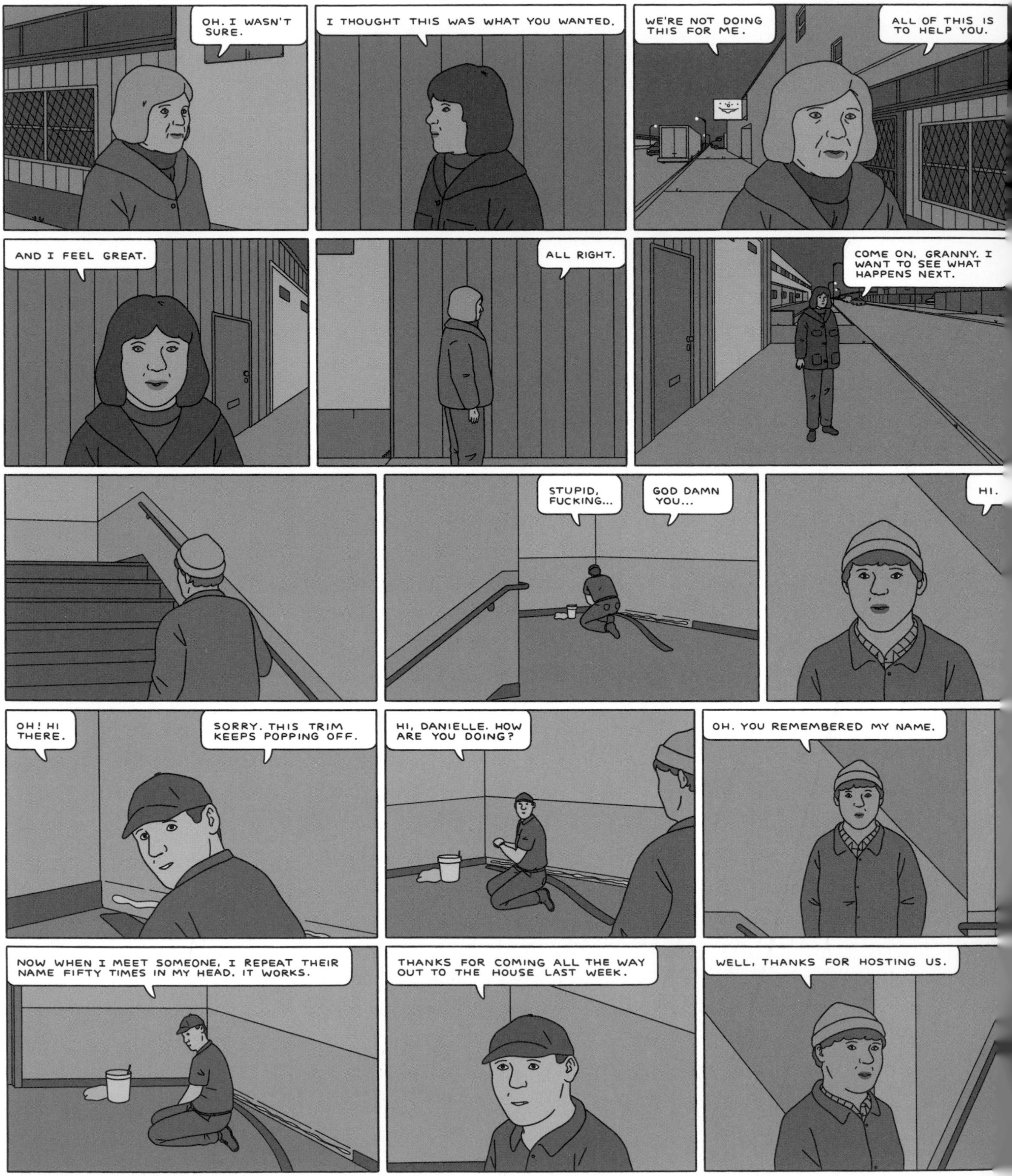
OH. I WASN'T SURE.
I THOUGHT THIS WAS WHAT YOU WANTED.
WE'RE NOT DOING THIS FOR ME.
ALL OF THIS IS TO HELP YOU.
AND I FEEL GREAT.
ALL RIGHT.
COME ON, GRANNY. I WANT TO SEE WHAT HAPPENS NEXT.
STUPID, FUCKING...
GOD DAMN YOU...
HI.
OH! HI THERE.
SORRY. THIS TRIM KEEPS POPPING OFF.
HI, DANIELLE. HOW ARE YOU DOING?
OH. YOU REMEMBERED MY NAME.
NOW WHEN I MEET SOMEONE, I REPEAT THEIR NAME FIFTY TIMES IN MY HEAD. IT WORKS.
THANKS FOR COMING ALL THE WAY OUT TO THE HOUSE LAST WEEK.
WELL, THANKS FOR HOSTING US.

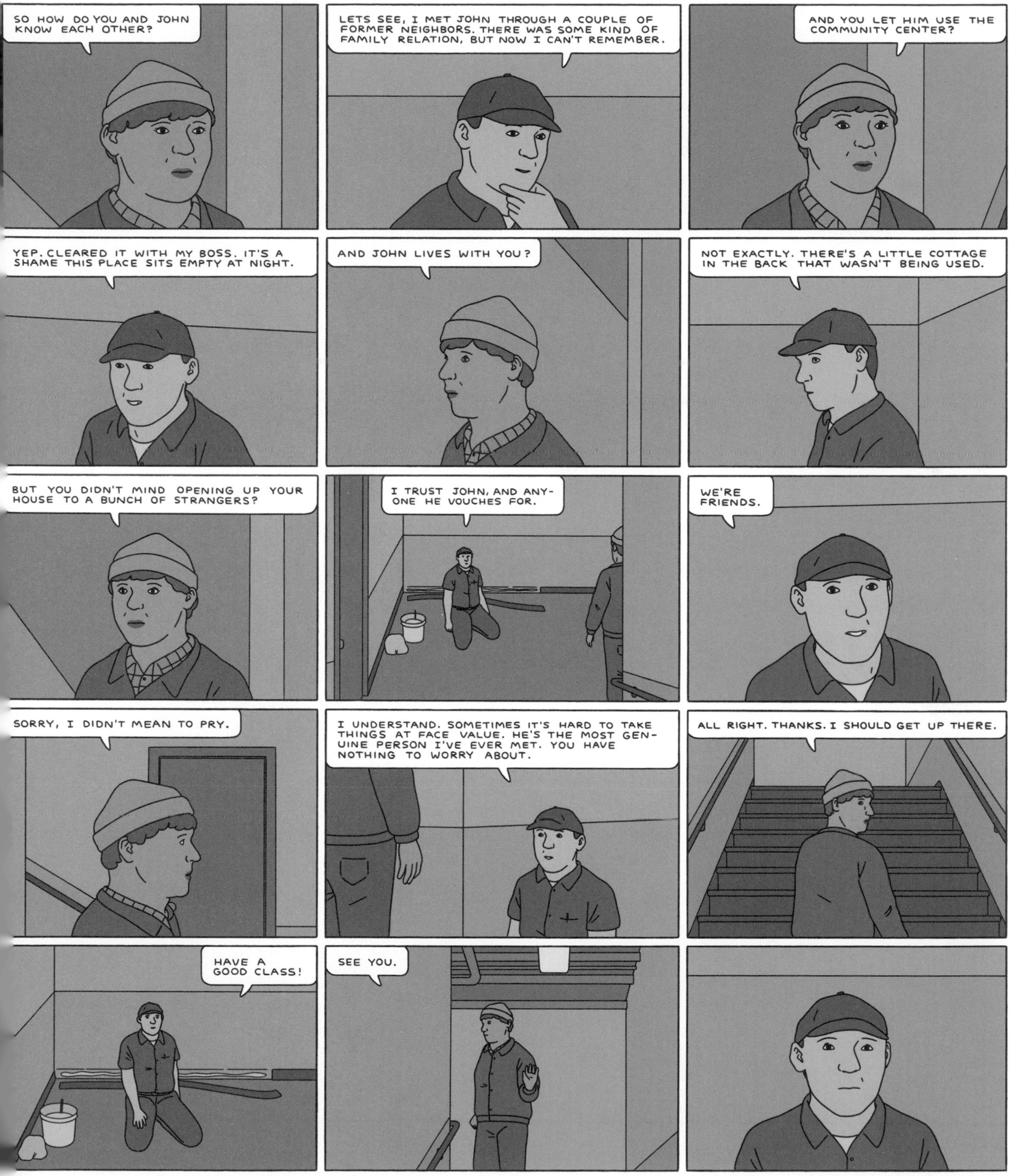
SO HOW DO YOU AND JOHN KNOW EACH OTHER?
LETS SEE, I MET JOHN THROUGH A COUPLE OF FORMER NEIGHBORS. THERE WAS SOME KIND OF FAMILY RELATION, BUT NOW I CAN'T REMEMBER.
AND YOU LET HIM USE THE COMMUNITY CENTER?
YEP. CLEARED IT WITH MY BOSS. IT'S A SHAME THIS PLACE SITS EMPTY AT NIGHT.
AND JOHN LIVES WITH YOU?
NOT EXACTLY. THERE'S A LITTLE COTTAGE IN THE BACK THAT WASN'T BEING USED.
BUT YOU DIDN'T MIND OPENING UP YOUR HOUSE TO A BUNCH OF STRANGERS?
I TRUST JOHN, AND ANYONE HE VOUCHES FOR.
WE'RE FRIENDS.
SORRY, I DIDN'T MEAN TO PRY.
I UNDERSTAND. SOMETIMES IT'S HARD TO TAKE THINGS AT FACE VALUE. HE'S THE MOST GENUINE PERSON I'VE EVER MET. YOU HAVE NOTHING TO WORRY ABOUT.
ALL RIGHT. THANKS. I SHOULD GET UP THERE.
HAVE A GOOD CLASS!
SEE YOU.

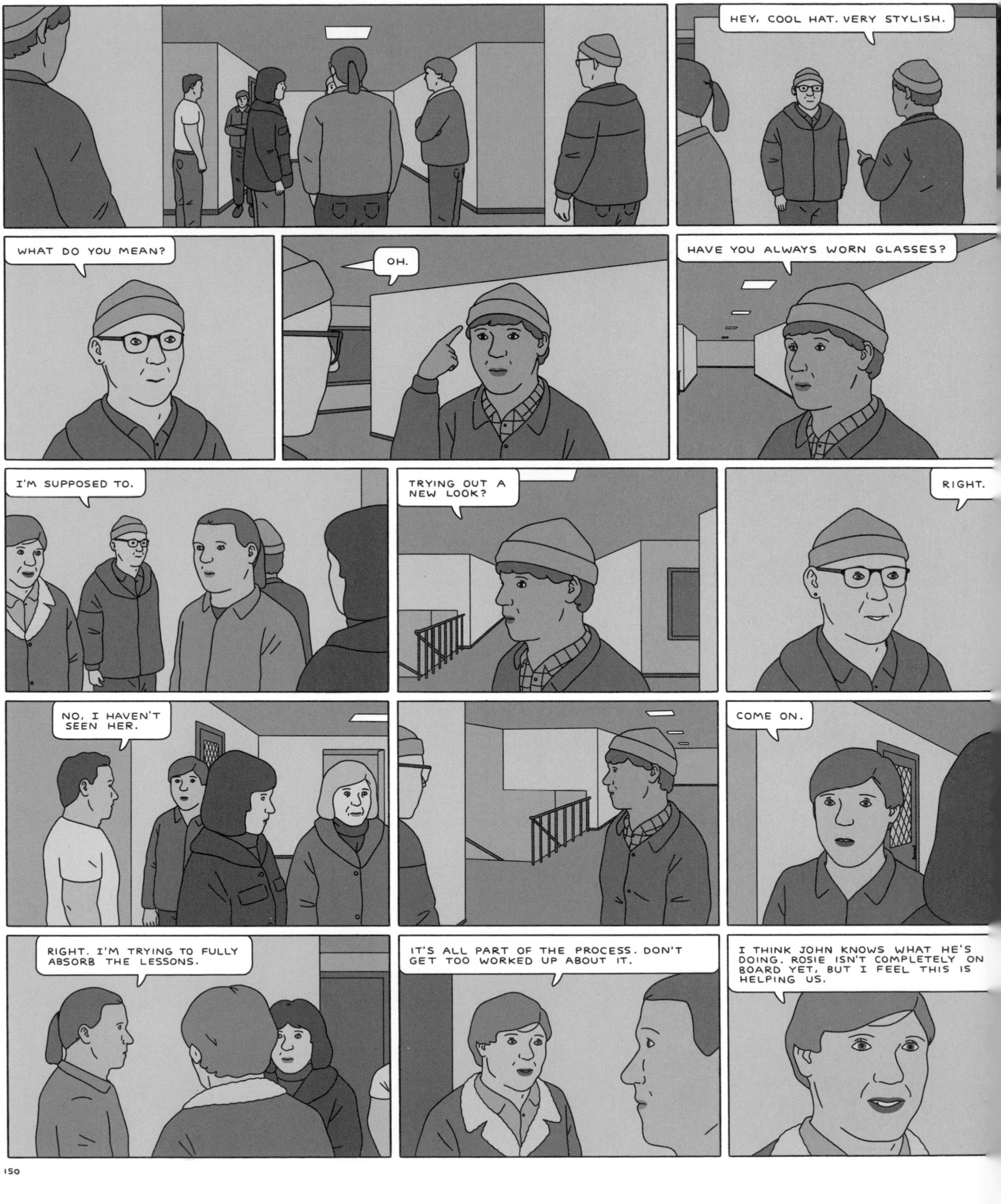
HEY, COOL HAT. VERY STYLISH.
WHAT DO YOU MEAN?
OH.
HAVE YOU ALWAYS WORN GLASSES?
I'M SUPPOSED TO.
TRYING OUT A NEW LOOK?
RIGHT.
NO, I HAVEN'T SEEN HER.
COME ON.
RIGHT. I'M TRYING TO FULLY ABSORB THE LESSONS.
IT'S ALL PART OF THE PROCESS. DON'T GET TOO WORKED UP ABOUT IT.
I THINK JOHN KNOWS WHAT HE'S DOING. ROSIE ISN'T COMPLETELY ON BOARD YET, BUT I FEEL THIS IS HELPING US.

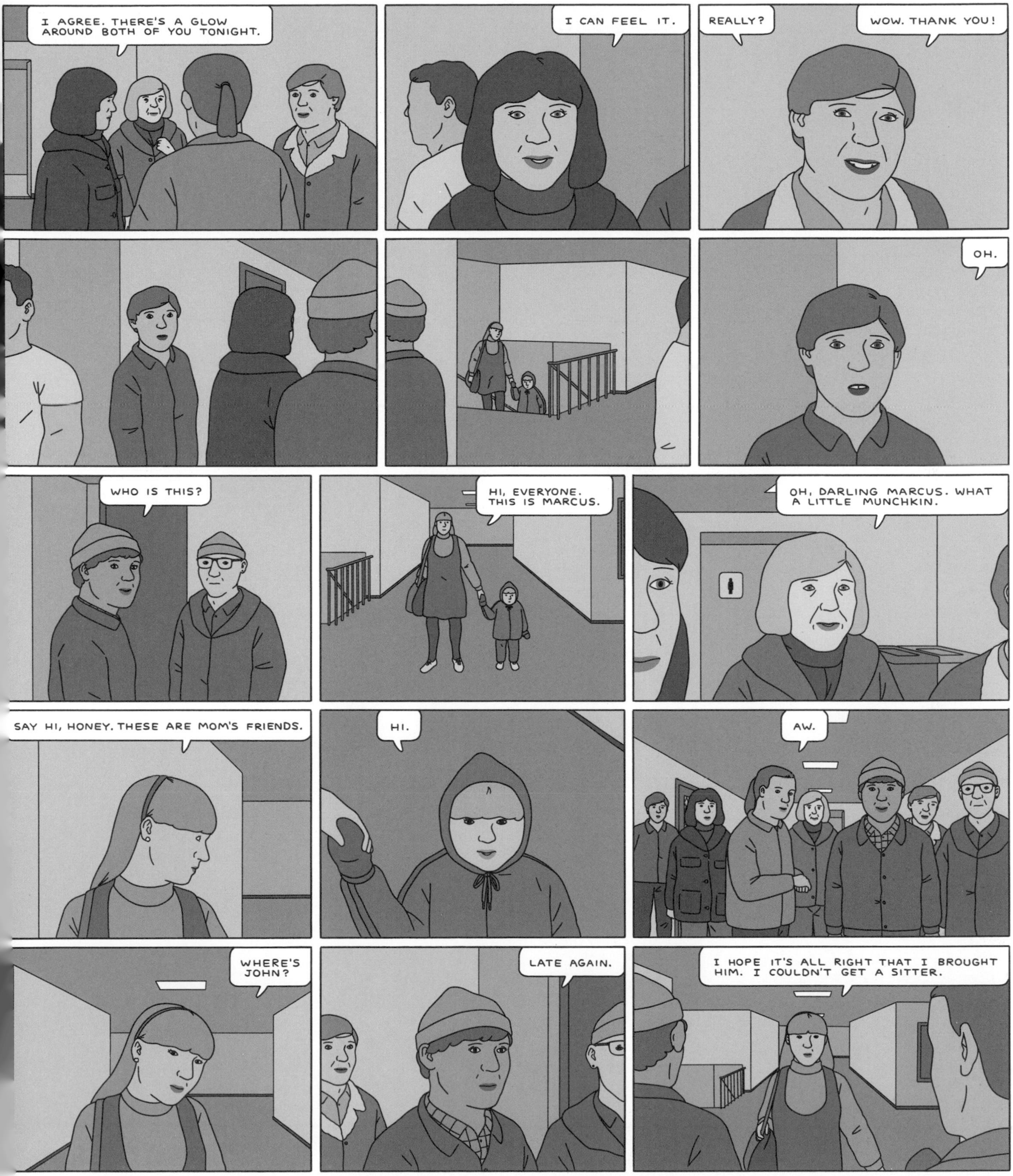
I AGREE. THERE'S A GLOW AROUND BOTH OF YOU TONIGHT.
I CAN FEEL IT.
REALLY?
WOW. THANK YOU!
OH.
WHO IS THIS?
HI, EVERYONE. THIS IS MARCUS.
OH, DARLING MARCUS. WHAT A LITTLE MUNCHKIN.
SAY HI, HONEY. THESE ARE MOM'S FRIENDS.
HI.
AW.
WHERE'S JOHN?
LATE AGAIN.
I HOPE IT'S ALL RIGHT THAT I BROUGHT HIM. I COULDN'T GET A SITTER.

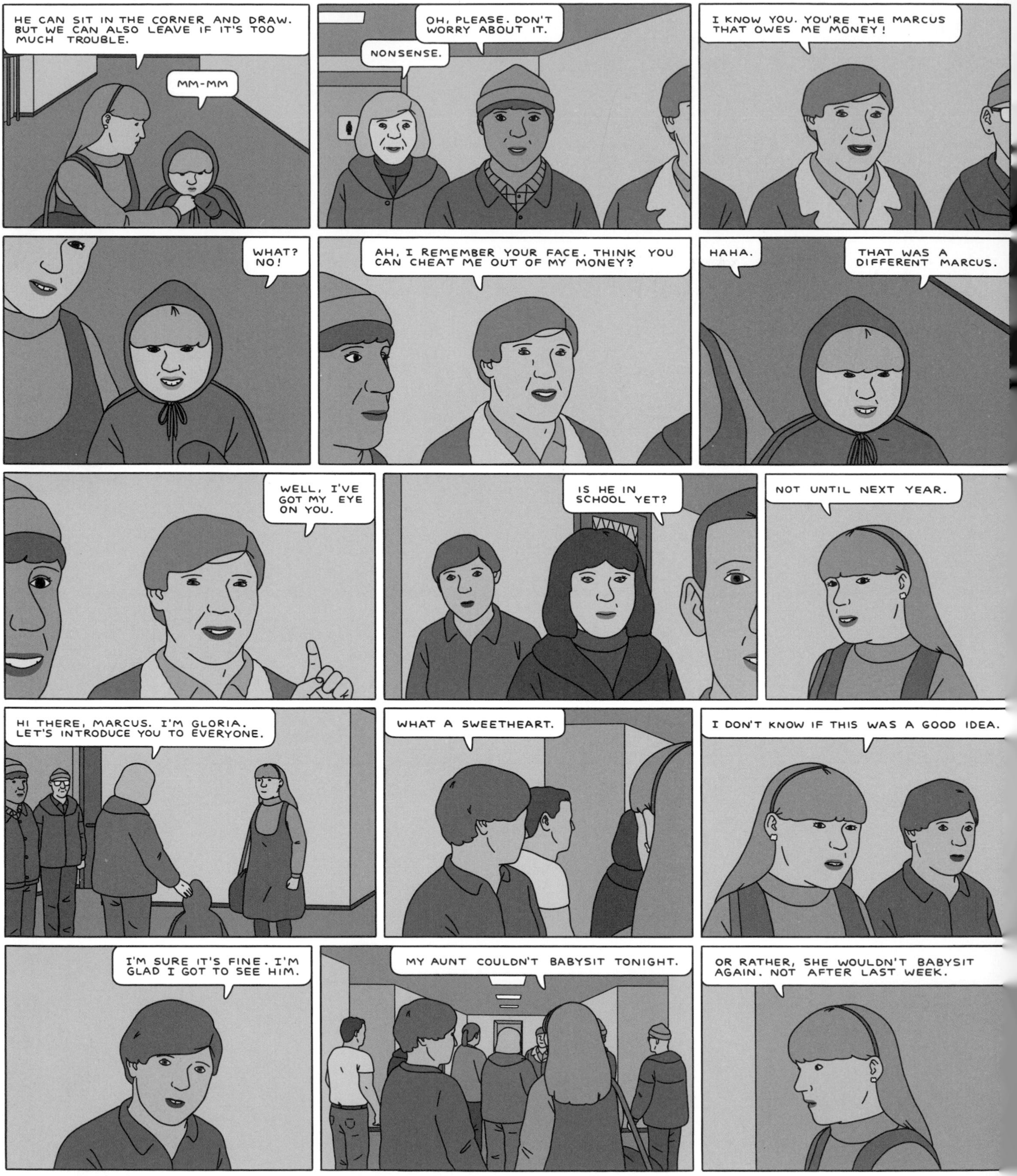
HE CAN SIT IN THE CORNER AND DRAW. BUT WE CAN ALSO LEAVE IF IT'S TOO MUCH TROUBLE.
MM-MM
OH, PLEASE. DON'T WORRY ABOUT IT.
NONSENSE.
I KNOW YOU. YOU'RE THE MARCUS THAT OWES ME MONEY!
WHAT? NO!
AH, I REMEMBER YOUR FACE. THINK YOU CAN CHEAT ME OUT OF MY MONEY?
HAHA.
THAT WAS A DIFFERENT MARCUS.
WELL, I'VE GOT MY EYE ON YOU.
IS HE IN SCHOOL YET?
NOT UNTIL NEXT YEAR.
HI THERE, MARCUS. I'M GLORIA. LET'S INTRODUCE YOU TO EVERYONE.
WHAT A SWEETHEART.
I DON'T KNOW IF THIS WAS A GOOD IDEA.
I'M SURE IT'S FINE. I'M GLAD I GOT TO SEE HIM.
MY AUNT COULDN'T BABYSIT TONIGHT.
OR RATHER, SHE WOULDN'T BABYSIT AGAIN. NOT AFTER LAST WEEK.

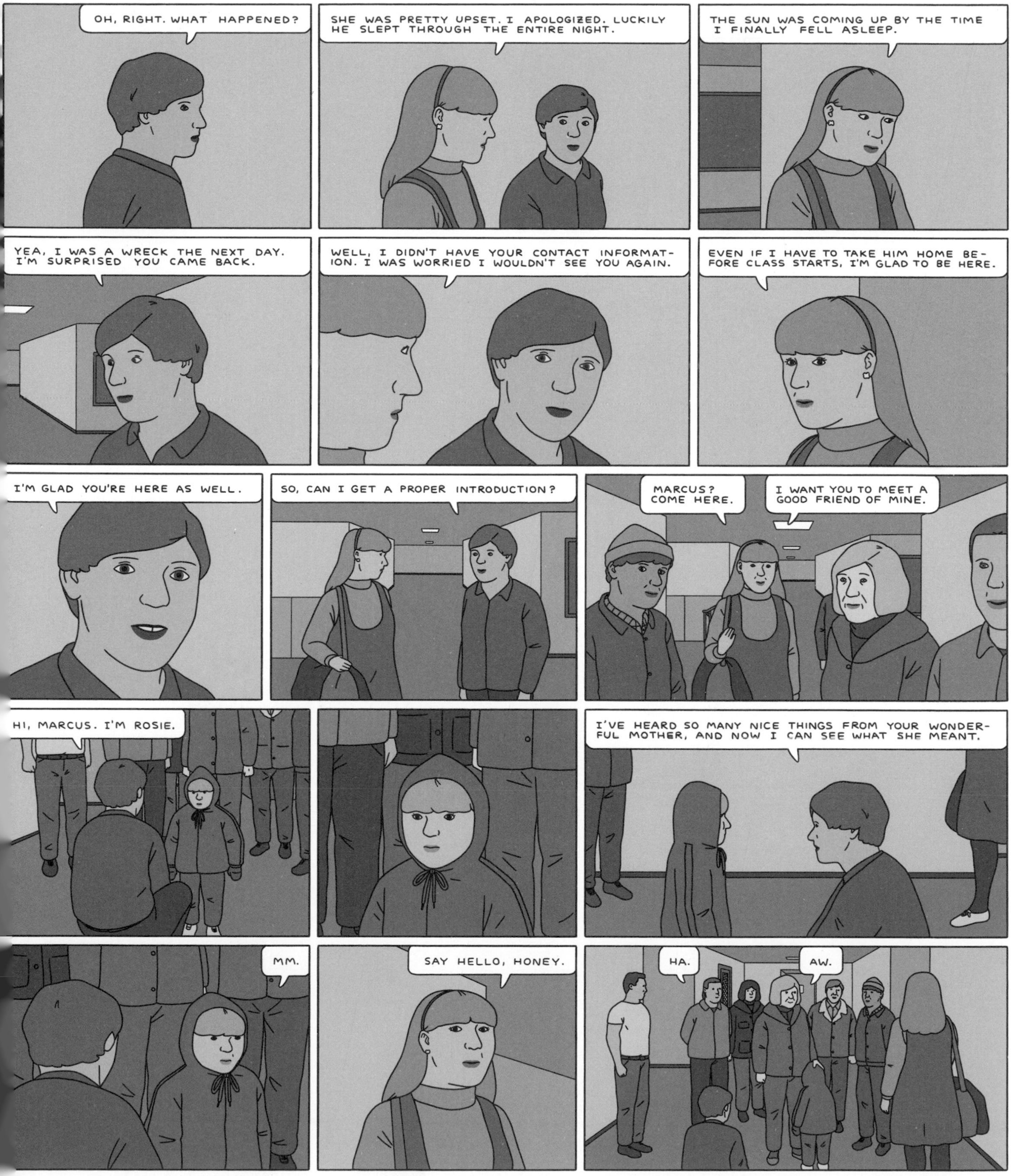

OH, RIGHT. WHAT HAPPENED?
SHE WAS PRETTY UPSET. I APOLOGIZED. LUCKILY HE SLEPT THROUGH THE ENTIRE NIGHT.
THE SUN WAS COMING UP BY THE TIME I FINALLY FELL ASLEEP.
YEA, I WAS A WRECK THE NEXT DAY. I'M SURPRISED YOU CAME BACK.
WELL, I DIDN'T HAVE YOUR CONTACT INFORMAT-ION. I WAS WORRIED I WOULDN'T SEE YOU AGAIN.
EVEN IF I HAVE TO TAKE HIM HOME BE-FORE CLASS STARTS, I'M GLAD TO BE HERE.
I'M GLAD YOU'RE HERE AS WELL.
SO, CAN I GET A PROPER INTRODUCTION?
MARCUS? COME HERE.
I WANT YOU TO MEET A GOOD FRIEND OF MINE.
HI, MARCUS. I'M ROSIE.
I'VE HEARD SO MANY NICE THINGS FROM YOUR WONDER-FUL MOTHER, AND NOW I CAN SEE WHAT SHE MEANT.
MM.
SAY HELLO, HONEY.
HA.
AW.

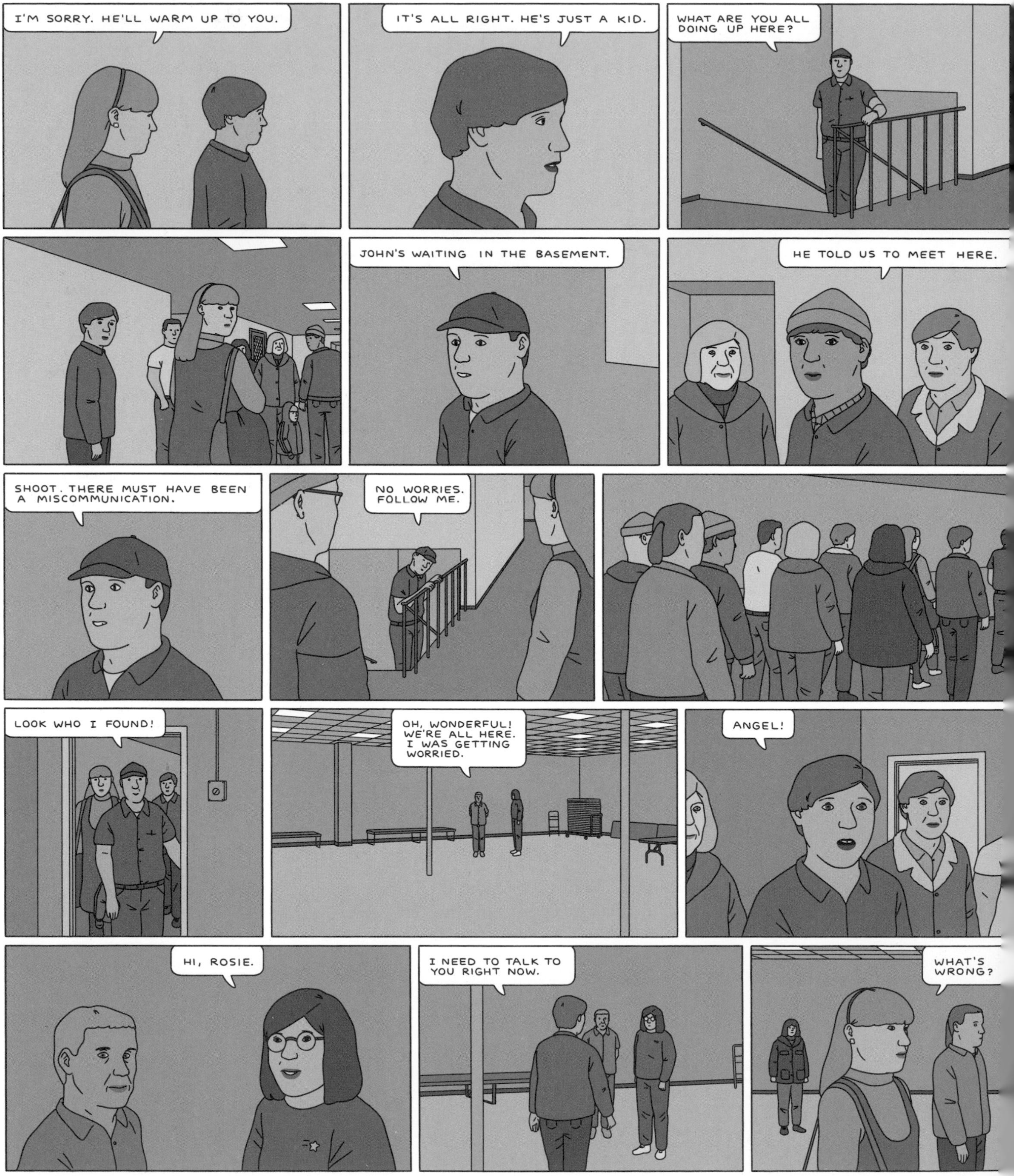
I'M SORRY. HE'LL WARM UP TO YOU.
IT'S ALL RIGHT. HE'S JUST A KID.
WHAT ARE YOU ALL DOING UP HERE?
JOHN'S WAITING IN THE BASEMENT.
HE TOLD US TO MEET HERE.
SHOOT. THERE MUST HAVE BEEN A MISCOMMUNICATION.
NO WORRIES. FOLLOW ME.
LOOK WHO I FOUND!
OH, WONDERFUL! WE'RE ALL HERE. I WAS GETTING WORRIED.
ANGEL!
HI, ROSIE.
I NEED TO TALK TO YOU RIGHT NOW.
WHAT'S WRONG?

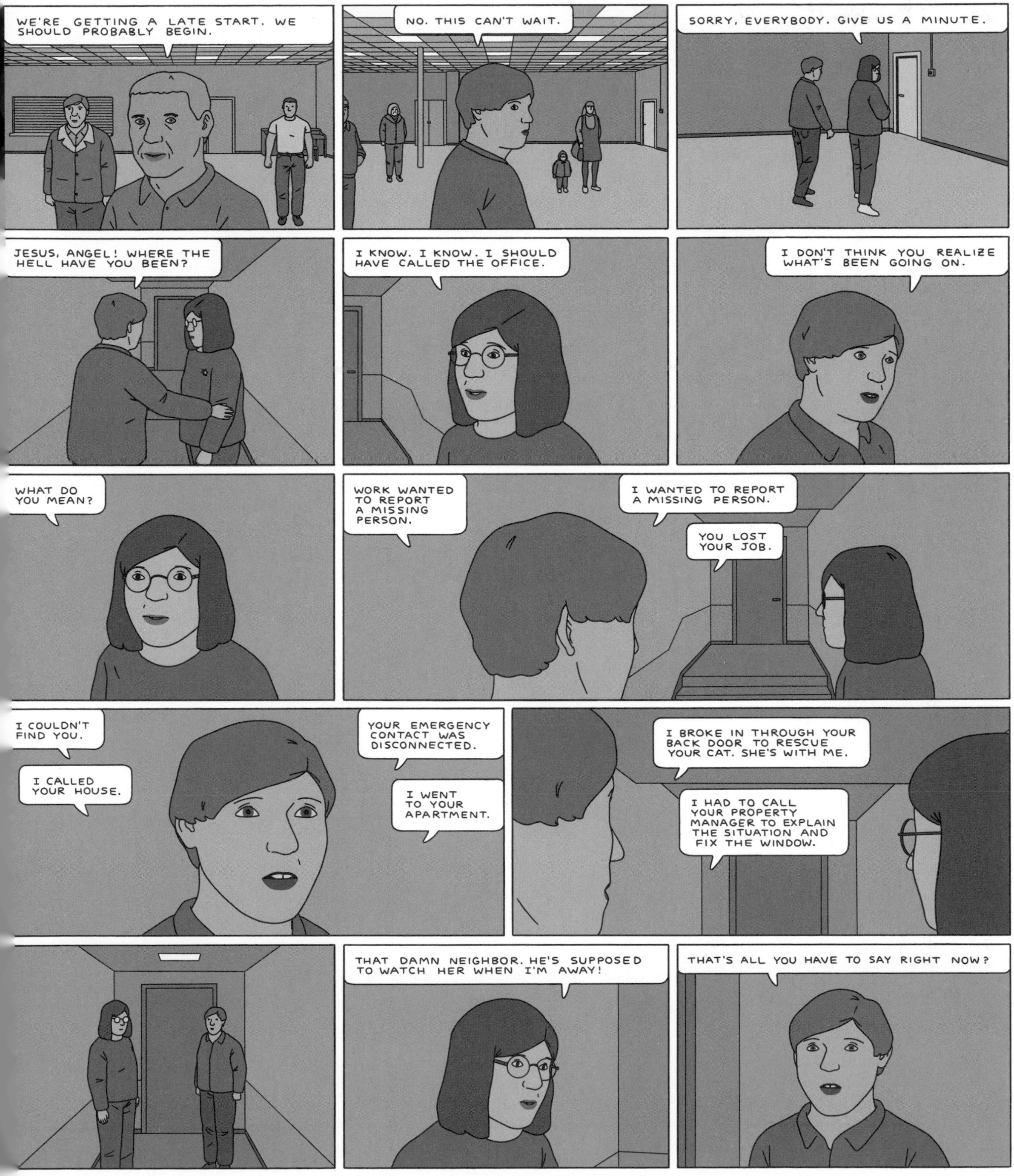

WE'RE GETTING A LATE START. WE SHOULD PROBABLY BEGIN.
NO. THIS CAN'T WAIT.
SORRY, EVERYBODY. GIVE US A MINUTE.
JESUS, ANGEL! WHERE THE HELL HAVE YOU BEEN?
I KNOW. I KNOW. I SHOULD HAVE CALLED THE OFFICE.
I DON'T THINK YOU REALIZE WHAT'S BEEN GOING ON.
WHAT DO YOU MEAN?
WORK WANTED TO REPORT A MISSING PERSON.
I WANTED TO REPORT A MISSING PERSON.
YOU LOST YOUR JOB.
I COULDN'T FIND YOU.
I CALLED YOUR HOUSE.
YOUR EMERGENCY CONTACT WAS DISCONNECTED.
I WENT TO YOUR APARTMENT.
I BROKE IN THROUGH YOUR BACK DOOR TO RESCUE YOUR CAT. SHE'S WITH ME.
I HAD TO CALL YOUR PROPERTY MANAGER TO EXPLAIN THE SITUATION AND FIX THE WINDOW.
THAT DAMN NEIGHBOR. HE'S SUPPOSED TO WATCH HER WHEN I'M AWAY!
THAT'S ALL YOU HAVE TO SAY RIGHT NOW?

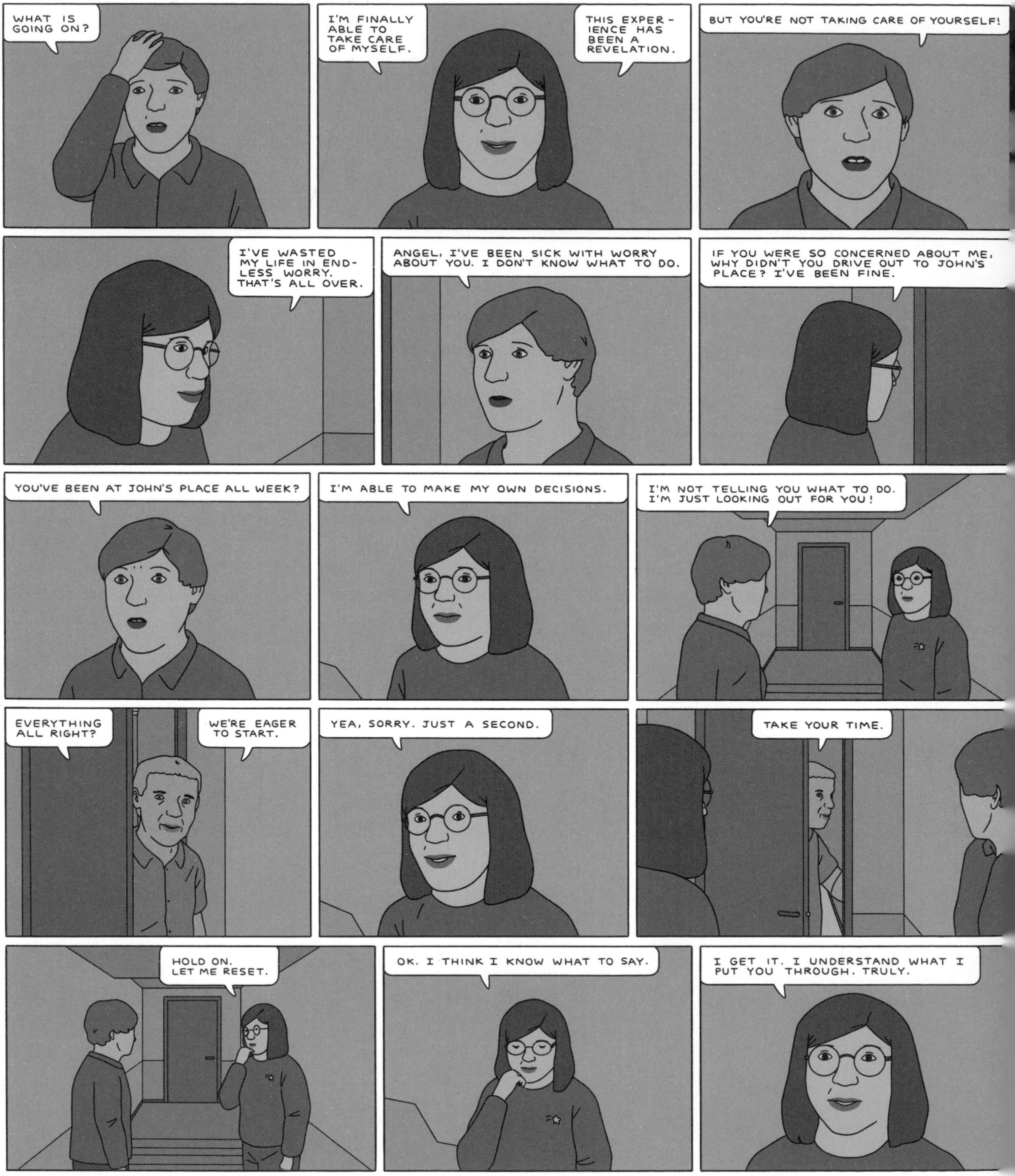
WHAT IS GOING ON?
I'M FINALLY ABLE TO TAKE CARE OF MYSELF.
THIS EXPERIENCE HAS BEEN A REVELATION.
BUT YOU'RE NOT TAKING CARE OF YOURSELF!
I'VE WASTED MY LIFE IN ENDLESS WORRY. THAT'S ALL OVER.
ANGEL, I'VE BEEN SICK WITH WORRY ABOUT YOU. I DON'T KNOW WHAT TO DO.
IF YOU WERE SO CONCERNED ABOUT ME, WHY DIDN'T YOU DRIVE OUT TO JOHN'S PLACE? I'VE BEEN FINE.
YOU'VE BEEN AT JOHN'S PLACE ALL WEEK?
I'M ABLE TO MAKE MY OWN DECISIONS.
I'M NOT TELLING YOU WHAT TO DO. I'M JUST LOOKING OUT FOR YOU!
EVERYTHING ALL RIGHT?
WE'RE EAGER TO START.
YEA, SORRY. JUST A SECOND.
TAKE YOUR TIME.
HOLD ON. LET ME RESET.
OK. I THINK I KNOW WHAT TO SAY.
I GET IT. I UNDERSTAND WHAT I PUT YOU THROUGH. TRULY.

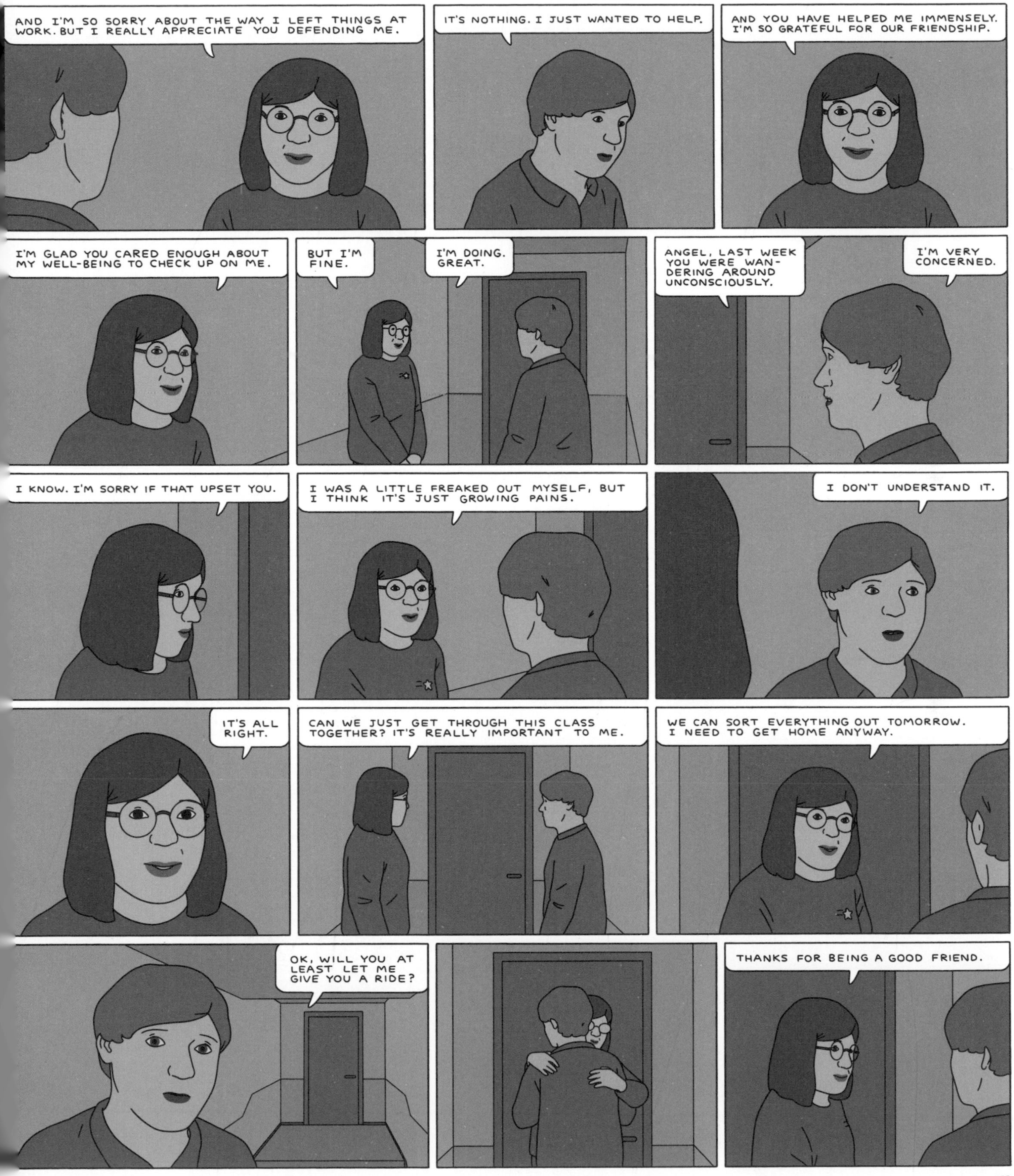
AND I'M SO SORRY ABOUT THE WAY I LEFT THINGS AT WORK. BUT I REALLY APPRECIATE YOU DEFENDING ME.
IT'S NOTHING. I JUST WANTED TO HELP.
AND YOU HAVE HELPED ME IMMENSELY. I'M SO GRATEFUL FOR OUR FRIENDSHIP.
I'M GLAD YOU CARED ENOUGH ABOUT MY WELL-BEING TO CHECK UP ON ME.
BUT I'M FINE.
I'M DOING. GREAT.
ANGEL, LAST WEEK YOU WERE WAN- DERING AROUND UNCONSCIOUSLY.
I'M VERY CONCERNED.
I KNOW. I'M SORRY IF THAT UPSET YOU.
I WAS A LITTLE FREAKED OUT MYSELF, BUT I THINK IT'S JUST GROWING PAINS.
I DON'T UNDERSTAND IT.
IT'S ALL RIGHT.
CAN WE JUST GET THROUGH THIS CLASS TOGETHER? IT'S REALLY IMPORTANT TO ME.
WE CAN SORT EVERYTHING OUT TOMORROW. I NEED TO GET HOME ANYWAY.
OK, WILL YOU AT LEAST LET ME GIVE YOU A RIDE?
THANKS FOR BEING A GOOD FRIEND.

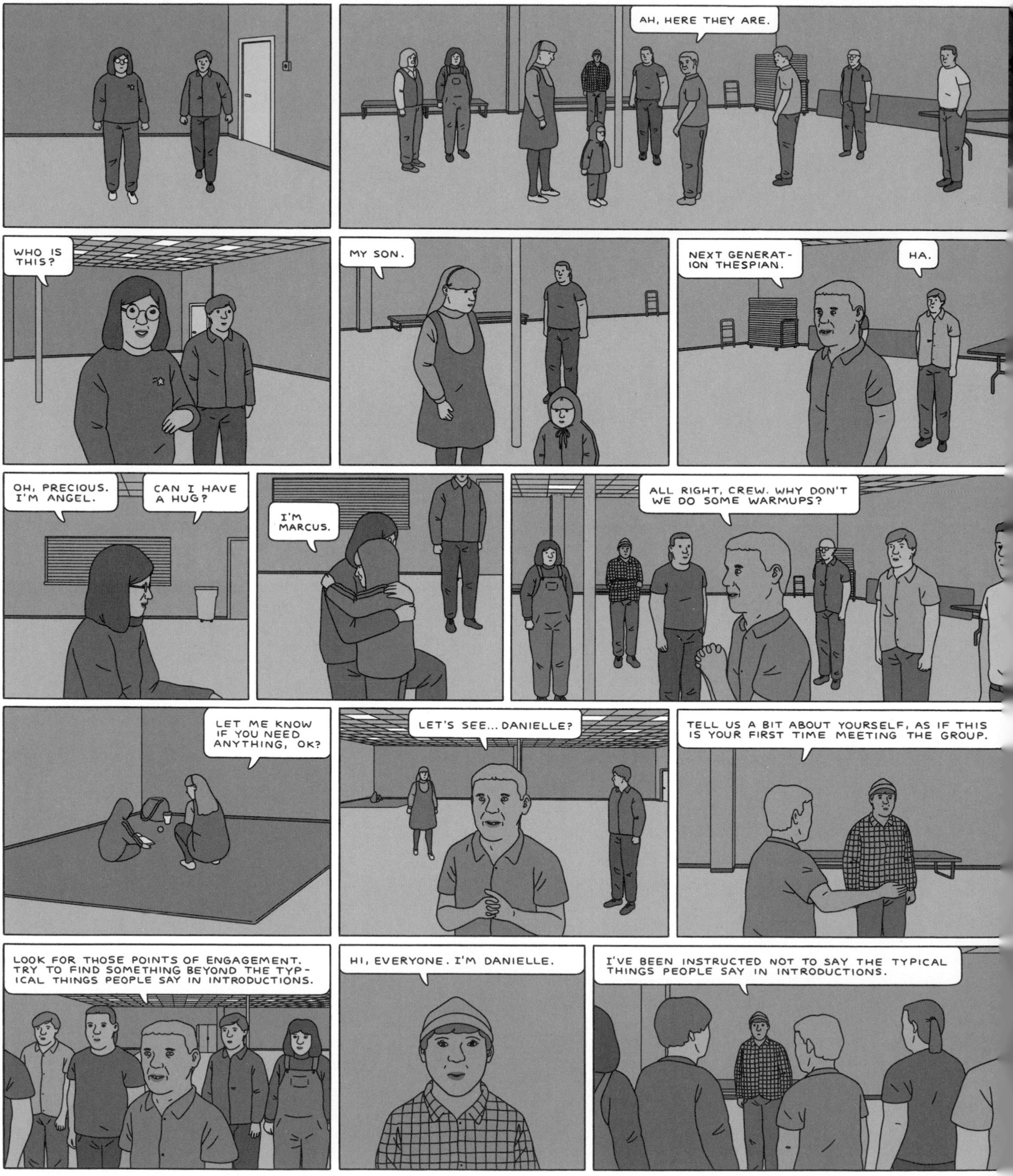
AH, HERE THEY ARE.
WHO IS THIS?
MY SON.
NEXT GENERATION THESPIAN.
HA.
OH, PRECIOUS. I'M ANGEL.
CAN I HAVE A HUG?
I'M MARCUS.
ALL RIGHT, CREW. WHY DON'T WE DO SOME WARMUPS?
LET ME KNOW IF YOU NEED ANYTHING, OK?
LET'S SEE... DANIELLE?
TELL US A BIT ABOUT YOURSELF, AS IF THIS IS YOUR FIRST TIME MEETING THE GROUP.
LOOK FOR THOSE POINTS OF ENGAGEMENT. TRY TO FIND SOMETHING BEYOND THE TYPICAL THINGS PEOPLE SAY IN INTRODUCTIONS.
HI, EVERYONE. I'M DANIELLE.
I'VE BEEN INSTRUCTED NOT TO SAY THE TYPICAL THINGS PEOPLE SAY IN INTRODUCTIONS.

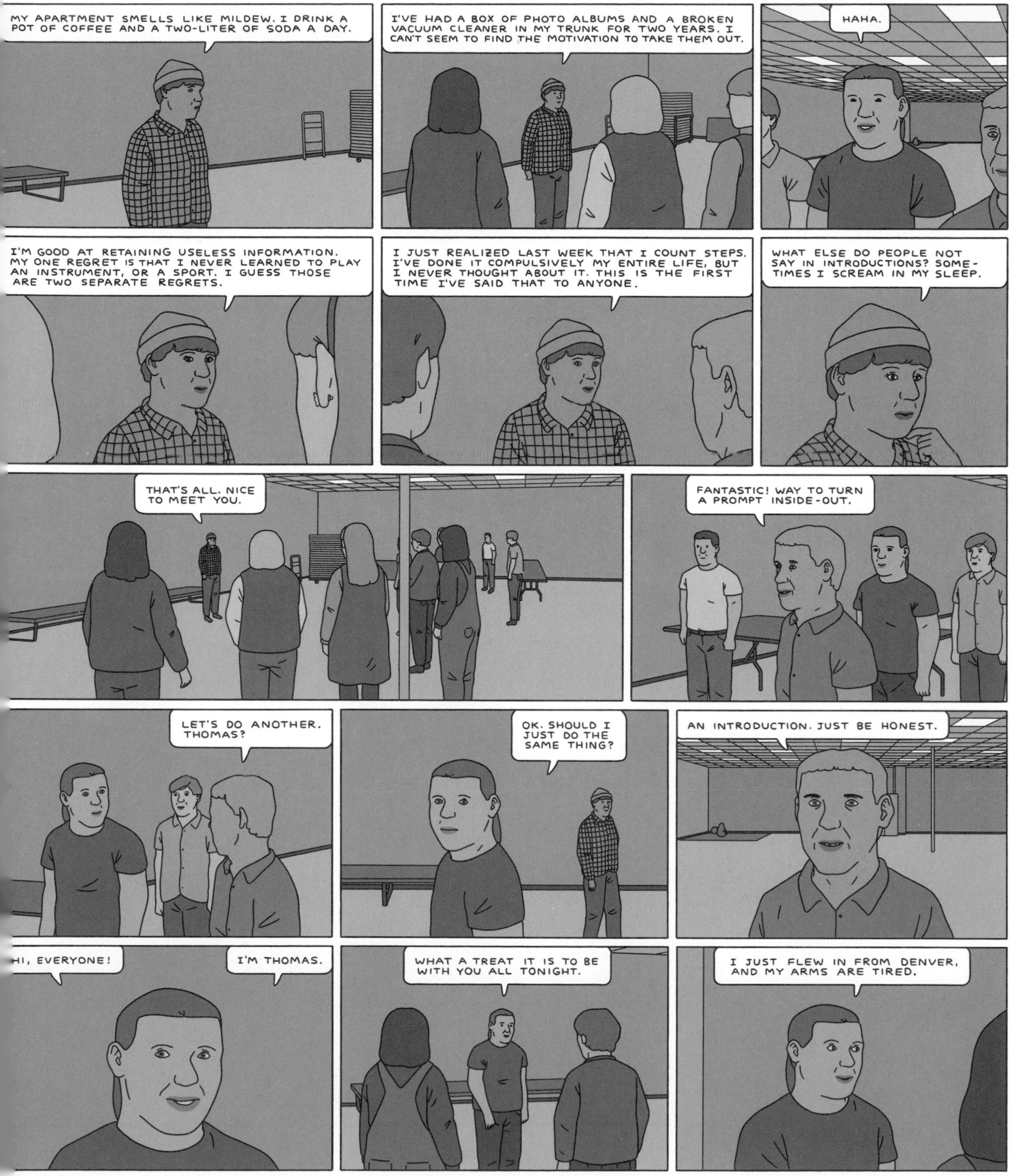
MY APARTMENT SMELLS LIKE MILDEW. I DRINK A POT OF COFFEE AND A TWO-LITER OF SODA A DAY.
I'VE HAD A BOX OF PHOTO ALBUMS AND A BROKEN VACUUM CLEANER IN MY TRUNK FOR TWO YEARS. I CAN'T SEEM TO FIND THE MOTIVATION TO TAKE THEM OUT.
HAHA.
I'M GOOD AT RETAINING USELESS INFORMATION. MY ONE REGRET IS THAT I NEVER LEARNED TO PLAY AN INSTRUMENT, OR A SPORT. I GUESS THOSE ARE TWO SEPARATE REGRETS.
I JUST REALIZED LAST WEEK THAT I COUNT STEPS. I'VE DONE IT COMPULSIVELY MY ENTIRE LIFE, BUT I NEVER THOUGHT ABOUT IT. THIS IS THE FIRST TIME I'VE SAID THAT TO ANYONE.
WHAT ELSE DO PEOPLE NOT SAY IN INTRODUCTIONS? SOMETIMES I SCREAM IN MY SLEEP.
THAT'S ALL. NICE TO MEET YOU.
FANTASTIC! WAY TO TURN A PROMPT INSIDE-OUT.
LET'S DO ANOTHER. THOMAS?
OK. SHOULD I JUST DO THE SAME THING?
AN INTRODUCTION. JUST BE HONEST.
HI, EVERYONE!
I'M THOMAS.
WHAT A TREAT IT IS TO BE WITH YOU ALL TONIGHT.
I JUST FLEW IN FROM DENVER, AND MY ARMS ARE TIRED.

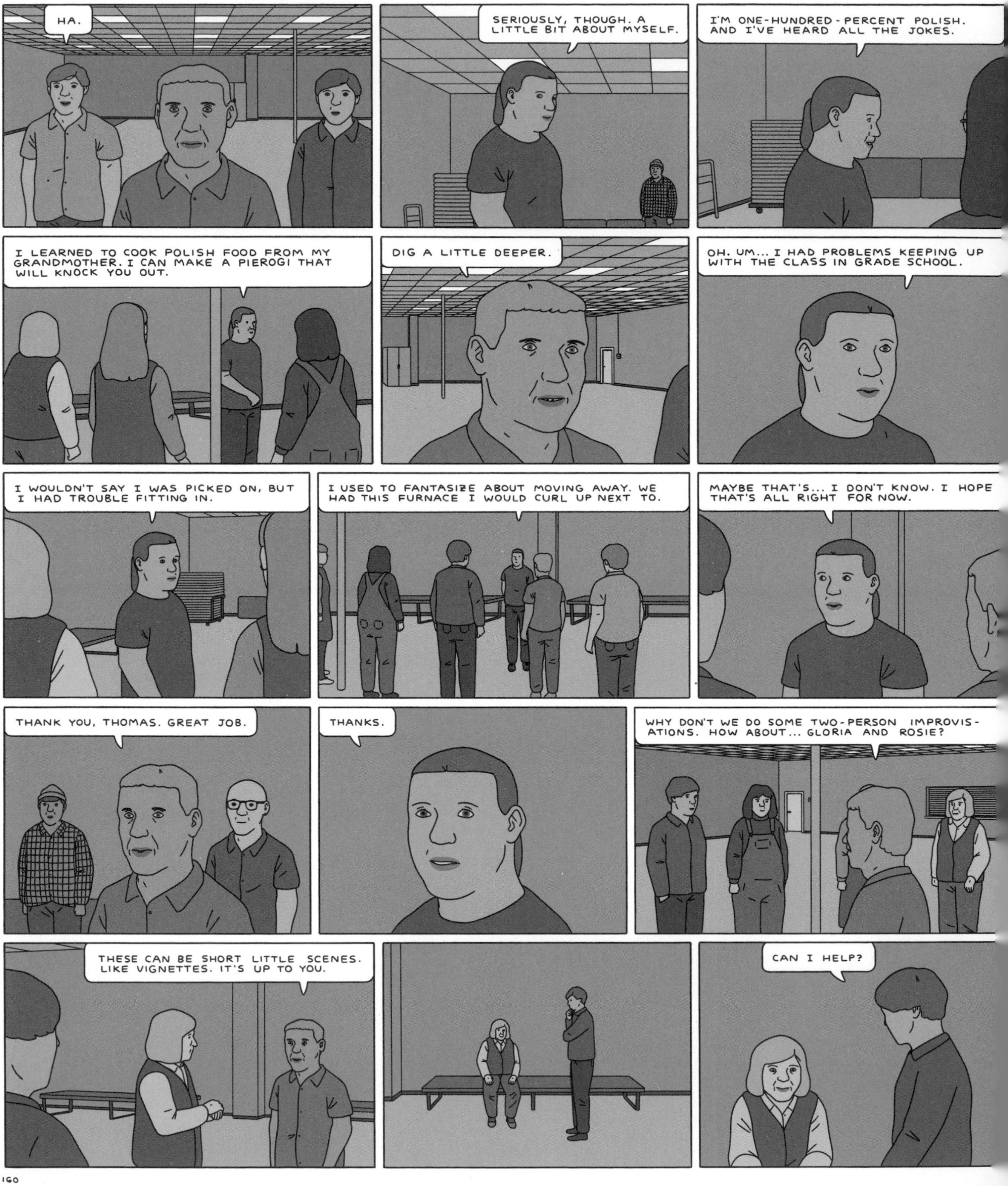
HA.
SERIOUSLY, THOUGH. A LITTLE BIT ABOUT MYSELF.
I'M ONE-HUNDRED-PERCENT POLISH. AND I'VE HEARD ALL THE JOKES.
I LEARNED TO COOK POLISH FOOD FROM MY GRANDMOTHER. I CAN MAKE A PIEROGI THAT WILL KNOCK YOU OUT.
DIG A LITTLE DEEPER.
OH. UM... I HAD PROBLEMS KEEPING UP WITH THE CLASS IN GRADE SCHOOL.
I WOULDN'T SAY I WAS PICKED ON, BUT I HAD TROUBLE FITTING IN.
I USED TO FANTASIZE ABOUT MOVING AWAY. WE HAD THIS FURNACE I WOULD CURL UP NEXT TO.
MAYBE THAT'S... I DON'T KNOW. I HOPE THAT'S ALL RIGHT FOR NOW.
THANK YOU, THOMAS. GREAT JOB.
THANKS.
WHY DON'T WE DO SOME TWO-PERSON IMPROVISATIONS. HOW ABOUT... GLORIA AND ROSIE?
THESE CAN BE SHORT LITTLE SCENES. LIKE VIGNETTES. IT'S UP TO YOU.
CAN I HELP?

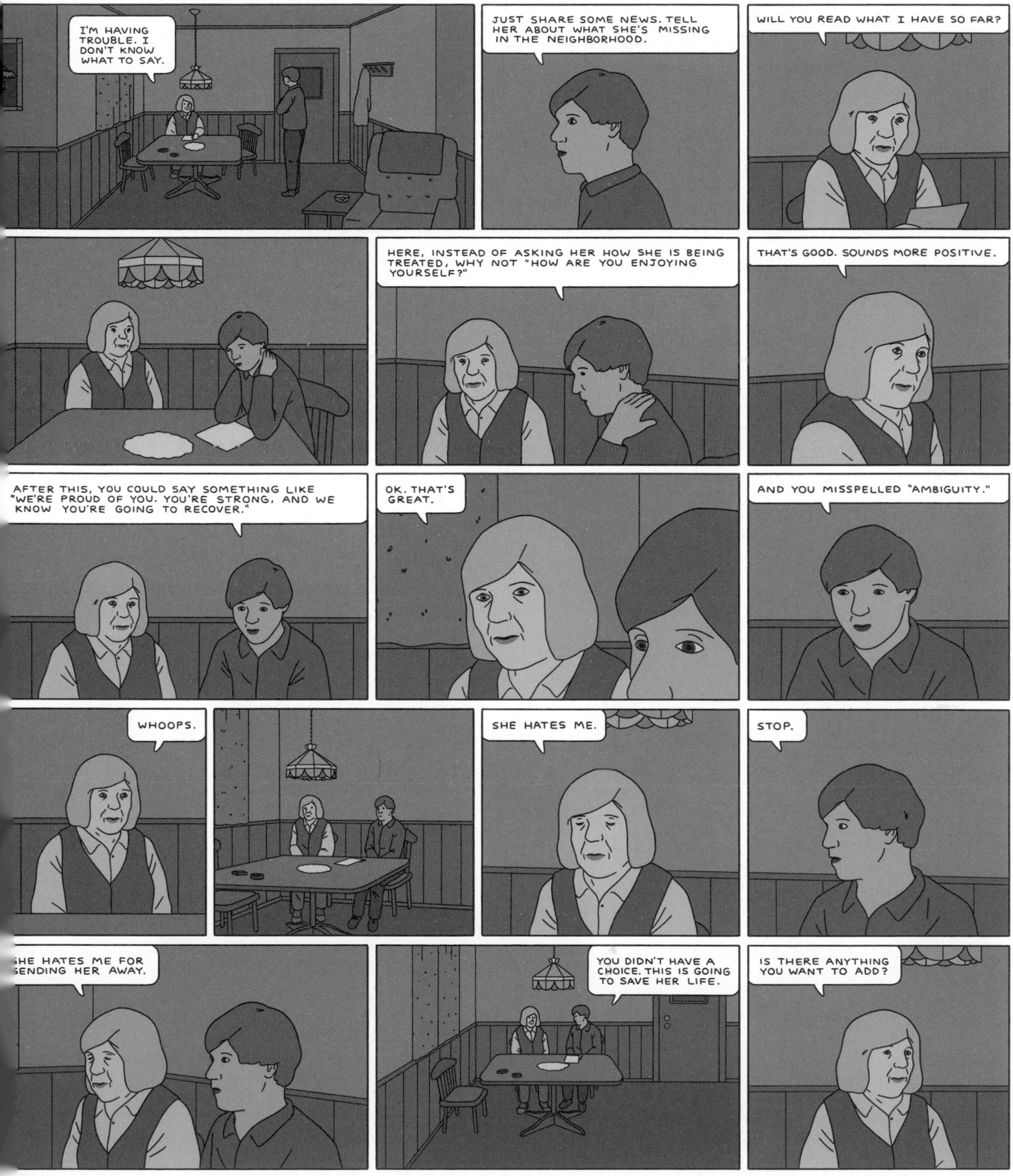
I'M HAVING TROUBLE. I DON'T KNOW WHAT TO SAY.
JUST SHARE SOME NEWS. TELL HER ABOUT WHAT SHE'S MISSING IN THE NEIGHBORHOOD.
WILL YOU READ WHAT I HAVE SO FAR?
HERE, INSTEAD OF ASKING HER HOW SHE IS BEING TREATED, WHY NOT "HOW ARE YOU ENJOYING YOURSELF?"
THAT'S GOOD. SOUNDS MORE POSITIVE.
AFTER THIS, YOU COULD SAY SOMETHING LIKE "WE'RE PROUD OF YOU. YOU'RE STRONG, AND WE KNOW YOU'RE GOING TO RECOVER."
OK. THAT'S GREAT.
AND YOU MISSPELLED "AMBIGUITY."
WHOOPS.
SHE HATES ME.
STOP.
SHE HATES ME FOR SENDING HER AWAY.
YOU DIDN'T HAVE A CHOICE. THIS IS GOING TO SAVE HER LIFE.
IS THERE ANYTHING YOU WANT TO ADD?

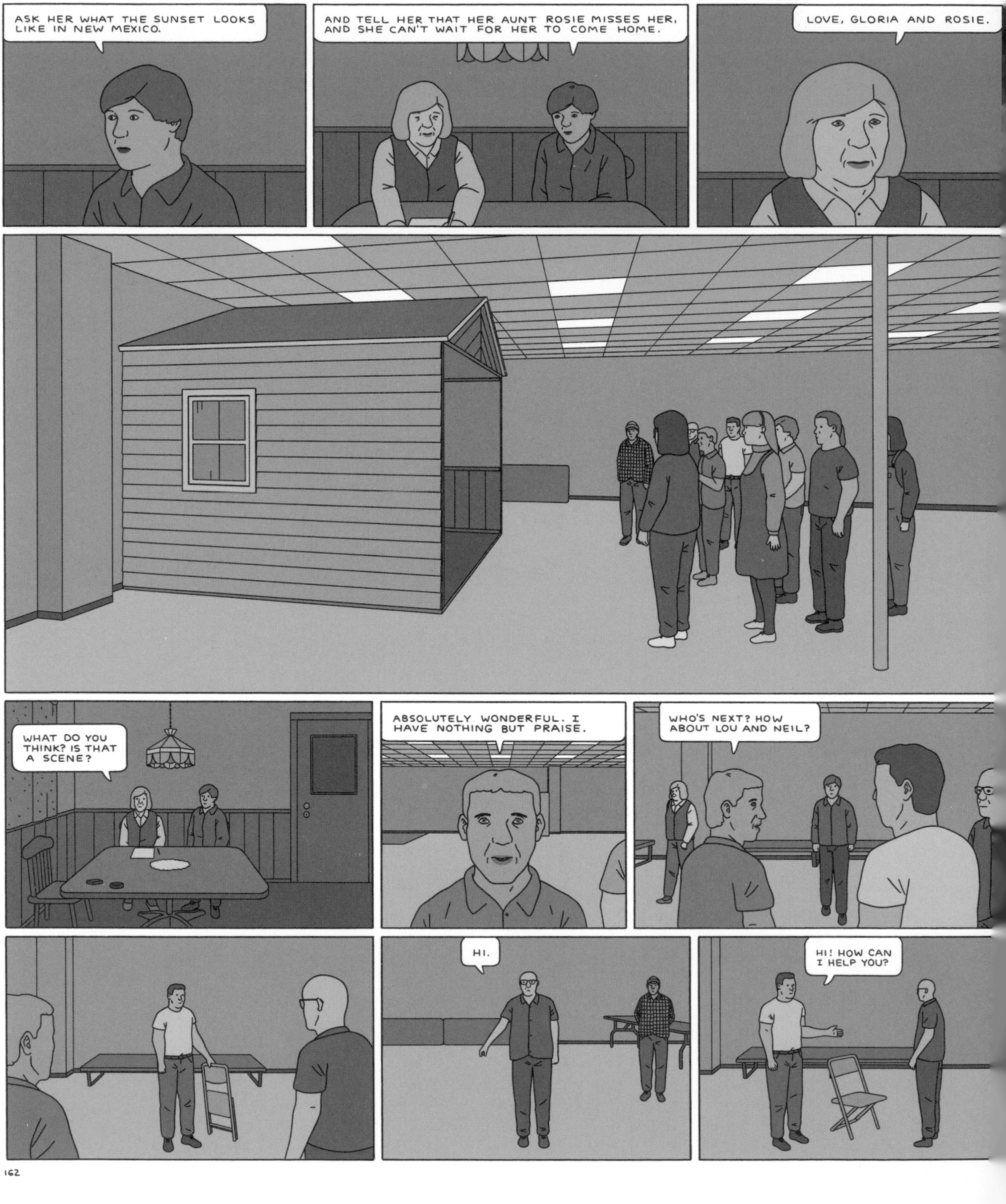
ASK HER WHAT THE SUNSET LOOKS LIKE IN NEW MEXICO.
AND TELL HER THAT HER AUNT ROSIE MISSES HER, AND SHE CAN'T WAIT FOR HER TO COME HOME.
LOVE, GLORIA AND ROSIE.
WHAT DO YOU THINK? IS THAT A SCENE?
ABSOLUTELY WONDERFUL. I HAVE NOTHING BUT PRAISE.
WHO'S NEXT? HOW ABOUT LOU AND NEIL?
HI.
HI! HOW CAN I HELP YOU?

I'M LOOKING TO GET A HAIRCUT.

CERTAINLY. LET'S SEE WHAT WE'RE WORKING WITH.

WOW, BEAUTIFUL. NICE AND THICK.

I WANT YOU TO SHAVE IT ALL OFF.

REALLY? THAT WOULD BE SUCH A SHAME. WANT ME TO STYLE IT FOR YOU?

NO. JUST BUZZ IT OFF. AND HOW ABOUT A SHAVE WHILE YOU'RE AT IT.

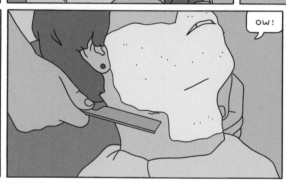

OW!

SORRY.

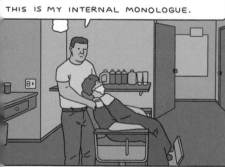

THIS IS MY INTERNAL MONOLOGUE.

EVERY DAY, THE SAME COMPLAINTS. THE SAME INSECURITIES.

"CUT MORE OFF. NO, THAT'S TOO MUCH!"

"IT'S TOO BUSHY ON THE SIDES."

"I HATE MY BALD SPOT."

I COULD END IT ALL RIGHT NOW.

ONE SLICE, AND THIS COULD BE MY LAST CUSTOMER. HIS LAST BREATH. MY LAST DAY ON EARTH.

I DON'T KNOW HOW LONG I'LL BE ABLE TO KEEP THIS UP.

WHAT A RELIEF JUST TO KNOW I HAVE THE OPTION.

YOU KNOW WHAT, I'LL KEEP MY HAIR THE SAME.

I WON'T ARGUE WITH YOU. IT LOOKS GOOD TO ME.

HERE'S A LITTLE EXTRA FOR YOUR TROUBLE.

HEY, THANKS A LOT.

TELL YOUR FRIENDS!

GREAT.

GREAT INTERNAL CONFLICT.

LET'S GET EVERYONE INTO THE MIX BEFORE WE START OUR NEXT EXERCISE.

HOW ABOUT ANOTHER TWO-PERSON VIGNETTE. RAYANNE AND BETH?

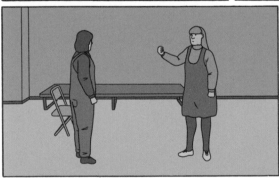

PUT THAT DOWN!

CLEAN UP YOUR TOYS. THIS ROOM IS A MESS.

OK.

HOW ABOUT FISH STICKS FOR DINNER?

MY FAVORITE.

COME HERE, HONEY.

OOF! YOU'RE GETTING BIG.

HAHA.

WHICH JIGSAW PUZZLE DO YOU WANT TO DO TONIGHT?

LET'S DO THE NEW YORK CITY SKYLINE.

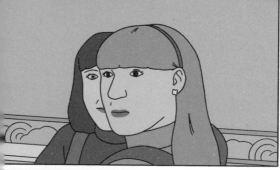

OK, LET ME DOWN.

WHAT'S WRONG?

JUST GIVE ME SOME SPACE, MOM!

SOMEONE'S CRANKY. IS IT TIME FOR BED?

I'M NOT CRANKY. I'M EXPRESSING MYSELF.

KEEP MISBEHAVING. YOUR FATHER WILL HEAR ABOUT THIS WHEN HE GETS HOME.

MY FATHER.

I DON'T WANT TO HEAR ANOTHER WORD ABOUT MY FATHER.

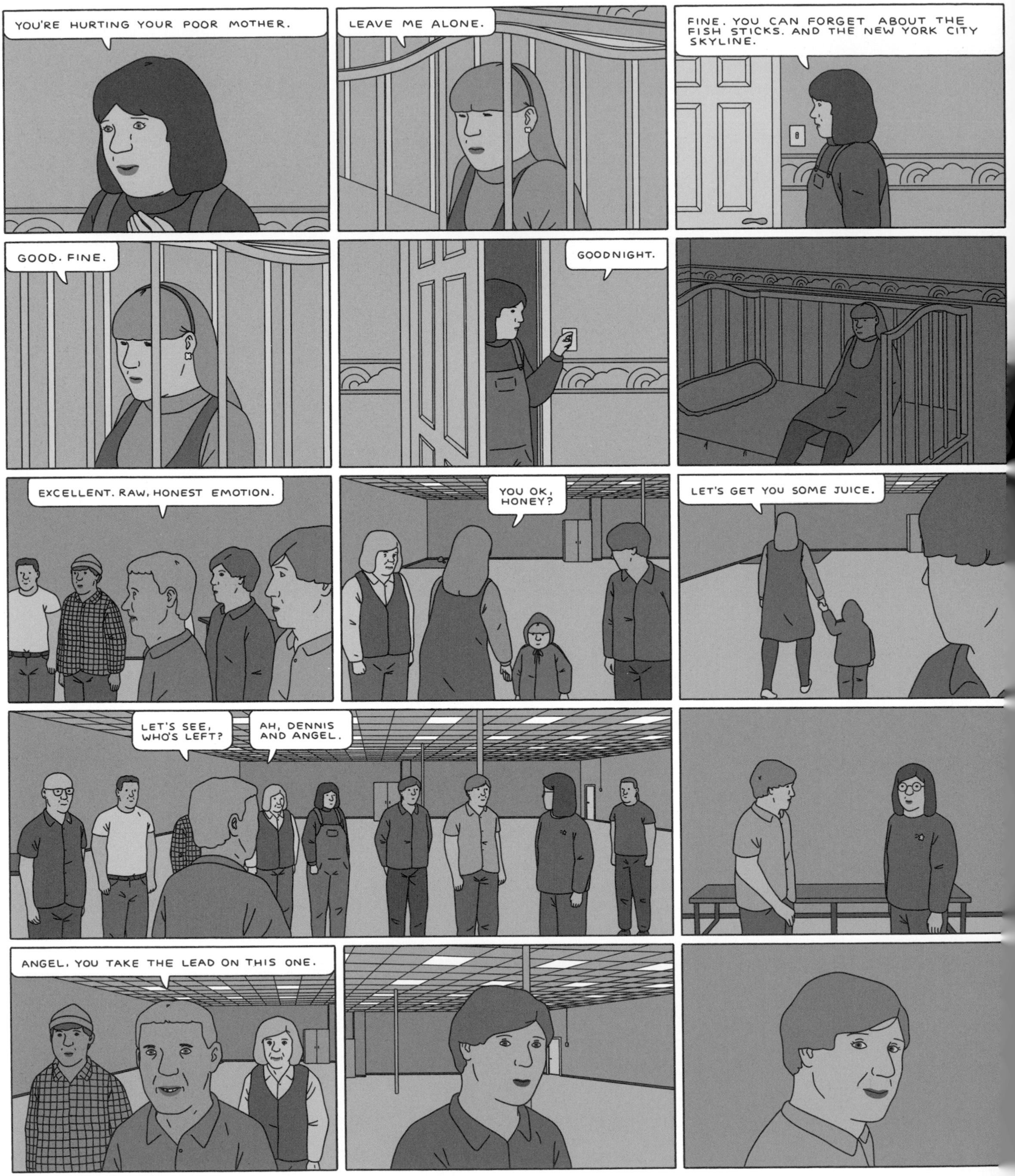
YOU'RE HURTING YOUR POOR MOTHER.
LEAVE ME ALONE.
FINE. YOU CAN FORGET ABOUT THE FISH STICKS. AND THE NEW YORK CITY SKYLINE.
GOOD. FINE.
GOODNIGHT.
EXCELLENT. RAW, HONEST EMOTION.
YOU OK, HONEY?
LET'S GET YOU SOME JUICE.
LET'S SEE, WHO'S LEFT?
AH, DENNIS AND ANGEL.
ANGEL, YOU TAKE THE LEAD ON THIS ONE.

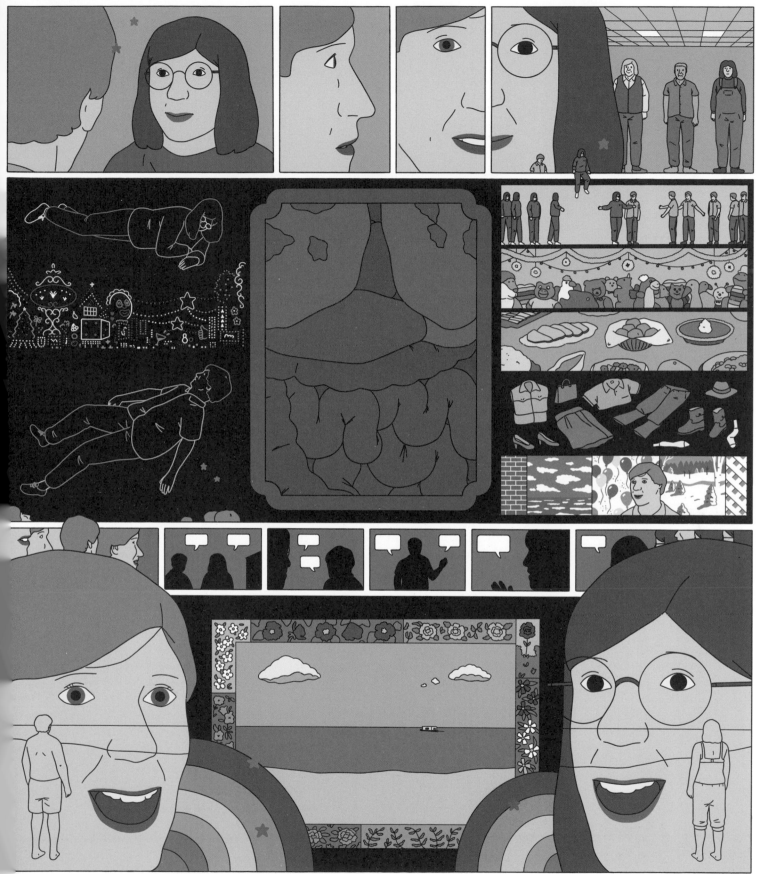

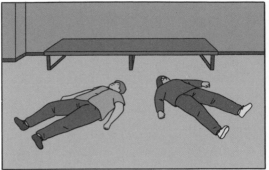

I LOVE IT. WAY TO SHAKE OFF YOUR INHIBITIONS.

I'M CONFUSED. WHY WERE THEY JUST ROLLING AROUND ON THE FLOOR?

IT WAS MORE OF AN INTERPRETIVE THING, WOULDN'T YOU SAY? LIKE AN INTERNAL EXERCISE.

GREAT JOB, EVERYONE. I APPRECIATE ALL OF YOUR OPENNESS AND VULNERABILITY. THAT'S THE KEY.

I HOPE YOU ALL RECOGNIZE THE PROGRESS YOU'VE MADE IN THREE SHORT WEEKS.

LET'S DO SOMETHING BASIC BEFORE WE GET INTO OUR MAIN LESSON.

THIS IS CALLED "WHAT YOU'RE SAYING MAKES ME FEEL."

IT'S ANOTHER TWO-PERSON EXERCISE. ONE PERSON BEGINS WITH A DECLARATION, A PROPOSITION, AN ACCUSATION. A STARTING POINT, BASICALLY.

IT COULD BE "I DON'T LOVE YOU ANYMORE." IT COULD BE SOMETHING MINOR LIKE "DO YOU KNOW WHICH WAY TO GO?"

PERSON TWO RESPONDS WITH "WHAT YOU'RE SAYING MAKES ME FEEL... FILL IN THE BLANK." THEN ADD A BIT MORE.

PERSON ONE REACTS TO THAT WITH "WHAT YOU'RE SAYING MAKES ME FEEL... BLANK." AND ADD A BIT MORE.

AND BACK AND FORTH. A SIMPLE EXERCISE THAT CAN CREATE A COMPELLING SCENE.

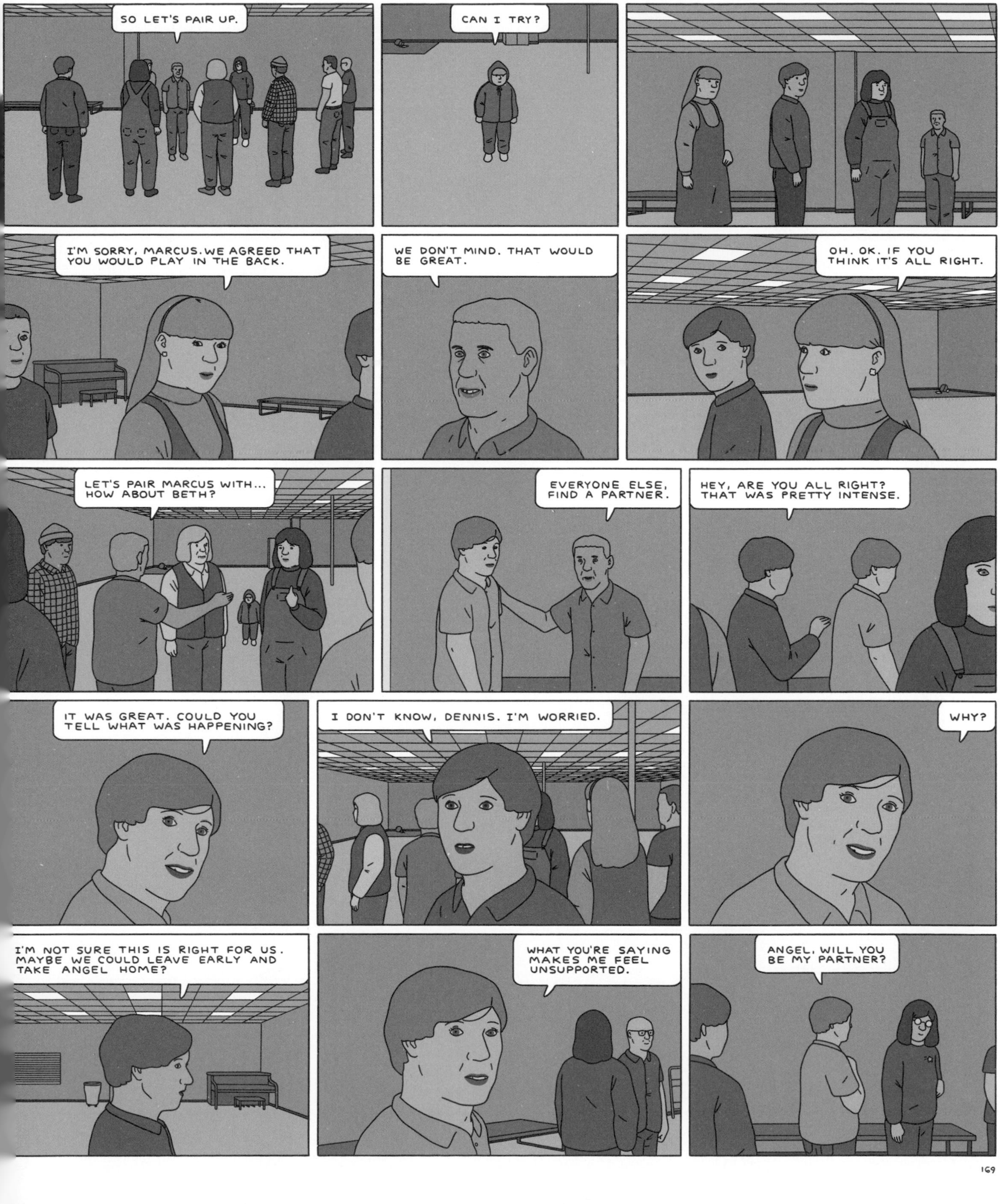
SO LET'S PAIR UP.
CAN I TRY?
I'M SORRY, MARCUS. WE AGREED THAT YOU WOULD PLAY IN THE BACK.
WE DON'T MIND. THAT WOULD BE GREAT.
OH. OK. IF YOU THINK IT'S ALL RIGHT.
LET'S PAIR MARCUS WITH... HOW ABOUT BETH?
EVERYONE ELSE, FIND A PARTNER.
HEY, ARE YOU ALL RIGHT? THAT WAS PRETTY INTENSE.
IT WAS GREAT. COULD YOU TELL WHAT WAS HAPPENING?
I DON'T KNOW, DENNIS. I'M WORRIED.
WHY?
I'M NOT SURE THIS IS RIGHT FOR US. MAYBE WE COULD LEAVE EARLY AND TAKE ANGEL HOME?
WHAT YOU'RE SAYING MAKES ME FEEL UNSUPPORTED.
ANGEL, WILL YOU BE MY PARTNER?

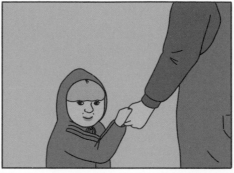

I DON'T HAVE A PARTNER.

OH. RIGHT.

WELL, I'M BREAKING MY OWN RULE, BUT WE CAN DO THIS ACTIVITY TOGETHER.

OK.

GREAT.

YOU CAN DO MORE THAN ONE ROUND. SWITCH THE ORDER. LOOSEN UP. THERE'S NO WRONG METHOD.

YOU SEEM TROUBLED.

YEA, IT'S JUST... OH, RIGHT.

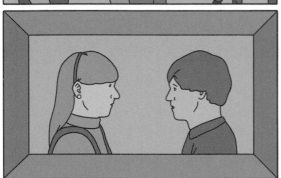

WHAT YOU'RE SAYING MAKES ME FEEL COMFORTED. I'M GLAD I CAN TALK TO YOU.

WHAT YOU'RE SAYING MAKES ME FEEL HOPEFUL. WE'RE GOING TO GET THROUGH THIS.

WHAT YOU'RE SAYING MAKES ME FEEL BONDED TO YOU. I DON'T KNOW WHAT I WOULD DO WITHOUT YOUR HELP.

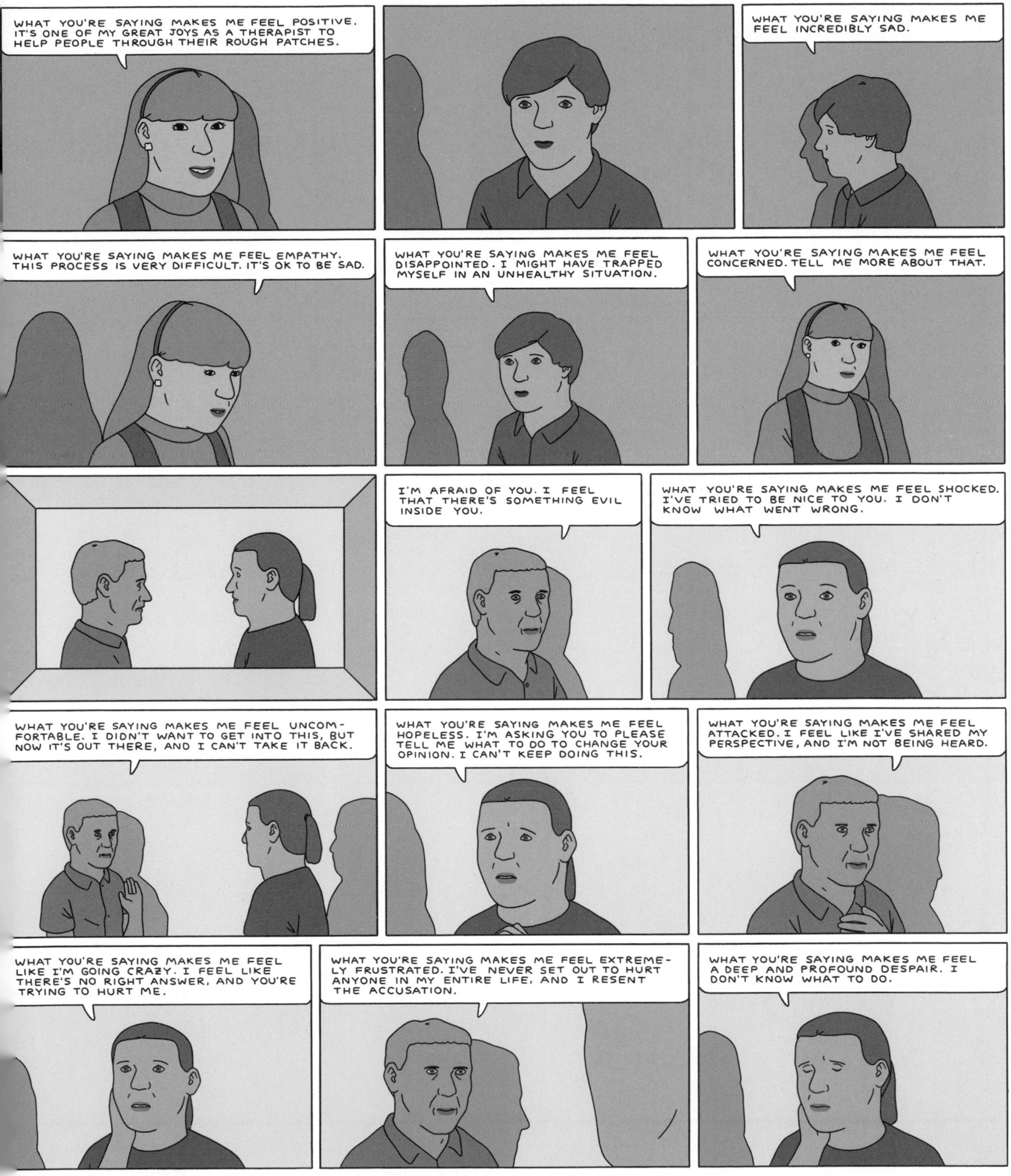
WHAT YOU'RE SAYING MAKES ME FEEL POSITIVE. IT'S ONE OF MY GREAT JOYS AS A THERAPIST TO HELP PEOPLE THROUGH THEIR ROUGH PATCHES.
WHAT YOU'RE SAYING MAKES ME FEEL INCREDIBLY SAD.
WHAT YOU'RE SAYING MAKES ME FEEL EMPATHY. THIS PROCESS IS VERY DIFFICULT. IT'S OK TO BE SAD.
WHAT YOU'RE SAYING MAKES ME FEEL DISAPPOINTED. I MIGHT HAVE TRAPPED MYSELF IN AN UNHEALTHY SITUATION.
WHAT YOU'RE SAYING MAKES ME FEEL CONCERNED. TELL ME MORE ABOUT THAT.
I'M AFRAID OF YOU. I FEEL THAT THERE'S SOMETHING EVIL INSIDE YOU.
WHAT YOU'RE SAYING MAKES ME FEEL SHOCKED. I'VE TRIED TO BE NICE TO YOU. I DON'T KNOW WHAT WENT WRONG.
WHAT YOU'RE SAYING MAKES ME FEEL UNCOM-FORTABLE. I DIDN'T WANT TO GET INTO THIS, BUT NOW IT'S OUT THERE, AND I CAN'T TAKE IT BACK.
WHAT YOU'RE SAYING MAKES ME FEEL HOPELESS. I'M ASKING YOU TO PLEASE TELL ME WHAT TO DO TO CHANGE YOUR OPINION. I CAN'T KEEP DOING THIS.
WHAT YOU'RE SAYING MAKES ME FEEL ATTACKED. I FEEL LIKE I'VE SHARED MY PERSPECTIVE, AND I'M NOT BEING HEARD.
WHAT YOU'RE SAYING MAKES ME FEEL LIKE I'M GOING CRAZY. I FEEL LIKE THERE'S NO RIGHT ANSWER, AND YOU'RE TRYING TO HURT ME.
WHAT YOU'RE SAYING MAKES ME FEEL EXTREME-LY FRUSTRATED. I'VE NEVER SET OUT TO HURT ANYONE IN MY ENTIRE LIFE, AND I RESENT THE ACCUSATION.
WHAT YOU'RE SAYING MAKES ME FEEL A DEEP AND PROFOUND DESPAIR. I DON'T KNOW WHAT TO DO.

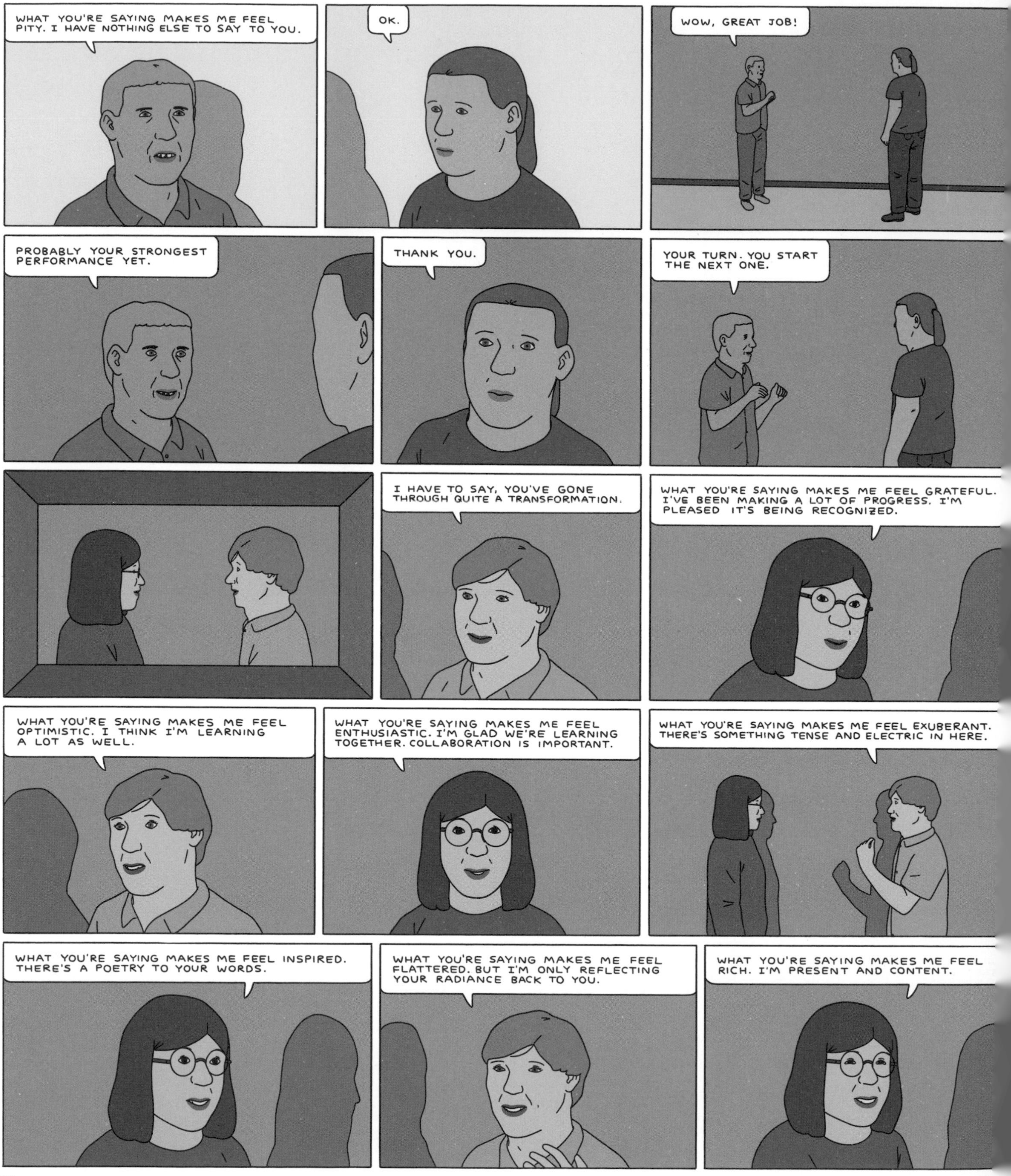
WHAT YOU'RE SAYING MAKES ME FEEL PITY. I HAVE NOTHING ELSE TO SAY TO YOU.
OK.
WOW, GREAT JOB!
PROBABLY YOUR STRONGEST PERFORMANCE YET.
THANK YOU.
YOUR TURN. YOU START THE NEXT ONE.
I HAVE TO SAY, YOU'VE GONE THROUGH QUITE A TRANSFORMATION.
WHAT YOU'RE SAYING MAKES ME FEEL GRATEFUL. I'VE BEEN MAKING A LOT OF PROGRESS. I'M PLEASED IT'S BEING RECOGNIZED.
WHAT YOU'RE SAYING MAKES ME FEEL OPTIMISTIC. I THINK I'M LEARNING A LOT AS WELL.
WHAT YOU'RE SAYING MAKES ME FEEL ENTHUSIASTIC. I'M GLAD WE'RE LEARNING TOGETHER. COLLABORATION IS IMPORTANT.
WHAT YOU'RE SAYING MAKES ME FEEL EXUBERANT. THERE'S SOMETHING TENSE AND ELECTRIC IN HERE.
WHAT YOU'RE SAYING MAKES ME FEEL INSPIRED. THERE'S A POETRY TO YOUR WORDS.
WHAT YOU'RE SAYING MAKES ME FEEL FLATTERED. BUT I'M ONLY REFLECTING YOUR RADIANCE BACK TO YOU.
WHAT YOU'RE SAYING MAKES ME FEEL RICH. I'M PRESENT AND CONTENT.

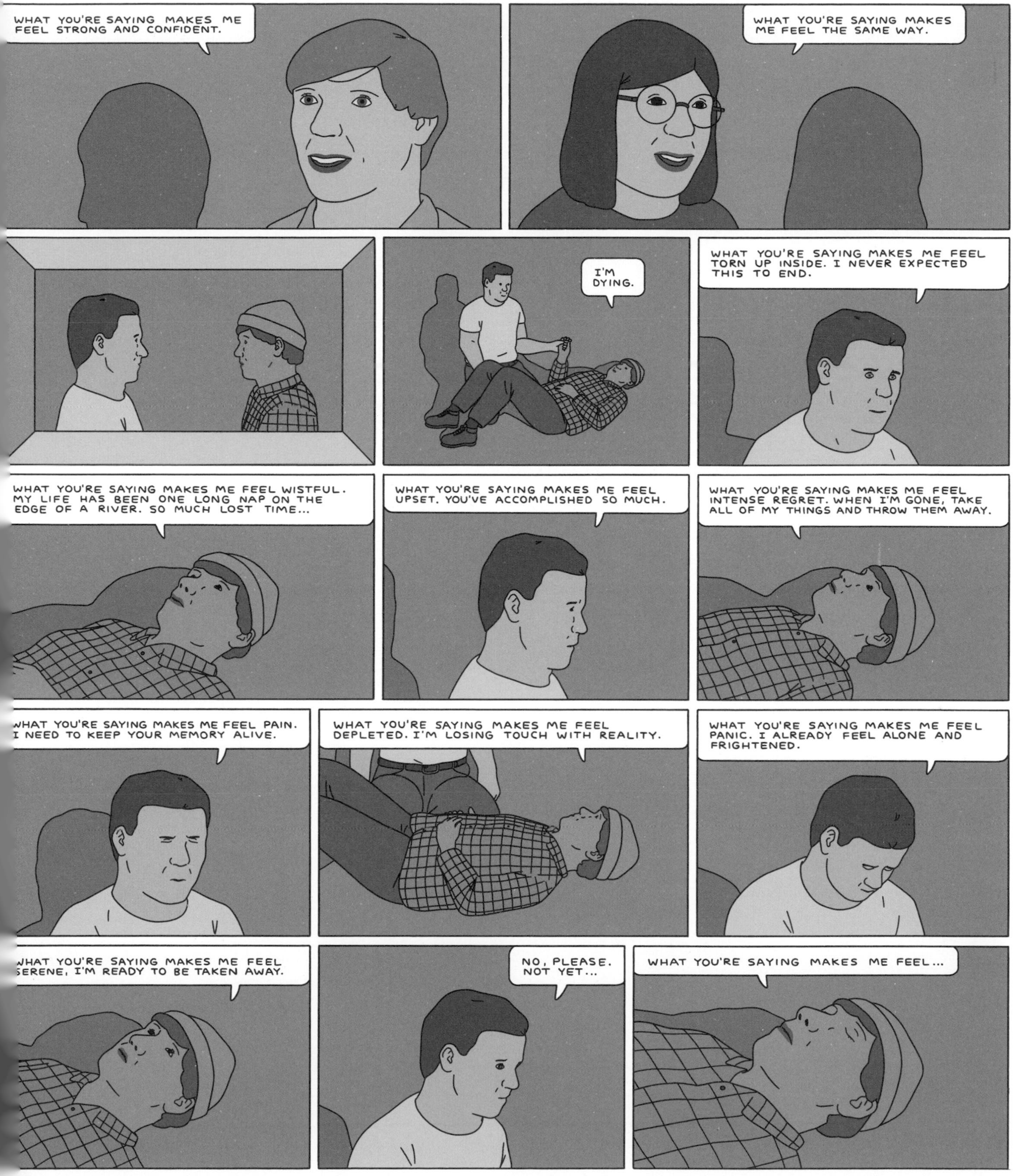
WHAT YOU'RE SAYING MAKES ME FEEL STRONG AND CONFIDENT.
WHAT YOU'RE SAYING MAKES ME FEEL THE SAME WAY.
I'M DYING.
WHAT YOU'RE SAYING MAKES ME FEEL TORN UP INSIDE. I NEVER EXPECTED THIS TO END.
WHAT YOU'RE SAYING MAKES ME FEEL WISTFUL. MY LIFE HAS BEEN ONE LONG NAP ON THE EDGE OF A RIVER. SO MUCH LOST TIME...
WHAT YOU'RE SAYING MAKES ME FEEL UPSET. YOU'VE ACCOMPLISHED SO MUCH.
WHAT YOU'RE SAYING MAKES ME FEEL INTENSE REGRET. WHEN I'M GONE, TAKE ALL OF MY THINGS AND THROW THEM AWAY.
WHAT YOU'RE SAYING MAKES ME FEEL PAIN. I NEED TO KEEP YOUR MEMORY ALIVE.
WHAT YOU'RE SAYING MAKES ME FEEL DEPLETED. I'M LOSING TOUCH WITH REALITY.
WHAT YOU'RE SAYING MAKES ME FEEL PANIC. I ALREADY FEEL ALONE AND FRIGHTENED.
WHAT YOU'RE SAYING MAKES ME FEEL SERENE, I'M READY TO BE TAKEN AWAY.
NO, PLEASE. NOT YET...
WHAT YOU'RE SAYING MAKES ME FEEL...

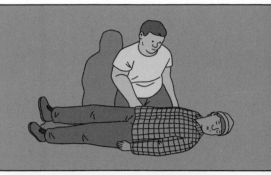

WELL, THAT WAS SOMETHING.

YOU WERE GREAT.

YOU TOO.

YOU START.

NO, YOU. YOU'RE THE GROWNUP.

WHAT YOU'RE SAYING MAKES ME FEEL EXTRA LARGE.

WHAT YOU'RE SAYING MAKES ME FEEL LIKE A SHOOTING STAR.

WHAT YOU'RE SAYING MAKES ME FEEL LIKE A WALL THAT NEEDS TO BE PAINTED.

WHAT YOU'RE SAYING MAKES ME FEEL LIKE A SHIP AT THE BOTTOM OF THE OCEAN.

WHAT YOU'RE SAYING MAKES ME FEEL LIKE A BOWL OF ROTTEN FRUIT.

WHAT YOU'RE SAYING MAKES ME FEEL LIKE AN ELEPHANT BEING LET OUT OF A ZOO.

WHAT YOU'RE SAYING MAKES ME FEEL WARM AND FUZZY, LIKE A TEDDY BEAR BURNING IN HELL.

WHAT YOU'RE SAYING MAKES ME FEEL LIKE A CAR GOING SO FAST THAT IT SHOOTS OFF THE EDGE OF THE PLANET AND INTO SPACE.

WHAT YOU'RE SAYING MAKES ME FEEL LIKE A GRAND PIANO THAT NO ONE KNOWS HOW TO PLAY.

WHAT YOU'RE SAYING MAKES ME FEEL LIKE I'M A HUNDRED YEARS OLD, I'M SO BORED TO DEATH.

WHAT YOU'RE SAYING MAKES ME FEEL LIKE A MONSTER HIDING UNDER YOUR BED.

WHAT YOU'RE SAYING MAKES ME FEEL LIKE A HAMMER THAT COULD KNOCK YOUR TEETH OUT IF IT WANTED TO.

WHAT YOU'RE SAYING MAKES ME FEEL LIKE A BABYSITTER.

I'M NOT A BABY!

HA-HA. YOU LOSE THE GAME.

I BROUGHT YOU A PRESENT.

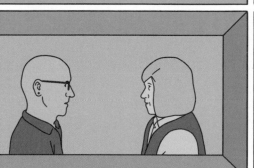

WHAT YOU'RE SAYING MAKES ME FEEL HAPPY. THAT'S SO THOUGHTFUL.

WHAT YOU'RE SAYING MAKES ME FEEL CONTENT. I LIKE DOING THINGS FOR OTHER PEOPLE.

WHAT YOU'RE SAYING MAKES ME FEEL GUILTY. I DIDN'T BRING ANYTHING FOR YOU.

WHAT YOU'RE SAYING MAKES ME FEEL SATISFIED. I WASN'T EXPECTING ANYTHING IN RETURN, BUT I APPRECIATE IT.

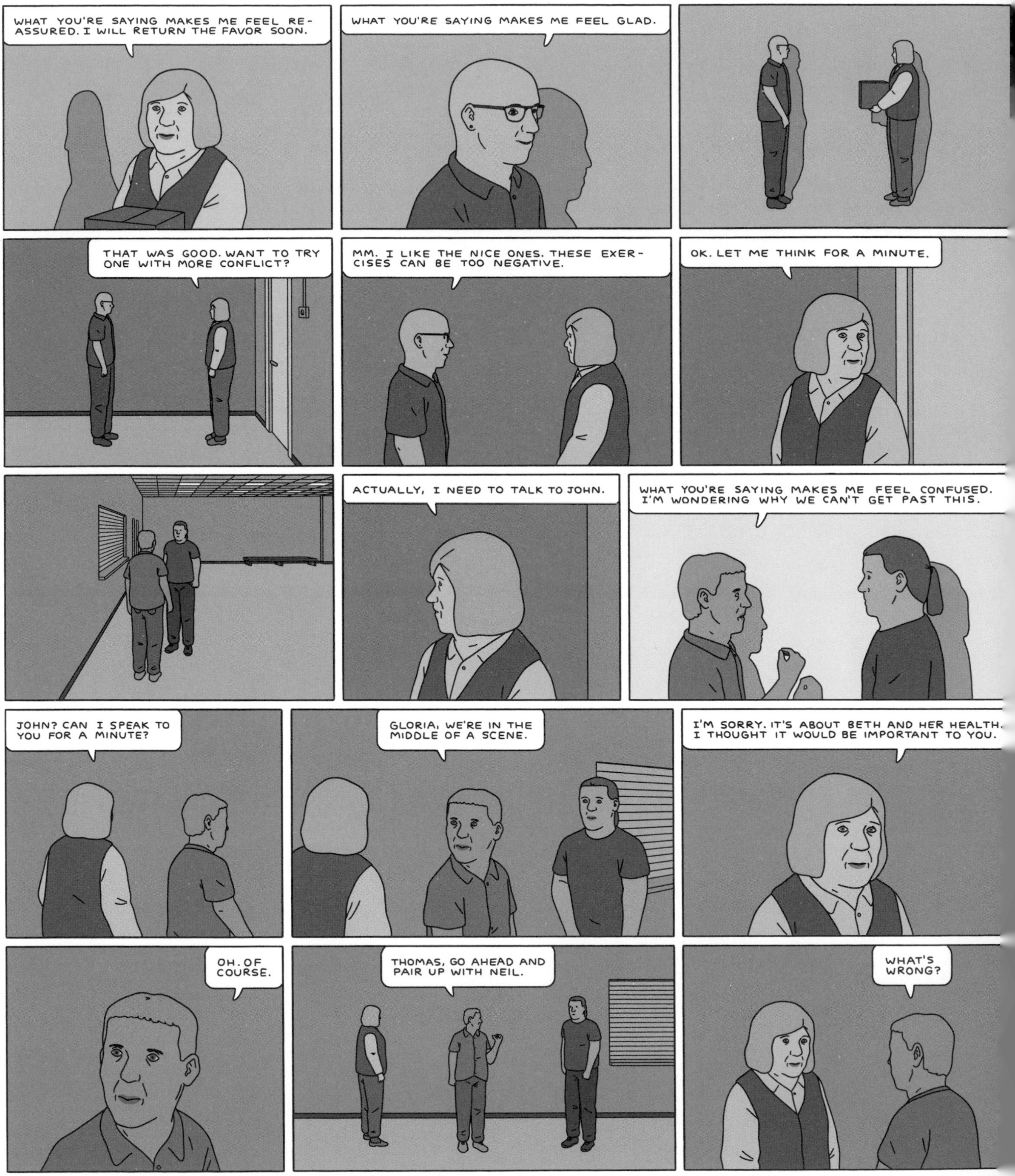
WHAT YOU'RE SAYING MAKES ME FEEL RE-ASSURED. I WILL RETURN THE FAVOR SOON.
WHAT YOU'RE SAYING MAKES ME FEEL GLAD.
THAT WAS GOOD. WANT TO TRY ONE WITH MORE CONFLICT?
MM. I LIKE THE NICE ONES. THESE EXER-CISES CAN BE TOO NEGATIVE.
OK. LET ME THINK FOR A MINUTE.
ACTUALLY, I NEED TO TALK TO JOHN.
WHAT YOU'RE SAYING MAKES ME FEEL CONFUSED. I'M WONDERING WHY WE CAN'T GET PAST THIS.
JOHN? CAN I SPEAK TO YOU FOR A MINUTE?
GLORIA, WE'RE IN THE MIDDLE OF A SCENE.
I'M SORRY. IT'S ABOUT BETH AND HER HEALTH. I THOUGHT IT WOULD BE IMPORTANT TO YOU.
OH. OF COURSE.
THOMAS, GO AHEAD AND PAIR UP WITH NEIL.
WHAT'S WRONG?

CAN WE TALK CANDIDLY?

YES. LET'S GET SOME PRIVACY.

I BROUGHT YOU A PRESENT.

WOW...

WHAT YOU'RE SAYING MAKES ME FEEL SO HAPPY. YOU HAVE NO IDEA HOW MUCH THIS MEANS TO ME.

WHAT YOU'RE SAYING MAKES ME FEEL PLEASED. I'VE DECIDED TO MAKE IT MY MISSION TO SPREAD LOVE AND POSITIVITY.

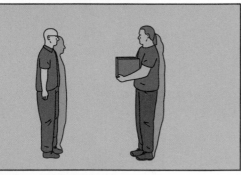

SHOULD I OPEN IT?

OH. YOU DON'T HAVE TO.

I'M TOO EXCITED. I WANT YOU TO SEE MY EXPRESSION.

IT'S EMPTY.

SO YOU COULD SEE WHY I WANTED TO SHARE MY CONCERNS WITH YOU.

ABSOLUTELY. THANK YOU.

177

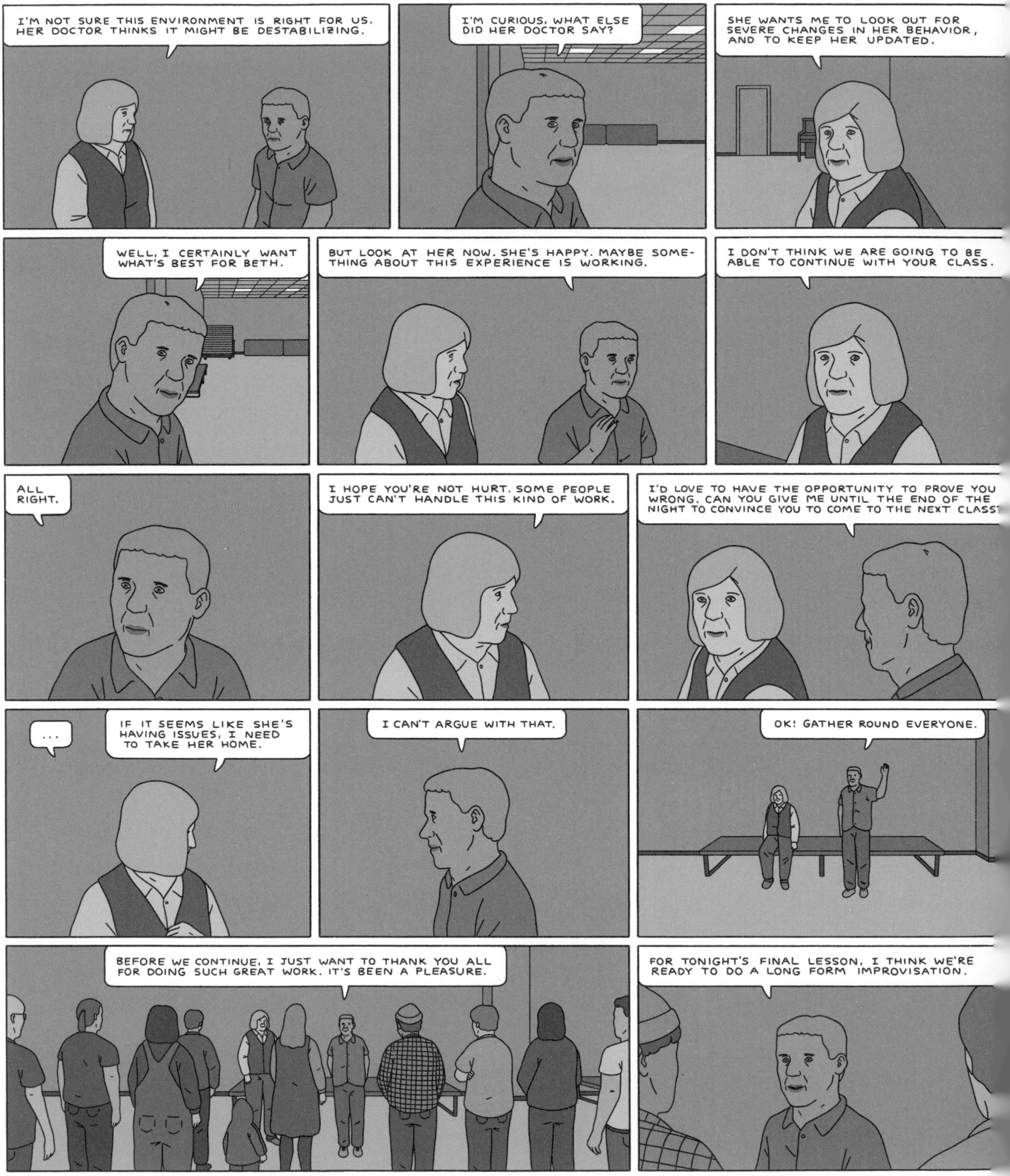
I'M NOT SURE THIS ENVIRONMENT IS RIGHT FOR US. HER DOCTOR THINKS IT MIGHT BE DESTABILIZING.
I'M CURIOUS, WHAT ELSE DID HER DOCTOR SAY?
SHE WANTS ME TO LOOK OUT FOR SEVERE CHANGES IN HER BEHAVIOR, AND TO KEEP HER UPDATED.
WELL, I CERTAINLY WANT WHAT'S BEST FOR BETH.
BUT LOOK AT HER NOW. SHE'S HAPPY. MAYBE SOME-THING ABOUT THIS EXPERIENCE IS WORKING.
I DON'T THINK WE ARE GOING TO BE ABLE TO CONTINUE WITH YOUR CLASS.
ALL RIGHT.
I HOPE YOU'RE NOT HURT. SOME PEOPLE JUST CAN'T HANDLE THIS KIND OF WORK.
I'D LOVE TO HAVE THE OPPORTUNITY TO PROVE YOU WRONG. CAN YOU GIVE ME UNTIL THE END OF THE NIGHT TO CONVINCE YOU TO COME TO THE NEXT CLASS
...
IF IT SEEMS LIKE SHE'S HAVING ISSUES, I NEED TO TAKE HER HOME.
I CAN'T ARGUE WITH THAT.
OK! GATHER ROUND EVERYONE.
BEFORE WE CONTINUE, I JUST WANT TO THANK YOU ALL FOR DOING SUCH GREAT WORK. IT'S BEEN A PLEASURE.
FOR TONIGHT'S FINAL LESSON, I THINK WE'RE READY TO DO A LONG FORM IMPROVISATION.

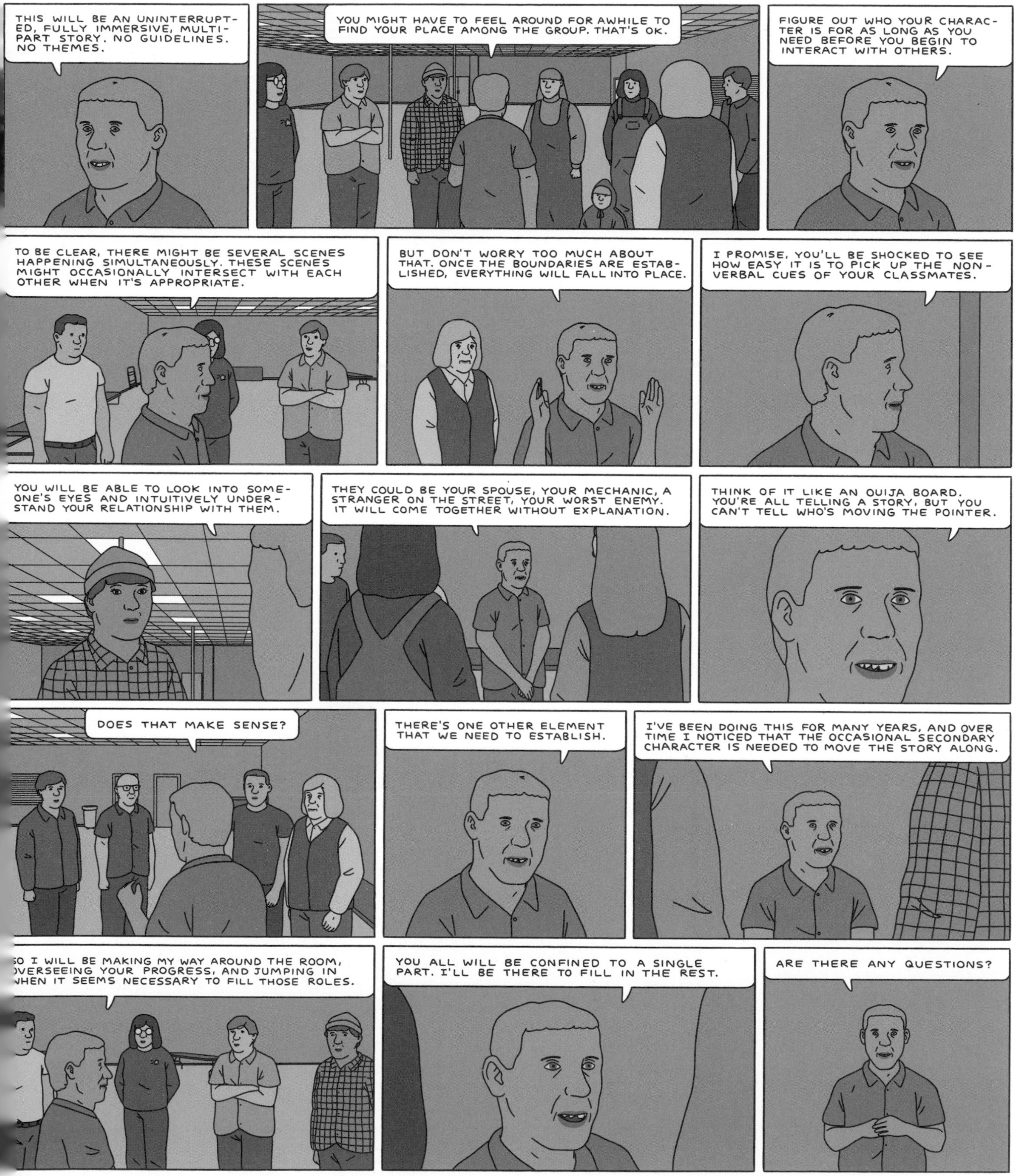
THIS WILL BE AN UNINTERRUPTED, FULLY IMMERSIVE, MULTI-PART STORY. NO GUIDELINES. NO THEMES.
YOU MIGHT HAVE TO FEEL AROUND FOR AWHILE TO FIND YOUR PLACE AMONG THE GROUP. THAT'S OK.
FIGURE OUT WHO YOUR CHARACTER IS FOR AS LONG AS YOU NEED BEFORE YOU BEGIN TO INTERACT WITH OTHERS.
TO BE CLEAR, THERE MIGHT BE SEVERAL SCENES HAPPENING SIMULTANEOUSLY. THESE SCENES MIGHT OCCASIONALLY INTERSECT WITH EACH OTHER WHEN IT'S APPROPRIATE.
BUT DON'T WORRY TOO MUCH ABOUT THAT. ONCE THE BOUNDARIES ARE ESTABLISHED, EVERYTHING WILL FALL INTO PLACE.
I PROMISE, YOU'LL BE SHOCKED TO SEE HOW EASY IT IS TO PICK UP THE NON-VERBAL CUES OF YOUR CLASSMATES.
YOU WILL BE ABLE TO LOOK INTO SOMEONE'S EYES AND INTUITIVELY UNDERSTAND YOUR RELATIONSHIP WITH THEM.
THEY COULD BE YOUR SPOUSE, YOUR MECHANIC, A STRANGER ON THE STREET, YOUR WORST ENEMY. IT WILL COME TOGETHER WITHOUT EXPLANATION.
THINK OF IT LIKE AN OUIJA BOARD. YOU'RE ALL TELLING A STORY, BUT YOU CAN'T TELL WHO'S MOVING THE POINTER.
DOES THAT MAKE SENSE?
THERE'S ONE OTHER ELEMENT THAT WE NEED TO ESTABLISH.
I'VE BEEN DOING THIS FOR MANY YEARS, AND OVER TIME I NOTICED THAT THE OCCASIONAL SECONDARY CHARACTER IS NEEDED TO MOVE THE STORY ALONG.
SO I WILL BE MAKING MY WAY AROUND THE ROOM, OVERSEEING YOUR PROGRESS, AND JUMPING IN WHEN IT SEEMS NECESSARY TO FILL THOSE ROLES.
YOU ALL WILL BE CONFINED TO A SINGLE PART. I'LL BE THERE TO FILL IN THE REST.
ARE THERE ANY QUESTIONS?

HOW WILL WE KNOW WHEN IT'S OVER?

I'LL END THE CLASS PROMPTLY THIS TIME. I PROMISE.

WHAT ABOUT MARCUS?

HM.

I CAN TAKE HIM HOME EARLY.

NO, NO. WHY DON'T YOU GO THROUGH THE LESSON AS MOTHER AND SON? THAT WAY YOU CAN BOTH PARTICIPATE AND YOU'LL BE ABLE TO KEEP AN EYE ON HIM.

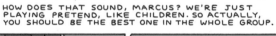

HOW DOES THAT SOUND, MARCUS? WE'RE JUST PLAYING PRETEND, LIKE CHILDREN. SO ACTUALLY, YOU SHOULD BE THE BEST ONE IN THE WHOLE GROUP.

THAT SOUNDS FUN.

GREAT. EVERYONE SPREAD OUT A BIT.

CLOSE YOUR EYES AND COUNT TO THIRTY. TAKE THAT TIME TO CLEAR YOUR MIND.

WHEN YOU OPEN YOUR EYES, THE PLAY HAS BEGUN.

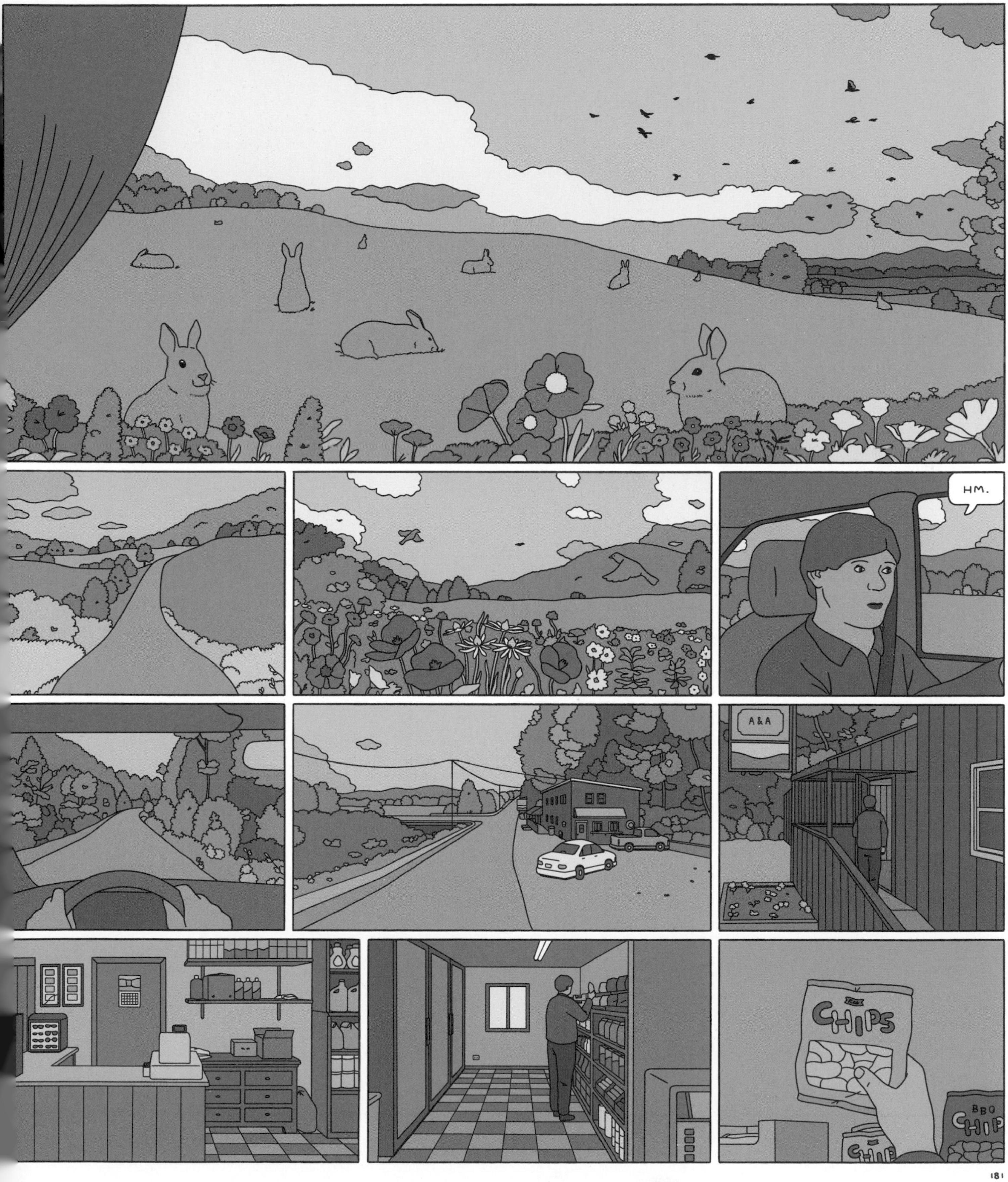
HM.
A&A
CHIPS
BBQ CHIP
CHIPS

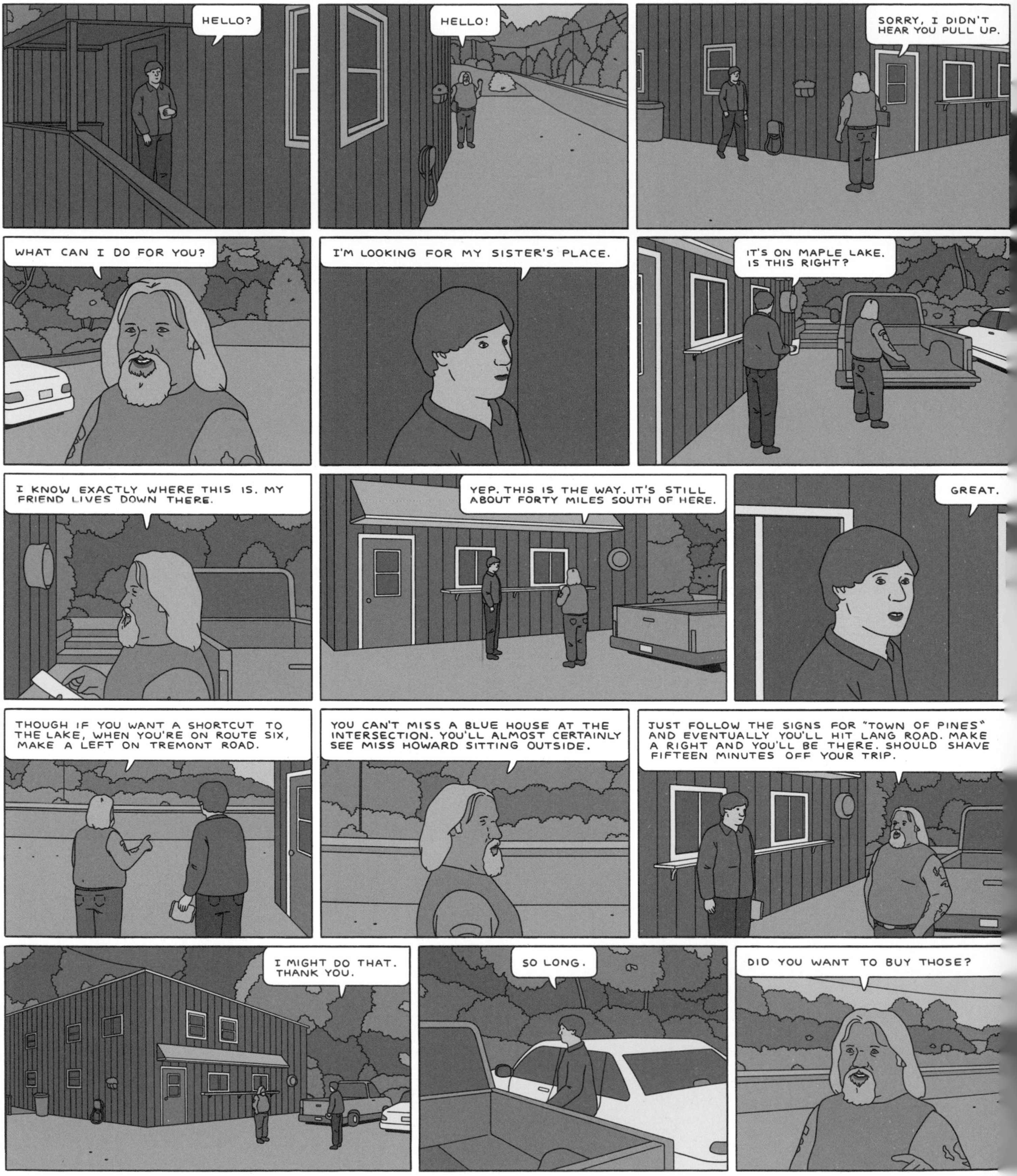

HELLO?
HELLO!
SORRY, I DIDN'T HEAR YOU PULL UP.
WHAT CAN I DO FOR YOU?
I'M LOOKING FOR MY SISTER'S PLACE.
IT'S ON MAPLE LAKE. IS THIS RIGHT?
I KNOW EXACTLY WHERE THIS IS. MY FRIEND LIVES DOWN THERE.
YEP. THIS IS THE WAY. IT'S STILL ABOUT FORTY MILES SOUTH OF HERE.
GREAT.
THOUGH IF YOU WANT A SHORTCUT TO THE LAKE, WHEN YOU'RE ON ROUTE SIX, MAKE A LEFT ON TREMONT ROAD.
YOU CAN'T MISS A BLUE HOUSE AT THE INTERSECTION. YOU'LL ALMOST CERTAINLY SEE MISS HOWARD SITTING OUTSIDE.
JUST FOLLOW THE SIGNS FOR "TOWN OF PINES" AND EVENTUALLY YOU'LL HIT LANG ROAD. MAKE A RIGHT AND YOU'LL BE THERE. SHOULD SHAVE FIFTEEN MINUTES OFF YOUR TRIP.
I MIGHT DO THAT. THANK YOU.
SO LONG.
DID YOU WANT TO BUY THOSE?

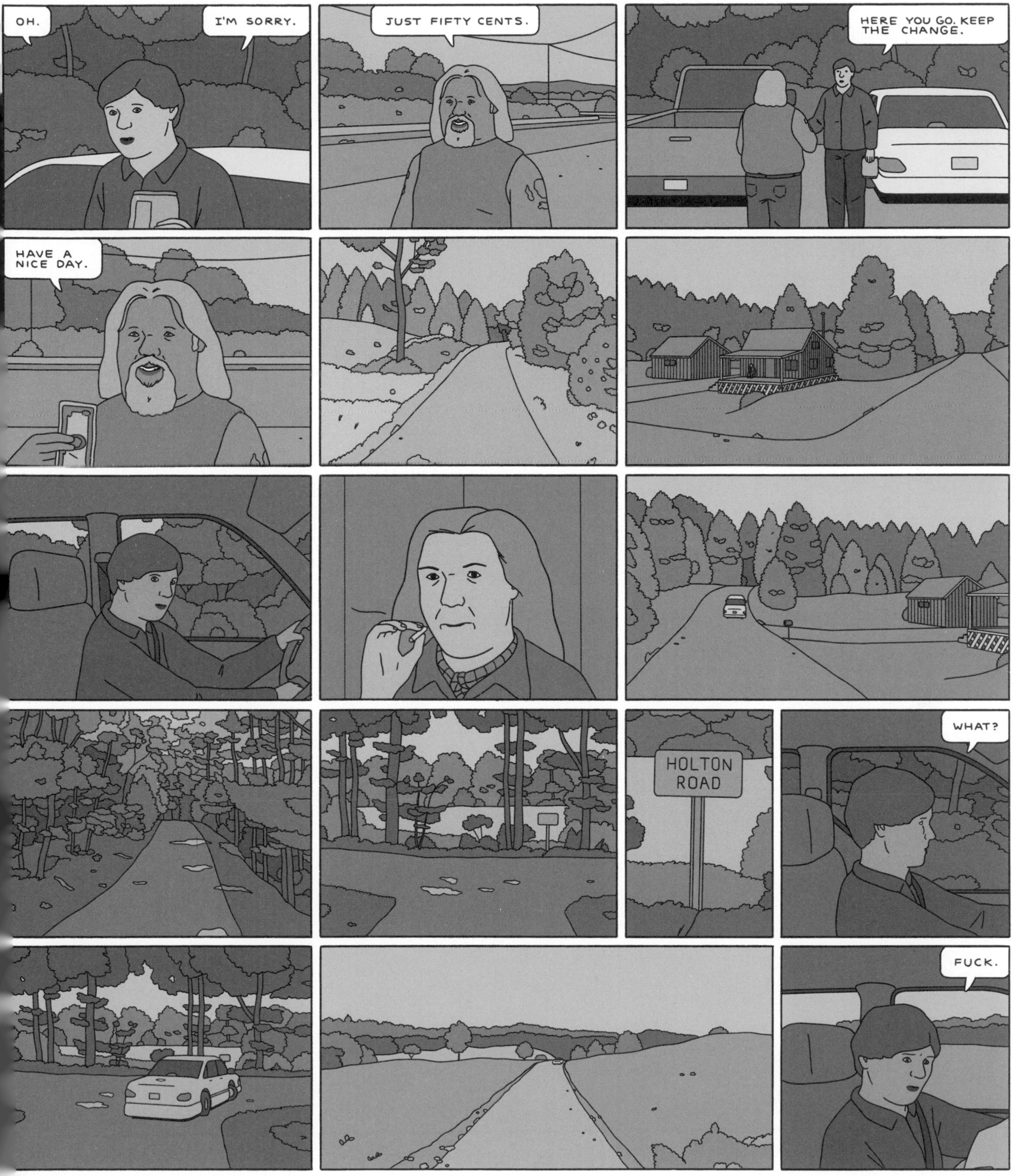
OH.
I'M SORRY.
JUST FIFTY CENTS.
HERE YOU GO. KEEP THE CHANGE.
HAVE A NICE DAY.
HOLTON ROAD
WHAT?
FUCK.

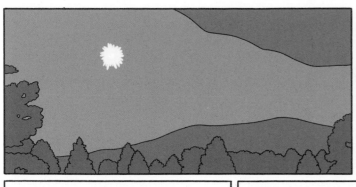

COULD YOU TELL ME WHERE TO FIND LANG ROAD?

LANG ROAD? THAT'S CLEAR ON THE OTHER SIDE OF THE LAKE.

KEEP GOING THIS WAY. TAKE A LEFT AT THE SIGN FOR RAMSEY BOAT RENTAL. TAKE ANOTHER LEFT AT PAULETTE ROAD. YOU'LL HIT LANG.

THANKS.

LANG ROAD

FUCKING ASSHOLE.

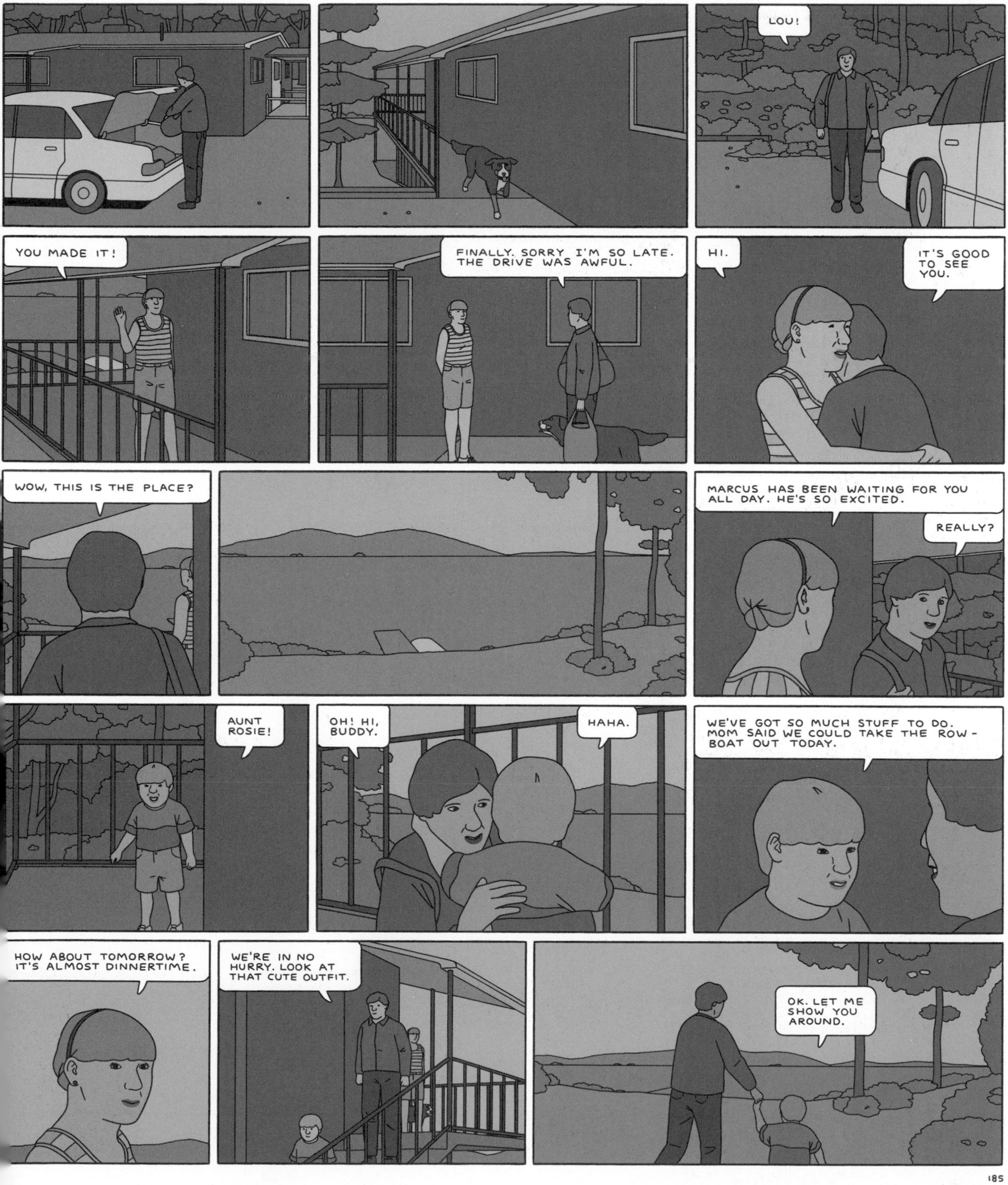
LOU!
YOU MADE IT!
FINALLY. SORRY I'M SO LATE. THE DRIVE WAS AWFUL.
HI.
IT'S GOOD TO SEE YOU.
WOW, THIS IS THE PLACE?
MARCUS HAS BEEN WAITING FOR YOU ALL DAY. HE'S SO EXCITED.
REALLY?
AUNT ROSIE!
OH! HI, BUDDY.
HAHA.
WE'VE GOT SO MUCH STUFF TO DO. MOM SAID WE COULD TAKE THE ROW-BOAT OUT TODAY.
HOW ABOUT TOMORROW? IT'S ALMOST DINNERTIME.
WE'RE IN NO HURRY. LOOK AT THAT CUTE OUTFIT.
OK. LET ME SHOW YOU AROUND.

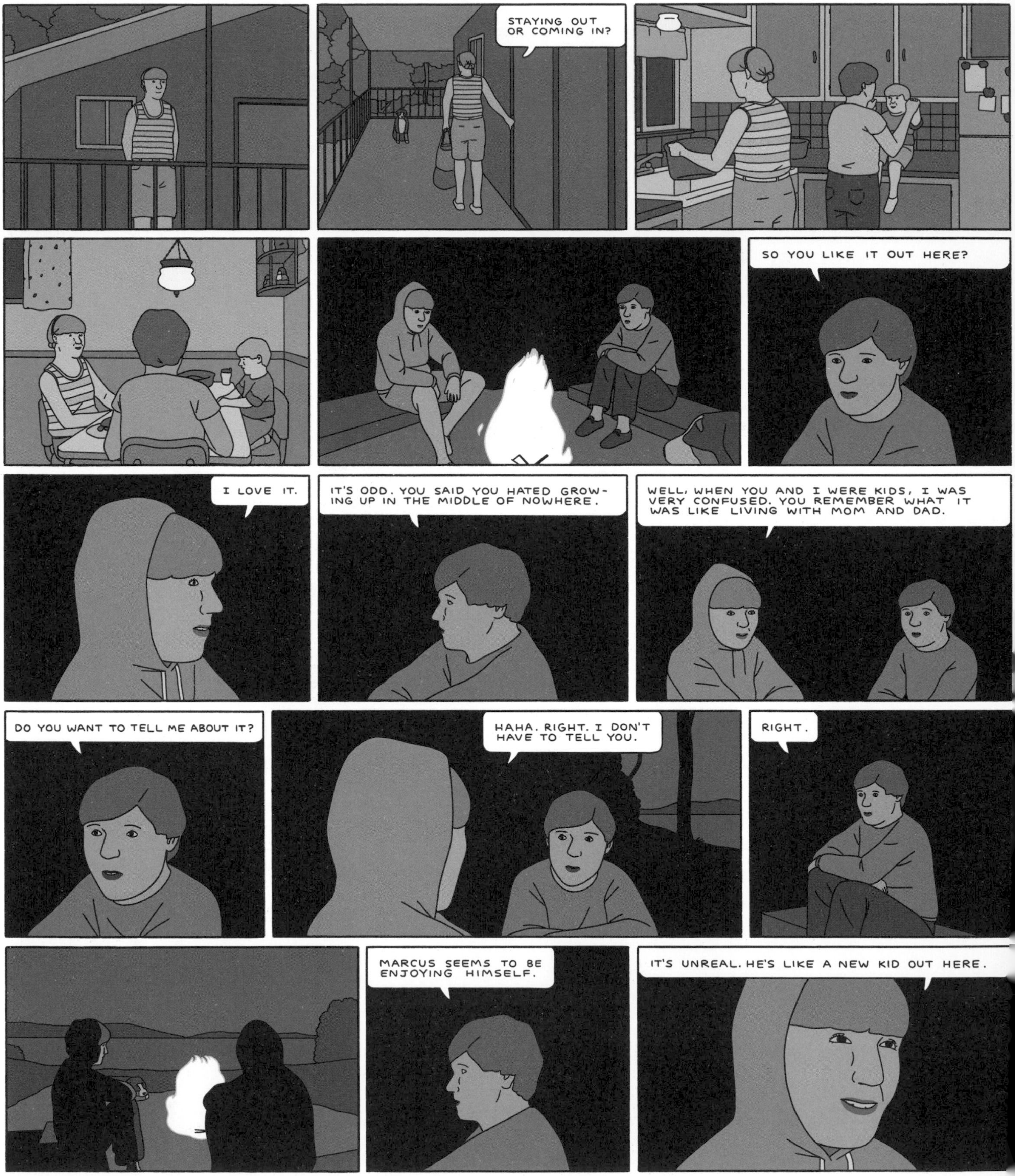
STAYING OUT OR COMING IN?
SO YOU LIKE IT OUT HERE?
I LOVE IT.
IT'S ODD. YOU SAID YOU HATED GROWING UP IN THE MIDDLE OF NOWHERE.
WELL, WHEN YOU AND I WERE KIDS, I WAS VERY CONFUSED. YOU REMEMBER WHAT IT WAS LIKE LIVING WITH MOM AND DAD.
DO YOU WANT TO TELL ME ABOUT IT?
HAHA. RIGHT. I DON'T HAVE TO TELL YOU.
RIGHT.
MARCUS SEEMS TO BE ENJOYING HIMSELF.
IT'S UNREAL. HE'S LIKE A NEW KID OUT HERE.

I GUESS THIS IS WHAT HE NEEDED.

WHAT DO YOU MEAN? THE NATURE? THE QUIET?

ALL OF IT.

WHAT ARE THOSE LIGHTS?

THERE ARE SOME BIG MANSIONS ON THE OTHER SIDE OF THE LAKE.

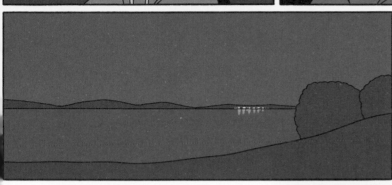

WEIRD. FROM HERE, IT LOOKS LIKE AN ENTIRE CITY WAY OFF IN THE DISTANCE.

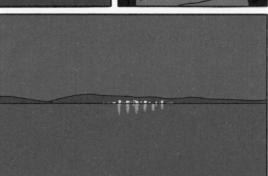

HOW ARE THINGS GOING WITH PETER?

PETER?

IT SEEMED LIKE YOU WERE GETTING SERIOUS.

OH.

I DON'T KNOW.

I THOUGHT YOU MIGHT WANT TO BRING HIM OUT HERE.

I DON'T FEEL VERY CLOSE TO HIM.

THAT'S TOO BAD.

YEA. IT IS TOO BAD.

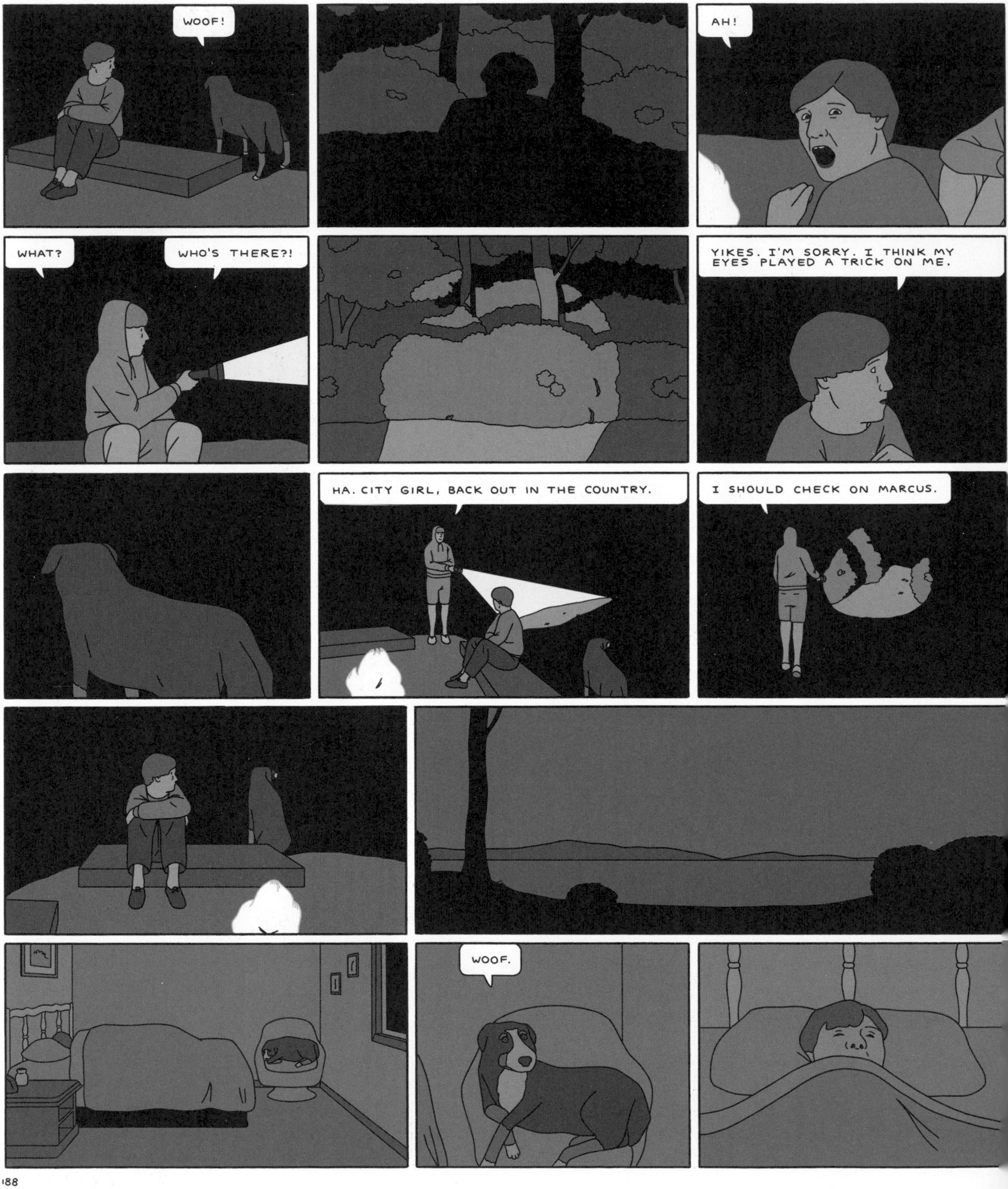
WOOF!
AH!
WHAT?
WHO'S THERE?!
YIKES. I'M SORRY. I THINK MY EYES PLAYED A TRICK ON ME.
HA. CITY GIRL, BACK OUT IN THE COUNTRY.
I SHOULD CHECK ON MARCUS.
WOOF.

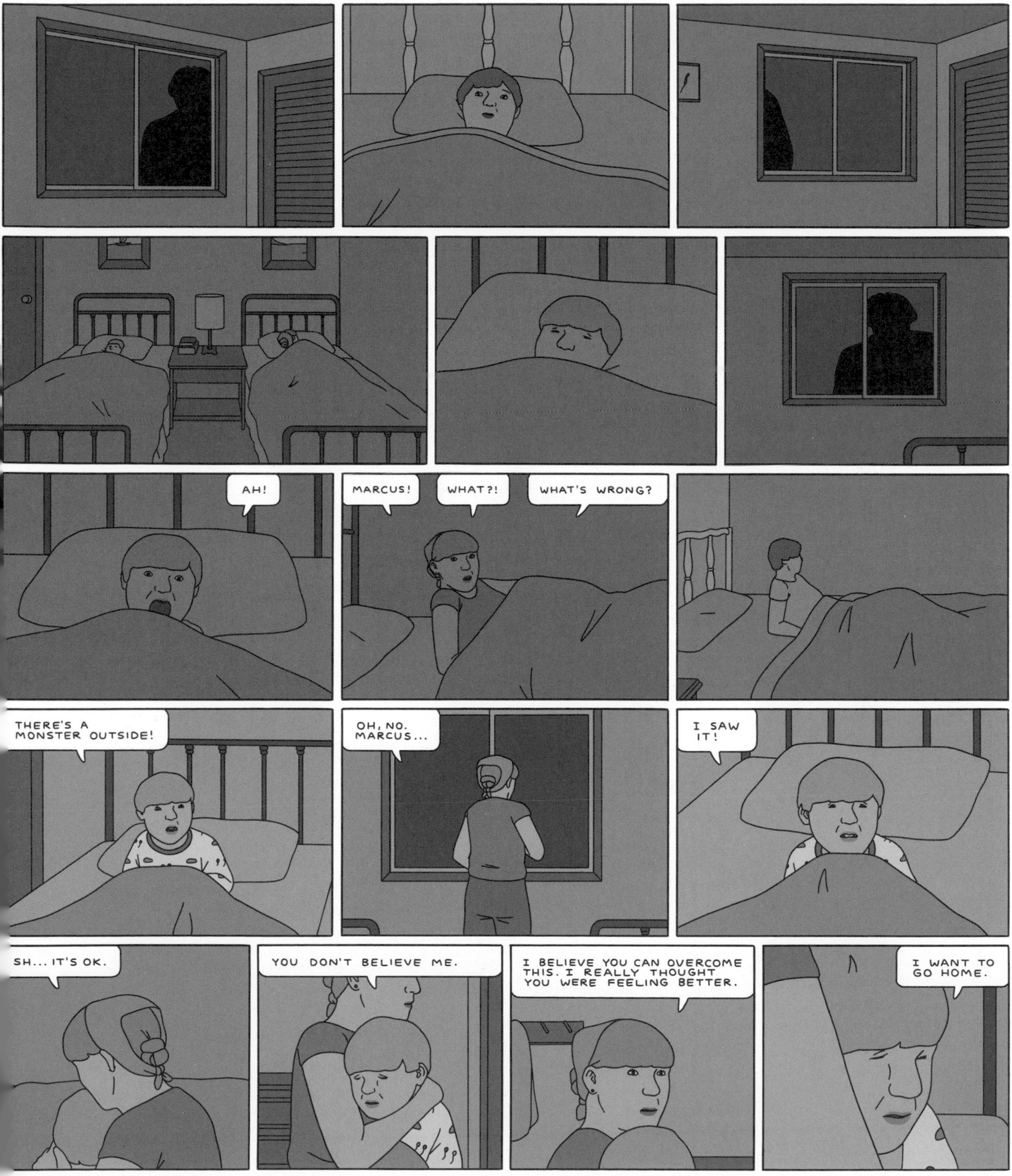
AH!
MARCUS!
WHAT?!
WHAT'S WRONG?
THERE'S A MONSTER OUTSIDE!
OH, NO. MARCUS...
I SAW IT!
SH... IT'S OK.
YOU DON'T BELIEVE ME.
I BELIEVE YOU CAN OVERCOME THIS. I REALLY THOUGHT YOU WERE FEELING BETTER.
I WANT TO GO HOME.

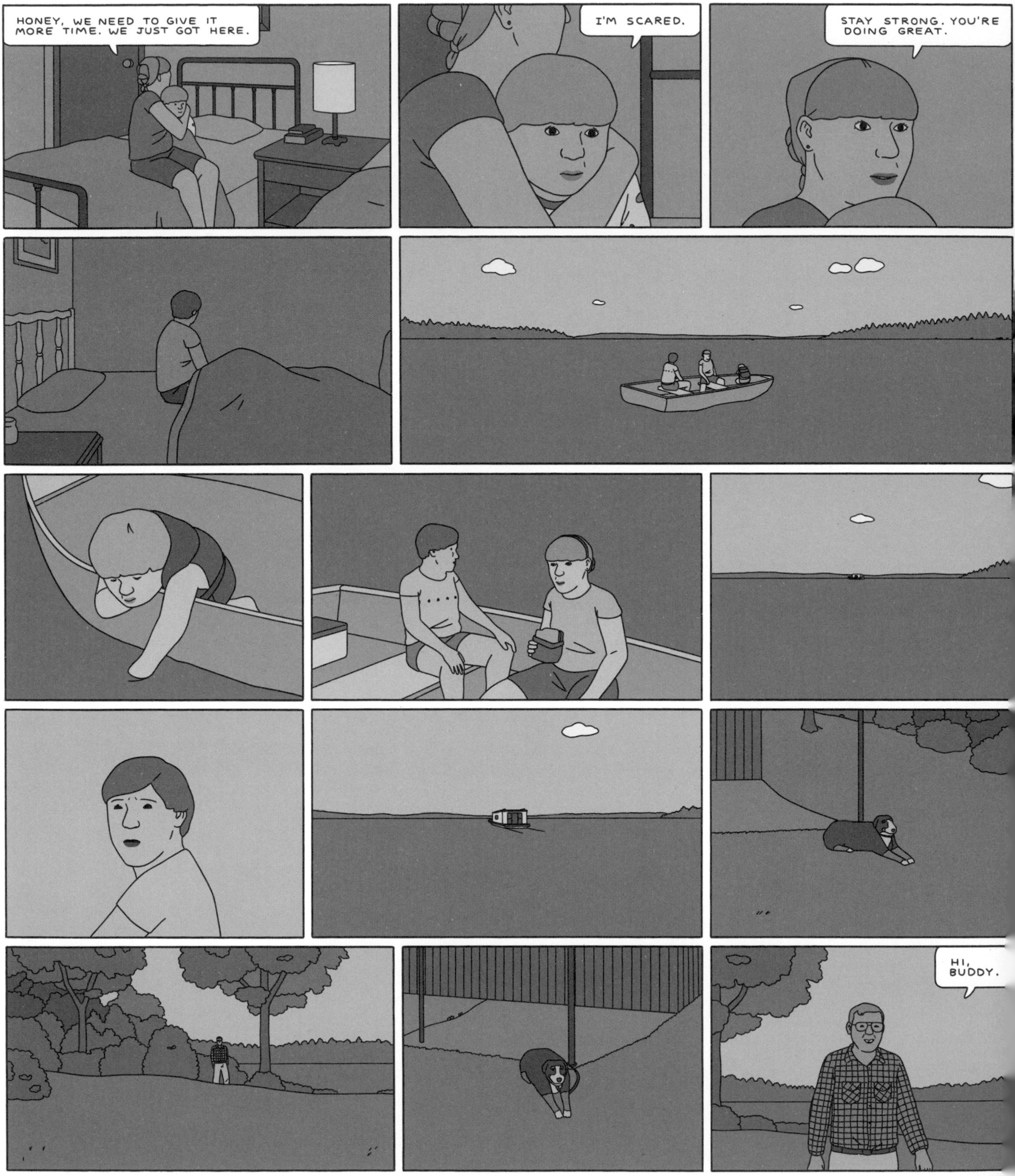
HONEY, WE NEED TO GIVE IT MORE TIME. WE JUST GOT HERE.
I'M SCARED.
STAY STRONG. YOU'RE DOING GREAT.
HI, BUDDY.

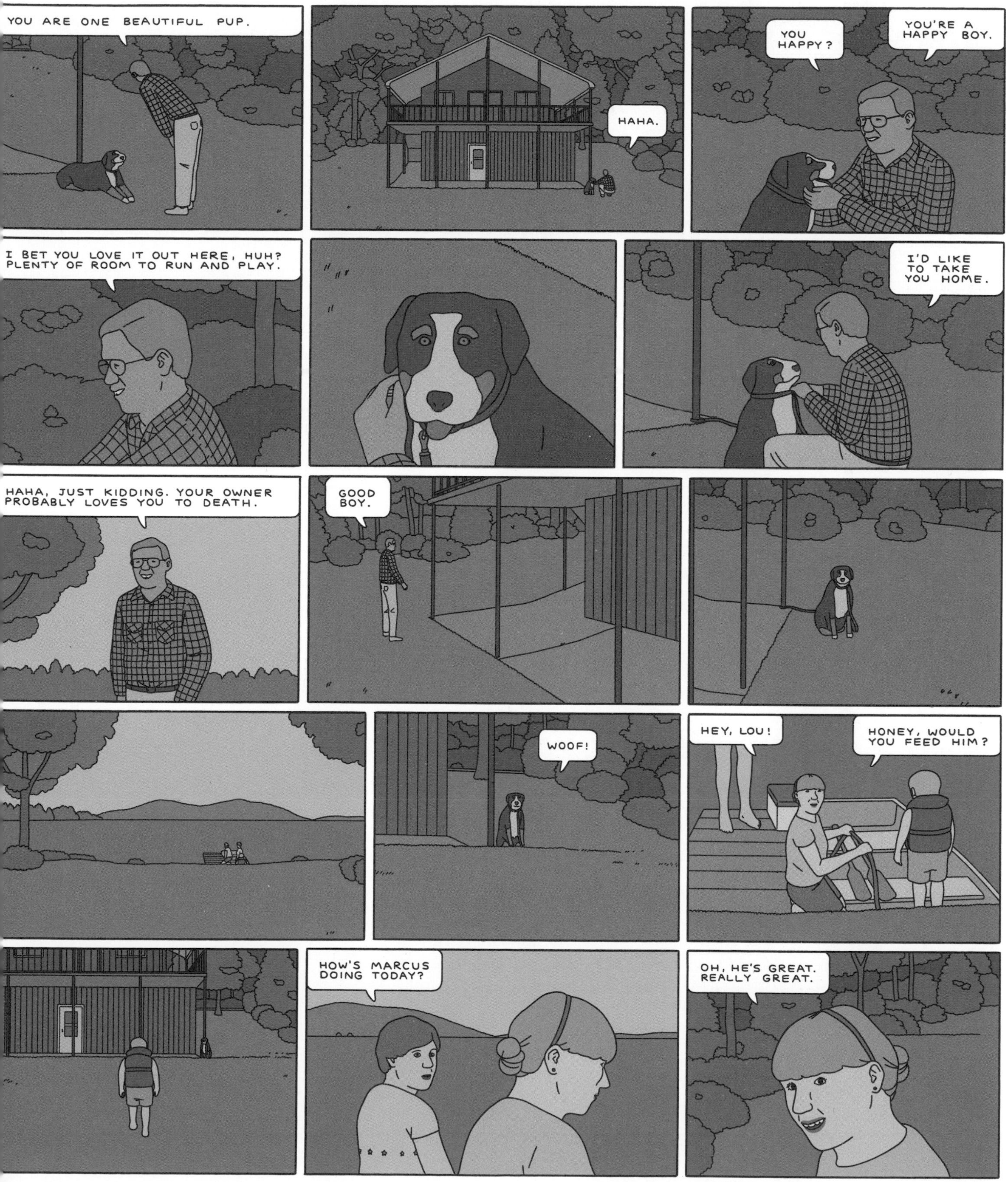
YOU ARE ONE BEAUTIFUL PUP.
HAHA.
YOU HAPPY?
YOU'RE A HAPPY BOY.
I BET YOU LOVE IT OUT HERE, HUH? PLENTY OF ROOM TO RUN AND PLAY.
I'D LIKE TO TAKE YOU HOME.
HAHA, JUST KIDDING. YOUR OWNER PROBABLY LOVES YOU TO DEATH.
GOOD BOY.
WOOF!
HEY, LOU!
HONEY, WOULD YOU FEED HIM?
HOW'S MARCUS DOING TODAY?
OH, HE'S GREAT. REALLY GREAT.

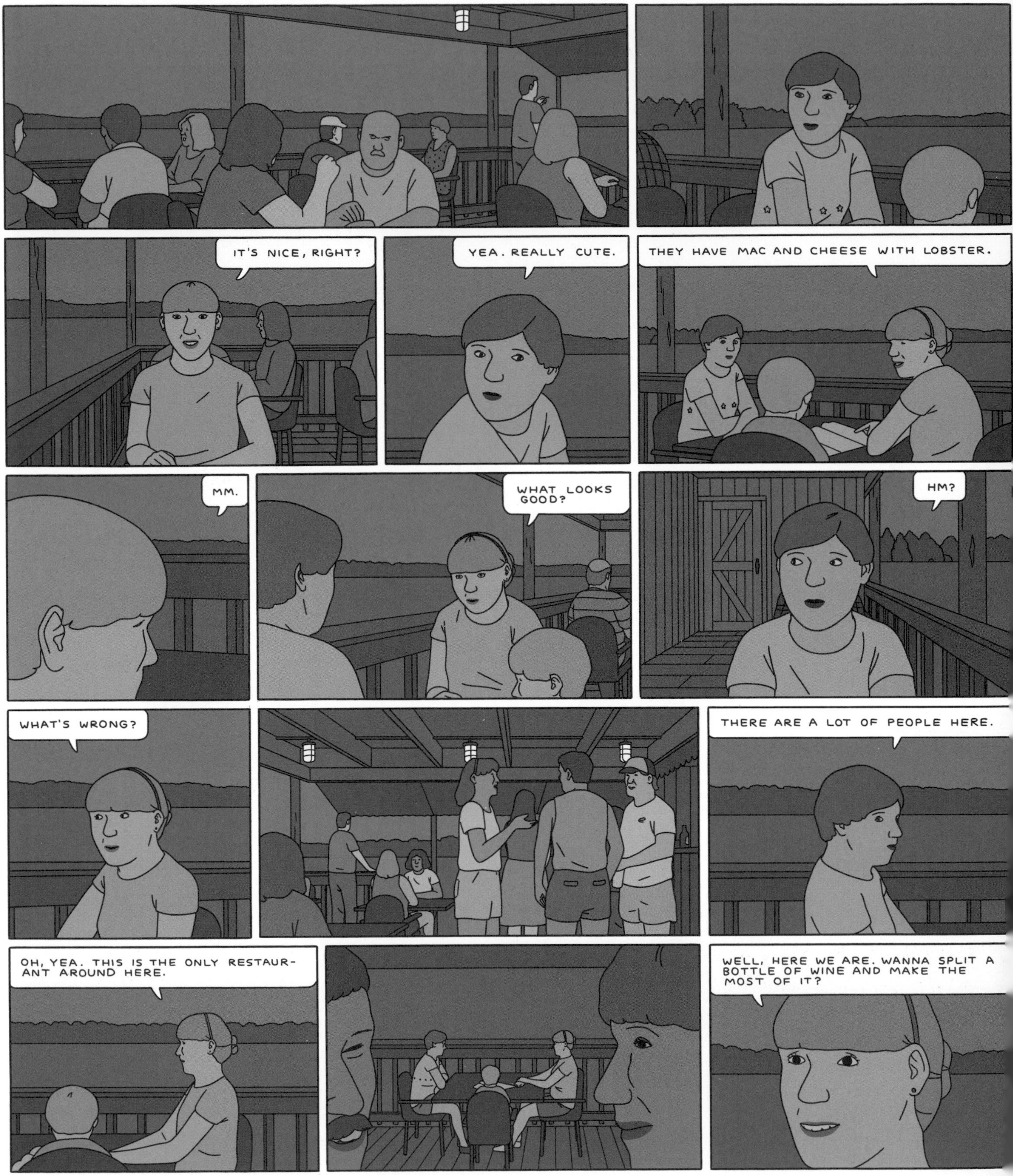
IT'S NICE, RIGHT?
YEA. REALLY CUTE.
THEY HAVE MAC AND CHEESE WITH LOBSTER.
MM.
WHAT LOOKS GOOD?
HM?
WHAT'S WRONG?
THERE ARE A LOT OF PEOPLE HERE.
OH, YEA. THIS IS THE ONLY RESTAURANT AROUND HERE.
WELL, HERE WE ARE. WANNA SPLIT A BOTTLE OF WINE AND MAKE THE MOST OF IT?

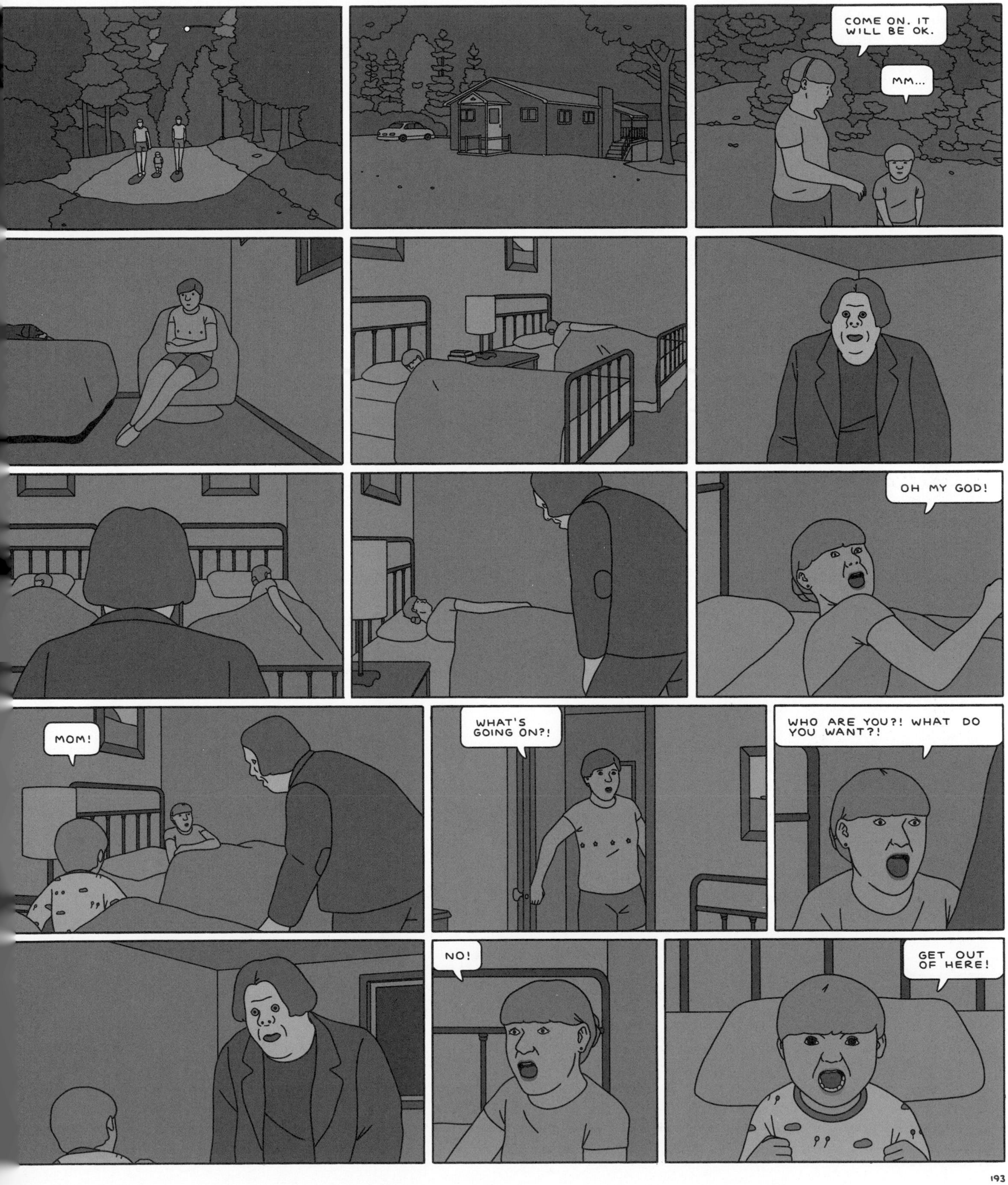
COME ON. IT WILL BE OK.
MM...
OH MY GOD!
MOM!
WHAT'S GOING ON?!
WHO ARE YOU?! WHAT DO YOU WANT?!
NO!
GET OUT OF HERE!

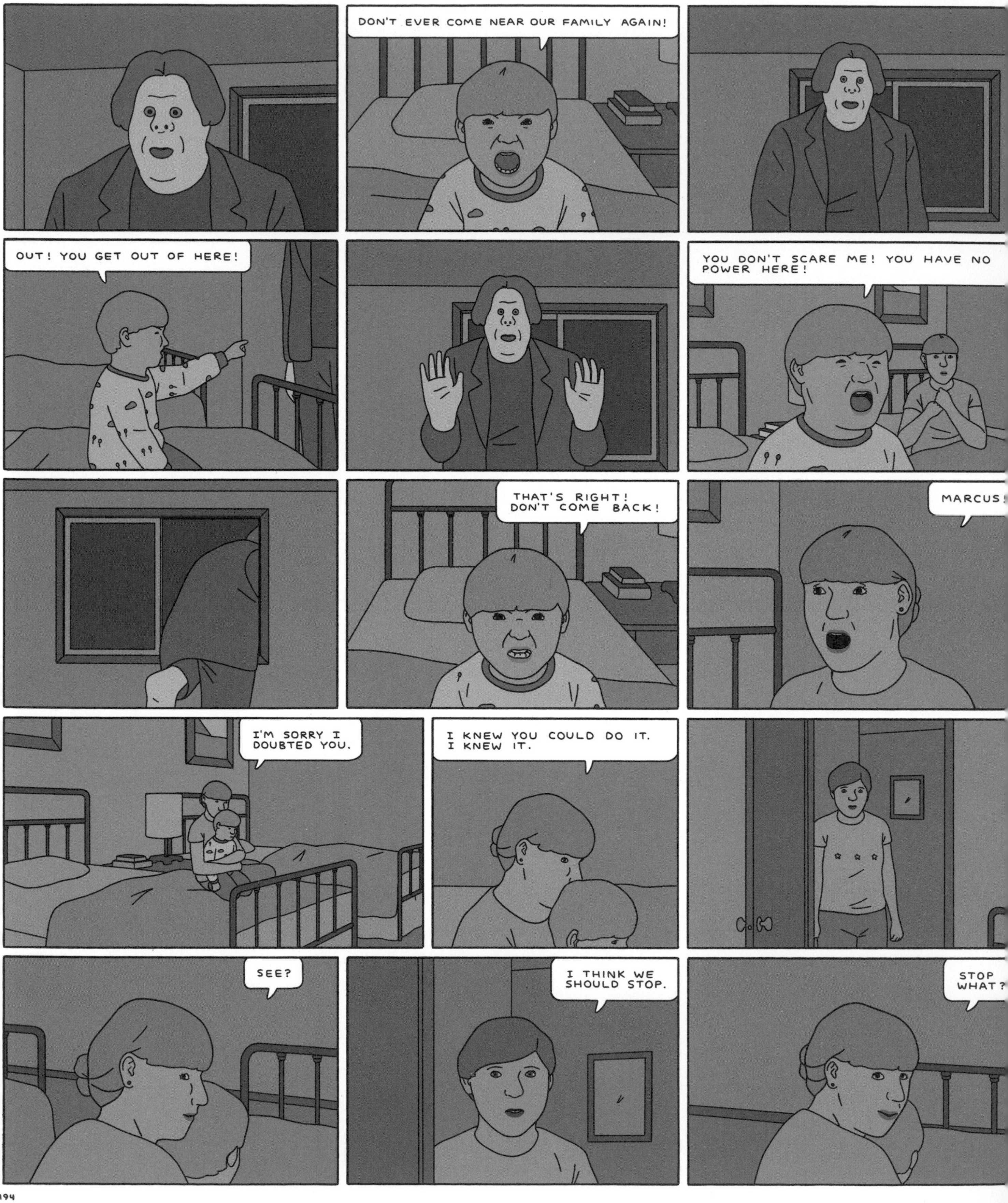
DON'T EVER COME NEAR OUR FAMILY AGAIN!
OUT! YOU GET OUT OF HERE!
YOU DON'T SCARE ME! YOU HAVE NO POWER HERE!
THAT'S RIGHT! DON'T COME BACK!
MARCUS!
I'M SORRY I DOUBTED YOU.
I KNEW YOU COULD DO IT. I KNEW IT.
SEE?
I THINK WE SHOULD STOP.
STOP WHAT?

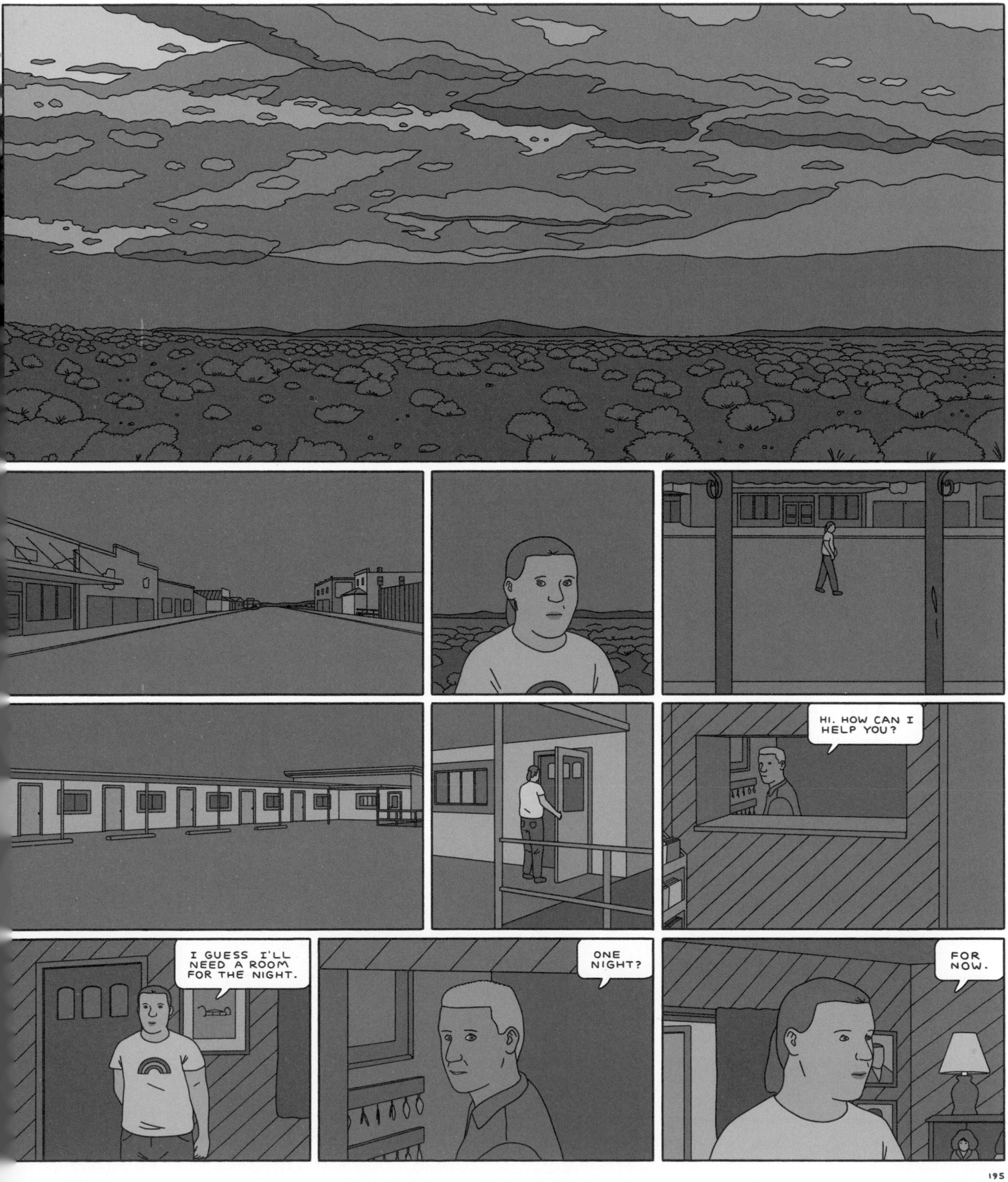
HI. HOW CAN I HELP YOU?
I GUESS I'LL NEED A ROOM FOR THE NIGHT.
ONE NIGHT?
FOR NOW.

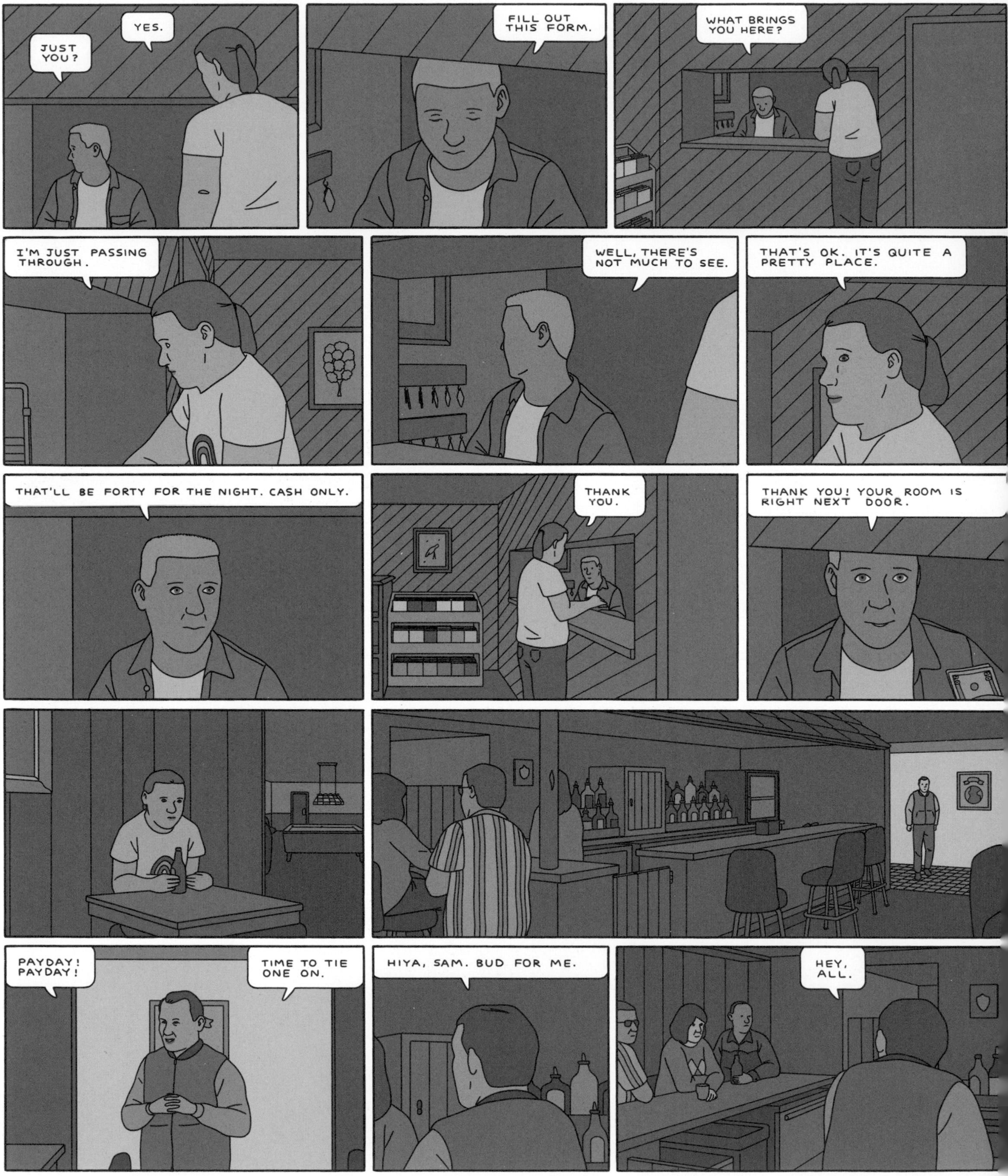
JUST YOU?
YES.
FILL OUT THIS FORM.
WHAT BRINGS YOU HERE?
I'M JUST PASSING THROUGH.
WELL, THERE'S NOT MUCH TO SEE.
THAT'S OK. IT'S QUITE A PRETTY PLACE.
THAT'LL BE FORTY FOR THE NIGHT. CASH ONLY.
THANK YOU.
THANK YOU! YOUR ROOM IS RIGHT NEXT DOOR.
PAYDAY! PAYDAY!
TIME TO TIE ONE ON.
HIYA, SAM. BUD FOR ME.
HEY, ALL.

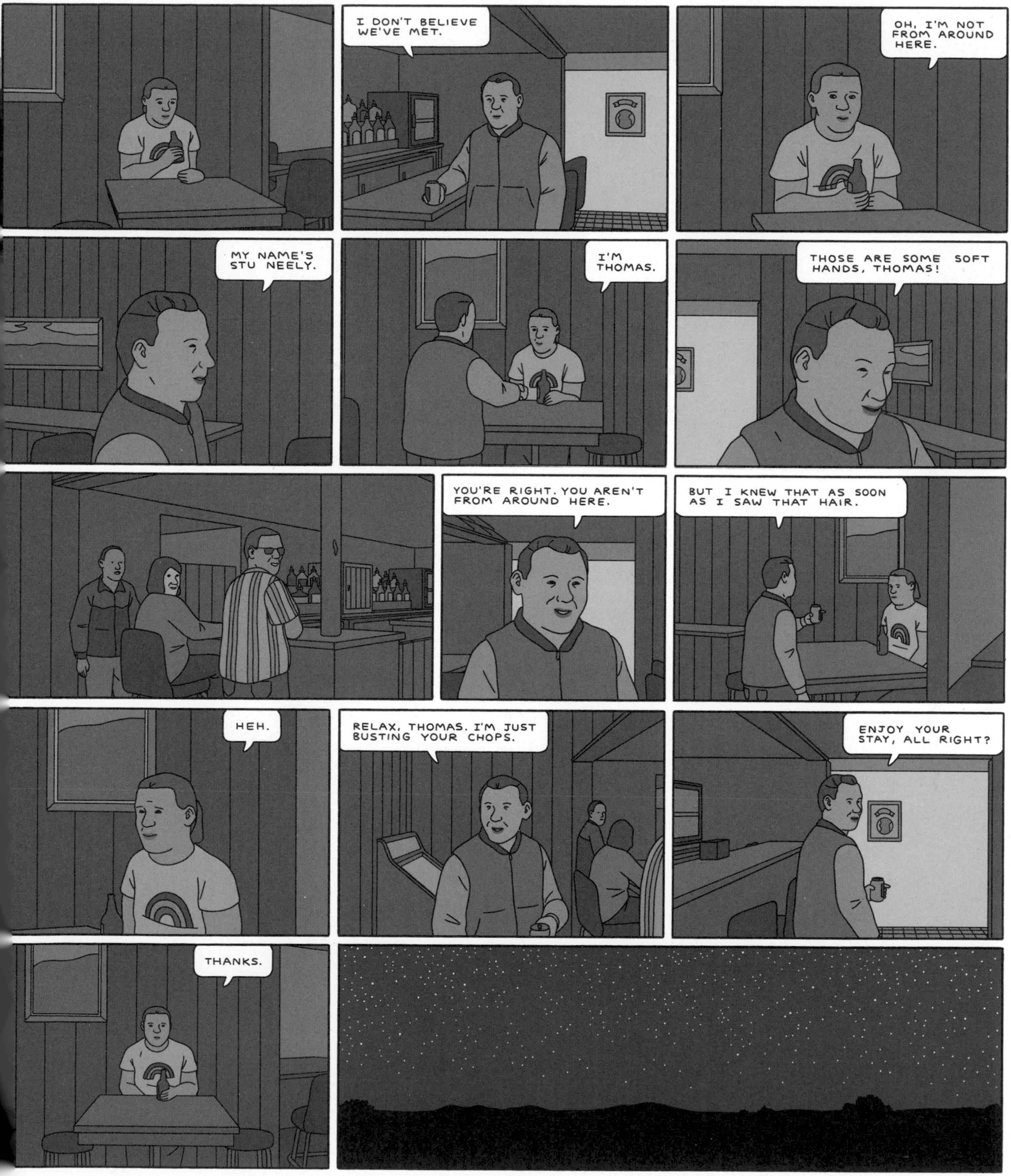
I DON'T BELIEVE WE'VE MET.
OH, I'M NOT FROM AROUND HERE.
MY NAME'S STU NEELY.
I'M THOMAS.
THOSE ARE SOME SOFT HANDS, THOMAS!
YOU'RE RIGHT. YOU AREN'T FROM AROUND HERE.
BUT I KNEW THAT AS SOON AS I SAW THAT HAIR.
HEH.
RELAX, THOMAS. I'M JUST BUSTING YOUR CHOPS.
ENJOY YOUR STAY, ALL RIGHT?
THANKS.

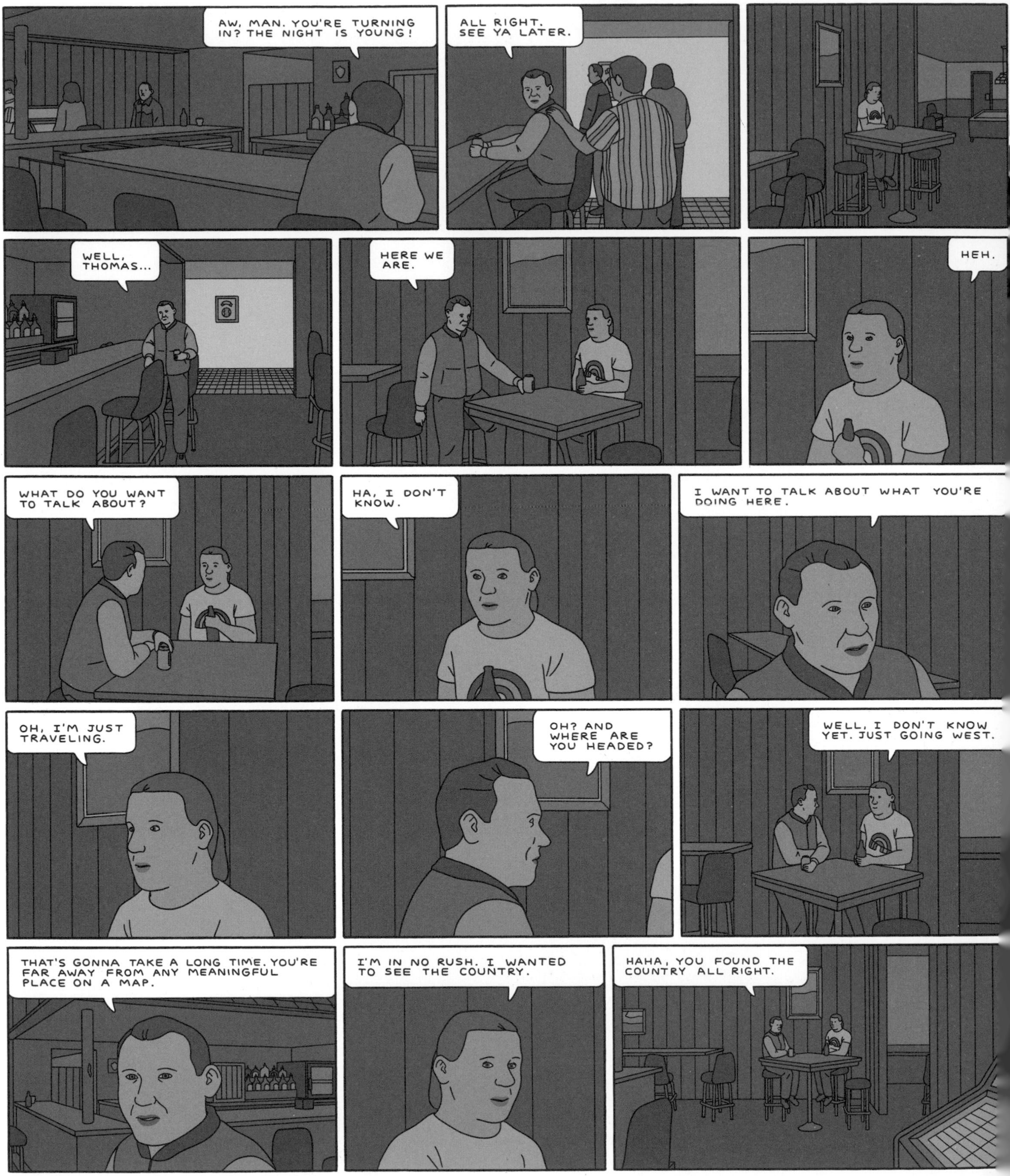
AW, MAN. YOU'RE TURNING IN? THE NIGHT IS YOUNG!
ALL RIGHT. SEE YA LATER.
WELL, THOMAS...
HERE WE ARE.
HEH.
WHAT DO YOU WANT TO TALK ABOUT?
HA, I DON'T KNOW.
I WANT TO TALK ABOUT WHAT YOU'RE DOING HERE.
OH, I'M JUST TRAVELING.
OH? AND WHERE ARE YOU HEADED?
WELL, I DON'T KNOW YET. JUST GOING WEST.
THAT'S GONNA TAKE A LONG TIME. YOU'RE FAR AWAY FROM ANY MEANINGFUL PLACE ON A MAP.
I'M IN NO RUSH. I WANTED TO SEE THE COUNTRY.
HAHA, YOU FOUND THE COUNTRY ALL RIGHT.

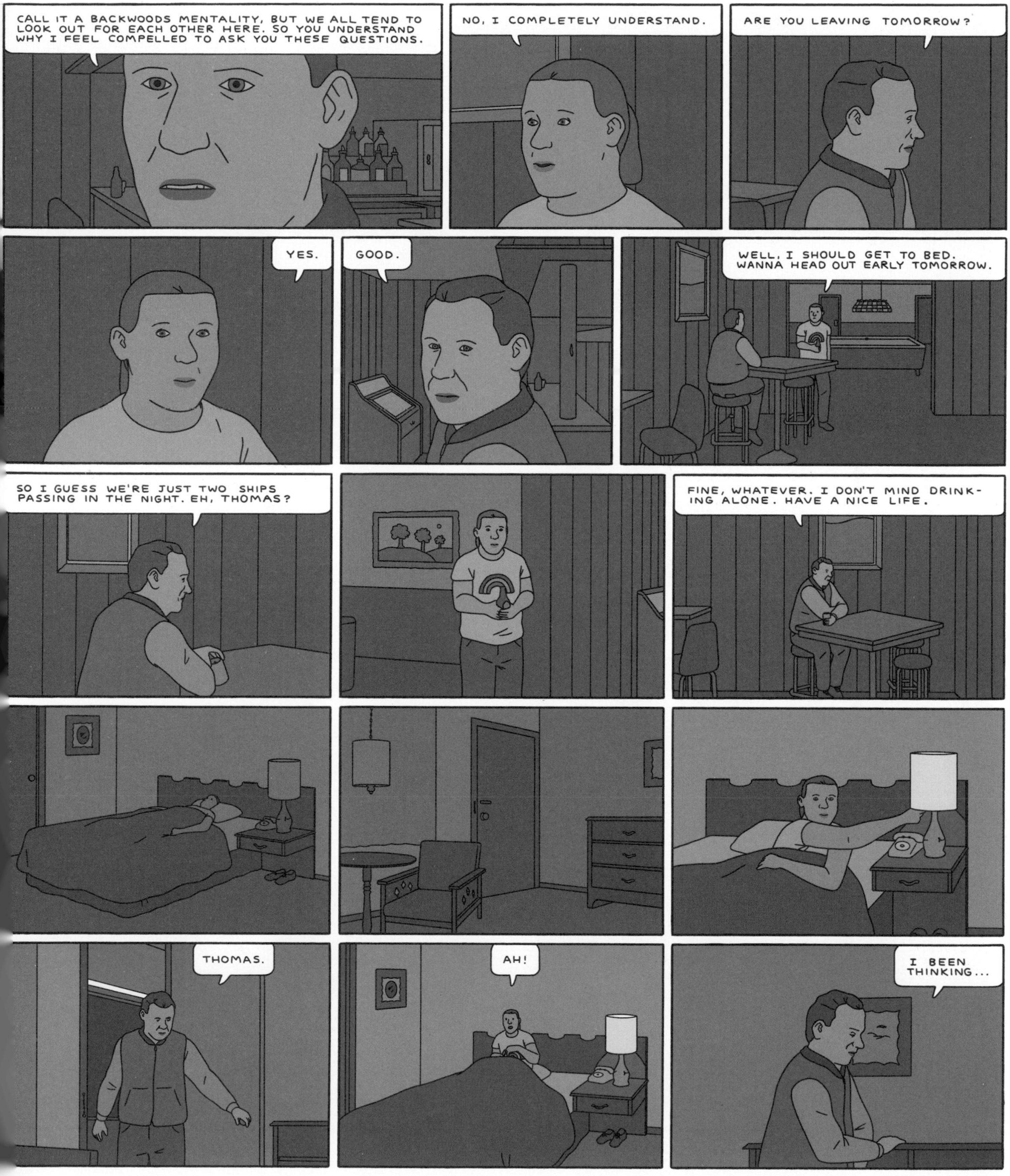
CALL IT A BACKWOODS MENTALITY, BUT WE ALL TEND TO LOOK OUT FOR EACH OTHER HERE. SO YOU UNDERSTAND WHY I FEEL COMPELLED TO ASK YOU THESE QUESTIONS.
NO, I COMPLETELY UNDERSTAND.
ARE YOU LEAVING TOMORROW?
YES.
GOOD.
WELL, I SHOULD GET TO BED. WANNA HEAD OUT EARLY TOMORROW.
SO I GUESS WE'RE JUST TWO SHIPS PASSING IN THE NIGHT. EH, THOMAS?
FINE, WHATEVER. I DON'T MIND DRINKING ALONE. HAVE A NICE LIFE.
THOMAS.
AH!
I BEEN THINKING...

 WHAT DO
YOU WANT?

 WAS I GETTING AN
ATTITUDE FROM
YOU EARLIER?

 NO, OF
COURSE NOT!

 THE WAY I SEE IT, YOU'RE
A GUEST IN OUR TOWN.

 IT'S A COURTESY THING. THERE'S A RESPECT
THING, AND I DIDN'T FEEL THAT FROM
YOU, AND I. DON'T. LIKE. IT.

 YOU'RE RIGHT. I'M SORRY.
I'M NOT WANTED HERE.

 HEH... YOU JUST NEED TO ACT RIGHT.

 OK. YOU'RE
RIGHT.

 GOD. YOU BASTARD.
ACT RIGHT!

 HEY! WHAT ARE YOU DOING?!

 ACT
RIGHT!

 AH!
NO!

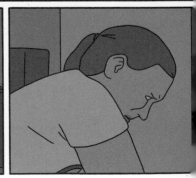

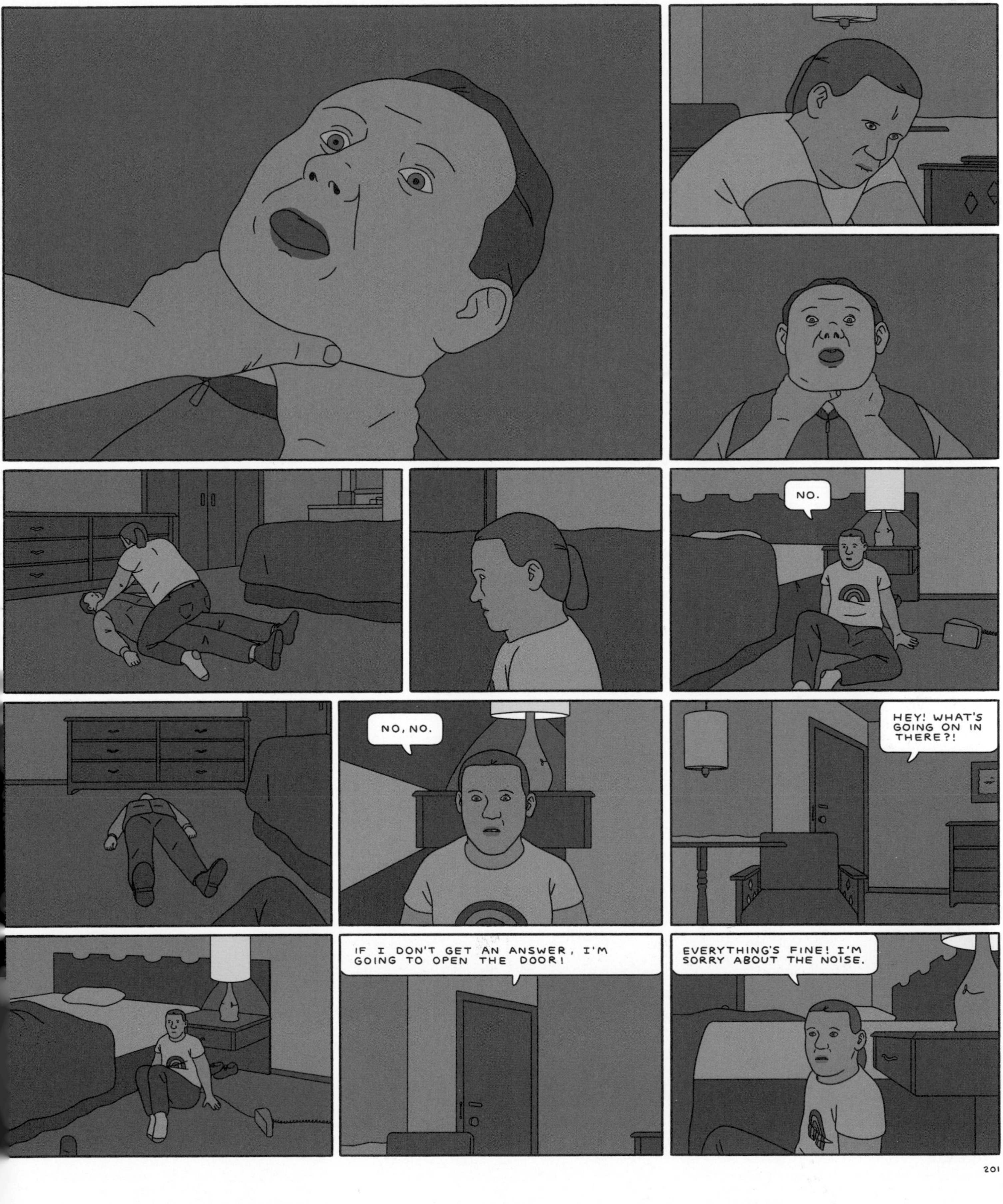
NO.
NO, NO.
HEY! WHAT'S GOING ON IN THERE?!
IF I DON'T GET AN ANSWER, I'M GOING TO OPEN THE DOOR!
EVERYTHING'S FINE! I'M SORRY ABOUT THE NOISE.

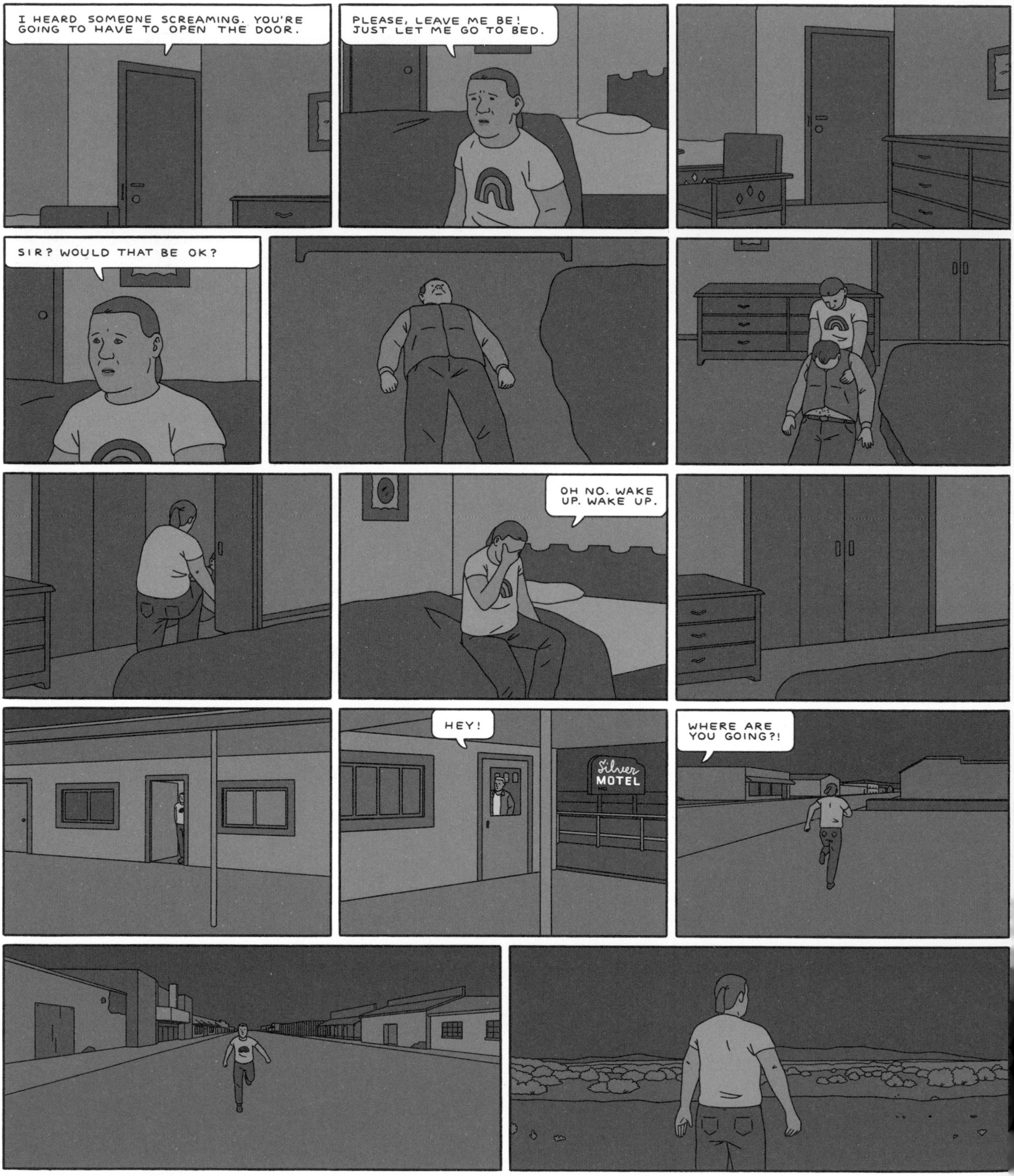
I HEARD SOMEONE SCREAMING. YOU'RE GOING TO HAVE TO OPEN THE DOOR.
PLEASE, LEAVE ME BE! JUST LET ME GO TO BED.
SIR? WOULD THAT BE OK?
OH NO. WAKE UP. WAKE UP.
HEY!
Silver MOTEL
WHERE ARE YOU GOING?!

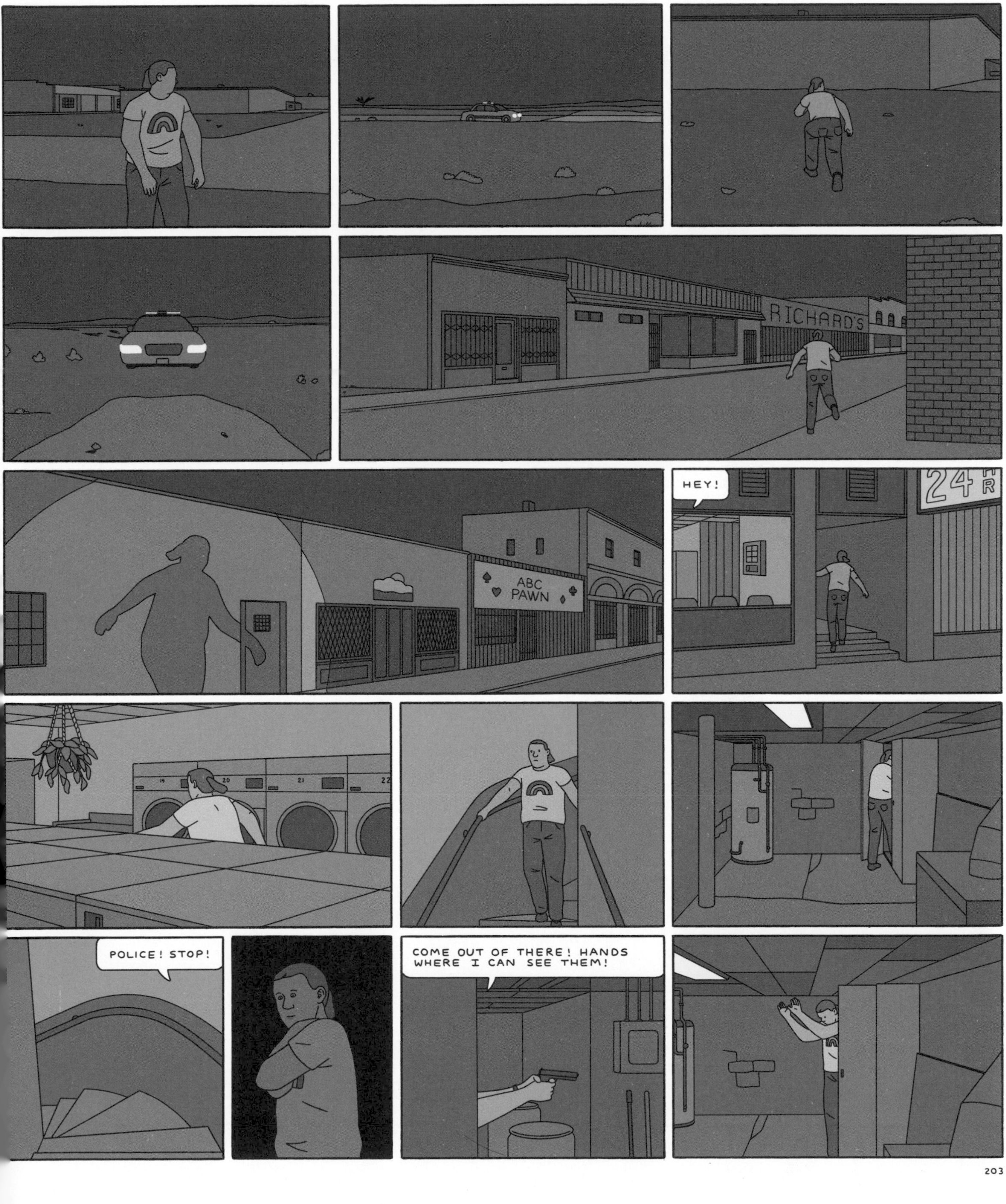
RICHARD'S
ABC PAWN
HEY!
24 HR
POLICE! STOP!
COME OUT OF THERE! HANDS WHERE I CAN SEE THEM!

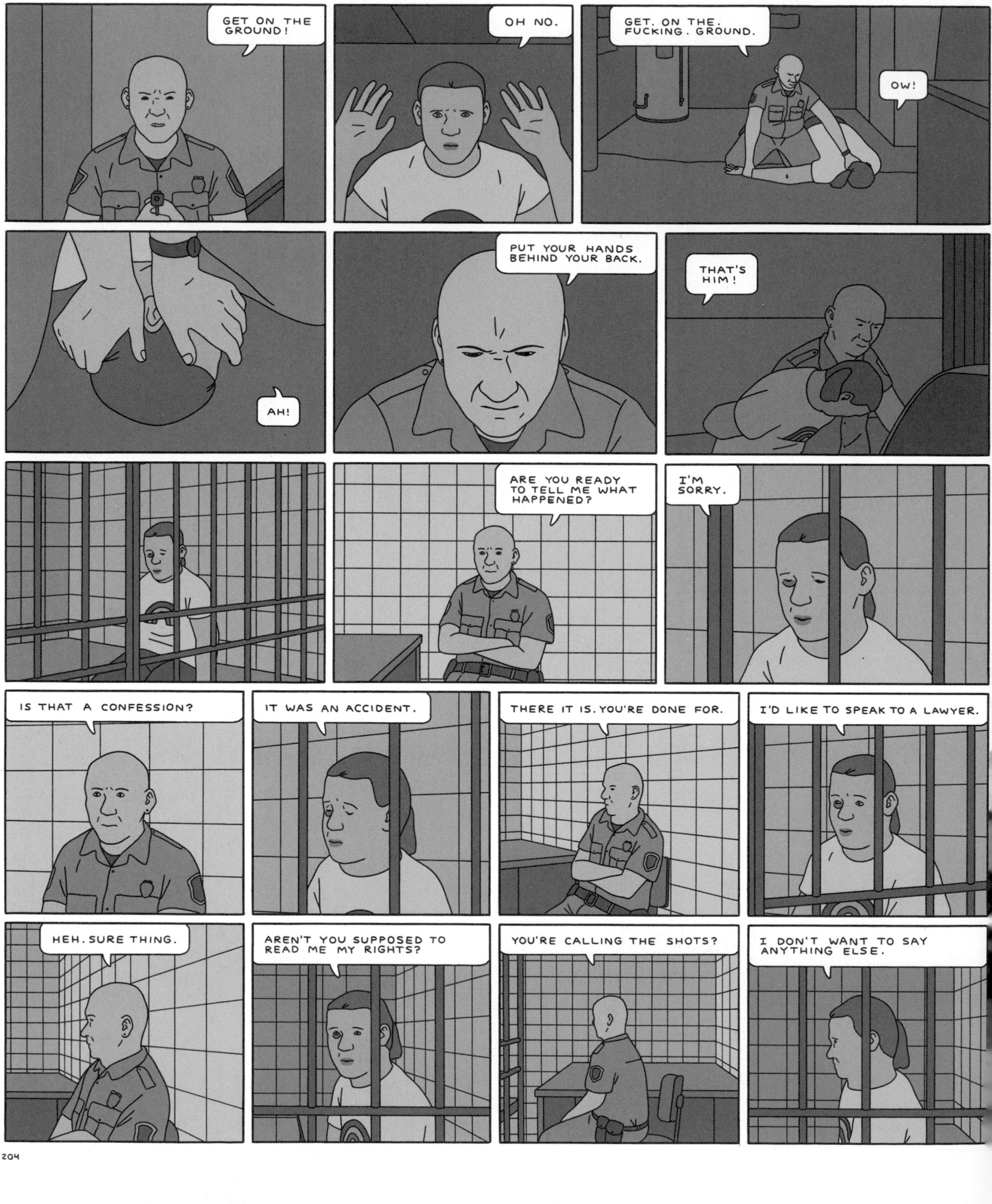
GET ON THE GROUND!
OH NO.
GET. ON THE. FUCKING. GROUND.
OW!
AH!
PUT YOUR HANDS BEHIND YOUR BACK.
THAT'S HIM!
ARE YOU READY TO TELL ME WHAT HAPPENED?
I'M SORRY.
IS THAT A CONFESSION?
IT WAS AN ACCIDENT.
THERE IT IS. YOU'RE DONE FOR.
I'D LIKE TO SPEAK TO A LAWYER.
HEH. SURE THING.
AREN'T YOU SUPPOSED TO READ ME MY RIGHTS?
YOU'RE CALLING THE SHOTS?
I DON'T WANT TO SAY ANYTHING ELSE.

IF YOU CHALLENGE MY AUTHORITY AGAIN, I'LL BLOW YOUR HEAD OFF AND SAY IT WAS SELF-DEFENSE.

OH GOD.

TAKE OFF YOUR CLOTHES.

WHAT?

I NEED TO DO AN INSPECTION. YOU'LL GET YOUR PRISON UNIFORM AFTER.

TOSS 'EM OVER HERE.

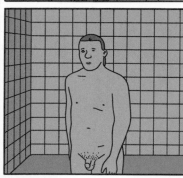

TURN AROUND. I NEED TO MAKE SURE YOU'RE NOT HIDING ANYTHING.

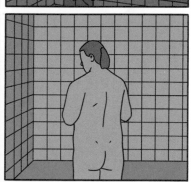

ALL RIGHT, THOMAS.

OFFICER CAMPOS.

SIR.

THIS IS THE GUY?

YES. I WAS JUST GETTING HIS UNIFORM.

COME HERE A MINUTE.

205

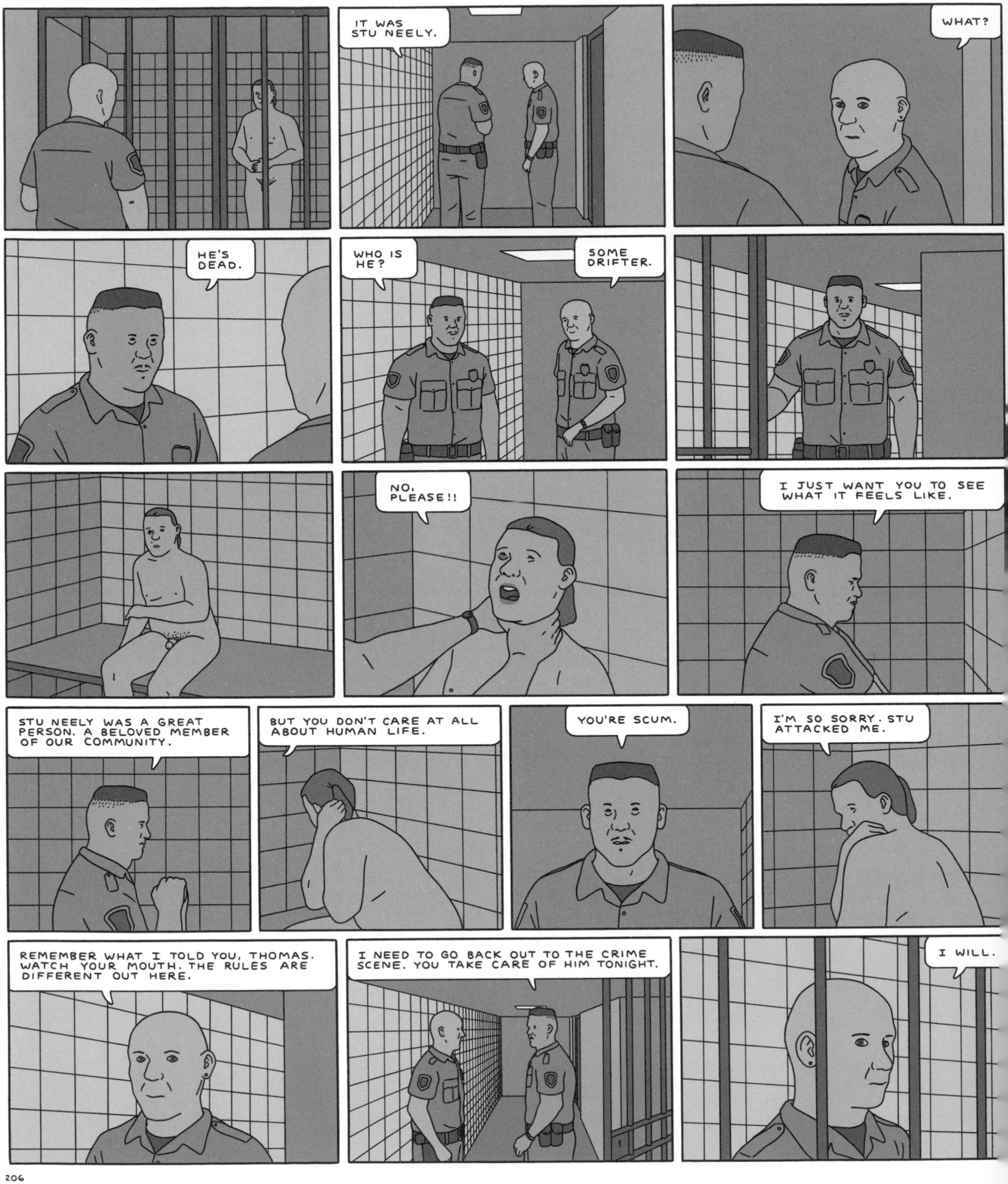
IT WAS STU NEELY.
WHAT?
HE'S DEAD.
WHO IS HE?
SOME DRIFTER.
NO, PLEASE!!
I JUST WANT YOU TO SEE WHAT IT FEELS LIKE.
STU NEELY WAS A GREAT PERSON. A BELOVED MEMBER OF OUR COMMUNITY.
BUT YOU DON'T CARE AT ALL ABOUT HUMAN LIFE.
YOU'RE SCUM.
I'M SO SORRY. STU ATTACKED ME.
REMEMBER WHAT I TOLD YOU, THOMAS. WATCH YOUR MOUTH. THE RULES ARE DIFFERENT OUT HERE.
I NEED TO GO BACK OUT TO THE CRIME SCENE. YOU TAKE CARE OF HIM TONIGHT.
I WILL.

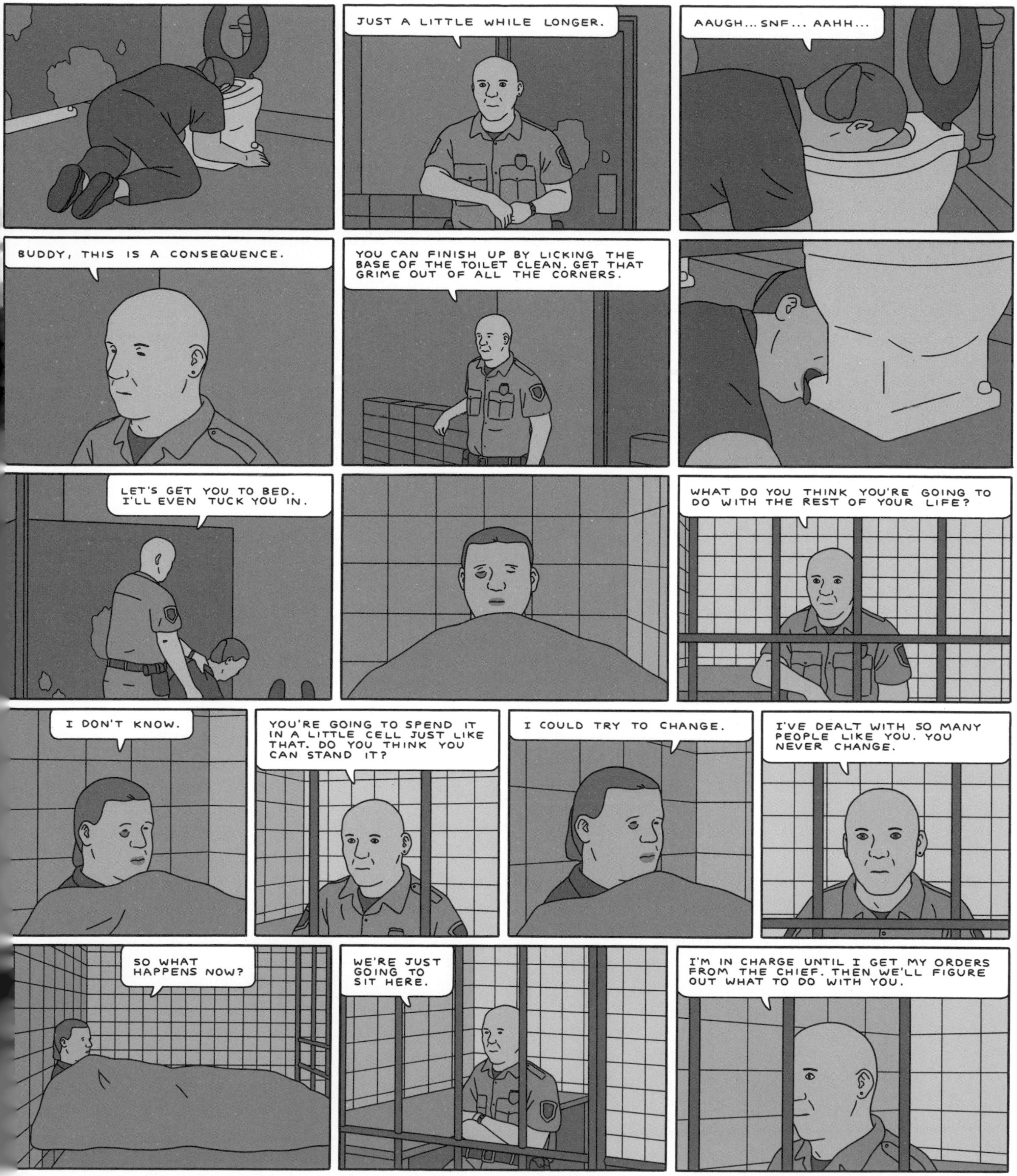
JUST A LITTLE WHILE LONGER.
AAUGH... SNF... AAHH...
BUDDY, THIS IS A CONSEQUENCE.
YOU CAN FINISH UP BY LICKING THE BASE OF THE TOILET CLEAN. GET THAT GRIME OUT OF ALL THE CORNERS.
LET'S GET YOU TO BED. I'LL EVEN TUCK YOU IN.
WHAT DO YOU THINK YOU'RE GOING TO DO WITH THE REST OF YOUR LIFE?
I DON'T KNOW.
YOU'RE GOING TO SPEND IT IN A LITTLE CELL JUST LIKE THAT. DO YOU THINK YOU CAN STAND IT?
I COULD TRY TO CHANGE.
I'VE DEALT WITH SO MANY PEOPLE LIKE YOU. YOU NEVER CHANGE.
SO WHAT HAPPENS NOW?
WE'RE JUST GOING TO SIT HERE.
I'M IN CHARGE UNTIL I GET MY ORDERS FROM THE CHIEF. THEN WE'LL FIGURE OUT WHAT TO DO WITH YOU.

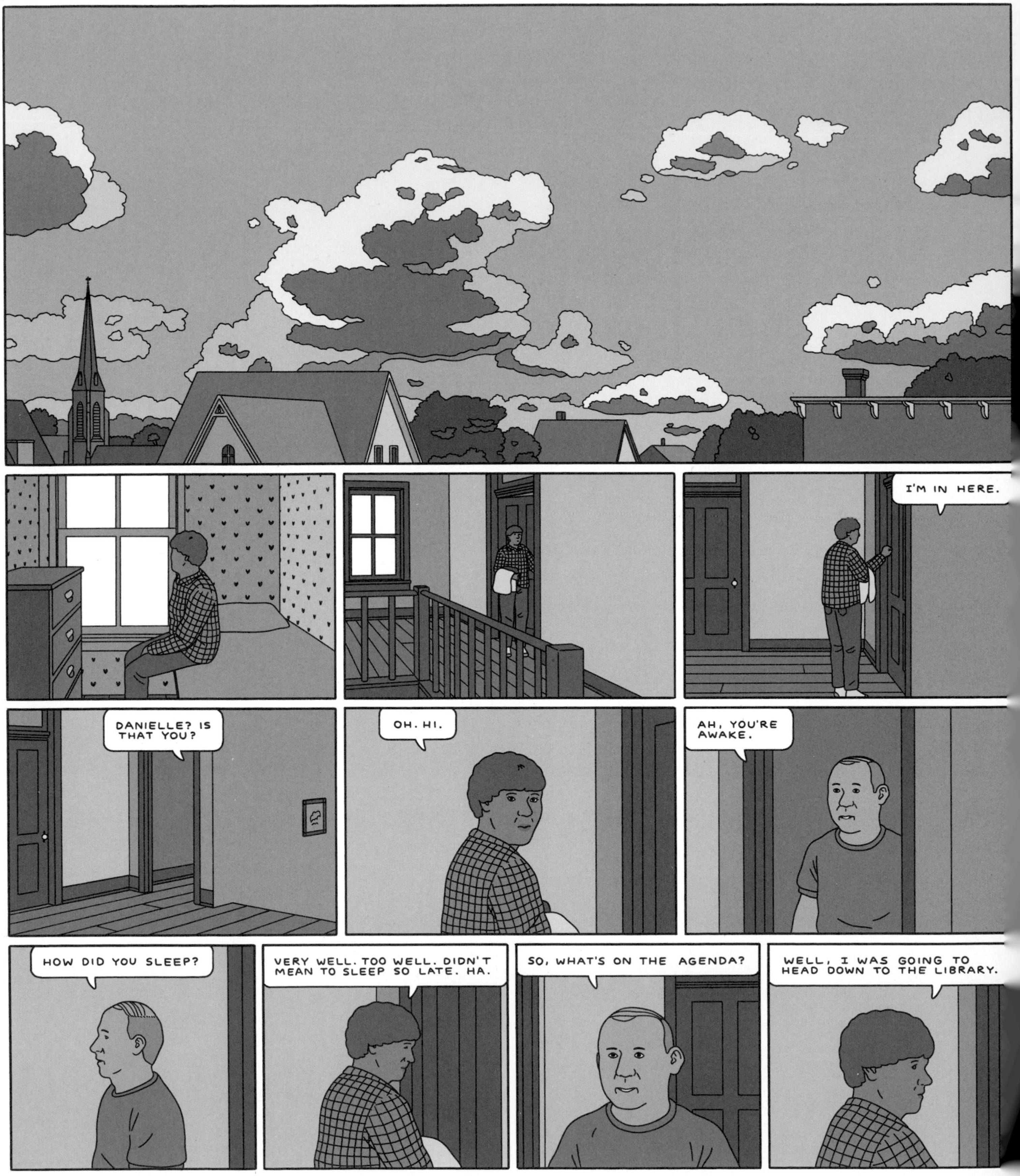
I'M IN HERE.
DANIELLE? IS THAT YOU?
OH. HI.
AH, YOU'RE AWAKE.
HOW DID YOU SLEEP?
VERY WELL. TOO WELL. DIDN'T MEAN TO SLEEP SO LATE. HA.
SO, WHAT'S ON THE AGENDA?
WELL, I WAS GOING TO HEAD DOWN TO THE LIBRARY.

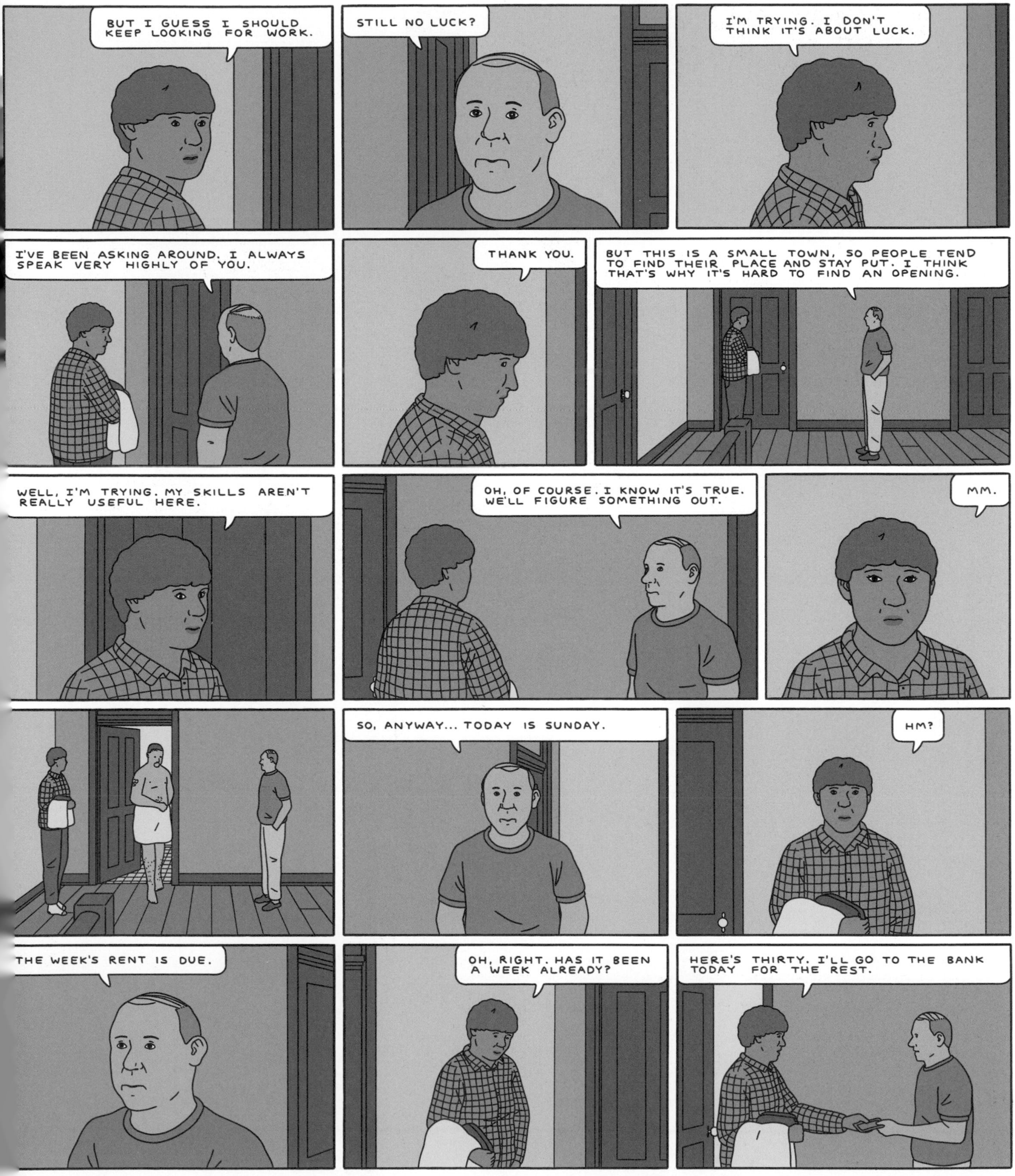
BUT I GUESS I SHOULD KEEP LOOKING FOR WORK.
STILL NO LUCK?
I'M TRYING. I DON'T THINK IT'S ABOUT LUCK.
I'VE BEEN ASKING AROUND. I ALWAYS SPEAK VERY HIGHLY OF YOU.
THANK YOU.
BUT THIS IS A SMALL TOWN, SO PEOPLE TEND TO FIND THEIR PLACE AND STAY PUT. I THINK THAT'S WHY IT'S HARD TO FIND AN OPENING.
WELL, I'M TRYING. MY SKILLS AREN'T REALLY USEFUL HERE.
OH, OF COURSE. I KNOW IT'S TRUE. WE'LL FIGURE SOMETHING OUT.
MM.
SO, ANYWAY... TODAY IS SUNDAY.
HM?
THE WEEK'S RENT IS DUE.
OH, RIGHT. HAS IT BEEN A WEEK ALREADY?
HERE'S THIRTY. I'LL GO TO THE BANK TODAY FOR THE REST.

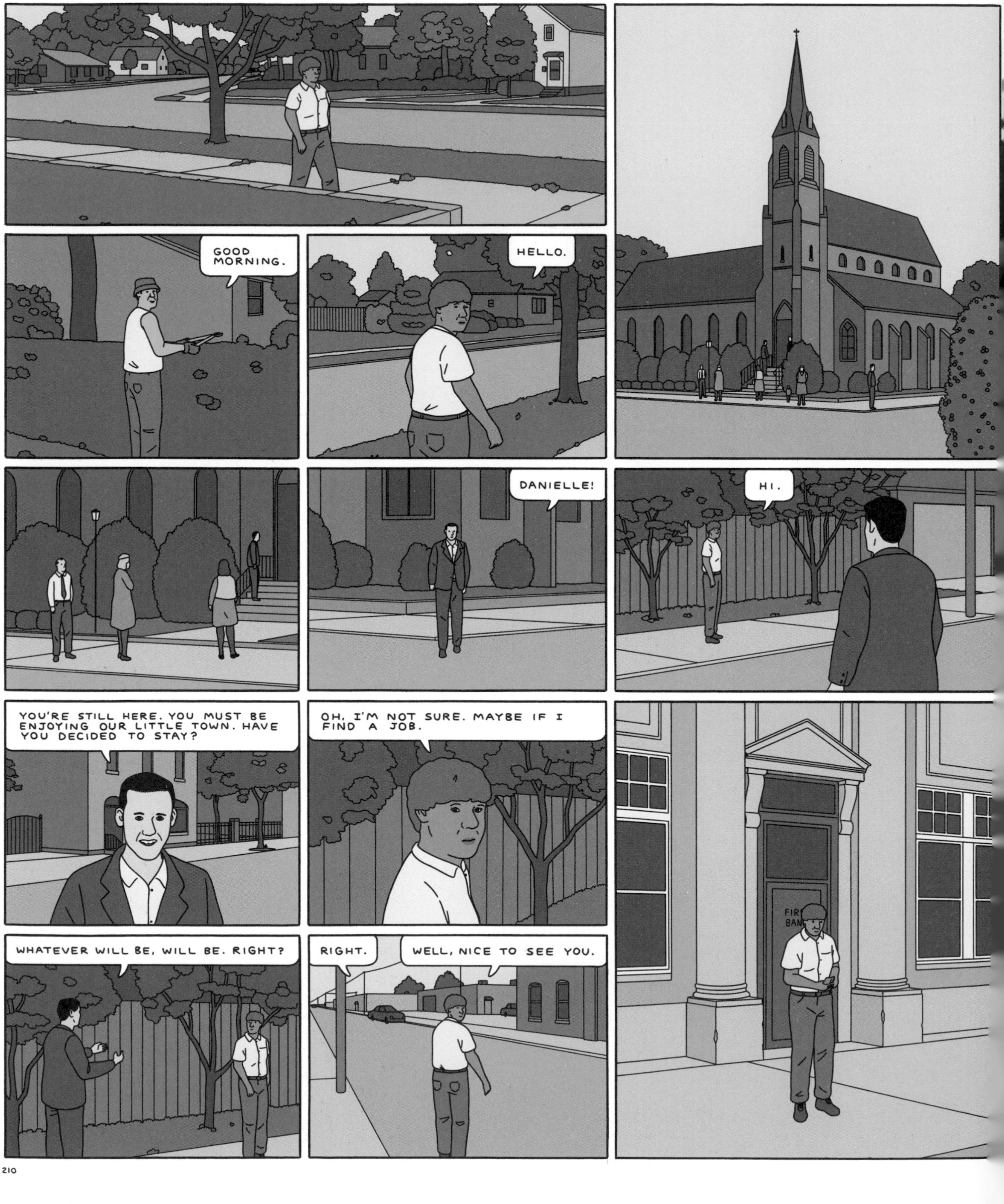
GOOD MORNING.
HELLO.
DANIELLE!
HI.
YOU'RE STILL HERE. YOU MUST BE ENJOYING OUR LITTLE TOWN. HAVE YOU DECIDED TO STAY?
OH, I'M NOT SURE. MAYBE IF I FIND A JOB.
WHATEVER WILL BE, WILL BE. RIGHT?
RIGHT.
WELL, NICE TO SEE YOU.

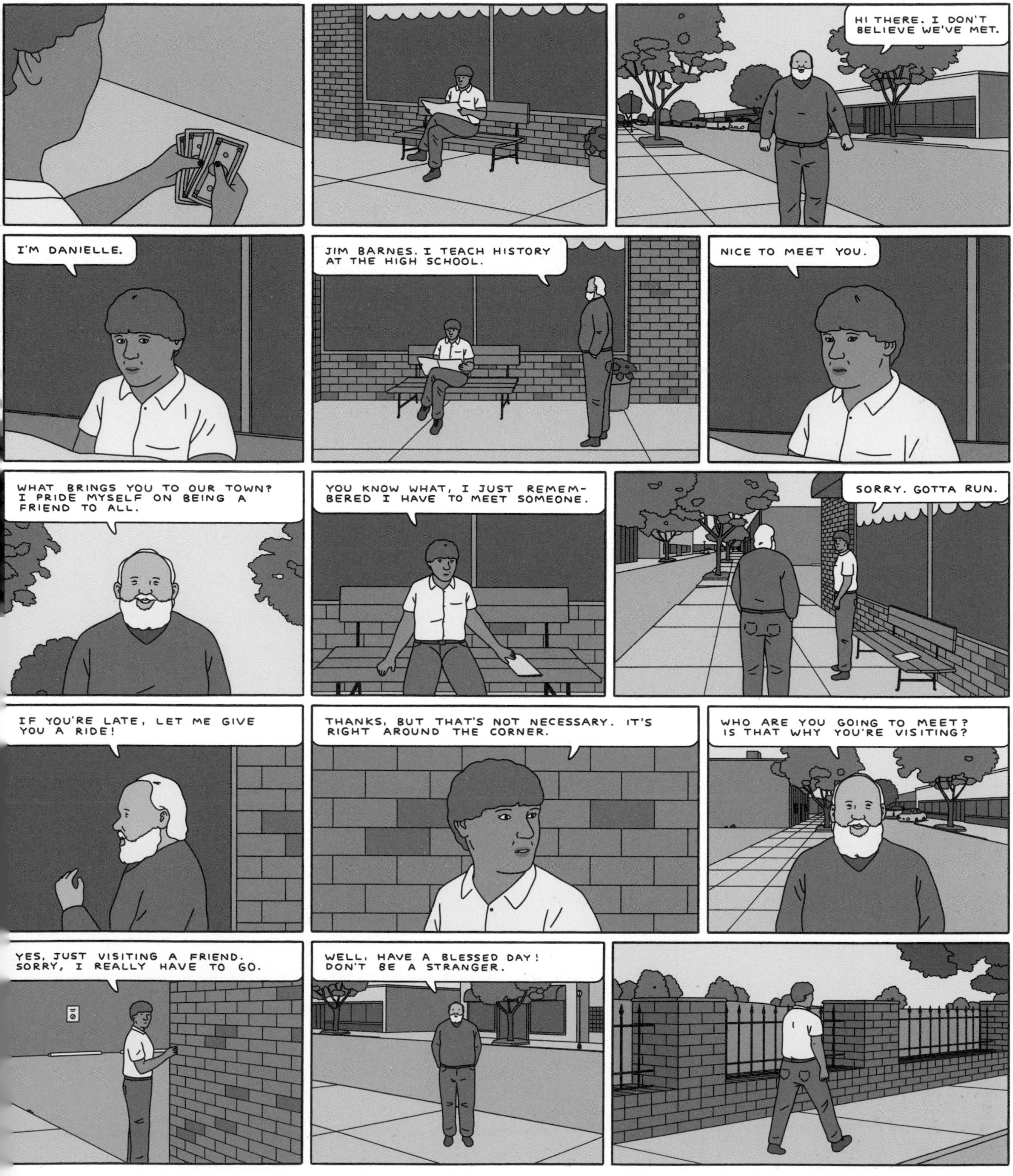
HI THERE. I DON'T BELIEVE WE'VE MET.
I'M DANIELLE.
JIM BARNES. I TEACH HISTORY AT THE HIGH SCHOOL.
NICE TO MEET YOU.
WHAT BRINGS YOU TO OUR TOWN? I PRIDE MYSELF ON BEING A FRIEND TO ALL.
YOU KNOW WHAT, I JUST REMEMBERED I HAVE TO MEET SOMEONE.
SORRY. GOTTA RUN.
IF YOU'RE LATE, LET ME GIVE YOU A RIDE!
THANKS, BUT THAT'S NOT NECESSARY. IT'S RIGHT AROUND THE CORNER.
WHO ARE YOU GOING TO MEET? IS THAT WHY YOU'RE VISITING?
YES, JUST VISITING A FRIEND. SORRY, I REALLY HAVE TO GO.
WELL, HAVE A BLESSED DAY! DON'T BE A STRANGER.

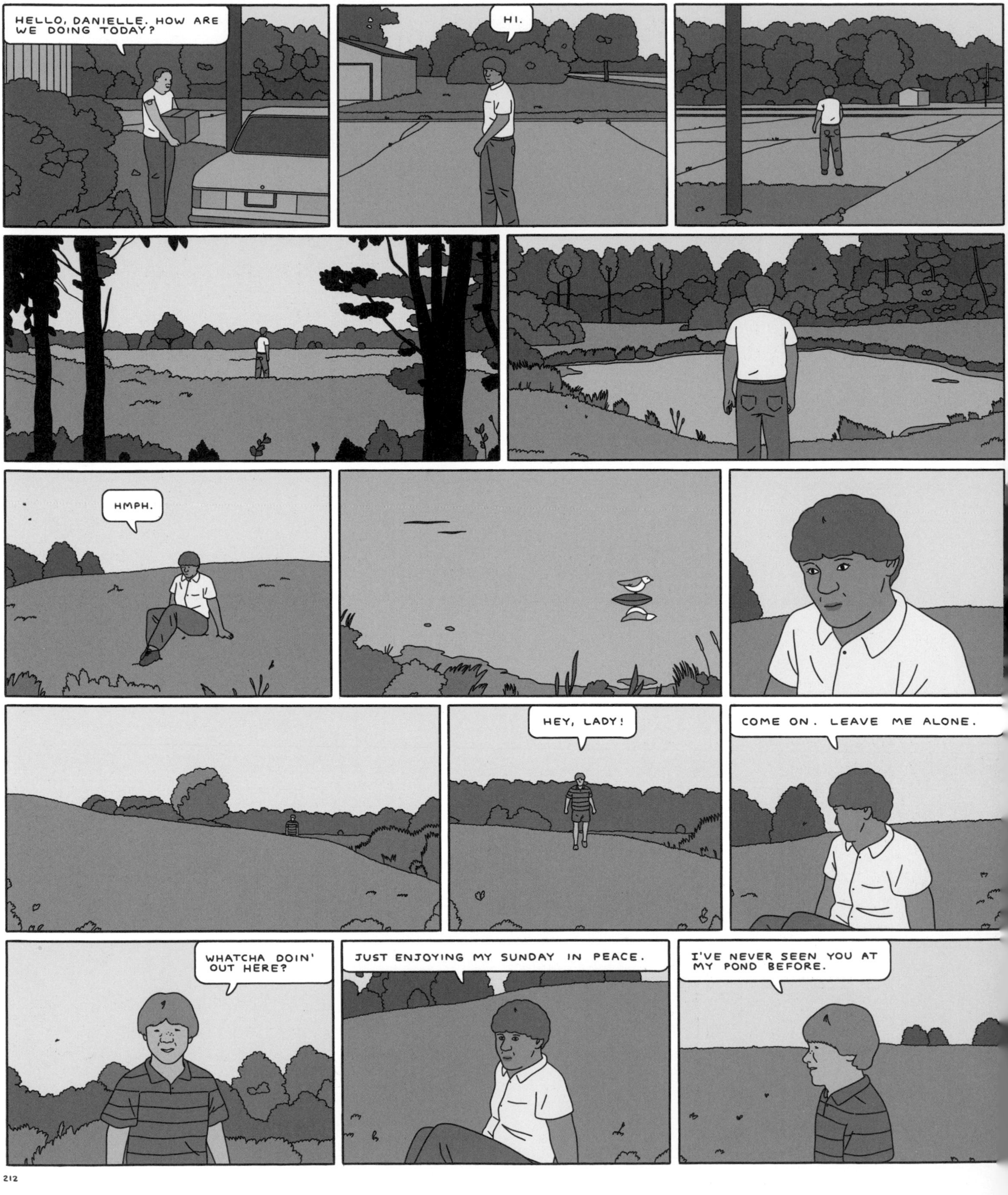
HELLO, DANIELLE. HOW ARE WE DOING TODAY?
HI.
HMPH.
HEY, LADY!
COME ON. LEAVE ME ALONE.
WHATCHA DOIN' OUT HERE?
JUST ENJOYING MY SUNDAY IN PEACE.
I'VE NEVER SEEN YOU AT MY POND BEFORE.

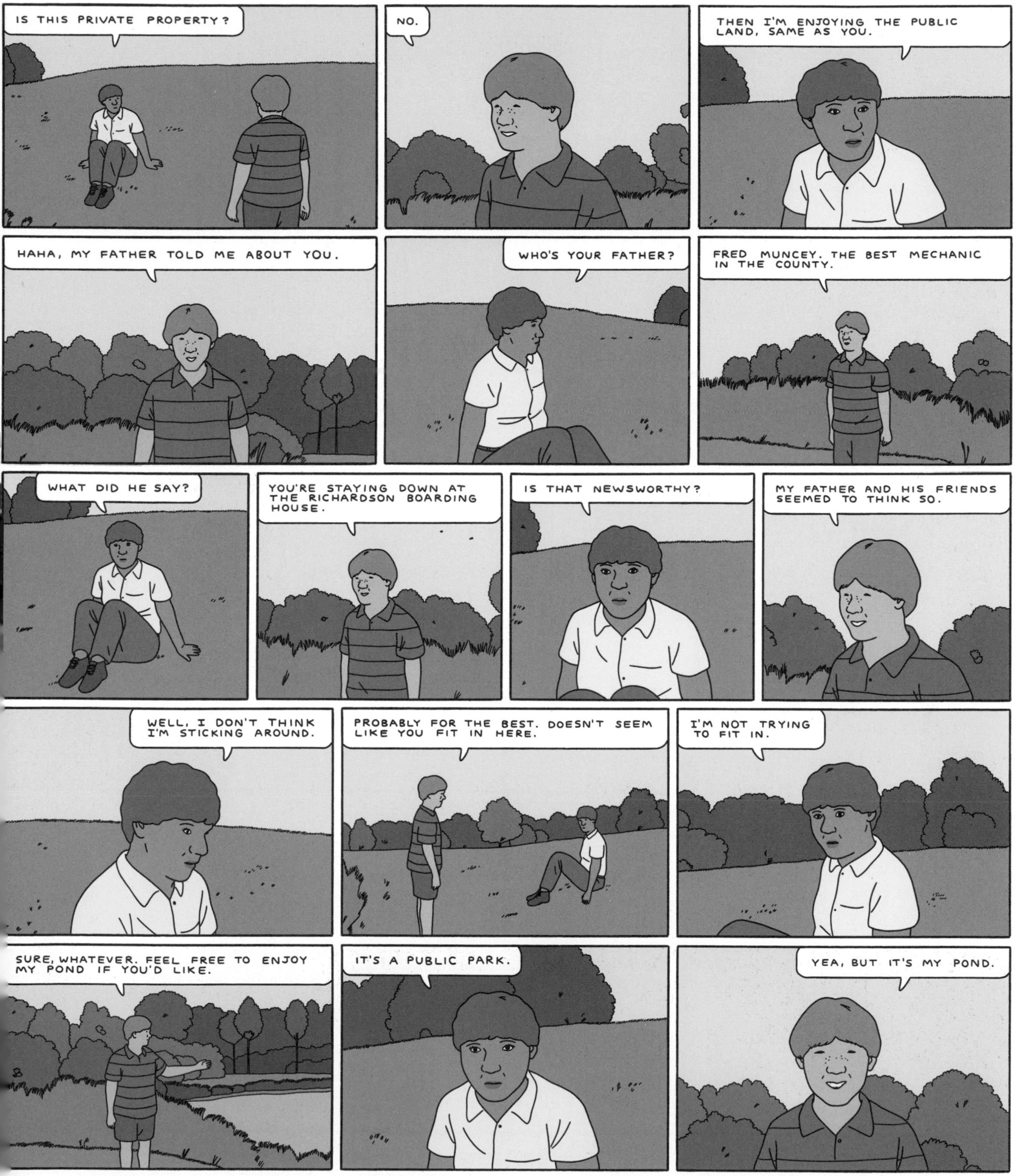
IS THIS PRIVATE PROPERTY?
NO.
THEN I'M ENJOYING THE PUBLIC LAND, SAME AS YOU.
HAHA, MY FATHER TOLD ME ABOUT YOU.
WHO'S YOUR FATHER?
FRED MUNCEY. THE BEST MECHANIC IN THE COUNTY.
WHAT DID HE SAY?
YOU'RE STAYING DOWN AT THE RICHARDSON BOARDING HOUSE.
IS THAT NEWSWORTHY?
MY FATHER AND HIS FRIENDS SEEMED TO THINK SO.
WELL, I DON'T THINK I'M STICKING AROUND.
PROBABLY FOR THE BEST. DOESN'T SEEM LIKE YOU FIT IN HERE.
I'M NOT TRYING TO FIT IN.
SURE, WHATEVER. FEEL FREE TO ENJOY MY POND IF YOU'D LIKE.
IT'S A PUBLIC PARK.
YEA, BUT IT'S MY POND.

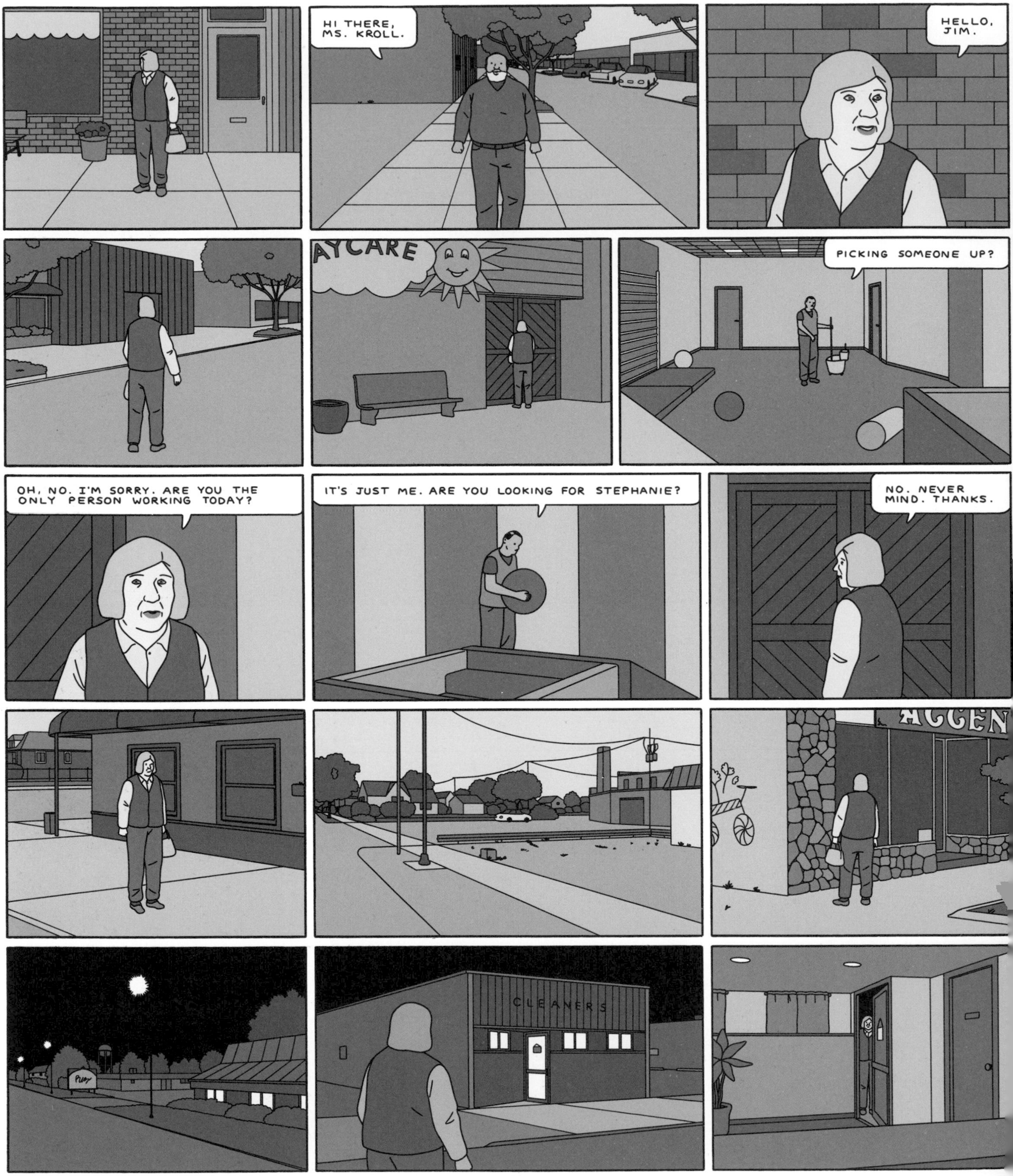
HI THERE, MS. KROLL.
HELLO, JIM.
AYCARE
PICKING SOMEONE UP?
OH, NO. I'M SORRY. ARE YOU THE ONLY PERSON WORKING TODAY?
IT'S JUST ME. ARE YOU LOOKING FOR STEPHANIE?
NO. NEVER MIND. THANKS.
ACCEN
CLEANERS

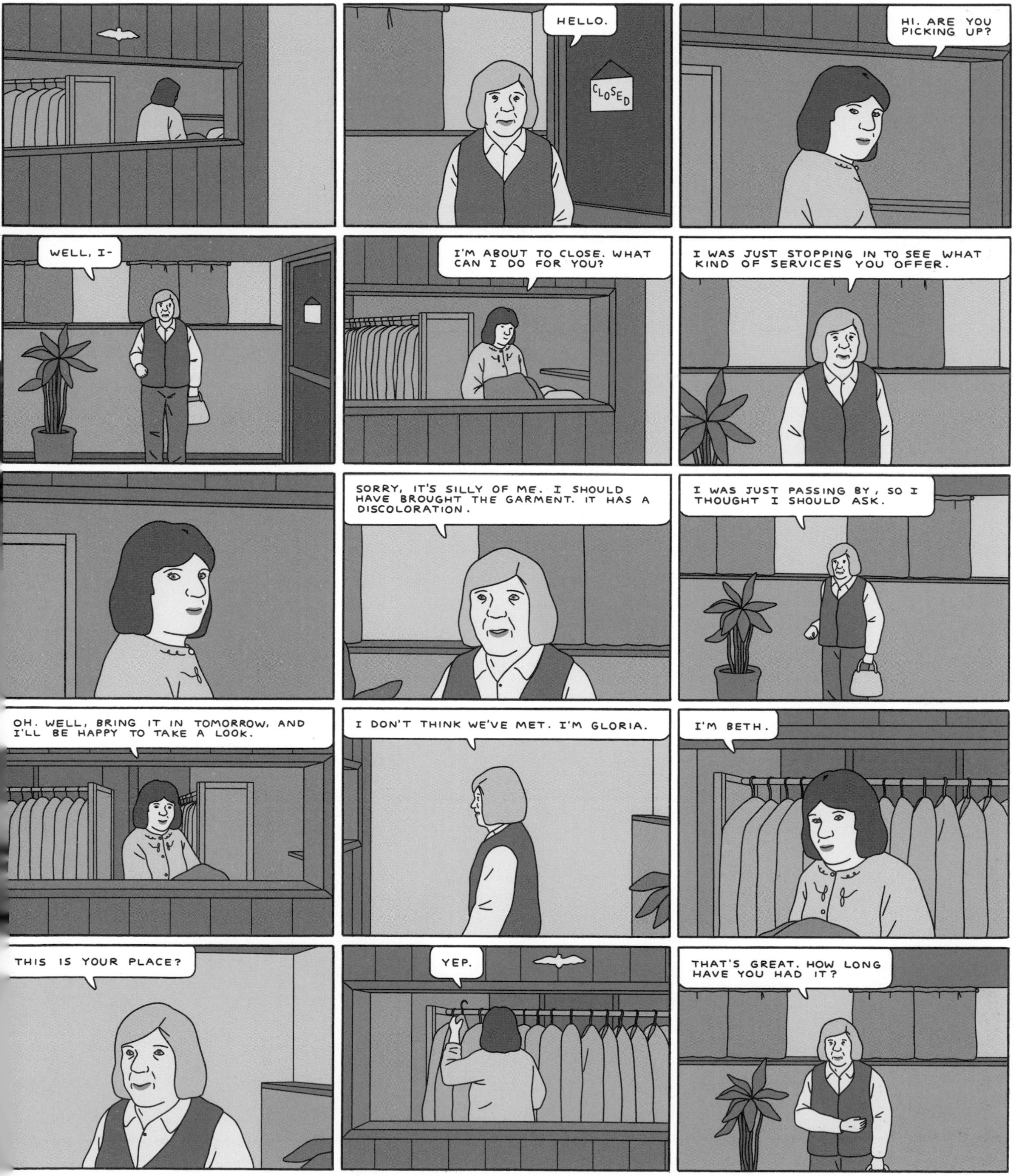
HELLO.
CLOSED
HI. ARE YOU PICKING UP?
WELL, I-
I'M ABOUT TO CLOSE. WHAT CAN I DO FOR YOU?
I WAS JUST STOPPING IN TO SEE WHAT KIND OF SERVICES YOU OFFER.
SORRY, IT'S SILLY OF ME. I SHOULD HAVE BROUGHT THE GARMENT. IT HAS A DISCOLORATION.
I WAS JUST PASSING BY, SO I THOUGHT I SHOULD ASK.
OH. WELL, BRING IT IN TOMORROW, AND I'LL BE HAPPY TO TAKE A LOOK.
I DON'T THINK WE'VE MET. I'M GLORIA.
I'M BETH.
THIS IS YOUR PLACE?
YEP.
THAT'S GREAT. HOW LONG HAVE YOU HAD IT?

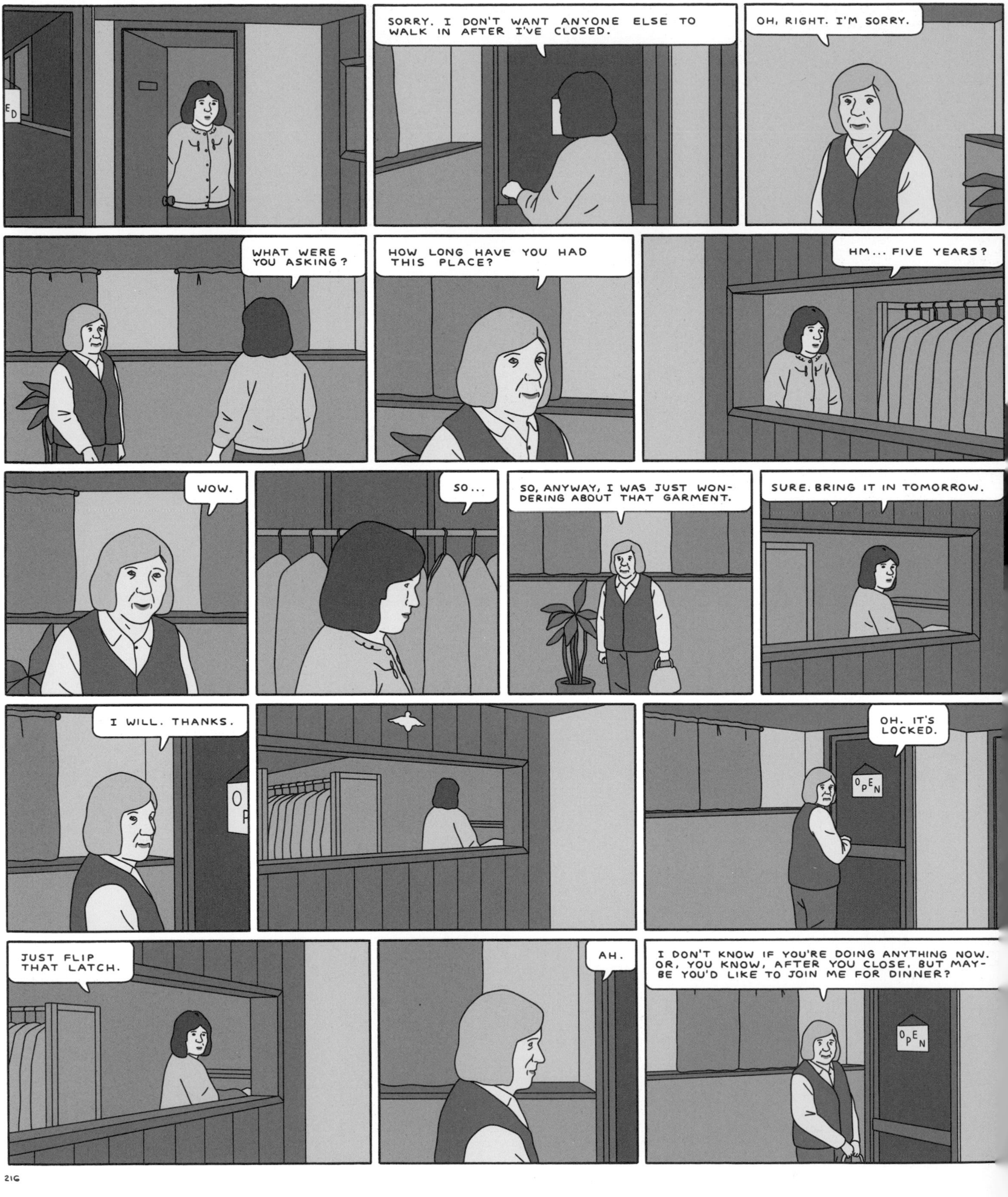
ED
SORRY. I DON'T WANT ANYONE ELSE TO WALK IN AFTER I'VE CLOSED.
OH, RIGHT. I'M SORRY.
WHAT WERE YOU ASKING?
HOW LONG HAVE YOU HAD THIS PLACE?
HM... FIVE YEARS?
WOW.
SO...
SO, ANYWAY, I WAS JUST WONDERING ABOUT THAT GARMENT.
SURE. BRING IT IN TOMORROW.
I WILL. THANKS.
OH. IT'S LOCKED.
OPEN
JUST FLIP THAT LATCH.
AH.
I DON'T KNOW IF YOU'RE DOING ANYTHING NOW. OR, YOU KNOW, AFTER YOU CLOSE, BUT MAYBE YOU'D LIKE TO JOIN ME FOR DINNER?
OPEN

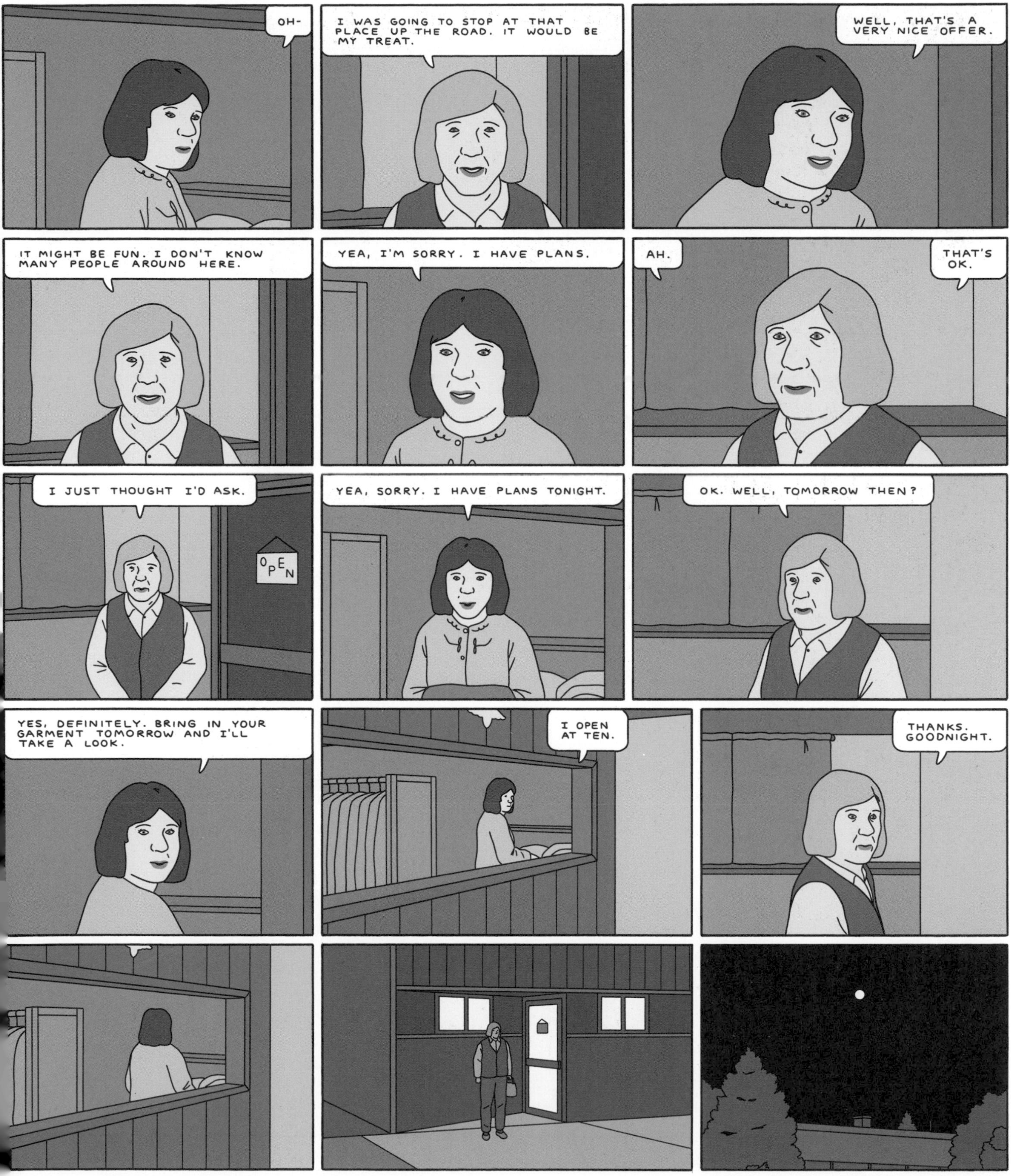
OH-
I WAS GOING TO STOP AT THAT PLACE UP THE ROAD. IT WOULD BE MY TREAT.
WELL, THAT'S A VERY NICE OFFER.
IT MIGHT BE FUN. I DON'T KNOW MANY PEOPLE AROUND HERE.
YEA, I'M SORRY. I HAVE PLANS.
AH.
THAT'S OK.
I JUST THOUGHT I'D ASK.
OPEN
YEA, SORRY. I HAVE PLANS TONIGHT.
OK. WELL, TOMORROW THEN?
YES, DEFINITELY. BRING IN YOUR GARMENT TOMORROW AND I'LL TAKE A LOOK.
I OPEN AT TEN.
THANKS. GOODNIGHT.

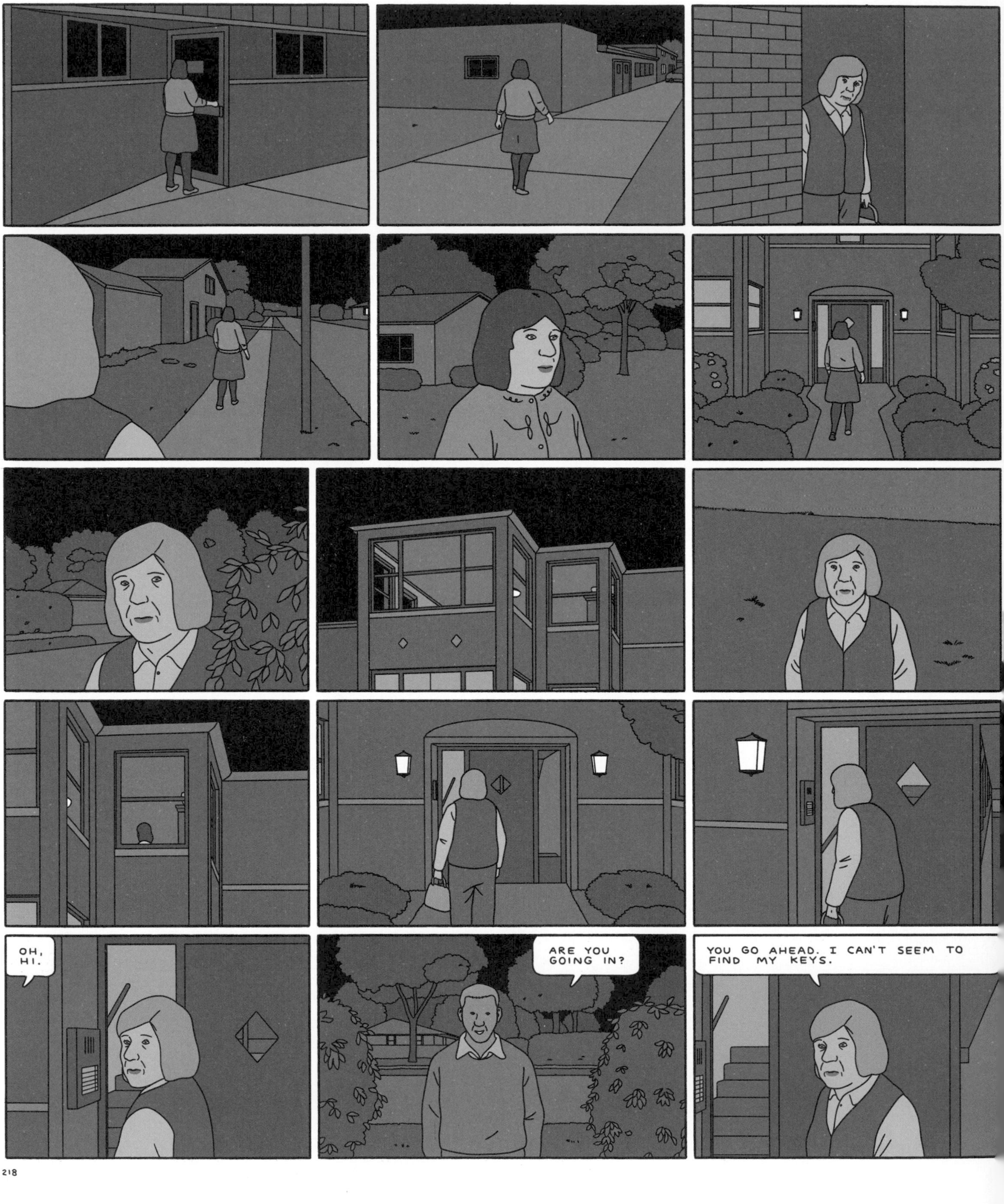
OH, HI.
ARE YOU GOING IN?
YOU GO AHEAD. I CAN'T SEEM TO FIND MY KEYS.

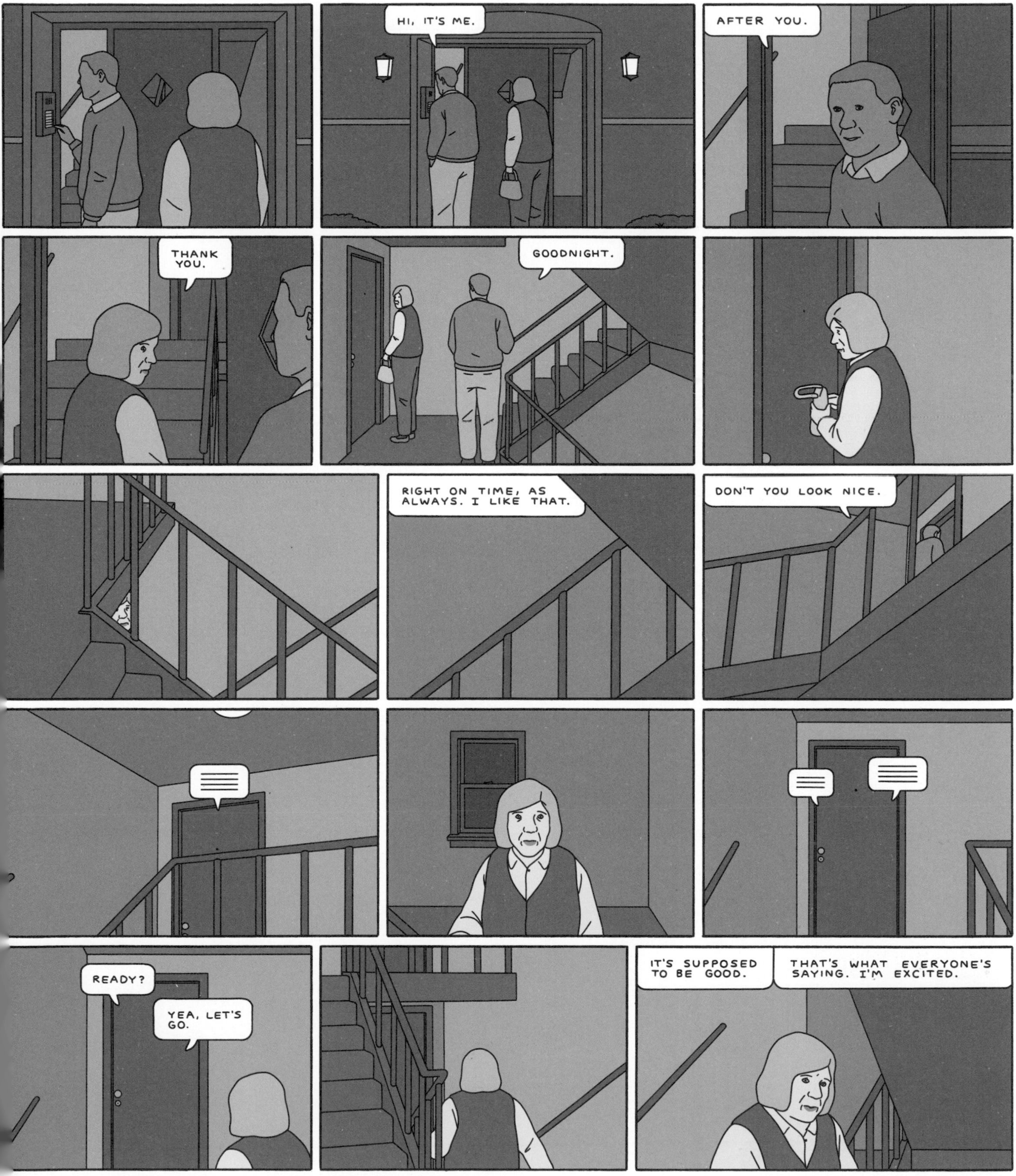
HI, IT'S ME.
AFTER YOU.
THANK YOU.
GOODNIGHT.
RIGHT ON TIME, AS ALWAYS. I LIKE THAT.
DON'T YOU LOOK NICE.
READY?
YEA, LET'S GO.
IT'S SUPPOSED TO BE GOOD.
THAT'S WHAT EVERYONE'S SAYING. I'M EXCITED.

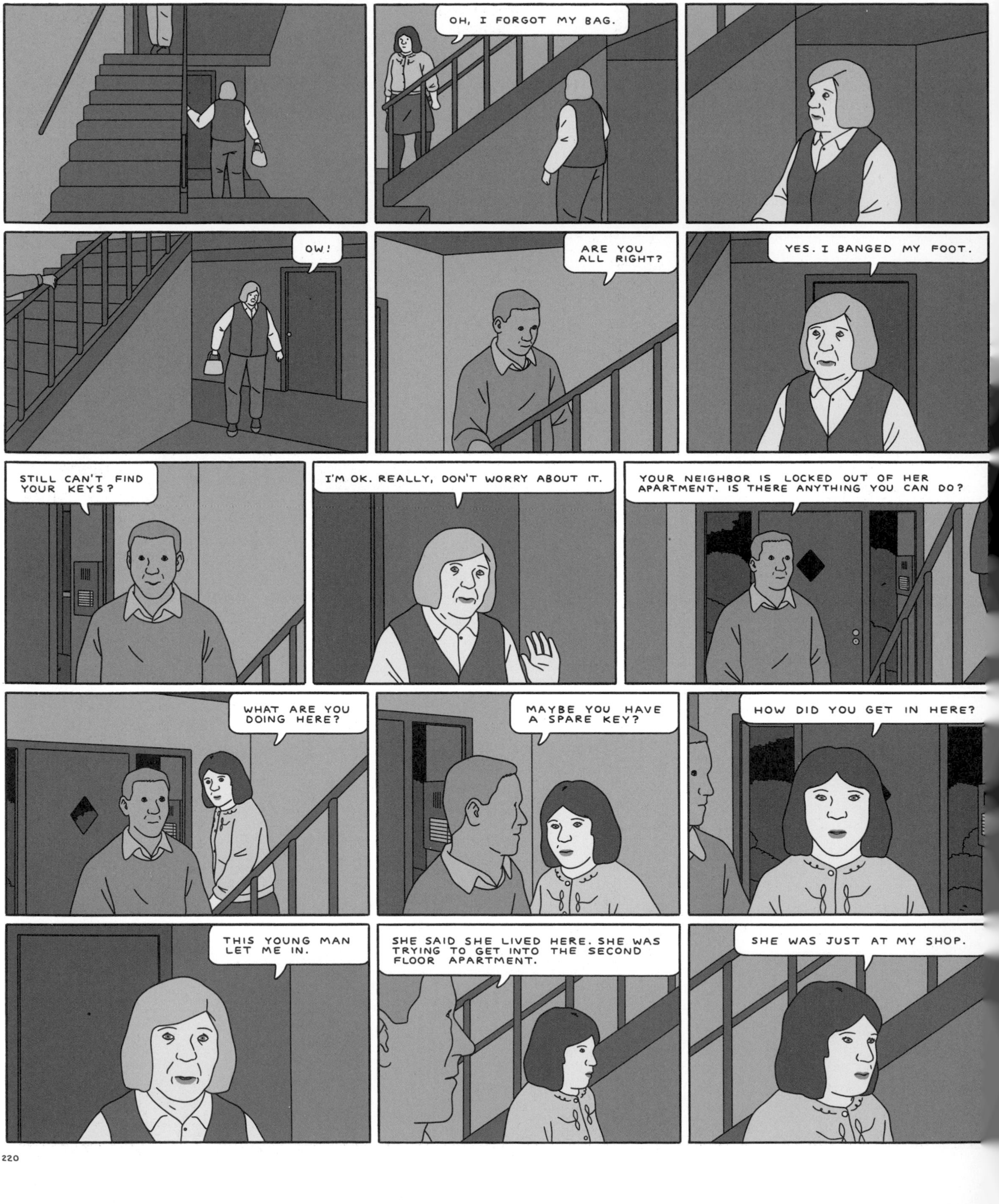
OH, I FORGOT MY BAG.
OW!
ARE YOU ALL RIGHT?
YES. I BANGED MY FOOT.
STILL CAN'T FIND YOUR KEYS?
I'M OK. REALLY, DON'T WORRY ABOUT IT.
YOUR NEIGHBOR IS LOCKED OUT OF HER APARTMENT. IS THERE ANYTHING YOU CAN DO?
WHAT ARE YOU DOING HERE?
MAYBE YOU HAVE A SPARE KEY?
HOW DID YOU GET IN HERE?
THIS YOUNG MAN LET ME IN.
SHE SAID SHE LIVED HERE. SHE WAS TRYING TO GET INTO THE SECOND FLOOR APARTMENT.
SHE WAS JUST AT MY SHOP.

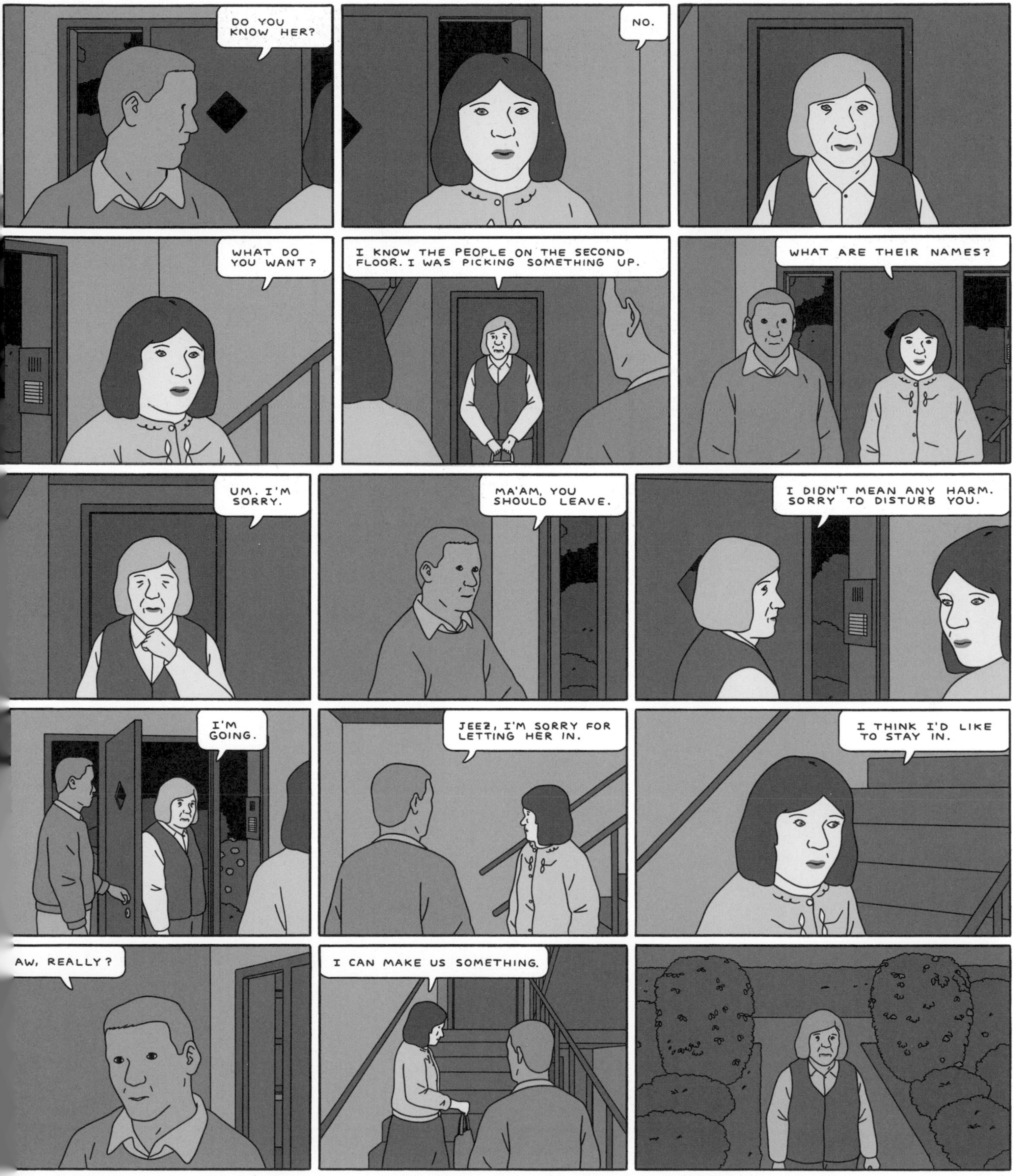
DO YOU KNOW HER?
NO.
WHAT DO YOU WANT?
I KNOW THE PEOPLE ON THE SECOND FLOOR. I WAS PICKING SOMETHING UP.
WHAT ARE THEIR NAMES?
UM. I'M SORRY.
MA'AM, YOU SHOULD LEAVE.
I DIDN'T MEAN ANY HARM. SORRY TO DISTURB YOU.
I'M GOING.
JEEZ, I'M SORRY FOR LETTING HER IN.
I THINK I'D LIKE TO STAY IN.
AW, REALLY?
I CAN MAKE US SOMETHING.

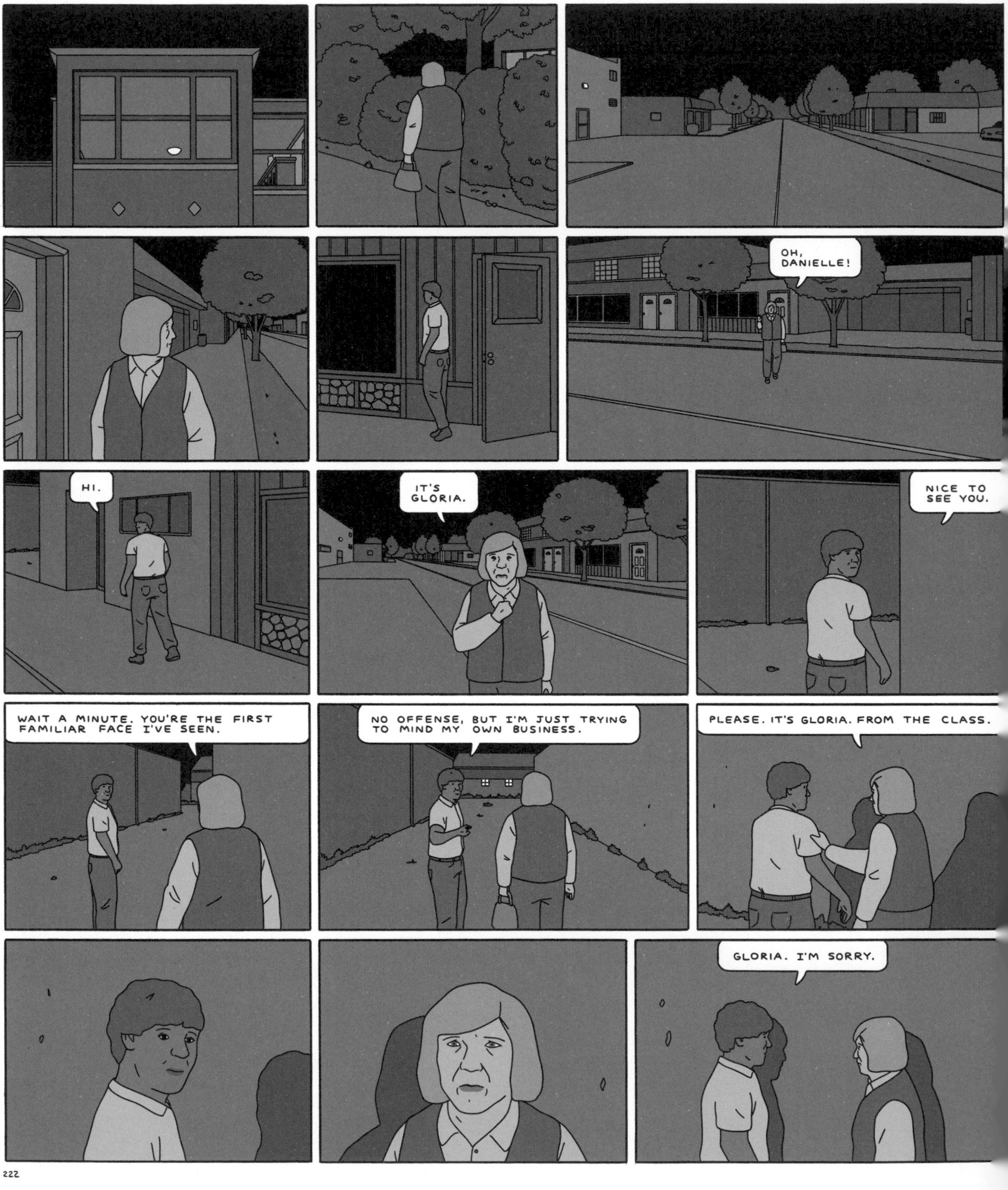
OH, DANIELLE!
HI.
IT'S GLORIA.
NICE TO SEE YOU.
WAIT A MINUTE. YOU'RE THE FIRST FAMILIAR FACE I'VE SEEN.
NO OFFENSE, BUT I'M JUST TRYING TO MIND MY OWN BUSINESS.
PLEASE. IT'S GLORIA. FROM THE CLASS.
GLORIA. I'M SORRY.

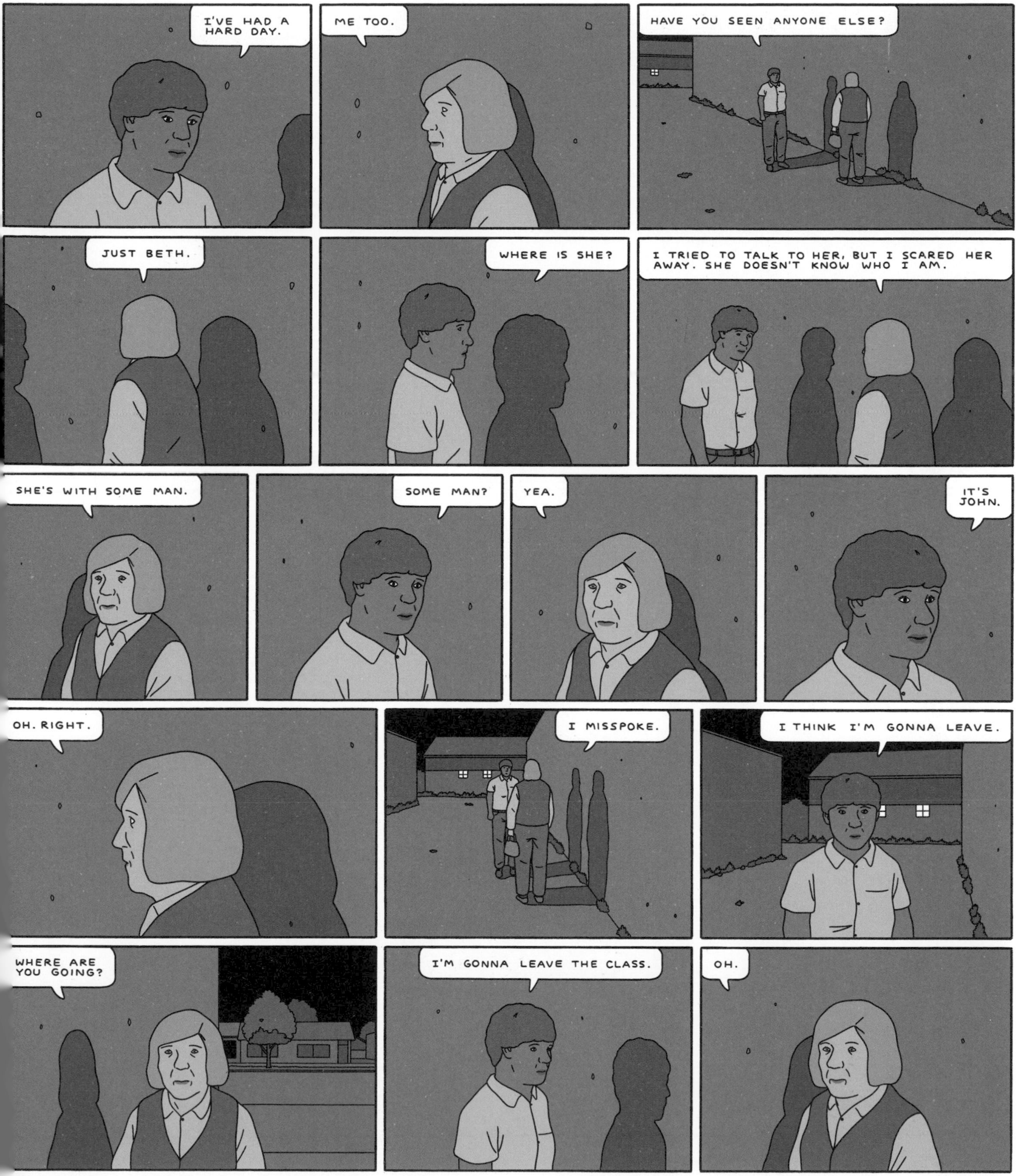
I'VE HAD A HARD DAY.
ME TOO.
HAVE YOU SEEN ANYONE ELSE?
JUST BETH.
WHERE IS SHE?
I TRIED TO TALK TO HER, BUT I SCARED HER AWAY. SHE DOESN'T KNOW WHO I AM.
SHE'S WITH SOME MAN.
SOME MAN?
YEA.
IT'S JOHN.
OH. RIGHT.
I MISSPOKE.
I THINK I'M GONNA LEAVE.
WHERE ARE YOU GOING?
I'M GONNA LEAVE THE CLASS.
OH.

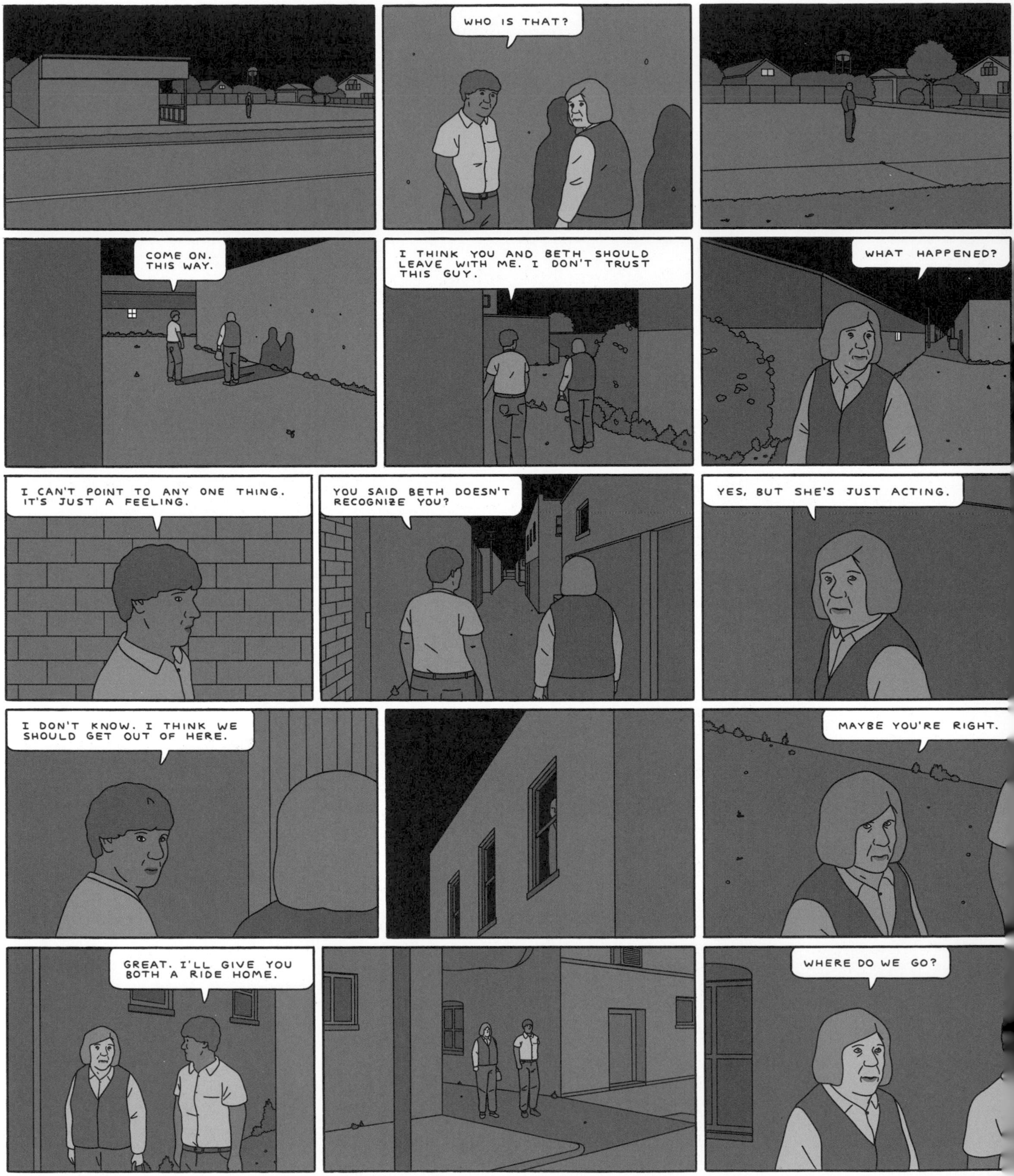
WHO IS THAT?
COME ON. THIS WAY.
I THINK YOU AND BETH SHOULD LEAVE WITH ME. I DON'T TRUST THIS GUY.
WHAT HAPPENED?
I CAN'T POINT TO ANY ONE THING. IT'S JUST A FEELING.
YOU SAID BETH DOESN'T RECOGNIZE YOU?
YES, BUT SHE'S JUST ACTING.
I DON'T KNOW. I THINK WE SHOULD GET OUT OF HERE.
MAYBE YOU'RE RIGHT.
GREAT. I'LL GIVE YOU BOTH A RIDE HOME.
WHERE DO WE GO?

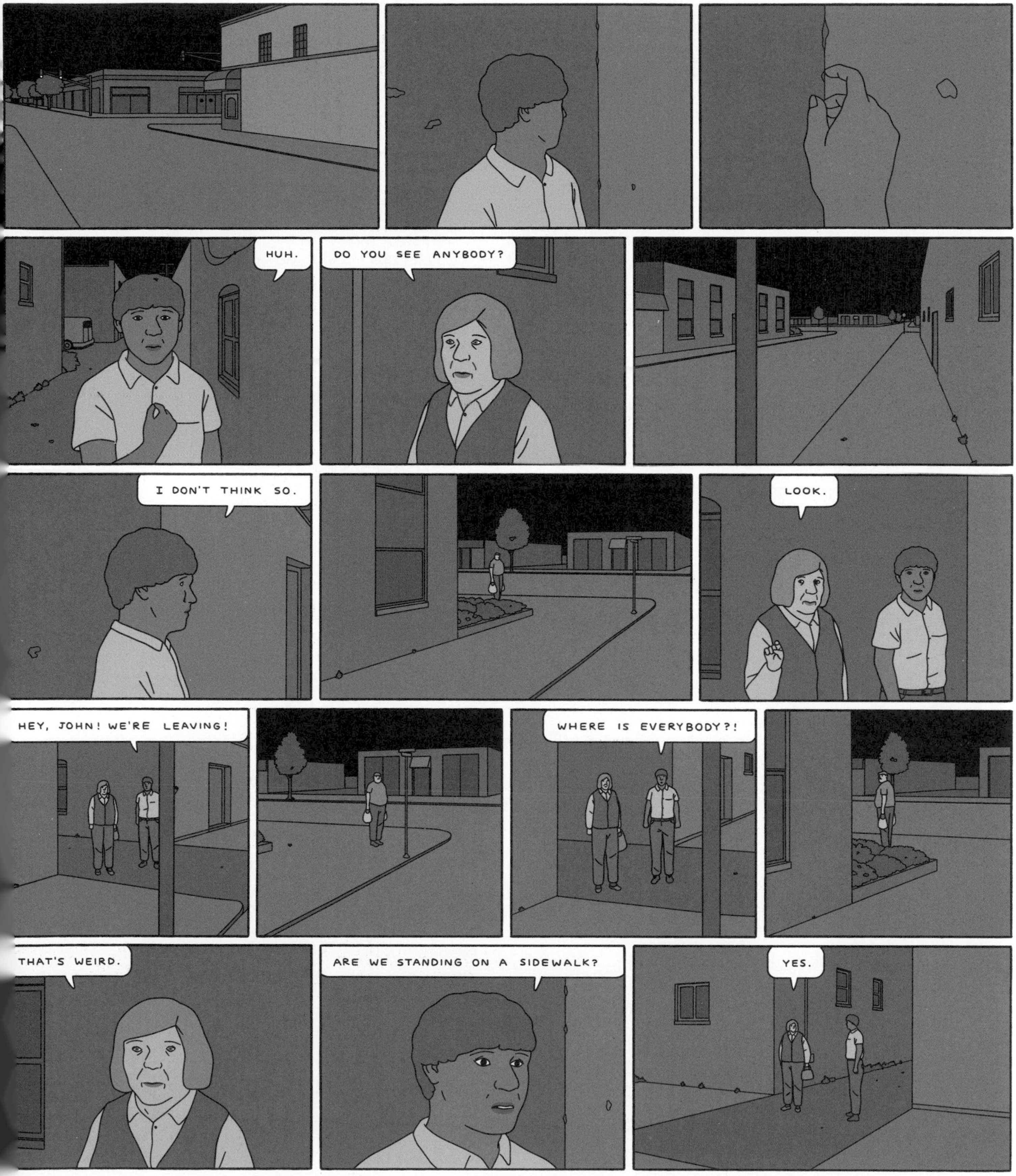
HUH.
DO YOU SEE ANYBODY?
I DON'T THINK SO.
LOOK.
HEY, JOHN! WE'RE LEAVING!
WHERE IS EVERYBODY?!
THAT'S WEIRD.
ARE WE STANDING ON A SIDEWALK?
YES.

 HOLD ON A SECOND.

 WHAT AM I POINTING AT?

 AN ICE CREAM SHOP.

 OH NO. WHAT HAPPENED?

 HOW DID WE GET HERE?

 WHAT DO YOU REMEMBER FROM WHEN WE BEGAN THE EXERCISE?

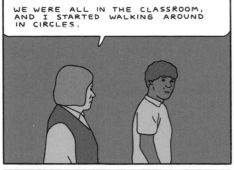 WE WERE ALL IN THE CLASSROOM, AND I STARTED WALKING AROUND IN CIRCLES.

 THEN I IMAGINED I WAS ON A TRAIN FOR A LONG TIME. THE SCENE STARTED TO GET FUZZY.

 THEN I WAS HERE.

 HOW LONG DO YOU THINK WE'VE BEEN DOING THIS?

 IT'S HARD TO TELL. WHAT DO YOU THINK?

 IT SEEMS LIKE IT'S BEEN A LONG TIME. HOW DID THIS HAPPEN?

 GOD, I DON'T KNOW.

 WE NEED TO TALK TO BETH. SHE'S VERY CONFUSED.

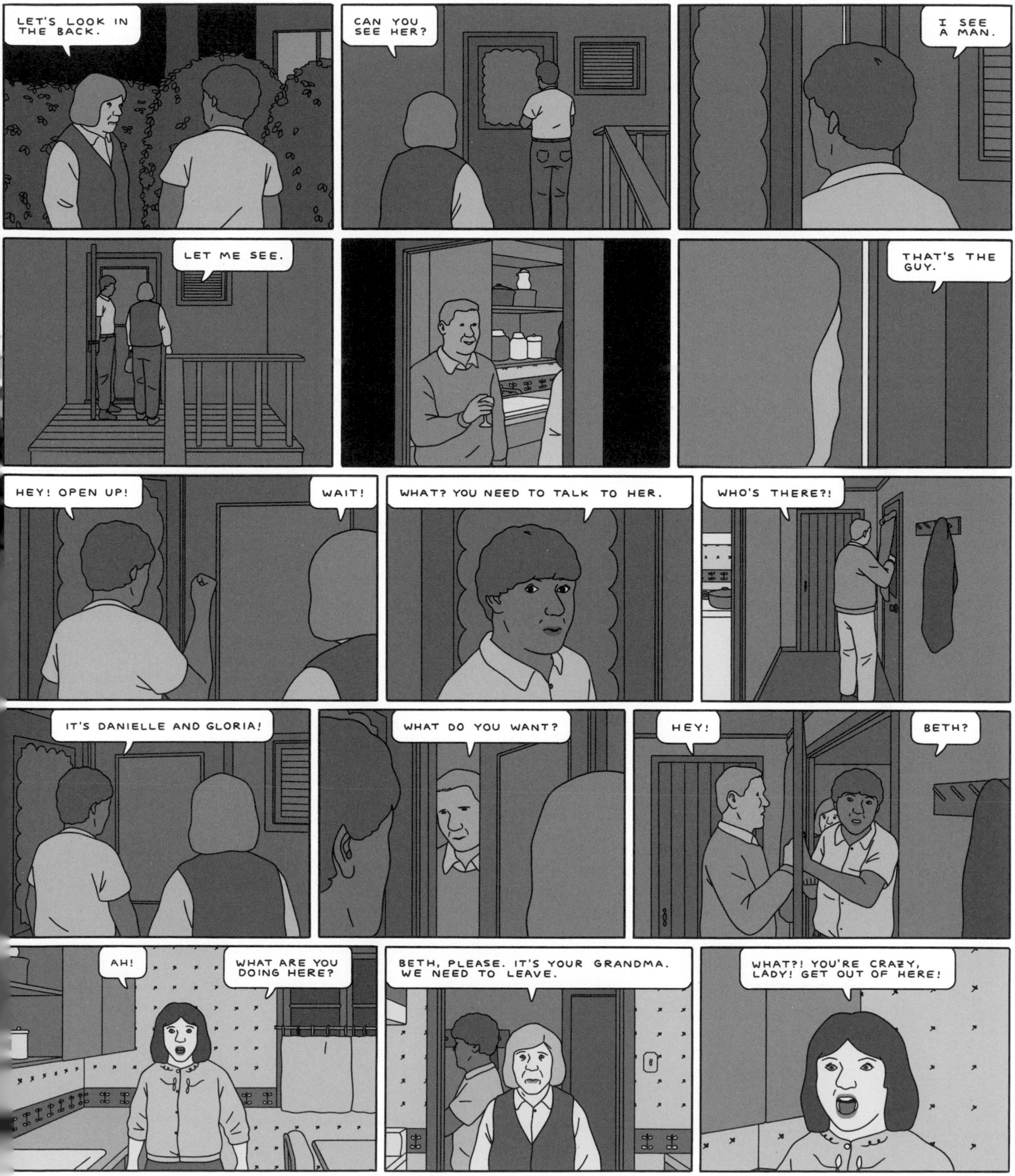
LET'S LOOK IN THE BACK.
CAN YOU SEE HER?
I SEE A MAN.
LET ME SEE.
THAT'S THE GUY.
HEY! OPEN UP!
WAIT!
WHAT? YOU NEED TO TALK TO HER.
WHO'S THERE?!
IT'S DANIELLE AND GLORIA!
WHAT DO YOU WANT?
HEY!
BETH?
AH!
WHAT ARE YOU DOING HERE?
BETH, PLEASE. IT'S YOUR GRANDMA. WE NEED TO LEAVE.
WHAT?! YOU'RE CRAZY, LADY! GET OUT OF HERE!

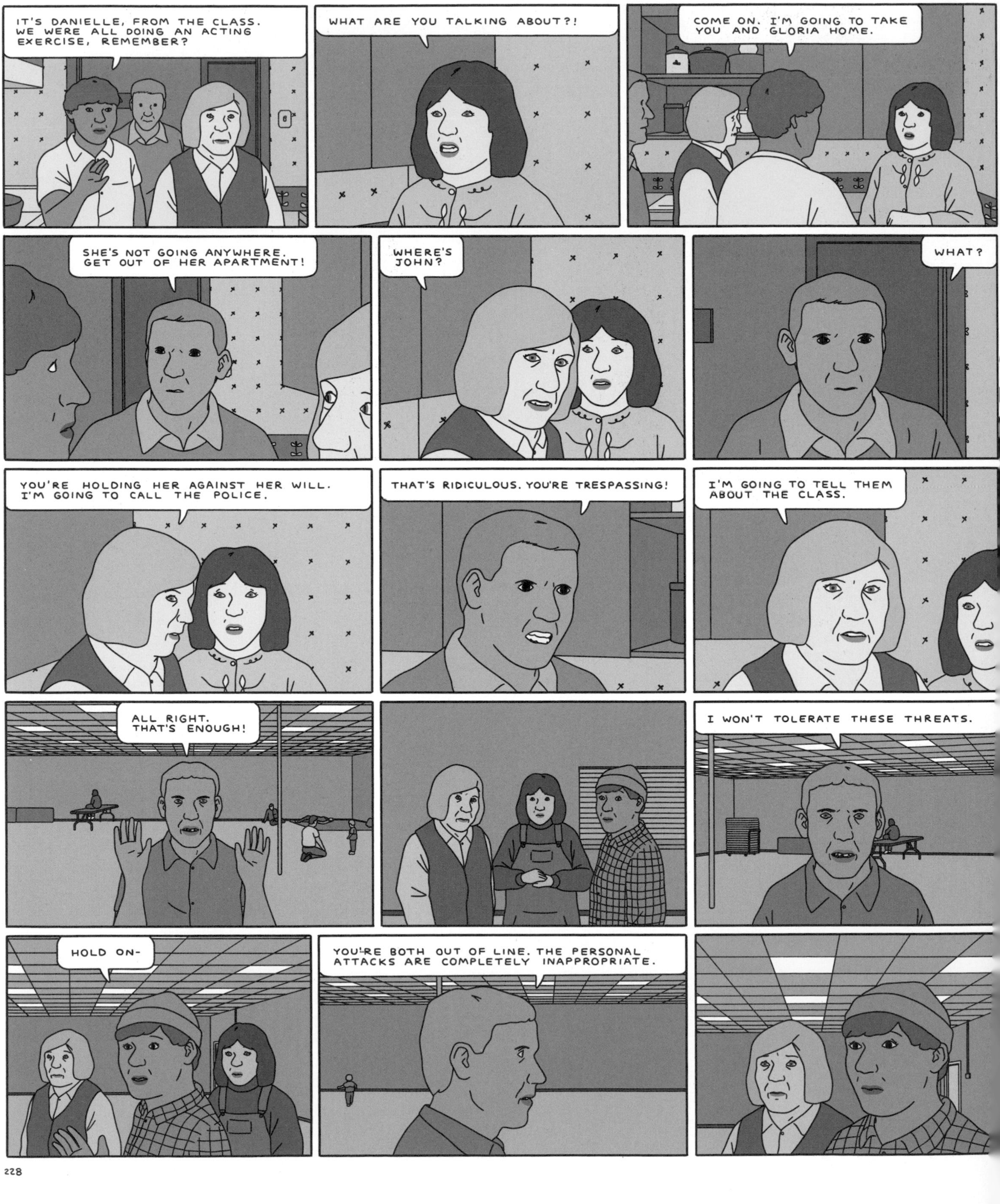
IT'S DANIELLE, FROM THE CLASS. WE WERE ALL DOING AN ACTING EXERCISE, REMEMBER?
WHAT ARE YOU TALKING ABOUT?!
COME ON. I'M GOING TO TAKE YOU AND GLORIA HOME.
SHE'S NOT GOING ANYWHERE. GET OUT OF HER APARTMENT!
WHERE'S JOHN?
WHAT?
YOU'RE HOLDING HER AGAINST HER WILL. I'M GOING TO CALL THE POLICE.
THAT'S RIDICULOUS. YOU'RE TRESPASSING!
I'M GOING TO TELL THEM ABOUT THE CLASS.
ALL RIGHT. THAT'S ENOUGH!
I WON'T TOLERATE THESE THREATS.
HOLD ON-
YOU'RE BOTH OUT OF LINE. THE PERSONAL ATTACKS ARE COMPLETELY INAPPROPRIATE.

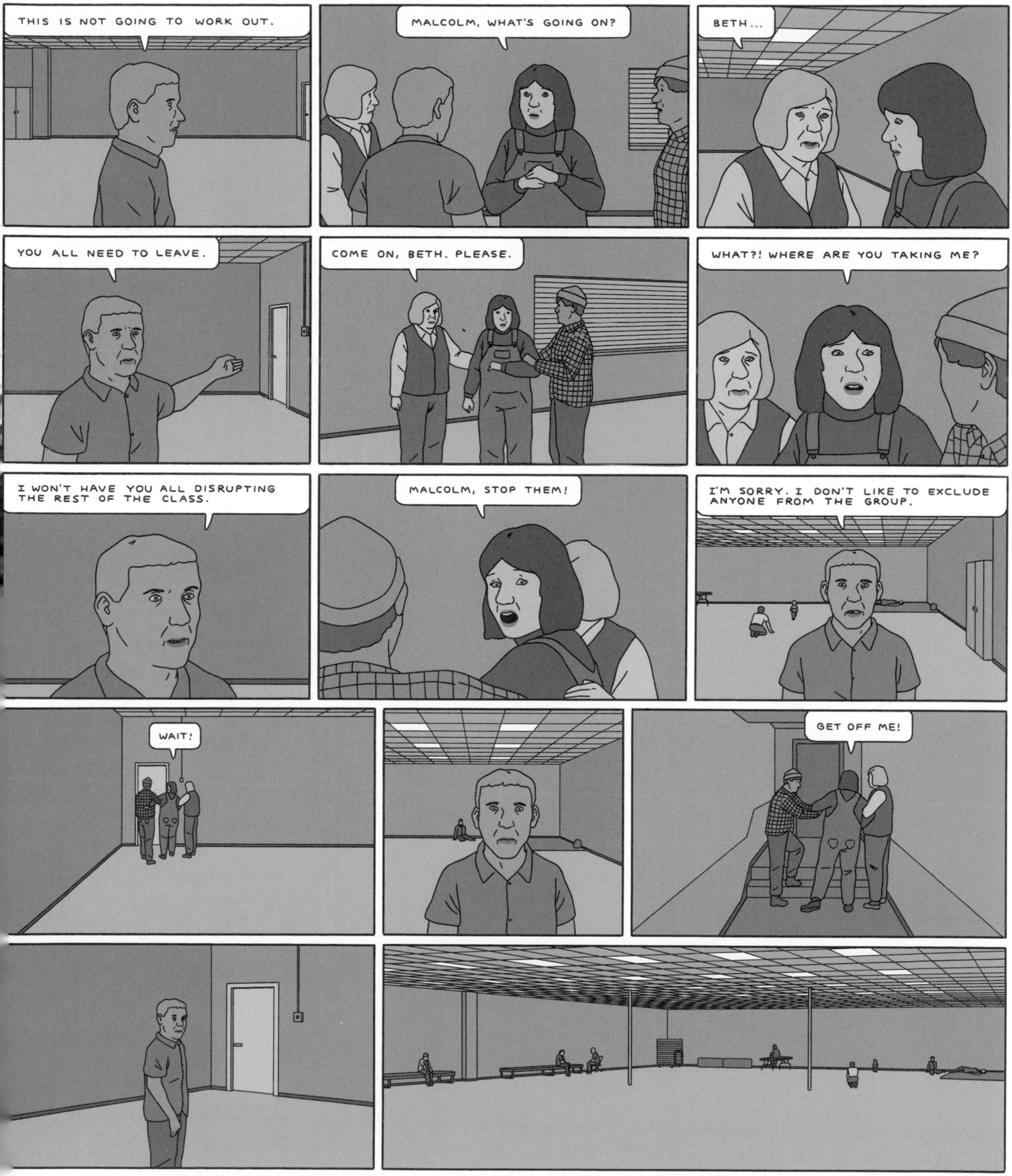
THIS IS NOT GOING TO WORK OUT.
MALCOLM, WHAT'S GOING ON?
BETH...
YOU ALL NEED TO LEAVE.
COME ON, BETH. PLEASE.
WHAT?! WHERE ARE YOU TAKING ME?
I WON'T HAVE YOU ALL DISRUPTING THE REST OF THE CLASS.
MALCOLM, STOP THEM!
I'M SORRY. I DON'T LIKE TO EXCLUDE ANYONE FROM THE GROUP.
WAIT!
GET OFF ME!

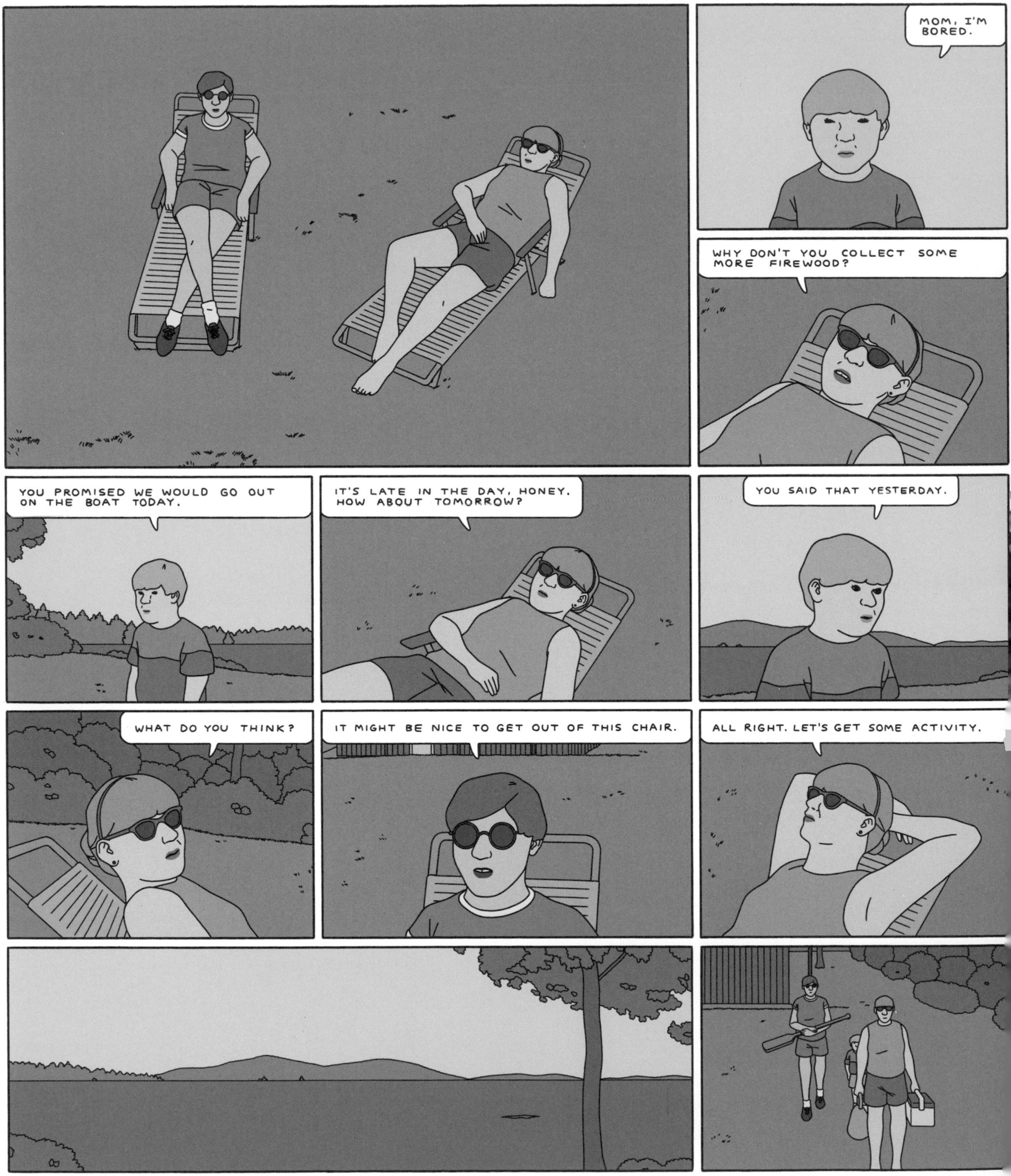
MOM, I'M BORED.
WHY DON'T YOU COLLECT SOME MORE FIREWOOD?
YOU PROMISED WE WOULD GO OUT ON THE BOAT TODAY.
IT'S LATE IN THE DAY, HONEY. HOW ABOUT TOMORROW?
YOU SAID THAT YESTERDAY.
WHAT DO YOU THINK?
IT MIGHT BE NICE TO GET OUT OF THIS CHAIR.
ALL RIGHT. LET'S GET SOME ACTIVITY.

WHAT ARE YOU DOING, LOU? COME ON, LET'S LEASH YOU UP.

CAN WE TAKE HIM WITH US?

WOOF!

I GUESS THAT WOULD BE FINE.

WHERE ARE WE GOING, CAPTAIN?

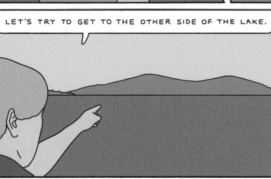

LET'S TRY TO GET TO THE OTHER SIDE OF THE LAKE.

AYE AYE.

THIS IS PRETTY PHYSICAL. I'VE BECOME LAZY ON THIS TRIP.

MOM, CAN I HAVE A SNACK?

WE JUST LEFT THE HOUSE. LET'S WAIT UNTIL WE'RE HALFWAY THERE.

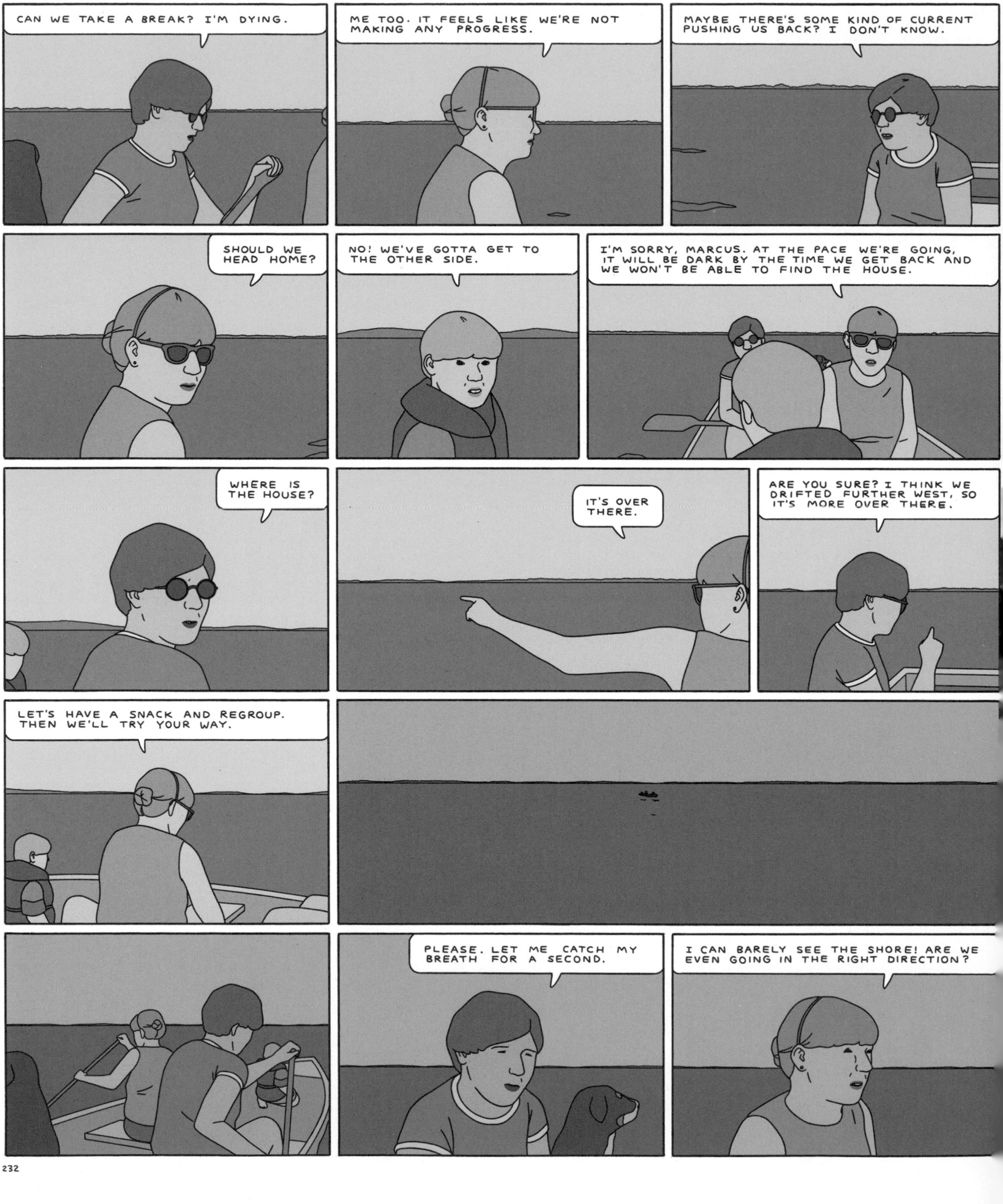
CAN WE TAKE A BREAK? I'M DYING.
ME TOO. IT FEELS LIKE WE'RE NOT MAKING ANY PROGRESS.
MAYBE THERE'S SOME KIND OF CURRENT PUSHING US BACK? I DON'T KNOW.
SHOULD WE HEAD HOME?
NO! WE'VE GOTTA GET TO THE OTHER SIDE.
I'M SORRY, MARCUS. AT THE PACE WE'RE GOING, IT WILL BE DARK BY THE TIME WE GET BACK AND WE WON'T BE ABLE TO FIND THE HOUSE.
WHERE IS THE HOUSE?
IT'S OVER THERE.
ARE YOU SURE? I THINK WE DRIFTED FURTHER WEST, SO IT'S MORE OVER THERE.
LET'S HAVE A SNACK AND REGROUP. THEN WE'LL TRY YOUR WAY.
PLEASE. LET ME CATCH MY BREATH FOR A SECOND.
I CAN BARELY SEE THE SHORE! ARE WE EVEN GOING IN THE RIGHT DIRECTION?

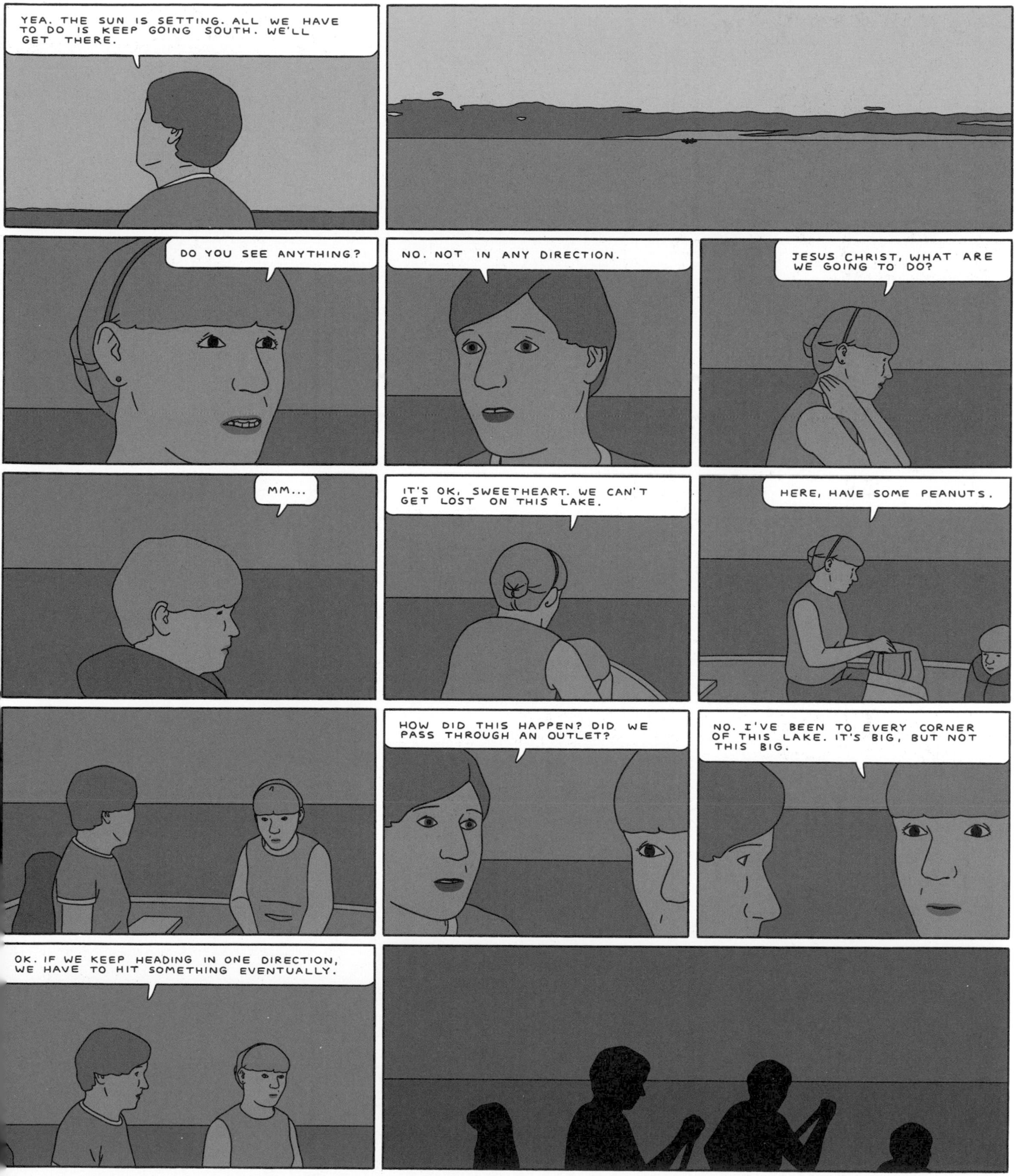
YEA. THE SUN IS SETTING. ALL WE HAVE TO DO IS KEEP GOING SOUTH. WE'LL GET THERE.
DO YOU SEE ANYTHING?
NO. NOT IN ANY DIRECTION.
JESUS CHRIST, WHAT ARE WE GOING TO DO?
MM...
IT'S OK, SWEETHEART. WE CAN'T GET LOST ON THIS LAKE.
HERE, HAVE SOME PEANUTS.
HOW DID THIS HAPPEN? DID WE PASS THROUGH AN OUTLET?
NO. I'VE BEEN TO EVERY CORNER OF THIS LAKE. IT'S BIG, BUT NOT THIS BIG.
OK. IF WE KEEP HEADING IN ONE DIRECTION, WE HAVE TO HIT SOMETHING EVENTUALLY.

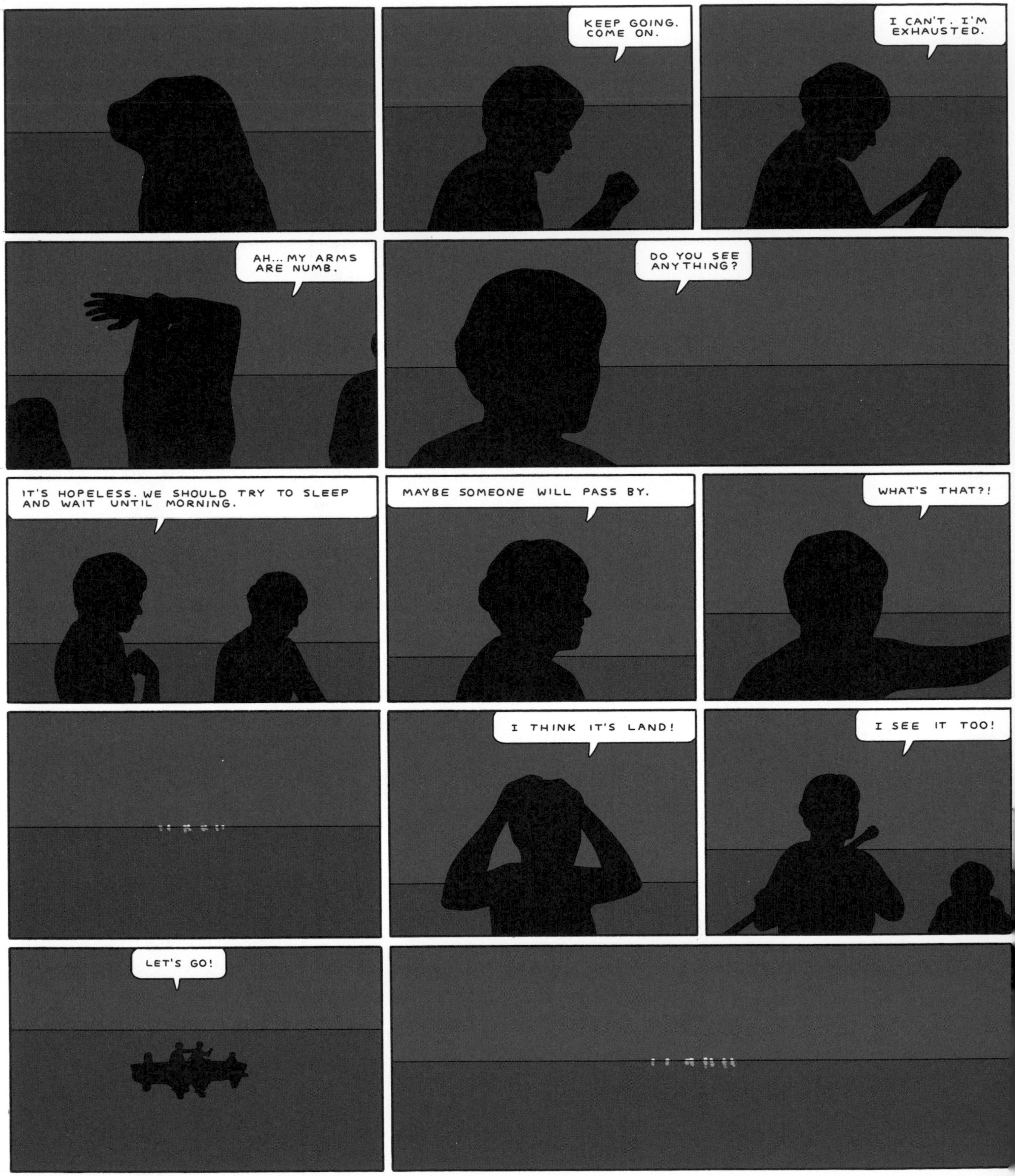
KEEP GOING. COME ON.
I CAN'T. I'M EXHAUSTED.
AH... MY ARMS ARE NUMB.
DO YOU SEE ANYTHING?
IT'S HOPELESS. WE SHOULD TRY TO SLEEP AND WAIT UNTIL MORNING.
MAYBE SOMEONE WILL PASS BY.
WHAT'S THAT?!
I THINK IT'S LAND!
I SEE IT TOO!
LET'S GO!

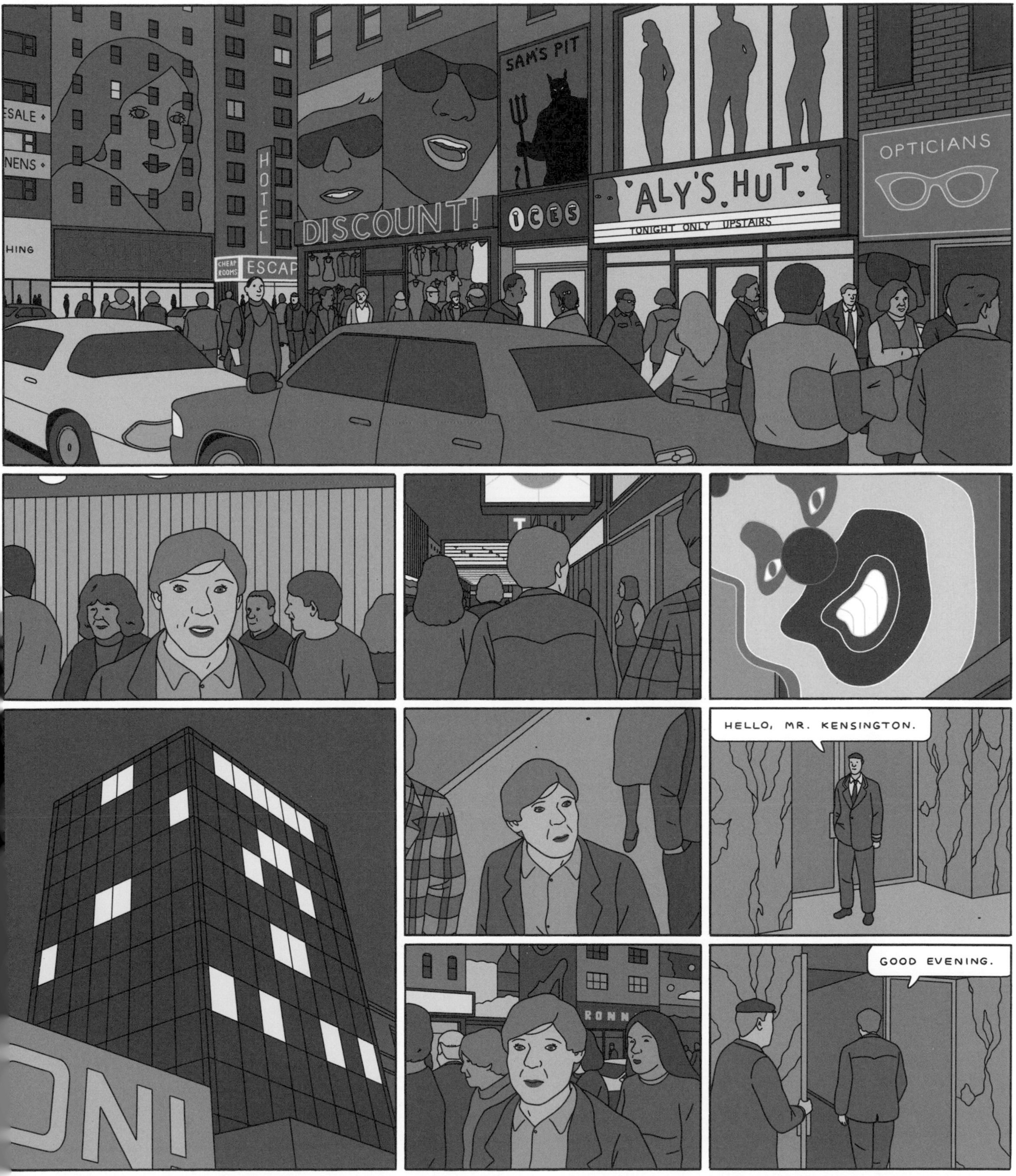
SAM'S PIT
ALY'S HUT
TONIGHT ONLY UPSTAIRS
OPTICIANS
DISCOUNT!
HOTEL
CHEAP ROOMS
ESCAP
SALE
NENS
HING
ICES
RONN
HELLO, MR. KENSINGTON.
GOOD EVENING.

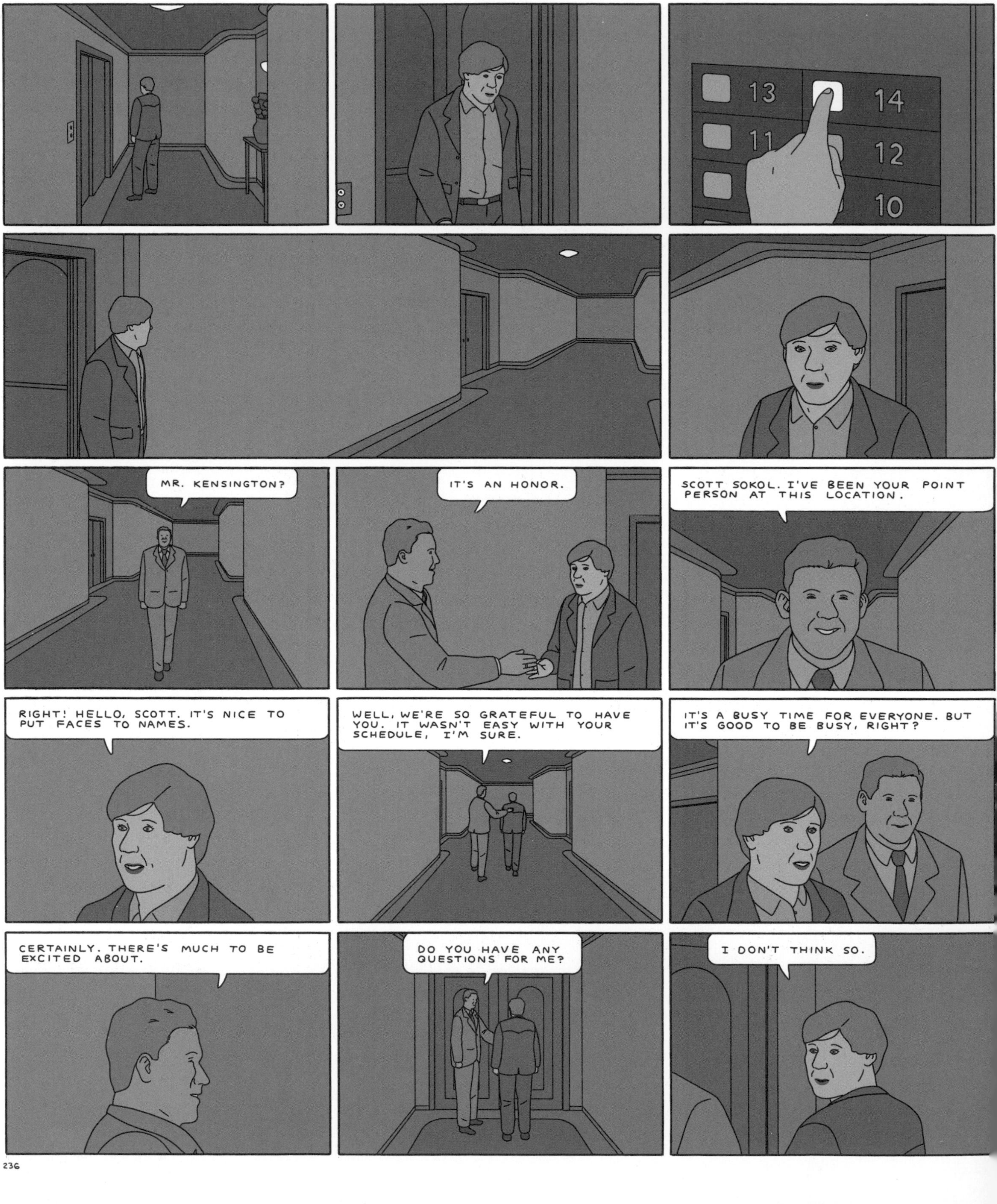
13
14
11
12
10
MR. KENSINGTON?
IT'S AN HONOR.
SCOTT SOKOL. I'VE BEEN YOUR POINT PERSON AT THIS LOCATION.
RIGHT! HELLO, SCOTT. IT'S NICE TO PUT FACES TO NAMES.
WELL, WE'RE SO GRATEFUL TO HAVE YOU. IT WASN'T EASY WITH YOUR SCHEDULE, I'M SURE.
IT'S A BUSY TIME FOR EVERYONE. BUT IT'S GOOD TO BE BUSY, RIGHT?
CERTAINLY. THERE'S MUCH TO BE EXCITED ABOUT.
DO YOU HAVE ANY QUESTIONS FOR ME?
I DON'T THINK SO.

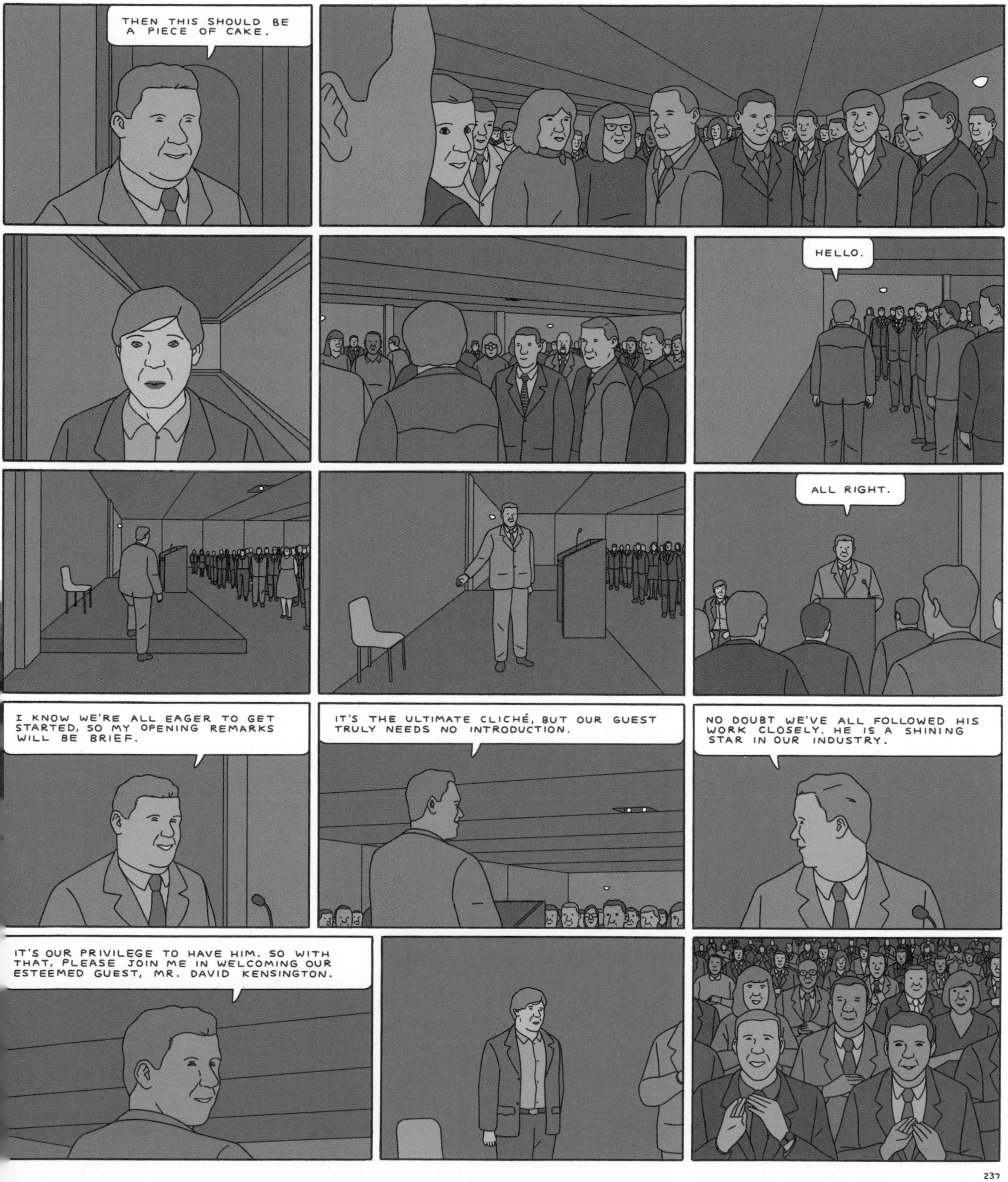
THEN THIS SHOULD BE A PIECE OF CAKE.
HELLO.
ALL RIGHT.
I KNOW WE'RE ALL EAGER TO GET STARTED, SO MY OPENING REMARKS WILL BE BRIEF.
IT'S THE ULTIMATE CLICHÉ, BUT OUR GUEST TRULY NEEDS NO INTRODUCTION.
NO DOUBT WE'VE ALL FOLLOWED HIS WORK CLOSELY. HE IS A SHINING STAR IN OUR INDUSTRY.
IT'S OUR PRIVILEGE TO HAVE HIM. SO WITH THAT, PLEASE JOIN ME IN WELCOMING OUR ESTEEMED GUEST, MR. DAVID KENSINGTON.

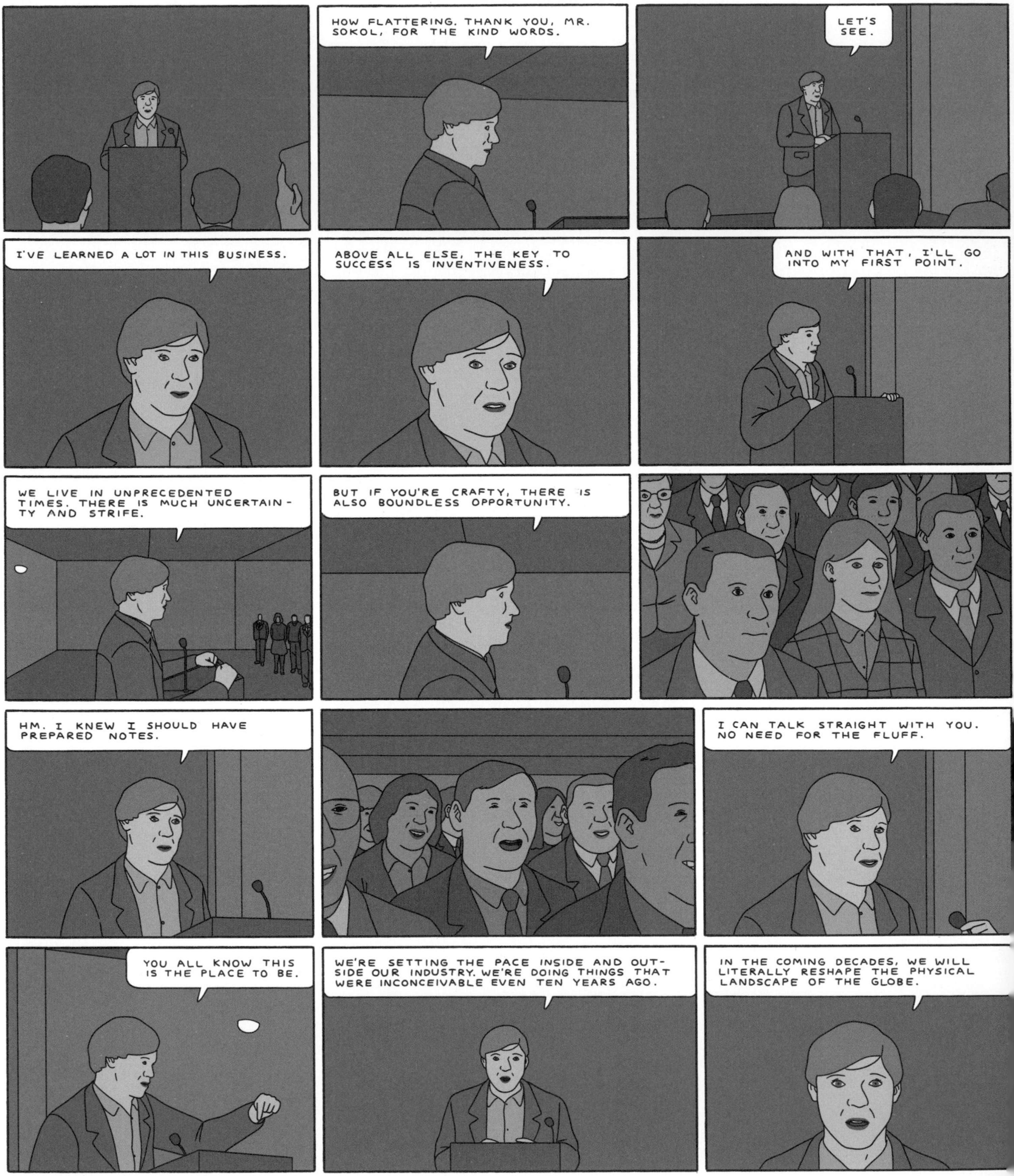
HOW FLATTERING. THANK YOU, MR. SOKOL, FOR THE KIND WORDS.
LET'S SEE.
I'VE LEARNED A LOT IN THIS BUSINESS.
ABOVE ALL ELSE, THE KEY TO SUCCESS IS INVENTIVENESS.
AND WITH THAT, I'LL GO INTO MY FIRST POINT.
WE LIVE IN UNPRECEDENTED TIMES. THERE IS MUCH UNCERTAIN-TY AND STRIFE.
BUT IF YOU'RE CRAFTY, THERE IS ALSO BOUNDLESS OPPORTUNITY.
HM. I KNEW I SHOULD HAVE PREPARED NOTES.
I CAN TALK STRAIGHT WITH YOU. NO NEED FOR THE FLUFF.
YOU ALL KNOW THIS IS THE PLACE TO BE.
WE'RE SETTING THE PACE INSIDE AND OUT-SIDE OUR INDUSTRY. WE'RE DOING THINGS THAT WERE INCONCEIVABLE EVEN TEN YEARS AGO.
IN THE COMING DECADES, WE WILL LITERALLY RESHAPE THE PHYSICAL LANDSCAPE OF THE GLOBE.

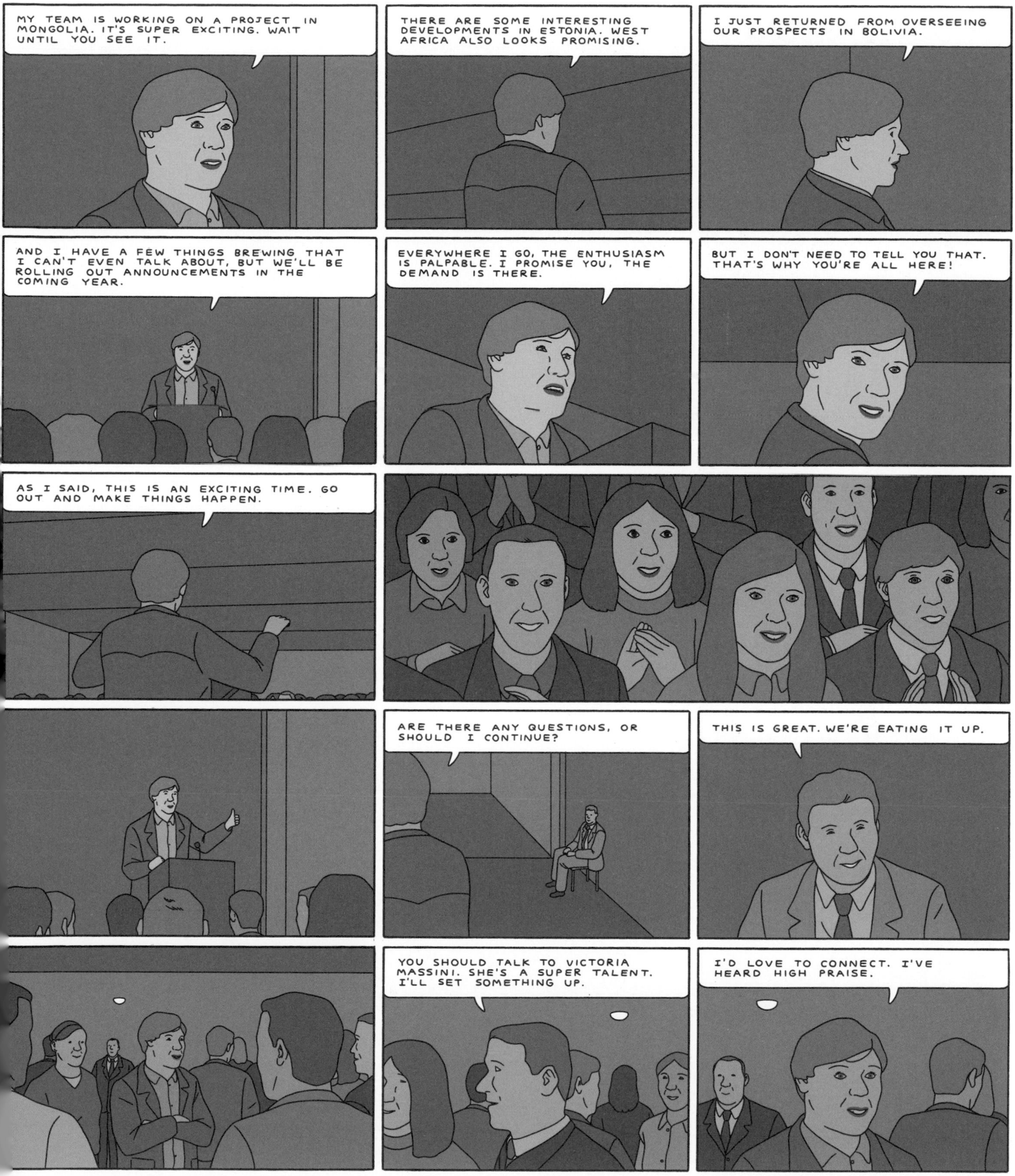
MY TEAM IS WORKING ON A PROJECT IN MONGOLIA. IT'S SUPER EXCITING. WAIT UNTIL YOU SEE IT.
THERE ARE SOME INTERESTING DEVELOPMENTS IN ESTONIA. WEST AFRICA ALSO LOOKS PROMISING.
I JUST RETURNED FROM OVERSEEING OUR PROSPECTS IN BOLIVIA.
AND I HAVE A FEW THINGS BREWING THAT I CAN'T EVEN TALK ABOUT, BUT WE'LL BE ROLLING OUT ANNOUNCEMENTS IN THE COMING YEAR.
EVERYWHERE I GO, THE ENTHUSIASM IS PALPABLE. I PROMISE YOU, THE DEMAND IS THERE.
BUT I DON'T NEED TO TELL YOU THAT. THAT'S WHY YOU'RE ALL HERE!
AS I SAID, THIS IS AN EXCITING TIME. GO OUT AND MAKE THINGS HAPPEN.
ARE THERE ANY QUESTIONS, OR SHOULD I CONTINUE?
THIS IS GREAT. WE'RE EATING IT UP.
YOU SHOULD TALK TO VICTORIA MASSINI. SHE'S A SUPER TALENT. I'LL SET SOMETHING UP.
I'D LOVE TO CONNECT. I'VE HEARD HIGH PRAISE.

GREAT PRESENTATION, MR. KENSINGTON.

MY FIRM WOULD LIKE TO TALK TO YOU ABOUT A PARTNERSHIP. WE'RE STARTING TO DEVELOP JUST OUTSIDE OF TULSA.

I THINK THE NUMBERS WOULD MAKE YOU VERY HAPPY.

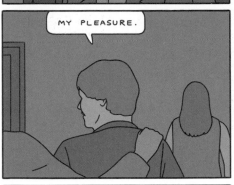

WE'LL SEE. WE'LL SEE. SET SOMETHING UP WITH MY OFFICE.

LET ME STEAL HIM FROM YOU.

THAT WAS FANTASTIC. WE REALLY APPRECIATE IT.

MY PLEASURE.

HERE'S A LITTLE BONUS FROM THE TOP BRASS.

THEY WANTED TO SHOW THEIR GRATITUDE.

WOW. TELL THEM "THANK YOU."

YOU MUST BE EAGER TO GET BACK TO THE HOTEL. I BELIEVE YOU HAVE AN EARLY DEPARTURE TOMORROW.

YES, YOU'RE PROBABLY RIGHT.

THE SUITE IS LOVELY, BUT IF THERE ARE ANY PROBLEMS, GIVE ME A CALL.

THANK YOU, SCOTT.

I'LL HAVE A CAR DOWNSTAIRS FOR YOU IN TEN MINUTES. TAKE YOUR TIME.

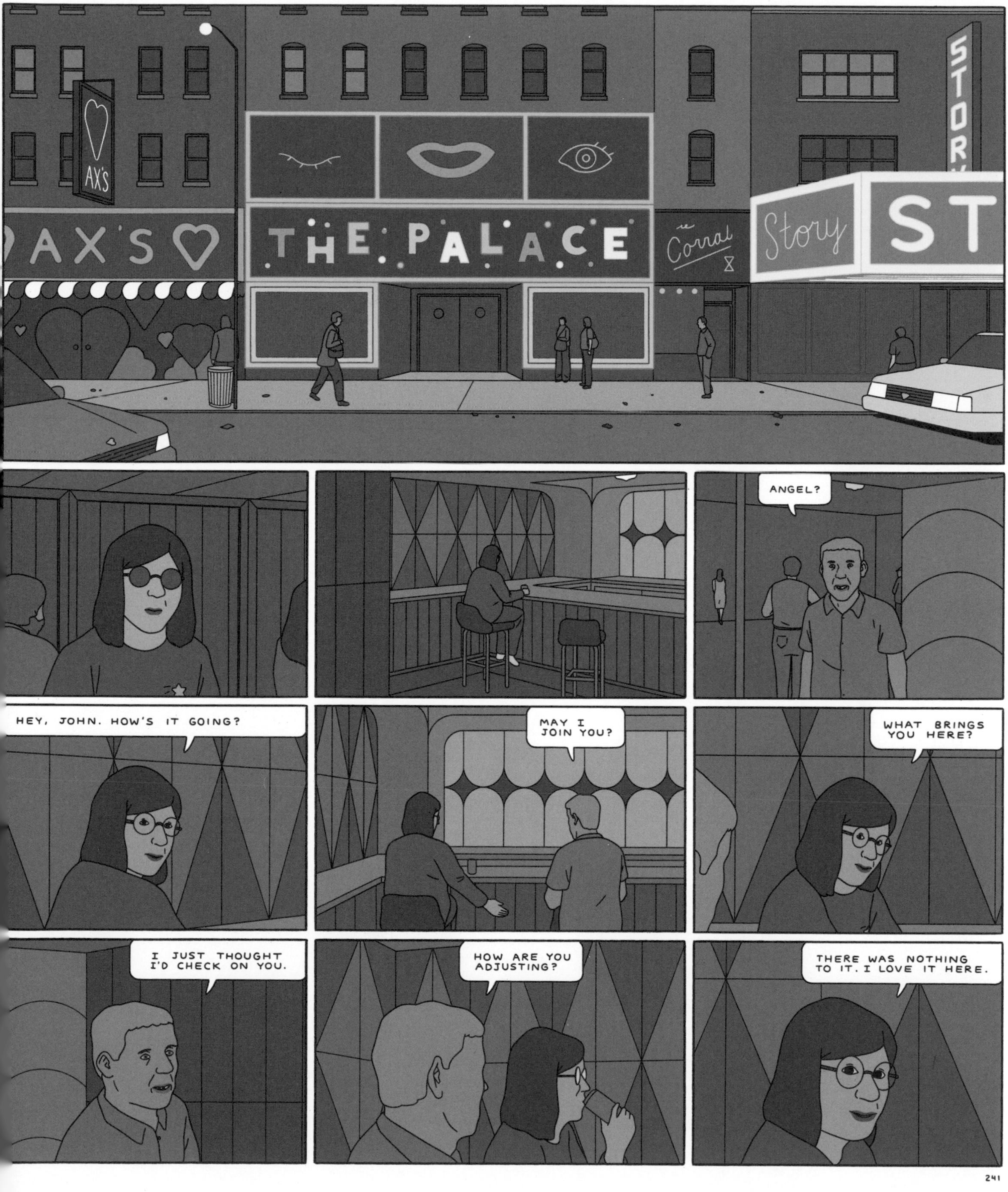
AX'S
AX'S
THE PALACE
Corral
Story
ST
STOR
ANGEL?
HEY, JOHN. HOW'S IT GOING?
MAY I JOIN YOU?
WHAT BRINGS YOU HERE?
I JUST THOUGHT I'D CHECK ON YOU.
HOW ARE YOU ADJUSTING?
THERE WAS NOTHING TO IT. I LOVE IT HERE.

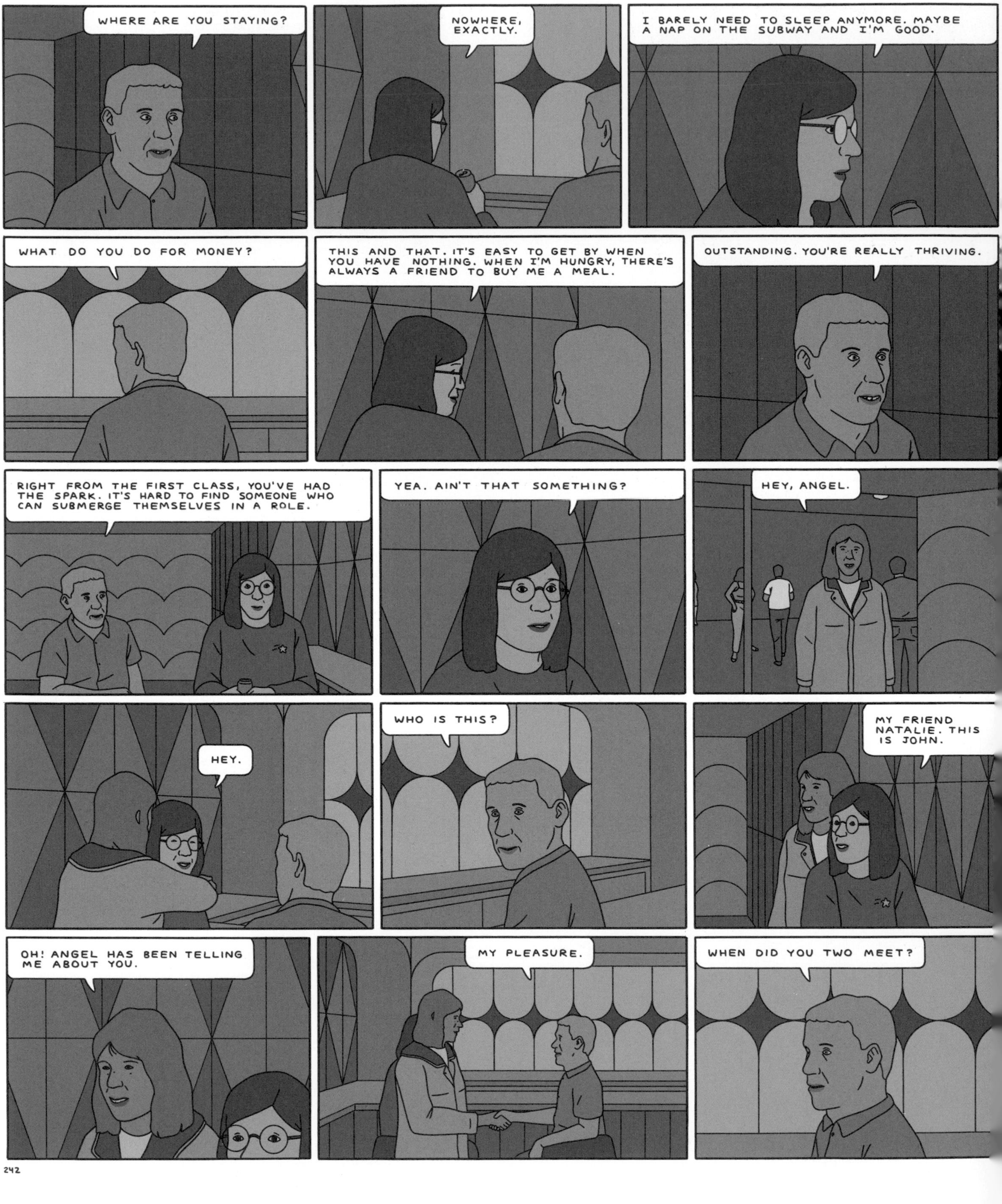
WHERE ARE YOU STAYING?
NOWHERE, EXACTLY.
I BARELY NEED TO SLEEP ANYMORE. MAYBE A NAP ON THE SUBWAY AND I'M GOOD.
WHAT DO YOU DO FOR MONEY?
THIS AND THAT. IT'S EASY TO GET BY WHEN YOU HAVE NOTHING. WHEN I'M HUNGRY, THERE'S ALWAYS A FRIEND TO BUY ME A MEAL.
OUTSTANDING. YOU'RE REALLY THRIVING.
RIGHT FROM THE FIRST CLASS, YOU'VE HAD THE SPARK. IT'S HARD TO FIND SOMEONE WHO CAN SUBMERGE THEMSELVES IN A ROLE.
YEA. AIN'T THAT SOMETHING?
HEY, ANGEL.
HEY.
WHO IS THIS?
MY FRIEND NATALIE. THIS IS JOHN.
OH! ANGEL HAS BEEN TELLING ME ABOUT YOU.
MY PLEASURE.
WHEN DID YOU TWO MEET?

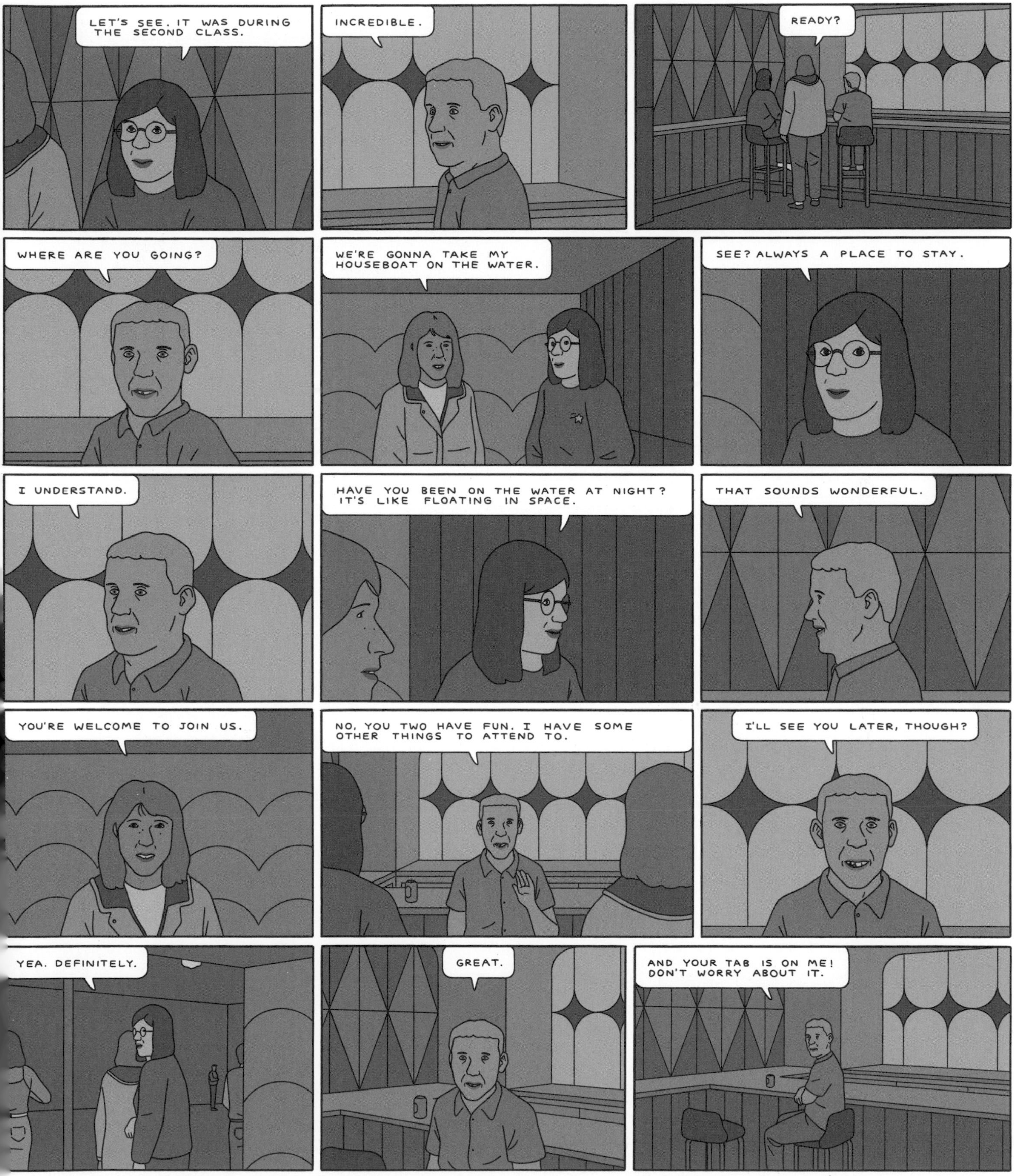
LET'S SEE. IT WAS DURING THE SECOND CLASS.
INCREDIBLE.
READY?
WHERE ARE YOU GOING?
WE'RE GONNA TAKE MY HOUSEBOAT ON THE WATER.
SEE? ALWAYS A PLACE TO STAY.
I UNDERSTAND.
HAVE YOU BEEN ON THE WATER AT NIGHT? IT'S LIKE FLOATING IN SPACE.
THAT SOUNDS WONDERFUL.
YOU'RE WELCOME TO JOIN US.
NO, YOU TWO HAVE FUN. I HAVE SOME OTHER THINGS TO ATTEND TO.
I'LL SEE YOU LATER, THOUGH?
YEA. DEFINITELY.
GREAT.
AND YOUR TAB IS ON ME! DON'T WORRY ABOUT IT.

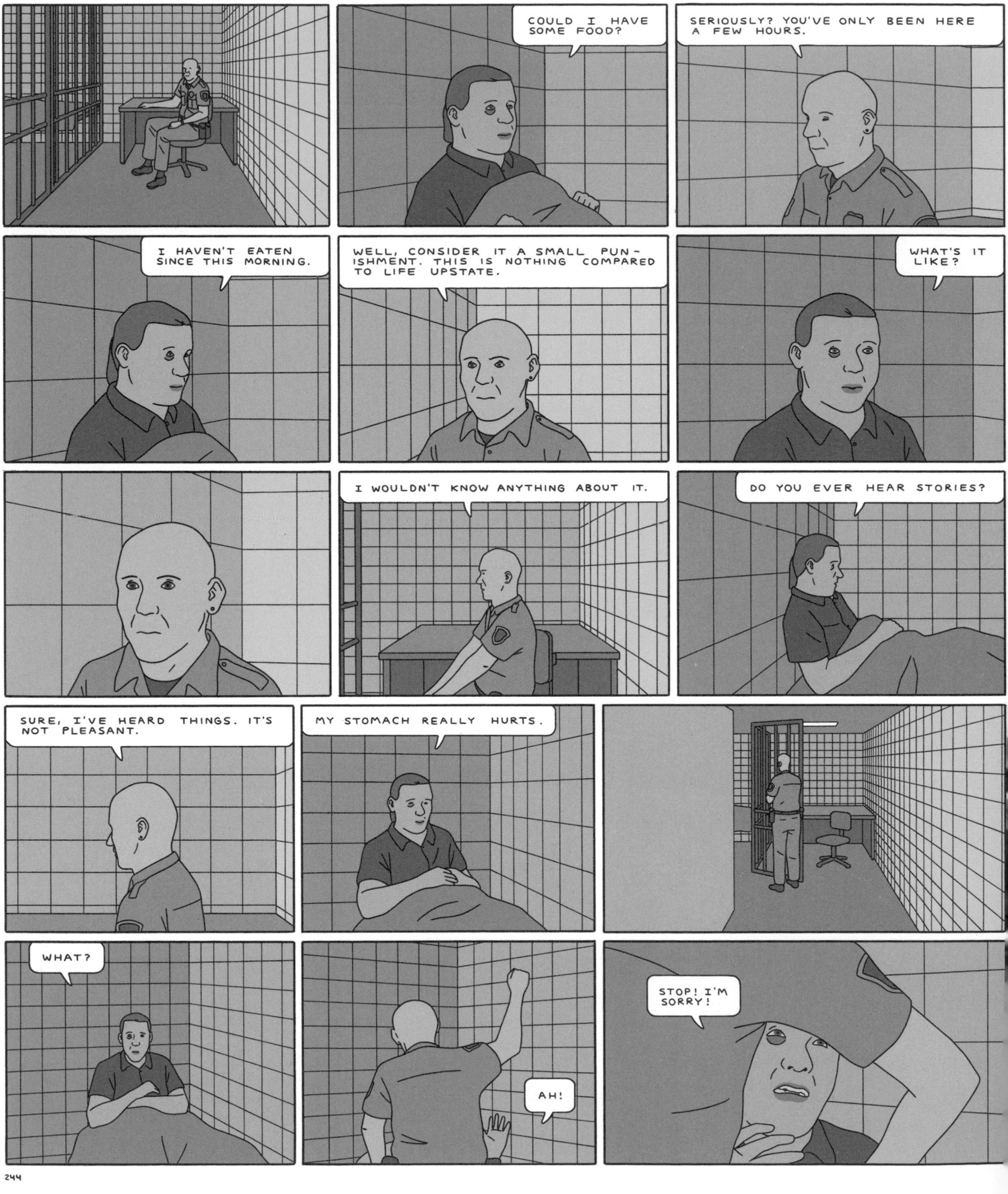
COULD I HAVE SOME FOOD?
SERIOUSLY? YOU'VE ONLY BEEN HERE A FEW HOURS.
I HAVEN'T EATEN SINCE THIS MORNING.
WELL, CONSIDER IT A SMALL PUN-ISHMENT. THIS IS NOTHING COMPARED TO LIFE UPSTATE.
WHAT'S IT LIKE?
I WOULDN'T KNOW ANYTHING ABOUT IT.
DO YOU EVER HEAR STORIES?
SURE, I'VE HEARD THINGS. IT'S NOT PLEASANT.
MY STOMACH REALLY HURTS.
WHAT?
AH!
STOP! I'M SORRY!

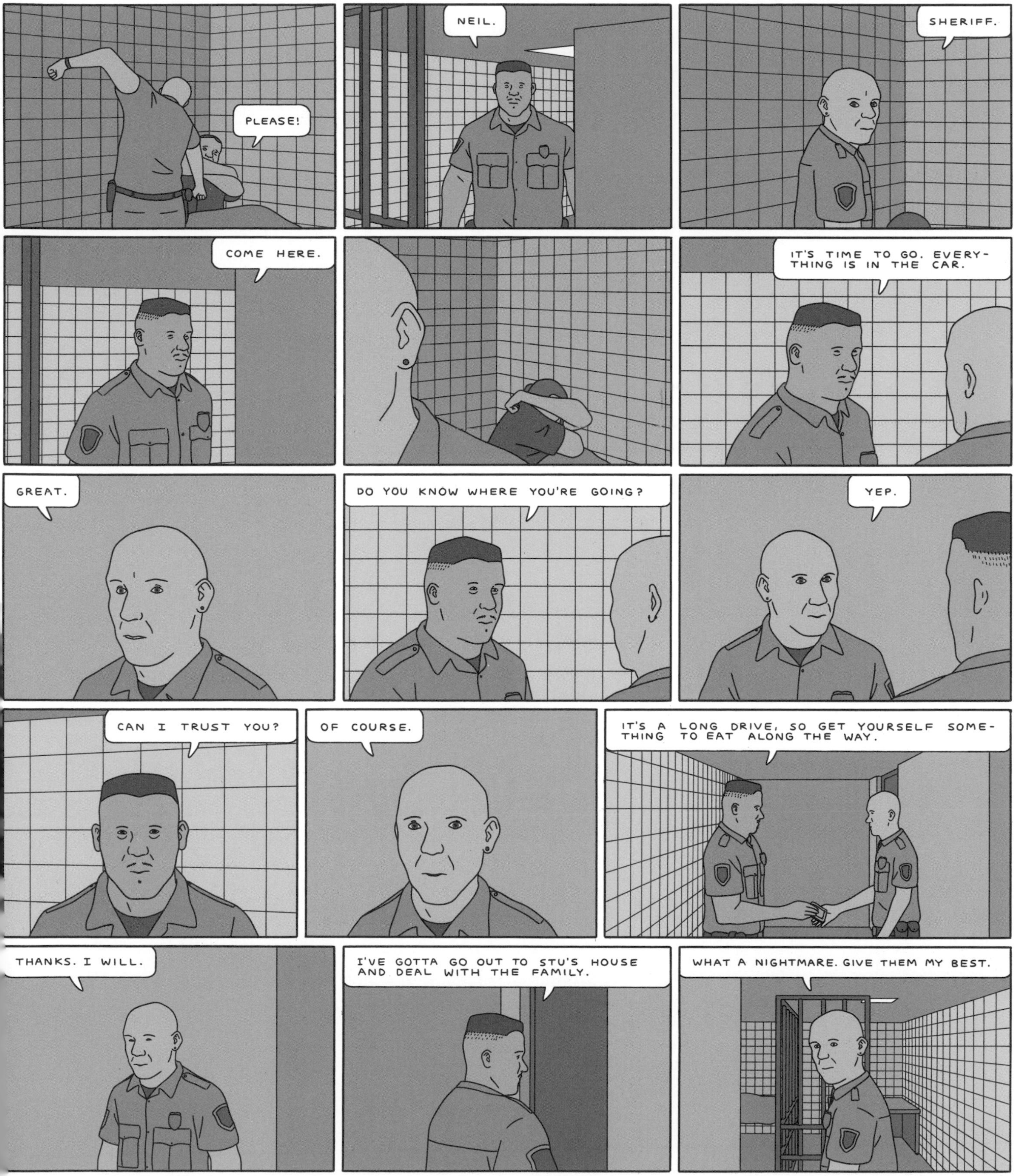
PLEASE!
NEIL.
SHERIFF.
COME HERE.
IT'S TIME TO GO. EVERYTHING IS IN THE CAR.
GREAT.
DO YOU KNOW WHERE YOU'RE GOING?
YEP.
CAN I TRUST YOU?
OF COURSE.
IT'S A LONG DRIVE, SO GET YOURSELF SOMETHING TO EAT ALONG THE WAY.
THANKS. I WILL.
I'VE GOTTA GO OUT TO STU'S HOUSE AND DEAL WITH THE FAMILY.
WHAT A NIGHTMARE. GIVE THEM MY BEST.

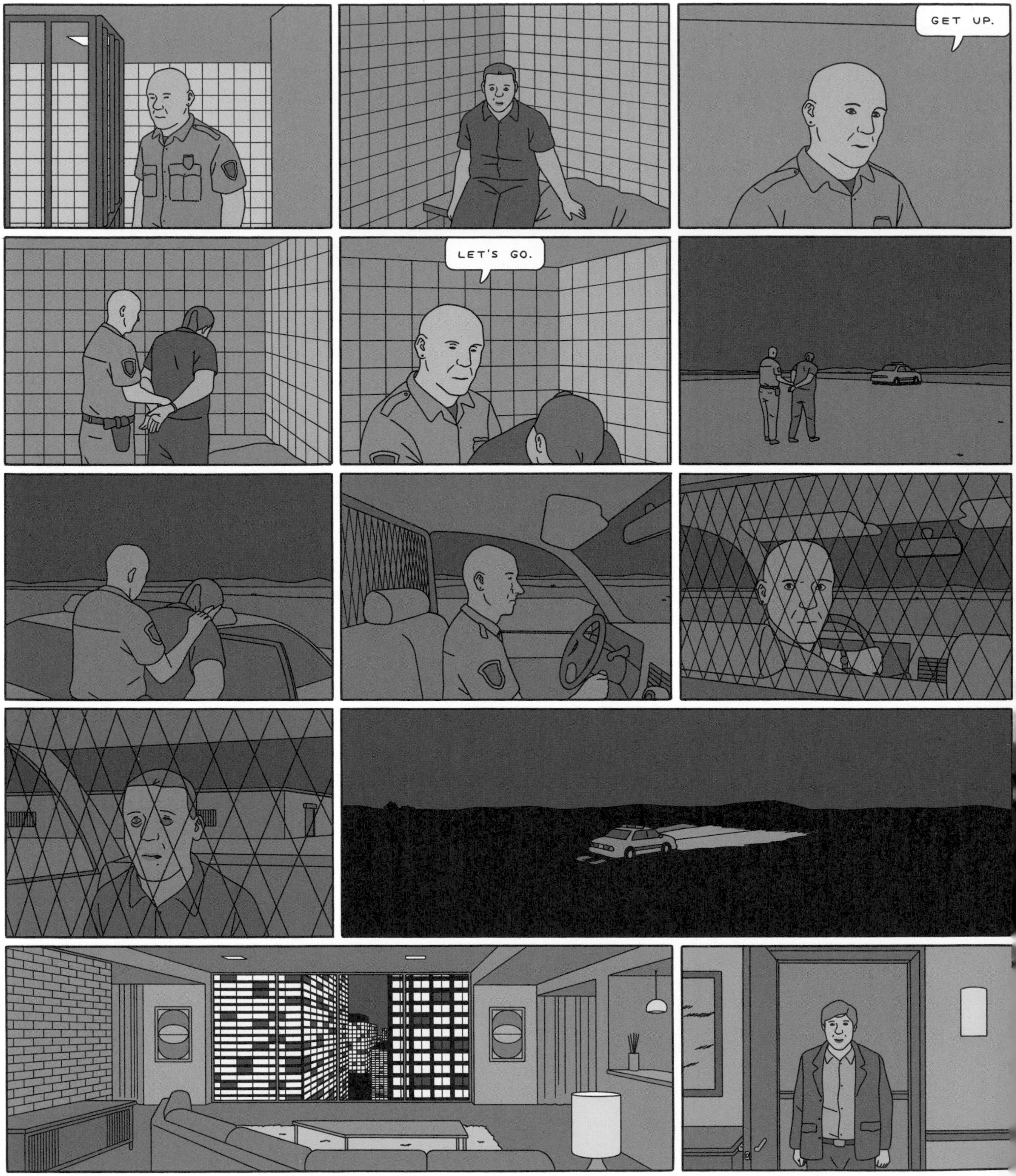
GET UP.
LET'S GO.

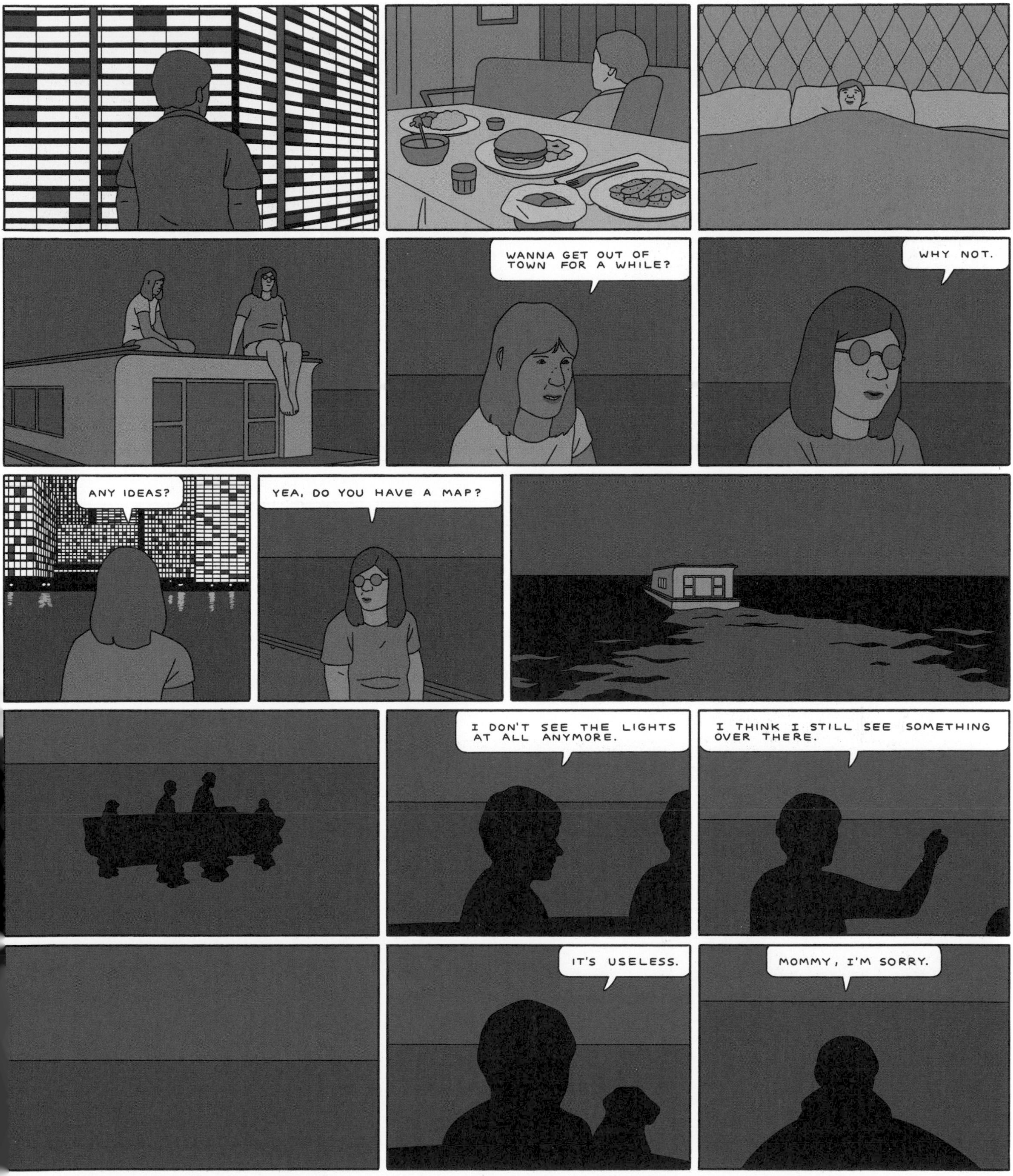
WANNA GET OUT OF TOWN FOR A WHILE?
WHY NOT.
ANY IDEAS?
YEA, DO YOU HAVE A MAP?
I DON'T SEE THE LIGHTS AT ALL ANYMORE.
I THINK I STILL SEE SOMETHING OVER THERE.
IT'S USELESS.
MOMMY, I'M SORRY.

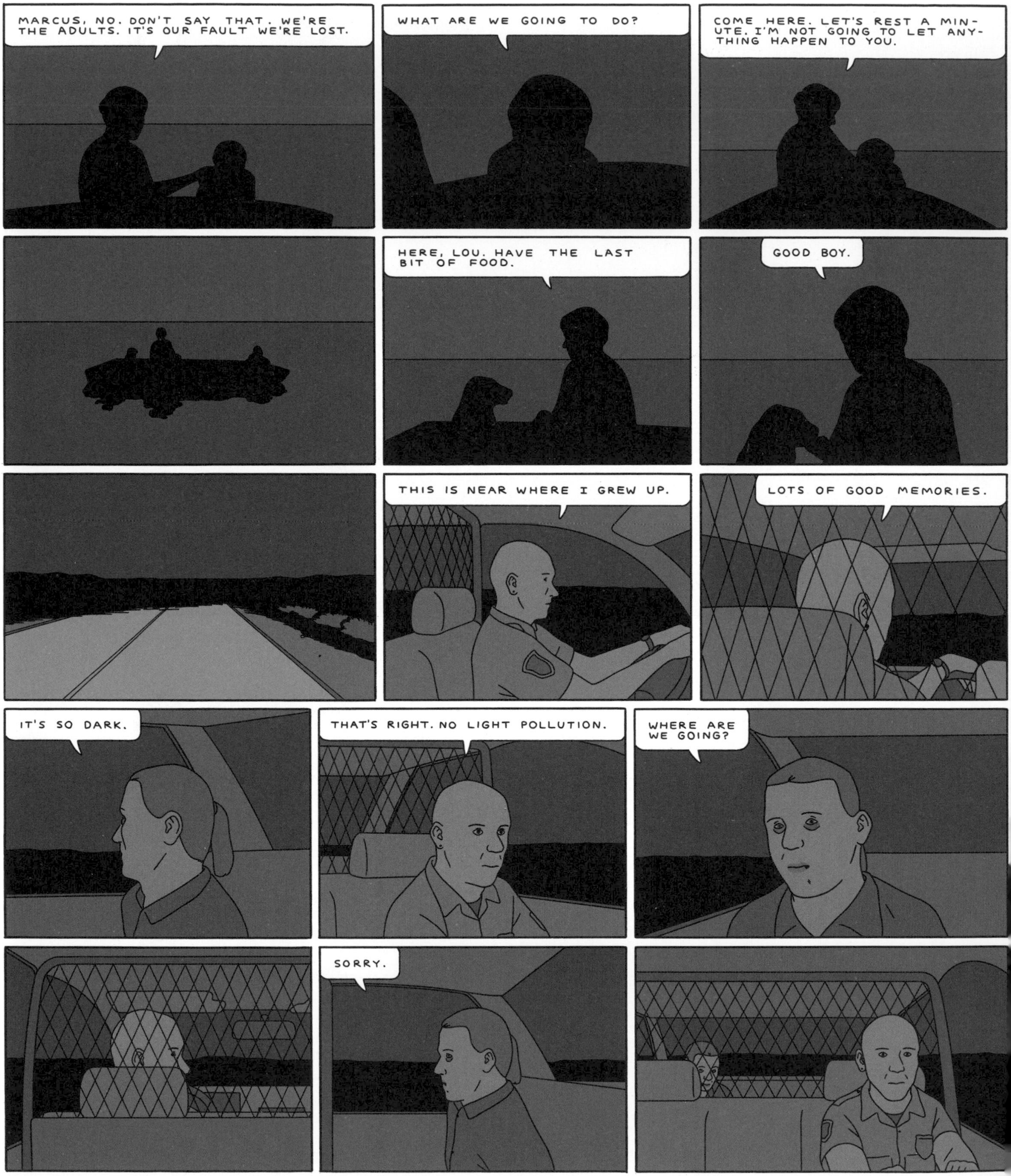
MARCUS, NO. DON'T SAY THAT. WE'RE THE ADULTS. IT'S OUR FAULT WE'RE LOST.
WHAT ARE WE GOING TO DO?
COME HERE. LET'S REST A MINUTE. I'M NOT GOING TO LET ANYTHING HAPPEN TO YOU.
HERE, LOU. HAVE THE LAST BIT OF FOOD.
GOOD BOY.
THIS IS NEAR WHERE I GREW UP.
LOTS OF GOOD MEMORIES.
IT'S SO DARK.
THAT'S RIGHT. NO LIGHT POLLUTION.
WHERE ARE WE GOING?
SORRY.

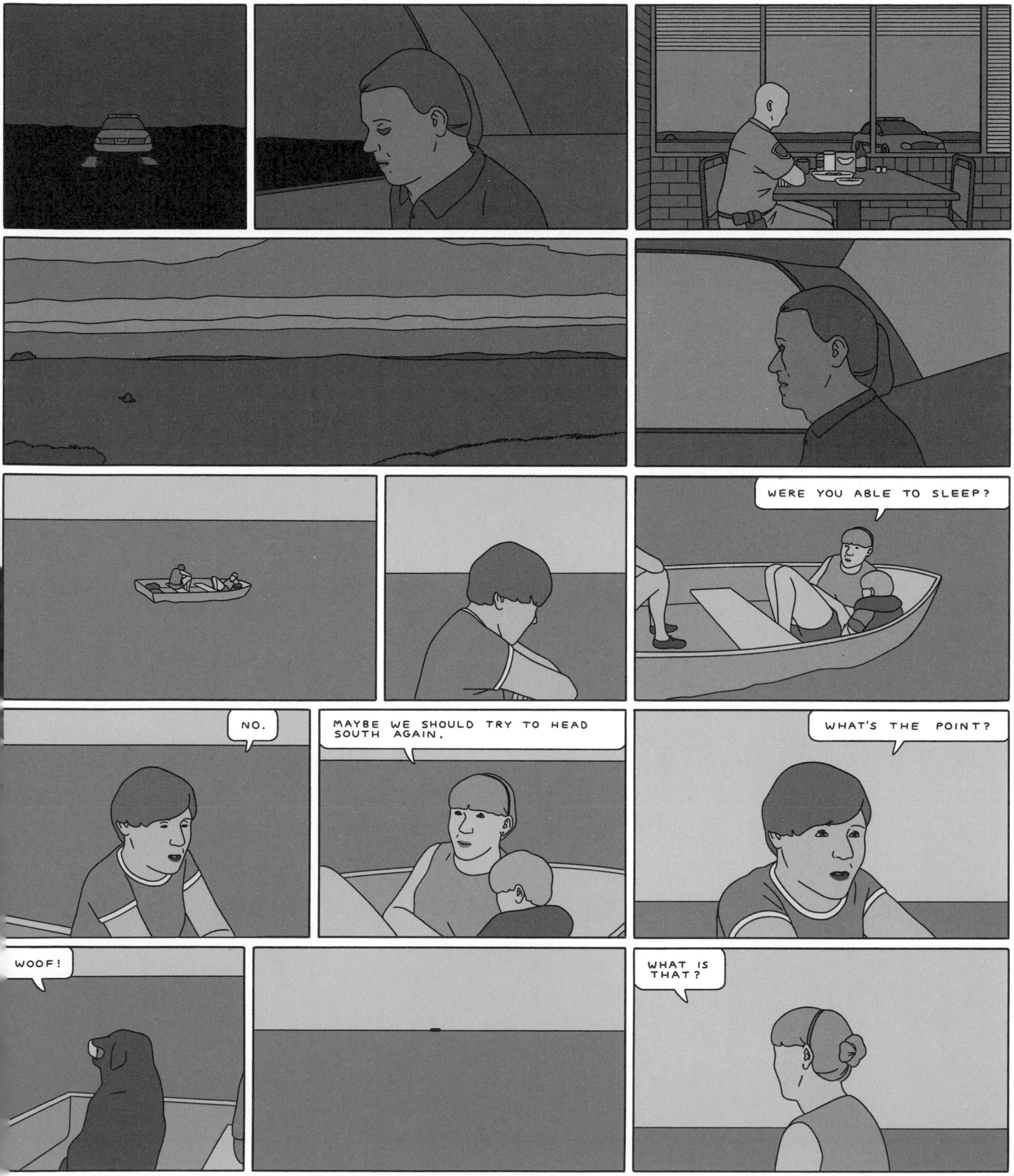
WERE YOU ABLE TO SLEEP?
NO.
MAYBE WE SHOULD TRY TO HEAD SOUTH AGAIN.
WHAT'S THE POINT?
WOOF!
WHAT IS THAT?

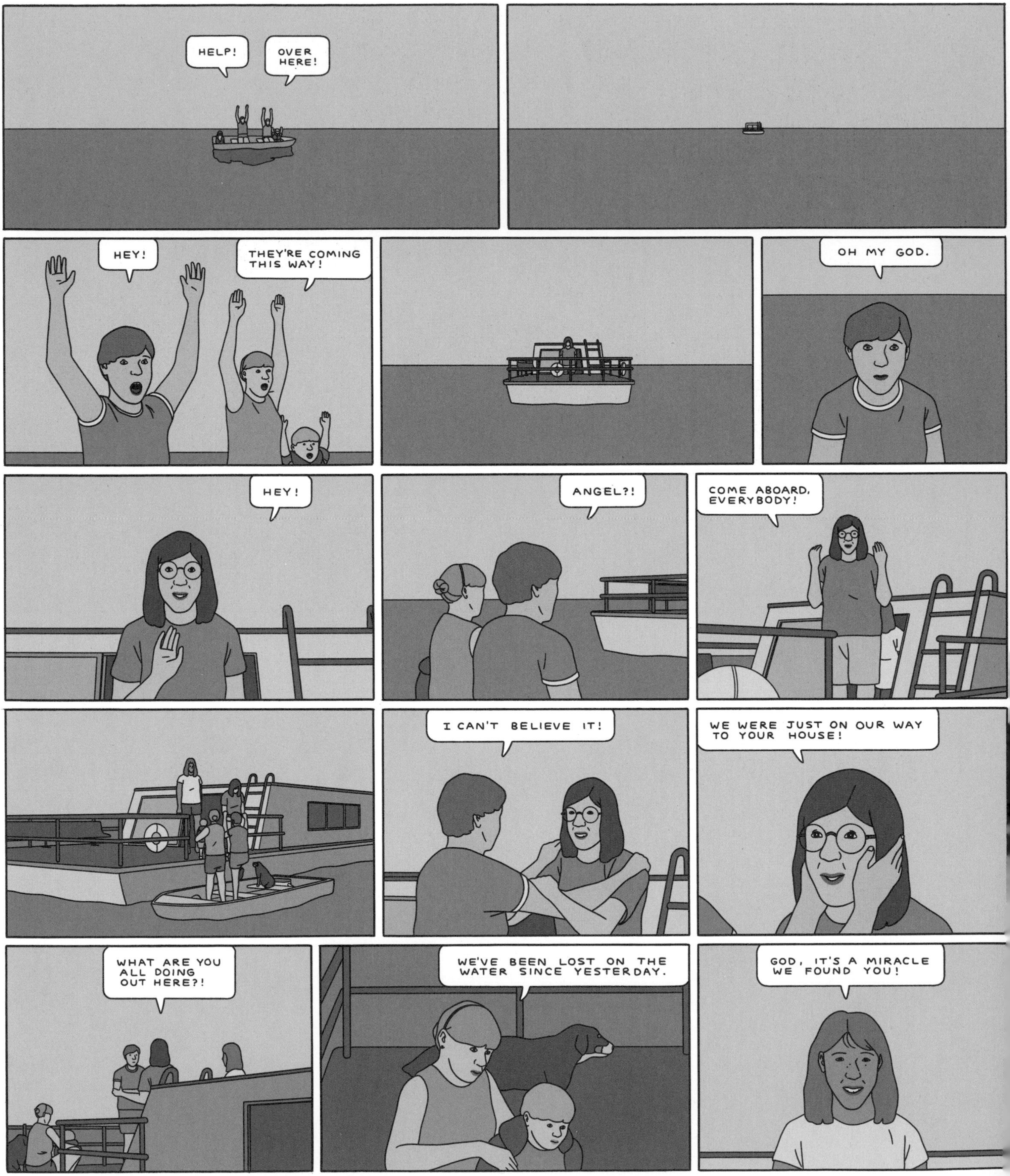
HELP!
OVER HERE!
HEY!
THEY'RE COMING THIS WAY!
OH MY GOD.
HEY!
ANGEL?!
COME ABOARD, EVERYBODY!
I CAN'T BELIEVE IT!
WE WERE JUST ON OUR WAY TO YOUR HOUSE!
WHAT ARE YOU ALL DOING OUT HERE?!
WE'VE BEEN LOST ON THE WATER SINCE YESTERDAY.
GOD, IT'S A MIRACLE WE FOUND YOU!

EVERYONE, MEET NATALIE. THIS IS HER BOAT.

THIS IS ROSIE, RAYANNE, MARCUS, AND LOU.

NICE TO FINALLY MEET YOU ALL.

YOU MUST BE HUNGRY. I'LL START BREAKFAST. WHO WANTS COFFEE?

THAT WOULD BE GREAT.

MAKE YOURSELVES COMFORTABLE. THERE'S A BATHROOM IN THE CABIN.

LEAVE EVERYTHING TO ME. WE'LL BE ON LAND IN NO TIME.

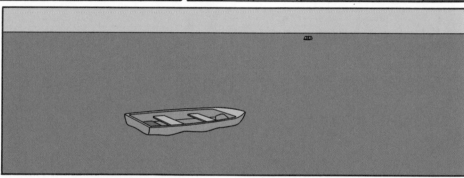

MR. KENSINGTON?

THAT'S ME.

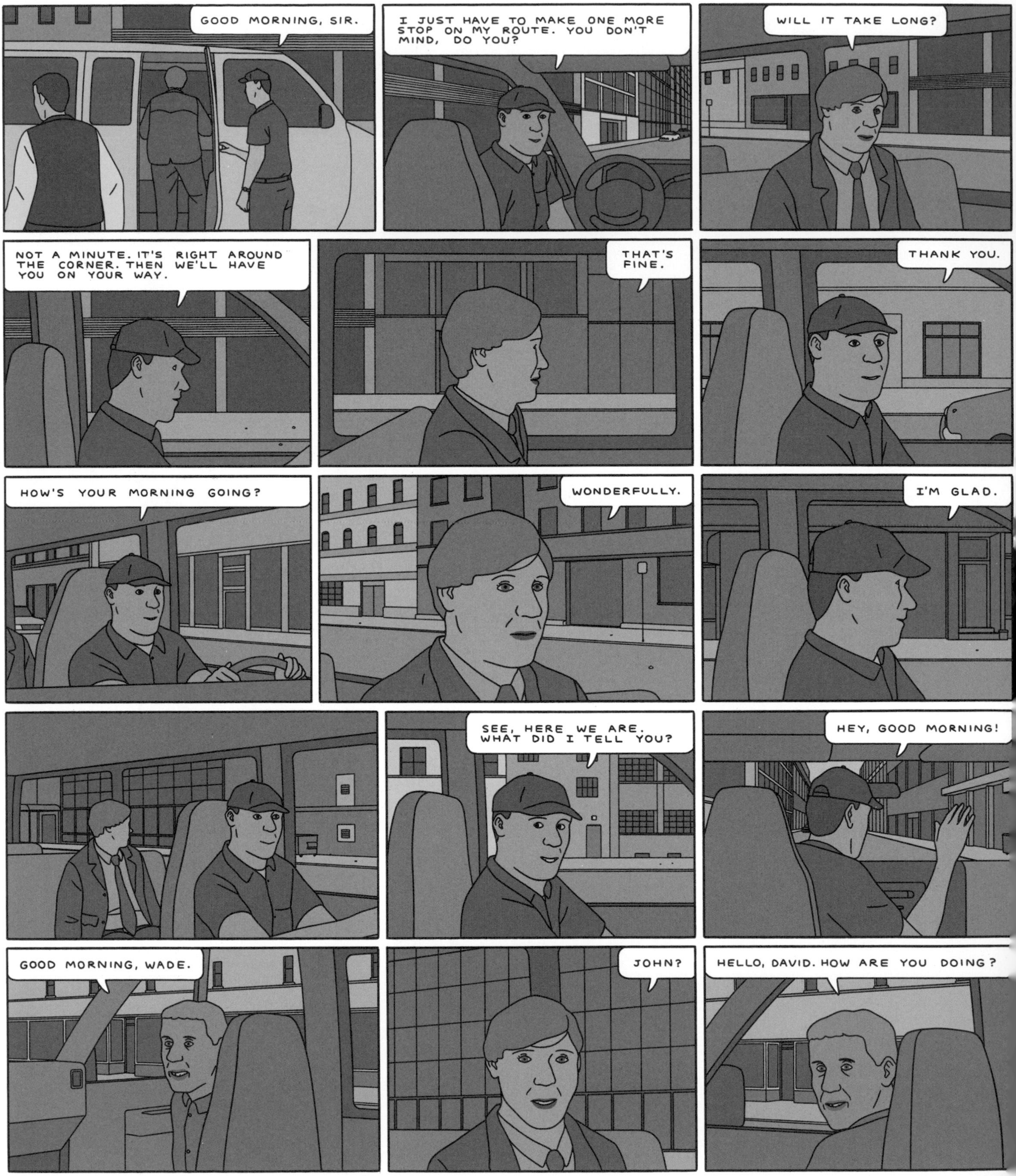
GOOD MORNING, SIR.
I JUST HAVE TO MAKE ONE MORE STOP ON MY ROUTE. YOU DON'T MIND, DO YOU?
WILL IT TAKE LONG?
NOT A MINUTE. IT'S RIGHT AROUND THE CORNER. THEN WE'LL HAVE YOU ON YOUR WAY.
THAT'S FINE.
THANK YOU.
HOW'S YOUR MORNING GOING?
WONDERFULLY.
I'M GLAD.
SEE, HERE WE ARE. WHAT DID I TELL YOU?
HEY, GOOD MORNING!
GOOD MORNING, WADE.
JOHN?
HELLO, DAVID. HOW ARE YOU DOING?

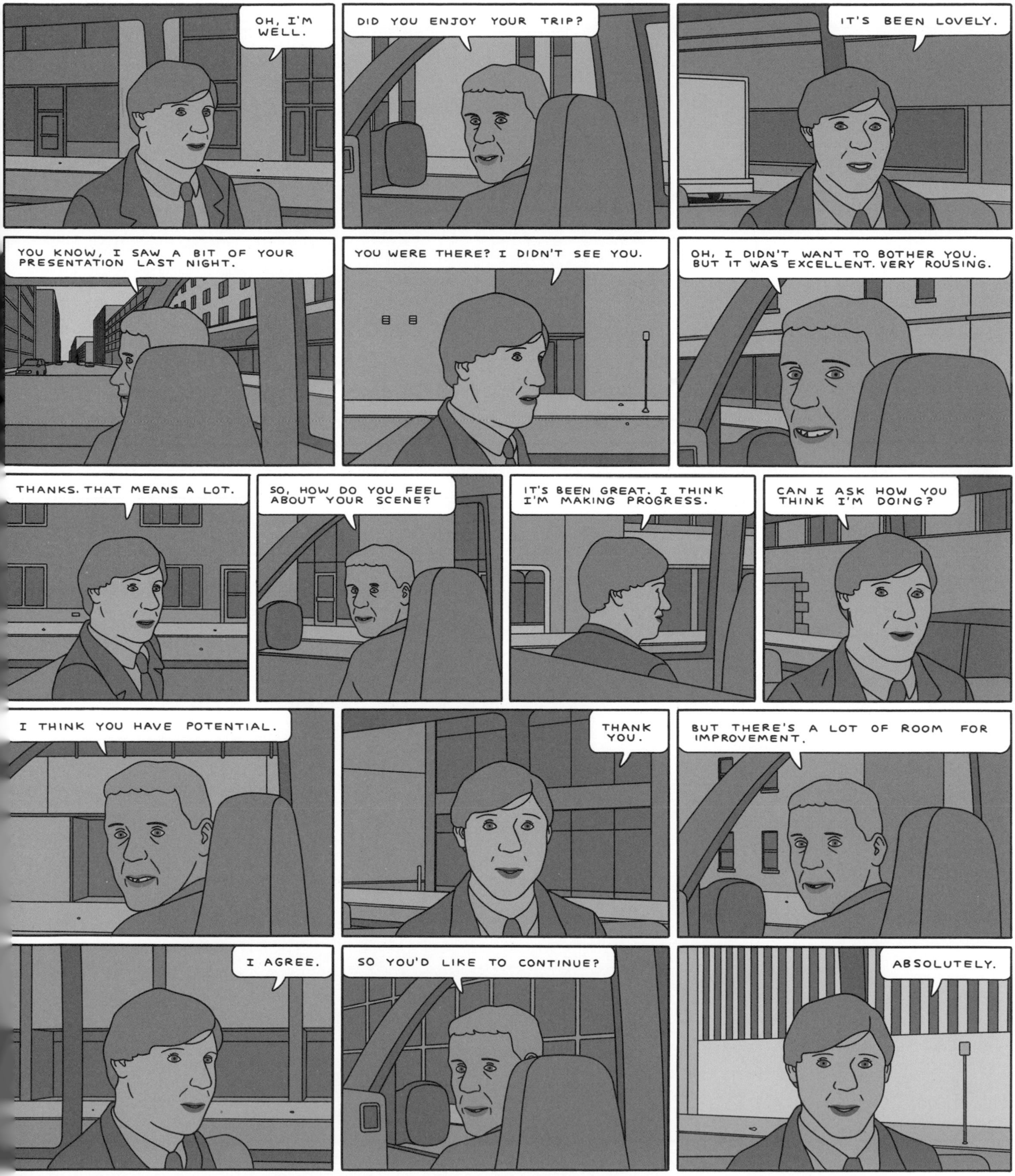
OH, I'M WELL.
DID YOU ENJOY YOUR TRIP?
IT'S BEEN LOVELY.
YOU KNOW, I SAW A BIT OF YOUR PRESENTATION LAST NIGHT.
YOU WERE THERE? I DIDN'T SEE YOU.
OH, I DIDN'T WANT TO BOTHER YOU. BUT IT WAS EXCELLENT. VERY ROUSING.
THANKS. THAT MEANS A LOT.
SO, HOW DO YOU FEEL ABOUT YOUR SCENE?
IT'S BEEN GREAT. I THINK I'M MAKING PROGRESS.
CAN I ASK HOW YOU THINK I'M DOING?
I THINK YOU HAVE POTENTIAL.
THANK YOU.
BUT THERE'S A LOT OF ROOM FOR IMPROVEMENT.
I AGREE.
SO YOU'D LIKE TO CONTINUE?
ABSOLUTELY.

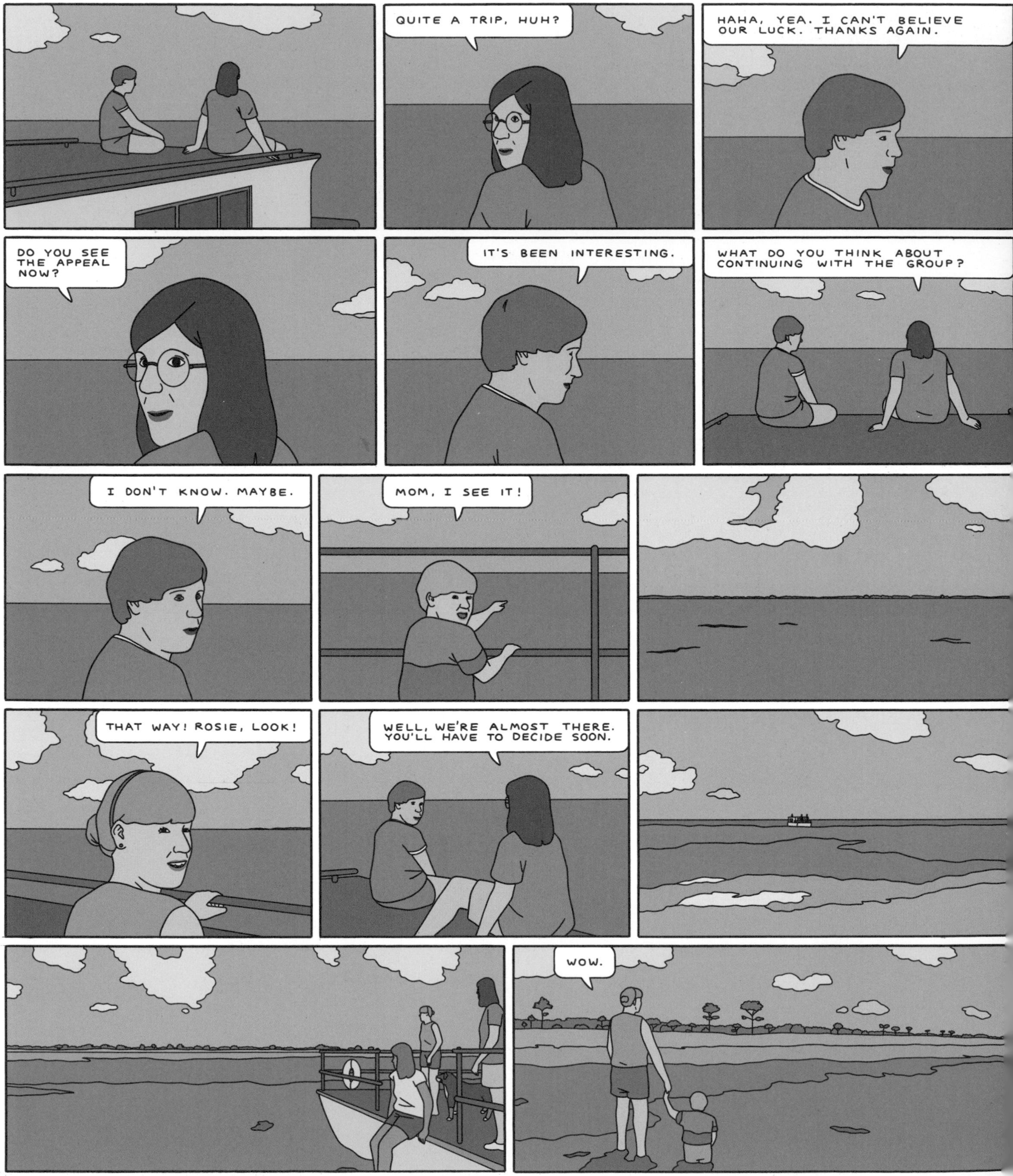
QUITE A TRIP, HUH?
HAHA, YEA. I CAN'T BELIEVE OUR LUCK. THANKS AGAIN.
DO YOU SEE THE APPEAL NOW?
IT'S BEEN INTERESTING.
WHAT DO YOU THINK ABOUT CONTINUING WITH THE GROUP?
I DON'T KNOW. MAYBE.
MOM, I SEE IT!
THAT WAY! ROSIE, LOOK!
WELL, WE'RE ALMOST THERE. YOU'LL HAVE TO DECIDE SOON.
WOW.

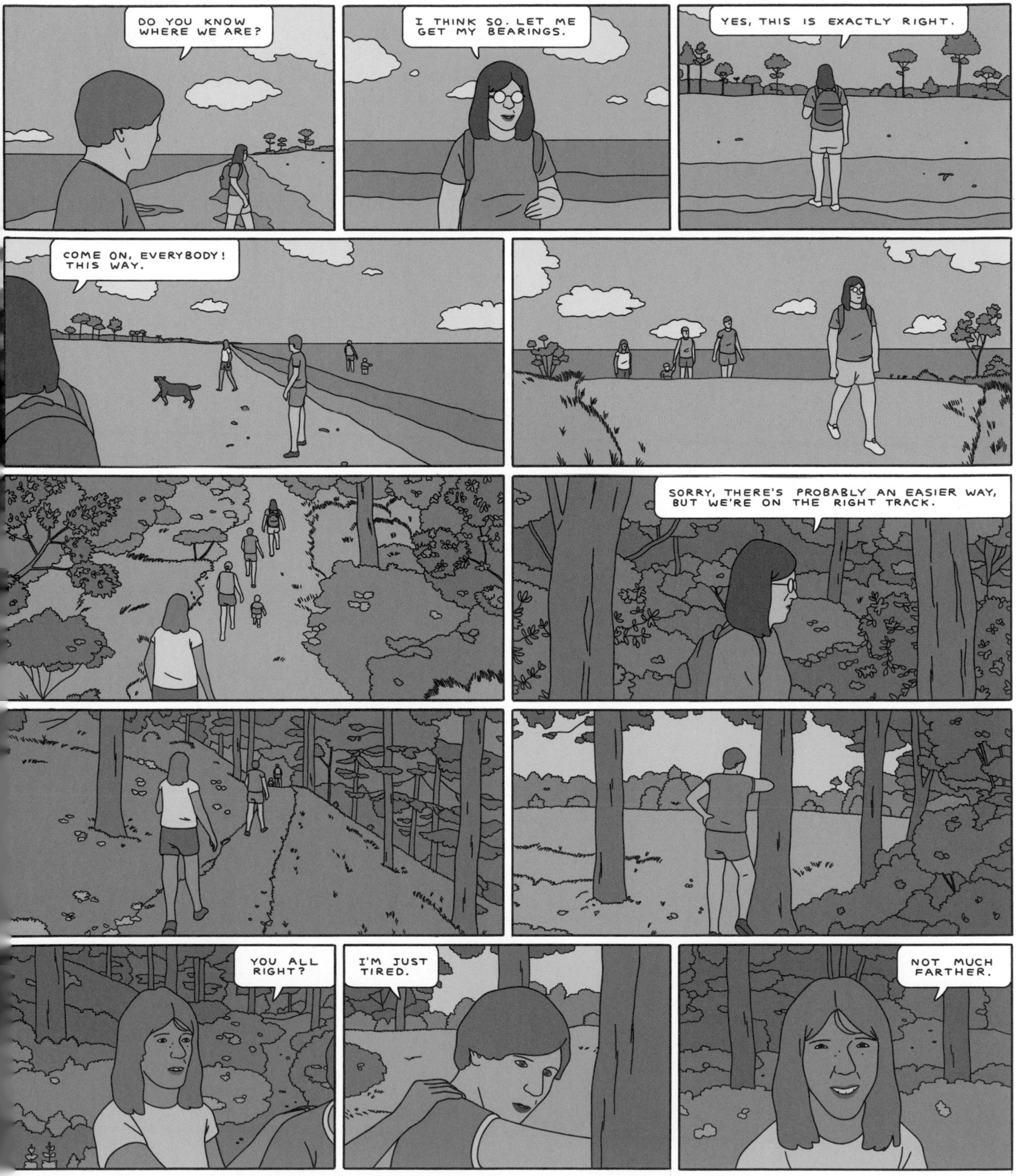
DO YOU KNOW WHERE WE ARE?
I THINK SO. LET ME GET MY BEARINGS.
YES, THIS IS EXACTLY RIGHT.
COME ON, EVERYBODY! THIS WAY.
SORRY, THERE'S PROBABLY AN EASIER WAY, BUT WE'RE ON THE RIGHT TRACK.
YOU ALL RIGHT?
I'M JUST TIRED.
NOT MUCH FARTHER.

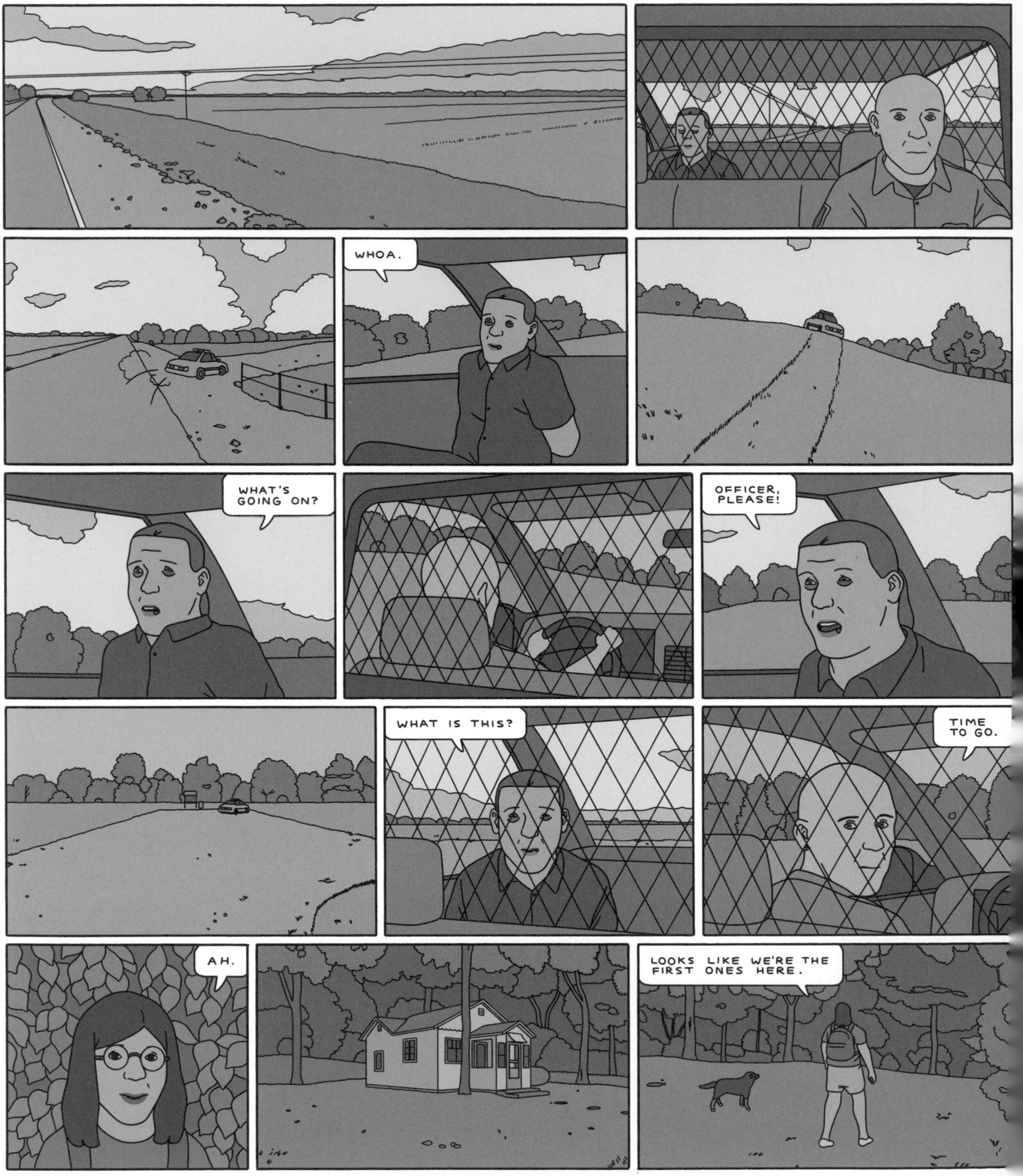
WHOA.
WHAT'S GOING ON?
OFFICER, PLEASE!
WHAT IS THIS?
TIME TO GO.
AH.
LOOKS LIKE WE'RE THE FIRST ONES HERE.

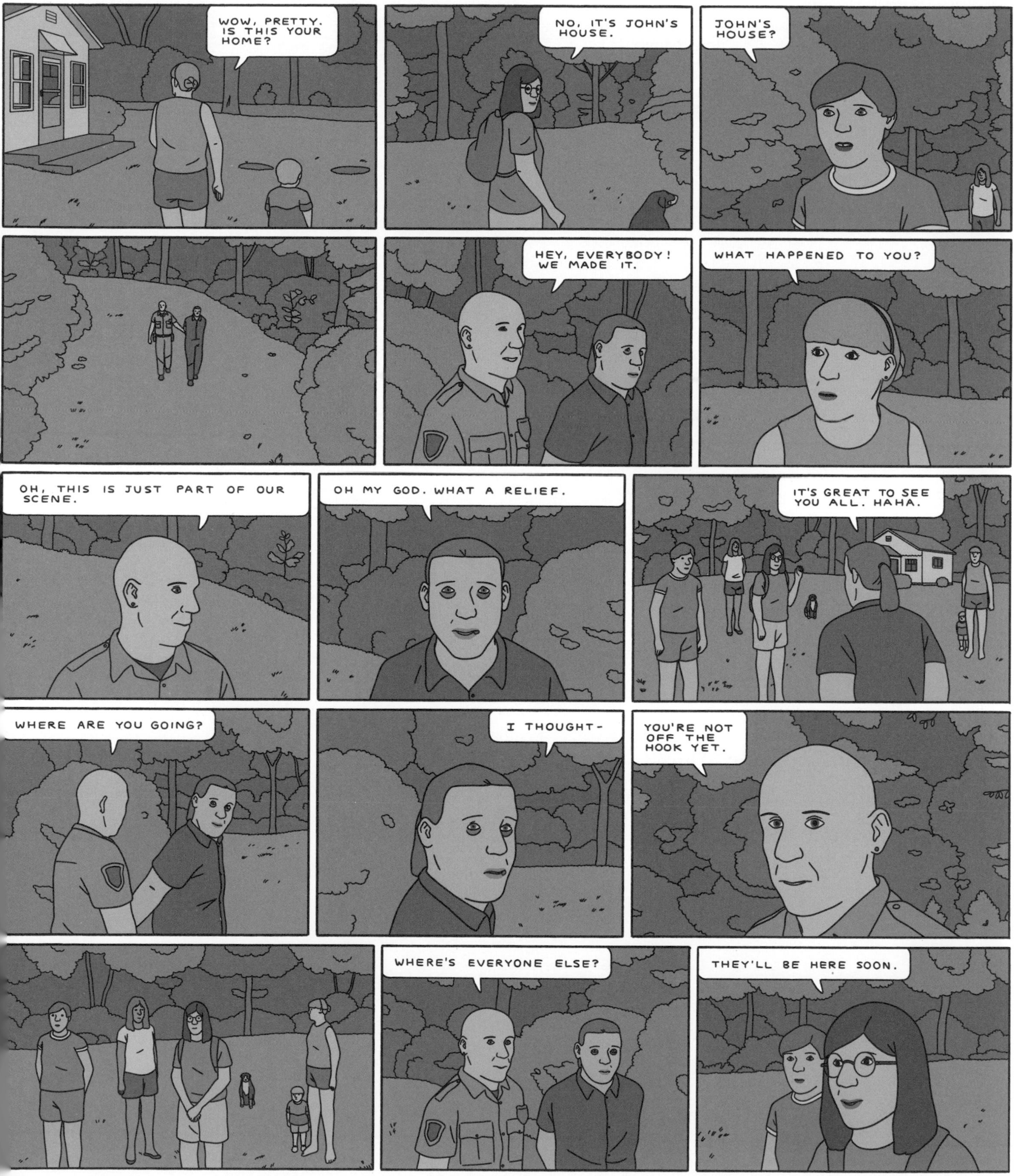
WOW, PRETTY. IS THIS YOUR HOME?
NO, IT'S JOHN'S HOUSE.
JOHN'S HOUSE?
HEY, EVERYBODY! WE MADE IT.
WHAT HAPPENED TO YOU?
OH, THIS IS JUST PART OF OUR SCENE.
OH MY GOD. WHAT A RELIEF.
IT'S GREAT TO SEE YOU ALL. HAHA.
WHERE ARE YOU GOING?
I THOUGHT-
YOU'RE NOT OFF THE HOOK YET.
WHERE'S EVERYONE ELSE?
THEY'LL BE HERE SOON.

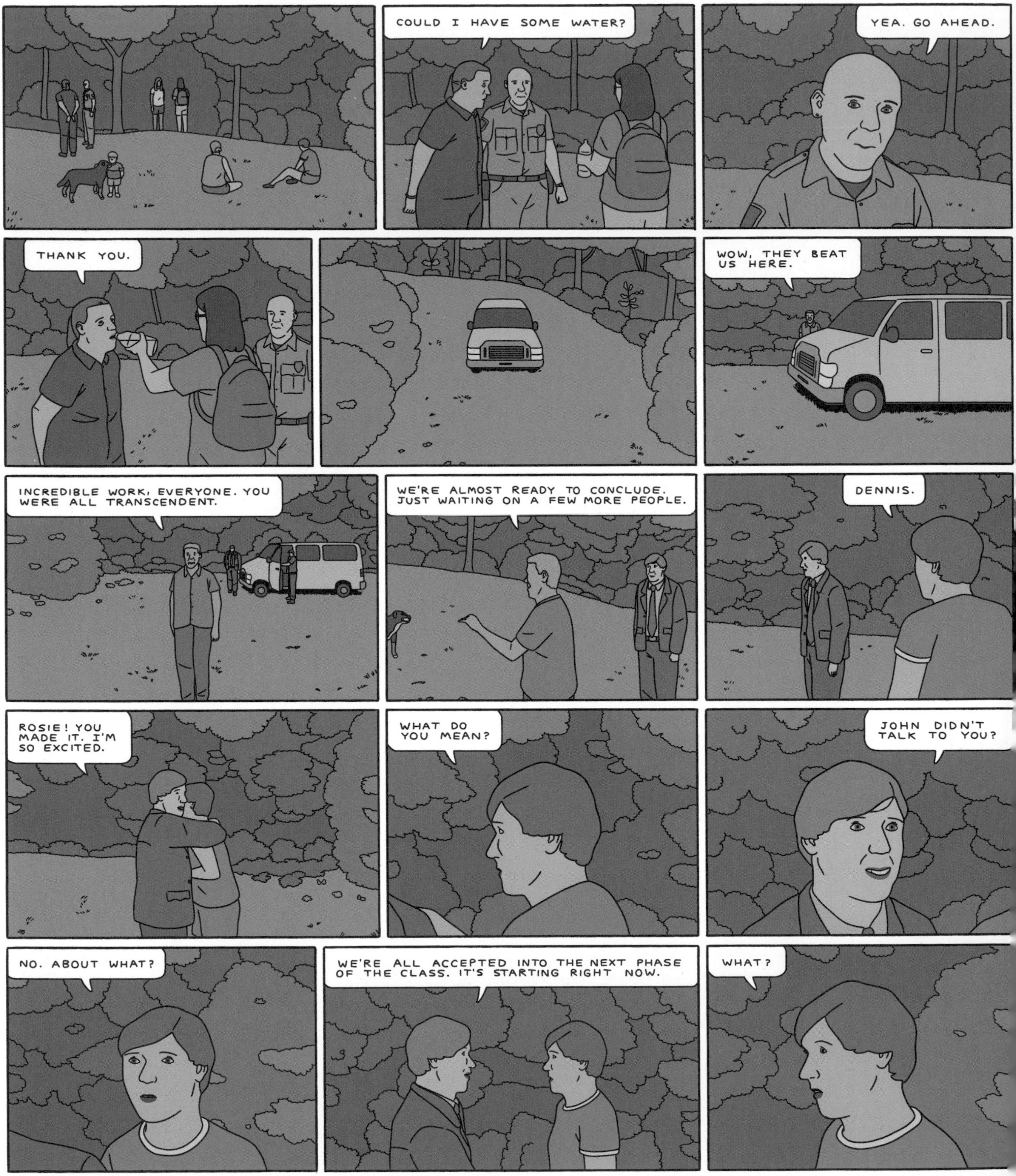
COULD I HAVE SOME WATER?
YEA. GO AHEAD.
THANK YOU.
WOW, THEY BEAT US HERE.
INCREDIBLE WORK, EVERYONE. YOU WERE ALL TRANSCENDENT.
WE'RE ALMOST READY TO CONCLUDE. JUST WAITING ON A FEW MORE PEOPLE.
DENNIS.
ROSIE! YOU MADE IT. I'M SO EXCITED.
WHAT DO YOU MEAN?
JOHN DIDN'T TALK TO YOU?
NO. ABOUT WHAT?
WE'RE ALL ACCEPTED INTO THE NEXT PHASE OF THE CLASS. IT'S STARTING RIGHT NOW.
WHAT?

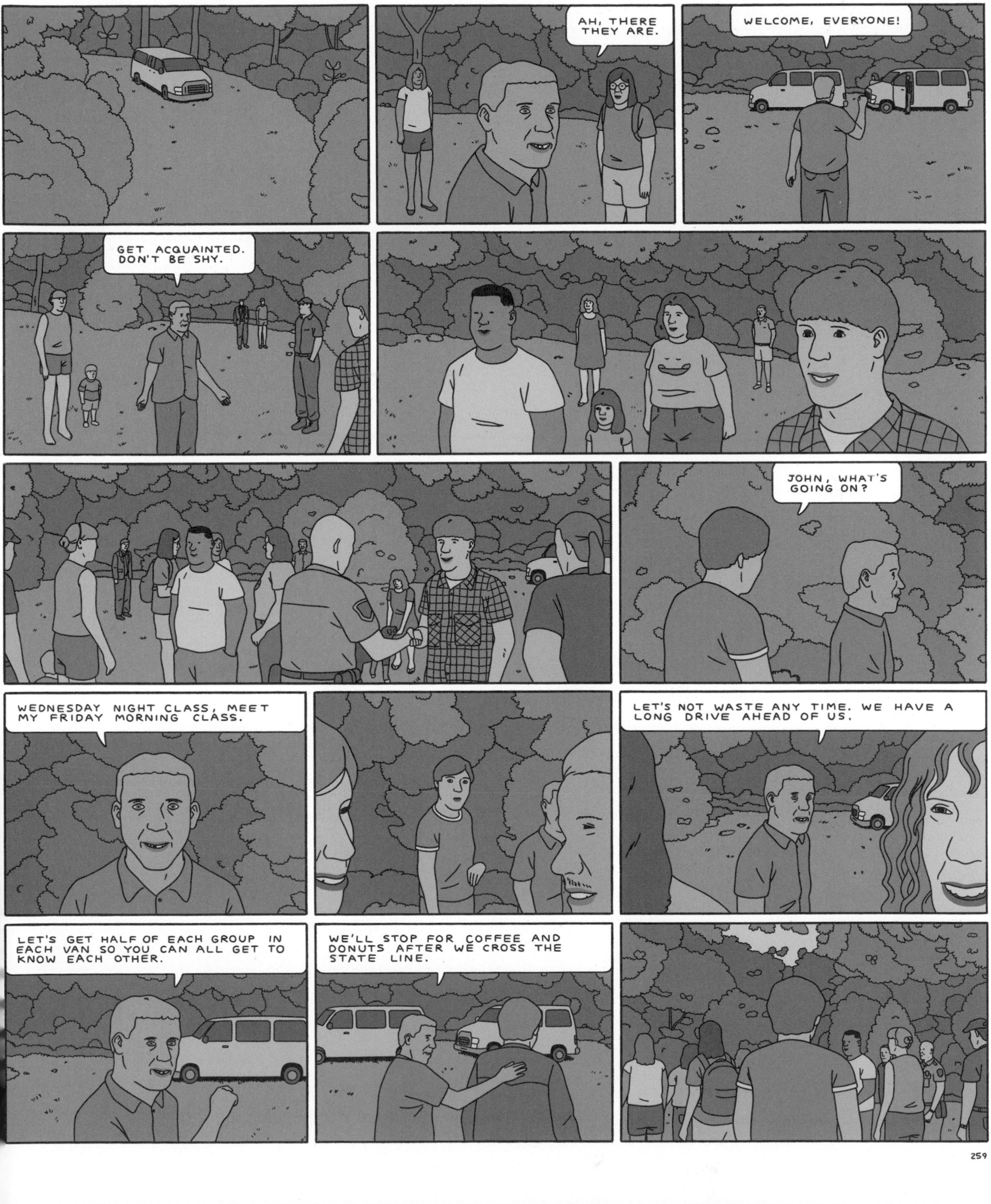
AH, THERE THEY ARE.
WELCOME, EVERYONE!
GET ACQUAINTED. DON'T BE SHY.
JOHN, WHAT'S GOING ON?
WEDNESDAY NIGHT CLASS, MEET MY FRIDAY MORNING CLASS.
LET'S NOT WASTE ANY TIME. WE HAVE A LONG DRIVE AHEAD OF US.
LET'S GET HALF OF EACH GROUP IN EACH VAN SO YOU CAN ALL GET TO KNOW EACH OTHER.
WE'LL STOP FOR COFFEE AND DONUTS AFTER WE CROSS THE STATE LINE.

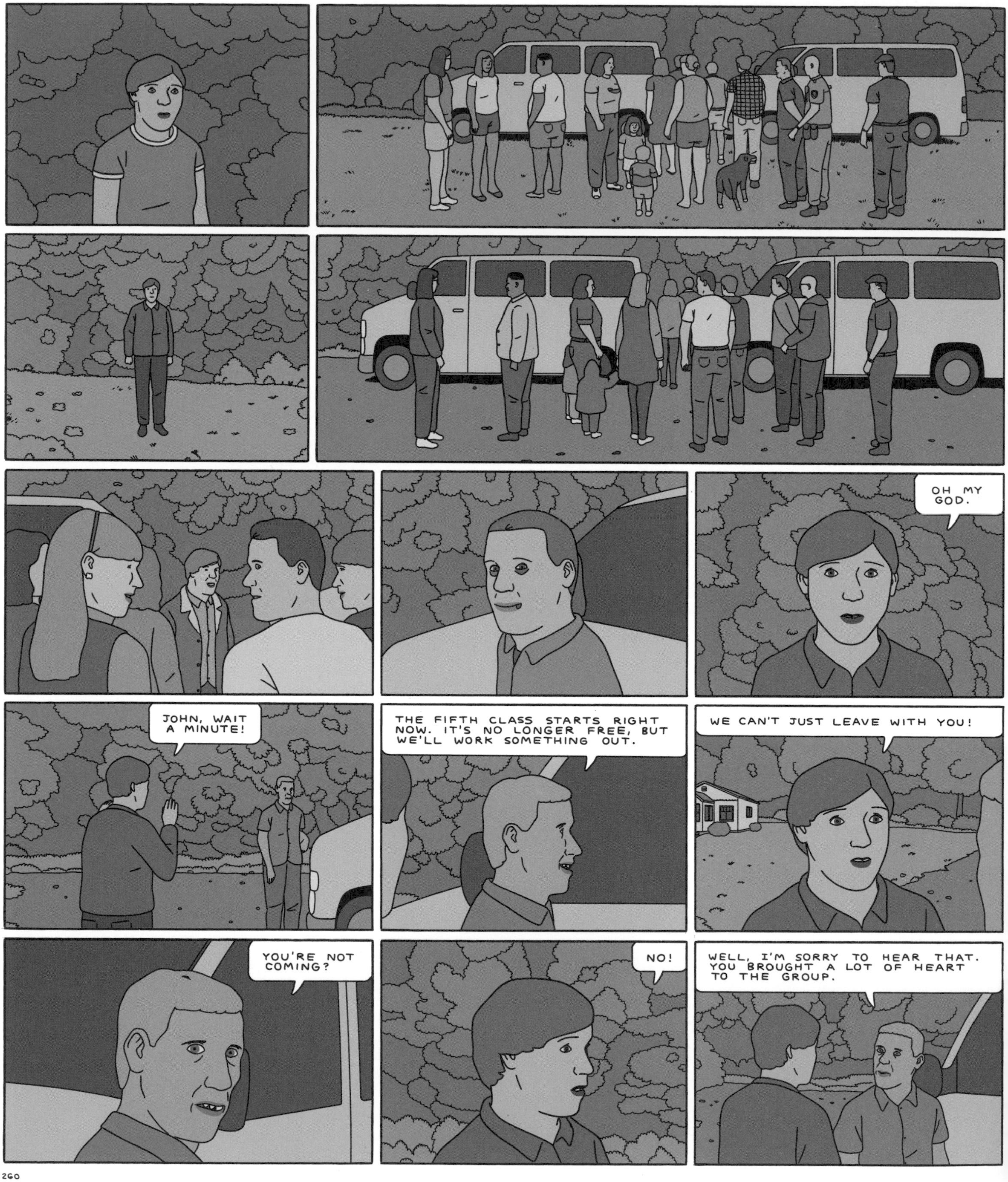
OH MY GOD.
JOHN, WAIT A MINUTE!
THE FIFTH CLASS STARTS RIGHT NOW. IT'S NO LONGER FREE, BUT WE'LL WORK SOMETHING OUT.
WE CAN'T JUST LEAVE WITH YOU!
YOU'RE NOT COMING?
NO!
WELL, I'M SORRY TO HEAR THAT. YOU BROUGHT A LOT OF HEART TO THE GROUP.

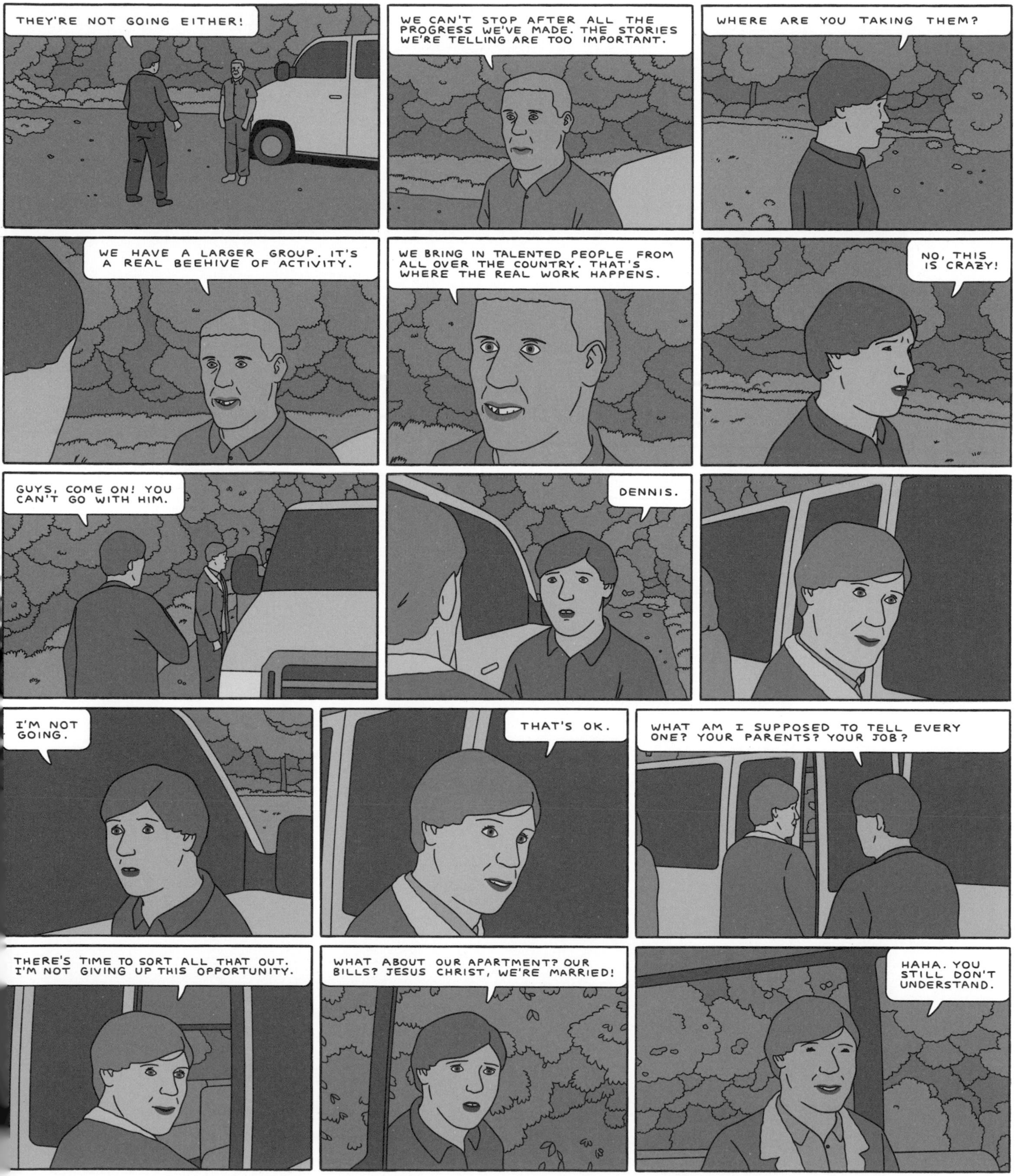
THEY'RE NOT GOING EITHER!
WE CAN'T STOP AFTER ALL THE PROGRESS WE'VE MADE. THE STORIES WE'RE TELLING ARE TOO IMPORTANT.
WHERE ARE YOU TAKING THEM?
WE HAVE A LARGER GROUP. IT'S A REAL BEEHIVE OF ACTIVITY.
WE BRING IN TALENTED PEOPLE FROM ALL OVER THE COUNTRY. THAT'S WHERE THE REAL WORK HAPPENS.
NO, THIS IS CRAZY!
GUYS, COME ON! YOU CAN'T GO WITH HIM.
DENNIS.
I'M NOT GOING.
THAT'S OK.
WHAT AM I SUPPOSED TO TELL EVERY ONE? YOUR PARENTS? YOUR JOB?
THERE'S TIME TO SORT ALL THAT OUT. I'M NOT GIVING UP THIS OPPORTUNITY.
WHAT ABOUT OUR APARTMENT? OUR BILLS? JESUS CHRIST, WE'RE MARRIED!
HAHA. YOU STILL DON'T UNDERSTAND.

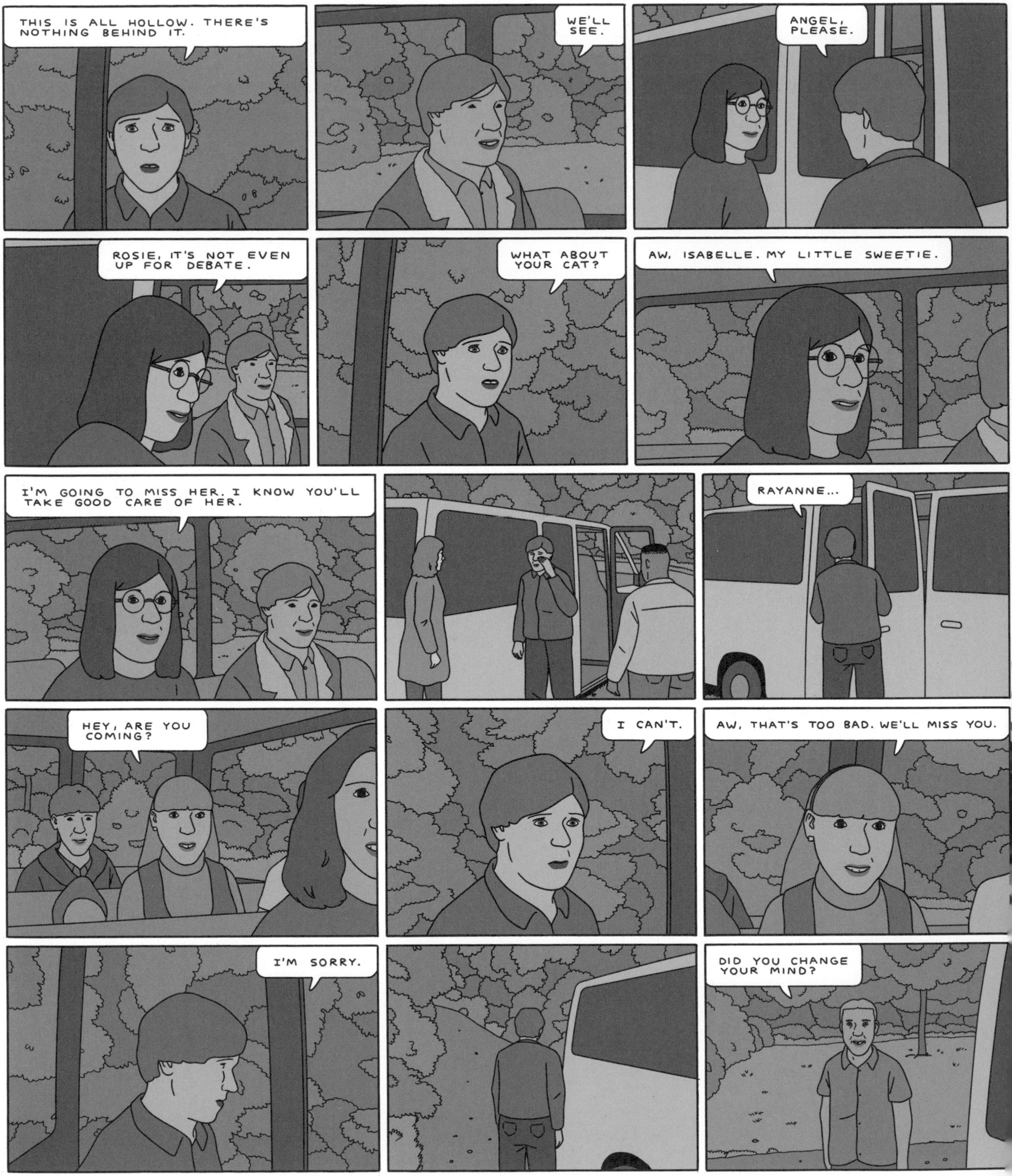
THIS IS ALL HOLLOW. THERE'S NOTHING BEHIND IT.
WE'LL SEE.
ANGEL, PLEASE.
ROSIE, IT'S NOT EVEN UP FOR DEBATE.
WHAT ABOUT YOUR CAT?
AW, ISABELLE. MY LITTLE SWEETIE.
I'M GOING TO MISS HER. I KNOW YOU'LL TAKE GOOD CARE OF HER.
RAYANNE...
HEY, ARE YOU COMING?
I CAN'T.
AW, THAT'S TOO BAD. WE'LL MISS YOU.
I'M SORRY.
DID YOU CHANGE YOUR MIND?

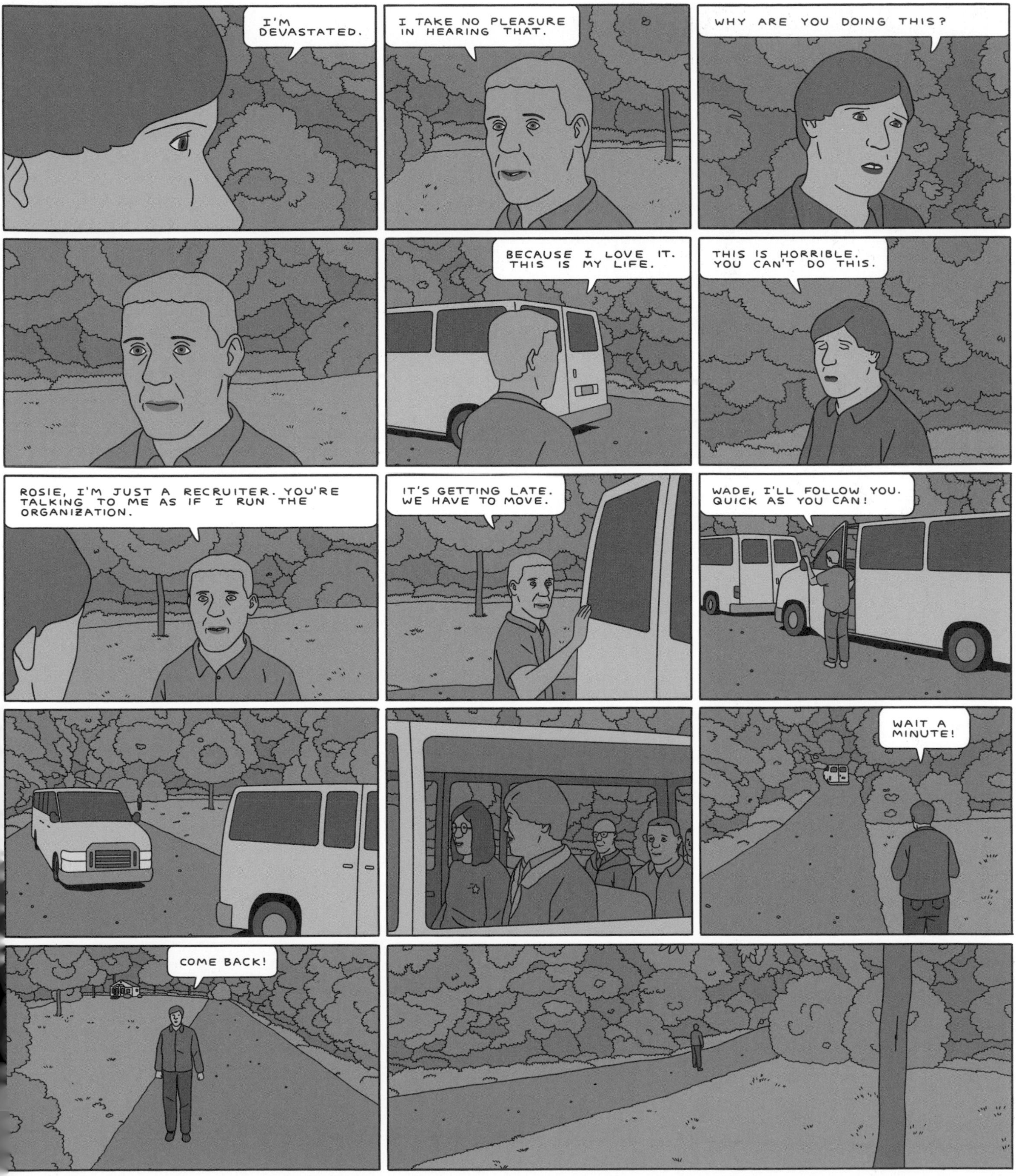
I'M DEVASTATED.
I TAKE NO PLEASURE IN HEARING THAT.
WHY ARE YOU DOING THIS?
BECAUSE I LOVE IT. THIS IS MY LIFE.
THIS IS HORRIBLE. YOU CAN'T DO THIS.
ROSIE, I'M JUST A RECRUITER. YOU'RE TALKING TO ME AS IF I RUN THE ORGANIZATION.
IT'S GETTING LATE. WE HAVE TO MOVE.
WADE, I'LL FOLLOW YOU. QUICK AS YOU CAN!
WAIT A MINUTE!
COME BACK!

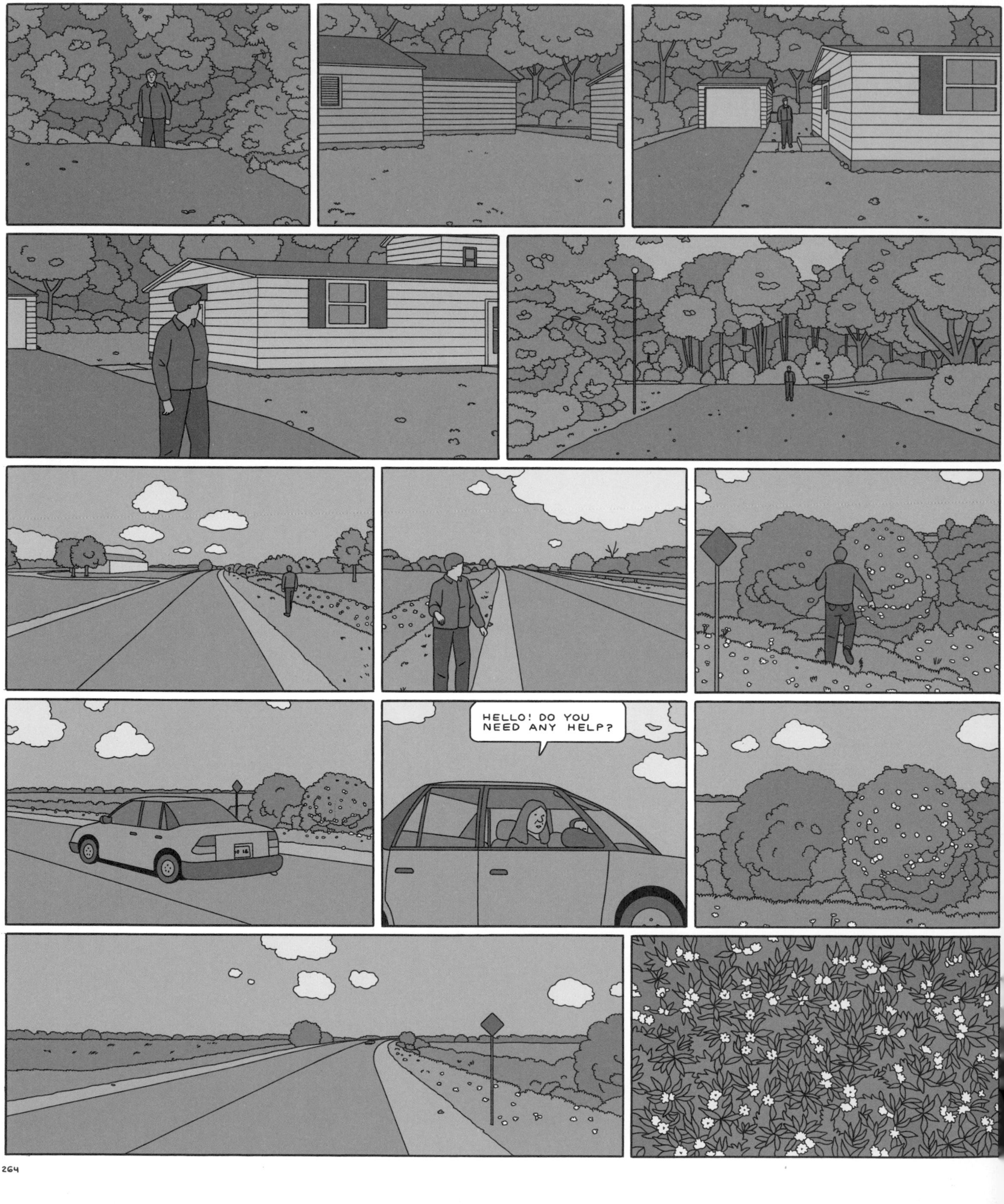
HELLO! DO YOU NEED ANY HELP?

WHAT DO YOU THINK?

I DON'T KNOW. IT'S A LOT OF MONEY.

WE CAN RUN THROUGH THE NUMBERS AGAIN. OVER THE COURSE OF YOUR LIFETIME YOU'LL MAKE THOUSANDS!

MY LIFETIME...

WHAT ARE YOU TWO TALKING ABOUT?

AN UNBELIEVABLE INVESTMENT OPPORTUNITY.

I DON'T KNOW. I DON'T KNOW.

BETH, I'VE ASKED YOU TO NOT GET HER WORKED UP WITH THESE GAMES.

HEATHER, LET'S GET YOU TO BED.

I'M SORRY, YOUR GRANDMA CALLED AND SHE WON'T BE VISITING TOMORROW.

AH.

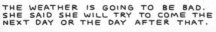
THE WEATHER IS GOING TO BE BAD. SHE SAID SHE WILL TRY TO COME THE NEXT DAY OR THE DAY AFTER THAT.

I'LL BE WAITING RIGHT HERE.

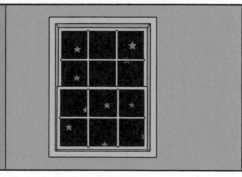

NICK DRNASO WAS BORN IN 1989 AND
GREW UP IN PALOS HILLS, ILLINOIS.
HE IS THE AUTHOR OF BEVERLY (2016)
AND SABRINA (2018). HIS WORK HAS
BEEN TRANSLATED INTO SIXTEEN
LANGUAGES. HE LIVES IN CHICAGO
WITH HIS WIFE AND THEIR TWO CATS.

THANKS: SARAH LEITTEN, TRACY
HURREN, LING MA, IVAN BRUNETTI,
MARGOT FERRICK, PEGGY BURNS,
JULIA POHL-MIRANDA, TOM DEVLIN,
ALISON NATURALE, MEGAN TAN,
SHIRLEY WONG, TRYNNE DELANEY,
KAIYA CADE SMITH BLACKBURN,
REBECCA LLOYD, LUCIA GARGIULO,
FRANCINE YULO, EMMA ALLEN,
CHRIS WARE, ROB SEVIER, JASON
RICHMAN, AND CHRIS OLIVEROS.

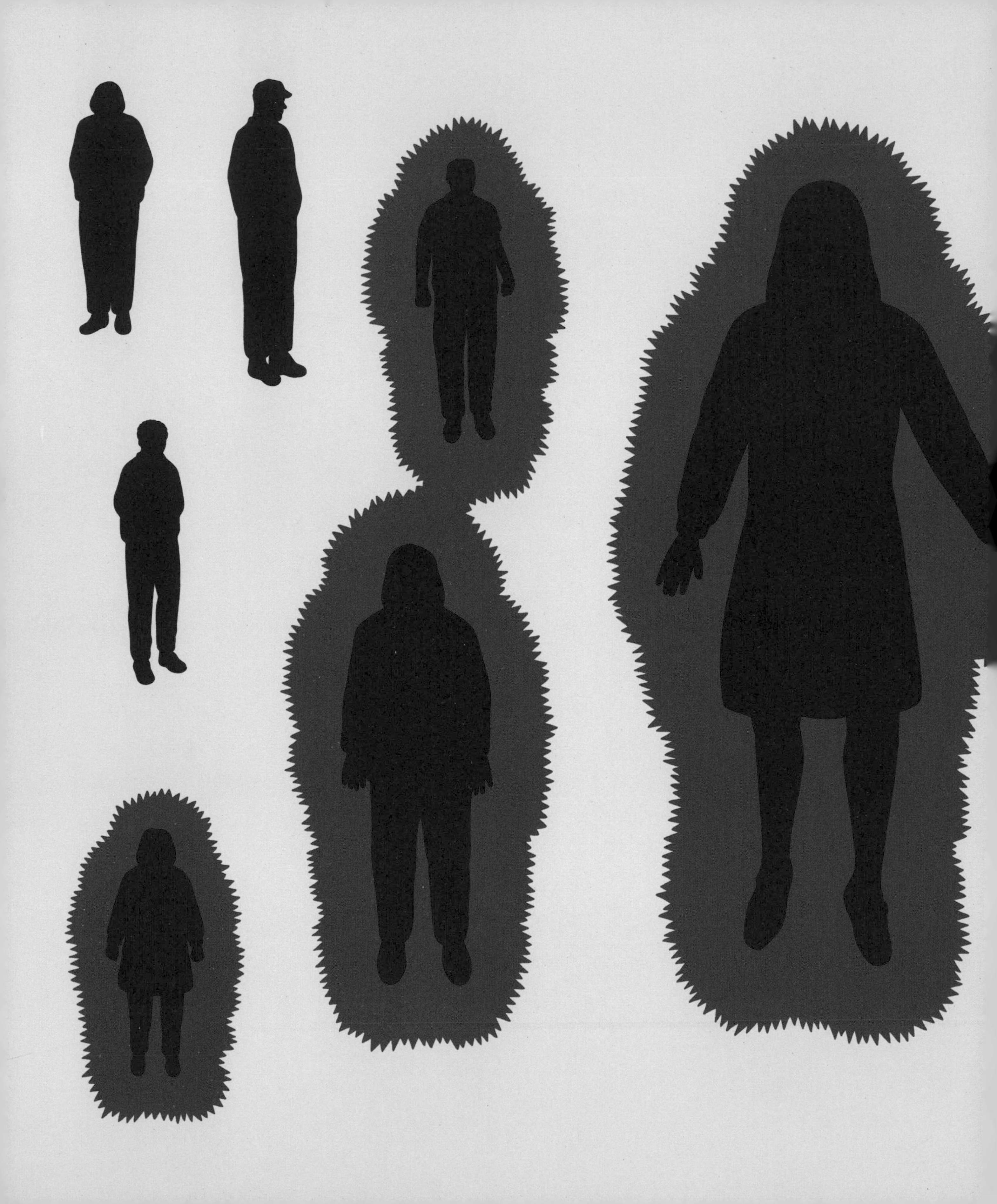